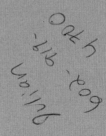

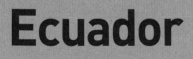

THE ROUGH GUIDE TO

Ecuador

This sixth edition updated by

Sara Humphreys and Stephan Küffner

roughguides.com

Contents

Introduction to
Ecuador

There's a well-known saying that Ecuador, one of the smallest states in South America, is actually four worlds rolled into one country. Straddling the equator, it boasts a mountainous Andean spine (the sierra) encrusted with glittering snowcapped volcanic peaks – the famed "Avenue of the Volcanoes" – and dotted with cobalt-blue lakes. To the east, vast emerald carpets of steamy Amazonian rainforest harbour a mind-boggling array of flora and flora (the Oriente), while the 2000 kilometre-long Pacific coastline entices visitors with its hidden coves, avian-rich mangroves and endless golden beaches lapped by warm waters. Then there is the country's most famous attraction, the other-worldly Galápagos Islands. Marooned 1000 kilometres from the mainland, and like nowhere else on the planet, this volcanic archipelago is renowned for its fearless wildlife – giant tortoises, penguins, marine iguanas and blue-footed boobies to name but a few – that inspired Charles Darwin's thinking on the nature of evolution.

The **cultural and ethnic make-up** of Ecuador is as fascinating and diverse as its landscapes and wildlife. Most of the country's sixteen million citizens are descendants of the various **indigenous groups** who first inhabited this territory 12,000 years ago, Incas who colonized the land in the late fifteenth century, Spaniards who conquered the Incas in the 1530s and African slaves brought by Spanish colonists. Although the mixing of blood over the centuries has resulted in a largely mestizo (mixed) population, indigenous cultures remain very strong, particularly among the Kichwa-speaking communities of the rural sierra and the ethnic groups of the Oriente. As in many parts of Latin America, social and economic divisions between *indígenas*, Afro-Ecuadorians, mestizos and a small elite class of white people remain fairly entrenched.

While Andean Quito is the **political and cultural heart** of Ecuador, the port city of Guayaquil is the pulse of the country's **economy,** exporting tonnes of bananas, shrimps, cocoa and coffee worldwide. Above all though, the country relies heavily on the export of oil: vast tracts of Amazonian rainforest in the Oriente have been transformed by oil multinationals, and although significant areas are officially protected, pollution and industrial accidents have had a devastating impact. That said, the accessibility of the rainforest and its abundant wildlife is one of Ecuador's main draws – due, ironically, to the transport infrastructure developed by and for the oil companies. Other threats to Ecuador's jungle come from **deforestation**, on account of logging, gold mining and clearing land for cultivation. These factors threaten not only the region's ecosystem, but also the numerous distinct indigenous groups – including the Siona, Waorani and Secoya – who live there. In recent years, indigenous rights groups and environmentalists have combined their efforts to resist the continued threat posed by government and multinationals to one of the most biodiverse landscapes on the planet.

The task of balancing human rights and environmental protection with the perceived needs of economic development belongs to Ecuador's charismatic leader, **President Rafael Correa.** Now into his third term of office after re-election in 2013, this left-leaning, US-trained economist has transformed the country's political and economic landscape by increasing social spending on education and health, reducing poverty levels and narrowing income inequalities. In doing so he has created a large middle class, though his critics accuse him of centralizing power and attacking freedom of expression.

What is not in doubt, however, is Correa's support for and investment in tourism: there are now an increasing number of ways to enjoy the country's diverse landscapes and interact with Ecuadorians: from kayaking or rafting down whitewater rivers, to climbing or mountain biking down snow-capped volcanoes; from experiencing the bustle of colourful highland markets, to learning traditional hunting methods with indigenous

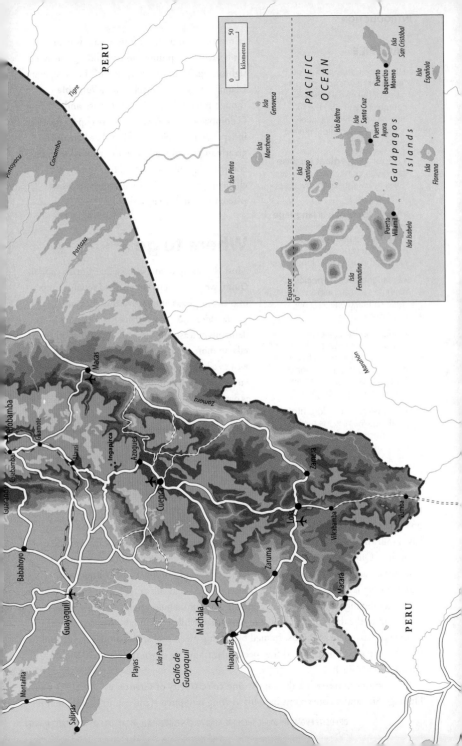

FACT FILE

• "Ecuador" is the Spanish for **"equator"**. It was chosen as the name of the newly independent country in 1830 after the alternatives, which included "Quito" and "Atahualpa", proved unpopular.

• The Galápagos **giant tortoise** can weigh up to 250kg, over four times the weight of the average adult human.

• Spanish is the official **language** of Ecuador, but there are more than 20 other native tongues, including several dialects of Kichwa, the language of the Incas.

• Ecuador has more **species** of mammals and amphibians per square metre than any other country on Earth.

• In 2015, at the age of 26, Vanessa Arauz, coach of Ecuador's women's football team, became the world's youngest national **football** coach at a FIFA World Cup – women's or men's.

• Chimborazo, Ecuador's **highest peak** at 6268m, is the furthest point from the centre of the Earth due to the planet's equatorial bulge.

rainforest communities; from whale-watching to birdwatching, zip-lining to paragliding, surfing to sightseeing. With the exception of the Galápagos Islands, the country is relatively **affordable** – though pricier than neighbours Peru and Colombia – and well set up for backpackers and independent travellers. Add to that Ecuador's greatly improved road network coupled with its compact size, and you'll find that the biggest challenge most travellers will face is deciding where to go and what to do first.

Where to go

Most visitors fly in to the lofty Ecuadorian capital, **Quito**, whose glorious colonial old town – a mix of pleasant plazas, impressive churches and monasteries and some fascinating museums – demands at least a day to explore. Add another to take in more art and culture in the new town as well as climbing to one of the city's many stunning viewpoints. North from Quito, the **northern sierra** is dappled with glistening lakes backed by volcanic peaks, a region famed for its **artesanías** – centres of native craftwork, leather goods and woodcarving – all within a short bus ride of each other. Of these, **Otavalo** is undoubtedly the biggest attraction, thanks to its enormous Saturday market – one of the continent's most renowned – and flourishing weaving industry. The region also offers plenty of scope for walkers and horse riders, who should consider splashing out on a stay in one of the beautifully converted **haciendas**, while an increasing number of community-based tourism initiatives provide opportunities to learn first-hand about highland life.

South of Quito, the **central sierra** is home to the most spectacular of the country's volcanoes, including the smoking snowcapped cone of **Cotopaxi** and **Chimborazo**, Ecuador's highest peak at 6268m (see box, p.37). Also in this rural region are some of the more exciting highland markets, at **Saquisilí** and **Zumbahua**, often combined with a side-trip to the dazzling crater lake of **Quilotoa**, while more established attractions include the spa town of **Baños**, framed by soaring green peaks, **Riobamba**, the central sierra's most appealing city, and the spectacular train ride down the **Nariz del Diablo** ("the Devil's Nose").

In the **southern sierra** lies the captivating colonial city of **Cuenca**, a UNESCO World Heritage Site and a convenient base for visiting **Ingapirca** – the country's only major

OPPOSITE FROM TOP YOUNG SHEPHERD NEAR VOLCÁN CHIMBORAZO; FRUIT FOR SALE AT A STREET MARKET

A BRILLIANT BIODIVERSITY

Ecuador's size belies a **stunning biodiversity**. The country has more than 25,000 plant species – ten percent of the world's total – compared to around 17,000 in North America. It is home to 1600 types of birds – about twice as many as in the whole of Europe, and almost half the total for all of South America. Ecuador's extraordinary concentration of wildlife is largely due to the country's unique geography, its position on the equator and the geologically recent appearance of Andean cordilleras, which divide the coastal and Amazonian basins and provide an array of habitats and isolated areas for the evolution of new species. Ecuador's highly **varied terrain** encompasses Andean mountains, parched semi-desert scrub, chilly high-altitude grasslands, subtropical cloudforests, tropical rainforests, dry forests, mangrove swamps, warm Pacific beaches and the unique environment of the Galápagos Islands.

Inca ruins – and **Parque Nacional El Cajas**, a starkly beautiful páramo wilderness. Further south is the charming city of **Loja**, renowned for its music and culture and a jumping-off point for visits to the **Parque Nacional Podocarpus**, whose humid lower reaches are particularly sumptuous, and to the relaxing village of **Vilcabamba**, nestled in a picturesque warm valley and a long-standing favourite with travellers wanting some downtime.

The **Oriente** encompasses one of Ecuador's greatest wildernesses, a thick carpet of **tropical rainforest** unfurling for almost 300km, which was home only to isolated indigenous groups and the odd Christian mission until the discovery of oil in the late 1960s. Since then, the region's infrastructure has developed apace, allowing easier access to the **Amazonian jungle** than in any other Andean country. Two of the country's largest wilderness areas – the **Reserva Faunística Cuyabeno** and the **Parque Nacional Yasuní** – and a number of private reserves protect substantial tracts of forest. Staying in a private jungle lodge is the most comfortable way to experience the thrill of this diverse and exciting habitat, or you can stay with an indigenous community for a glimpse into the lives of the jungle's residents. The Oriente towns of **Macas** and **Tena** are two of the best places to organize such stays.

A couple of hours' drive northwest of Quito on the way to the coast, a number of **private reserves** showcase the country's beautiful **cloudforests** – otherworldly gardens of gnarled and tangled vegetation, wrapped in mosses and vines, and drenched daily in mist – and provide accommodation and guides for exploring or birdwatching. The village of **Mindo**, enveloped in richly forested hills, is the country's birding capital.

OPPOSITE FROM TOP HIKERS IN THE ANDES; GREEN SEA TURTLE, GALÁPAGOS; FRAILEJONES

Author picks

Our authors have bussed, trekked, cycled, climbed and sailed the length and breadth of Ecuador. These are some of their favourite travel experiences.

Encounters with animals Get up close to the creatures of the Galápagos Islands (p.330), where you can snorkel or scuba dive with sea lions, turtles, penguins and even sharks.

Views of Quito Quito has several excellent viewpoints, notably the TelefériQo cable car (p.73), El Panecillo hill (p.41) and the vertiginous Basílica del Voto Nacional (p.72).

Coastal cuisine It's hard to resist the country's coastal culinary treats (p.32): try *encocado de pescado*, fresh fish cooked in spices and coconut milk, served with rice and crispy *patacones* – deep-fried plantain chips – accompanied by an ice-cold beer.

Hiking trails Ecuador has no shortage of great trails but the 4km route through the dry tropical forest of Parque Nacional Machalilla (p.328) to the gorgeous Playa de los Frailes is one of the most enjoyable, taking in golden- and black-sand beaches and fabulous coastal views.

Volcanoes Beside the iconic snowcapped volcanoes of Cotopaxi (p.137) and Chimborazo (p.168), El Altar (p.170) is often overlooked, but the sight of the jagged snow-powdered peaks that form this natural amphitheatre is truly breathtaking.

Páramo landscapes The otherworldliness of the páramo is at its most apparent in the Reserva Ecológica El Ángel (p.125), where frailejones – tall, spiky, furry-leaved plants that are endemic to the Andes – loom out of the mist.

> Our author recommendations don't end here. We've flagged up our favourite places – a perfectly sited hotel, an atmospheric café, a special restaurant – throughout the guide, highlighted with the ★ symbol.

Westwards, Ecuador's varied coastline begins at the Colombian border in a profusion of mangrove swamps, protected by the **Reserva Ecológica Manglares Cayapas-Mataje**. The surrounding **north coast**, however has long been known for its beaches; now increasingly overdeveloped with apartment blocks and high-rises, many visitors now sidestep the brash and boisterous **Atacames,** and the neighbouring sands of **Súa**, **Same** and **Muisne**, in search of a mellower beach scene and more attractive coastline further south, at the low-key surfing resort of **Mompiche**, in laidback **Canoa**, which offers daytime beach tranquillity and night-time partying, or at the self-proclaimed eco-resort of **Bahía de Caráquez**. Among the chief attractions of the **southern coast** is **Parque Nacional Machalilla**, with its dry and humid forests, superb beaches and impressive birdlife on its offshore island, **Isla de la Plata**, which is also a prime spot for some spectacular whale-watching (June–Sept).

Further down the coast, take your pick between the delightful beach hideaway of **Ayampe**, the hedonistic, surfing and backpacker magnet of **Montañita** and **Salinas,** the country's most prestigious seaside resort. **Guayaquil**, the region's humid main port and the largest city in Ecuador, showcases some impressive examples of urban regeneration and is deservedly emerging as a tourist destination, while quieter attractions include the mangrove forests of the **Reserva Ecológica Manglares Churute**, the picturesque hill village of **Zaruma** and the petrified forest of **Puyango**.

The **Galápagos Islands** are for many visitors the initial lure to the country, and arguably the most compelling wildlife destination in the world. Ever since Darwin dropped anchor at these forbidding volcanic islands, they have enchanted all who come with their unworldly landscapes and unique flora and fauna. Beyond gawping at fearless land

animals, there are great opportunities to get closer to the archipelago's abundant marine life: swimming with turtles and sharks, peering through a glass-bottomed boat and looking out for dolphins and whales.

When to go

There's no real summer and winter in Ecuador, and its **weather** generally varies by regional geography, with temperatures determined more by altitude than by season or latitude. The warmest and driest months in the **sierra** are June to September, though this is complicated by various microclimates found in some areas. Outside these months, typical sierra weather offers sunny, clear mornings and cloudy, often wet, afternoons. In the **Oriente**, you can expect it to be warm, humid and rainy throughout the year, though there are often short breaks from the daily rains from August to September and December to February. In the **lowlands** it can get particularly hot on clear days, with temperatures easily topping 30°C. The **coast** has the most clearly defined wet and dry seasons, and the best time to visit is from December to April, when frequent showers alternate with blue skies and temperatures stay high. From May to November it's often overcast and relatively cool, especially in the south, with less chance of rainfall. The **Galápagos** climate sees hot, sunny days interspersed with the odd heavy shower from January to June, and dry and overcast weather for the rest of the year, when the garúa mists are prevalent. **El Niño** years can bring enormous fluctuations in weather patterns on the coast and in the Galápagos archipelago, when levels of rainfall can be many times the norm.

AVERAGE TEMPERATURES AND RAINFALL

	Jan	Feb	Mar	Apr	May	Jun	Jul	Aug	Sep	Oct	Nov	Dec
QUITO (SIERRA)												
Max/min (°C)	19/10	19/10	19/10	19/11	19/11	19/9	19/9	19/9	20/9	19/9	19/9	19/10
Max/min (°F)	66/50	66/50	66/50	66/52	66/52	66/48	66/48	66/48	68/48	66/48	66/48	66/50
Rainfall (mm)	114	130	152	175	124	48	20	25	79	127	109	104
GUAYAQUIL (COAST)												
Max/min (°C)	31/23	31/24	32/24	32/24	31/23	29/22	29/21	29/21	30/21	29/22	30/23	31/23
Max/min (°F)	88/73	88/75	90/75	90/75	88/73	84/71	84/70	84/70	86/70	84/72	86/73	88/73
Rainfall (mm)	224	279	287	180	53	18	3	0	3	3	3	30
TENA (ORIENTE)												
Av daily (°C)	29/19	28/18	28/18	28/18	28/19	27/18	27/18	28/18	29/18	29/19	29/19	29/19
Av daily (°F)	83/66	83/65	83/65	82/65	82/65	81/65	81/64	83/64	84/65	84/66	84/66	84/66
Rainfall (mm)	268	258	364	448	445	488	474	307	328	345	322	300
PUERTO AYORA (GALÁPAGOS)												
Max/min (°C)	28/23	30/23	31/23	30/23	28/22	26/21	25/20	24/19	24/19	25/20	26/20	27/21
Max/min (°F)	82/73	86/73	88/73	86/73	82/72	79/70	77/68	75/66	75/66	77/68	77/68	80/70
Rainfall (mm)	44	56	80	73	70	49	25	8	10	11	11	41

21

things not to miss

It's not possible to see everything that Ecuador has to offer in one trip – and we don't suggest you try. What follows is a selective and subjective taste of the country's highlights, including fun festivals, outstanding beaches, spectacular wildlife and extraordinary landscapes. All highlights are colour-coded by chapter and have a page reference to take you straight into the Guide, where you can find out more.

1

1 OTAVALO MARKET

Page 106

Few travellers can resist the fabulous handicrafts and weavings at one of South America's largest and most colourful artesanía markets.

2 QUITO

Page 52

A mixture of church spires, tiled roofs and skyscrapers glinting in the sunlight against the brooding backdrop of Volcán Pichincha, Quito is an enthralling blend of urban and traditional indigenous cultures.

3 CANOA

Page 283

The perfect laidback spot to enjoy sun, surf and sundowners, before partying on the sand into the early hours.

4 WHALE-WATCHING

Pages 275, 287, 319 & 327

Don't miss the heart-stopping sight of a 36-tonne humpback breaching and flopping back into the ocean amid towers of spray.

5 PARQUE NACIONAL MACHALILLA
Page 328

Ecuador's only coastal national park is home to a dazzling array of wildlife.

6 MALECÓN 2000
Page 299

A triumph of urban renewal, this riverside walkway is the cultural heart of Guayaquil.

7 NARIZ DEL DIABLO
Page 174

Starting in leafy Alausí, this is one of the world's greatest train journeys.

8 LA COMPAÑÍA
Page 62

Quito's centre is packed with magnificent churches, but few can match La Compañía.

9 ORCHIDS
Pages 247, 260 & 262

A miracle of biodiversity, Ecuador has more orchid species than any other country on Earth.

10 CEVICHE
Page 32

The bright, zesty flavours and tender textures of ceviche have made it a national obsession.

11 BAÑOS
Page 152

Wallow in thermal baths at this charming spa town, or go hiking, biking or canyoning nearby.

12 CLIMB A VOLCANO
Pages 136, 116 & 122

Even novices, if fit, fully acclimatized and under professional guidance, can have a crack at conquering a volcano – Iliniza Norte, Cotacachi or Imbabura are all over 4500m.

13 MUSEO NACIONAL DEL ECUADOR
Page 69

Ecuador's top museum exhibits more than 5000 years of culture, including some of the oldest artefacts discovered on the continent.

14 INGAPIRCA
Page 181

Ecuador's best-preserved Inca ruins exhibit the fine stonemasonry and trapezoidal doorways that were the hallmarks of the empire's architecture.

15 LAGUNA QUILOTOA
Page 145

This glittering crater lake sits at the heart of the Quilotoa Loop, a popular scenic diversion through the rural central highlands.

16 JUNGLE OBSERVATION TOWERS
Pages 234 & 235

Several jungle lodges feature observation towers that rise above the vegetation to give unbeatable views across the forest canopy.

17 CONTEMPORARY ART
Pages 73, 76, 185, 300 & 398

Ecuador's great modern artists are influential social commentators, whose work shouldn't be missed.

16

17

20

21

Itineraries

The following itineraries feature a combination of popular and off-the-beaten-track attractions, from historic colonial cities to the heart of the Amazon. Even if you don't have the time to complete a whole itinerary, it will still give you an insight into Ecuador's stunning diversity.

THE GRAND TOUR

You'll need four to five weeks to complete this trip around Ecuador; many travellers spend at least seven nights on a cruise of the Galápagos Islands alone.

❶ **Quito** High in the Andes, Ecuador's capital has an atmospheric old town, filled with wonderfully preserved Spanish colonial architecture. **See p.52**

❷ **Otavalo** This town is famous for its world-renowned Saturday market, which attracts craft producers from across the country and beyond. **See p.104**

❸ **Parque Nacional Cotopaxi** One of the highest active volcanoes on Earth, with a perfect cone shape, Cotopaxi is part of the dramatic "Avenue of the Volcanoes". **See p.137**

❹ **Baños** A subtropical resort town in a verdant location, Baños offers a wide range of outdoor activities, including a vertigo-inducing swing. **See p.152**

❺ **The Oriente** The huge swath of Amazon rainforest in the Oriente region of eastern Ecuador is home to a dizzying array of flora and fauna. **See p.212**

❻ **La Nariz del Diablo train ride** "The Devil's Nose" train ride follows a spectacular route, zigzagging down a sheer rock face. **See p.174**

❼ **Cuenca** The most beautiful city in Ecuador with an array of narrow, cobbled streets, hidden courtyards and whitewashed churches and monasteries. **See p.183**

❽ **Canoa** Once a sleepy fishing village, now a chilled-out beach resort, Canoa has a stunning stretch of coast that attracts both surfers and sun-seekers. **See p.283**

❾ **The Galápagos Islands** This archipelago is the world's premier destination for spotting wildlife, from blue-footed boobies to giant tortoises. **See p.330**

WILDLIFE AND NATURE

You'll need around four weeks to complete this tour, though, if you have the time, there are plenty of potential side trips to add on.

❶ **The Galápagos Islands** Observing the unique and famously fearless wildlife of the archipelago is a real once-in-a-lifetime experience. **See p.330**

❷ **Parque Nacional Machalilla** Blue-footed, red-footed and masked boobies are all found at Isla de la Plata, while humpback whales can be spotted in the waters around Puerto López. **See p.328**

❸ **Mindo** Surrounded by cloudforest, Mindo is a good base for some superb birdwatching – there are some 370 species in the area. **See p.262**

❹ **Quilotoa Loop** A spectacular tour that takes in an emerald-coloured lake, mountainous terrain and a real sense of isolation. **See p.144**

ABOVE SWING, NEAR BAÑOS

❺ **Volcán Chimborazo** Aim for the top if you can, although most visitors are happy just to reach the second refuge. **See p.168**

❻ **Parque Nacional Podocarpus** This protected area houses an incredible range of species – you might even spot a spectacled bear. **See p.204**

❼ **Parque Nacional Yasuní** Ecuador's largest national park is home to a wealth of wildlife, as well as indigenous Waorani communities. **See p.233**

TRADITIONAL CULTURE

This itinerary takes around two weeks, though you may want to extend it to take in a range of the different festivals.

❶ **Quito's museums** The Museo Nacional del Ecuador and the newer Casa del Alabado both have extensive collections of pre-Columbian artefacts in stone, gold and ceramics. **See p.69 & p.64**

❷ **Otavalo** The town hosts several fascinating festivals, including the Fiesta del Yamor, which takes place in the first two weeks in September. **See p.107**

❸ **Mama Negra fiestas** The town of Latacunga explodes into life every September and November with the Mama Negra fiestas. **See p.142**

❹ **Craft villages around Cuenca** In the countryside around Cuenca, several small towns and villages – including Chordeleg, Sigsig and Gualaceo – specialize in producing handicrafts. **See p.196**

❺ **Homestays in the Oriente** Experience a completely different way of life by staying with an indigenous community in the jungle. **See p.219, p.227, 236, 243 249 & p.252**

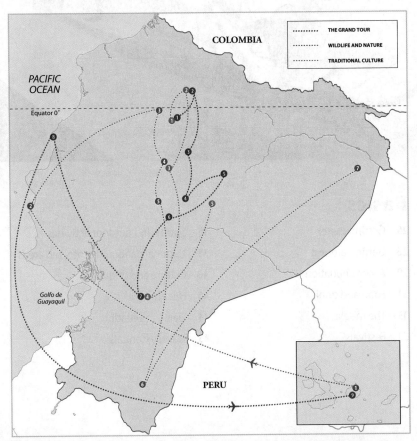

DUGOUT CANOE ON THE RÍO NAPO

Basics

Getting there

Direct flights to Ecuador's international airports in Quito and Guayaquil depart from a relatively small number of places. Higher prices are likely in the July to September high season and during the Christmas holiday season.

If you're planning to include Ecuador as part of a South American tour, consider an **"open-jaw"** ticket, which lets you make your own way overland between your arrival and departure points.

Ecuador is too small to warrant its own **airpass**, but is included in larger networks, such as the LAN airpass (Ⓦlan.com), which links LAN destinations and offers further discounts if you have a transatlantic ticket with them.

It's also possible to enter Ecuador **by bus** from neighbouring Peru and Colombia.

Flights from the US and Canada

While there are few direct routes to Ecuador, it's easy to pick up connecting flights to the main hubs. **From the US**, direct routes to Quito and Guayaquil are operated by American Airlines (Ⓦaa.com), Delta (Ⓦdelta.com), LAN (Ⓦlan.com) and United (Ⓦunited.com) from Atlanta, Houston and Miami. Avianca (Ⓦavianca.com), Copa Airlines (Ⓦcopaair .com) and Insel Air (Ⓦfly-inselair.com) have indirect flights via cities such as Bogotá, Panama City and San Salvador (El Salvador). There are no direct flights **from Canada** to Ecuador; Canadian travellers generally have to travel via the US.

Approximate **flying times** from the US to Quito without stops are around four hours from Miami, and around five hours from Houston and Atlanta. Prices are roughly $500–700 return from Miami, $600–800 from Houston and Atlanta, and CAN$700–900 from Toronto, but shop around, as prices can vary greatly.

Flights from the UK and Ireland

There are no direct flights to Ecuador **from the UK and Ireland**, but there are plenty of indirect flights

to both Quito and Guayaquil involving a change of plane in either a European or American city. The US airlines fly via their respective hubs (see above), while Iberia (Ⓦiberia.com) routes via Madrid, and KLM (Ⓦklm.com) via Amsterdam. Other possibilities include taking a flight to a South American hub, such as Bogotá or Lima, from where connections to Ecuador can be made.

Typical **journey times** are between 15 and 17 hours. You can expect to pay around £700–900 return in low season and £800–1100 in high, though prices can vary widely.

Flights from Australia, New Zealand and South Africa

There are no direct flights to Ecuador **from Australia or New Zealand**. The most straightforward route is with Qantas/LAN (Ⓦqantas.com and Ⓦlan.com) from Sydney to Quito and Guayaquil, stopping in Auckland and changing in Santiago. Alternatively, you can travel via the US, or fly to Buenos Aires with Aerolineas Argentinas (Ⓦaerolineas.com.ar) and pick up a connection from there. Typical **travel times** are around 25 to 40 hours. Expect to pay at least around A$2000 from Australia, and NZ$2100 from New Zealand.

To get to Ecuador **from South Africa**, you're best off flying to a South American hub, such as São Paulo, Buenos Aires, Santiago or Lima, from where there are ongoing services to Quito. Johannesburg to São Paulo with South African Airlines (Ⓦflysaa .com) is a ten-hour flight costing from ZAR6000. Ecuadorian state airline Tame flies to São Paulo several times a week (6 hours) and is the only direct option, but booking can be complicated and service poor.

Buses from neighbouring countries

It is possible to enter Ecuador **by bus from Peru** via Macará (see p.210) or Huaquillas (see p.316), or **from Colombia** via Tulcán (see p.126). However, the region around the border with Colombia is

---

A BETTER KIND OF TRAVEL

At Rough Guides we are passionately committed to travel. We believe it helps us understand the world we live in and the people we share it with – and of course tourism is vital to many developing economies. But the scale of modern tourism has also damaged some places irreparably, and climate change is accelerated by most forms of transport, especially flying. All Rough Guides' flights are carbon-offset, and every year we donate money to a variety of environmental charities.

unsettled and may be unsafe – check the latest security situation before attempting this route. It's also worth noting that cross-border buses are notorious hunting grounds for pickpockets and bag-snatchers; keep a very close eye on your belongings (see p.45). Be aware, too, that scams are common – spurious stories along the lines of "the road is closed" or "there are protests" can be ploys to get travellers into the scammers' vehicles or to an isolated place with the aim of robbing them.

AGENTS AND OPERATORS

Abercrombie & Kent US ☎ 1 888 611 4711, UK ☎ 01242 547 760, Australia ☎ 03 9536 1800, New Zealand ☎ 0800 441 638; Ⓦ abercrombiekent.com. Top-end tours of Ecuador and the Galápagos Islands.

Adventure Associates Australia ☎ 02 4758 9922, Ⓦ adventureassociates.com. A variety of mainland tours involving markets, the Devil's Nose train ride, Amazon lodges, volcanoes and Galápagos cruises.

Adventure Center US ☎ 1 844 227 9087, Ⓦ adventurecenter.com. Hiking and "soft adventure" specialists with a number of tours to Ecuador and Galápagos.

Andean Treks US ☎ 1 800 683 8148, Ⓦ andeantreks.com. For Ecuador, Andean Treks offers customized tours including one or more of four "segments": Amazon, highlands and haciendas, cities and the Galápagos Islands.

Austral Tours Australia ☎ 03 93706621, Ⓦ www.australtours.com. Central and South American specialist offering trips to *Kapawi Lodge* and Galápagos cruises.

Dragoman Overland UK ☎ 1 855 273 0866, Ⓦ dragoman.com. Small-group overland trips in a special truck with several routes across South America that take in Ecuador.

Intrepid Travel UK ☎ 1 510 285 0640, Ⓦ intrepidtravel.com. Small-group tours with the emphasis on cross-cultural contact and low-impact tourism.

Journey Latin America UK ☎ 0203 3582 8684, Ⓦ journeylatinamerica.co.uk. Specialists in flights, packages, adventure tours and tailor-made trips to Latin America.

Kellie Worldwide UK ☎ 07887 642 897, Ⓦ kellieworldwide.com. Agent for Galápagos cruises on a selection of top-class boats, with extensions to the Andes and Amazonia.

Metropolitan Touring UK ☎ 203 371 7096, US ☎ 1 888 572 0166, Ⓦ metropolitan-touring.com. Ecuador's leading travel company, with three Galápagos vessels and luxury lodge *Mashpi* in Andean cloudforest.

Mountain Travel Sobek US ☎ 1 888 831 7526, Ⓦ mtsobek.com. Galápagos cruises.

Myths and Mountains US ☎ 1 800 670 6984, Ⓦ mythsandmountains.com. Socially responsible tours visiting indigenous communities in the highlands and Oriente.

Naturetrek UK ☎ 01962 733 051, Ⓦ naturetrek.co.uk. Specializes in birdwatching and botanical holidays, with cloudforest tours and trips to the Amazon and Andean páramo.

North South Travel UK ☎ 01245 608 291, Ⓦ northsouthtravel.co.uk. Competitive travel agency, offering discounted fares worldwide. Profits are used to support projects in the developing world.

On the Go Tours UK ☎ 020 7371 1113, Ⓦ onthegotours.com. Runs two different group-only tours to Ecuador and the Galápagos, from 13 to 37 days in length.

Ornitholidays UK ☎ 01794 519 445, Ⓦ ornitholidays.co.uk. Specialist birding tours of Ecuador and the Galápagos.

Quasar Expeditions US ☎ 1 866 481 7790, UK ☎ 0800 883 0827, Ⓦ galapagosexpeditions.com. Well-respected Galápagos specialist, owning a range of luxury and first-class yachts. Also arranges high-quality tailor-made land tours.

Reef and Rainforest UK ☎ 01803 866 965, Ⓦ reefandrainforest.co.uk. Trips to the Galápagos, plus birding groups in the Amazon basin and cloudforests.

Select Latin America UK ☎ 020 7407 1478, Ⓦ selectlatinamerica.co.uk. Specializes in Galápagos cruises on a variety of yachts, but can combine these with treks and jungle trips.

Sunbird UK ☎ 01767 262 522, Ⓦ sunbirdtours.co.uk. Specialist birdwatching tours to Ecuador, the Oriente, Podocarpus and the Santa Elena peninsula.

Tribes UK ☎ 01728 685 971, US ☎ 1 800 608 4651; Ⓦ tribes.co.uk. Environmentally and culturally sensitive operator offering a range of small-group and special-interest tours around Ecuador.

Wilderness Travel US ☎ 1 800 368 2794, Ⓦ wildernesstravel.com. Established adventure company offering Galápagos trips combined with hiking, kayaking and snorkelling options, plus trips to the highlands.

Getting around

Ecuador's inexpensive and generally reliable buses are the country's preferred form of public transport, and trundle along just about anywhere there's a road. By contrast, the train network covers only a small fraction of the country, and is mainly used for tourist excursions, rather than as a way of getting from "A" to "B".

Road coverage is limited by North American and European standards, but expanding and improving all the time, though you can expect a bumpy ride off the main routes. The **Panamericana** (Panamerican Highway, often called *la Pana* by locals) forms the backbone of the country's road network, linking all the major highland towns and cities from Tulcán, by the northern border with Colombia, to Loja and on to Peru. A handful of other good roads spill down the Andes to important coastal cities including Guayaquil, Manta and Esmeraldas, while in the Oriente the road system is the least developed and exists almost entirely to serve the needs of the local oil industry.

The network's biggest problem has always been the **weather**, with floods and landslides both common, knocking out roads sometimes for weeks on end. Even in fine conditions, rough terrain means that travelling in the country's highland regions is often much slower than you might expect.

By bus

Ecuador's comprehensive bus service makes getting around simple. Hundreds of companies ply the country's roads, transporting people at relatively little cost to all but the remotest regions. Levels of comfort can vary widely between companies: some have fleets of a/c buses with TV, toilet and on-board snacks, while others run beaten-up old monsters. As a general rule, **luxury buses** (ask for an *autobús de lujo*) travel the most popular long-distance routes, and require passengers to have a pre-booked ticket. They won't allow standing passengers on board, and only stop at scheduled destinations, reducing journey times.

The further into the backwaters you go, the more the comfort level is likely to drop. **Standard buses** will stop anywhere for anyone who wants to get on until all available space has been filled. At the margins of the bus network, pick-up trucks (**camionetas**), minibuses (**busetas**) and open-sided trucks converted to hold wooden benches (**rancheras** or **chivas**) often fill the vacuum. For reasons of safety, **avoid travelling at night** on buses, when hold-ups and accidents are more likely.

Larger towns usually have a main **bus terminal** (*terminal terrestre*), where all the long-distance bus companies are based. In smaller towns, company offices and departure points may be scattered around the place. Out of town, it's easy to hail non-luxury buses if you stand in a place where they have plenty of time to spot you; the standard gesture to flag one down is to point to the ground in the middle of the road next to you.

You can buy **fares** from the conductor (*ayudante*) on board, who will come and collect it. Overcharging is uncommon, but keep an eye on what others are paying. To get off, make for the door and say "*bajo*" or "*gracias*". If possible, buy your ticket in advance at the company office to guarantee a seat, something you can do on all long-distance buses.

Local **city buses** in the larger towns generally carry a board in the window showing their route, with a list of street names and key landmarks, and cost 25 cents. Local buses often stop to pick up and put down anywhere on request, though in some city centres proper **bus stops**, marked "*parada*", are respected. Guayaquil and Quito have buses on dedicated lanes.

For bus timetables, check the scheduling website Ⓦ horariodebuses.com/EN/ec.

By train

A train ride here is a real treat, with several routes offering excellent views, but it's not an efficient way to travel the country. The network is currently limited to upscale tourist-oriented excursions (see p.78, p.108, p.124, p.140, p.151, p.166, p.174 & p.306), topped by a luxury "rail cruise", a multi-day affair running from Quito to Guayaquil; check Ⓦ trenecuador.com for the latest.

By air

Flying within Ecuador is a quick, convenient and relatively inexpensive way of avoiding the country's serpentine and often clogged roads. Those short on time can cut an all-day bus journey down to a 30-minute hop – and if the weather's clear, enjoy wonderful aerial views of volcanoes and rainforests on the way. **Domestic carriers** include Avianca (Ⓦ avianca.com), LAN (Ⓦ lan.com) and Tame (Ⓦ tame.com.ec), plus a number of small-scale and local charter companies, particularly in Cuenca and in the Amazon. With the exception of services to the Galápagos (see p.341), internal flights can be pretty inexpensive, but prices vary depending on the type of ticket, how far in advance you purchase it, and the popularity of the route – generally starting from $100 for a round-trip, including taxes. Busier routes should be booked days, if not weeks, in advance of holidays. The weather can be a problem, particularly in Quito and the Amazon, resulting in fairly frequent delays, cancellations or diversions.

By car

If you intend to zoom around the country in a short space of time, or want to get to really off-the-beaten-track destinations, **renting a car** is a worthwhile, but potentially stressful option. You will need to be at least 21 years old (extra charges may be payable if you are under 25) and have a major credit/debit card for the deposit. Theoretically, you only need your national licence to rent a vehicle, but you're strongly advised to bring an **international licence** as well – the Ecuadorian police, who frequently stop drivers to check their documents, are much happier when dealing with international licences. The national **speed limit** is 90kmh on highways (or less if indicated), and usually around 50kmh in towns or urban areas. There are draconian penalties for some minor **motoring offences**, such as not wearing your seat belt; driving the wrong way down a one-way street is supposedly punishable by a 14-day mandatory jail sentence, and speeding 20km faster than the limit can also get you three days in jail.

Rental outlets, costs and vehicles

For convenience's sake, you might want to arrange your car rental in advance through your nearest branch of an international rental company, but it nearly always works out cheaper to sort it out when you get there, typically at the airport in Guayaquil or Quito. Expect to pay from around $50 a day for a small hatchback, and $100 a day for a 4WD, including **insurance** and IVA (value-added tax, or VAT) – always check whether the price quoted includes insurance, IVA and unlimited mileage. Check, too, what the **excess** is on the insurance – known as "*el deducible*" – as it is usually frighteningly high. It's a good idea to use agencies such as Ⓦinsurance4carhire.com, which provide year-long cover for rental vehicles, pay all excess costs and cover anyone named on the rental agreement.

When choosing which type of vehicle to rent, remember that 4WDs, or at least high clearance and sturdy tyres, definitely come in handy on unpaved roads, but aren't necessary for the big cities and better-maintained parts of the road network.

On the road

Ecuadorian drivers tend to be undisciplined and sometimes downright dangerous; aggressive overtaking is particularly common, as is abruptly veering over to the wrong side of the road to avoid potholes. As long as you **drive defensively** and keep your wits about you, however, it's perfectly possible to cover thousands of kilometres without running into problems. **Never drive at night** if you can avoid it, as this is when most accidents occur, in part due to the absence of decent road markings, lighting and the lack of signs alerting drivers to hazards. In addition, although **ambushes** against drivers are extremely rare, when they do happen it's most often at night.

Never leave valuables in your car, or your car on the street overnight, as it will almost certainly be broken into; try to stay in hotels with a garage, or else leave your vehicle overnight in a securely locked *parqueadero* (car park).

In the event of an **accident**, try to come to an agreement with the other party without involving the police if you can. This will not be possible if it is serious, and the upshot is often that both parties are detained until one admits liability. Unsurprisingly, hit and runs are common in Ecuador.

Hitchhiking

Hitching is not recommended as a safe way of getting about, but it's widely practised by Ecuadorians in rural areas. For backpackers, the bus service is such that you'll only really need to hitch in the remoter places – you're most likely to get a ride in the back of a pick-up truck. The etiquette is to ask "*¿Cuánto le debo?*" ("How much do I owe you?") at the end of the journey, at which point you may be asked to pay a small amount, rarely more than the bus fare would have been, or let off for free.

By taxi

Most towns in Ecuador have a fleet of yellow **taxis** – in rural areas, green-and-white **camionetas** (pick-up trucks) take their place. In tropical areas, you may also come across **mototaxis** – motorbikes with small trailers converted to take passengers, who sit on a couple of makeshift benches. Since 2014 it has been compulsory across Ecuador for taxi drivers to have a taximeter, though a small percentage are still without one. The new law has led to fares for some journeys going up and others going down, with the result that some passengers and drivers still prefer to negotiate a price. In Guayaquil, most taxi drivers still refuse to use the taximeter, even when they have one (see p.306). The minimum fare is usually $1–2, depending on the size of the town or city, and is higher at night, with a standard short journey, outside Quito or Guayaquil, typically costing $1.50–4. Most drivers are honest, but where drivers refused to use the taximeter, the best way to avoid being ripped off is to ask locals what the standard fares are to various destinations. Always agree on the price with the driver beforehand, and don't be

ADDRESSES

Written **addresses** appear as a street and a number (Sucre 353), a street and the nearest intersecting street (Sucre y Olmedo) or all three (Sucre 353 y Olmedo). The number is often hyphenated – such as Sucre 3-53 – so that there's no confusion between the first digits (the block number) and the last digits (the house number). Some out-of-the-way places don't have a numbered address, which is then written *s/n* for "*sin número*". Note that the ground floor (US first floor) is known as the *planta baja*, while the first floor (US second floor) is the *primer piso*.

afraid to haggle. Tipping isn't necessary, but it's common to round up fares.

Taxis are also sometimes the best way of getting to out-of-the-way places such as national parks or mountain refuges, particularly if you're in a group and can share the cost. Hiring a taxi for the day costs from about $60.

By boat

The most likely place you'll end up travelling by boat is in the **Oriente**, where the best of the jungle is often a boat ride away. On the **coast**, a highway runs the entire length of the Ecuadorian seaboard, meaning you're less likely to need to travel by boat, but it's still fun to tour through the mangroves around San Lorenzo or Muisne.

Unless you're on a private boat transport to a smart jungle lodge, seats are invariably wooden and thoroughly uncomfortable. Bring something to sit on and keep food and water with you, as the bulk of your luggage will usually be put under wraps at the front of the boat.

A **chartered boat** (*flete*) is more expensive than going on a public one, though you can reduce costs by gathering a group. Travel around the Galápagos Islands is almost exclusively by boat (see p.342).

By bicycle

Even if Ecuador's chaotic roads don't always make the ideal cycleways, **cycling** can offer unrivalled closeness to the land and its people. Besides, cycling is growing in popularity within the country – president Rafael Correa is an enthusiast – and there are a growing number of cycleways in the major cities and along the coast, most notably the 21-kilometre route between Canoa and Bahía de Caráquez (see p.283). For proper **cycle touring**, you're better off bringing your own bike and equipment from home. The best cycling is off the busy main roads, so you'll need wide tyres, decent pannier clearance, plenty of low gears and preferably 36-spoke wheels. It's good to know that once you're out of the scrum of Quito, the busy Panamericana is often paralleled by less-travelled asphalt and cobbled roads. A good rack, fully waterproof panniers and a secure bike lock are essential. Bicycle **repair shops** (*talleres de bicicletas*) are fairly widespread, but outside major cities will only have parts for rudimentary repairs – bring a comprehensive toolkit and a selection of essential spares. When **planning your route**, don't forget to take account of the altitude.

In the UK, the CTC (Cyclists'Touring Club; ☎01483 238 337, ⓦctc.org.uk), is an excellent source of information and has a great website.

Accommodation

Ecuador provides good value for money across the accommodation spectrum. At the high end, you'll find beautiful haciendas and well-known international luxury hotel chains. Mid-range hotels are as good as any in North America or Europe, while travellers on a tight budget can find a decent budget hotel or hostel in just about every town in Ecuador.

Supply is such that it's unlikely you'll have any trouble getting a cheap room, though coastal resorts can get very crowded during holidays, and city accommodation tends to fill up for major fiestas. Except for the Galápagos Islands, the top jungle lodges and the most popular seaside resorts, there's not much of a price difference between **seasons**, but broadly speaking the high season is mid-June to August and December to January, and at beach resorts during national holidays. Choices at the top end are always fewer, so if you're on a higher budget, it's a good idea to book ahead. **Discounts** are sometimes negotiable out of season too and midweek in places that are mainly weekend destinations, such as Otavalo. The more expensive hotels are likely to add **22 percent** onto your bill: 12 percent for the IVA, plus a 10 percent service charge. We have included the total amount in the price where relevant.

Hotels masquerade under a variety of names in Ecuador; generally, in increasing order of comfort, they are: *pensión*, *residencial*, hostal, hotel and hostería. Beware of anything calling itself a *motel*, which in Ecuador indicates the sort of place that charges by the hour. Some *hoteles* are as bad as the worst *pensiones*, however, and there's no substitute for having a good look round yourself before you sign in.

There are differences between the highlands and lowlands, too. In the highlands, you'll get **hot water** in all but the cheapest joints, but in the lowlands, where people sometimes consider it unnecessary, only the smarter places will offer it. Conversely, **a/c** and fans are more common at a cheaper level in the lowlands than in the highlands. **Mosquito nets** are usually only in evidence on the coast and in jungle lodges – consider bringing one from home.

ACCOMMODATION PRICES

The **accommodation prices** in this book refer to the cheapest en-suite double room in high season, and include all taxes (see p.29), but not breakfast, unless otherwise stated. They should only be treated as approximations however; room rates fluctuate significantly, often depending on how busy a hotel is at any particular time, while haggling and booking online can often secure you a discount or a cheaper deal. Note also that some coastal destinations will hike their prices even higher for holiday periods such as Christmas, Carnaval or Easter.

Pensiones and residenciales

The humblest type of accommodation is the **pensión**, usually a simple family home around a small courtyard with a couple of basic rooms and a cold-water shared bathroom. At $10–15 for a double, this is about as cheap as you can go without being in a tent. At these prices *pensiones* tend to be either great value or uninhabitable. **Residenciales** are larger, slightly more comfortable versions of the *pensión*, on the whole offering simple, modestly furnished rooms, often arranged around a courtyard or patio. They usually contain little more than a bed, and most, but not all, have shared bathrooms.

Hostales and hoteles

A **hostal** or **hotel** can be anything from an attractive nineteenth-century family house, with waxed wooden floorboards, floor-to-ceiling windows and courtyards draped with flowers, to a generic, uninspiring hotel block, or a fabulous luxury chain hotel. Facilities, on the whole, are better than in a *residencial*, with more likelihood of private bathrooms, hot water, clean towels, soap and cable TV. They can cost anywhere between $15 and $100 for a double. Rooms should be well kept, clean and fresh, have good mattresses, phone, cable TV, air conditioning (in the lowlands) and all-day hot water powered by a *calefón* (water heater) rather than an electric shower – a terrifying-looking contraption bolted on to the shower head with wires dangling around everywhere (touching the pipes can give you a mild shock when it's on). The best luxury hotels have all you'd expect of such places anywhere in the world and charge prices to match.

TOP 5 BOUTIQUE HOTELS

Casa Gangotena Quito. See p.82
Finch Bay Puerto Ayora. See p.349
Hacienda Cusín Otavalo. See p.112
Hotel Casa del Águila Cuenca. See p.189
Mansión del Río Guayaquil. See p.306

Ecuador has numerous **hostels** (note, these are not that same as hostales) several of which are accredited with Hostelling International (HI). They're often quite comfortable, with dorms as well as double rooms. Prices are often a bit more expensive than perfectly adequate non-hostel accommodation, but hostels usually have advantages such as a social atmosphere and organized events.

Haciendas and lodges

Among the accommodation treats of highland Ecuador are the **haciendas**, grand farming estates of colonial times converted into magnificent, out-of-the-way hotels – and some are still also working farms. Many are truly luxurious, with period details, such as open fires in each room, augmented by modern comforts, including plush carpets and thundering hot-water showers. They're sometimes called **hosterías**, which signifies a large country hotel, but this category also includes the far less charming out-of-town tourist complexes.

Lodges are normally found in forested regions and serve as bases for exploring the surrounding environment. The top-end ones have all the modern comforts allowed by their isolated locations. Most, though, won't have electricity, and some are lodges only in name, perhaps little more than open-sided shelters with raised platforms, mattresses and mosquito nets. Lodges usually consist of a collection of **cabañas**, simple cabins with thatched roofs and wooden walls and floors. These are also popular on the coast.

Camping

With so few designated campsites in the country and accommodation being so cheap, few people bother with **camping**, unless they're out exploring Ecuador's wildernesses. Generally, you are allowed to pitch a tent inside most parks and reserves, where you can sometimes use the facilities of a nearby guard post or refuge, but on the whole you'll have to be entirely self-sufficient. Camping near towns is uncommon and not particularly safe.

A few hotels allow you to pitch a tent on their grounds and use their facilities at low rates.

Food and drink

You can eat well for little money in Ecuador, though standard restaurant meals throughout the country tend to be the same – either fish, chicken or beef served with rice, chips and/or *patacones* (fried plantain), topped off with a bit of salad.

Eating out

Ecuador's restaurants range from those charging Western prices for top-class international cuisine to grimy roadside diners serving chicken, rice and little else. The majority of **restaurants**, however, are clean but modest and offer decent food at low prices. Most of them simply call themselves **restaurantes**, but others you might encounter are **cevicherías** (for ceviche), **asaderos** (usually roast chicken), **pizzerías** (pizzas), **marisquerías** (seafood), **comedores** (usually for cheap set meals), **picanterías** (cheap snacks and sometimes spicy food), **parrilladas** (grill-houses) and **paradores** (roadside stophouses). The Chinese restaurant, or **chifa**, is to Ecuador what the curry house is to the UK.

Vegetarian food

Vegetarians are likely to become well acquainted with *pizzerías* and *chifas* for their *tallarines con verduras* (noodles and veg), among the few hot veggie meals available across the country. There's no shortage of vegetarian food in the main tourist centres, but away from those, the cry of *"soy vegeteriano"* or *"vegeteriana"* for a woman ("I'm a vegetarian"), will sometimes be met with offers of fish or chicken. A quick discussion with the staff usually ends with them finding something appropriate for you, even if it's just egg, chips and rice.

Costs

Eating out can be very economical if you stick to **set menus**; at **lunch** this is called almuerzo and at **dinner** merienda, and consists of two or three courses and a drink for about $3–5. **À la carte** and individual **main courses** (*platos fuertes*) are typically $6–9 – you're probably in a smart place if it's much more than $9. Remember, many places will add twelve percent **tax** (IVA) and ten percent service to your bill; prices in this book include all relevant taxes. At some restaurants (usually at the cheaper end of the scale) you will only be charged IVA if you ask for an itemized bill.

Markets and street food

Markets are among the cheapest sources of food, not only because of the nutritious fruits and produce on offer, but also for the makeshift restaurants and **stalls** doling out fried meats, potatoes and other snacks. Although some stallholders may not be overly scrupulous on the hygiene front, sizzling-hot food prepared and cooked in front of you should be fine. **Street vendors** also offer **snacks** such as *salchipapas*, a bag of chips propping up a sausage. Vendors often sell their wares on buses – as you haven't seen how or where these have been prepared, you should probably resist their advances.

Comida típica

Ecuador's three geographical regions produce a startling array of foods, including unusual exotic fruits, and distinct regional styles of cooking. It's easy to tire of Ecuador's standard restaurant cuisine, so look out on menus for the more exciting **comida típica**, the traditional food of each region.

Highland cuisine

In the **highlands**, a typical meal might start off with a *locro*, a **soup** of potato, cheese and corn with half an avocado tossed in for good measure. Its relative, the *yaguarlocro*, swaps the avocado for a sausage of sheep's blood, tripe and giblets. Other soups include *caldo de patas*, cattle hoof soup, and *caldo de gallina*, chicken soup. A number of different grains, such as *morocho*, similar to rice, and quinoa are also thrown into soups, along with whatever meat and vegetables are available. Other **starters**, or snacks, include empanadas, corn pasties filled with vegetables, cheese or meat.

For a **main course** you might go for *llapingachos*, cheesy potato cakes often served with chorizo (sausage), *lomo* (steak) or *pollo* (chicken) and fried eggs. The famous *cuy*, guinea pig roasted whole, has been for centuries a speciality of the indigenous highlanders. Another traditional dish is *seco de chivo*, a stew usually made out of mutton in the highlands, and goat on the coast. The unappetizing-looking *guatita*, pork stomach smothered in peanut sauce, is much better than it sounds.

Mote, a hard corn peeled with calcium carbonate solution and then boiled in salt water, is frequently served as an accompaniment to main courses, particularly *fritada*, seasoned pork deep-fried in lard, and *hornado*, pork slow-roasted in the oven.

TOP 5 ECUADORIAN RESTAURANTS

HJ Gourmet & Grill Bahía de Caráquez.
See p.287
La Mirage Cotacachi. See p.116
Tiestos Cuenca. See p.191
Urko Quito. See p.84
Zazu Quito. See p.84

Motepillo is a Cuenca speciality, in which the *mote* is mixed with eggs to make corn-filled scrambled eggs. Another common side dish is *tostado*, toasted maize, or *canguil*, popcorn that often comes with soups and ceviches.

For **pudding**, there's *morocho de leche*, similar to rice pudding; *quesadillas*, baked cheese doughballs brushed with sweet syrup; *humitas*, ground corn mixed with cheese, sugar, butter and vanilla, wrapped in banana leaves and steamed; or *quimbolitos*, which are similar but more spongey. *Higos con queso*, figs with cheese, is another common highland dessert.

Coastal cuisine

Coastal delicacies, unsurprisingly, centre on **seafood**. The classic **ceviche** is prepared by marinating raw seafood in lime juice and chilli, and serving it with raw onion. It can be dangerous to eat uncooked seafood, so it's worth knowing that shrimps (*camarones*) and king prawns (*langostinos*) are usually boiled for ten minutes before they're marinated. If a *cevichería* (ceviche restaurant) looks unhygienic, skip it. On the north coast, *encocados* are fantastic fish dishes with a Caribbean flavour, cooked in a sauce of coconut milk, tomato and garlic and often served with a huge mound of rice. Bananas and plantain may replace the potato, appearing in many different forms. *Patacones* are fried thick-cut plantains served with plenty of salt, while *chifles* are thinly cut plantains cooked the same way. *Bolón de verde* is a rather stodgy ball of mashed baked plantain, cheese or baked pork and coriander traditionally served as a snack with coffee. The cuisine of Manabí is particularly fabled for creativity, while that of Esmeraldas has the strongest African influence.

Amazon cuisine

The **Oriente** has rather less well-defined speciali-ties, but you can count on *yuca* (a manioc similar to yam), alongside rice, bananas and river fish. As a guest of a forest community, you may eat game such as wild pig or *guanta*, a large rodent not that different from *cuy*. You will also see *chontacuro* – a thick edible larva eaten live or, more palatably as a kebab, tasting a bit like smoked sausage.

Drinks

Ecuador has more types of **fruit** than you can imagine – certainly far more than there are English names for – and just about all of them are made into mouthwatering **juices** (*jugos*). The most common fruit juices are made from *maracuyá* (passion-fruit), *tomate de árbol* (tree tomato, also known in the West as tamarillo; it's orange and more fruity than a tomato), *naranjilla* (native to Ecuador, sweet and tart at the same time), *piña* (pineapple), *naranja* (orange), *guanábana* (a very sweet white fruit), *taxo* (another kind of passion-fruit), *mora* (blackberry) and *babaco* (indigenous relative of the papaya, juicy and slightly acidic), but there are many others. Juices can come pure (*puro*) or mixed with water (make sure it's purified). When they're mixed with milk they're called *batidos*. **Fizzy drinks** (*colas* or *gaseosas*) can be obtained all over Ecuador, as can bottled **mineral water**: still is "*sin gas*", sparkling is "*con gas*".

Hot drinks

Considering Ecuador is a major **coffee**-producing country, it's a shame there's not more of the real stuff about. Most cafés and restaurants will have a jar of Nescafé on the table, though a few places have *esencia de café*, a liquid coffee distillate. You'll get a cup of hot milk if you ask for *café con leche*, and hot water for black coffee if you specify *café negro* (*tinto*). Only in smarter places are you likely to get a *café pasado* or filter coffee. **Tea** (*té*) is served without milk and usually with a slice of lemon. Asking for *té con leche* is likely to get you a cup of hot milk and a teabag. For just a dash of milk, it's best not to say anything until your (milkless) tea arrives, and then ask for a little milk. **Herbal teas** (*aromáticas* or *aguas de viejas*) are widely available.

Alcohol

Apart from the output of a few small microbreweries in the biggest cities, Ecuadorian **beer** essentially comes in two forms: Pilsener is the people's beer, weak, light and in big bottles; Club is a bit stronger, a bit more expensive and comes in a green bottle; Club "rojo" ambers and "negra" and new "chocolate" stouts are periodically available. Latin American imports like Brahma and Corona are increasingly common, while European and US beers are pricey, as are beers from the booming local craft beers scene. You'll find good Chilean and Argentine **wine** in the better restaurants for much more than you'd pay at home.

The local tipple, especially in the sierra, is **chicha**, a fermented corn drink of which there are many varieties. Buckets – literally – of the stuff do the rounds at all highland fiestas. In the Oriente, the *chicha* is made from *yuca*, which is chewed up, spat in a pot and allowed to ferment. *Aguardiente* (also called *caña* or *punta*) is a sugar-cane **spirit**, sharper than rum (*ron*), that will take off the roof of your mouth. In fiestas they might mix it with fruit juices, or in the sierra drink it as *canelazo*, adding sugar, cinnamon (*canela*), naranjilla juice and hot water. On the coast it stars in many cocktails, the most ubiquitous being *caipiriña*.

The sale of alcohol, except during daytime hours in restaurants, is illegal on Sundays except in restaurants until 6pm, though this law isn't always adhered to.

The media

The media in Ecuador are divided between its two great cities, with ownership of the main national and television stations based in Quito and Guayaquil. Even on the televised nightly news, coverage is split equally between newsdesks based in each city. Under the Correa administration, media have become largely polarized between independent private companies subject to government harassment, according to human rights organizations, and publicly funded outlets supporting the government.

Newspapers run the gamut from national broadsheets offering in-depth reporting to tabloids revelling in lurid tittle-tattle. **Television**, on the whole, has a smattering of quality programmes, but is dominated by imports, soaps and game shows. Ecuador has many local **radio** stations, which are considered the glue that binds remote communities together.

Newspapers

Ecuador produces several high-quality daily **newspapers**. Leaders of the pack are the Quito-based *El Comercio*, a traditional **broadsheet** that has good coverage of home and international news, and El Universo, with Ecuador's widest circulation, from Guayaquil. There are a number of **regional newspapers** too, such as Guayaquil's *Expreso* and *El Mercurio* in Cuenca, and *La Hora*, with numerous regional editions.

A few **English-language** city guides and magazines are published in Quito, including *This is Ecuador* (ⓦthisisecuador.com) and Ñan (ⓦnanmagazine.com), which has an app. Imported news magazines are usually only found in the tourist centres, where you're also likely to get copies of the *International New York Times* and the overseas edition of the *Miami Herald*.

Radio

Radio is an important part of community life, particularly in the rural regions. **Religious broadcasting** from evangelical Christians is also widespread. With a smartphone and near-ubiquitous wi-fi or a local 4G SIM card, radio apps get you broadcasts from around the globe.

Television

Ecuador has several private and public **national television** broadcasters, and numerous other **regional channels**. Of the nationals, Ecuavisa and Teleamazonas are the most highbrow, providing the best news bulletins and the occasional quality imported documentary. At the other end of the spectrum, there's government-run Gamavision, which has a penchant for screening soaps (*telenovelas*). **Cable** and satellite TV have made big inroads, and even budget hotels often have it, with programming in Spanish and English.

Festivals

Ecuador has a long tradition of festivals and fiestas, dating from well before the arrival of the Spanish. Many of the indigenous festivals, celebrating, for example, the movements of the sun and the harvests, became incorporated into the Christian tradition, resulting in a syncretism of Catholic religious imagery and older local beliefs. Most national holidays mark famous events in post-Conquest history and the standard festivals of the Catholic Church.

For most Ecuadorians, big fiestas are community-wide events that define local and national identity. If you get the chance, you should get to a fiesta at some point during your stay; these are among the most memorable and colourful expressions of Ecuadorian culture.

Carnaval is one of the more boisterous national festivals, culminating in an orgy of water fights before Lent. **Local fiestas** can also be rowdy, and are reasonably frequent. Most towns and villages have a foundation day or a saint's day festival, and then maybe another for being the capital of the canton (each province is divided into several cantons). Provincial capitals enjoy similar festivals. You can expect anything at these celebrations: music, dance, food, drink, gaudy parades, beauty pageants, bullfights, marching bands, tournaments and markets. In the remoter highland communities, they can be very local, almost private affairs, yet they'll usually welcome the outsider who stumbles in. Local people will be much more wary of ogling, snap-happy intruders – sensitivity is the key.

Public holidays and festivals

On public holidays just about all shops except malls and facilities are closed all day.

JANUARY

New Year's Day (Año Nuevo), January 1. Public holiday.
Epiphany (Reyes Magos), January 6. Celebrated mainly in the central highlands, most notably at Píllaro in Tungurahua, but also in Montecristi on the coast.

FEBRUARY/MARCH

Carnival (Carnaval; Monday and Tuesday are public holidays). The week before Lent is marked by nationwide high jinks, partying and water-throwing. In Ambato, it's celebrated by the grand *Fiesta de las Frutas y las Flores*, with parades, dancing, bullfights and sporting events – water-throwing is banned here.

MARCH/APRIL

Holy Week (Semana Santa; Maundy Thursday and Good Friday are public holidays). Religious parades take place across the country during Holy Week, when lots of people head to the beach. The big processions in Quito are on Good Friday.

MAY

Labour Day (Día del Trabajo), May 1. Public holiday.
Battle of Pichincha (La Batalla del Pichincha), May 24. Public holiday commemorating the 1822 battle that secured independence from Spain.

JUNE

Corpus Christi A moveable festival sometime in mid-June, on the first Thursday after Trinity Sunday. Celebrated in the central sierra, particularly Salasaca and Pujilí, with *danzantes* (masked dancers), wonderful costumes and, in the latter town, 5–10m poles people climb to get prizes at the top; also notable in Cuenca.
Festival of the Sun (Inti Raymi), June 21 and onwards.
A pre-Conquest festival celebrated on the solstice at important ancient sites such as Cochasquí. Also subsumed into the Catholic festivals of

San Juan, San Pedro and San Pablo, collectively known as "Los San Juanes" in the Otavalo and Cayambe regions.
San Juan June 24. St John the Baptist's day, celebrated particularly heartily in the Otavalo region, beginning with ritual bathing in Peguche and ending with *tinku* – ritual fighting – in San Juan on the outskirts of Otavalo (now discouraged). Outsiders should avoid these two activities.
San Pedro and San Pablo June 29. Celebrated across the country, particularly in Cayambe and the northern sierra.

JULY

Foundation of Guayaquil July 25. Local celebrations featuring parades, preceded by three weeks of cultural events and assorted festivities.

AUGUST

Independence Day (Día de la independencia) August 10. Public holiday commemorating the nation's first independence (and thwarted) uprising in Quito in 1809.
Festival of the Virgin of El Cisne August 15. The effigy of the virgin is paraded 72km from El Cisne to Loja followed by thousands of pilgrims.

SEPTEMBER

Yamor Festival A big shindig in Otavalo for the first two weeks of September.
Mama Negra de la Merced September 24. The religious one of two important fiestas in Latacunga, focusing on the Virgen de la Merced.

OCTOBER

Independence of Guayaquil October 9. Big celebrations in Guayaquil. Public holiday.
Columbus Day (Día de la Raza), October 12. Marks the discovery of the New World. Rodeos held in Los Ríos, Guayas and Manabí provinces.

NOVEMBER

All Souls' Day/Day of the Dead (Día de los Difuntos) November 2. Highland communities go to cemeteries to pay their respects with flowers, offerings of food and drink, and incantations. Public holiday.
Independence of Cuenca November 3. The city's largest celebration, which merges into the preceding holidays. Public holiday.
Mama Negra First Friday or Saturday of November. Famous fiesta in Latacunga with colourful parades and extravagant costumes, centred around the Mama Negra – a blacked-up man in woman's clothing – thought to be related to the town's first encounter with black slaves. Events continue up to November 11 celebrating the independence of Latacunga (possibly subject to the Cotopaxi eruptive process).
Festival of the Virgin of El Quinche November 21. Pilgrims celebrate at the baroque Quinche church outside Quito.

DECEMBER

Foundation of Quito December 6. Festivities across the capital over the preceding week, with parades, dances, bullfights and sporting events. Public holiday.
Christmas Day (Navidad), December 25. Public holiday.
New Year's Eve (Nochevieja), December 31. *Años viejos*, large effigies of topical figures representing the old year are burnt at midnight.

Sports and outdoor activities

Having so much untamed wilderness within easy striking distance of major population centres, Ecuador is a superb destination for outdoor enthusiasts. Traditionally it's been a target for climbers, as it boasts ten volcanoes over 5000m, including the beautifully symmetrical Cotopaxi, and the point furthest from the centre of the Earth, the summit of Chimborazo. Ecuador has also made a name for itself in international rafting and kayaking circles, while hiking, mountain biking, surfing, diving, fishing and horse riding are all possible. Birdwatching is another big draw, with Ecuador having more than 1600 species of bird, more than a sixth of the world's total.

Climbing

Ecuador's "Avenue of the Volcanoes", formed by the twin range of the Andes running the length of the country, offers numerous **climbing** opportunities, from relatively easy day-trips for strong hill-walkers to challenging technical peaks for experienced climbers. The most popular **snow peaks**, requiring full mountaineering equipment, include **Cotopaxi** (5897m), **Chimborazo** (6268m), **Cayambe** (5790m) and **Iliniza Sur** (5248m). Lower, less demanding climbs, not requiring special equipment and suitable for acclimatizing or simply enjoying them in their own right, include **Guagua Pichincha** (4794m), **Sincholagua** (4893m), **Corazón** (4788m), **Rumiñahui** (4712m), **Imbabura** (4609m) and **Pasochoa** (4200m).

Not all the higher peaks require previous mountaineering **experience**; many (physically fit) beginners make it up Cotopaxi, for instance. Others, such as **El Altar** (5319m), are technically difficult and should only be attempted by experienced climbers. It's essential that climbers with limited mountaineering experience should be accompanied by an experienced and reliable **guide**, whose first concern is safety. Ecuador's best-trained mountain guides are certified by an organization called ASEGUIM (Asociación Ecuatoriana de Guías de Montaña, Pinto E4-385 and J.L. Mera in Quito ☎02 2234109, ⓦaseguim.org), whose members have to pass exams and take courses spread over a three-year period before receiving the *Diploma de Guía*. It's always worth paying extra for an ASEGUIM guide –

even relatively straightforward, non-technical climbs carry an inherent risk, and your life may depend on your guide. More experienced climbers should also consider ascending with a guide, whose intimate knowledge of the route options, weather patterns, avalanche risks, glaciers and crevasses can make all the difference to the safety and success of an expedition, especially when the rapid melting of the glaciers is changing routes and climbing conditions at a pace. Recommended guides are listed in the relevant chapters (see p.80, p.142 & p.167).

Practical considerations

December and January are generally considered the **best months** to climb, followed by the dry summer months of June to August. March, April and May are the worst months, but because of the topography and microclimates of the land, several mountains, such as Cotopaxi, are more or less climbable throughout the year. The **weather** is highly changeable, as are snow and glacier conditions. Unlike their alpine counterparts, Ecuadorian **glaciers** do not follow normal patterns of ablation and accumulation in summer and winter months respectively. Instead, glacier conditions can change from day to day, meaning the technical difficulty is also constantly changing; all the more reason to employ a properly trained guide who knows the mountain and its variable conditions well.

All your **equipment** will be provided by the guiding company if you're going with one, or can be **rented** from the listed companies. If you have your own plastic mountaineering boots, bring them with you; they will invariably be in better condition than most of the rental boots. Check the equipment over very carefully before deciding which company to sign up with. Guides also provide all **food** on the climb, but you should take your own snacks to keep energy levels up, as well as your own water bottle. **Accommodation** is usually in mountain refuges, which serve as the starting point of the climbs. You will typically only get three or four hours' sleep before a big climb, as it's common to set off around midnight or 1am to arrive at the summit around dawn, and descend before the sun starts to melt the snow.

One point that cannot be stressed forcefully enough is the **importance of acclimatizing** before attempting the higher peaks. This should involve spending a few days at the altitude of Quito (2800m), taking a combination of rest and moderate exercise, followed by at least four or five days around 3500–3800m, interspersed with day-walks up some lower peaks. If you ignore this warning and try to shoot up Cotopaxi after a couple of days' hill-climbing around Quito, you may find yourself suffering from **altitude sickness** (see p.42) as you ascend, or simply feeling too dizzy and nauseous to leave the refuge. A couple of good bases for acclimatizing include the walker's refuge at Urbina (3620m), near Riobamba (see p.167), hotels in and around Cotopaxi National Park (see p.139), and the tiny village of Salinas (3500m), near Guaranda (see p.162).

Several popular, though potentially hazardous, climbs are on **active volcanoes** – particularly Guagua Pichincha, Reventador, Sangay, Cotopaxi and Tungurahua and you should be fully aware of the current situation before you ascend. You can check the latest volcanic activity news on the Instituto Geofísico website Ⓦigepn.edu.ec, or contact the South American Explorers (SAE), (see p.79) for up-to-date climbing conditions. At time of writing, Reventador, Cotopaxi, and Tungurahua summits were off limits to climbers.

Hiking

Ecuador's great wilderness areas and striking landscapes offer fantastic opportunities for **hiking**, though a general absence of well-marked trails and decent trekking maps does mean a little effort is required to tap into the potential.

The widest choice of hikes is found in the sierra, where numerous trails lead into the mountains and up to the páramo, providing access to stunning views and exhilarating, wide-open spaces. The country's best-known long-distance hike is in the southern sierra: the **Inca Trail to Ingapirca** (see p.182), a three-day hike ending up at Ecuador's most important Inca ruins. Also down in the south, **Parque Nacional El Cajas** (see p.193) provides some of the best hiking in the country, in a landscape strongly reminiscent of the Scottish highlands, while **Parque Nacional Podocarpus** offers a fabulous two-day hike across the páramo to the Lagunas del Compadre (see p.205).

Elsewhere in the sierra, rewarding possibilities include day-hikes in the area around **Laguna Quilotoa** (see p.145), and a wonderful two-day hike to El Placer hot springs in **Parque Nacional Sangay** (see p.171). There are fewer options for hiking in the **Oriente**; but hikes descending from highlands to lowlands, such as the one from **Oyacachi to El Chaco** (see p.104), are good for revealing Ecuador's various habitats and landscapes. **Cotopaxi** (see p.137) and **Machalilla** (see p.328) national parks also present good hiking possibilities, as do the highlands.

Guided hikes

One way of getting around logistical difficulties is by **hiring a guide**, usually through a local tour operator. This solves the problem of arranging transport to the trailhead, and means there's far less danger of getting lost. A good guide can also enhance your enjoyment of the hike by sharing his or her knowledge of local flora and fauna with you, or of the history, legends and customs associated with the area. A bad one, however, can really sour the whole experience. When booking a tour, it's always a good idea to ask to meet the person who will be guiding you before parting with your money, and it's essential to make clear what level of difficulty you're willing to tackle, and what pace you want to go at. In many national protected areas, hiring of an official guide is mandatory for groups.

Rafting and kayaking

Whitewater rafting combines the thrill of riding rapids with the chance to reach some spectacular landscapes that otherwise can't be visited.

HIKING EQUIPMENT

If you're thinking of going long-distance hiking without a guide, you should be competent at route finding and map reading, and equip yourself with the necessary IGM **topographical maps** (1:50,000 is the most useful scale) before you leave Quito (see p.48). You will also need a **compass** (GPS is also useful) and – for multi-day hikes – a waterproof **tent**, a warm **sleeping bag** (which needs to be good for –5°C in the sierra), a reliable **stove**, **candles** and waterproof **matches**. Other **equipment** essential for hiking in the sierra – whether you're on a day-hike or long-distance hike, and with or without a guide – includes: strong, water-resistant hiking boots; thermal underwear; warm layers such as a fleece or down jacket; waterproof jacket, trousers and gaiters; hat and gloves; water purification tablets; sunglasses; sunscreen; spare boot laces; and medical kit. You might also consider taking **rubber boots** for wading through the deep mud that commonly blights mountain paths after rainfall. As a general rule, weather conditions in the sierra are driest from June to September and wettest from February to April.

VOLCANOES

Ecuador is one of South America's most volcanically active areas. Its highlands are studded with snow-crested cones either side of a broad central valley, grandly described by explorer Alexander von Humboldt as the "Avenue of the Volcanoes". The **volcanoes** here include the furthest point from the centre of the Earth (Chimborazo); the highest point on the equator (Cayambe); and one of the world's highest active peaks (Cotopaxi) – they attract mountaineers from across the globe.

Although many of Ecuador's 55 volcanic peaks are **extinct**, eight remain **active**, while a further nine have erupted in the last few thousand years and are classified as "potentially active". In recent years the volcanoes causing most disruption have been Cotopaxi and Guagua Pichincha near Quito, Reventador in the Oriente, and Tungurahua, which has been threatening the town of Baños for years. These are not the only active volcanoes in the country; you can keep abreast of any volcanic activity at Ecuador's Instituto Geofísico website ⓦ igepn.edu.ec (in Spanish), the Smithsonian Global Volcanism Program ⓦ volcano.si.edu (in English), or through local media, authorities and your embassy.

A small number of whitewater rafting and **kayaking** companies, mainly based in Quito, Tena and Baños, organize trips to dozens of rivers. Not far from Quito, on the way to Santo Domingo, the **ríos Blanco** and **Toachi** offer a selection of popular runs suitable for beginners and old hands alike. A high density of rivers around **Tena** has brought the town to the fore as a centre for the sport in Ecuador. Among the most popular is the **Upper Napo (Jatunyacu)**, a typical beginner's run, while the nearby **Río Misahuallí** is suitable for more advanced paddlers; it weaves through a stunning canyon in a remote section of rainforest, described as the best rafting trip in the country. Other options from Tena and Baeza include the **Río Hollín**, **Río Anzu** and the **Río Quijos** and tributaries. In the southern Oriente, the **Río Upano** is one of the best runs, involving a trip of several days with the spectacular Namangosa Gorge on the itinerary.

Rapids are categorized according to a **grading system**: beginners can happily handle waters of Class II and III rating, which usually involve substantial sections of quiet paddling between rougher and more exciting rapids; Class V runs are very difficult, sometimes dangerous, and can be terrifying for the non-expert.

Safety

Safety is the prime consideration before you choose to go whitewater rafting or kayaking. Rainfall can have a dramatic effect on a river, and an easy Class II in the dry months can turn into a swollen torrent too dangerous to run in the rainy season. A good rafting company will be on top of the situation and will not attempt to run unsafe water. A few shoddy outfits with untrained guides and inappropriate equipment do exist; only go rafting with a reputable company, those that have fully trained guides who know first aid, can supply good-quality life jackets and helmets and employ a safety kayak to accompany the raft on the run. For runs around Quito, try Yacu Amu rafting (see p.81). Rafting companies in Baños are not as highly regarded as those listed in Tena (see p.239) and Quito. General **information** can be obtained from the Ecuadorian Rivers Institute (ERI), based in Tena (ⓣ 06 288 7438, ⓦ kayakecuador.com).

Birdwatching

With roughly as many species as North America and Europe combined crammed into a country smaller than Nevada, Ecuador has the **best birding in the world**, including hundreds of endemic species. The greatest **diversity** is in the transition zone habitats and montane forests, most famously on the **western flank** of the Andes, part of the Chocó bioregion. **Mindo**, west of Quito, is internationally recognized as an Important Bird Area, and there are several fine private reserves in the northwestern forests renowned for their birdlife (see pp.259–267).

On the **eastern slopes of the Andes** (see pp.222–223) the Cosanga and Baeza areas are recommended, and, in the south, Podocarpus national park and the areas around Loja, Zamora and Vilcabamba. The most convenient way to watch birds in the **Oriente** is at one of the lodges, where ornithologist guides and bird lists, some recording well over 500 species, are provided. There are four main groupings of jungle lodges, each with slightly different species lists: the Cuyabeno area; around Misahuallí and Tena on the upper Río Napo or in Sumaco-Galeras reserve; on the lower Río Napo; and in Pastaza and the Southern Oriente. The best **highland and páramo** habitats are usually found in the national parks, for example El Ángel and Cajas, and the highland sections of Cotacachi-Cayapas and Cayambe-Coca reserves. On the **coast**, Parque Nacional Machalilla and Cerro Blanco hold interesting areas of dry forest and hints of Galápagos birdlife, while the saltpans on the Santa Elena peninsula attract hundreds of sea and shore birds.

It's always worth hiring a local **guide**, who will know where to look and have a knack for picking out birds amid the undergrowth and greenery. Most of the better lodges and private reserves have in-house guides, often trained ornithologists, or will be able to find one for you.

Mountain biking

Mountain biking is more widespread in the sierra than in the lowlands. Several specialist biking operators, mainly based in Quito (see p.80), also arrange mountain-biking tours of various parts of the sierra, such as Cotopaxi National Park, the Papallacta area or the Otavalo region, with both cross-country and downhill routes available. Riobamba (see p.167) also offers good mountain biking. Being at altitude means that some trips can be hard work, but a reasonable level of fitness is generally all that's required. Always check that the bike is in good working order before setting off. The better operators will be able to provide helmets.

Horse riding

Ecuador's sierra region offers numerous opportunities for **horse riding**, particularly at the many haciendas that have been converted into country inns, where riding has been a way of life for

centuries. Riding up to the region's sweeping páramos framed by snowcapped volcanoes is undoubtedly a memorable experience. Ecuadorian **horses** are very tough, capable of climbing steep slopes and trotting and cantering at high altitudes.

Most haciendas and reputable tour companies provide healthy, well-looked-after horses, but it's not unusual for cheaper outfits to take tourists out on neglected, overworked animals. If you sign up to a riding tour and your horse looks lame or ill, refuse to ride it and ask for another one. Check that the saddle is securely fitted, with the girth pulled tight, and take time to adjust your stirrups to the right length – they should be level with your ankles if you let your legs hang freely. Ecuadorian riding outfits rarely provide protective hats.

Two highly recommended **riding operators** are: the German-run Green Horse Ranch, north of Quito (☎08 6125433, ⊛horseranch.de); and the excellent British-run, Quito-based Ride Andes (⊛rideandes .com). Other outfits and guides are detailed throughout the text, including: *Hacienda Guachalá* (see p.101), *Hacienda Cusín*, *Hacienda Pinsaquí* (p.112), *Hacienda Zuleta* (see p.112) and *Hostería La Ciénega* (see p.140).

Diving and snorkelling

Ecuador's top **scuba-diving** spots are in the Galápagos, where there are great opportunities to see large sea fish as well as spectacular endemic reef fish. Most people arrange diving tours before arrival, but there are several operators on the islands who can arrange trips for you there and then (see p.344 & p.348). The Galápagos is not the easiest place for

---

MAGIC BIRDING CIRCUIT

While many birding lodges in Ecuador will organize day-trips to other reserves or lodges to ensure you get to explore a range of habitats and increase your chances of spotting the birds on your wish list, the Magic Birding Circuit (☎02 2247549, ⊛eco-lodgesanjorge.com) is the first of its kind in South America to have its own series of reserves and lodges covering eleven different eco-systems, from high barren plains, through cloudforest, to upper lowland tropical forest and scarce dry tropical forest – all within a two-hour radius from Quito.

Accommodation ranges from the charming old hacienda and former Jesuit monastery, **San Jorge Eco-Lodge and Botanical Reserve** (see p.83), perched above Quito, to the vast-windowed mountainside retreat that is **San Jorge de Tandayapa Lodge** (see p.261), and the capacious bamboo cabañas at **San Jorge de Milpe Orchid and Bird Reserve**, around 12km northwest of Mindo (see p.266). Birding tours from 1–15 days are available, costing around $275–350 per person per day (inclusive of all transport, food, accommodation and bilingual guiding services); budget $195–225 per person for a day-tour from Quito, and from around $1,375 for a five-day tour. Though primarily aimed at serious birders, all the lodges make delightful retreats for more casual nature lovers for a couple of nights, offering high-quality food, stunning views, trails and wonderful wildlife viewing opportunities. They can be booked individually on a nightly basis, though prior notice is needed.

novices to learn to dive – mainly due to strong currents and cold temperatures – but it is possible.

Snorkelling is likely to be an important part of a Galápagos cruise: bring your own gear if you have it; even though most boats can provide it, there may not be enough to go round and what there is may not fit. A **wet suit** is recommended between July and December. Off the mainland coast, there's not a lot of scuba diving or snorkelling, apart from tours arranged in Puerto López (see p.327) for dives and snorkelling around the Isla de la Plata.

Surfing

There are scores of **surfing** spots on the Ecuadorian coast with the greatest concentration in Manabí and Guayas provinces between Playas and Manta. Laidback Montañita in Guayas province has the reputation of being the leading surf centre, though quieter Canoa, and Mompiche to the north, also have a loyal, less hippy-ish following. There are some keen surfers on the Galápagos Islands, particularly on San Cristóbal island. In all these locations, you'll be able to find places to hire a board and get a lesson. The surf **season** is at its height from December to March, when the waves are usually at their fiercest and the water at its warmest.

Paragliding

Paragliding is free flight using a fabric "wing", which resembles a parachute, under which the pilot is suspended by a harness. It is a sport that has had a following in **Quito** (try the Escuela Pichincha de Vuelo Libre at Carlos Endara Oe3-60 and Amazonas; ☎02 2256592) for some time, but which is now spreading to other highland towns, such as **Ibarra** (see p.119) and **Baños** (see p.157), where there are good cliffs and ledges nearby from which to launch. Coastal destinations such as **Canoa** (see p.283) and **Montañita** (see p.323) are also becoming popular places to practise the sport. A few agencies offer tandem flights for beginners, as well as courses.

Fishing

Fishing (*pesca deportiva*) for trout (*trucha*) in the lakes of the sierra is a widespread local hobby. A couple of the national reserves are well-known fishing spots, namely El Ángel in the north and Cajas in the south. Few tours to the **Oriente** forgo the chance of fishing for piranhas, with nothing more sophisticated than a line, hook and bait. Take care when de-hooking Oriente fish: some have

poisonous spines discreetly tucked into their fins. **Deep-sea fishing** is less widespread, with Salinas and Manta the main centres.

National parks and protected areas

Almost nineteen percent of Ecuador's territory is protected within forty national parks, reserves, refuges and recreation areas, including 97 percent of the Galápagos Islands, plus an ample marine reserve surrounding them. Encompassing mangrove swamps, dry and wet tropical coastal forests, cloud- and montane forests, tropical rainforests, páramo and volcanoes, the protected areas represent a cross section of the country's most outstanding natural landscapes and habitats.

Some are so important they have earned international recognition – such as Sangay, a World Natural Heritage Site; Yasuní, a World Biosphere Reserve; and the Galápagos Islands, which are both. Few parks, however, have much in the way of tourist facilities; some parks have rudimentary refuges and a few trails, but for the most part these are pure wildernesses – areas that are primarily protected by virtue of their remoteness and inaccessibility – and exploring them is only possible with a guide and camping equipment or the logistical help of a tour operator.

Visiting national parks

No **permit** is needed to visit Ecuador's national parks, which are all free except the Galápagos Islands ($100), though at the time of writing the government was considering reintroducing park fees. The *guardaparques* are the best people to speak to if you want **information**; they can also put you in touch with a good local guide, if not offer their own services. Alternatively, try the Ministerio del Ambiente office in the nearest town, which should have small leaflets (*trípticos*) about the park and basic maps. The ministry also has a Spanish–English smartphone app, Áreas Protegidas Ecuador, with basic information on all of them, including contact details. Finally, there's the head office in Quito (on the 8th floor of the Ministerio de Agricultura y Ganadería building on avenidas Amazonas and Eloy Alfaro; ☎02 2563429, ⊛ambiente.gob.ec), which keeps information on all the parks.

Few parks have provision for **accommodation**. Wardens are happy to let you **camp**, but there's rarely a designated camping area or camping facilities. Some reserves have a basic **refuge** (*refugio*); most of the volcanoes popular with climbers have these within a day's climb of the summit, usually a hut with a couple of rooms full of bunks, some simple cooking facilities and running water. You should bring your own sleeping bag.

Private reserves

There is also a growing number of smaller **private reserves**, which have been set up for conservation, scientific or ecotourism projects and managed by philanthropists, environmentalists or ecological foundations. Generally, these places are much better geared to receiving tourists than the national parks and many have a purpose-built **lodge** or accommodation within the main research station. They will often also have clear trails, equipment to borrow, guides and information, such as bird lists. Some of the best options are the cloudforest reserves of northwestern Ecuador (see p.258) and the jungle lodges in the Oriente (see pp.234–235).

Culture and etiquette

A little politeness goes a long way in Ecuador, by nature a conservative and generally good-mannered country. An exchange of greetings is de rigueur before conversation, no matter how short or banal the subject; say buenos días before noon, buenas tardes in the afternoon, and buenas noches after nightfall. Shake hands with people you meet, and if it's for the first time, say *mucho gusto* ("pleased to meet you"); it's quite normal to shake hands again when saying goodbye. A more familiar greeting between women or between a man and a woman is a peck on the cheek.

Say *buen provecho* ("enjoy your meal") to your companions before a meal (not before your host if being cooked for), or to fellow diners when entering or leaving a restaurant, and use *con permiso* ("with permission") if squeezing past someone in a crowd.

Clothing and appearance

Neatness in **dress** will always earn respect, particularly in the highlands, where sartorial norms are more formal than on the coast. Men should remove hats or caps indoors, and shorts or skirts shouldn't be worn inside churches, where scruffiness of any sort will be frowned on: shorts for men on the coast are more acceptable. Skimpy dress for women will probably draw unwanted attention (see p.51), while topless or nude bathing on beaches is out of the question.

Dealing with bureaucracy

Politeness and tidy dress are particularly important when dealing with police or officials. Ecuadorian **bureaucracy** can be frustrating, but it's vital to maintain good humour; losing your temper will quickly turn people against you.

While corruption is widely condemned in Ecuador, low-level bribery is routinely practised, with minor officials sometimes asking for "a little something for a cola" (as the cliché goes) in return for a favour or to speed up paperwork. It's an art best left to locals; if you need a special favour, ask an Ecuadorian friend for advice on how to proceed and leave the negotiating up to them if possible. Never openly offer a bribe to anyone or you could end up in serious trouble.

Cultural tips

If arranging to meet someone or inviting someone out, remember **punctuality** obeys the laws of *"la hora ecuatoriana"* ("Ecuadorian time"), meaning Ecuadorians will usually arrive late, up to an hour being well within the bounds of politeness. The person making an invitation is usually expected to pay for everything, especially if it's a man entertaining a woman.

Pointing at people (not objects) with your finger is considered impolite; use your whole hand or chin instead. Beckon people towards you by pointing your hand downwards and towards you.

See Travel Essentials (see pp.45–51) for information on gay and lesbian travellers, travelling with children, tipping and women travellers.

Health

Ecuador has its fair share of scary-sounding tropical diseases, but there's no reason to be paranoid. Most are rare and pose much more of a threat to residents – especially

those from poorer communities – than to tourists. The two illnesses you should be especially vigilant against, however, are stomach upsets caused by contaminated food and water, and malaria. You can dramatically cut the risks of getting either through simple, practical steps.

Standards in Ecuador's health care system are variable. Public **hospitals** and **clinics** are free, but you generally get better quality care in the private sector, where you have to pay before you receive treatment (though costs are lower than in North America and Europe). While there are plenty of good health care options in the bigger cities, your choices are often severely limited in rural areas.

Vaccinations

The only **inoculation** you are legally required to have for Ecuador is yellow fever – but only if you're coming from a tropical African or South American country, when (in theory, at least) you're supposed to show a vaccination certificate. It's a good idea to have the jab anyway if you're planning to visit the Amazon, where the disease is rare but present. Ask your doctor at least two months before travelling whether you need any other vaccinations or malaria prophylaxis, and make sure you're up to date with your vaccinations and boosters for polio, tetanus, diphtheria, hepatitis A and typhoid. Additional jabs to consider are rabies, tuberculosis and hepatitis B, while those consistently exposed to wild rodents for long periods in Loja, Tungurahua or Cañar provinces should ask their health professionals about a plague vaccine.

Food and water

The traveller's commonest health complaint is an **upset stomach**, usually caused by **contaminated food or water**. Except Quito and Cuenca, tap water is unsafe to drink in Ecuador; bottled water and soft drinks, widely available in all but the remotest places, are safe alternatives, but always check that the seal is intact. Wash your hands before meals and use bottled or boiled water to clean your teeth. You can also pick up stomach upsets from swimming in unclean water.

Things to **avoid** include: ice made from tap water; fruit juices with tap water added; raw vegetables and salads; undercooked, partly cooked or reheated fish, crustaceans, meat or eggs; dairy products and ice cream made from unpasteurized milk; and food that's been lying around uncovered. Food that's freshly prepared and hot, and fruit and vegetables that you can peel yourself, rarely cause any harm.

If you want to avoid relying on bottled water, you can **purify your water**. Bringing water to a good rolling boil for a minute (3 minutes at altitude) is extremely effective, though anyone travelling without cooking equipment will find that chemical purification is simpler. Chemical and iodine tablets are small, light and easy to use, and iodine tincture is particularly effective against amoebas and giardia; iodine is unsafe for pregnant women, babies and people with thyroid complaints. Portable water purifiers give the most complete treatment but are expensive and bulky.

Diarrhoea

A bout of **diarrhoea**, sometimes accompanied by vomiting and stomach cramps, is an annoyance most travellers suffer at one time or another. In most cases it passes within a couple of days and is best remedied by resting and drinking plenty of fluids. Avoid milk, alcohol and caffeine-based drinks; still drinks are preferable to fizzy. Rehydration salts are widely available in pharmacies, or you can make your own solution by adding a generous pinch of salt and three to four tablespoons of sugar to a litre of clean water – aim to drink at least three litres a day if you're unwell, or a couple of glasses for every loose movement. Current medical opinion is that you should continue to eat normally, if you feel like eating, rather than fasting. Anti-diarrhoeal drugs only suppress symptoms rather than solving the problem, but can be useful if you're on the move.

Consult a doctor if symptoms last for longer than five days, there is blood in your stools, you also have a high fever or if abdominal pain is severe and constant. Most towns have facilities for testing stool samples; tests often only take a matter of hours, cost a few dollars and are invaluable for diagnosis. Diarrhoea caused by bacteria can be treated with a course of **antibiotics** like Ciprofloxacin (available over the counter in most pharmacies).

Amoebic dysentery and giardia

Ciprofloxacin does not work against **amoebic dysentery** (amoebiasis), which can become very serious if it's not treated with metronidazole (Flagyl), or against **giardia**, a parasitic infection that induces sudden, watery and extra-bad-smelling diarrhoea, bloating, fatigue and excessive rotten-egg-smelling gas. Symptoms wax and wane but can last for weeks if left untreated with a course of metronidazole or tinidazole (Fasigyn); you should avoid alcohol if taking either of these medications.

Cholera

Cholera – transmitted through contaminated water – occasionally breaks out in rural areas, but tends to be very localized and restricted to poor communities with inadequate sanitation. It's unlikely you'll go anywhere near these places, but if you suspect you're infected (symptoms include profuse watery diarrhoea, explosive vomiting and fever), it's easy to treat, provided you get to a doctor immediately and keep rehydrating by drinking large quantities of bottled or boiled water.

Insect-borne diseases

Heavy rains can trigger a sharp increase in **insect-borne diseases**, particularly malaria, dengue fever, and chikungunya. The best way of avoiding such diseases is to not get bitten in the first place. Use insect repellent, cover up as much as possible and sleep in screened rooms with a mosquito net, preferably treated with permethrin repellent.

Hundreds of people contract **malaria** every year in Ecuador, about a third of them with the very serious *falciparum* variety. The worst-affected areas are below 1500m, especially in or around population centres. Above 1500m the risk falls substantially, and above 2500m the malaria mosquito cannot survive. Quito and the Galápagos Islands are malaria-free, and the risk is extremely small in the highlands. The malarial *Anopheles* mosquito bites between dusk and dawn, so dress and protect yourself appropriately before sunset and sleeping.

Consult your doctor if travelling in malarial areas and follow a course of **prophylactic medication**. There are chloroquine-resistant strains of malaria in Ecuador, meaning you'll probably use Lariam (mefloquine), Malarone (atovaquone and proguanil) or Vibramycin (doxycyline). These drugs do not completely wipe out the risk of the disease, and you should always take care to avoid being bitten. Symptoms include fever, diarrhoea, joint pain, shivering and flu-like symptoms; if you suspect you've caught the disease, see a doctor immediately and have a blood test. Symptoms can appear several months after leaving a malarial area. **Dengue fever** is a painful and debilitating disease spread by the *Aedes* mosquito, which bites during the day. There's no vaccine and there's not a lot you can do should you contract it, except resting and taking painkillers (avoid aspirin) and plenty of fluids. Symptoms include headaches, severe joint pain and high fever, though it's usually only fatal if caught repeatedly.

Avoiding insect bites will also provide you with protection against a number of rarer diseases such as: **leishmaniasis**, a parasitic disease spread by the bite of infected sand flies present in lowland Ecuador; **river blindness** (onchocerciasis), spread by the bite of black flies found around fast-moving water, mainly in parts of Esmeraldas province; and **Chagas disease**, which is carried by bugs found in rural mud, thatch and adobe buildings in coastal areas, and transmitted when the bug's faeces are unwittingly rubbed into its bite wound.

Altitude issues

If you've flown to Quito from sea level, you may feel a bit woozy, sleepless and lethargic – normal symptoms of the acclimatization process the body undergoes over a few days as it adjusts to reduced levels of oxygen at **altitude**. Symptoms, which might also include breathlessness, needing to urinate frequently, fatigue and strange dreams, will abate naturally if you rest and avoid alcohol and sleeping pills.

Acute Mountain Sickness

Acute Mountain Sickness (AMS), known as *soroche* in Ecuador, occurs when your acclimatization process does not keep pace with your rate of ascent. It's a debilitating and potentially dangerous condition caused by the reduced oxygen levels and atmospheric pressure at high elevations, and if you're going to go much above 3000m you should be aware of the risks. Your gender and fitness have no bearing on whether you will develop AMS, but children are known to be more susceptible than adults, and, if young, may not be able to tell you they're feeling sick, in which case they shouldn't be taken to high altitudes at all. Teenagers and young adults are also more susceptible and should allow extra days for acclimatization. Symptoms include headaches, nausea and extreme tiredness, dizziness, insomnia, confusion and a staggering gait. The best way to relieve the condition is to **lose altitude**.

You can minimize the risks of developing AMS by ascending to high elevations slowly and allowing yourself to **acclimatize** – don't whizz straight up the nearest volcano without spending a night or two at altitude first. You should also avoid alcohol and salt, and drink lots of water or try the local remedy for altitude sickness, **coca-leaf tea** (*mate de coca*). A course of acetazolamide (Diamox) speeds up the acclimatization process, but this is a prescription-only drug in most countries, as it can be dangerous for people with heart conditions. It's unlikely you'll need this drug in Ecuador, but if you're planning to go to very high elevations, you might consider it as a precaution.

If you develop AMS, it is essential you do not ascend any further. Your condition will worsen and may become life-threatening. There are two severe forms of AMS. **HAPO** (high altitude pulmonary oedema) is caused by a build-up of liquid in the lungs. Symptoms include fever, an increased pulse rate and coughing up white fluid; sufferers should descend immediately, whereupon recovery is usually quick and complete. Rarer, but more serious, is **HACO** (high altitude cerebral oedema), which occurs when the brain gets waterlogged with fluid. Symptoms include loss of balance and coordination, severe lassitude, weakness or numbness on one side of the body and a confused mental state. If you or a fellow traveller displays any of these symptoms, descend immediately, and get to a doctor; HACO can be fatal within 24 hours.

Decompression sickness is a more oblique problem associated with gaining altitude quickly. If you have been scuba diving in the Galápagos or on the coast, wait at least 24 hours before coming to the highlands or flying.

Hypothermia

Another concern for people at altitude is **hypothermia**, an underestimated enemy responsible for more deaths among trekkers and climbers than anything else. Brought on by exposure to cold and when the body loses heat faster than it can generate it, hypothermia is greatly accelerated when you're wet, tired and in the wind. Because early symptoms can include an almost euphoric sense of sleepiness and disorientation, your body's core temperature can plummet to danger level before you know what has happened. Other symptoms are violent shivering, erratic behaviour, slurred speech, loss of coordination and drowsiness, and are much easier to spot in other people than in yourself. Victims should be given dry clothes, warm drinks (slowly) and kept awake and warm.

The sun

It's not a good idea to strip off and soak up the rays of the **equatorial sun**. Serious sunburn and sunstroke are real risks, particularly at altitude, when the temperature is not necessarily that high but the thin air amplifies the harm done by the sun's ultraviolet rays. Jungle and coastal boat rides can also be dangerous, as cool river or sea breezes disguise the effects of the sun as it is reflected off the water. Use a high-factor sunscreen (very expensive if bought locally) reapplying after bathing or exertion, and wear a wide-brimmed hat. Drink plenty of water, and consider taking a rehydration solution or adding more salt to your food to counterbalance the effects of excessive sweating.

Bites and stings

At some point you're bound to come across unfriendly **dogs**, as they're often used in rural communities to deter thieves. If a dog snarls and bares its teeth at you, back off slowly, without turning your back on it, staring at it or showing any fear. Picking up a stone and pretending to throw it sometimes works, but you don't want to provoke an attack either. **Rabies**, though only a remote risk, does exist in Ecuador: if you get bitten or scratched by a dog, cat or most other mammals you should wash the affected area thoroughly with soap and clean water and seek medical attention *immediately*. This is particularly relevant in the southeast Amazon, where vampire bats can transmit rabies.

Stings and bites from other creatures such as scorpions, spiders and snakes are very uncommon but can be terribly painful and, in rare cases, fatal. It's good practice to go through your clothes, socks and shoes before dressing, and to check your bedclothes and under lavatory seats. In the rainforests, watch where you put your feet and hands, and don't lean against trees. Walking around barefoot is an invitation to get bitten or stung and opens the door to hookworm. In tropical areas, mosquitoes can transmit dangerous diseases like dengue, malaria and the Zika virus, which saw an outbreak across South America in 2015 and has been linked to neurological disorders in babies. Pregnant women planning a trip to Ecuador should check ⓦcdc.gov for the latest advice on travel.

Ecuador has its share of venomous **snakes**, but bites are rare, and even if they do strike, there's every chance they won't inject any venom. In the unlikely event of snakebite, keep still. If possible, get someone to kill the snake for identification purpose and seek medical help as quickly as possible. In remote rainforest communities, following local knowledge may sometimes be better than spending hours getting to a hospital. Village doctors (*curanderos*) may know effective antidotes, and be able to prepare them quickly.

Other health hazards

Sexually transmitted diseases are as much a threat here as in any country. **Condoms** (*condones* or *preservativos*) are not as widely available as in Western countries – it's a good idea to take your own supply if you're worried about the safety of unfamiliar brands.

Car crashes cause more injuries to travellers in Ecuador than anything else. Minimize risks by only travelling during the day, wearing seatbelts in cars or helmets on motorbikes, avoiding overloaded buses and changing vehicle if you think the driver is drunk, fatigued or unduly reckless.

MEDICAL RESOURCES

Canadian Society for International Health ☎ 613 241 5785, Ⓦ csih.org. Extensive list of travel health centres.

CDC ☎ 1800 232 4636, Ⓦ cdc.gov/travel. Official US government travel health site.

Hospital for Tropical Diseases Travel Clinic UK Ⓦ www.thehtd .org. UK NHS website with advice on tropical diseases and travel.

International Society for Travel Medicine US ☎ 1404 373 8282, Ⓦ istm.org. Has a full list of travel health clinics.

MASTA (Medical Advisory Service for Travellers Abroad) UK Ⓦ masta.org. See website for the nearest clinic.

The Travel Doctor – TMVC ☎ 1300 658 844, Ⓦ tmvc.com.au. Lists travel clinics in Australia, New Zealand and South Africa.

Tropical Medical Bureau Ireland ☎ 1850 487 674, Ⓦ tmb.ie.

Living in Ecuador

There's plenty of scope for spending fruitful time in Ecuador other than travelling. A huge number of possibilities exist for prospective volunteers, and Ecuador is also one of the top choices on the continent for learning Spanish.

Volunteering

Many opportunities exist for **volunteers**, though most require you to pay your own way for food and accommodation and to stay for at least a month. Reasonable Spanish skills will usually be needed for any kind of volunteer work with communities, and a background in science for research work.

Someone without these skills should still be able to find places with no trouble, especially in areas of conservation work demanding a degree of hard toil, such as reforestation or trail clearing in a reserve. In fact, short-term, unskilled volunteering has evolved into a kind of tourism in its own right in Ecuador, so-called "**voluntourism**". You can arrange to volunteer either from home – probably better for more formal, long-term posts – or on arrival in Ecuador, which is simpler and more convenient. The SAE in Quito (see p.79) keeps files on dozens of organizations looking for volunteers. We've listed below a few popular ones based in Ecuador, plus useful organizations abroad. If the **main purpose** of

your trip is volunteering, you will need to have the appropriate **visa** before you go (see p.46); those planning to work with children should allow enough time for Ecuadorian authorities to carry out checks before travel.

The Volunteer South America website (Ⓦ volunteersouthamerica.net) has a useful list of free and low-cost volunteering opportunities across the continent.

VOLUNTEER CONTACTS IN ECUADOR

AmaZOOnico ☎ 09 980 0463, Ⓦ amazoonico.org. Volunteers needed to help tend to rescued forest animals and show guests around a jungle rehabilitation centre on a tributary of the Río Napo (see p.245). Best to book six months in advance.

Bosque de Paz El Limonal, Imbabura ☎ 06 2648692, Ⓦ bospas .org. This organic, family farm in northwestern Ecuador (see p.124) welcomes volunteers to learn about sustainable farming, clear and maintain trails, and occasionally to show visitors around.

Centro de Investigaciones de los Bosques Tropicales ☎ 08 460 0274, Ⓦ reservaloscedros.org. This organization manages the beautiful and remote Los Cedros reserve (see p.260) and needs volunteers to work on reforestation, trail maintenance and general upkeep of facilities.

Centro de la Niña Trabajadora Huacho 150 and José Peralta, Quito ☎ 02 2654260, Ⓦ cenitecuador.org. An NGO that helps children and families, especially working girls and women, overcome extreme poverty in Quito. Volunteers work in schools, a medical centre, a production workshop or with outreach projects.

Cofán Survival Fund Mariano Cardenal N74-153 and Joaquín Mancheno, Carcelén Alto, Quito ☎ 02 2470946, Ⓦ cofan.org. Volunteers are needed at Cofán communities deep in the Oriente for help on a number of ongoing projects.

Ecuador Volunteer Yánez Pinzón N25-106 and Colón, Quito ☎ 02 2557749, Ⓦ ecuadorvolunteer.com. Organizes placements in social, community, ecological and educational projects.

FEVI San Pedro s/n, Quito ☎ 9980 2640, Ⓦ fevi.org. Volunteers work on projects providing care and education to disadvantaged children, and promoting community development and protection of the environment.

Fundación Ecológica Arcoiris Segundo Cueva Celi 03-15 and Clodoveo Carrión, Loja ☎ 02 2572926, Ⓦ arcoiris.org.ec. Based in Loja, this foundation is concerned with conservation and community projects in southern Ecuador.

Fundación Jatún Sacha Teresa de Cepeda N34-260 and República, Quito ☎ 02 2432240, Ⓦ jatunsacha.org. The foundation manages seven biological stations or reserves around the country, which require volunteers for conservation, education, maintenance, research and agriculture projects.

Fundación Maquipucuna Baquerizo E9-153 and Tamayo, Quito ☎ 02 2507200, Ⓦ maqui.org/ecotourism. Researchers and volunteers are welcome at this reserve in the western flank cloudforests (see p.259) for work on conservation, maintenance, agriculture or education projects.

Río Muchacho Organic Farm Guacamayo Tours, Bolívar 902 and Arenas, Bahía de Caráquez ☎ 05 2691107, ⓦ riomuchacho.com. Volunteers are needed to work on this ecological farm near the coast in Manabí province for reforestation, education in the local school and agriculture (see p.284).

Santa Lucía Cloud Forest Reserve ☎ 02 2157242, ⓦ santaluciaecuador.com. Based in northwestern Ecuador (see p.260), this organization protects community-owned cloudforest, establishes sustainable sources of income and educates local people. Volunteers help with agroforestry, trail clearing, teaching English and other projects.

Yachana Foundation Vicente Solano E12-61 and Av Oriental, Quito ☎ 02 2523777, ⓦ yachana.org.ec. Operates Yachana Lodge (see p.246) and works with Oriente communities to develop medical care, ecotourism, sustainable agriculture and education programmes, all with a view to conserving the rainforest. Needs volunteers to help with all these projects.

Language schools

One-to-one **Spanish lessons** arranged in Ecuador generally cost less than $10 an hour, offering tremendous value for money to prospective learners. Most language schools are based in Quito (see box, p.89), with a few in Cuenca (see box, p.192) and the other main tourist centres. You'll normally have lessons for the morning or afternoon, and there are often social activities arranged in the evenings and at weekends. To immerse yourself totally in the language, **homestays** arranged through language schools are a good idea. You can arrange Spanish courses in Ecuador from home, but it's unlikely to be as cheap as doing it when you get there.

More adventurous linguists could also have a stab at learning an indigenous language, such as **Kichwa**, which a few schools offer on the side. The reaction you'll get from native speakers, even with some elementary knowledge, is well worth the effort.

Work

Unless you have something arranged in advance, you're unlikely to find much paid work in Ecuador. As an English-speaker, the only type of job you can expect to get with relative ease is as an **English-language teacher**, especially in Quito or Guayaquil. Don't expect to be paid very much, unless you have a TEFL (Teaching English as a Foreign Language) or similar qualification. You'll need a work visa, too, which can be expensive to get – enough to put most people off in the first place (see p.46). If you have any training in ecology, biology, ornithology and the like, you could contact the jungle lodge operators asking if they need a **guide**. Fluent English-speakers with such qualifications are often in demand.

Travel essentials

Costs

Although prices have risen since dollarization, those on a really tight budget should be able to get by on about $30–40 per day, with the occasional treat. Spending $50–80 daily will get you accommodation in more comfortable hotels, better food and the occasional guided tour. Those spending over $150 a day (travelling independently) are likely to find themselves in the country's better hotels and restaurants.

The most widespread **hidden cost** is **IVA** (*Impuesto al Valor Agregado*), a tax of 12 percent added to most goods and services. In lower-end restaurants and hotels it's taken for granted that IVA is included in the quoted price. Other places will add it to the end of the bill, often in tandem with a further ten percent service charge, making the final total 22 percent more than you might have bargained for, although more and more restaurants are including these charges upfront in menus. Car rental is almost always quoted without IVA. If in doubt, always clarify whether prices for anything from souvenirs to room rates include IVA.

Crime and personal safety

Ecuador's reputation for being one of the safer Latin American countries has in recent years been tested by rising crime levels. Still, there's no need to be paranoid if you take sensible precautions.

Pickpockets and **thieves** favour crowded places, typically bus stations, markets, city centres, public transport, crowded beaches, fiestas and anywhere lots of people congregate, providing them with cover. When out and about, carry as little of value as you possibly can, and be **discreet** with what you have. Secret pockets or money belts are useful, but don't reveal hiding places in public. Split up your reserves in different places, making it less likely that you'll lose everything in one go.

On buses, keep close watch on your **bags**; don't put them under your seat or in overhead storage. The same goes for in restaurants – wrap the bag straps around your chair or leg. Be wary of people approaching you in the street, no matter how polite or smartly dressed. It's a common trick to use **distraction** to take your mind off your belongings; spilling something messy on you is a perennial favourite. Take care when using **ATMs**; you are particularly vulnerable from both robbers and card scammers if using machines on the street. Use machines inside banks and buildings where possible, during business hours.

Travelling at night, whether in your own vehicle or on public transport, is a bad idea. This is especially true in Guayas and southern Ecuador, where hold-ups have been an ongoing problem, as well as Esmeraldas province and the border regions with Colombia. In the big cities, especially Quito, always take a **taxi** at night rather than wandering the streets; it's safest to call a registered taxi through your hotel or a taxi app rather than hail one in the street.

Armed robbery is a problem throughout the country, and is on the rise in Quito's Mariscal district. Other danger spots are parts of the old town, the walk up to El Panecillo (always take a cab), Rucu Pichincha and Cruz Loma volcanoes (*not* including the TelefériQo complex itself), and parques El Ejido and La Carolina. Security in Guayaquil is improving, but nevertheless you should be extra vigilant in the downtown areas, the dock and the bus terminal.

Never accept food, drinks, cigarettes or other objects from people you don't know well, to minimize the risk of **drugging**. Chemicals have even been suffused into leaflets and paper, which when handled make victims compliant.

Border areas and crossings are always places to be extra vigilant. **Drug smuggling** and Colombian **guerrilla activity** along the northern border have made certain (remote) parts of Sucumbíos (capital Lago Agrio), Carchi (capital Tulcán) and Esmeraldas (capital Esmeraldas) provinces unsafe. San Lorenzo in the north has a problem with gun crime and "express kidnappings" have been reported in Huaquillas and Macará on the southern border. The Cordillera del Cóndor, southeast of Zamora, a region long involved in a border dispute with Peru, still contains unmarked **minefields** and should be avoided altogether.

Stay informed by referring to your government's website for the latest **travel advice** (see p.50).

Drugs

The possession of **drugs** is a serious offence in Ecuador. While tolerance of small amounts is a hot political issue, people who've been charged may have to contend with the country's dilapidated and overcrowded prisons for more than a year before they're even brought to trial, not to mention being at the mercy of corrupt officials. If offered drugs in the street, walk away. Don't take any chances with drugs or drug dealers – setups have happened and raids are common in "druggie" places such as Montañita and certain Quito clubs. It's simply not worth the consequences.

Police

The only contact you're likely to have with the **police** (*policía*) are at road **checkpoints** at various places around the country, where you may be registered. Generally the police are polite and helpful, particularly the specially designated **tourist police** who patrol areas popular with travellers.

It's rare, but there are reports of corrupt or false police planting drugs in bags – the idea being to extract a large "fine" from the terrified tourist. Plain-clothes "police" should always be dealt with cautiously; pretending you don't understand and walking away is a strategy.

If you are the victim of a crime, you should go to the police as soon as possible to fill out a report (*denuncia*). In an emergency, call ☎911 in Quito, Guayaquil and Cuenca, or ☎101 elsewhere.

Electricity

110V/60Hz is the standard supply, and sockets are for two flat prongs. Fluctuations in the supply are common so use a surge protector if you're plugging in expensive equipment.

Entry requirements

Most nationals, including citizens of the EU, US, Canada, Australia and New Zealand, do not need a tourist visa, and only require a passport valid for more than six months; in theory, you are also supposed to have a return ticket and proof of having enough money for the duration of the stay too, but these are rarely checked. Your passport will be stamped on arrival and you'll be issued with a **T-3 embarkation card**, which you should keep – it will be collected when you leave the country. The T-3 gives you **90 days** in Ecuador. If you want to extend your stay, you will probably need to apply for a visa. People who **overstay** are likely to be fined and banned from Ecuador for six months.

Visas

If you plan to stay in Ecuador for more than ninety days or are visiting for some purpose other than tourism, you'll need a **visa**. Visas are divided into those for immigrants (10-I to 10-VI) and non-immigrants (12-I to 12-X), including those for study (12-V), work (12-VI), volunteering (12-VII), cultural exchanges (12-VIII) or business and tourism (12-IX and 12-X). Each has its own application procedure and **fee**, which varies from $30 to $200 depending on type, plus $30 for the application form. For details, check the Ecuadorian Ministerio de Relaciones Exteriores website Ⓦ www.cancilleria .gob.ec.

The rules for **extending a T-3 embarkation card** are confusing and change regularly. The latest information is that a T-3 cannot be renewed, though there are reports that it's possible to leave and re-enter the country and be issued with a new T-3 for another 90 days –however, this doesn't seem completely reliable and there have been cases of people being refused new cards. Stays longer than 180 days a year are impossible without one.

The other option is to get a 12-IX or 12-X visa from the Dirección General de Asuntos Migratorios y Extranjería, Edificio Solís, Av 10 de Agosto 21-255 and Carrión in Quito (Ⓣ 02 2227025). Allow at least a week, preferably more, on your T-3 card to obtain the visa. Whichever way you extend your visit, you will only be allowed to stay a total of **180 days** in any 12-month period.

Once in Ecuador, visa holders must **register** at the Dirección General de Extranjería at the corner of San Ignacio 207 and San Javier (Ⓣ 02 2221817; Mon–Fri 8am–12.30pm) in Quito, or the Sub-Dirección General de Extranjería in Guayaquil (Ⓣ 04 2322692) within 30 days of arrival in order to get a **censo** (resident identity card). The process takes several days. Holders of immigrant visas will also need to get a *cédula* (national identity card); ask at the Extranjería for details.

If you're seeking to become a **long-term resident**, it pays to do plenty of research beforehand and to find a reputed immigration lawyer to help you through the complicated legal process. Costs run to $400–800 for a visa. Information and assistance can be found on the website Ⓦ pro-ecuador.com.

Identification

The law requires you to carry "**proper identification**" at all times – for foreigners this means a **passport**. Visa holders will also need to carry their identification card (*cédula*) and any other relevant documentation. Photocopies of the stamps and important pages are usually sufficient, so you can keep the original in a safe place. In the Oriente and border areas, only the originals will do. If the authorities stop you and you can't produce identification, you can be detained.

ECUADORIAN EMBASSIES ABROAD

Australia 6 Pindari Crescent, O'Malley, Canberra, ACT 2606
Ⓣ 02 6286 4021, Ⓦ australia.embajada.gob.ec
Canada 50 O'Connor St, Office 316, Ottawa, Ontario K1P 6L2
Ⓣ 613 563-8206, Ⓦ embassyecuador.ca
Ireland 27 Library Rd, Dun Laoghaire, Dublin Ⓣ 01 280 5917,
Ⓔ ececudublin@mmrree.gov.ec

New Zealand Level 9, 2 Saint Martins Lane, Auckland Ⓣ 09 303 0590, Ⓔ elanglinks@aix.co.nz
UK Flat 3b, 3 Hans Crescent, London SW1X 0LS Ⓣ 020 7584 1367, Ⓦ ecuadorembassyuk.org.uk
US 2535 15th St NW, Washington, DC 20009 Ⓣ 202 234-7200, Ⓦ ecuador.org

Gay and lesbian travellers

Ecuador took a leap forward in **gay and lesbian rights** by reforming its constitution in 1998 to outlaw discrimination on the basis of sexuality, and again in 2008 to allow same-sex civil unions. Yet it's still a very macho society and public attitudes have a fair bit of catching up to do. There is a blossoming gay scene in Quito and Guayaquil, but gay couples in Ecuador tend to avoid revealing their orientation in public places. Gay and lesbian travellers are probably best off following their example – overt displays of affection are likely to be met with stern disapproval, even abuse.

A good source of **information** on gay life in Ecuador, and in Quito in particular, is the website Ⓦ quito.queercity.info.

Insurance

It's essential to take out an **insurance policy** before travelling to Ecuador to cover against theft, loss and illness or injury. A typical policy usually provides cover for the loss of baggage, tickets and – up to a certain limit – cash or cheques, as well as cancellation or curtailment of your journey. Most of them exclude so-called dangerous sports unless an extra premium is paid: in Ecuador this can mean scuba diving, whitewater rafting, mountaineering and trekking. Many policies can be chopped and changed to exclude coverage you don't need. If you do take medical coverage, ascertain whether benefits will be paid as treatment proceeds or only after your return home, and whether there is a 24-hour medical emergency number. When securing baggage cover, make sure the per-article limit – typically under £500/$750 – will cover your most valuable possession. If you need to make a claim, you should keep receipts for medicines and medical treatment. In the event you have anything stolen, you must obtain an official statement (*denuncia*) from the police.

Internet

In recent years there has been a rapid expansion of **internet** facilities across the country. Fierce competition keeps prices as low as $0.50–1 for an hour online in Quito and Guayaquil, and even in areas further afield it's rare to be charged more than $2–3 per hour. This means that unless you are staying for a long time or keeping to the cities and hotels where wi-fi coverage is common, it's probably not worth the bother and risk of bringing your own **computer** to Ecuador. Smartphones and tablets are lightweight options to stay in touch, but don't bring more than one of each due to tight customs regulations.

Laundry

Most large towns and tourist centres will have an inexpensive **laundry** (*lavandería*) that charges by the kilo. Washing and drying are done for you and your clothes are neatly folded ready for collection. In other areas, dry cleaners or laundries that charge by the item, which work out to be expensive, are more common. Many hotels and hostels also offer a laundry service.

Mail

Letters and postcards **sent from Ecuador** can take from five days to a month to reach their destination, though they're often faster to North America. If you need to send something of value or urgently, you're better off using a **courier**, such as DHL (check ⓦ dhl.com.ec for the nearest branch), though this is much more expensive. Alternatively, try Servientrega (ⓦ servientrega.com) a fair-priced domestic courier.

You can receive **poste restante** at just about any post office in the country. Have it sent to "*Lista de Correos*, [the town concerned], Ecuador", and make sure your surname is written clearly, as it will be filed under whatever the clerk thinks it is; you'll need to have photo ID to pick it up. In Quito, *Lista de Correos* mail usually ends up at the main office on Espejo and Guayaquil in the old town; if marked "Correo Central", it could well go to the head office in the new town on Eloy Alfaro 354 and Avenida 9 de Octubre.

American Express card holders can make use of AmEx offices for mail services, and some **embassies** also do poste restante. **SAE** (see p.79) will also take mail for members.

Maps

For Ecuador, the rise of the smartphone app means that it's easier than ever to find your way around with up-to-date digital maps you can use to plot your travels all the way down to walks or bike trips. Waze provides live traffic data, while apps like maps .me or Forever Map based on the Open Streetmap platform tend to be slightly superior to those from Apple or Google.

The widest selection of paper **maps** covering Ecuador is published by the Instituto Geográfico Militar (ⓣ 02 3975100, ⓦ igm.gob.ec) in Quito, up on the hill overlooking the Parque El Ejido at Senierges and Paz y Miño (you'll need to bring your passport or ID along), which has maps on a variety of scales. The most useful maps for **trekking** are their 1:50,000 series, which show accurate contour markings and geographic features and cover most of the country except for remote corners of the Oriente. Unfortunately, popular maps are often sold out, in which case you'll be supplied with a difficult-to-read black-and-white photocopy. Maps are also available in a 1:250,000 series for the whole country, and a 1:25,000 series for approximately half of it. You may need a supporting letter from a government agency if you require maps of sensitive border areas and the Amazon.

Money

The **US dollar** is the official currency of Ecuador. Bills come in denominations of $1, $5, $10, $20, $50 and $100. Coins come in a mixture of US- and Ecuadorian-minted 1, 5, 10, 25 and 50 cent pieces, plus $1 coins only minted in the US; Ecuadorian coins can't be used abroad. The $50 and $100 bills are rarely accepted at most shops and restaurants, and small change is often in short supply.

Take a mixture between cash in US dollars (other currencies are difficult to change) and credit/debit cards (or pre-paid cash cards). **ATMs** are widespread in the cities and larger towns, though less so in more remote places. Many machines are connected to the worldwide Visa/Plus and MasterCard/Cirrus/Maestro systems and a smaller number accept American Express and Diners Club cards. Usually, you won't be able to withdraw more than around $300–500 from an ATM in a day (depending on the bank).

Travellers' cheques are difficult to change, even in Quito, Guayaquil and Cuenca, where few banks accept them; *casas de cambio* are your best bet, though the commission is sometimes high.

Discount cards

Full-time students should consider getting the **International Student ID Card**, or "ISIC card" (W isic .org), which is the only widely recognized student identification in Ecuador and entitles the bearer to a range of discounts. The same organization offers the **International Youth Travel Card** to those who are 26 or younger and the **International Teacher Card** for teachers, offering similar discounts. Check with local tourism offices in major cities for discounts cards for major attractions.

Opening hours

Most **shops** open Monday to Saturday from 9am to 6pm. Many occupy the family home and, outside the biggest cities, open every day for as long as someone is up. Opening hours of **public offices** are generally from 9am to 5 or 6pm Monday to Friday, with an hour or so for lunch. In rural areas, the working day often starts earlier, say at 8am, and a longer lunch of a couple of hours is taken.

Banks do business from 8 or 9am to 1.30–2pm, Monday to Friday, and a few also open on Saturday mornings in shopping malls. Some banks extend business to 6pm during the week, though with reduced services. **Post offices** are open Monday to Friday 8am–7pm, and 8am–noon on Saturdays, while **telephone offices** open daily 8am–10pm; in rural regions and smaller towns, expect hours to be shorter for both services. **Museums** are usually closed on Mondays.

Phones

Although there are more mobile phones than residents in the country, many Ecuadorians still make their calls from the numerous public phone offices in every town and city in the country, which are usually the cheapest and most convenient places for you to make local and national calls too. The nationalized telephone service is operated by **CNT** (Corporación Nacional de Telecomunicaciones), though you might still find offices with the old livery of Andinatel (in the north) and Pacífictel (in the south and Galápagos); and Etapa for Cuenca. Inside the phone office you'll normally be allocated a cabin (*cabina*) where you make the call, and then you pay afterwards.

In many cities, the nationalized phone offices are quickly being superseded by **private offices**, which often have longer opening hours and lower rates. The mobile phone companies Movistar and Claro (see below) also operate phone offices and card-operated phone kiosks, which can receive incoming calls; cards specific to each company can be bought at nearby shops. These only tend to be economical, however, if calling mobile phones of the same company.

International calls with CNT cost less than $0.50 per minute for most countries, though Skype and other internet-based telephone services are by far the cheapest option for calling home.

Phoning from hotels is convenient, but usually involves a big surcharge; check prices before using a hotel phone.

Mobile phones

The three Ecuadorian networks use GSM 850 (Movistar and Claro) and GSM 1900 (CNT), as well as 3G 850 and 1700/2100Mhz for LTE (4G), the latter is slowly being rolled out. However, roaming is not cheap, so if you expect to use your **mobile phone** often, you should consider buying a local SIM card; take identification. In addition, note that the SAE (see p.79) sells secondhand phones.

> ### CALLING HOME FROM ABROAD
>
> The initial zero in omitted from the area code when dialling the UK, Ireland, Australia and New Zealand from abroad.
> **Australia** international access code + 61
> **New Zealand** international access code + 64
> **UK** international access code + 44
> **US and Canada** international access code + 1
> **Republic of Ireland** international access code + 353
> **South Africa** international access code + 27

USEFUL PHONE NUMBERS

Police, fire, emergencies ☎ 911
National operator ☎ 100
International operator ☎ 116 & ☎ 117

ECUADORIAN AREA CODES

Only use the prefix when calling from outside the area or when using a mobile phone. Drop the zero if calling from outside Ecuador.

☎ **02** Quito and Pichincha, Santo Domingo
☎ **03** Bolívar, Chimborazo, Cotopaxi, Tungurahua, Pastaza
☎ **04** Guayaquil and Guayas, Santa Elena
☎ **05** Manabí, Los Ríos, Galápagos
☎ **06** Carchi, Imbabura, Esmeraldas, Sucumbíos, Napo, Orellana
☎ **07** Cuenca and Azuay, Cañar, El Oro, Loja, Morona-Santiago, Zamora-Chinchipe
☎ **09** Mobile phones
☎ **593** Ecuador country code

Photography

If you're using a **non-digital** camera, consider bringing fast film (400 ASA and above) for the gloom of jungles and forests, while 200 ASA is more appropriate for the brighter conditions elsewhere. It's best to bring your own film and batteries from home, but both are available in the bigger cities; check the expiry dates before purchase. You can transfer pictures taken with a **digital camera** onto disk or have them printed in the larger tourist centres to free up space on memory cards. Rechargeable batteries are ideal, as the shelf-life of batteries bought in the Amazon or on the coast is often badly affected by heat and humidity.

You'll get best results when the sun is lowest in the sky, as you'll lose detail and nuance in the high contrasts cast by harsh midday light, though you can reduce heavy shadows using fill-in flash. In the Andes, sunlight is most likely between 6am and 10 am. Mountaineers with digital cameras should take their batteries out while climbing and carry them somewhere warm under their clothes; cold batteries lose power in seconds, usually just when you want to take that spectacular mountaintop sunrise. Always respect people's **privacy** and never take someone's photograph without asking first; usually they will be flattered or they may ask for a small fee.

Time

Ecuador is five hours behind GMT (the same as US Eastern Standard Time, falling back an hour during daylight savings time), and the Galápagos Islands are six hours behind GMT (or one hour behind US EST).

Tipping

In smarter places, a ten percent service charge will automatically be added to your bill; **tipping** above this is only warranted for exceptional service. Cheaper restaurants will not usually expect you to leave a tip, although it's very welcome if you do. Airport and hotel porters should be tipped, as should the people who watch your car for you if you've parked in a street. Taxi drivers don't normally get a tip, but will often round up the fare. Guides are tipped depending on the length of your stay or trip, from a couple of dollars to over ten. Tour crews in the Galápagos also receive tips (see box, p.342).

Toilets

In **toilets**, the bin by your feet is for your toilet paper – apart from at smarter hotels, the plumbing can't generally cope with it being flushed. Public toilets are most common at bus terminals, where you'll see them signposted as *baños* or *SS HH* (the abbreviation for *servicios higiénicos*); women are *damas* or *mujeres* and men *caballeros* or *hombres*. Often there's an attendant who sells toilet paper at the door. It's a good idea to carry some paper (*papel higiénico*) with you, wherever you are.

Tourist information

There's a Ministry of Tourism (Ⓦecuador.travel) **information office**, sometimes labelled "iTur", in every provincial capital and the main tourist centres. Some offices won't have an English-speaker on hand, but almost all have rudimentary maps, lists of hotels and restaurants, leaflets and probably basic information on any sites of interest in the area. Many regional centres also have tourist offices run by the municipality, which can be as good or better than their government counterparts.

TRAVEL WEBSITES

Ⓦ ecuador.com
Ⓦ ecuador-travel-guide.org
Ⓦ ecuadortimes.net
Ⓦ exploringecuador.com
Ⓦ goecuador.com
Ⓦ ingalapagos.com
Ⓦ inquito.com
Ⓦ quito.com

GOVERNMENT WEBSITES

Australian Department of Foreign Affairs Ⓦ dfat.gov.au, Ⓦ smartraveller.gov.au.

British Embassy in Quito Ⓦ ukinecuador.fco.gov.uk.
British Foreign & Commonwealth Office Ⓦ gov.uk/fco.
Canadian Department of Foreign Affairs Ⓦ voyage.gc.ca.
Ecuador Tourism Ministry Ⓦ ecuador.travel.
Irish Department of Foreign Affairs Ⓦ foreignaffairs.gov.ie.
New Zealand Ministry of Foreign Affairs Ⓦ mft.govt.nz.
South African Department of Foreign Affairs Ⓦ dfa.gov.za.
US State Department Ⓦ travel.state.gov.

Travelling with children

Ecuadorians love children and usually go out of their way to make life as easy as possible for those travelling with children. Tourists can be a bit of a puzzle to the many Ecuadorians who have never left the country, but parents and their children represent something everyone understands – a **family**. Foreign children are something of a novelty, particularly outside the big cities, and will usually quickly attract the attention of local kids, who'll want to have a look and a chat. Before long, the whole family will be out too, and social barriers will quickly crumble.

You and especially your children will get the most out of such openness if you take some time to learn some **Spanish**. Children can pick it up very quickly when immersed for a week or three, and most language schools are very accommodating of their needs. You'll be amazed at the heart-melting effect it will have on even the surliest Ecuadorian when they hear your child speak in their own tongue.

Ecuadorian **food** doesn't tend to be a big issue for children; old favourites like fried chicken or breaded fish and French fries are available just about everywhere.

Child discounts

For most **travel**, children pay half-price, and on a few things, such as **trains**, they go for free. Long-distance **buses** are an exception and full fares have to be paid for each seat, though if the trip isn't too long and the child not too big, they can sit on your lap without charge and even be plonked on a chair whenever the bus clears. Longer bus journeys can be wearisome for children, so try to break up any lengthy hauls into smaller chunks, which will also allow you to see more on the way. If a big trip is unavoidable, consider taking an internal **flight** as these are relatively cheap for adults, while children under 12 go for half-price and under-2s pay just ten percent. In rural areas, you'll often find people will offer you a ride, through kindness, when they see you walking with a child.

Children will also regularly get half-price rates for their **accommodation**, and occasionally be let off for free, particularly if young.

Travellers with disabilities

South America is not the friendliest of destinations for **travellers with disabilities**, and, sadly, Ecuador is no exception. In all but the very newest public buildings, you're unlikely to find much in the way of ramps, widened doorways or disabled toilets. Pavements are often narrow and full of obstructions.

About 12 percent of Ecuadorians have a disability, and many manage with the assistance of others. Some of the smarter city hotels do cater for disabled guests and Quito's segregated bus systems afford access too, at least outside rush hour when it's not too crowded to get on in the first place. Travelling further afield in Ecuador is likely to throw up difficulties, and you may have to forego the idyllic rustic cabañas in the middle of nowhere for a luxury chain hotel, or substitute local buses for taxis or internal flights.

Women travellers

Travelling as a **lone woman** in Ecuador presents no major obstacles and can be very rewarding – if you are prepared to put up with the occasional annoyance and take a few simple precautions. **Unwanted attention** is the most common irritation and has to be borne most often by fair-haired women or those who most obviously look foreign; dressing or behaving provocatively is only likely to make the situation worse. Being whistled, hissed or kissed at is part of the territory, but these situations are more a nuisance than a danger and the accepted wisdom is to pointedly ignore the perpetrators – shouting at them will only encourage them.

More serious cases of **sexual assault** are a concern in Ecuador for lone women; minimize the risks by treating known danger situations with caution. Beaches are regarded as unsafe for women alone; generally anyone, even in groups, should stay off beaches at night. Avoid walking alone after dark anywhere and hiking alone. If you become the victim of rape or sexual assault, report the incident immediately to the police and your embassy in Quito. It must be stressed that most Ecuadorians are friendly and respectful of solo female travellers, and few experience problems while travelling through the country.

Sanitary protection comes most commonly in the form of towels, with tampons being hard to get hold of outside the cities.

Quito

BARRIO PALUCO AT SUNRISE

1

Quito

High in the Andes, Ecuador's capital unfurls in a long north–south ribbon, more than 50km top to bottom and on average just 5km wide – and even narrower in places. To the west, Quito is dramatically hemmed in by the steep green walls of Volcán Pichincha, a benign-looking but active volcano that in 1999 sent a giant mushroom cloud of ash into the sky. Eastwards, the city abruptly drops away to the wide suburban valleys of Los Chillos and Tumbaco, before the Andes surge again to the snow-capped Antisana, Cotopaxi and Cayambe volcanoes. It's a superb setting, although during most of the year, the "four seasons in a day" means bright mornings are followed by noon clouds, afternoon thunderstorms and chilly nights.

Rivalled only by Guayaquil in size and economic clout, Quito is Ecuador's political and cultural heart. With a population of more than 2.5 million, it's a busy transit hub and, despite the inevitable pollution and screeching horns, is an easy and appealing place to spend time in. Central Quito is divided into two distinct parts. The compact **old town**, known as the *centro histórico*, is the city's undisputed highlight, a jumble of narrow streets and wide, cobbled plazas lined with churches, monasteries, mansions and colourful balconied houses. A UNESCO World Heritage Site, the old town contains some of the most beautiful Spanish colonial architecture on the continent and the frenetic crowds of *indígenas* and mestizos that throng its streets give it a tremendous energy. The neighbouring **new town** has beautiful parks and modern conveniences including numerous hotels, restaurants, bars, banks, shops and tour operators.

Quito's **altitude** (2800m) can leave you feeling breathless and woozy when you first arrive – most people adjust in a couple of days, often by resting, drinking plenty of water and avoiding alcohol.

Brief history

Little is known about the indigenous people who, until the fifteenth century, inhabited the terrain that Quito now occupies. Archaeologists believe that by about 1400 a number of *señoríos étnicos* ("lordships" or "chiefdoms"), including that of the obscure **Quitus**, from whom the modern city takes its name, inhabited the Quito basin, which was an important trading centre. In the late fifteenth century, the last great Inca emperors, **Huayna Capac** and his son **Atahualpa**, made Quito a political and ceremonial centre of the northern part of their empire, though on a smaller scale than Tomebamba (now Cuenca).

The arrival of the Spanish

The Spanish chose Quito as the capital of their newly acquired territory, despite the Inca leader Rumiñahui burning it to the ground five days before its capture in 1534. The colonial city was founded as **San Francisco de Quito** on August 28, 1534, and its governor **Sebastián de Benalcázar** established the proper workings of a city on

Highlights

❶ **Colonial Quito** Quito's magnificent historic centre has some of the continent's best-preserved and most beautiful Spanish colonial architecture. **See p.57**

❷ **Basílica del Voto Nacional** Quito's concertinaed terrain lends itself to stunning views, but few are as exciting as those from the breathtaking ledges of this quirky neo-Gothic church. **See p.72**

❸ **TelefériQo** A swish cable car ride that effortlessly whizzes passengers high up the slopes of Volcán Pichincha above the capital. **See p.73**

❹ **Guápulo** Walk down the steep slope and through a lovely colonial neighbourhood, a route followed by the Spanish explorers on their way to discover the Amazon. **See p.74**

❺ **Good Friday** Evocative spectacle in which hundreds of purple-robed penitents parade through the city's historic core, providing a striking glimpse of its Spanish religious heritage. **See p.87**

HIGHLIGHTS ARE MARKED ON THE MAP ON P.56

1

December 6 of that year. Within thirty years, the **catedral** was finished, and by the end of the sixteenth century, most of the great churches, monasteries and public buildings were in place, making Quito one of the great cities of Spanish America and the capital of an audiencia (a legal district).

The city was nonetheless for removed from the epicentres of the colonies, its quiet pace of life interrupted only by the petty quarrels and rivalries between clerics, creoles (Spanish born in the Americas) and public officials. Periodically however, earthquakes

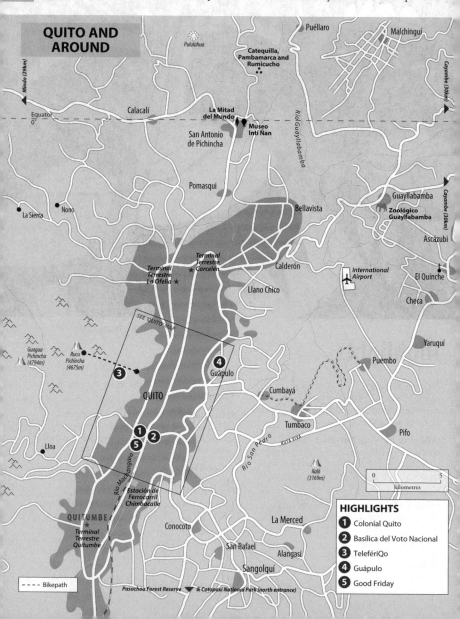

QUITO AND AROUND

Mindo (29km)

Pululahua

Puéllaro

Malchinguí

Catequilla, Pambamarca and Rumicucho

Equator 0°

Calacalí

La Mitad del Mundo

Museo Inti Ñan

San Antonio de Pichincha

Río Guayllabamba

Coyambe (30km)

Pomasqui

Guayllabamba

Zoológico Guayllabamba

La Sierra

Nono

Bellavista

Ascázubi

El Queche

International Airport

Terminal Terrestre Carcelén

Calderón

Terminal Terrestre La Ofelia

Llano Chico

Checa

SEE QUITO MAP

Yaruquí

Guagua Pichincha (4794m)

Rucu Pichincha (4675m)

3

4

Guápulo

Puembo

QUITO

Cumbayá

Tumbaco

Pifo

1 **2**

5

Río San Pedro

RUTA VIVA

Lloa

Río Machángara

Ilaló (3169m)

0   5
kilometres

Estación de Ferrocarril Chimbacalle

QUITUMBE

Terminal Terrestre Quitumbe

Conocoto

San Rafael

La Merced

Alangasí

HIGHLIGHTS

1 Colonial Quito

2 Basílica del Voto Nacional

3 TelefériQo

4 Guápulo

5 Good Friday

Sangolquí

- - - Bikepath

Pasochoa Forest Reserve ▼ & Cotopaxi National Park (north entrance)

ORIENTATION IN QUITO

Quito is shaped like a long, narrow strip. Approximately in the middle is the **old town** (*centro histórico*), focused on three large squares: **Plaza Grande** (or Plaza de la Independencia), **Plaza San Francisco** and **Plaza Santo Domingo**. The street grid around these squares comprises a small, compact urban core dominated to the south by the hill of **El Panecillo**, which is crowned by a large statue of the winged **Virgen de Quito**. Fanning north from old Quito towards the new town is a transitional stretch around **Parque La Alameda**, while the **new town's** central area begins a few blocks further north at **Parque El Ejido**. Known as **Centro Norte** (Centre North), this area stretches all the way north to the former airport, but the parts you're most likely to visit are the central areas between **La Mariscal**, just north of Parque El Ejido, where many accommodation and tourist facilities are located, and the business district further north, around **Parque La Carolina**. The south of Quito holds few attractions, but the main bus terminal, Terminal Terrestre Quitumbe, is located here.

and volcanic eruptions shattered the calm, but nothing was to compare with the events of the fight against Spain.

Revolution and independence

Quito in the early **nineteenth century** was one of the places that started the tide of revolution sweeping over the continent. Major events marking Ecuador's struggle for **independence** took place in or around Quito, and in 1830 the city became the capital of the new **Republic of Ecuador**. But it had paid a heavy toll. War and disease left the population at just 28,000 by 1858, a generation after the war, compared with 61,000 in 1779.

As Quito entered the **twentieth century** it finally outgrew its original boundaries and slowly expanded. The construction of new buildings became easier with the arrival, in 1909, of the **Quito–Guayaquil railway**, which facilitated the transport of heavy building materials and new machinery to the capital. As late as 1945, there had still been little fundamental change to Quito's long-standing physical and social landscape: the wealthy still lived in the colonial centre, the working class occupied a barrio (neighbourhood) near the railway station to the south, and farms and countryside still surrounded most of the city.

The banana and oil booms

The city changed dramatically in the **post-war** years, fuelled initially by the **banana boom** of the 1940s, which turned Ecuador into a top exporter and gave it the resources to pay for new infrastructure in Quito. When the city's wealthy moved out to the fashionable new barrio of Mariscal Sucre (commonly known as **La Mariscal**), Quito's social geography fundamentally changed too. Further transformations followed the **oil boom** of the 1970s, which funded the construction of high-rise offices, new residential districts and public buildings. Rural Ecuadoreans flocked to the capital in search of work and services. Accordingly, the population exploded and passed the **one million** mark in 1990. Since then, Quito's boundaries have been spreading farther outwards, stretching the city's resources to their limits; at more than 2.5 million people and rising, the current population boom shows no signs of fading. Despite this, the authorities have made real progress in developing a cross-city bus system and rejuvenating the historic centre. As a result, Quito is today, more than ever, a city to explore and enjoy.

The old town

Quito's chief attraction is the **old town** and its dazzling array of churches, monasteries and convents, which date from the early days of the colony. Known

1

QUITO

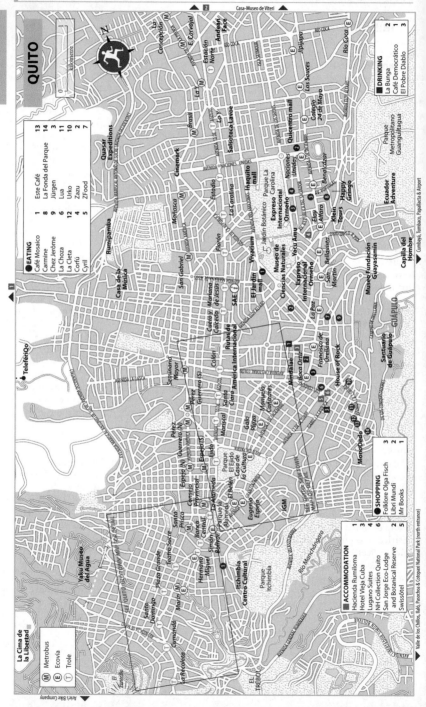

EATING
Café Mosaico	1	Este Café	13
Carmine	8	La Fonda del Parque	14
Chez Jerôme	9	Jürgen	3
La Choza	6	Lua	11
La Cleta	12	Urko	10
Corfú	4	Zazu	2
Cyril	5	ZFood	7

Quasar Expeditions

DRINKING
La Bunga	2
Café Democrático	1
El Pobre Diablo	3

SHOPPING
Folklore Olga Fisch	3
Libri Mundi	1
Mr Books	5

ACCOMMODATION
Hacienda Rumiloma	1
Hotel Vieja Cuba	3
Lugano Suites	4
NH Collection Quito	6
San Jorge Eco-Lodge and Botanical Reserve	2
Swissôtel	5

Metrobus (M)
Ecovia (E)
Trole (T)

to Quiteños as **el Centro Histórico**, the old town falls into a fairly small area that can be comfortably covered on foot in a day; trying to take in the forty-odd churches and assorted museums will quickly leave you feeling swamped and exhausted, so try to single out a few highlights. These should definitely include the three main squares – **Plaza Grande**, **Plaza Santo Domingo** and **Plaza San Francisco** – as well as the charming little **Plaza del Teatro**. Of the city's churches, the most impressive are **San Francisco**, **La Compañía** and **La Merced**, along with **El Sagrario** and **San Agustín**.

The old town's most rewarding museum is the excellent **Museo de la Ciudad**, while the **Museo Alberto Mena Caamaño** and its waxworks set in evocative surroundings is also worth a visit. A short walk away is the **Museo Manuela Sáenz**, which gives an insight into the love between two of South America's heroes of the Independence era, and the **Museo Camilo Egas**, a permanent retrospective of one of Ecuador's greatest-ever artists – both are fascinating. For a glimpse inside the best-preserved old-town houses, head for the **Casa de María Augusta Urrutia** or the **Casa de Sucre**, while for sweeping views of the city, a short taxi ride outside of the centre is highly recommended (see p.71).

Orientation in the old town can sometimes be confusing, as many streets have two different street names: the official name on green plaques, and the historical one painted on ceramic tiles. Only the official names appear on the maps and in the text of this guide.

Plaza Grande and around
In the centre of the old town, bounded by Chile, García Moreno, Eugenio Espejo and Venezuela

The **Plaza Grande**, also known as the **Plaza de la Independencia**, was first laid out with a string and ruler in 1534 and still preserves its original dimensions. Surrounded by the city's most important civic and religious buildings – the cathedral, Government Palace, Archbishop's Palace and City Hall – the plaza has always been the city's focus. On Sundays, when traffic is prohibited from the surrounding streets (9am–4pm), the square is at its best, offering a chance for great **people-watching**, especially the permanent array of dapper old men out for a stroll in their Sunday best, and the schoolchildren, grandmothers and sweethearts sitting on benches amid the spindly palm trees and flowerbeds. An elaborate, albeit twenty first-century changing of the guard happens on Monday mornings around 11am, with president Rafael Correa often presiding from the upper balcony of Palacio de Carondelet.

Catedral metropolitana
Plaza Grande • Mon–Sat 9am–5.15pm • $2 • ☎ 02 2570371

The sturdy horizontal outline of the **catedral metropolitana**, with its gleaming white walls, grey-stone portals and terracotta-tiled roof, takes in the entire south side of Plaza Grande. Initially built in the 1560s, the present building stems from the second

---

QUITO ADDRESSES
Quito is caught between two **street-numbering** systems. A few years ago, an attempt was made to modernize **addresses**, whereby north–south streets would be prefixed by the letter N (for *norte*) if north of Calle Rocafuerte at the edge of the old town, while addresses on east–west streets would be prefixed by E (*este* – east) or Oe (*oeste* – west) to indicate their orientation to Avenida 10 de Agosto. Following these letters come street number, a dash and then house number. However, both old and new systems are currently in use, so throughout the chapter we provide the form of address used by the establishments themselves.

1

half of the seventeenth century. Its Baroque interior contains the remains of historical figures including independence hero **Field Marshal Antonio José de Sucre** (see p.387), as well as presidents Juan José Flores and Gabriel García Moreno. More interesting are the details of the sensational murder that took place here during the Good Friday Mass of 1877, when the Bishop of Quito was poisoned with strychnine dissolved in the holy wine.

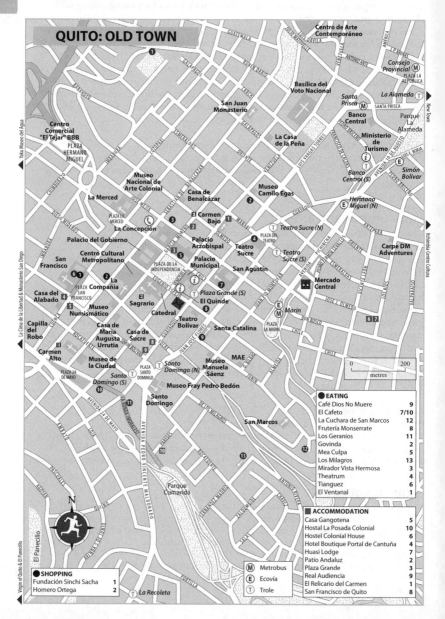

QUITO: OLD TOWN

● EATING

Café Dios No Muere	9
El Cafeto	7/10
La Cuchara de San Marcos	12
Frutería Monserrate	8
Los Geranios	11
Govinda	2
Mea Culpa	5
Los Milagros	13
Mirador Vista Hermosa	3
Theatrum	4
Tianguez	6
El Ventanal	1

■ ACCOMMODATION

Casa Gangotena	5
Hostal La Posada Colonial	10
Hostel Colonial House	6
Hotel Boutique Portal de Cantuña	4
Huasi Lodge	7
Patio Andaluz	2
Plaza Grande	3
Real Audiencia	9
El Relicario del Carmen	1
San Francisco de Quito	8

● SHOPPING

Fundación Sinchi Sacha	1
Homero Ortega	2

M Metrobus
E Ecovía
T Trole

1

Palacio de Gobierno (Carondelet)

Plaza Grande • Mon 3pm–7pm Tues–Fri 9am–7pm, Sat 9am–10pm, Sun 9am–4pm • Free with ID, 45min tours every 15min • ☎ 02 3827000

Perpendicular to the cathedral on the west side of the plaza, the **Palacio de Gobierno** (Government Palace) was also the site of a dramatic murder when, in 1875, Dictator Gabriel García Moreno was macheted to death (see p.388); a blue inscription marks the spot below the exterior first-story balcony, above a line of traditional shops. This white-stuccoed, perfectly symmetrical building – fronted by a long row of columns – is both the seat of government and the presidential palace and named Palacio de Carondelet after a late colonial president of the Quito audiencia. Most of the building stems from the late-colonial and early-republican periods.

Palacio Arzobispal

The grand and dazzlingly white **Palacio Arzobispal** (Archbishop's Palace), a two-storey Neoclassical building taking up most of the north side of the Plaza Grande, accommodates a string of shops and restaurants. Free events are sometimes staged in the **Patio Cultural**, one of its two covered courtyards inside.

Palacio Municipal

The concrete **Palacio Municipal** (City Hall), which was built between 1968 and 1973, occupies the east side of the Plaza Grande. Controversial for its modernity, it still blends in surprisingly well with the neighbouring colonial buildings, thanks to its low, horizontal design, tiled roof and white-painted walls. The main Quito Turismo tourist office is based here (see p.79).

Centro Cultural Metropolitano

García Moreno and Espejo • Tues–Sun 9am–4.30pm • Centro Cultural free; Museo Alberto Mena Caamaño $1.50 • ☎ 02 2584363, ⓦ centrocultural-quito.com

The **Centro Cultural Metropolitano** is the focus of cultural life in the old town, housing gallery space for temporary exhibitions, lecture rooms, the municipal library and a museum, as well as elegant, glass-covered courtyards and a café.

The building occupies a site rich in history, supposedly the location of one of Atahualpa's palaces before becoming a Jesuit university in the early colonial period, then a military barracks, and once more a university – which in 1830 hosted the signing of the Act of Constitution of the Independent State. Its most infamous moment came in 1810, when a group of revolutionaries was executed in a cell inside the building. This gruesome incident and other milestones of Ecuador's journey to independence are commemorated in waxwork displays, which form part of the **Museo Alberto Mena Caamaño**, located within. The rest comprises a collection of colonial, republican and contemporary art.

El Sagrario

García Moreno • Mon–Fri 7.30am–5.30pm, Sat 7.30am–6pm, Sun 7.30am–1pm & 5–6pm • Free • ☎ 02 2284398

Opposite the Centro Cultural Metropolitano, just off the Plaza Grande and adjoining the catedral, is **El Sagrario**, a seventeenth-century church topped by a pale-blue dome, whose colourful Baroque interior features turquoise walls embellished with bright geometric designs and stone pillars painted dark coral. The underside of the main dome is covered with swirling multicoloured frescos, while the altar is often festooned with fresh white lilies.

Teatro Bolívar

Espejo 0e2-43 • ☎ 02 2582486, ⓦ teatrobolivar.org

The flamboyant **Teatro Bolívar**, built in 1933, was lavishly refurbished in 1997 but gutted two years later by a fire that started in a neighbouring pizza place. A second

1

restoration took place, and the theatre now hosts a variety of dance and theatrical performances. Night-time tours are also sometimes offered. Half a block down from the theatre, at Espejo and Juan José Flores, is the **Monasterio Santa Catalina**, Quito's most colourful religious building.

South of Plaza Grande

Past Espejo on the southern, cathedral side of Plaza Grande lie the three other grand squares of the historic centre – San Francisco, Santo Domingo, and 24 de Mayo – and two of Latin America's most spectacular churches. The area also features many little traditional stores selling crafts, herbs and vegetables, some in the atmospheric neighbourhoods of La Ronda and San Marcos.

La Compañía

García Moreno Oe5-133 and Sucre • Mon–Thurs 9.30am–6.30pm, Fri 9.30am–5.30pm, Sat 9.30am–4.15pm, Sun 12.30–4.15pm; groups can also arrange night-time visits • $4 • ☎ 02 2584175, ⓦ fundacioniglesiadelacompania.org.ec

The most opulent of a string of churches on Calle García Moreno (also known as the "Street of the Seven Crosses" after the large stone crucifixes lining its route), **La Compañía** was built by Jesuits between 1605 and 1765 and completed just two years before Spain expelled the order from the continent. Boasting an extraordinary Baroque facade of carved volcanic stone, the church is piled high with twisted columns, sacred hearts, cherubs, angels and saints. Inside, any thoughts of restraint vanish amid the wild extravagance of gold leaf – there's a reputed seven tonnes of it covering the altars, galleries, Moorish tracery and pulpit. The building was beautifully restored after a fire in 1996, the only testament to the damage being the smoke-blackened face of an angel, deliberately left uncleaned, peering down from the inner circle of the cupola. Go early to see the sun light up the facade. The opulent Neoclassical building to its north was formerly the central bank and, ironically for a country that dropped its currency, houses a nostalgic numismatic museum, including pre-Columbian spondylus shells.

Casa de María Augusta Urrutia

García Moreno 760 • Tues–Sat 10am–6pm, Sun 9.30am–5pm • $2 • ☎ 02 2580103

The **Casa de María Augusta Urrutia** is a fine nineteenth-century mansion built around three inner patios. It was occupied by philanthropist Doña María who was widowed at an early age and lived alone with her 24 servants until her death in 1987. Many of the rooms have been left virtually untouched, and provide a fascinating glimpse of the tastes of Quito's upper classes in the twentieth century. The house is now owned by a religious charity Doña María founded in the 1930s, which aims to alleviate poverty in Quito and Guayaquil by building low-price housing.

Casa de Sucre

Venezuela and Sucre • Tues–Fri 8am–4pm, Sat 8.30am–1pm • $1 • ☎ 02 2952860

The nineteenth-century **Casa de Sucre** was once the property of Ecuador's liberator, Field Marshal Sucre. Unless you're into military history, however, the battle plans, weapons, uniforms, standards and portraits of generals exhibited are not that exciting, though the building itself is a beautiful example of a late-period Spanish colonial house.

Museo de la Ciudad

García Moreno S1-47 and Rocafuerte • Tues–Sun 9.30am–5.30pm; last entry 4.30pm • $3 • ☎ 02 2283879, ⓦ museociudadquito.gov.ec

Housed in a former hospital, the dynamic **Museo de la Ciudad** uses replicas, scale models, mannequins, friezes and sound effects to illustrate the city's development. Exhibits include a scale model of the construction of the Iglesia San Francisco, with hundreds of miniature workers toiling away; a reconstruction of the inside of a sixteenth-century house; and another of a workshop belonging to a Quito School artist. The old hospital's church is also worth a look, for its blazing red-and-gold interior and exuberant Baroque altarpieces.

Convento del Carmen Alto

García Moreno at Rocafuerte • Tues–Sun 9.30–5.30pm (last entry 4.30pm) • $3 • ☎ 02 2881513

The eighteenth-century **Convento del Carmen Alto** is home to a group of Carmelite nuns, who still live in complete isolation. That hasn't stopped them from transforming part of the convent into a museum showcasing their history going back to 1653 at this site, with painting and sculpture going back four centuries. The exposition highlights the life of local saint Mariana de Jesús, whose famous quote "Ecuador won't disappear because of earthquakes but because of bad governments" is certainly apocryphal. The nuns also sell honey, herbs and wine, as do the nuns of seventeenth-century Santa Clara, on the square of the same name at Cuenca and Rocafuerte. Crossing García Moreno is the eighteenth-century Arco de la Reina, which was built as a rain shelter for the local Mass-goers.

Plaza San Francisco and around

The vast, cobbled **Plaza San Francisco**, bounded by calles Cuenca, Simon Bolívar, Benalcázar and Sucre, is one of Quito's most beautiful squares. Its monochrome shades and sweeping proportions are accentuated by the absence of trees and benches, giving it an empty, slightly melancholy air and providing quite a contrast to the cheerful leafiness of the Plaza Grande.

Iglesia y Monasterio de San Francisco

Plaza San Francisco • Mon–Sat 7am–noon & 3–5.30pm, Sun 7am–noon • Free • ☎ 02 2281124

Stretching across the plaza's western side is the monumental **Iglesia y Monasterio de San Francisco**, whose horizontal whitewashed walls are dominated by the twin bell towers and carved-stone portal of the church's entrance. Hidden behind this facade are the extensive buildings and seven courtyards that make San Francisco the largest religious complex in South America.

From the square, a broad flight of stone steps leads up to the front entrance of the **church**, whose construction began in 1536 shortly after the founding of Quito. Once your eyes become accustomed to the shadows you'll notice that the walls, altars, pillars and pulpit are encrusted with gilt, almost rivalling the theatricality of La Compañía. The main altar fills a large, domed area and is adorned by Bernardo de Legarda's famous winged carving of the **Virgen de Quito**, which inspired the giant statue on El Panecillo (see p.71).

Capilla de Cantuña

Plaza San Francisco • Tues–Thurs 8am–5pm • Free • ☎ 02 2281124

To the left of the entrance of the Iglesia de San Francisco is the door to the **Capilla de Cantuña** (Cantuña Chapel). Inside you'll find a splendid altar and many paintings and carvings produced by the Quito School (see box, p.66). According to legend, the chapel was built by an Indian named **Cantuña**, whom the Devil helped to complete the work. When the time came to hand over his soul, however, Cantuña was saved on discovering that a single stone was missing from the structure.

Museo de San Francisco

Plaza San Francisco • Mon–Sat 9am–5pm, Sun 9am–1pm • $2 • ☎ 02 2952911

Next to the entrance of the Iglesia de San Francisco is the door to the **Museo de San Francisco** which displays an impressive collection of religious sculpture, paintings and furniture in a gallery off the monastery's main cloister. If you take advantage of the free guide service available at the entrance (a small tip is expected), you can see the otherwise locked **coro** (choir) of the church, housed in a raised gallery overlooking the

1

central nave, which features a spectacular carved *mudéjar* (Moorish-style) ceiling and a row of 36 painted wooden carvings of Franciscan martyrs on the walls, above the choir stalls. Just outside there's a so-called **whispering corridor**, where two people speaking into diagonally opposite corners can hear each other's voices.

Casa del Alabado
Cuenca and Rocafuerte, just off Plaza San Francisco • Tues–Sat 9.30am–5.30pm, Sun 10am–4pm • $4, audio guides $2 • ⓦ alabado.org

A must-see private museum housed in a delightfully restored colonial building, the **Casa del Alabado** showcases around 500 beautifully crafted pieces of pre-Columbian stone, ceramic and gold. Exhibits are displayed to stunning effect in a series of intimate, whitewashed rooms with subtly lit display cabinets. As well as highlighting the exquisite artistry of Ecuador's early civilizations, the museum provides detailed insights into the ritualistic and symbolic significance of many of the pieces, the meanings of recurrent artistic motifs and how they related to pre-Columbian cosmology. Emphasis is also given to the traditional role of shamans and their practices as they mediated between the world of ancestral spirits and the material world of the living. There is a small café and a gift shop – a good place to pick up some unusual and high-quality souvenirs.

Capilla del Robo
24 de Mayo between Cuenca and Imbabura • Thurs 4pm–6pm, Sun 6am–4pm • Free

For such a large plaza, the architectural highlight of Plaza 24 de Mayo is the smallish and relatively simple 1650 Capilla del Robo. The "chapel of the theft" marks the spot where a silver-clad tabernacle stolen from the convent of Santa Clara was found (the robbers were also identified, hanged and quartered). It's separated from the plaza by a small courtyard, and its transept is covered by a cupola clad in the typical ceramic tiles of other churches in the centre. On the inside, the centre of the cupola is painted with a typical indigenous motif, the sun, brightly lit by side windows.

Plaza Santo Domingo and around

In early colonial times, except for the monastery of San Diego, the city ended along the sloping Plaza 24 de Mayo that was once a ravine and is now often a location for free weekend concerts. Below the arch of a bridge at its bottom starts La Ronda, the old town's most evocative narrow alley, which meanders down to a modern public sporting facility, Parque Cumandá. Past Santo Domingo lies the quieter, charming neighbourhood of San Marcos.

La Ronda
Just south of Plaza Domingo, off Calle Guayaquil • Free

One block south from Plaza Domingo, Calle Guayaquil crosses a narrow, pedestrianized section of Calle Morales still known by its original name of **La Ronda**. Lined with thick-walled, whitewashed buildings with wrought-iron balconies and billowing flags, this picturesque cobblestoned alley is one of Quito's oldest streets, and one of the few remaining stretches of eighteenth-century working-class and artisanal housing. In the early twentieth century it was the bohemian and artistic heart of the capital, but years of neglect left it a notorious haunt of thieves and lowlifes. A regeneration project has restored its charms: many of the houses have been converted into galleries, cafés and shops, and numerous games (including table football and hoopla) have been put out on the street for passers-by to play with.

Iglesia Santo Domingo
Plaza Santo Domingo • Mon–Fri 9am–5pm, Sat–Sun 9am–1pm • Free • ⓣ 02 2282695

The graceful **Iglesia Santo Domingo** was built by Dominicans in the sixteenth century. Unfortunately, an ill-conceived interior remodelling took place in the nineteenth century, leaving the church with an altar that looks more like a miniature Gothic castle. Still, you can't help but be impressed by the Moorish-influenced tracery on the ceilings. On the outside, note the arch over Rocafuerte Street. The **Museo Fray Pedro Bedón** contains a large collection of Dominican religious art from the sixteenth to eighteenth centuries, but at time of writing it was closed for renovations.

Capilla de los Milagros

Fernando Madrid N1-113 and Vicente Rocafuerte • Tues–Sun 11am–6pm • Free • ☎ 02 295 5691

A few blocks south of Santo Domingo, uphill from the end of La Ronda in the Loma Grande sector, lies a Baroque jewel well off the beaten track. The little-known seventeeth-century chapel strikes a fine balance between the gaudy red and gold of the high altar with the blue-green and tan backgrounds of the walls, ceilings and arches, featuring numerous paintings and frescos all around – one case where the nineteenth-century painting doesn't overshadow the seventeenth-century altar. It can be accessed during the opening hours of the *Los Milagros* restaurant in its gardens.

Museo Manuela Sáenz

Junín 709 and Montúfar • Mon–Fri 8am–noon & 2–4pm • $0.80 • ☎ 02 2958321

A short walk northeast of Plaza Santo Domingo, the **Museo Manuela Sáenz** is set in an imposing colonial house. The museum is primarily dedicated to the life of Manuela Sáenz (1797–1856), the lover of Simón Bolívar, and for a brief period one of the most influential women in Latin American history – the so-called Liberator's liberator – who died in exile, penniless. On display are their love letters, as well as many of their personal belongings, including Bolívar's silver dagger, revolver, sabre and, well, his chamber pot. Another key figure in Ecuador's struggle for independence, Field Marshal Sucre, is also well represented by his gem-encrusted spurs and dozens of portraits. Other rooms show coins, antique weaponry, religious art and carved ivory from Africa and China.

Museo Archivo de Arquitectura del Ecuador

Junín and Ortíz Bilbao • Tues–Sat 10am–5.30pm • $0.50 • ☎ 02 2280446

A three-block walk north of Santo Domingo along Flores leads to Calle Junín, which heads eastward, forming the backbone of the San Marcos quarter. Amid a number of cultural sites here, the **Museo Archivo de Arquitectura del Ecuador** is the best place to get an understanding of Quito's architecture post-1880 (though descriptions are in Spanish only). Picking out key architects and buildings, it offers an overview of the capital's architectural development, mainly through text, photos and the occasional model. The various rooms are brought together on the ground floor, which shows a scale reconstruction of the historic centre and facsimile maps of Quito from 1573 to the present day.

North of the Plaza Grande

The area uphill from the Plaza Grande is more compact to explore, featuring some often overlooked and beautiful churches but also museums and theatres, including Teatro Bolívar and Teatro Sucre, amid the commercial bustle of the centre.

Iglesia de la Merced

Chile • Mon–Fri 8am–noon & 2–4pm • Free • ☎ 02 2280743

The **Iglesia de La Merced**, built between 1701 and 1747, features a wonderfully over-the-top Baroque and Moorish interior that is one of the highlights of the old town. Its ceilings and walls offer a confection of white, lace-like plaster relief against a sugary-pink background, looking like icing on a cake, with the side walls further adorned by dozens of oil paintings set in immense gilt frames. The main altar, carved

1

by Bernardo de Legarda in 1751, and two side altars are resplendent with gold leaf, while the choir, on a raised gallery at the back of the church, is ablaze with yet more gilding. The clock tower contains a 5.7-tonne bronze bell, Quito's largest. You can also visit the adjoining **convent**, built around a huge central patio enclosed within beautiful arched cloisters.

Iglesia San Agustín

Chile and Guayaquil • Mon–Fri 9am–12.30pm & 2–4pm, Sat 9am–1pm • $1 • ☎ 02 2955525

The imposing **Iglesia San Agustín** dates from the sixteenth century but was substantially rebuilt in 1880 after an earthquake, and features a massive 37m bell tower crowned by a statue of St Augustine. Its dark, neo-Gothic interior contains a series of enormous paintings by the distinguished seventeenth-century artist, Miguel de Santiago, depicting the life of the church's namesake. The adjoining **Convento de San Agustín** has survived intact since its completion in 1627, and contains a fine cloister with two levels of thick stone columns. It was in the convent's chapter house (*sala capítular*) where fledgling patriots signed the Act of Independence on August 10, 1809, and the great hall also boasts an intricately painted, highly ornate ceiling and glittering gold-leaf altar. On the second floor of the convent, a **museum** houses a large, dusty collection of religious paintings attributed to artists of the Quito School.

Museo Nacional de Arte Colonial

Cuenca and José Mejía • ☎ 02 2822297 • Tues–Sat 9am–5pm • $2 (students $1)

The **Museo Nacional de Arte Colonial** is based inside a restored sixteenth-century colonial house built around a colonnaded courtyard with a fountain. Dedicated almost exclusively to **religious art**, particularly oil paintings and carved, polychrome statuary, the museum contains some impressive work by Quito School artists

---

COLONIAL RELIGIOUS ART AND THE QUITO SCHOOL

After the conquest, the Spanish Crown was faced with the task of colonizing its new territories and subsuming their indigenous populations into its empire. The Spanish used conversion to Catholicism to consolidate their power, and **religious art and architecture** took on an enormous importance: splendid monasteries and cathedrals instilled awe in the natives, while artwork was used both for visual religious instruction and to replace former idols.

Initially religious art was imported from Spain, but the need to disperse large quantities of it around the continent prompted the growth of home-grown **artists' workshops** and **guilds** where Spanish teachers trained *indígenas* and mestizos. This resulted in a unique blend of indigenous and European elements: for example, carvings of biblical characters were frequently clothed in native dress and sometimes given indigenous traits and colouring.

Over time, Quito artists became known for their mastery of **polychromy** (decorative colouring) made out of cedar or red oak. Characterized by bold colours and exuberant decoration, the style found its greatest expression between 1660 and 1765, when the proliferation of high-quality Quiteño artists gave rise to the **Quito School** of art.

Led by **Miguel de Santiago** and **Bernardo de Legarda** in the early eighteenth century, and later by Manuel Chili (known as **Caspicara**), the Quito School's most delicate and beautiful creations were its polychrome carvings, often of the Virgin, covered in sumptuous attire and exposing only the head, face, hands and feet. One of the most peculiar aspects of the style was the use of human hair and false eyelashes, nails and glass eyes. The school's paintings were characterized by vivid shades of red against darker, duller tones.

The movement began to wane towards the end of the eighteenth century, when secular subjects such as landscapes and town scenes began to replace religious ones, and finally died out after Ecuador's independence in 1822.

(see box opposite). The first two rooms are devoted to the art of the sixteenth and seventeenth centuries, but the bulk of the collection, filling three rooms, is made up of eighteenth-century works.

Casa de Benalcázar
Olmedo Oe5-74 and Benalcázar • Mon–Fri 9.30am–1pm, 3.30pm–7pm • $1 • ☎ 02 2952860

The eighteenth-century **Casa de Benalcázar**, run by the Ecuadorian Institute for Hispanic Culture, showcases a typical colonial mansion with a glass-covered courtyard. One of the first historic renovations, it holds a collection of Baroque sculpture and sparked the idea to revitalize the whole centre in the 1960s, although it was probably never the site of the home of the namesake conquistador, Sebastián de Benalcázar.

Plaza del Teatro
One of the most charming squares in the city is the intimate **Plaza del Teatro**, bounded by calles Flores, Manabi and Guayaquil, and with a seated bronze statue of popular actor Ernesto Albán. Often a venue for open-air jazz concerts, it's surrounded by meticulously restored buildings, including the white, temple-like **Teatro Sucre** (see p.88). The theatre was built between 1879 and 1887 (symbolically on the site of the city slaughterhouse) and its glorious facade features six Corinthian columns and bas-reliefs of human figures representing music, drama and poetry. Perpendicular to it is the smaller Teatro de Variedades, originally from 1914. A block west, at Olmedo and Venezuela, stands the lovely stone **Iglesia del Carmen Bajo**.

Museo Camilo Egas
Venezuela and Esmeraldas • Tues–Fri 9am–5pm, Sat 10am–4pm • $1 • ☎ 02 2572811

The **Museo Camilo Egas** offers an excellent overview of the paintings of Camilo Egas (1889–1962), one of Ecuador's most important twentieth-century artists. The early works from the mid-1920s, romanticized depictions of native people in everyday life, are perhaps the most charming and accessible and became instant classics in Ecuador, helping to foster the *indigenismo* movement. His less optimistic later works traverse styles from Social Realism to Surrealism, neo-Cubism and finally Abstract Expressionism.

The new town

The heart of Quito's **new town**, officially called **Mariscal Sucre** but known locally as **La Mariscal** or the Centro Norte, is roughly bound by avenidas Patria in the south, Orellana in the north, 12 de Octubre in the east and 10 de Agosto in the west. The main commercial artery, **Avenida Amazonas**, is lined with banks, tour operators and souvenir shops, but the social focus is the **Plaza del Quinde** (also called Plaza Foch), at the intersection of Reina Victoria and Foch, where bars, clubs, restaurants and cafés are often thronged with people in the evenings. The jumble of colonial-style town houses, Art Deco villas and functional 1970s blocks means La Mariscal isn't particularly attractive, but it is where most visitors base themselves.

The new town benefits from several precious green spaces, including the triangular **Parque La Alameda** and the pleasant expanse of **Parque El Ejido**. There are no outstanding attractions in the new town proper, save the first-rate **Museo Nacional del Ecuador**. Yet there is plenty of good stuff to do if you're willing to take a short taxi ride outside the centre (see p.71).

1

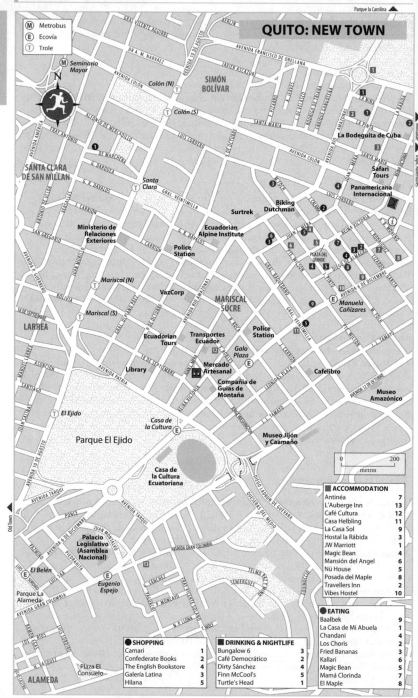

QUITO: NEW TOWN

M Metrobus
E Ecovía
T Trole

N

Seminario Mayor

Colón (N)
Colón (S)

SIMÓN BOLÍVAR

La Bodeguita de Cuba

Safari Tours

Panamericana Internacional

SANTA CLARA DE SAN MILLAN

Santa Clara

Biking Dutchman

Surtrek

Ecuadorian Alpine Institute

Ministerio de Relaciones Exteriores

Police Station

PLAZA DEL QUINDE

Mariscal (N)

VazCorp

MARISCAL SÚCRE

Mariscal (S)

Manuela Cañizares

LARREA

Ecuadorian Tours

Transportes Ecuador

Police Station

Galo Plaza

Library

Mercado Artesanal

Compañía de Guías de Montaña

Cafelibro

Museo Amazónico

El Ejido

Casa de la Cultura

Parque El Ejido

Museo Jijón y Caamaño

Casa de la Cultura Ecuatoriana

0   200
metres

Palacio Legislativo (Asamblea Nacional)

El Belén

Eugenio Espejo

Parque La Alameda

Plaza El Consuelo

ALAMEDA

ACCOMMODATION

Antinéa	7
L'Auberge Inn	13
Café Cultura	12
Casa Helbling	11
La Casa Sol	9
Hostal la Rábida	3
JW Marriott	1
Magic Bean	4
Mansión del Angel	6
Nü House	5
Posada del Maple	8
Travellers Inn	2
Vibes Hostel	10

EATING

Baalbek	9
La Casa de Mi Abuela	1
Chandani	4
Los Choris	2
Fried Bananas	3
Kallari	6
Magic Bean	5
Mamá Clorinda	7
El Maple	8

SHOPPING

Camari	1
Confederate Books	2
The English Bookstore	4
Galería Latina	3
Hilana	5

DRINKING & NIGHTLIFE

Bungalow 6	3
Café Democrático	2
Dirty Sánchez	4
Finn McCool's	5
Turtle's Head	1

Parque La Alameda

Southwest end of 6 de Deciembre • **Observatorio Astronómico** Mon–Fri 9am–12.30pm & 2.30–5.30pm • $1

North of the old colonial centre lies a transitional area between the old and the new, featuring the triangular **Parque La Alameda**, which goes back as far as 1596. It's marked by a statue of Simón Bolívar at its southern end, and a boating lake and the **Observatorio Astronómico** in the middle. Built in 1873, the latter is reputed to be the oldest observatory in South America. It houses a glorious brass telescope and an array of other astronomical devices collected during its long history. Across Av 12 de Octubre is the restored, early twentieth-century **Teatro Capitol**. The park's north side features El Churo (The Curl), a popular spiral stone outlook, and, across the street, is El Belén, a colonial chapel, site of the first Mass held in Quito in 1534. Two blocks north is the 1956 legislature or Asamblea Nacional, with a frieze carved by Luis Mideros on the north side and guided tours Monday to Friday featuring a massive Guayasamín mural (☎02 3991487).

Parque El Ejido

Just north of the legislature, off 6 de Deciembre, is **Parque El Ejido**, a pleasant expanse of foliage with monuments to liberal leader Eloy Alfaro, murdered in the old jail, whose body was dragged to be burnt here on January 8, 1912, and José María Velasco Ibarra, appropriately leaning on a railing (the moustachioed populist boasted "give me a balcony in each town and I'll be president"). It's also the site of a weekend **art market**, where artists line the edge of the park along Calle Patria with paintings. Mideros built the triumphal Arco de la Circasiana on its north side in the first half of the twentieth century.

Casa de la Cultura Ecuatoriana Benjamín Carrión

6 de Deciembre • Free entry to building; see website for programme of events • ☎ 02 2223258, ⓦ casadelacultura.gob.ec

On the north side of Parque El Arbolito, the **Casa de la Cultura Ecuatoriana Benjamín Carrión** is a complex of museums, theatres, auditoriums, exhibition spaces and a cinema, all housed in two buildings. The original, a distinguished Neocolonial house built in 1946 and embellished inside with murals by Oswaldo Guayasamín and others, now contains the national cinema archive and rooms for temporary exhibitions; it is somewhat overshadowed by the modernist, circular glass and concrete successor, designed in the 1950s but not completed until 1992, primarily to house the excellent **Museo Nacional,** scheduled to reopen before the end of 2016.

Museo Nacional del Ecuador

Inside the Casa de la Cultura Ecuatoriana • Side museums open Tues–Sat 9.30am–1pm, 2–4.30pm • Free

Ecuador's premier museum and one of the city's key attractions, the **Museo Nacional** has an incomparable collection of pre-Columbian ceramics and gold artefacts going back thousands of years, as well as colonial, republican (nineteenth-century) and modern art totalling some 5000 works. At time of print, the Museo Nacional was undergoing a full renovation of its twenty-year-old exhibition halls. The collection will stay the same when it reopens, and some works may be on display even as restoration proceeds.

Ceramics and artefacts

The collection includes some of the western hemisphere's oldest known ceramics crafted by the **Valdivia** culture (3500–1500 BC). It features remarkable female figurines and examples of **Chorrera** ceramics (900–300 BC), most famously the **whistle-bottles** in the form of various creatures, which mimic animal noises when water is poured into them. Also included in the collection are large, seated humans known as the **Gigantes de Bahía**, the work of the **Bahía** culture (500 BC–650 AD), which range from 50 to 100cm in height and show men and women sitting with their legs crossed or outstretched, wearing fine ornaments and elaborate headdresses. Perhaps most eye-catching are the pots and

1

figurines of the northern coast's **La Tolita** culture (600 BC–400 AD), comprising fantastical images including fanged felines with long, unfurling tongues. The Tolita culture produced one of the most iconic works of art of Ecuador, a stunning, sun-like image of a mythical face sprouting dozens of twisted rays tipped by monkeys and snakes. Other beautiful works of prehistoric gold displayed here including masks, breastplates, headdresses, assorted jewellery and ceremonial bowls, are both exquisite and exotic, with recurring motifs of cats, serpents and birds of prey.

Colonial, republican and modern art and sculpture

The museum's collection of Baroque colonial painting and sculpture is mostly religious in theme. It features works by the most celebrated artists of the Quito School (see box, p.66), including Caspicara and Bernardo de Legarda. Although these **paintings** and **polychrome carvings** are brilliantly executed and wonderfully expressive, the most striking aspect is the gory and macabre nature of Hispanic colonial religious art: countless images of lacerated Christs dying in agony on the cross and in one piece a decapitated San Dionisio standing with his head in his hands.

Around the time of independence, humanist, secular "republican" themes emerged, starting with portraits of revolutionary heroes and moving through landscapes and images of fruit-sellers, workers and festival dancers. The discovery of ordinary life led to *indigenismo*, a twentieth-century movement that set out to highlight the plight of indigenous people amid demands for social progress. The collection highlights Ecuadorian painters led by Oswaldo Guayasamín, Eduardo Kingman and Diógenes Paredes.

Exhibitions open during renovation

A side entrance provides access to separate permanent collections and temporary exhibitions housed in the main building. The **Museo de Instrumentos Musicales Pablo Traversari** has a collection of 540 lutes, flutes, guitars and other string instruments reaching back as far as 5000 years, but also of Baroque and nineteenth-century European instruments, many in fascinating, exotic forms. Past the collection of instruments, the small **ethnographic exhibition** is not at the same level as the Mindalae and Abya Yala collections except for a remarkable introduction into shamanic practices in a darkened chamber. Press a button alongside one of the displays and a quasi-hologram video of a Tsáchila, Kichwa or Shuar shaman will appear, carrying out a brief ceremony.

Museo Abya Yala

12 de Octubre 23-116 and Wilson • Mon–Fri 8.30am–1pm, 2–5.30pm • $2 • ☎ 02 396 2800

This museum specializes in archaeology and ethnology of Ecuador's seven separate Amazon indigenous cultures – Achuar, Cofán, Siona, Secoya, Waorani, Kichwaand, above all, the Shuar: it features a collection and careful explanation of these rainforest warriors' tradition of shrinking heads of defeated enemies into tzantzas. The museum also describes the troubling impact the oil industry has had on their livelihoods going back to its beginnings in the 1960s. Run by Universidad Politécnica Salesiana, it has a leading Spanish-language ethnography bookshop.

Mindalae

Reina Victoria N26-166 and La Niña • Mon–Sat 9.30am–5.30pm • $3 • ☎ 02 2230609

In a striking modern building that belies the timelessness of the crafts inside, **Mindalae** (or the Museo Etnohistórico de Artenasías del Ecuador) provides a comprehensive picture of indigenous life and culture, beautifully displayed over five floors. Peoples from the coast, highlands and Amazon of Ecuador are represented in exhibits of clothing, weavings, ceramics, jewellery, musical instruments and tools of everyday life; other areas explain ancient solar astronomy, indigenous rituals and shamanism.

A *mindala* (hence the museum's name) was a pre-Inca travelling merchant – fitting, then, that the museum includes a handicrafts shop and Fairtrade café.

Outside the centre

There are several attractions located outside the centre of Quito, most notably the ever-popular **TelefériQo**, a ski-lift-type gondola which swoops up to a lofty vantage point west of the capital. Another highlight is the buzzing **Parque La Carolina**, where among the trees and cycle paths you'll find a botanical garden, a natural science museum and the **Vivarium**, which houses snakes and amphibians.

A number of the sights outside the centre offer stupendous views of the old town from all cardinal points, two of the best being the **Basílica del Voto Nacional** and **Parque Itchimbía**; both can be reached on foot from the centre, while others are reachable via public transport or a short taxi ride. The panorama from the viewing platform of **El Panecillo**, just south of the old town, is particularly memorable. On the high ground east of town, the **Museo Fundación Guayasamín** and the associated **Capilla del Hombre** showcase the powerful works of Ecuador's most famous twentieth-century artist, while nearby **Guápulo** has the feel of a sleepy village.

Monasterio San Diego

Calicuchima 117 and General Farfán • Daily 9.30am–1pm & 2.30–5.30pm • $2 • Take a taxi ($2 from the old town), as the surrounding neighbourhood is unsafe

Just northwest of El Panecillo is the **Monasterio San Diego**, a beautiful early-colonial Franciscan monastery of quiet, cloistered courtyards, a refectory with a painting of Christ sitting down to eat *cuy* (guinea pig) at the Last Supper, simple whitewashed walls and the fragments of some restored murals. The complex offers a taste of both colonial and contemporary monastery life, with secret doors and old pit tombs, as well as views over the old town from the top of the bell tower; only the modest living quarters of the monastery's current occupants remain off-limits. The church features an exquisite **pulpit** thought to be the second oldest in South America, and a modest art collection.

Yaku Parque – Museo del Agua

El Placer Oe11-271, west of the old town • Tues–Sun 9am–5.30pm, last entry 4.30pm • $3 • Guided tours free in Spanish; $1 in English • ☎ 02 2511100, ⓦ yakumuseoagua.gob.ec • Take Metrobús Q to the Seminario Mayor stop on Avenida América (at Colón), then catch the "El Placer" bus, which will drop you outside the museum • A taxi from the old town costs $2

A few blocks west of San Francisco and steeply uphill, **Yaku Parque – Museo del Agua** is set in Quito's old water-treatment plant – a monolithic metal structure standing in the foothills of Volcán Pichincha. Guided tours take in the squares, fountains, vaults and exhibition rooms of the complex while the journey of Quito's water supply and the importance of water conservation is explained. The natural water sources in the mountainside here are said to have been the site of the Inca Atahualpa's ceremonial and purification baths. Whatever the truth of that legend, it's an impressive spot, commanding fine views down to the old town and across to neighbouring El Panecillo.

El Panecillo

At the southern end of the old town • A bus service (every 15–30min; 45min) runs between El Panecillo and La Mitad del Mundo (see p.90), but muggings are common on the steps up to El Panecillo from the end of García Moreno, so take a taxi instead ($2–4 from the old town) • **Virgen de Quito** Daily 9am–7pm • $2

Rising over the southern edge of the old town is the hill known as **El Panecillo** ("the little bread loaf"), crowned by a magnificent, 30m-high statue of the Virgin. The summit –

which is patrolled by guards between 9am and 7pm – offers exhilarating views down to the city, spread out below like pearl-white miniature houses enclosed by green hills. In contrast to the toy-town views, the winged **Virgen de Quito** is colossal up here, standing on an orb with a serpent curled around her feet, gazing serenely down to the city. You can climb the fifty-odd steps up the small tower on which she's standing to a **viewing platform**.

Parque La Carolina

A kilometre north of La Mariscal, between Av de la República and Av de los Shyris, is the southern tip of the large and leafy **Parque La Carolina**, the most popular green space in the city and always buzzing with football games, joggers, cyclists, hyperactive kids and strolling families. It's located in a swanky part of town, flanked by a wealthy barrio full of smart high-rises to the east and brilliant views of Pichincha to the west.

Museo Ecuatoriano de Ciencias Naturales
Parque La Carolina • Mon–Fri 8am–1pm & 1.45–4.45pm, Sat 9am–1pm • $2 • ☎ 02 2449824, ⓦ www.mecn.gob.ec

The **Museo Ecuatoriano de Ciencias Naturales** in the middle of Parque La Carolina, may suffer from a lack of cash, but it does boast some fascinating exhibits, including the 7m skeleton of an anaconda, the gigantic cranium of a blue whale and a chilling display of enormous spiders.

Jardín Botánico de Quito
Parque La Carolina • Mon–Fri 8am–4.45pm, Sat–Sun 9am–4.45pm • $3.50 • ☎ 02 333 0828

Next door to the Museo Ecuatoriano de Ciencias Naturales is the **Jardín Botánico de Quito**, where you can see a good cross-section of native Andean plants on meandering paths through reconstructed habitats, from cloudforest to páramo to dry mountain scrub. The highlights are the "crystal palaces", two greenhouses devoted to Ecuadorian orchids and tropical plants – giving a taste of the country's extraordinary floral colour and diversity.

Vivarium
Amazonas 3008 and Rumipamba • Tues–Sun 9.30am–5.30pm • $3 • ☎ 02 2271799, ⓦ vivarium.org.ec

At the edge of Parque La Carolina is one of Quito's most unusual attractions, the **Vivarium**, part of an NGO that promotes public education about Ecuador's native fauna and tries to improve conditions in the nation's zoos. On show in glass cabinets are 44 species of **reptiles** and **amphibians** – highlights include an **Equis**, one of the country's deadliest snakes, and a 5m king cobra.

La Cima de la Libertad

De los Libertadores • Tues–Fri 9am–5pm, Sat 10am–2pm • $1 • ☎ 02 2288733 • You'll need to take a taxi up here (about $8–10 for the return journey from the old town, including waiting time)

The sweeping hilltop views are part of the pleasure of visiting **La Cima de la Libertad**, a military museum on a foothill of Volcán Pichincha, marking the site of the victorious **Battle of Pichincha** that sealed Ecuador's independence from Spain on May 24, 1822. The Temple of the Fatherland museum houses a large collection of nineteenth-century uniforms, weapons and other military paraphernalia, enlivened by some **murals** of key characters and events. Easily the most impressive is Eduardo Kingman's enormous 200-square-metre mural, which explores the nation's historical roots.

Basílica del Voto Nacional

Venezuela • **Towers** daily 9am–5pm • $2 • **Church** Mon–Sat 7–8am & 6–7.30pm • Free

Perched on Calle Venezuela, eight blocks uphill of the Plaza Grande, the **Basílica del Voto Nacional** is the tallest church in Ecuador, thanks to its two imposing 115m

1

towers, plainly visible from much the city. Built in a flamboyant, neo-Gothic style begun in 1892, it's a wild concoction of spires, flying buttresses, turrets, parapets, arches, gables and elaborate stained-glass windows. The **gargoyles**, based on Ecuadorian fauna such as monkeys and jaguars, are a contemporary departure from the traditional representations of mythical creatures.

Don't miss the fantastic **views** from two vantage points accessed by a lift and then some vertiginous metal ladders: an unnerving buckling roof on the northern steeple, and a higher spot way up on the east tower, past the third-floor café, then on stairs and ladders past the clock machinery and belfry to an artificial floor made only of wide steel grille. From here, those with a head for heights can squeeze out onto tiny ledges on the spire's exterior for a genuine thrill.

Centro de Arte Contemporáneo

Montevideo and Luis Dávila • Daily 9.00 am–5.30 pm • $2 • ☎ 02 3946990

A short walk north of the Basílica del Voto Nacional is the **Centro de Arte Contemporáneo**, a triumphant rehabilitation of Quito's crumbling old Military Hospital into an impressive new exhibition and cultural centre – a bold project undertaken to commemorate the bicentenary of Quito's 1809 revolution (see p.387). For all its whitewashed colonnades, cobbled patios, tall windows and airy wards and corridors, the building (constructed between 1900 and 1929) seems uniquely well suited to house three large exhibition spaces dedicated to both visual and performing arts. Eventually the complex will also hold a library and auditorium, but till then it only presents temporary exhibitions: to find out what's on ask at a tourist office (see p.79) or check the website ⓦcentrodearte contemporaneo.gob.ec. The museum also has a fine view of northern Quito.

Itchimbía Centro Cultural

Iquique s/n, east of the old town • Tues–Sun 9am–6pm • Free • ☎ 02 2584362, ⓦ centrocultural-quito.com

On a hilltop directly southeast of the Basílica is the **Itchimbía Centro Cultural**, a stunning nineteenth-century market hall, reinvented as an art gallery and the centrepiece of the **Parque Itchimbía**, a green space commanding wonderful views over Quito. The glass-and-metal structure, featuring an imposing octagonal cupola which looks particularly impressive when floodlit by night, was imported from Hamburg in 1889 and originally located in the old town, before its removal and re-inauguration as an exhibition space 115 years later. Once you're up here you'll see there are charming places to refuel close by, above all *Café Mosaico* (see p.83), as well as an attractive park with reforestation in native Andean plants.

TelefériQo

Off avenidas Occidental and La Gasca, west of Mariscal Sucre • Daily 8am–7.30pm • $8.50 • ☎ 02 2222996 • Take a taxi (around $7 from the new town) or a TelefériQo minibus from the northern Ecovía terminal at Río Coca; the CCI, Quicentro and El Jardín malls; or the Estación Norte

A modern cable-car system, the **TelefériQo** transports six-person cabins from a base station at 2950m on the lower slopes of Volcán Pichincha, up to the antennae-barbed peak of Cruz Loma at 4053m. It opened in 2005 to great fanfare, and instantly became Quito's most popular attraction for sunny days and clear evenings. The 2.5km ride glides by in around eight minutes, wafting noiselessly above the treetops and over into the páramo moorlands of the high Andes to arrive at a series of lookouts, which give grand views over the capital ringed by the Cayambe, Antisana and Cotopaxi volcanoes.

From the top of the cable car, short trails lead up to lookout points. Signs tell you to take it easy as you ascend and if you've arrived in Quito within a couple of days this is good advice, as you'll definitely feel the thin air. You should also bring warm clothing,

1

as it can be bitingly cold up here. Beyond the complex, the trail continues up to the summit of **Rucu Pichincha** (4627m); however, there have been a number of robberies and assaults here, so give the hike a miss unless on a tour (see p.80).

Although the TeleferiQo is highly recommended, there's also an awful lot of flimflam – souvenir stores, food courts, even a dedicated amusement zone, VulQano Park – to circumnavigate while you're here. At weekends and on sunny afternoons, the whole place can get very crowded – it's quietest on weekday mornings.

Guápulo
Around 1km west of Parque La Carolina • Best reached by taxi (around $4–7 from the Mariscal)

The outdoor terrace of the Fundación Guayasamín and the Capilla del Hombre afford views down to the picturesque village of **GUÁPULO**, which is perched on the steep slopes on the east side of town. Its narrow, cobbled streets and terracotta-roofed, whitewashed houses have the look of a Mediterranean village, and feel far removed from the hurly-burly of the capital, particularly its spacious new park.

Santuario de Guápulo
Plazoleta de Guápulo • **Museum** Mon–Fri 8am–noon & 3–6pm • $1.50 • ☎ 02 2235576

Aside from the quaint streets, charming houses and relaxed atmosphere, the principal attraction here is the magnificent **Santuario de Guápulo**, a beautiful seventeenth-century church with an impressive pulpit and monastery. A fine museum inside, the **Museo Franciscano Fray Antonio Rodríguez**, displays some of the best pieces from the church's collection of colonial art, such as Quito School paintings by Miguel de Santiago and elegantly carved ecclesiastical furniture.

Parque Metropolitano Guanguiltagua
The main entrance is on C Juan Guanguiltagua in El Baltán Alta • Daily 6am–5.30pm • Free • A taxi from the Mariscal costs around $4

Running north–south along a ridge skirting the eastern edge of Quito, the **Parque Metropolitano Guanguiltagua** is often ignored by tourists but is the capital's most impressive green space, popular with middle-class Quiteños for walking their dogs or jogging. Although a magnet for families at weekends, it's easy to escape the crowds amid the sweet-smelling eucalyptus, although efforts are under way to reforest with native Andean trees. The park affords spectacular city and mountain views (including, on a clear day, of Pichincha, Cotopaxi, Cayambe and Antisana and, if really lucky, all the way to Chimborazo) and the chance for a serious hike, cycle or run in the fresh air, away from the traffic-filled streets below. There are trails of varying lengths and a 10km cycle route.

Casa-Museo de Viteri
Juncal N64-196 and Ambrosi beyond Parque Bicentenario (the old airport) • $10; visits must be arranged in advance • ☎ 02 2473114, 🖥 oswaldoviteri.com • A taxi from the Mariscal costs around $7

It's a rare privilege to be able to visit the home and studio of a celebrated painter, and thanks to the open invitation issued by **Oswaldo Viteri**, Ecuador's greatest living contemporary artist, you can do exactly that at the **Casa-Museo de Viteri**. He or his wife, Marta, will guide you around their formidable **art collection**, one of the best and most interesting in the country. Spanning the centuries from pre-Columbian times to the present day, the works are ingeniously displayed to emphasize *mestizaje*, the mixing of races, cultures and traditions underpinning Ecuador's cultural identity. Among the many treasures are a model of the *Santa María*, one of Columbus's three ships, sailing on a sea of pre-Columbian axe-heads; an exquisite eighteenth-century representation of the Virgin of Quito; and engravings by Goya and Picasso.

FROM TOP LA MITAD DEL MUNDO (P.90); MULTICOLOURED POSTCOLONIAL HOUSES, QUITO (P.57) >

1

The creative engine room is Viteri's **studio**, filled with paints and brushes, works in progress, antique tomes and the sharp smell of oils and white spirit. Viteri's boldness and versatility with the brush are unmistakable in striking portraits such as *Autorretrato con Amigos* (*Self-portrait with Friends*). But he is perhaps best known for his **assemblages**, including the astounding *Ojo de Luz* (*Eye of Light*), mixed-media works combining colourful dolls made by Ecuador's indigenous communities with material such as sackcloth or ornate Catholic livery.

Parque Arqueológico y Ecológico Rumipamba

Mariana de Jesús and Occidental • Wed–Sun 8am–4.30pm • Free • ☏ 02 2957576 • A taxi from the Mariscal costs around $5

The **Parque Arqueológico y Ecológico Rumipamba**, on the western slopes of the city, is just a short hop from La Mariscal. The 32-hectare park shows vestiges of a prehistoric agriculturalist village dating back three thousand years. The site wasn't continuously occupied, thanks to eruptions from Pululahua and Pichincha which destroyed parts of the village between 600 and 900 AD, but also surviving here are pre-Inca stone walls, thought to be the oldest in Quito. A small museum exhibits some of the prodigious quantities of ceramics found in the park.

Museo Fundación Guayasamín

Bosmediano 543 and José Carbo, northeast of Mariscal Sucre • Daily 10am–5pm, closed on national holidays • $4 • ☏ 02 2446455, ⓦ guayasamin.org • Best reached by taxi (around $5–7 from the Mariscal)

East of Parque La Carolina, in the hilltop barrio of Bellavista Alto, the **Museo Fundación Guayasamín** houses one of Quito's most compelling collections of art. The pre-Columbian pieces and colonial carvings and paintings are excellent, but the main attraction is the work of the late **Oswaldo Guayasamín**, Ecuador's most renowned contemporary artist.

Beginning with Guayasamín's early work from the 1940s, dealing mainly with "the struggle of the Indian", the collection moves through to his series *La Edad de la Ternura* (*The Age of Tenderness*), with his famous moon-faced, round-eyed women and children shown in close, tender embraces – a tribute to his and all mothers. Guayasamín's great triumph is his disturbing **Edad de la Ira** (*Age of Anger*) series, where massive canvases feature repetitive images of giant clenched hands, faces screaming in agony, skeletal figures that look utterly defeated and bodies in positions of torture.

Capilla del Hombre

Mariano Calvache and Lorenzo Chávez • Tues–Sun 10am–5.30pm • $4 • The chapel is a 10min walk from the Museo Guayasamín; go a short distance uphill and turn right onto José Carbo and follow the road along to the chapel

Overlooking the capital, close to the Museo Fundación Guayasamín, is the **Capilla del Hombre**, which was begun in 1995 but only completed in 2002, three years after Guayasamín's death. It is a secular "chapel" dedicated to humanity itself. The two-storey gallery serves as both a memorial to the suffering of the oppressed and victims of war and torture, and a celebration of Latin American identity and the positive aspects of human nature. The scope of the works is as ambitious as it is affecting, from the agonies of workers in the silver mines of **Potosí**, Bolivia, where eight million people perished over three centuries, to the poignancy of motherhood and the family, in the famous *La Ternura* (*Tenderness*), to the uncharacteristically light-hearted *Bull and the Condor*, representing the tensions between Andean and Spanish traditions. On the lower floor, an **eternal flame** flickers for the cause of human rights – though it was initially broken on the gallery's inaugural night when a child dropped a cola bottle on it. Above the chapel in the grounds of Guayasamín's house are sculptures, a Honduran Maya stela and the memorial **Tree of Life**, where the artist's ashes were deposited.

1

BUS COMPANIES IN QUITO

Expreso Internacional Ormeño Av Los Shyris 11-68 and Portugal ☎ 02 2456630.
Destinations include Lima, Cali, Bogotá, Caracas, La Paz, Sao Paulo, Santiago and Buenos Aires.

Flor del Valle Manuel Larrea and Asunción ☎ 02 2527495, ⦿ flordelvalle.com.ec.
Destinations Cayambe and Mindo.

Flota Imbabura Manuel Larrea 1211 and Portoviejo ☎ 02 2236940, ⦿ flota-imbabura.com.
Destinations Cuenca, Guayaquil, Manta and Tulcán.

Panamericana Internacional Colón 852 and Reina Victoria ☎ 02 2557133, ⦿ panamericana.ec.
Domestic destinations Atacames, Cuenca,

Huaquillas, Machala, Loja, Guayaquil, Manta and Esmeraldas.
International destinations Caracas, Máncora, Cali, Bogotá, Medellín, Lima, Piura.

Transportes Ecuador Juan León Mera N21-44 and Jorge Washington ☎ 02 225315, ⦿ transportes ecuador.
Destinations Major coastal cities including Guayaquil.

Transportes Rutas de América Internacional Selva Alegre Oe1-70 and 10 de Agosto ☎ 02 2503611, ⦿ rutasenbus.com.
Destinations Bogotá, Buenos Aires, Caracas, La Paz, Lima and Montevideo.

ARRIVAL AND DEPARTURE QUITO

Quito is at the heart of Ecuador's national transport network and offers **bus** access to just about every corner of the country, along with regular domestic **flights** and limited tourist **train** services. Arrival in Quito can be a little unnerving, with huge crowds pressing around the exit gate at the airport, and a confusing layout and sometimes intimidating atmosphere at the bus terminals. The best thing to do is to get a **taxi** straight to your accommodation, where you can orientate yourself.

BY PLANE

Quito's new international airport (⦿ aeropuertoquito .aero) is near the village of Tababela, around 18km east of the city. The journey to the old town/La Mariscal (30min–1hr during the rush hours) costs $25–30 by taxi. Shuttle buses (every 30min; $8) run throughout the day and night between the old airport, 6km from La Mariscal ($5–7 by taxi), and the new one. For more than one person, a taxi is a much better deal, and the old airport is unsafe for arrivals after dark. Slower but less expensive public buses ($2) also run into town from the new airport, but it is far safer and faster to use the shuttle (during daylight hours) or a taxi. As well as numerous international connections, there are daily flights to destinations throughout Ecuador.

BY BUS

Most regional and long-distance journeys from Quito are likely to be by bus, and the city has two main stations: Terminal Quitumbe (mainly for destinations to the south of Quito) and Terminal Carcelén (mainly for destinations to the north of Quito). A few buses use the much smaller Terminal Ofelia, and a number have ticket offices in the new town (see box above). Be aware of pickpockets and bag-snatchers in and around all the terminals, and on public transport to and from the terminals. Taking a taxi to and from the terminals is the safest option, especially if you have luggage or are travelling after dark; if heading to a terminal, ask to be dropped off inside the complex rather than on a street outside. Also bear in mind that bus timetables are notoriously prone to change.

TERMINAL TERRESTRE QUITUMBE

Quito's main bus terminal (☎ 02 2907 005; ext. 31222 for bus schedules) is about 10km south of the old town at Avenida Cóndor Ñan and Avenida Mariscal Sucre. The Trole (see p.78) connects the terminal with the old and new towns, but a taxi (around $12–14 to the centre-north, a bit less to the old town; the journey can take well over an hour) is a much better option. There's a 20 cent usage fee charged when you buy your ticket.

Destinations Alausí (4 daily at 7.25am, 9.25am, 12.15pm & 5.25pm; 5hr); Ambato (every 5–15min; 2hr 30min); Atacames (6 daily; 6hr 30min); Baeza (every 30min–1hr; 3hr); Bahía de Caráquez (4 daily at 8.30am, 10.30am, 3.15pm & 11.30pm; 8hr); Baños (every 15–30min; 3hr 15min); Coca (25 daily; 10hr); Cuenca (every 15–30min; 11–12hr); Esmeraldas (every 20–30min; 6hr); Guaranda (every 20–30min; 4hr 30min); Guayaquil (every 10–20min; 8hr); Huaquillas (15 daily; 11hr); Lago Agrio (every 30min–1hr; 8hr); Latacunga (every 10–20min; 2hr); Loja (around 25 daily; 14–16hr); Macará (3 daily at 2pm, 4pm & 6pm; 15hr); Macas (10 daily; 10hr); Machala (21 daily; 10hr); Manta (every 15–30min; 8hr 30min); Papallacta (every 30min–1hr; 1hr 30min); Pedernales (19 daily; 5hr); Pujilí (every 15–30min; 2hr); Puyo (23 daily; 5hr); Quevedo (20 daily; 4hr 30min); Riobamba (every 15–30min; 4hr); Salinas (5 daily at 9.30am, 8.50pm, 9.20pm, 9.50pm & 10.20pm; 10hr); San Lorenzo (1 daily at 9.15pm; 7hr); San Vicente (4 daily at 1pm, 5pm, 7pm & 11.30pm; 9hr); Santo Domingo (every 10–15min; 3hr); Saquisilí (10 daily; 1hr 30min); Sigchos (4 daily at 8am, 9am, 10am & 2pm; 5hr); Tena (25 daily; 5hr); and Tulcán (every 10–20min; 5hr).

1

TERMINAL TERRESTRE CARCELÉN

Quito's second busiest bus terminal (☎ 02 3961600) is in the far north of the city on Avenida Eloy Alfaro. Frequent public buses connect the terminal with the Ecovía network, but a taxi (around $10 to the new town, a bit more to the old town; 30–50min) is a better option.

Destinations Atacames (5 daily at 8am, 9.10am, 11.10am, 1.30pm, 11.15pm; 7hr); El Ángel (19 daily; 4hr); Cotacachi (4 daily at 11.30am, 3.40pm, 6.40pm & 9.30pm; 2hr 20min); Esmeraldas (9 daily; 7hr); Ibarra (every 15–20min; 2hr 30min); Otavalo (every 10min; 2hr); San Gabriel (17 daily; 4hr 15min); San Lorenzo (8 daily; 7hr); and Tulcán (every 10–20min; 5hr).

TERMINAL TERRESTRE LA OFELIA

Some buses to destinations northwest of Quito depart from the small Terminal La Ofelia, which is in the north of the city on Diego Vásquez de Cepeda, off Avenida de la Prensa. A taxi here to the Mariscal costs around $15 (30–40min), and about $4 more to the old town; Metrobús services also connect the terminal with the rest of Quito, though a taxi is a better option at night or if you have luggage with you.

Destinations Cayambe (every 5–10min; 1hr 20min), Mindo (Mon–Fri 8am, 9am, 3pm & 4pm, Sat–Sun 7.40am, 8.20am, 9.20am, 2pm & 4pm; 1hr 30min–2hr) and La Mitad del Mundo (every 15min–1hr; 30–45min).

BY TRAIN

Ecuador's railway has been partially restored purely as an excursion and tourism service. The luxury, multi-day Tren Crucero package connecting Quito and Guayaquil is the only way to arrive or depart by rail. The indefinite threat of a major eruption of Cotopaxi means that departures and arrivals from the charming Chimbacalle station near the historic centre may go ahead by bus, with train service only between Latacunga and Guayaquil. Daily excursions at the time of printing were available from Quito to El Boliche near Cotopaxi for $50, but could be suspended at short notice if volcanic activity increases. Tickets are available online at ⊕ trenecuador.com (☎ 1800 873 637).

GETTING AROUND

The various forms of **public transport** make for easy access between the old and the new towns, although traffic can be slow; consider walking from the Basílica down to the centre. **Taxis** are also inexpensive, convenient and plentiful; at night, or if you are carrying valuables or luggage, you should use nothing else. Only use legally marked taxis (see opposite).

BY TROLE, ECOVÍA AND METROBÚS

Three wheelchair-accessible Buss Rapid Transit networks service Quito, running north–south on broadly parallel routes. The systems are segregated from the general chaos of ordinary traffic and provide a fast (if crowded) ride. The flat fare is $0.25; pay the fare into the machine by the entrance barrier, or buy a book of tickets at slightly discounted rates from one of the kiosks. Each system is augmented by feeder buses (*alimentadores*), which branch off into the suburbs from the main terminals. Broadly speaking, services run 5/6am–9.30pm/midnight.

BY TROLE

The Trole (⊕ trolebus.gob.ec) is a little different from the other two lines in that it uses electric trolleybuses. It runs for about 16km from its northern terminus (Terminal Norte) along the Avenida 10 de Agosto into the heart of the old town and then deep into southern Quito, finishing at Terminal Quitumbe. Not every trolleybus serves the entire line, with different route numbers and colour codes indicating where they begin and end, but unless you're travelling outside the central areas – including the old town and La Mariscal – it shouldn't make any difference which bus you take. There's a one-way system through the old town: southbound buses go along Guayaquil, while those returning north use Flores and Montúfar.

BY ECOVÍA

The Ecovía runs for 9km between La Marín in the old town and the Río Coca transfer station in the north, mainly along the Avenida 6 de Diciembre, and operates in much the same manner as the Trole, except that it uses a fleet of articulated, low-emission buses *ecológicos*.

BY METROBÚS

The Metrobús is the newest part of the system, running similar *buses ecológicos* between La Marín in the old town and Carcelén in the north, passing the airport and the La Ofelia bus terminal, mainly by way of avenidas América and de la Prensa.

BY BUS

Quito's ordinary buses operate from about 6am to 9pm and screech to a halt whenever anyone wants to get on or off. There's no route map available to make sense of the 130-plus lines, but main stops and final destinations are marked on the front window. The flat fare is usually $0.25, but there are a few beaten-up *populares* that are a bit cheaper; pay with coins or small-denomination notes. Although there are designated bus stops, it's normally possible to flag down a bus wherever you are, and to get off at any street corner (shout "*en la esquina, por favor*" or "*parada*"). Green interparroquial buses service outlying suburbs and districts. Many city buses pass through La Marín, a stretched-out, chaotic and none-too-safe bus station between old town and the La Tola neighbourhood.

BY CAR

Although you're unlikely to need (or want) to drive in Quito, numerous car rental companies have offices in the city, including: Avis, Av de los Granados E11-26 and 6 de Diciembre (02 6016000, avis.com.ec); Budget at Eloy Alfaro S40-153 and José Queri (02 2244095, budget-ec.com), also offers half-day taxi service for $38. For more on renting a vehicle in Ecuador, check out Basics (see p.28).

BY TAXI

Quito has thousands of yellow taxis, but make sure you pick one with a four-digit or five-digit code on a green sticker on its doors and windscreen, which signifies that it's legal. Quito is the only city in Ecuador where taxis regularly use a meter (*taxímetro*), and fares are pretty cheap, minimum $1.45; if the driver doesn't turn it on, a polite "*ponga su taxímetro, por favor*" should jolt his memory. Even though they're legally required to do so at all hours, many taxi drivers don't use their meters at night, so agree a price beforehand.

Taxi companies If you want to book a taxi, try Americantaxi (02 2222333), City Taxi (02 2633333) or Taxi Amigo (02 2222222). Easy Taxi and OK Taxi are reliable taxi apps.

BY BICYCLE

Ciclopaseos are held on Sundays (8am–2pm), when about 30km of key streets are closed off to traffic so cyclists (and pedestrians) can traverse the city north to south on car-free roads; visit ciclopolis.ec for more details. For rentals and tours, contact the agencies listed (see p.80). For a mountain city, the north–south area is flat enough to bike, and the number of bike lanes is growing.

INFORMATION

Quito Turismo Maps, leaflets, brochures on Quito, English-speaking staff and an informative website (quito.com.ec), as well as several information offices around the city. It also has a useful IOS and Android app. The head office, El Quinde, is in the old town in the Palacio Municipal (02 2572445; Mon–Fri 9am–6pm, Sat 9am–8pm, Sun 10am–5pm), and there are other offices: in La Mariscal at Ecuador Gourmet, Reina Victoria N24-263 and Lizardo García (02 2239469; Mon–Fri 9am–6pm, Sat–Sun 11am–7pm); at the airport (02 2818363; daily 8am–midnight); and at Terminal Terrestre Quitumbe (02 3824815; daily 8am–7pm).

Ministerio de Turismo At the edge of the old town opposite the Parque Alameda at Av Gran Colombia and Briceño, the national Ministerio de Turismo (Mon–Fri 8.30am–5pm; 02 3999333, ecuador.travel) has a small office on the ground floor, equipped with glossy brochures and maps of Quito and Ecuador.

South American Explorers (SAE) At Mariana de Jesús Oe3-32 and Ulloa, travel NGO South American Explorers (02 2227235, saexplorers.org; Mon–Fri 9.30am–5pm, Sat 9.30am–1pm) is a good source of information. Non-members can pop in for basic advice, while members (see the website for details on joining) receive a much wider range of benefits including detailed travel reports, weekly activities, mail and luggage storage, tours and discounts on accommodation and services.

TOURS

There's no shortage of **tour operators** in Quito, with many of them located in La Mariscal, particularly along Amazonas, Juan León Mera and their adjoining streets. Almost all offer everything from half-day city tours to week-long trips into the jungle or cruises around the Galápagos Islands. **Prices** can vary wildly, so it's worth shopping around.

QUITO CITY TOURS

General tours Standard city tours (around $30–50) last about three hours and usually include a mix of riding in a vehicle and walking around the old town, visiting a few churches and museums and then taking a trip to the top of El Panecillo. Many operators also make tours of the old town by night, when the churches and monuments are illuminated. Casa 1028 runs old town lunch ($38; full day $65) and dinner ($43) tours aboard a bus (02 26035143, casa1028.com).

Walking tours Quito Turismo (02 2572445, quito.com.ec) runs a variety of interesting and inexpensive walking tours ($4–15) of the old town, including one at night and others aimed at children. Book at the main office in the Palacio Municipal off the Plaza Grande or by phone.

TOURS FROM QUITO

Standard day-trips (generally $30–100) from Quito offered by general operators include visits to the Mitad del Mundo monument (see p.91), Otavalo (see p.104), Saquisilí (see p.143), Zumbahua (see p.145) and Parque Nacional Cotopaxi (see p.137). Many also offer birding tours to cloudforest reserves close to the capital, or trips based around stays in luxurious haciendas. The larger companies can put together complete customized packages, and almost all of the agencies are agents for Galápagos Islands cruise companies. Many also offer adventure tours, such as whitewater rafting, mountain biking, horse riding and trekking. When comparing prices, always check what is included, particularly with regards to equipment, food, accommodation and the

1

availability of English-speaking guides. For multi-day trips, try to meet your guide beforehand.

GENERAL TOUR OPERATORS

Campus Trekking J. Vargas 99 and A. Calderón, Conocoto ☎ 02 2340601, ⓦ campus-trekking.com; map p.58. A Dutch–Ecuadorian company that is particularly strong on trekking, as well as climbing, cultural, Galápagos and adventure trips.

CarpeDM Adventures Antepara E4-70 and Los Ríos ☎ 02 2954713, ⓦ carpedm.ca; map p.60. A professional Canadian-run agency with a social and environmental conscience: carbon offsetting is used and a percentage of profits goes to local charities. It offers excellent tours of all types throughout Ecuador, and can also help with volunteer placements.

Ecuador Adventure Manuel Sotomayor E17-105 and Flores Jijón ☎ 02 26046800, ⓦ ecuadoradventure.ec; map p.58. An all-rounder offering culture tours of the big sights in and around Quito, and many adventure tours, including trekking, kayaking, mountain biking and whitewater rafting.

Ecuadorian Tours Amazonas N21-33 and Jorge Washington ☎ 02 2560488, ⓦ ecuadoriantours.com; map p.68. Founded in 1947, this experienced and reliable agency provides all the usual sierra tours, plus a wide choice of programmes in other parts of the country, including the southern coast.

Happy Gringo Travel Edificio Catalina Plaza, Catalina Aldaz N34-155 & Portugal ☎ 02 5123486, ⓦ happygringo.com; map p.68. A well-run Anglo-Dutch tour operator that offers everything from day-trips showcasing the "real" side of Quito life to Amazon and Galápagos trips. Staff are helpful and the agency gets consistently good reports from travellers.

Klein Tours/Go Galápagos Eloy Alfaro N34-151 and Catalina Aldaz ☎ 02 2267000, ⓦ kleintours.com; map p.58. One of Quito's most established and polished operators offering something for everyone, from wildlife to cultural tours all over the country, focused on Galápagos cruises and tailor-made packages.

Metropolitan Touring De las Palmeras N45-74 and De las Orquídeas ☎ 02 2988200, ⓦ metropolitan-touring .com; map p.58. Huge travel agent and operator, with branches across Ecuador and a wealth of resources, offering top-notch tours and packages throughout the country and elsewhere in South America.

Quasar Expeditions José Jussieu N41-28 and Alonso de Torres ☎ 02 2446996, ⓦ galapagosexpeditions.com; map p.58. A recommended top-end operator providing customized tours of the whole country, using luxury accommodation. Also an excellent Galápagos cruise operator (see p.344).

Safari Tours Av del Establo 118, Cumbayá,

☎ 02 2552505, ⓦ safari.com.ec; map p.68. A British– Ecuadorian-run operator with a wide choice of tours, including custom trekking, climbing and Jeep trips. Also offers women-only tours, with female drivers and guides, and has information on many Galápagos boats.

Surtrek San Ignacio E10-114 and Plácido Caamaño ☎ 02 2500660, ⓦ surtrek.com; map p.68. Excellent and long-established top-end operator specializing in customized tours across Ecuador, including Galápagos cruises and diving trips, stays in Amazonian ecolodges and trips along the coast. Highly recommended.

Tropic Ecological Adventures La Niña E7-46 and Reina Victoria ☎ 02 2225907, ⓦ tropiceco.com; map p.68. Award-winning ecologically and culturally sensitive operator offering tours in the sierra and western cloudforests, and above all to the Amazon, as well as Floreana in the Galápagos (see p.368).

CLIMBING AND TREKKING OPERATORS

If you're going climbing, don't cut costs – while many of the climbs near Quito are not technically difficult, the potential hazards are very serious. Check that your operator uses only guides qualified by ASEGUIM (Asociación Ecuatoriana de Guías de Montaña), and take a close look at its equipment before signing up. Ideally, the company should provide one guide for every two climbers. If you need to buy climbing equipment, try MonoDedo (☎ 02 2904496, ⓦ monodedo .com), which has a climbing and mountaineering shop (Mon–Fri 11am–7pm, Sat 9.30am–1.30pm), and a climbing gym, at Larrea N24-36 and Av Coruña. All the companies listed below also offer trekking tips.

Andean Face Luis Coloma N44-81 and El Inca ☎ 02 22437611, ⓦ andeanface.com; map p.58. Socially responsible Dutch–Ecuadorian company specializing in high-altitude mountaineering and trekking. Also offers glacier training and bespoke climbing expeditions.

Compañía de Guías de Montaña 6 de Diciembre N20-50 and Jorge Washington ☎ 02 2901551, ⓦ companiadeguias.com; map p.68. Very reliable outfit run by a group of experienced Ecuadorian and Swiss mountain guides who take climbers up all the main snow peaks and on trekking trips across the sierra.

Ecuadorian Alpine Institute Ramírez Dávalos 136 and Amazonas, office 102 ☎ 02 2565465, ⓦ volcano climbing.com; map p.68. As well as guiding up all the main peaks and doing treks, this company runs a climbing school teaching basic mountaineering skills to beginners.

CYCLING AND RAFTING OPERATORS

Biking tours typically start from a high point and hurtle downhill on mountain bikes to a pick-up point from where you are shuttled home. That's not to say it's all coasting; you'll get uphill stretches on many itineraries. Whitewater rafting (and kayaking) trips are also on offer.

Arie's Bike Company Av Interoceánica Km22.5 vía Pifo, La Libertad, Calle de Los Hongos, LT5 ☎02 2380802, ⓦariesbikecompany.com; map p.58. Offers bike tours of one to fourteen days, which might include descents down volcanoes, into jungle from Papallacta or Baños and rides throughout the sierra.

Biking Dutchman La Pinta E-731 and Amazonas ☎02 2568323, ⓦbikingdutchman.com; map p.68. The original bike-tour operator in Ecuador – run, appropriately enough, by a pedalling Dutchman – with a wide range of mainly downhill biking tours from one to eight days.

Yacu Amu Checoslovaquia E10-137 and 6 de Diciembre ☎02 2461511, ⓦyacuamu.com; map p.58. Largest and longest-established whitewater rafting and kayaking specialist in Ecuador, offering runs on the best routes (grades II–V) in the Blanco, Quijos, Napo and Upano watersheds. Also does tours that combine rafting with caving, biking, hiking and the like, and runs a kayaking school.

ACCOMMODATION

Quito has a huge range of accommodation, in all price ranges. Most people stay in the **centre-north**, especially in the Mariscal area, where you'll find innumerable cafés, restaurants, bars and clubs, and most of the banks and travel agencies. Many streets are noisy, however, so it's always worth asking for a back room. Staying in the **old town**, which is benefiting from an ongoing regeneration, is a much more atmospheric option, especially if you have the money to splash out on one of the luxurious colonial conversions. You're also close to most of the city's sights, though you can't really explore safely beyond the blocks around the Plaza Independencia after dark. Wherever you stay, it's always best to take a taxi from your arrival point straight to your hotel and to avoid wandering the streets with your luggage.

THE NEW TOWN

Antinéa Juan Rodríguez 175 ☎02 2506838, ⓦhotelantinea.com; map p.68. Elegant French-run villa on a central leafy street, containing a mix of en-suite rooms, suites and mini-apartments, all tastefully furnished. There's also a pretty interior patio, a gym and a sauna. A sizeable French-style breakfast is included. **$75**

L'Auberge Inn Colombia 1138 and Yaguachi ☎02 2552912, ⓦauberge-inn-hostal.com; map p.68. Situated between old and new towns, this pleasant Swiss-owned joint has clean and comfortable rooms equipped with firm mattresses and shared or private bathrooms, as well as a soothing garden patio, kitchen facilities, a restaurant and luggage storage. Breakfast included. **$35**

Café Cultura Robles 513 and Reina Victoria ☎02 2564956, ⓦcafecultura.com; map p.68. Exuberantly decorated old house with high ceilings, big stone fireplaces, and bright walls with frescos of parrots, flowers, dolphins and cherubs. The rooms on the ground and first floors are the best, along with the three suites (each of which has a Victorian cast-iron bath). There's a good restaurant too, and breakfast is included. **$100**

★**Casa Helbling** Veintimilla E8-152 and 6 de Diciembre ☎02 2226013, ⓦcasahelbling.de; map p.68. Relaxed, German-Ecuadorean bed and breakfast with excellent service and better quality than more expensive places, including double glazing to keep the street noise out. There's a garden to the back, kitchen facilities and a roofed sitting area around a huge palm tree. Breakfast $3.80–6.90. Dorms **$12**; doubles **$21**

★**La Casa Sol** Calama 127 and 6 de Diciembre ☎02 2230798, ⓦlacasasol.com; map p.68. Lovely guesthouse with comfortable en suites set around a pretty little courtyard. It's run by cheerful staff, mainly from the Otavalo region, who are unfailingly polite and helpful. Facilities include a sitting room with a fireplace, luggage storage, book exchange and a TV lounge. Breakfast included. **$60**

Hostal la Rábida La Rábida 227 and Santa María ☎02 2222169, ⓦhostalrabida.com; map p.68. This charming Italian-owned hotel, on a quiet residential street, has the feel of a period house, with its wooden floors, crackling fire and elegant rooms. Service is excellent, and there's a fine restaurant too. Breakfast included. **$92**

Hotel Vieja Cuba La Niña N26-202 and Diego de Almagro ☎02 2906729, ⓦhotelviejacuba.com; map p.68. Located a short walk away from the heart of La Mariscal, this attractive little mid-range hotel offers bright en suites with wooden floors and fittings, a pretty flower garden and a Cuban restaurant. Breakfast included. **$87**

JW Marriott Orellana 1172 and Amazonas ☎02 2972000, ⓦmarriott.com; map p.68. Unmistakeable ziggurat of cream stone and green glass, the *Marriott* has stately en suites with all the mod cons you'd expect; try to get one with a mountain view. Facilities include a gym, spa, pool and a quality restaurant. Discounted rates are available at weekends and online. Breakfast included. **$159**

Lugano Suites Suiza N33-132 and Checoslovaquia ☎02 3331900, ⓦluganosuiteshotel.com; map p.68. A great option for families, groups or couples planning to self-cater, *Lugano Suites* has a collection of economical apartments with bedrooms, bathrooms and kitchenettes (the latter feature stoves, microwaves, fridges and coffee-makers, as well as pots and pans). There's also a terrace with barbecue equipment. Breakfast included. **$98**

Magic Bean Foch E5-08 ☎02 2566181, ⓦmagicbeanquito.com; map p.68. The coffee shop and café of the same name (see p.84), *Magic Bean* has a handful of compact dorms and neat and tidy en-suite rooms (one of which has its own kitchenette). Breakfast for overnight guests $2.50. Dorms **$14.50**; doubles start at **$35**

1

LONG-TERM ACCOMMODATION

The best place to look for **long-term accommodation** is in the classified section of the daily newspaper *El Comercio*, especially on Sundays. You might also try the notice boards of South American Explorers (see p.79), which also keeps a list of homestays. **Rates** are around $300–450 per month for a two-bedroom apartment in the new town, though foreigners are often charged inflated prices; try to get a local friend to come along to negotiate the price. For medium-term stays **apart-hotels** are a good option. They're a bit more expensive than renting your own apartment, but are comfortable, furnished and easy to arrange. Try *Antinéa* or *Lugano Suites* (see p.81). You can also check online rental site ⓦ **airbnb.com**.

Mansión del Angel Wilson E5-29 ☎02 2557721, ⓦmansiondelangel.com.ec; map p.68. This elegant boutique hotel is housed in an old mansion lavishly decorated with crystal chandeliers, gilt cornices, chaises longues and dark oil paintings. Most rooms have four-poster beds. Breakfast included. $150

NH Collection Quito Cordero 444 and 12 de Octubre ☎02 2233333, ⓦnh-collection.com/hotel/nh-collection -quito-royal; map p.68. Modernized lobby, restaurants and rooms make the hotel one of Quito's top choices. While directly connected to the World Trade Centre office complex, the *NH Quito* offers competitive rates. There's a fully fitted gym and health club and a large business centre. Weekend discounts available online. Breakfast included. $110

Nü House Foch E6-12 and Reina Victoria ☎02 2557845, ⓦnuhousehotels.com; map p.68. Slick boutique hotel with two restaurants in the centre of La Mariscal – the location is convenient for night owls, though not the most peaceful. The minimalist en suites come with queen-sized beds, stone-wall bathrooms with vessel sinks and 32-inch TVs. Breakfast included. $119

Posada del Maple Juan Rodríguez E8-49 ☎02 2544507, ⓦposadadelmaple.com; map p.58. Straddling the line between hostel and B&B, *Posada del Maple* has a range of spick and span private rooms, some of which are en suite, as well as a dorm. There's a communal kitchen (with free tea and coffee), plus a patio and roof terrace. The owners also run the slightly smarter *Alcalá* (Luis Cordero E5-48 and Reina Victoria). Breakfast included. Dorms $10; doubles $32

Swissôtel 12 de Octubre 1820 and Luis Cordero ☎02 2567600, ⓦswissotel.com; map p.58. This five-star is an excellent choice: service is friendly and efficient, rooms are spacious and well kitted out, there's a small pool, a tennis court, a wonderful gym and spa complex and several high-quality restaurants. Breakfast included. $178

Travellers Inn Joaquín Pinto E4-435 ☎02 2556985, ⓦtravellersecuador.com; map p.68. This inexpensive hotel is fairly quiet by Quito standards. Based in a renovated townhouse, it has welcoming staff and clean and comfortable rooms with either shared or private bathrooms. Good for couples or groups, though not the most sociable for single travellers. Breakfast included. $48

Vibes Hostel Joaquín Pinto 132 and 6 de Diciembre ☎02 2555154, ⓦvibesquito.com; map p.68. Popular hostel with a lively, sociable atmosphere, though it's not the quietest place. It has four- and six-bed dorms, private rooms with shared bathrooms, a big communal kitchen, a pool table, a well-stocked DVD collection, regular happy hours at the in-house bar and Sunday all-you-can-eat barbecues. Breakfast included. Dorms $9; doubles $25

THE OLD TOWN

★**Casa Gangotena** Bolívar Oe6-41 and Cuenca ☎02 4008000, ⓦcasagangotena.com; map p.60. While expensive, *Casa Gangotena* is a fittingly luxurious place to stay. An opulent boutique hotel in a restored historic mansion on Plaza San Francisco, it has regal en suites (not all have plaza views), a wood-panelled library, a garden and terrace overlooking the plaza, and an excellent gourmet restaurant. The starting rack rate is given here, but cheaper deals are often available online. Breakfast, afternoon coffee service and evening presentations for guests included. $450

Hostal La Posada Colonial J Paredes S1-49 and Rocafuerte ☎02 2282859, ⓦlaposadacolonial.com; map p.60. A family-run hotel in a 1930s home near Santo Domingo with a selection of simple rooms of varying shapes and sizes. They all retain original features such as wooden floors, and most are en suite: no.15 is probably the pick of the bunch. There's also a roof terrace and a lounge area. Breakfast $2.50. $24

Hostal Colonial House Olmedo 432 and Los Ríos ☎02 23161810, ⓦcolonialhousequito.com; map p.60. In the La Tola neighbourhood, this hostel is a reliable option, with clean dorms and private rooms (though the showers could be hotter and more powerful). There's a communal kitchen, helpful staff and activities such as Spanish lessons on offer. Breakfast $3. Dorms $10; doubles $20

Hotel Boutique Portal de Cantuña Bolívar Oe6-105 and Cuenca ☎02 2282276, ⓦhotelportaldecantuna .com; map p.60. This family-run hotel, based in an atmospheric old townhouse just off Plaza San Francisco, is impeccably decorated, with rooms set around a gorgeous central atrium. All the rooms are en suite and feature artwork and local crafts and rugs; one even has its own attached living room. Staff are incredibly friendly too. Breakfast included. $83

Huasi Lodge Olmedo E4-74 and Los Ríos ☎ 02 3161644, ⓦ huasilodge.com; map p.60. Between old town and Itchimbía, excellent for backpackers, with both dorms and private rooms. There's a communal kitchen, TV lounge, pool table, plenty of information and perks such as the thrice-weekly free rum and Coke nights. Breakfast included. Dorms $5; doubles $16

Patio Andaluz García Moreno N6-52 and Olmedo ☎ 02 2280830, ⓦ hotelpatioandaluz.com; map p.60. In a fabulous old building – parts of which date from the sixteenth century – with colonnaded courtyards and balconies, *Patio Andaluz* has elegant, if rather pricey en suites, a great restaurant, a library and a gift shop. Breakfast included. $270

★ **Plaza Grande** García Moreno N5-16 and Chile ☎ 02 2510777, ⓦ plazagrandequito.com; map p.60. This luxury hotel in a restored Neoclassical building enjoys an unrivalled location on the Plaza Grande. All the rooms are suites (three of them overlook the square) and come with hot tubs and hefty price tags, though they are undoubtedly gorgeous. The restaurant serves sumptuous food too. The rack rate is given here, but cheaper deals can often be found online. Breakfast included. $450

Real Audiencia Bolívar Oe3-18 and Guayaquil ☎ 02 2952711, ⓦ realaudiencia.com; map p.60. Although rather old-fashioned, this mid-range hotel has sizeable en suites with TVs, phones and writing desks – they're comfortable, but not the most stylish. Some rooms – and the third-floor restaurant – have wonderful views over Plaza Santo Domingo. Breakfast included. $80

El Relicario del Carmen Venezuela 1041 and Olmedo ☎ 02 2289120, ⓦ hotelrelicariodelcarmen.com; map p.60. A warm welcome awaits you at this atmospheric hotel, in a sensitively renovated building dating from 1705. The attractive rooms vary in size and shape, but all

are comfortable and have plenty of colonial features such as beamed ceilings and patterned tiles. Breakfast included. $150

San Francisco de Quito Sucre 217 and Guayaquil ☎ 02 2287758, ⓦ sanfranciscodequito.com.ec; map p.60. A beautiful colonial building, *San Francisco de Quito* has modest but clean and comfortable en-suite rooms set around a charming, geranium-filled courtyard with a fountain. There's also a communal TV lounge and a terrace. Breakfast included. $62

AROUND QUITO

If the hurly-burly of the city centre is too daunting, you could consider staying at one of the hotels on the outskirts of town, where you'll have the benefits of a more peaceful and spacious setting, but still be within range to visit the city sights.

Hacienda Rumiloma Obispo de la Madrid s/n, on the slopes of Pichincha ☎ 02 3200953, ⓦ rumiloma.com; map p.58. This luxurious hacienda combines a tranquil location with easy access (10–15min by car) to central Quito. Each of the adobe-walled rooms is spacious and tastefully decorated with antiques, crafts and traditional Ecuadorian furnishings. The views are stunning, and there's a superb restaurant, an Irish-style pub, and a well-stocked wine cellar. Breakfast included. $270

San Jorge Eco-Lodge and Botanical Reserve 4km west of Av Occidental on the Nono road ☎ 02 3390403, ⓦ eco-lodgesanjorge.com; map p.58. About 20min after you escape the traffic of the Centre-North of Quito, this eighteenth-century hacienda on the northeastern foothills of Volcán Pichincha was once a presidential retreat and is now surrounded by a 230-acre private nature reserve which is ideal for birdwatching, hiking, studying plant and wild orchids. Accommodation is provided in cosy rooms with wooden beams. There's a bar-restaurant and delightful patio. Full board. $220

EATING

Quito boasts the best and most varied choice of restaurants and cafés in the country, from humble canteens to classy outfits offering a wide range of **world cuisines**, as well as tasty **seafood** restaurants and typical **Ecuadorian** and **Latin American** restaurants. In Quito, *comida típica* generally comprises hearty food based around a fatty meat dish, such as roasted or fried pork (*hornado* or *fritada*), delicious cheesy potato cakes (*llapingachos*) and a range of soups (*caldos* or *locros*) and stews (*secos*). Restaurants here are markedly more expensive than those outside the capital, but even the priciest are cheaper than their equivalents in Europe or North America. **Set-menu meals**, called almuerzos at lunch and meriendas at dinner, are even better value, sometimes consisting of two or three courses for a dollar or two.

THE NEW TOWN

The greatest concentration of restaurants is in the Mariscal area of the new town, and many specifically target foreigners – anything on Plaza Foch is likely to be overpriced. Some of the best restaurants, which cater to Quito's moneyed classes, are outside the main tourist zone, and well worth the taxi ride. In addition, many of the smarter hotels have good restaurants.

CAFÉS

Café Mosaico Manuel Samaniego N8-95 and Antepara ☎ 02 2542871, ⓦ cafemosaico.com.ec; map p.58. Run by a Greek-American-Ecuadorian family, *Café Mosaico*'s cuisine ($8–25) draws inspiration from all three countries. The terrace balcony is a fabulous spot for a sunset cocktail or two overlooking the old town (though you'll have to get here early or book ahead to bag a mosaic-topped table).

1

Mon–Wed 4pm–11pm, Thurs–Sat 1–11pm, Sun 1–10.30pm.

La Cleta Lugo N24-250 and Guipuzcóa ☎02 2233505; map p.58. This funky café-bar is aimed firmly at cyclists – there's bicycle-themed graffiti, light fittings fashioned from pedals and chains, and seats made from tyre rims. It's a good place for a coffee or beer and pizza ($7–15), and the friendly English-speaking owners can provide plenty of information on cycling in Ecuador. Mon–Sat 11am–11pm.

Corfú Portugal E9-59 and Los Shyris, east of Parque La Carolina ☎02 2460690, ⓦcorfuecuador.com; map p.58. This café serves up some of the best ice cream and *helados de paila* (fruit sorbets) in Quito, as well as excellent lattes and cappuccinos, and tempting pastries. There are nine other branches around town, and the same owners also run the Cyrano bakery next door. Ice cream $1–3. Mon–Sat 10am–8pm.

Cyril Irlanda E10-124 and 6 de Diciembre ☎02 2452511, ⓦcyril-boutique.com; map p.58. Exquisite works of art that simply dissolve in your mouth are created in this sublime Belgian chocolaterie-pâtisserie, which has a small patio *salon de thé* attached. The ornate cakes (around $3–5), delicious ice creams and alluring chocolates provide an unparalleled sensory experience, though at a price. Mon–Sat 8am–8pm, Sun 8am–7pm.

Jürgen Holanda E9-37 and Luxemburgo ☎02 2242415, ⓦjurgencafe.com; map p.58. Near La Carolina, this fourth-generation Dutch bakery and café-restaurant serves pricey but top-quality breakfasts with coffee refills ($7.50–19) and snacks ($7–14). Its berry pancakes are a sweet and sour delight. *Jürgen* has a second branch at La Coruña and Whymper. Mon–Sat 7am–8pm, Sun 7am–2pm.

★Kallari Wilson E4-266 and Juan León Mera ☎02 2236009, ⓦkallari.com; map p.68. Run by a cooperative of Kichwacommunities of the Tena region, this café serves breakfasts, lunches and organic home-grown coffee and hot chocolate ($1.50–2). Groups of six or more can book a special "cultural dinner" ($7.50/person). An attached shop sells crafts from the Tena region. Mon–Fri 9am–6pm.

Magic Bean Foch E5-08 ☎02 2566181, ⓦmagicbeanquito.com; map p.68. Deservedly popular café-restaurant with a pleasant little garden and an extensive backpacker-friendly menu: hearty breakfasts, organic salads, sandwiches, pancakes, pizzas, pastas and much more besides, as well as innumerable hot, cold and alcoholic drinks (including great juices and smoothies). Mains around $7.50–16. Daily 7am–11pm.

ECUADORIAN AND LATIN AMERICAN RESTAURANTS

La Casa de Mi Abuela Juan León Mera 1649 and La Niña ☎02 2565667; map p.68. This place really does feel like a granny's house, with its brown carpet and black

wooden chairs. A short menu – steak, chorizo, roast chicken and ravioli (around $12–15) – but the quality is good and the service very friendly. Mon–Sat 11am–3.30pm & 7–10pm, Sun 11am–3.30pm.

Los Choris González Suárez N27-189 and Muros ☎02 2500888, ⓦloschoris.com; map p.58. Affordable beef makes this Quito's most popular haunt of carnivores as well as a good place to watch major football matches, with five other locales besides the original across from *Hotel Quito*. Wear warm clothing after dark as parts of the restaurant are open to the sidewalk. Mains are $10–15. Mon–Thurs noon–midnight, Fri–Sat noon–1am, Sun noon–10pm.

La Choza 12 de Octubre N24-551 and Cordero ☎02 022230839; map p.58. Popular with the local business crowd, this ample, high-ceilinged restaurant is set well away from the noisy avenue. It serves up dishes from around the country, including combined regional sample platters ($14). The decorations are folkloric but sparse enough to be tasteful rather than touristy. Mon–Sat noon–4.30pm & 6.30–9.30pm, Sun noon–4.30pm.

Fried Bananas Foch E4-150, between Amazonas and Cordero ☎02 2235208, ⓦnewfriedbananas.com; map p.68. Look beyond the twee decor – religious iconography, plastic flowers on the tables, pan pipes on the walls – and you'll find a welcoming and good-value restaurant. The menu features tasty dishes ($5–9) such as baked trout, cream of avocado soup and shrimps with rice. Mon–Fri 12.30–8.30pm, Sat 12.30–4.30pm.

Lua Pontevedra N24-422 and Francisco Salazar ☎02 5112570, ⓦluarestaurante.com; map p.58. Tucked away in a Neocolonial house in hip La Floresta, this top-end restaurant serves up superb Latin American cuisine d'auteur, led by fish and seafood dishes, including Peruvian-style *tiraditos* and ceviches (mains $28–42) Mon–Sat 12–11pm.

Mamá Clorinda Reina Victoria 1144 ☎02 2544362; map p.68. Friendly restaurant serving tasty and good-value Ecuadorian dishes (mains $8–12) such as *llapingacho* (mashed potato patties with fried egg and chorizo) and *caldo de gallina* (chicken soup). Regularly hosts live music. Mon–Sat noon–10pm, Sun noon–9pm.

★Urko Isabel La Católica N24-862 and Coruña ☎02 5112570, ⓦurko.rest; map p.58. Launched by young Ecuadorean chefs, this restaurant has burst onto the vibrant restaurant scene of Isabel la Católica. *Urko* stands out for its thought-out, creative Ecuadorean cuisine, with excellent quality for the price (mains $7–15; 1.5hr tasting menu $50). See the hyperactive chefs at work from the bar. Tues–Sat 1–6pm & 9–11pm, tasting menu Thurs–Sun 8–11pm.

★Zazu Mariano Aguilera 331 and La Pradera ☎02 2543559, ⓦzazuquito.com; map p.58. Quite simply one of the best restaurants in Ecuador. *Zazu*'s award-winning

Peruvian chef brings great flair and international depth to traditional Latin American cuisine (mains $10–29). The super-fresh seafood (in particular the ceviche) is a real highlight. Reservations are advised. Mon–Fri 12.30pm–midnight, Sat 7pm–midnight.

INTERNATIONAL RESTAURANTS

Baalbek 6 de Deciembre N23-103 and Wilson ☎02 2552766, ⓦrestaurantbaalbek.com; map p.68. Excellent, authentic Lebanese restaurant offering a mix of mezze dishes (around $5–10) such as baba ghanoush and hummus, tasty spiced kebabs and sweet, sticky desserts. The fresh juices are well worth a look too. Sun–Tues noon–5pm, Wed–Sat noon–10.30pm.

Carmine Catalina Aldaz N34-208 and Portugal ☎02 3332829, ⓦcarmineristorante.com; map p.58. Excellent but expensive Italian restaurant with delicious pizza, pasta and seafood, as well as plenty of surprises on the menu, such as sauteed rabbit liver (mains around $18–25). Attentive waiters and the steady flow of guests give the place a good atmosphere. Mon–Sat noon–11pm, Sun 12.30–5pm.

Chandani Juan León Mera 1333 and Cordero ☎02 2221053; map p.68. Small, simple and unfussy canteen serving keenly priced Indian/Pakistani cuisine (mains $5–8), though the dishes can be a little mild for some tastes. Plenty of vegetarian options. Mon–Sat noon–10pm.

Chez Jerôme Whymper N30-96 and Coruña ☎02 2234067, ⓦchezjeromerestaurante.com; map p.58. Top-notch French restaurant that uses local ingredients to create both classic and more contemporary Gallic dishes ($15–30); the desserts are particularly tasty. The food is beautifully presented and service is good, and it has an artisanal Swiss bakery in the entrance garden called Hay Pan. Mon–Fri 12.30–3pm, 7.30–11pm; bakery Mon–Sat 7.30am–3pm.

Este Café Mallorca N24-266 and Guipúzcoa ☎09 98498594, ⓦestecafe.com; map p.58. In a charming old house, this cosy café is good for $6.50 two-course lunches and stone-baked pizzas ($10–14), as well as daily specials, either indoors or in a front patio with a fountain. Mon–Sat 12.30–11pm.

La Fonda del Parque Madrid 440 on the Parque de la Floresta roundabout ☎09 84055275; map p.58. One of Ecuador's best Mexican restaurants, lovingly prepared by chef Sergio and his team. If you know your Mexican food, ask for what might not be on the menu, like authentic *mole poblano* ($2 per taco, or $6 mains). Tues–Sun 12–8pm.

El Maple Corner of Foch and Diego de Almagro ☎02 2290000, ⓦelmaple.com; map p.68. Vegetarians aren't exactly spoilt for choice in Quito so this reliable, if not especially exciting, non-meat restaurant, is a handy place for a meal. The menu features dishes ($4–10) from around the world, including an Indian thali, stir fries, burritos and

pastas, as well as a few Andean-inspired concoctions. Mon–Tues 8am–9pm, Wed–Sat 8am–11pm, Sun 8am–6pm.

ZFood Pescadería Coruña N30-135 and Whymper ☎02 2236425; map p.58. Small and wildly popular fish and seafood restaurant with modern-rustic decor serving snacks (fish tacos) to mains (tuna steaks) for $7–20. Mon–Sat 11am–11pm.

THE OLD TOWN

Places to eat in the old town aren't as plentiful as those in the new, and its few long-established restaurants are primarily geared to providing locals with traditional Ecuadorian food. At one end of the spectrum you can sample classic, national home-cooking at several little places tucked away in La Ronda (see p.64), or indulge yourself with some of the most becoming dining rooms and accomplished menus in the capital, not least at the restaurants of the luxury hotels *Plaza Grande* (see p.83) and *Patio Andaluz* (see p.83).

CAFÉS

Café Dios No Muere Junín and Flores; map p.60. This atmospheric corner café, in the same building as the Santa Catalina monastery, is a delightful oddity. Spread across three narrow floors filled with knick-knacks (from old telephones to carnival masks), it has a menu reflecting the chef's Louisiana background: huge New Orleans "po boy" sandwiches ($5–8), a boozy bread and butter pudding and fresh lemonade, as well as home-made yucca chips and organic coffee. Mon–Sat noon–8/9pm.

El Cafeto Chile 930 and Flores ☎02 2572921; map p.60. This great little coffee shop uses only organic Ecuadorian beans (you can buy bags to take away with you too). As well as coffee (around $2–4), it serves teas, hot chocolate, sandwiches, snacks and cakes. Mon–Sat 8am–8pm.

Frutería Monserrate Espejo Oe2-12 and Flores ☎02 2583408; map p.60. A quirky café with a bizarre retro feel: the decor includes tiny seats, exposed brickwork, a giant industrial rusted staircase and a water fountain. The fresh juices (around $1.50) are excellent, and there's also a range of breakfast options, snacks, cakes, pastries and sundaes. Mon–Fri 8am–7.30pm, Sat–Sun 9am–6.30pm.

La Guanga Pedro Calixto 5-17 and Chile; map p.60. Two enterprising Colombians have transformed the former cockpit (cockfighting arena) of the La Tola neighbourhood into a café/bar featuring fine coffee and craft brews. DJs play Latin music on Tues and Wed nights. Snacks $2–6. Mon–Sat 8am–8pm, Sun 9am–3.30pm.

RESTAURANTS

Bandido Brewery Olmedo E1-136 and Fermín Cevallos, opposite the Mercado Central ☎02 2286504;

1

map p.60. A leader among Quito's upstart craft breweries, with seven flavourful US-style types of beer on tap and German-style brews by the bottle. Housed in a small former monastery, it has a rustic, old-world atmosphere and good pizzas. Mon–Fri 4–11pm, Sat 1–11pm.

Govinda Esmeraldas 0e3-119 and Venezuela ☎02 2957849; map p.60. A useful spot for vegetarians and bargain-hunters alike, this Hare Krishna-run restaurant serves huge portions of food at a negligible cost (set lunch $2, main meals around $3). Samosas, vegetable fried rice, spaghetti, salads and soups are among the dishes on offer. Mon–Sat 8am–4pm.

Mea Culpa Upstairs inside the Palacio Arzobispal, Chile and García Moreno ☎02 2951190, ⓦmeaculpa .com.ec; map p.60. Beautiful restaurant overlooking the graceful porticoes of the Plaza Grande, summoning a colonial grandeur only fractionally undermined by the Muzak. The food and wine, though expensive (mains $14–26), is eclectic and delicious – ostrich fillet flambéed in brandy with an apple, soy and maple sauce, for example. Dress up, as anyone in shorts or trainers will be turned away. Mon–Fri 12.30–3.30pm & 7–11pm, Sat 7–11pm.

Mirador Vista Hermosa Mejía 0e4-51 and García Moreno ☎02 2951401; map p.60. The main selling point of this place is the panoramic view from the roof terrace on the sixth floor, which is particularly enchanting after dark. The food is a bit overpriced (mains from $10) so some just come up here for a drink. There's live music Thurs–Sat. Mon–Sat 1.30pm–11.45pm.

Octava de Corpus Junín E2-164 ☎02 2952989, ⓦoctavadecorpus.com; map p.60. Owner Jaime Burgos combines charm and a love for good food in his cosy restaurant, tucked away in the San Marcos quarter. His restaurant, decorated with innumerable paintings, serves up fine international cuisine well worth the prices (mains $20–$30) and accompanied by wines from his carefully managed wine cellar. Mon–Thurs 12.30–10.30pm, Fri–Sat 12.30–11.45pm, Sun by reservation only.

★**Theatrum** Inside the Teatro Sucre, Manabí and Guayaquil ☎02 2289669, ⓦtheatrum.com.ec; map p.60. Sophisticated restaurant with high ceilings, brass chandeliers, lush red padded screens, black chairs and crisp white tablecloths. Grilled octopus or grouper and slow-cooked veal shin are among the dishes on offer. Make sure

you save room for dessert – the baby bananas wrapped in filo pastry and served with chocolate sauce and ice cream are a real highlight. Mains $14.50–25. Mon–Fri 12.30–3pm & 7–11pm, Sat–Sun 7–11pm.

Tianguez Plaza San Francisco ☎02 2570233, ⓦtianguez.org; map p.60. Lovely restaurant beneath the stone platform on which the Iglesia de San Francisco stands, where you can eat traditional Ecuadorian food. It's aimed at tourists and a little overpriced (mains $7.50–12), but the outside tables on the plaza can't be beaten for atmosphere. An excellent crafts shop is attached. Live music Wed–Sun evenings. Mon–Tues 9.30am–6.30pm, Wed–Sun 9.30am–11.30pm.

El Ventanal Carchi and Nicaragua ☎02 2572232, ⓦelventanal.ec; map p.60. Vast glass windows and a heated terrace afford this chic restaurant, inside a converted cable-car station, unparalleled panoramic views across colonial Quito and the valley of the volcanoes. Plus the fine dining is top-notch with a creative menu – try the fish carpaccio with ginger and gooseberry vinaigrette – and extensive wine list. Mains $17–21. Tues–Sat noon–3pm & 6–10pm, Sun noon–4pm.

OUTSIDE THE CENTRE

Brauhaus Páramo Calle Santa Rosa, Puembo ☎02 23895435, ⓦparamo.com.ec. Alongside his upstart craft brewery, German-Ecuadorian brewer Uli Hahl has set up an ultra-authentic Biergarten and German-style pub, the only place of its kind in Quito. The menu features good, hearty sausage and pork dishes (mains from $12). Fri–Sat noon–11pm, Sun noon–4pm.

Cats Manabí 216, off Parque de Cumbayá, Cumbayá ☎099 9942182, ⓦcats-restaurante.com. This long-running rock bar serves excellent, French-inspired pub grub (mains $9–18). It's right on Cumbayá's charming main square, and often features live rock music. Tues–Sat 7pm–2am.

Mucki's Restaurant Barrio San José, El Tingo ☎02 2861789, ⓦmuckis.com. Hard to find and pricey, but well worth visiting this superlative German restaurant, which also serves up French and Ecuadorean-influenced dishes. In a garden setting at the foot of Ilaló in the valley of Los Chillos, Mucki's serves excellent sausage platters, plus dishes like escargots and delicious Provençal-style lamb cutlets (mains $25–30). Wed–Sun noon–5pm, Fri till 11pm.

DRINKING AND NIGHTLIFE

The focus of Quito's **nightlife** is still La Mariscal, particularly the streets north of Wilson between Juan León Mera and Diego de Almagro. It's not all ear-shattering volumes and seething dancefloors, though; plenty of **bars** are geared more for drinking and chatting, while others put on live music (see opposite). In addition to those listed below, many restaurants (see p.83) are good for just a drink, although licensing rules won't make this possible everywhere. Some bars and clubs have small cover charges or a *consumo mínimo* policy which requires you to spend a specified amount at the bar. Always take a **taxi** when travelling around Quito at night.

1

BARS AND CLUBS

La Bunga Francisco de Orellana 899 and Yánez Pinzón ☎02 2904196; map p.68. Popular dance venue for 20-somethings, favouring rock (particularly by Spanish-language bands) and Latin rather than dance. Vintage bands like the Cure sometimes also get airtime, and there's occasional live music. Wed–Sat 8pm–3am.

Bungalow 6 Diego de Almagro and Calama ☎02 2547957; map p.68. This American-run bar/club is extremely popular with travellers and expats, as well as a fair number of locals, as the long queues outside testify. Expect a raucous atmosphere and a mix of dance, pop, Latin, reggaeton and hip-hop. Wed is ladies' night. Wed–Sat 8pm–3am.

Café Democrático Lizardo García E7-41 and Diego de Almagro ☎02 6034775; map p.68. The successor to the fabled *Aguijón*, this relaxed club plays alternative rock, funk, reggae and salsa, with occasional live acts. Serves snacks. Wed–Sat 6pm–3am ($5 cover past 8pm).

Dirty Sánchez Pinto E7-38 and Diego de Almagro ☎02 2551810, ⓦdirtysanchezbar.com; map p.68. Tiny Swiss-owned bar is among the best in La Mariscal, with live

DJ events and reasonably priced drinks and snacks. Mon 5–10pm; Tues–Thurs 2pm–12am; Fri–Sat 2pm–2am.

Finn McCool's Diego de Almagro N24-64 and Joaquin Pinto ☎02 2521780, ⓦirishpubquito.com; map p.68. Lively Irish pub with a good range of drinks (including Guinness in cans), live sport on the TV and decent pub grub (including Irish stew and shepherd's pie), plus a charity quiz night every Tuesday. Daily 11am–3am.

El Pobre Diablo Isabel La Católica E12-06 and Galavis ☎02 2235194, ⓦelpobrediablo.com; map p.58. This mellow restaurant-bar is one of the best places in Quito for live music. A diverse range of groups play here – check the website to see what's on. The food is also pretty good (though service isn't always a strong point). Mon–Sat noon–3pm & 7pm–2/3am.

Turtle's Head La Niña E4-57 and Juan León Mera ☎02 2565544; map p.68. This Scottish-owned pub has its own microbrewery, which produces its own excellent draught beer, including a Guinness-style creamy stout. There's British and American food on offer, as well as darts, table football, pool and live sport on the TV. Mon–Wed 5pm–1am, Thurs–Sat 5pm–2am, Sun 5–11pm.

ENTERTAINMENT

Culture in Quito is thriving and thanks to the regeneration, renovation or reinvention of some key institutions, including the **Teatro Sucre**, the artistic scene has been enlivened throughout the city. There are some great *peñas* and *salsotecas* if you're looking for a dance, and plenty of bars are geared towards **live music**, often Cuban, rock, jazz and especially salsa.

LIVE MUSIC, PEÑAS AND SALSOTECAS

La Bodeguita de Cuba Reina Victoria 1721 ☎02 2542476; map p.68. Predominantly a restaurant, but on Thursday to Saturday nights its live Cuban music draws a friendly crowd of all ages. The owners also run the nearby, and equally good, *Varadero* bar/club (Reina Victoria 1751 and La Pinta). Tues–Fri noon–4pm & 7pm–10/11pm, Sat–Sun noon–midnight.

Cafelibro Carrión 243 between Leonidas Plaza and Tamayo ☎02 2250321, ⓦcafelibro.com; map p.68. Arty

bookshop/café that in the evenings stages live music (including jazz, salsa and tango), dance events, poetry readings and sometimes theatrical performances. Check the website to see what's on. Mon–Fri noon–2pm & 5pm–midnight/1am, Sat 6pm–midnight/1am.

La Casa de la Peña García Moreno 1713 and Galápagos ☎02 2284179; map p.60. A popular *peña* housed in a historic building with a timber-beamed roof near the Basílica, this venue is great place to check out some live Ecuadorian folk music. Thurs–Sat 9pm–midnight/2am.

FIESTAS IN QUITO

Aside from the national public holidays and mischief of Carnaval (see Basics, p.34), Quito features several of its own colourful **fiestas** that are worth a look if you're in town. The city's most prominent religious festival is **Good Friday**, when hundreds of barefooted penitents solemnly cross through the old town in mourning, many dressed in purple robes with pointed hoods, others dragging huge crucifixes and a few even wearing crowns of thorns. Another major event comes on **May 24**, honouring the day in 1822 that the colony finally threw off the Spanish yoke at the Battle of Pichincha, when Quito erupts in a spectacle of booming cannons and military parades. The biggest fiesta of the year kicks off at the beginning of December and lasts for a week until **December 6**, marking the city's foundation. Celebrations include street parties, music and dancing, processions, bullfights at the Plaza de Toros, the election of the *Reina de Quito* (beauty queen) and general high spirits. December is generally regarded by Quiteños as a party month, topped off on **New Year's Eve** with a street parade of *años viejos* – effigies, often of current political figures, which are burnt at midnight.

1

House of Rock Isabel La Católica and Coruña ☎0981422507; map p.58. Cover bands at this lively venue play English and Spanish-language rock to raucous sing-alongs. Don't be surprised that the tables go almost all the way to the stage. It's relatively small, so reservations are a good idea. Thurs–Sat 7pm–1am.

Salsoteca Lavoe Iñaquito E2-17 and Naciones Unidas ☎02 243 5429, ⓦ salsotecalavoe.com; map p.58. Large, popular *salsoteca* in the Centro Norte. Classic salsa favourites on Wednesdays and professional dancers on hand to teach you to sharpen your moves on Friday nights. Wed–Sat 8pm–3am.

THEATRE AND DANCE

Ballet Andino Humanizarte Based at the Teatro Humanizarte, Leonidas Plaza N24-226 and Lizardo García ☎02 2226116. This ballet company stages innovative contemporary theatre and dance productions. It also specializes in folk ballets: flamboyant traditional dance shows with colourful costumed dances from Ecuador's diverse cultural groups. Tickets can be booked by phone or at the Teatro Humanizarte.

Casa de la Cultura 6 de Diciembre N16-224 and Patria ☎02 2902272, ⓦ casadelacultura.gob.ec. The national centre for the arts, the Casa de la Cultura is a leading theatre, dance and classical music venue, showcasing international performers and home-grown talent, with frequent appearances from its own choral group and ballet company, as well as international film screenings.

El Patio de Comedias 18 de Septiembre E4-26 and 9 de Octubre ☎02 2561902, ⓦ www.elpatiodecomedias.org. An innovative theatrical group that has performed across Latin America (as well as in the US) and presents new shows here every month, along with numerous other events.

Teatro Bolívar Espejo 847 and Guayaquil ☎02 2951661, ⓦ teatrobolivar.org. The restored Art Deco Teatro Bolívar, which was originally built in 1933, stages a wide variety of dance, theatre and cinematic shows.

Teatro Sucre Plaza del Teatro ☎02 2951661, ⓦ teatrosucre.org. The elegant, nineteenth-century Teatro Sucre is a pleasure to visit regardless of what's on. As Ecuador's national theatre, the shows are almost always of a very high standard and regularly feature international drama, dance and music companies from classical to pop. Diagonally across the square is its smaller sister venue, the Teatro Variedades.

FILM

Cinemark Plaza de las Américas at avenidas América and República ☎02 2260301, ⓦ www.cinemark.com.ec. This branch of the international cinema chain has huge screens and shows predominantly Hollywood blockbusters (mostly dubbed, but often in English with Spanish subtitles).

Ocho y Medio Valladolid N24-353 and Vizcaya ☎02 2904720, ⓦ ochoymedio.net. This excellent independent cinema specializes in showing world cinema and art-house productions from Quito and much further afield, and also stages mini film festivals.

CLASSICAL MUSIC

Casa de la Música Valderrama s/n and Avenida Mariana de Jesús ☎02 2261965, ⓦ casadelamusica.ec. The Casa de la Música is a high-spec, purpose-built hall with superb acoustics, which attracts top-quality musicians and orchestras from across the globe. It's also the home of the Orquesta Filarmónica del Ecuador.

Orquesta Sinfónica Nacional ☎02 2502814, ⓦ sinfonicanacional.gob.ec. Ecuador's national symphonic orchestra gives regular concerts at venues throughout Quito (and indeed Ecuador as a whole), including the Teatro Sucre. Check the website to see what's on.

SHOPPING

Quito has a huge range of **handicrafts** on offer, so you can do all your shopping here rather than haul a bagful of souvenirs around the country – and prices aren't usually much higher than at the point of production. For general goods, locals head to Quito's **malls**, where the best supermarkets, electronic goods and brand-name clothes chains are, or its street **markets**.

ARTS, CRAFTS AND CLOTHING

Camari Marchena 0e2-38 and Versalles ☎02 2906552; map p.68. A Fair Trade store that provides an outlet for a number of small-scale producers. Lots on offer, from organic coffee and chocolate, to handicrafts, stationery and musical instruments. Mon–Sat 9.30am–6.30pm.

Folklore Olga Fisch Colón E10-53 and Caamaño ☎02 2541315, ⓦ olgafisch.com; map p.58. A top-end art and craft boutique and small museum that was run by the late Olga Fisch, a renowned artesanía collector. The quality of the pieces on sale is a notch above the rest (as are the prices): there are a couple of other outlets around town

(check the website for details). Mon–Fri 9am–7pm, Sat 10am–6pm.

Fundación Sinchi Sacha Café Tianguez on Plaza San Francisco ☎02 2570233, ⓦ tianguez.org; map p.60. This shop is run by an NGO that aims to promote fair trade and provide indigenous people with an outlet for their products. It stocks a wide variety of good-quality crafts, clothes, jewellery, chocolates and coffee, as well as Ecuadorian cuisine. Daily 9.30am–6.30pm, restaurant until 11pm Thurs–Sat.

★**Galería Latina** Juan León Mera N23-69 and Veintimilla ☎02 2221098, ⓦ galerialatina-quito.com;

LEARNING SPANISH

Quito is a popular place to learn Spanish, thanks in large part to the fact that Quiteños speak the language much more clearly here than in many other countries (or even in Guayaquil and the coast). Some schools will encourage you to sign up for seven hours a day, but most students find that exhausting – four hours a day is a better bet, whether studying for just a few days or several weeks. The majority of schools can also organize **homestays**, **day-trips and tours**, as well as activities such as cookery and dance classes. The following institutions are established and reputable; South American Explorers (see p.79) and many embassies (see p.90) can also supply lists of language schools.

LANGUAGE SCHOOLS

Academia Latinoamericana de Español Noruega 156 and 6 de Diciembre ☎02 2250946, ⊛latinoschools.com.

Amazonas Jorge Washington 718 and Amazonas, Edificio Rocafuerte, third floor ☎02 2504654, ⊛eduamazonas.com.

Bipo & Toni's Carrión E8-183 and Leonidas Plaza ☎02 2547090.

Galápagos Spanish School Amazonas 884 and Wilson, first floor ☎02 2565213, ⊛galapagos .edu.ec.

Instituto Superior de Español Darquea Terán 1650 and 10 de Agosto ☎02 2223242, ⊛instituto -superior.net.

La Lengua Colón 1001 and Juan León Mera, Edificio Ave María, eighth floor ☎02 2501271, ⊛la-lengua.com.

Ruta del Sol 9 de Octubre N21-157 and Roca, Edificio Santa Teresita, third floor ☎02 2562956.

Simón Bolívar Mariscal Foch E9-20 and 6 de Diciembre ☎02 2544558, ⊛simon-bolivar.com.

South American Language Center Amazonas N26-59 and Santa María ☎02 2544715, ⊛southamerican.edu.ec.

map p.68. This pricey store has one of the best selections of handicrafts, jewellery and fine knitwear in Quito. Mon–Sat 10am–7.30pm, Sun 11am–6pm.

Hilana 6 de Diciembre N24-385 and Baquerizo Moreno ☎02 2540714, ⊛hilana.com.ec; map p.68. Sells wool and alpaca clothing and blankets woven with typical pre-Hispanic motifs – very attractive and not too expensive. Mon–Sat 9.30am–6.30pm.

Homero Ortega & Hijos Just off Plaza San Francisco at Benalcázar N2-52 and Sucre ☎02 2953337, ⊛homeroortega.com; map p.60. A very good Panama-hat shop run by a Cuenca family, who have been in the business for five generations. Mon–Fri 9.30am–6.30pm, Sat 9.30am–2pm.

Mercado Artesanal La Mariscal Jorge Washington and Juan León Mera; map p.68. Huge artesanía market housing many of the vendors who used to clutter the streets of La Mariscal. Definitely worth a look for the sheer range, though the quality is not always of the highest level. Mon–Sat 9/10am–5/6pm.

SHOPPING MALLS

El Jardín Amazonas and República ☎02 2980300; map p.58. This modern mall, conveniently located beside Parque La Carolina, has a huge food court as well as innumerable shops. Mon–Sat 10am–8.30pm, Sun 10am–7.30pm.

Quicentro Av Naciones Unidas and 6 de Diciembre ☎02 2464526, ⊛quicentro.com; map p.58. A smart mall, boasting lots of designer clothing stores – it's a favourite of Quito's well-heeled fashionistas. Mon–Sat 8.30am–9pm, Sun 9am–2pm.

BOOKS

Confederate Books Calama 410 and Juan León Mera ☎02 2527890; map p.68. An American-run bookshop with a well-ordered selection of secondhand English-language books (both fiction and non-fiction) to buy or exchange. Mon–Sat 10am–7pm.

The English Bookstore Corner of Calama and Diego de Almagro ☎02 2543996; map p.68. This secondhand bookshop has a good selection of titles in English, as well as a few in German and French, to buy or trade. Daily 10am–6.30pm.

Libri Mundi Quicentro ⊛librimundi.com; map p.68. Small collection of English-, French-, German- and Italian-language books, including a number of travel titles, as well as many more in Spanish. There are several other branches dotted around town (see the website for details). Mon–Fri 10am–7.30pm, Sat–Sun 9am–2pm & 3–6pm.

Mr Books El Jardín Mall ☎02 2980281, ⊛mrbooks .com; map p.58. Large bookshop with a good choice of both English- and Spanish-language books, including guidebooks. Mon–Sat 10am–8.30pm, Sun 10am–7.30pm.

1

DIRECTORY

Embassies and consulates Australians can get assistance at the Canadian embassy; Canada, Amazonas 4153 and Unión Nacional de Periodistas, Edificio Eurocenter, 3rd floor (☎02 2455499, ⓦcanadainternational.gc.ca /ecuador-equateur/); Colombia, 12 de Octubre N24-528 and Luis Cordero, Edif WTC (☎02 2236463); Ireland, Establo 50 Torre III, Cumbayá (☎02 3801 345); Peru, República de El Salvador 495 and Irlanda (☎02 2468410); UK, Naciones Unidas and República de El Salvador, Edif Citiplaza, 14th floor (☎02 2970800, ⓦukinecuador.fco .gov.uk); US, Av Avigiras E12-170 and Eloy Alfaro (☎02 3985000, ⓦecuador.usembassy.gov).

Emergencies ☎911, police ☎911, fire ☎102, ambulance ☎131.

Hospitals Hospital Metropolitano, Av Mariana de Jesús s/n and Nicolás Arteta (☎02 3998000, ⓦhospital metropolitano.org); Hospital de Clínicas Pichincha, Veintimilla E3-30 and Páez (general ☎02 2998700, emergency ☎02 2998777, ⓦhcp.com.ec); Hospital Voz Andes, Villalengua 0e2-37 and 10 de Agosto (☎02 2262142, ⓦhospitalvozandes.org).

Money and exchange There are innumerable ATMs throughout Quito, though most of the banks – including Banco del Austro (Amazonas and Santa María), Banco de Guayaquil (Reina Victoria and Colón) and Banco del Pacífico, Amazonas (N22-94 and Veintimilla) – are in the Centro Norte. Preferably use those that are fully indoors. Currency exchanges (casas de cambio) are also generally found in the new town: try VazCorp, Amazonas 21-169 and Roca (☎02 2529169, ⓦvazcorpsf.com). Note that very few places in Ecuador will change travellers' cheques.

Pharmacies Fybeca has numerous stores, including a 24hr branch at La Coruña N26-108 and San Ignacio. Call ☎1800 392 322 or visit ⓦfybeca.com to find your nearest branch.

Police Policía Nacional Servicio de Seguridad Turística, Reina Victoria N21-208 and Roca (daily 8am–7pm; ☎02 2543983), is dedicated to tourist incidents. See also "Emergencies" (above).

Post offices The main office is behind the CCI mall at Japón N36-153 and Av Naciones Unidas, but there are over twenty other branches. The most convenient for La Mariscal is at Reina Victoria and Colón. The old town branch is at Guayaquil 935 and Espejo.

Around Quito

The most dramatic attraction **around Quito** may be the looming outline of the potentially explosive **Volcán Pichincha**, but the best-known, busiest and most developed is **La Mitad del Mundo**. Almost directly north of the city, it's a complex celebrating, and positioned (almost) on, the equator. Nearby is another museum, **Inti Ñan**, and a prehistoric site, **Catequilla**, which are both exactly on the equator. Also in this area is the volcanic crater **Pululahua**, one of very few inhabited craters anywhere.

Northeast of Quito are **Guayllabamba**, home of the capital's zoo, and **El Quinche**, an important religious centre. Southeast of the capital in Los Chillos are the market town **Sangolquí; San Rafael**, with its excellent museum on artist **Eduardo Kingman**; and the **Refugio de Vida Silvestre Pasochoa**, a woodland refuge surrounding a volcanic crater.

La Mitad del Mundo

Around 20km north of central Quito · Mon–Thurs 9am–6pm, Fri–Sun 9am–7pm · $2; $3 extra for the La Mitad del Mundo monument/ Ethnographic Museum; $1.50 extra for the planetarium · ☎02 2394803, ⓦmitaddelmundo.com

At 2483m on the fringes of the dusty suburb of San Antonio de Pichincha, lies the colonial-styled complex of whitewashed buildings, gift shops, snack bars and museums known as **LA MITAD DEL MUNDO** (The Middle of the World), straddling the line that divides the earth's northern and southern hemispheres and gives the country its name – the **equator** (latitude of 0º 0' 0"). **Charles-Marie de La Condamine** and his geodesic mission first ascertained its exact demarcation in 1736–44, and a monument to this achievement was raised across the line in 1936. Deemed not grand enough, it was replaced in 1979 with the current one. Modern GPS readings have revealed that even the new monument is seven seconds of a degree south of the true equator, roughly 240m adrift, but the finding has done little to dent the popularity of the attraction – local crowds flock to the site, particularly on Sundays and holidays, when music and dance performances are held in the afternoons.

The Mitad del Mundo monument and the Ethnographic Museum

From the entrance to the site, a cobbled street, lined with busts of La Condamine's expedition members, leads up to the thirty-metre-tall **Mitad del Mundo monument**, a giant concrete monolith topped off with a large metal globe. From its base, a line representing the equator extends outwards – even running down the middle of the aisle (and altar) of the church within the complex. Inside is the **Ethnographic Museum**, accessed via a lift. Once at the top, you descend by stairs through the museum, which displays region-by-region exhibits on Ecuador's indigenous populations and their customs, with fine exhibits of native dress and artefacts.

The rest of the complex

Among the other sites in the complex are various **national pavilions**, representing the countries that took part in La Condamine's expedition, each with its own little museum. A **planetarium** on site offers rather unimpressive hourly shows, but the more stimulating **Fundación Quito Colonial**, contains richly detailed miniature models of Guayaquil, Cuenca and Quito – featuring their own artificial sunrise and sunset. Also within the complex is a **post office**, gift shops, an ATM, restaurants and snack bars. Pig out – and then try the weighing scales here, knowing you've actually lost a little weight while on the equator. Thanks to the earth's own bulging waistline, gravity is weaker here, so you weigh less; unfortunately, your mass will be the same. Just south of the complex is the rather modern headquarters of the UNASUR organization of South American nations, a modern structure reminiscent of two gigantic square cannons.

Museo Inti Ñan

Around 20km north of central Quito, next to La Mitad del Mundo • Daily 9.30am–5pm • $4 • ☎ 02 2395122, ⓦ museointinan.com.ec

If you find the Mitad del Mundo complex a little dry, try the enjoyable **Museo Inti Ñan**, which – as calculated by GPS – really does lie on the equator. It houses an idiosyncratic collection of equator-related experiments and curios and exhibits on indigenous cultures and their beliefs. The tone is light-hearted: having shot a blow dart into a pumpkin, you can try to win a certificate for balancing an egg on a nail on the equator. To reach the museum, head north along the main highway from the entrance of leaving the Mitad del Mundo complex and walk a few hundred metres uphill, then follow signs left again down a short driveway.

ARRIVAL AND DEPARTURE   **LA MITAD DEL MUNDO AND MUSEO INTI ÑAN**

By bus To get to the La Mitad del Mundo from Quito, take the Metrobús northwards to the terminal and catch a bus marked "Mitad del Mundo" (every 15min–1hr; about 30–45min). At weekends a special bus service runs every fifteen to thirty minutes between the complex and El Panecillo in the old town (see p.71): it takes around 1hr.

By taxi A taxi from Quito costs around $25 one-way or about $40 return including waiting time.

Tours Most tour operators (see p.79) in Quito arrange trips (around $30) to La Mitad del Mundo and Museo Inti Ñan, as well as to Pululahua (see p.92) and to the various archeological sites around the area.

Catequilla, Pambamarca and Rumicucho

3–4km northeast of La Mitad del Mundo • No fixed opening times • $1 for each site (though there's not always someone there to collect it); the sites can be visited on a tour with Calimatours (☎ 02 2394796, ⓦ mitaddelmundotour.com), whose office is inside the Mitad del Mundo complex – a 2.5hr tour costs from $15

Long before La Condamine came to Ecuador, native cultures understood that the equator passed through this region and, some might say, with far greater accuracy than the Enlightenment explorer. On a dusty hill the extraordinary **Catequilla** (or Kati-Killa), a huge and ancient circular platform bisected by the equator pays testament to the astronomical sophistication of the pre-Columbian Quitu-Cara culture, who built it around 800 AD. Along with **Pambamarca**, a large undeveloped ceremonial site connected

1

to the December solstice, and the impressive **Rumicucho**, a terraced ruin on a dramatic ridge-top, both nearby, this trio of ancestral ruins sounds a refreshing note of gravitas to counter the enjoyable, but rather hollow tackiness of the Mitad del Mundo complex.

Pululahua

About 4km north of La Mitad del Mundo • No fixed opening times • Free

A visit to the Mitad del Mundo is commonly combined with a trip up to the rim of the extinct volcano of **Pululahua**, whose 34-square-kilometre **crater** – one of the continent's largest – has been protected since 1966 as a **geobotanical reserve**. Its unusual topography and associated microclimates not only support rich, cultivated land on the valley floor, but also lush cloudforests, 260 types of plants and a large variety of orchids. Outlooks on the rim – including the Ventanillas viewpoint – afford **views** over bucolic scenery within the crater, beautiful networks of fields and small settlements squeezed around the two volcanic cones of Pondoña and Chivo, all cradled by the thickly forested and deeply gullied crater walls. It's best to get up here early in the morning as thick clouds engulf the crater later in the day.

ARRIVAL AND TOURS   PULULAHUA

There are **two points of access**. The first is 4km from La Mitad del Mundo heading north on the Calacalí highway (1hr walk), then turning right onto a **paved road** that climbs to a car park (30min walk) at the Ventanillas viewpoint, from where a steep trail leads down to the crater settlements below (30min down, 1hr back up; horses are sometimes available). The second access is more suitable for **independent motorists**; turn right near the petrol station about 3km further along the Calacalí highway onto a track leading up to the Moraspungo guard post; from here an 8km track winds down to the crater floor.

By bus Buses heading to Calacalí pass the Ventanillas turn-off.
A taxi A taxi will take you from the Mitad del Mundo to the viewpoint and back for about $5.
Tours Most people visit on an organized tour (around $30)

from Quito that also takes in La Mitad del Mundo and several other nearby sights. Alternatively, note that Calimatours (see p.91) offer shorter trips to the crater from La Mitad del Mundo for $8.

ACCOMMODATION AND EATING

El Cráter On the edge of the crater, near the Ventanillas viewpoint ☎ 02 2398132, ⓦ elcrater.com. In a beautiful location, this hotel has modern en-suite rooms (though not all have views of the crater), smart service and a spa, restaurant and bar. Horse riding, bike trips and massages can all be arranged. $95

Pululahua Hostal Inside the crater, just beyond the Ventanillas viewpoint ☎ 0999466636, ⓦ pululahua hostal.com. This peaceful, eco-friendly lodge in a dramatic location is a great option. You can camp (equipment provided) at two sites nearby or stay in simple cabins with shared facilities, or opt for more comfortable en-suite cabins. There's a jacuzzi, and staff can arrange birdwatching,

cycling, hiking and star-gazing trips. Doubles $30; camping $24

La Rinconada Inside the crater, 2.5km beyond Ventanillas ☎ 02 2520575, ⓦ hosteriarolandovera .com. This guesthouse/restaurant is tucked away in the northern corner of the crater, the retirement bolt-hole of Ecuador's most famous long-distance runner, Rolando Vera. As well as getting a good square meal here (mains around $7–10), you can camp (equipment provided) or stay in one of the simple rooms in the hacienda and hire horses to explore the crater. Make contact first, and they will pick you up from the bottom of the Ventanillas descent. Doubles $30; camping $3

Zoológico Guayllabamba (Quito Zoo)

In Guayllabamba, 32km from Quito • Tues–Fri 8.30am–5pm, Sat & Sun 9am–5pm • $4.50 • ☎ 02 2368898, ⓦ quitozoo.org • Buses to Cayambe (every 5–10min) from the Terminal Ofelia in Quito usually stop at or just outside Guayllabamba (45min–1hr) from where it's a 30min walk (or a short taxi ride) to the zoo.

Beyond Calderón, the Panamericana sweeps 700m down into the dry Guayllabamba gorge and plain. Stalls laden with jumbo avocados and exotic fruits line the main road

EL CHAQUIÑÁN AND ILALÓ

Urban planning has replaced the rail line that once meandered northeast from Quito with an attractive, hiking/biking route, **El Chaquiñan**, stretching for 20.5km between Cumbayá and Puembo, both suburban towns to the east of the capital proper. Open daily 6am–6pm, the route, named for the Kichwa word for pathway, makes for a mostly intersection-free, insightful option for exploring the **Tumbaco valley**, heading past new housing developments, some traditional architecture, and along the semi-arid, dramatic **Chiche river canyon**. Near its starting point, the main square of **Cumbayá** has a pretty neo-Baroque church on one side and restaurants and pubs along the others, many of which are branches of well-known downtown locales. Puembo, at the other end, is more low-key.

The ride, mostly over packed earth and gravel, doesn't require any technical expertise, but does involve some climbing from its lowest point, the Chiche river bridge, at 2,385m. Along the Chiche, the route offers **beautiful views**, particularly climbing towards Puembo, of Pichincha and Cotopaxi. That section also traverses several unlit railway tunnels, where pedalling in the dark provides a little excitement. Periodically along the trail, white, tile-roofed waystations offer water and fruit juices, and there's a **hacienda-style restaurant** open weekends and holidays at the Chiche river crossing.

South of El Chaquiñan rises **Ilaló**, an extinct volcano separating the Tumbaco valley to the north from the Valle de los Chillos to the south. Its cross-topped summit reaches an altitude of 3,091m. Several hiking trails lead to the top from Tumbaco in the north and from El Tingo in the south, the most commonly used ascent, and the area is also popular with mountain bikers. El Tingo has a wildly popular thermal pool with waterslides remodelled in 2008 ($2.50; Tues–Sun 6.30am–3pm), but the village's numerous eateries are prone to food scandals.

into **Guayllabamba**, 32km from the capital and home to Quito's attractive **zoo**, the largest in the country. The **Zoológico en Guayllabamba** puts the emphasis on crowd-pleasing native fauna, such as the Andean spectacled bear, pumas and condors, with successful breeding programmes. Many of the animals were rescued from the illegal wildlife trade.

El Quinche

About 7km southeast of Guayllabamba lies the village of **EL QUINCHE**, famous for its outsized **church**. For pilgrims, its most important feature is the wooden image of **El Virgen del Quinche**, carved at the end of the sixteenth century by artist and architect **Diego de Robles**, who was saved from tumbling hundreds of feet into the Río Oyacachi by a thorn snagging on his clothes. Since Robles cheated death, the Virgin has been credited with countless other miracles, depicted by paintings inside the church and plaques on the walls. Visitors make their way from across the country to venerate her, especially during the **festival** in the third week of November, climaxing on November 21, and throngs of people receive blessings all year round.

ARRIVAL AND DEPARTURE   EL QUINCHE

By bus There are regular buses (every 15–30min; 45min–1hr) to El Quinche from the Río Coca Ecovía stop in Quito, as well as equally frequent buses (10min) from Guayllabamba to the village.

Sangolquí

The most important town in the Valle de Los Chillos, **SANGOLQUÍ**, 15km southeast of the capital, has an impressive **church** with an imposing facade and grand bell tower. It's much better known, however, for its **market**, which runs all week, but is at its peak on Sundays (and to a lesser extent, Thursdays) when it expands from its three dedicated market squares to fill much of the town. It's a hard-edged and busy affair, perhaps

1

lacking the charm of a highland-village market, but the energy of the local commerce is compelling, and being so close to Quito it makes an easy day-trip for those with limited time.

ARRIVAL AND DEPARTURE

By bus Buses to Sangolquí leave regularly from Plaza Marín in the old town (every 15–30min; 25min).

ACCOMMODATION AND EATING

Hacienda La Carriona 2.5 km vía Sangolquí–Amaguaña ☎ 02 2332004, ⊛ haciendalacarriona.com. Sangolquí is easy to visit as a day-trip from Quito, but if you want to stay nearby, try this attractive, converted hacienda which dates from the early 1800s. It has a grand cobbled courtyard, colourful gardens, swimming pool and spa, well-appointed rooms and delicious food. A range of activities – including guided horseback tours to Pasochoa (see below) – can be arranged. Online discounts often available. **$140**

Museo de la Casa de Kingman

Porto Viejo and Dávila, San Rafael • Thurs–Fri 10am–4pm, Sat & Sun 10am–5pm • $2 • ☎ 02 2861065, ⊛ fundacionkingman.org • Buses (every 15–30min; 20–30min) from Quito to Sangolquí pass right by San Rafael's park, from where the museum is a short walk away; a taxi from Quito costs around $15–20

Easily combined with a trip to nearby Sangolquí, the unassuming town of **San Rafael** has little of inherent interest, except the excellent **Museo de la Casa de Kingman**. Occupying a peaceful spot high on the banks of the Río San Pedro, this was the house of **Eduardo Kingman**, one of Ecuador's greatest twentieth-century artists. He is best known for depicting the privation of Ecuador's indigenous peoples, often capturing their plight in the expressiveness of their hands – a technique he later taught Oswaldo Guayasamín. There are some wonderful pieces exhibited here that support Kingman's considerable reputation, as well as some colonial and republican art.

Refugio de Vida Silvestre Pasochoa

30km southeast of Quito • Mon–Fri 8am–4pm, Sat & Sun 6am–6pm • $10 • ☎ 02 2877835 • Hiking guides from $10 (call the reserve to book a guide in advance)

The luxuriant **Refugio de Vida Silvestre Pasochoa** is a dense forest spread over **Cerro Pasochoa** (4210m), an extinct volcano whose western side collapsed in an eruption more than 100,000 years ago. The inaccessibility of the terrain, hemmed in by the crater's remaining walls, has left the forest largely undisturbed, despite its proximity to Quito. Six **trails** lead through the forest, rich in beautiful native **trees** and **plants** – including Andean cedars, orchids and podocarpus (Ecuador's only native conifer), as well as 126 species of **birds**. One trail, Las Pantzas, rises out of the forest and heads up across the páramo, following the outer slopes of the crater rim. It's a six- to eight-hour hike up to the **summit** of Cerro Pasochoa, requiring a guide. Note that access may be restricted due to Cotopaxi's activity.

ARRIVAL AND DEPARTURE

By bus and camioneta From Plaza La Marín in Quito's old town, take one of the frequent buses to the small town of Amaguaña (every 15–30min; 25min) and then a camioneta (around $8; arrange a pick-up for the return journey) from Amaguaña's main plaza to the reserve entrance. Alternatively, you can walk from Amaguaña in less than two hours along a 7km cobbled access road leading south from town, though you will have to keep asking for directions as it's poorly signposted.

ACCOMMODATION AND EATING

Reserve facilities ☎ 02 3317457. Inside the reserve there are several accommodation options: private en-suite rooms, dorm beds in a basic refuge and a campsite (bring your own tent). Wherever you stay you will need to bring all

1

VOLCANIC ACTIVITY

Surrounded as it is by active volcanoes, Quito has periodically suffered the onslaught of an eruption. Pichincha experienced renewed **volcanic activity** since the late 1990s, after more than three centuries of near silence. In early 2015, Cotopaxi, always considered active but usually calm for a century and a half between eruptive activity, became restless, and from August began continuously to issue ash and steam. To the northeast, Reventador is highly active and in 2002 brought the capital to a standstill thanks to a major eruption. The main risk from Cotopaxi is high-speed avalanches, or lahars, that threaten parts of the suburban valleys and Latacunga. The volcano is therefore constantly and closely monitored.

your food and drink with you, though there are kitchen and barbecue facilities available. It's also worth bringing a sleeping bag to provide a bit more comfort. Camping $\overline{\$5}$; dorms $\overline{\$6}$; doubles $\overline{\$10}$

Volcán Pichincha

Rising over the west side of Quito, the broad-based, emerald-sloped **Volcán Pichincha** has two main peaks: the slightly lower, serene-looking and extinct **Rucu ("Old") Pichincha** (4675m) lies just beyond the hilltops; **Guagua ("Child") Pichincha** (4794m), 10km west of the city centre and often covered in snow early in the morning, is a highly active volcano, which erupted spectacularly in 1999, dusting Quito with ash.

Hiking to the top of Pichincha's summits has something of a poor reputation because of some muggings, but security has been improved. That said, the hikes shouldn't be done alone, but tours are plentiful. Check with South American Explorers (see p.79) for the latest situation. Turn back immediately if a thunderstorm threatens as walkers are highly exposed to lightning. **Rucu Pichincha** is most easily accessed from Cruz Loma, the end point of the TelefériQo (see p.73).

Guagua Pichincha is best reached from the village of Lloa, southwest of Quito, from where a signposted dirt track leads up to a **refuge** just below the summit (about 5–6hr walk).

TOURS AND ACCOMMODATION   VOLCÁN PICHINCHA

Tours Most climbing operators in Quito (see p.80) offer the Guagua climb as a day tour, including 4WD transport to the refuge (see below).

Refuge accommodation The refuge at Guagua Pichincha is very basic; if you stay here (climbing operators can sort out the practicalities for you) you should bring all your own food and drink, as well as a sleeping bag, as it can get very cold at night. $\overline{\$5}$

The northern sierra

LLAMAS NEAR COCHASQUÍ

The northern sierra

A magnificent sequence of volcanoes, sparkling crater lakes and patchwork scenery, the northern sierra extends northeast from Quito for 140 kilometres to the Colombian border. Down on the ground along the Panamericana, the main transport artery, this translates as 250km of highway snaking between cloud-piercing mountain peaks, windblown hilltop passes, warm valleys bursting with fruit orchards and flower plantations, and a couple of major ecological reserves. For many visitors, the prime lure has long been the region's vibrant markets, and although many key destinations are within easy reach of Quito, wandering from the bus-laden Panamericana will quickly take you into seldom-visited countryside.

Leaving the capital, the first town of any significant size you reach is **Cayambe**, set at the foot of **Volcán Cayambe** – the highest point in the world on the equator. Close by are the pre-Inca ruins of **Cochasquí**, the **Quitsato equator monument** and the bone-warming hot springs of **Oyacachi**, an idyllic village nestled in the high forests of the vast **Reserva Ecológica Cayambe-Coca**. The main attraction of the region, however, just forty minutes from Cayambe and two hours from the capital, is **Otavalo**'s famous artesanía market. It's at its best on Saturday but good throughout the week, bursting with an irresistible array of weavings, garments, carvings, ceramics, jewellery and assorted knick-knacks. The weaving tradition in the Otavalo valley predates even the Incas, and virtually all of its towns and villages specialize in a particular area of craftwork, from embroidery and woven belts to bulky knitted socks, with the nearby community of **Cotacachi** being the national centre for leather goods. The town also provides access to **Laguna Cuicocha**, tucked in the southernmost corner of the striking **Reserva Ecológica Cotacachi-Cayapas**, which gives a taster of the wildernesses unfurling westward, not least the teeming cloudforests of the **Intag region** beyond.

The largest city in the northern sierra, **Ibarra**, 30km north of Otavalo, charms with its elegant, whitewashed buildings and its relaxed atmosphere. Once the point of departure for a famously hair-raising **train** ride to the coast at San Lorenzo, Ibarra now sits at the head of a new road providing the country's fastest highway link between the sierra and the sea, descending through dramatic scenery from highlands to cloudforests to coast. A few kilometres north of Ibarra, the old road to the Colombian border branches off from the Panamericana and climbs to **El Ángel**, the 3000-metre-high entry point to the remote **Reserva Ecológica El Ángel**, where undulating páramo grasslands are speckled with rare frailejones plants. Meanwhile, the Panamericana ascends the dry and dusty **Chota valley**, one of the few places where African and Andean traditions

HACIENDA ZULETA

Highlights

① Haciendas Enjoy colonial luxury at several distinguished estates around Otavalo and Cayambe, some of which are still working farms. **See p.101 & p.112**

② Otavalo Saturday market One of the most intense, colourful and enjoyable shopping experiences in Ecuador, where you can find everything from dolls and tapestries to a brood of chickens. **See p.106**

③ Lagunas de Mojanda This trio of picturesque highland lakes, watched over by brooding volcanic peaks, makes a great day-hike. **See p.114**

④ Intag valley Delight in the sub-tropical Intag valley's forested hills and reserves, then luxuriate in Nangulví's hot springs while watching butterflies and hummingbirds. **See p.117**

⑤ Reserva Ecológica El Ángel Remote, windswept páramo with singular vegetation: armies of surreal, velvety frailejones, and pockets of papery polylepis forest. **See p.125**

⑥ Tulcán's topiary gardens The extraordinary topiary gardens are an unexpected delight in an otherwise drab border town. **See p.127**

HIGHLIGHTS ARE MARKED ON THE MAP ON P.100

have blended, on its way to **Tulcán**, a frontier town close to Colombia that plays unlikely host to some remarkable topiary gardens.

Cayambe and around

Although there's little to see in **Cayambe** itself, the town makes a good base for exploring the area and serves as the launch pad for climbing its volcanic namesake, which towers over it to the east. It also provides access to the western, highland section of the **Reserva Ecológica Cayambe-Coca**, in particular to the community of **Oyacachi**, known for its thermal springs and burgeoning ecotourism. A journey there takes you past the intriguing **Quitsato equator monument** and can be combined with lunch at nearby *Hacienda Guachalá*. To the west of Cayambe,

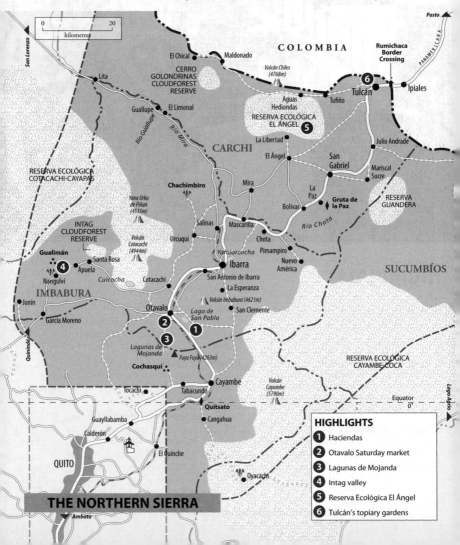

HIGHLIGHTS

1. Haciendas
2. Otavalo Saturday market
3. Lagunas de Mojanda
4. Intag valley
5. Reserva Ecológica El Ángel
6. Tulcán's topiary gardens

THE NORTHERN SIERRA

an easy half-day trip beckons to explore the fascinating pre-Columbian archeological site of **Cochasquí**.

Cayambe

Overshadowed by the eponymous volcano, **CAYAMBE** (2850m) is worth a quick visit for its renowned home-made *queso de hoja* – a salty, white cheese boiled and wrapped in *achira* leaves and **bizcochos** – buttery biscuits that locals carry around by the bagful, which you can buy from small factory-shops dotted round the town. Cayambe has a lively Sunday **market** and is a regional centre for Ecuador's **flower industry** (one of the country's main exports), evident in the shimmer of plastic-sheeted greenhouses gleaming across the valley.

ARRIVAL AND DEPARTURE   CAYAMBE

By bus From Quito's Ofelia terminal, Flor del Valle buses (⍟flordelvalle.com.ec) arrive in Cayambe at the two roundabouts next to the bullring, on the main road, 5min walk from the *parque central*. The Flor del Valle office in Cayambe is on Montalvo and Junín (☎02 2360094), from where buses to Quito depart. Other buses leave from the temporary bus terminal by the main market, nine blocks north of the *parque central*, but pick up in town and at the

roundabouts on the Panamericana Norte, where through buses also deposit passengers.

Destinations Cangahua (6am–7pm, every 15min, last return bus 6.30pm; 1hr); Ibarra (change in Otavalo); Otavalo (every 15–20min, last bus 8pm; 50min); Oyacachi (daily 3pm, from Oyacachi daily 4.30am; plus Sun at 7.30am, returning 3pm; 1hr 30min); Quito (Ofelia terminal; every 15min until 9pm; 1hr 20min).

GETTING AROUND AND INFORMATION

On foot Cayambe is a very small town, easy to walk around. The main park is only four blocks east up Bolívar from the main bus stop on the Panamericana Norte.

By taxi Taxis – cars and camionetas – wait in Cayambe's *parque central*, though cheaper camionetas can be hired outside the market.

Tourist office The very helpful I-Tur office (☎02 2361832 ext 126, ⍟cayambeturismo.gob.ec; Mon–Fri 8am–5pm),

on the corner of Bolívar and Rocafuerte at the *parque central*, can provide a map and information about various attractions in the area, including a number of community-based tourism initiatives. They can also help put you in contact with qualified mountain guides should you wish to conquer Volcán Cayambe, which is not for the novice climber.

ACCOMMODATION

La Gran Colombia Natalia Jarrín and Calderón ☎02 2361238. More business-oriented than the other lodgings listed here, this rather smart spot also has a popular on-site restaurant (7am–9pm). **$30**

Hacienda Guachalá 10km south of Cayambe, 2km up the road to Cangahua off the Panamericana at Km70 ☎02 2363042, ⍟guachala.com. One of Ecuador's oldest and most affordable haciendas, boasting ageing en-suite rooms with fireplaces around a cloistered, cobbled courtyard. Charming grounds are dotted with agapanthus

and alpacas, and there's a pool, games room, lounge and library plus a good restaurant (mains around $12) open to visitors. **$72**

Hostal Cayambe Bolívar 107 and Montalvo ☎02 2360400. The cheapest centrally located hotel offers rooms with sparkling, white-tiled floors and cable TV. **$14**

Hostal Mitad del Mundo Natalia Jarrín and Argentina ☎02 2360226. Adequate, inexpensive en-suite rooms, plus a heated indoor pool, sauna and steam room (Sat & Sun; $5). **$22**

THE FIESTAS OF CAYAMBE

For much of the year Cayambe is a quiet provincial town that most travellers skip on their way from Quito to Otavalo. During the **fiestas** of late June, however, things really get busy when *indígenas* descend from the surrounding villages for singing, dancing, parades and bullfights. The celebrations kick off with **Inti Raymi** (Kichwa for "sun festival"), which heralds the summer solstice and continues for several days until it merges with the **Fiesta de San Pedro** on June 29, honouring the town's patron saint. At the end of July folk head to the village of Juan Montalvo, on the outskirts of Cayambe, for **Las Octavas** and yet another explosion of colourful costumes, parades, dancing and general merrymaking, in celebration of the harvest.

EATING

Aroma Bolívar and Ascázubi ☏ 02 2361773. Slightly set back from the street, with a pleasant patio, this popular spot serves good traditional food and decent breakfasts. Specializes in beef dishes and splendid fancy cakes. Mains $5–9.50. Mon, Tues & Thurs–Sat 8am–8pm; Wed & Sun 8am–4pm.

KATY Jarrín and Bolívar, at the roundabout on the Panamericana ☏ 02 2110822. Gleaming tiles and large windows provide a cheerful setting for regular, inexpensive desayunos and almuerzos, ($2.50–6), which inevitably involve the local *bizcochos*. Mon–Fri 6.30am–8pm, Sat & Sun 6.30am–10pm.

Cochasquí

About 24km west of Cayambe and 70km north of Quito • Daily 8am–4.30pm • $3 • ☏ 02 3994405, ☏ 0999195952 • Take any bus along the Tabacundo road, which heads west out of town along Bolívar, and get off at one of the turnings for Cochasquí, from where it's an 8km uphill walk • A taxi from Cayambe costs $15–25 (including waiting time), or use a Quito or Otavalo tour operator (see p.79 & p.108)

The ruins of **Cochasquí** are one of the country's most significant pre-Inca archeological sites. Built at the base of Mount Fuya Fuya (3100m) by the Cara or Cayambi people around 900 AD, the site comprises fifteen flat-topped pyramids with long ramps constructed from blocks of compressed volcanic soil (*cangahua*), now coated in grass.

Cochasquí is now thought to have been both a **fortress**, given its strategic hilltop location, and an **observatory**; excavations have revealed the remnants of circular platforms, thought to be calendars of the sun and moon. Holes drilled nearby probably held pillars that would have cast shadows over sundials, and the site is also aligned with the summit of Cayambe volcano, over 30km away, and the Puntiazil site (in the town of Cayambe), another ancient monument used for gauging celestial movements; shamans still congregate at the site around the solstices and equinoxes to perform spiritual rites. Although many of the pyramids are now little more than overgrown mounds, the eerie atmosphere, roaming llamas and striking **views** merit a visit.

Tucked away behind the ruins are two reconstructions of ancient **Cara houses** (circular structures with thatched-grass roofs built around a living tree), a **medicinal plant garden** and a small **museum** exhibiting artefacts recovered from the site. Good Spanish-speaking **guides** at the site – one of whom also speaks English – can show you around (1hr; free, but tips appreciated).

Quitsato equator monument

7km south of Cayambe, just before the turn-off to Cangahua and *Hacienda Guachalá*, at Km70 on the Panamericana • Free • ⓦ quitsato.org • On the Cayambe to Cangahua bus route • A taxi from Cayambe costs $4–5.

The **Quitsato** equator monument, frequently billed as the true equator monument, takes the form of a **giant sundial** (*reloj solar*) spanning 54 metres across, with a ten-metre-high cylinder placed exactly on the equator as its gnomon to cast a shadow. The words "quitsa to" mean "centre of the world" in the language of the Tsáchila people (see box, p.267), reflecting one of the monument's goals, namely to link Ecuador's modern identity as an equatorial nation to the ancient cultures of the region, who well understood these techniques of charting celestial movements and knew the position of the equator to a degree (pardon the pun) that is only just becoming clear. The interesting on-site **museum** provides further information.

Reserva Ecológica Cayambe-Coca

East of Cayambe • Daily 7am–6pm • Free, but ID is required

East of Cayambe, the vast **Reserva Ecológica Cayambe-Coca** protects over 4000 square kilometres of land, from Cayambe's ice-covered peak of 5790m to just 600m above sea level, down in the Oriente. This huge range in altitude spans ten ecological zones that harbour a staggering number of plant and animal species, including nine hundred birds (among them the condor, mountain toucan and Andean cock-of-the-rock), and rare

---

ALTERNATIVE ACCESS POINTS TO THE RESERVA ECOLÓGICA CAYAMBE-COCA

There are several other points of access to the Cayambe-Coca reserve, mostly in the Oriente (see chapter 5). The road from Papallacta to Baeza and Lago Agrio borders the easily accessed southern and eastern edges of the reserve, with three common points of entry: from the car park for the thermal baths at Papallacta (see p.221); El Chaco (see p.224); and Lumbaquí, 60km west of Lago Agrio.

2

mammals, such as the spectacled bear and dwarf deer. Also living within the reserve are **Kichwa**-language speakers at **Oyacachi**, a village renowned for its hot springs, and the **Cofán** people, in the far northeast of the reserve at **Sinangoé**. Both communities welcome visitors as part of their community-based tourism initiatives (see ⓦoyacachi.org.ec – though note that the contact details are out of date – and ⓦcofan.org, respectively).

Volcán Cayambe

The reserve's highest point is the summit of **Volcán Cayambe** (5790m), Ecuador's third-highest mountain. Just south of the summit is the **highest point** on the equator, reputed to be the only place on the planet where the latitude and average temperature are both zero degrees. There's a **refuge** at about 4700m (see below); the **climb** from here to the summit (6–7hr) is regarded as more dangerous than either Cotopaxi or Chimborazo due to its many crevasses, risk of icefall, strong winds and frequent bouts of poor weather, though many agencies in Quito (see p.80) can arrange guides, equipment and transport, as can the tourist office in Cayambe (see p.101).

ARRIVAL AND DEPARTURE   VOLCÁN CAYAMBE

By car "Nevado Cayambe" is signposted as you enter Cayambe; from here it's a 25km drive to the refuge (4WD necessary).

By camioneta There is no public transport to the refuge, but camionetas can be picked up in the *parque central* in Cayambe, or more cheaply at the market (around $80 return) – high clearance 4WD essential. If you're hiring a guide to climb the summit (about $180/small group), transport will be arranged and included in the fee.

ACCOMMODATION AND EATING

Volcán Cayambe Refuge 25km from Cayambe. Administrator ☎0959559765. The volcano's recently renovated refuge has bunks, fireplaces, electricity and running water. Limited supplies are available for purchase, but kitchen facilites were not available at the time of writing; the nightly rate includes breakfast and dinner, but a boxed lunch is $10 extra. You'll need to bring your own sleeping bag. **$30**

Oyacachi

Nestled at 3200m in the crook of a cloudforested valley, the village of **OYACACHI** lies at the high end of one of the oldest routes into the Oriente, very likely the one Gonzalo Pizarro used during his ill-fated search for El Dorado (see box, p.231). Its main attraction is **thermal baths** (daily 6am–6pm; $3), deliciously empty midweek, and where you can wallow while admiring the surrounding scenery.

The community of around 600 abides by the reserve's regulations, which prevent them from developing or cultivating the surrounding terrain, but grant them generous plots of communal and individual land nearby. Trout farming, cheese production and **woodcarving** bolster the local economy. Several places in the village offer simple lodgings (around $10/person) and a couple of restaurants serve the delicious local trout. While village regulations ban alcohol and tobacco consumption within the community, tourists are allowed to bring both with them, although discretion should be exercised.

At the time of writing, a major **landslide** had all but destroyed the village (though not the baths). Work was already under way, though, to rebuild homes and revive tourism; check with the community tourism office for developments (see box, p.104).

2

TRAILS FROM OYACACHI

An ancient **trail** from Oyacachi follows the Río Oyacachi down to El Chaco in the Oriente (see p.224), a stunning **two- to three-day hike** traversing the cloudforest of the Cayambe-Coca Reserve. Another good **hike** begins at Las Puntas checkpoint and crosses the highland parts of the reserve through páramo and past glittering lakes southwards to **Papallacta** (see p.221).

   Guides are recommended ($40/day) and readily available in Oyacachi: ring the community tourist office (☎06 2991852; daily 7am–4pm) and ask for Héctor Parión (in Spanish). They can provide mules (around $15/day), though you need to bring your own **tent**, sleeping bag and provisions. On foot the Papallacta hike will take two days, but the route is passable by 4WD vehicles, taking less than an hour ($2 community fee).

   Either way, you will need permission from the Ministerio del Ambiente office in Cayambe (☎02 2110370, ✉werner.barrera@ambiente.gob.ec), at Once and Rocafuerte, opposite the CAMAL building at the south end of town. A **permit** is free but entails giving the name of the guide, the names and passport details of hikers or drivers and the registration plate if travelling in a vehicle.

ARRIVAL AND DEPARTURE   **OYACACHI**

By bus The daily village bus leaves at 4.30am, returning from Cayambe's local bus terminal by the wholesale market (*mercado mayorista*) at around 3pm. In addition there is a Sunday departure from Cayambe at 7.30am, returning 3pm (1hr 30min).

By camioneta A taxi or camioneta (which needs to be 4WD) from Cayambe costs around $80 for a full day, including waiting time.

Otavalo

Positioned between the peaks of Cotacachi and Imbabura, only two hours' bus ride from Quito, **OTAVALO** (2535m) is one of Ecuador's top attractions, thanks largely to its world-renowned **Saturday market**. For hundreds of years, *indígenas* from surrounding villages have brought their crafts and produce down from the hills for a day of frenzied barter and sale here. Nowadays, producers from across Ecuador and Colombia, plus hundreds of visitors, also flood the town's streets every weekend. Although much of the business is still local – including an animal market that's as authentic as they come – substantial sections of the market are devoted to tourists, with a mind-boggling range of carvings, clothing, craftwork, musical instruments, ceramics and souvenirs. It's most famous, though, for **weavings**, sold mainly at the **Plaza de Ponchos** in the heart of the tourist zone, a dizzying labyrinth of colourful hanging tapestries and garments. On Sunday afternoons (about 3–4pm) the plaza occasionally hosts a brisk game of **pelota de mano**, in which two opposing teams hit a tiny leather ball high into the air across the square with their bare hands.

   Otavalo's environs are far prettier than the town itself, which has few landmarks and attractions beyond the neatly laid-out **parque central**, dominated by an imposing bust of **Rumiñahui**, the valiant Inca general who led a fierce resistance against the Spanish. The park is set off by the elegant **municipio** building and the Iglesia de **San Luis**, which is less striking than Otavalo's other major church, **El Jordán**, two blocks east at Calderón and Roca, and home to an ornate gilded altar. The main place of interest, beyond the town's various markets, is the new "living museum" in the former hacienda and textile factory of San Pedro (see p.107).

   To get a good view of the town head southeast up La Piedrahita and follow the steep cobblestone road to **El Lechero**, a solitary sacred tree on a hilltop, said to possess magical healing properties. For a slightly more demanding walk, continue further along the road down to **Lago San Pablo**, a cobalt-blue lake 4km southeast of Otavalo, which you pass on the way from Quito. Its shoreline is dotted with **weaving villages**, such as La Compañía and Huaycupungu.

Brief history

Otavaleños have been accomplished weavers since pre-colonial times, when they traded textiles for *achiote* (a red dye) and cotton with peoples from the Oriente. The **Incas** finally took control of the region in 1495, beginning almost five hundred years of exploitation of the Otavaleños' skills. The Incas brought llamas and alpacas with them for wool, which was easier to weave and dye than cotton, and extracted tribute from the weavers. The locals, meanwhile, adopted Inca clothing, a form of which can still be seen in the traditional dress of native women; it reputedly resembles Inca dress more closely than that of any other indigenous people of the Andes (see box, p.106).

2

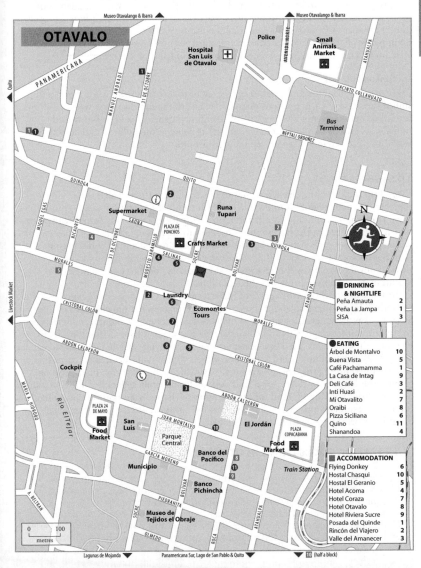

OTAVALO

Museo Otavalango & Ibarra

Police

Hospital San Luis de Otavalo

Small Animals Market

Bus Terminal

Supermarket

Runa Tupari

PLAZA DE PONCHOS

Crafts Market

Laundry

Ecomontes Tours

Cockpit

PLAZA 24 DE MAYO

Food Market

San Luis

Parque Central

El Jordán

PLAZA COPACABANA

Food Market

Municipio

Banco del Pacífico

Banco Pichincha

Train Station

Museo de Tejidos el Obraje

0 100 metres

■ DRINKING & NIGHTLIFE
Peña Amauta	2
Peña La Jampa	1
SISA	3

● EATING
Árbol de Montalvo	10
Buena Vista	5
Café Pachamamma	1
La Casa de Intag	9
Deli Café	3
Inti Huasi	2
Mi Otavalito	7
Oraibi	8
Pizza Siciliana	6
Quino	11
Shanandoa	4

■ ACCOMMODATION
Flying Donkey	6
Hostal Chasqui	10
Hostal El Geranio	5
Hotel Acoma	4
Hotel Coraza	7
Hotel Otavalo	8
Hotel Riviera Sucre	9
Posada del Quinde	1
Rincón del Viajero	2
Valle del Amanecer	3

Colonial times

The Incas only ruled for forty years before the **Spanish** swept in, soon establishing infamous **obrajes**, forced-labour sweatshops in which men, women and children were put to work for endless hours in atrocious conditions. With the introduction of silk, the spinning wheel and the treadle loom, Otavaleños began producing large quantities of quality textiles, supplying Spanish aristocrats all over the colonies. However, once the Industrial Revolution in Europe developed the mass production of textiles, the *obrajes* went into decline. The oppressive *huasipungo* system (see p.386) that was then introduced brought little change to the living conditions of the weavers, who continued to work on a small scale in the traditional styles – often using old techniques, such as the backstrap loom – to satisfy local demand. This changed in 1917 with the adaptation of techniques used to make Scottish tweeds. The new fabrics, known as *casimires*, proved hugely popular in Ecuador and rekindled the industry, but it wasn't until the **Agrarian Reform Law** of 1964, when the *huasipungo* system was outlawed and the great estates were broken up, that *indígenas* could finally own land and profit from their talents.

Tourism and textiles

The rise of regional tourism opened up the Otavalo valley to the outside world and spread the word of its marvellous textiles. Thanks to the success of the weaving industry, the Otavaleños are now one of the most prosperous and well-travelled indigenous groups in South America, as well as being at the political and cultural forefront of the country's under-represented peoples.

The markets

Every Friday afternoon, Otavalo comes to life as pick-up trucks laden with merchandise and vendors bent double under great blocks of textiles stream into town from the surrounding countryside, preparing for the fabulous **Saturday market**, which includes one of the largest and most colourful artesanía markets on the continent. If you can't visit on a Saturday, note that this crafts market has become such big business that most of the town's weaving and artesanía shops stay open throughout the week; you'll find stalls on the Plaza de Ponchos every day, and on **Wednesdays** it's almost as busy as the real thing.

The **Plaza de Ponchos** is the centre of the **artesanía** activity, where *indígenas* dressed in all their finery offer a splendid choice of clothes, textiles, hammocks and weavings, as well as jewellery, ceramics, dolls and many other craftworks – though an increase in the use of synthetic materials and chemical dyes has made it hard to find top-quality weavings these days, so you'll fare better visiting the outlying weaving villages of Peguche (see p.112), Agato, Ilumán and Carabuela, which all maintain textile workshops that can be visited during the day and are easily reachable by bus from the main terminal.

Amid the mounds of cloth, you'll find **vegetable** and **grain sellers** and a row of pans and cauldrons cooking up food for local shoppers. The stalls spill off the square in all directions, especially up Sucre, all the way to the *parque central*, and by 7am on a Saturday morning the market is already abuzz.

TRADITIONAL CLOTHING IN OTAVALO

Many Otavaleños still wear traditional clothing, as it is closely associated with their cultural identity, even as they own gleaming pick-up trucks, electric looms and modern hotel blocks. **Women** can often be seen in embroidered white blouses (*camisas*), shawls (*rebozos*), black-wrap skirts (*anakus*), gold-coloured bead necklaces (*walkas*) and red-bead bracelets (*maki watana*), with their hair wrapped up in strips of woven cloth (*cintas*). **Men** sport dapper blue ponchos (*ruwanas*) and mid-calf-length white trousers (*calzones*), with their hair braided (*shimba*) beneath felt hats (*sombreros*). Both wear *alpargatas*, sandals made from the fibre of the *penko* cactus.

2

FESTIVALS IN OTAVALO

Otavalo hosts several major **festivals**, including **San Juan** on June 24, which is celebrated with bonfires and fireworks as *indígenas* from the surrounding villages parade in costumes and masks, dancing and singing their way to the church of San Juan, west of town. The festivities last for several days, blending with the **Inti Raymi** celebration of the solstice on June 21 and those for **San Pedro** on June 29; the three are collectively known as "Los San Juanes", providing a Christianized gloss to what was doubtless a pre-Columbian celebration. The San Juan fiesta once involved a kind of ritual fighting (*tinku*) between rival villages, but today the ceremonies are largely confined to ritual bathing in the Peguche waterfall, followed by shindigs in the outlying communities.

Another important event, the **Fiesta del Yamor**, during the first two weeks of September, is a twentieth-century celebration – evident from the annual beauty pageant – and primarily mestizo, which sees bullfights, music, dancing and traditional food and drink, including *yamor* itself, a *chicha* made from seven types of corn and prepared over twelve hours. Among the smaller events are **Mojanda Arriba** (Oct 30 & 31), a two-day walk from Quito to Otavalo over the Mojanda hills, stopping at Malchinguí and marking the foundation of the town, and **Diciembre Mágico**, a minor arts festival in the weeks leading up to Christmas.

Although the sales patter is not aggressive, you will be expected to **haggle**, which should result in discounts of 25 percent or more. If you want to take a **photo** of someone, always ask first, or better still, buy something then ask. Also, take heed that Otavalo's markets can get very crowded, providing perfect cover for **pickpockets** and **bag slashers**, so protect your belongings.

The livestock market

On Saturdays, on the other side of the Panamericana (head west along Calderón and cross the river), is the town's **livestock market** (5–10am), a packed field of herds of animals bellowing through the early-morning mists, with their busily negotiating owners. A second **animal market** by the bus station deals with fowl, *cuyes* (guinea pigs), puppies and kittens – and other small creatures, thankfully not all destined for the kitchen.

The food market

The town's main **food market** (daily) is located around the Plaza 24 de Mayo (there's more at the Plaza Copacabana too), a covered square that has all the bustle of an eastern bazaar, and is charged with the smell of whole hogs roasting on spits, steaming vats of crab soup and the sizzle of meat and potatoes. Nearby, on 31 de Octubre, is the **cockfighting arena** (*gallera municipal*), where many traders head for a flutter once the stalls have been packed up for the day.

Museo Otavalango

Antigua Fábrica San Pedro, Vía Antigua a Quiroga • Fri–Sun 9am–5pm; other days by appointment • $5 • ☎ 06 2903879, ☎ 0993853344, ⓦ otavalango.org • $2 taxi ride from Otavalo

Located in the crumbling shell of a two-hundred-year-old hacienda and former textile factory, the **Museo Otavalango**, a locally owned and operated "living museum", is well worth a visit. The entry fee includes an informative tour (in Spanish) of the exhibits, which comprise a collection of modern and traditional clothing, musical instruments, agricultural tools and other artefacts central to the important rituals, festivals and everyday life of Kichwa-Otavaleño culture. An adjacent room serves as a workshop, where you can observe weavers and embroiderers perfecting their craft. The products of their labours – all made of natural materials – can be purchased in the **shop**. Across the courtyard, a second building serves as a cultural centre, offering language, dance and art classes, as well as housing a small permanent art exhibition.

Museo de Tejidos el Obraje

Sucre 6-08 and Piedrahita • Mon–Sat 9am–noon & 3–5pm • $2

A block and a half south of the *parque central* is the family-run **Museo de Tejidos el Obraje**, where lifelong weavers Luis and Luzmaría Maldonado demonstrate traditional methods of local textile production, from cleaning and carding wool to spinning, drying and weaving it on pedal and backstrap looms.

ARRIVAL AND DEPARTURE   OTAVALO

By bus The bus terminal, on Atahualpa and Ordoñez at the northeastern edge of the town, is served by Trans Otavalo and Trans Los Lagos from Quito, and is the home of Otavalo's reliable cooperative, Imbaburapak. If riding on other interprovincial bus lines, you'll probably be dropped off at the Panamericana, at the far southern end of Atahualpa, from where it's at least a six-block walk north to the nearest accommodation, a journey best not made at night.

Destinations Apuela (5 daily, last bus 3pm; 2hr 30min); Cayambe (every 15–20min until 7pm; 50min); Cotacachi (every 10min until 8pm; 20min); Ibarra (every 10min; 40min); Peguche (every 20min; 15min); Quito (every 10min until 7pm – thereafter, through buses can be flagged down on the Panamericana; 2hr); San Pablo del Lago (every 10min; 30min).

GETTING AROUND

On foot Otavalo is easy to navigate on foot, and walking across the town centre (Plaza de Ponchos to the *parque central*) only takes five minutes.

By taxi Taxis are available around the terminal and at the *parque central*, and should all have metres. Minimum fare $1.25.

By bicycle Mountain bikes can be hired from the tour operator Ecomontes (see below) and at the *Valle del Amanecer* hostel (see opposite), and there are four downloadable cycle route maps available on the town's tourist website (see below).

INFORMATION AND TOURS

INFORMATION

Tourist office For information and tours, head for the I-Tur office on Quiroga, in the northwest corner of Plaza de Ponchos (Mon–Sat 8am–6pm, ☎06 2927230, ⊛otavalo.travel).

TOUR OPERATORS

Otavalo's tour operators all offer similar out-of-town tours; typically, these are day-trips (around $30–75) to weaving villages and the homes of artisans in the area, to the nearby lakes Cuicocha and Mojanda, and trekking or horse riding up Imbabura. They can also organize volunteer placements. Taxi tours from the *parque central* to the lakes and villages are about $12–15/hour for two or three people, though the "guiding" won't be as proficient.

All about EQ Los Corazas and Juan de Albarracín, by the Panamericana ☎06 2923633, ⊛all-about-ecuador.com. Highly recommended organization which works with quality local guides, and specializing in adventure tourism and community projects, offering interesting multi-day itineraries, such as hiking across the páramo from the Lagunas de Piñan down into the Intag valley.

Ecomontes Corner of Sucre and Morales ☎06 2916244, ⊛otavaloguide.com. Offers the usual day tours with bilingual guides plus more adventure-focused options:

rafting ($45–65), mountain biking (from $40) and a two-day camping trip in the Intag cloudforest ($75). The company also has an office in Quito.

Runa Tupari Sucre and Quiroga on the Plaza de Ponchos ☎06 2925985 and ☎0999590646, ⊛runatupari.com. Intercultural exchanges with local indigenous communities, offering accommodation in "rural lodges" ($84 including breakfast and dinner, for two sharing a room), as well as standard day tours of the area and a variety of one- to four-day excursions led by an indigenous guide.

Wanderlust Sucre and Quiroga ☎06 2924098 and ☎0986989049, ⊛wanderlust.ec. Operated by Héctor Tipan, who works at the tourist office, this relatively new operator, which previously supplied the equipment for several of the other agencies, offers an array of hiking, horse riding, mountain biking and kayaking activities ($35–75/person for 1–4 people).

TRAIN

A beautifully restored diesel train now undertakes scenic day-trip excursions to Salinas, in the Chota valley, joining up with the train from Ibarra (see box, p.124) and visiting a wood-carving workshop in San Antonio de Ibarra en route. The train departs from the station on Guayaquil and Montalvo (☎06 2928172, ⊛trenecuador.com; Fri–Sun & hols 8am; 10hr; $50).

ACCOMMODATION

Otavalo has more than its fair share of hotels, though most of them are virtually empty during the week so prices can often be negotiated. Even so, things can get busy on Friday nights, so **reserve in advance**, especially in high season. If it's peace you're after, there's almost as much choice in the countryside around town (see p.111). **Campers** should head for *Hostal Aya Huma* in Peguche (see p.114); *Rose Cottage* and *La Luna*, 3–4km on the way to the Lagunas de Mojanda (see p.114), also offer scenic sites to pitch a tent.

Flying Donkey Corner of Calderón and Bolívar ☎06 2928122, ☻flyingdonkeyotavalo.com. Friendly new hostel with cheerfully decorated doubles, triples and dorms (though curtains are thin), a pleasant kitchen-dining area, decent beds, spotless bathrooms with good, hot showers and a splendid under-utilized rooftop terrace with views of Imbabura. Dorms $11; doubles $26

★**Hostal Chasqui** Piedrahita 141 and Guayaquil ☎06 2923199, ☻hostalchasqui@yahoo.com. Excellent inexpensive choice with a helpful host and spotless, comfy en-suite rooms with piping hot showers, use of kitchen and laundry facilities and a bar, plus a hammock-strewn terrace with great views. $28

Hostal El Geranio Ricaurte 1-01 and Morales ☎06 2920185, ☻hostalelgeranio.com. Quiet, popular, out-of-the-way budget choice in two buildings: slightly more expensive units in a modern concrete pile, and cheaper rooms in a rickety but endearing wooden addition at the back. Use of kitchen and breakfast included. $28

Hotel Acoma Salinas 07-57 and Ricaurte ☎06 2926570, ☻acomahotel.com. Striking hotel of "highland-colonial" design with plenty of wood, natural light and whitewashed walls, built and owned by a family of local musicians. Comfortable rooms with cable TV, optional en-suite bathrooms and handsome suites available. Breakfast included. Doubles $55; suites $85

Hotel Coraza Corner of Calderón and Sucre ☎06 2921225, ☻hotelcoraza.com. Clean, modern hotel offering excellent value for money with comfortable, carpeted en-suite accommodation (doubles, triples and family rooms), decent hot showers, cable TV, café and parking. Breakfast included. $37

★**Hotel Riviera Sucre** García Moreno 3-80 and Roca ☎06 2920241, ☻rivierasucre.com. Charming old hotel featuring greenery cascading down from balustrades and an abundant garden: it has simple rooms (shared bathroom $15 less) with cable TV, plus a games room and small living room warmed by a fire on chilly nights – much needed as the rooms can get cold. $35

★**Posada del Quinde** Quito and Egas ☎06 2920750, ☻posadaquinde.com. The best place to stay in Otavalo. Hospitable and lavishly decorated with plants and fine weavings, it features comfortable, heated rooms, and spacious, much pricier suites with views over a colourful garden towards Volcán Imbabura. Substantial breakfast included. Doubles $92; suites $134

Rincón del Viajero Roca 10-17, between Quito and Quiroga ☎06 2921741, ☻hostalrincondelviajero.com. Run by a hospitable Ecuadorian–US family, this popular budget hotel has tiny, clean and safe doubles with optional en-suite bathrooms, dorm beds, a sitting room with fireplace and a roof terrace with games area, pool table and hammocks. There's a good restaurant, and breakfast is included in private room rates. Dorms $10; doubles $30

Valle del Amanecer Corner of Quiroga and Roca ☎06 2920920, ☻valledelamanecer.com. Popular backpackers' hostel with small bamboo-thatched rooms around a cobbled courtyard shaded by palms and hammocks. On-site laundry, book exchange, board games, bike rental, hot water and restaurant. Shared bathrooms for $5 less. Owner Ramiro Buitrón also arranges tours to Playa de Oro (see p.273) and to the Intag region (see p.117). $37

EATING

Otavalo's **restaurants** feature a wide choice of cuisines, though prices are a bit higher than in other provincial towns. Cheap fresh fruit and vegetables are available at the produce **market**, where the vendors also offer high-cholesterol meals of *chicharrón* and *llapingachos* for a few dollars, and there's also a new supermarket on Plaza de Ponchos.

CAFÉS

★**La Casa de Intag** Colón between Sucre and Bolívar. Great place for breakfast and light lunches – crêpes, freshly made sandwiches and cakes accompanied by the café's signature organic, Fair Trade shade-grown coffee any which way. You can sip your cappuccino safe in the knowledge you're helping support Intag communities. Artesanía and beauty products produced by some of the area's cooperatives are also for sale. Mon–Sat 8am–6.30pm.

Deli Café Quiroga and Bolívar ☻delicaferestaurant.com.

Cosy venue with bright wooden furniture offering a range of international food, especially Tex-Mex fajitas and burritos, pizza and pasta plus some veggie options and local snacks such as tamales and *quimbolitos*. Daily 9.30am–9.30pm.

Oraibi Sucre and Colón ☎06 2921221. Serves good vegetarian food including quinoa soup, quiche and spinach lasagne in its pleasant little courtyard. Wed–Sat 8am–8pm.

Shanandoa Salinas and Jaramillo. Also known as *The Pie Shop* and a choice spot for juices, milkshakes, sandwiches and, above all, tasty home-baked pies with

2

several fruity fillings that are best appreciated with a dollop of ice cream. A Plaza de Ponchos stalwart, in business for thirty years. Mon–Fri & Sun 11am–9pm, Sat 9am–9pm.

RESTAURANTS

★**Árbol de Montalvo** Montalvo 4-44, at Doña Esther ☎ 06 2920739. Attractive restaurant serving quality Mediterranean cuisine with organic vegetables. The speciality is crispy thin-crust pizza cooked in a large wood-burning oven that dominates the dining room. Tues–Thurs & Sun 6–9pm, Fri & Sat 6–10pm.

Buena Vista Salinas 5-09 ☎ 06 2925166, ⓦ buenavistaotavalo.com. The balcony of this reliable first-floor restaurant presides over the Plaza de Ponchos with a standard, inexpensive menu of meat, fish, chicken and pasta, plus a fair few vegetarian options. Also a choice spot to chill out, with comfy seats, inexpensive drinks, book exchange and occasional midweek film showings. Mon & Sun 1–10pm, Wed & Thurs 10am–10pm, Fri 11am–11pm, Sat 9am–11pm.

Café Pachamama Posada del Quinde, Quito and Egas ☎ 06 2920750. Decent restaurant using as much local organic produce as possible; the tomatoes burst with flavour in the lasagne. The varied menu comprises plenty of vegetarian and gluten-free dishes (mains from $10) – and the blazing log fire and comfy lounge area make for cosy dining.

Occasional live music on busy Fridays. Daily 7.30am–8.30pm.

Inti Huasi Jaramillo and Quiroga ☎ 06 2922944. Nicely presented restaurant with tablecloths and napkins. It does the standard platos típicos well, in big portions, with efficient service and at a good price (from around $7). Popular with locals and foreigners alike. Mon & Sun 8.30am–5pm, Tues–Sat 8.30am–9pm.

Mi Otavalito Sucre 11-13 and Morales ☎ 06 2920176. Cosy cellar-like restaurant offering tourist-priced traditional food. The best value is the substantial and superior menu del día (for lunch or dinner) for $8. There's an extensive choice, including options for kids, but the piped music can grate. Daily noon–9pm.

Pizza Siciliana Morales and Sucre ☎ 06 2925999. Popular pizzeria noted for its excellent live music on Fridays and Saturdays. Huddle round the log fire and tuck into their pizzas cooked in a wood-fired oven; from $8, depending on size – even the small ones are large – and toppings, which include vegetarian options. Regular pasta dishes also on offer. Daily noon–10pm.

★**Quino** Roca and García Moreno ☎ 06 2924994. Colourful restaurant specializing in tasty seafood dishes, including fish stew, trout and shrimp, which go well with a glass of mulled wine on a chilly night. Most mains $7–11 but with a couple of budget options under $6. Tues–Sun noon–10.30pm.

DRINKING AND NIGHTLIFE

The energy and excitement the market generates finds an outlet on Friday and Saturday nights at Otavalo's discos and peñas, some of which feature **live music**. Previously most peñas featured folklórica, traditional Andean folk songs accompanied by rondador (small pan pipes), quena (wooden flute), charango (a lute, sometimes made from armadillo shell) and guitars. Currently, Peña Amauta is the only spot dedicated to folk music though you'll find folk groups playing in the restaurants round town. For a trawl of Otavalo's **nightclubs** head for the incipient Zona Rosa, which is establishing itself along 31 de Octubre between Quito and the Panamericana.

★**Peña Amauta** Jaramillo and Morales ☎ 06 2922435. Friendly, long-established peña consistently popular with visitors, showcasing good, established folklórica groups. Try the guayusa cocktails, hot infusions of the eponymous leaves from the Oriente, topped off with a healthy slug of sugar-cane spirit. Food is also available at the upstairs restaurant. Cover charge $2. Live music from 10pm. Fri &

Sat 8pm–2am.

Peña La Jampa 31 de Octubre and the Panamericana ☎ 06 2922988. The most popular venue of the moment, featuring a large dancefloor overlooked by two galleries and a good mixed crowd. Live music on Saturdays from folklórica to salsa and merengue. Cover charge from $6 depending on the entertainment. Fri & Sat 9pm–3am.

ENTERTAINMENT

SISA Abdón Calderón 4-09 and Sucre, upstairs ☎ 06 2920154. Arts complex on three floors containing a café, a cinema showing both arthouse and Hollywood films, and a

couple of restaurants, one with a pleasant bar area, offering live music on Fridays, Saturdays and over Sunday lunch. Daily 8am–10.30pm.

Around Otavalo

There's plenty to do around Otavalo. The nearby village of **Peguche**, within walking distance northeast of the town, has a cooperative that features weaving demonstrations and there's a secluded waterfall nearby, while the **Lagunas de Mojanda**, three lakes surrounded

> ### FIESTAS AROUND OTAVALO
> The villages lining the shores of Lago de San Pablo celebrate colourful **fiestas** including the banner-waving processions of **Los Pendoneros**, held in San Rafael and San Roque on October 15. San Rafael also hosts the costume ritual of **El Coraza** on August 19, in which one of the village's wealthiest men appears in a feathered hat that hung with so much gold chain and jewellery that his face is concealed. The festival of **Pawkar Raimi** held in Peguche and Agato (Feb & March) usually includes plenty of music-making and concerts open to all.

2

by brooding, cloud-hung peaks south of town, are set in ideal country for hiking and horse riding. Another popular excursion is to **Cuicocha**, a lake on the edge of the huge **Cotacachi-Cayapas reserve**, extending from the páramo down to tropical forests in the coastal Esmeraldas province. The lake is best reached from **Cotacachi**, 11km north of Otavalo, a smart little town famous for its market, leather goods and boutiques. A more adventurous destination within the reserve is the starkly beautiful and remote páramo region of **Las Lagunas de Piñan**, most easily accessed via the more northerly town of Ibarra (see p.119).

ACCOMMODATION   AROUND OTAVALO

There are several fine **haciendas** in the Otavalo region, originally built to oversee local *obrajes*; they generally cost more than accommodation in town, but are worth it for their character, colonial architecture and beautiful grounds. Whatever the newer **country hotels** lack in historical charm, they make up for in comfort and location. Most places listed offer horse riding and other excursions. There are also many good upmarket places to stay around Otavalo, in the nearby

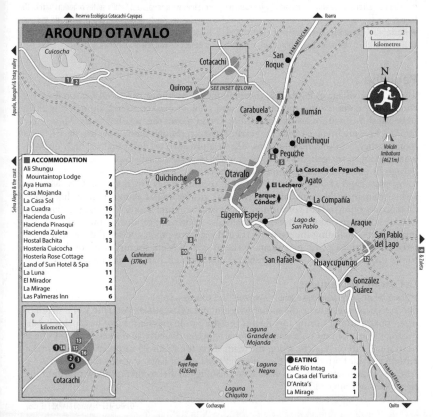

AROUND OTAVALO

■ **ACCOMMODATION**
Ali Shungu Mountaintop Lodge	7
Aya Huma	4
Casa Mojanda	10
La Casa Sol	5
La Cuadra	16
Hacienda Cusín	12
Hacienda Pinasquí	3
Hacienda Zuleta	9
Hostal Bachita	13
Hostería Cuicocha	1
Hostería Rose Cottage	8
Land of Sun Hotel & Spa	15
La Luna	11
El Mirador	2
La Mirage	14
Las Palmeras Inn	6

●**EATING**
Café Río Intag	4
La Casa del Turista	2
D'Anita's	3
La Mirage	1

2

weaving village of **Peguche** (see below), around **Cotacachi** (see p.115) and near the **Lagunas de Mojanda** (see p.114), all close enough to get an early start at the Saturday market. Most require a minimum two-night stay. All include breakfast, unless stated otherwise.

Ali Shungu Mountaintop Lodge 5km west of Otavalo ☎ 06 2920750 and ☎ 0989509945, ⍟ alishungumountaintoplodge.com. This peaceful lodge, perched on a hilltop and backed by the forests of its private reserve, offers mesmerizing views of Imbabura and Lago San Pablo. Its four cosy, self-contained guesthouses, popular with North American visitors, have wood-burning stoves, kitchenettes, gardens, huge windows and plenty of recreational material should the weather turn bad. Prices include breakfast and dinner in a superb restaurant. Two-night minimum stay. **$195**

★**Hacienda Cusín** 9km southeast of Otavalo, on the edge of San Pablo del Lago ☎ 06 2918013, ⍟ haciendacusin.com. Beautiful, early seventeenth-century hacienda, set amid tranquil gardens with cobbled courtyards bursting with flowers, roaming peacocks and llamas. Choose from rooms, suites or cottages offering striking views of the estate, some with fireplaces and beamed ceilings. The complex includes a library, games room and an excellent restaurant. Doubles **$146**; cottages & suites **$183**

★**Hacienda Pinsaquí** Panamericana Norte, Km5 ☎ 06 2946116, ⍟ haciendapinsaqui.com. Historic eighteenth-century hacienda, which formerly hosted Simón Bolívar. Stately residence with huge fireplaces, courtyards with trickling fountains and luxurious but simple bedrooms evoking a bygone age. Equine-related trappings and trophies abound, particularly in the snug bar. All rooms cost the same, though they vary in size. **$138**

Hacienda Zuleta Outside Zuleta, 12km east of Lago de San Pablo ☎ 02 2662182, ⍟ zuleta.com. A hospitable working dairy farm and hacienda dating from 1690 and former home of Ecuadorian president Galo Plaza Lasso, set in bucolic countryside. It has fifteen comfortable guest rooms with garden views, and the farm produces delicious organic fruit, vegetables, trout and dairy products. Minimum two-night stay required. Full board. **$486**

Las Palmeras Inn Just south of Quichinche ☎ 06 2668067, ⍟ laspalmerasinn.com. A 150-year-old hacienda affording great views of Cotacachi and Imbabura, offering a range of affordable accommodation in garden cottages with fireplaces, family suites or rooms within the main house. Plenty of activities are on offer and the main lodge includes a games room, restaurant, two lounges, internet café and reference library. **$75**

Peguche

The weaving village of **PEGUCHE**, three kilometres northeast of Otavalo, is a quiet community comprising a central square and a few unmarked streets, though it is likely to be subsumed within an ever-expanding Otavalo over the next few years. Most families here are involved with the textile business, though many now use electric looms rather than traditional means. The best places to see and purchase high-quality **weavings** are at the galleries of José Cotacachi (⍟ josecotacachi.com) and José Ruiz Perugachi (⍟ artesaniaelgrancondor.com), both close to the main square. If you want to try your hand at weaving or embroidery, consider a day's workshop at Casa Matico (✉ huarmimaqui@hotmail.com; $10/person), run by an indigenous family, that also offers courses in Andean cuisine and where you can purchase textiles made by Huarmi Maqui, a women's cooperative. Peguche is also known for producing **musical instruments**, including the *rondador* (Ecuadorian pan pipe), and for the talented *folklórica* musicians who play them. Seek out Ñanda Mañachi just north of the plaza for an impressive selection of instruments and some enchanting demonstrations.

La Cascada de Peguche
1km southeast of Peguche • Mon & Tues 8.30am–1.30pm, Wed–Sun 8.30am–6pm • $2

Set in a eucalyptus grove, the sacred waterfall of **La Cascada de Peguche** is the site of ceremonial bathing during Inti Raymi and the San Juanes fiestas (see box, p.107), but for the rest of the year it's a popular picnic spot, particularly at weekends. **To walk here**, head south out of Peguche along the main street for about 15 minutes from where the entrance is signposted. From Otavalo, walk east out of town towards the rail tracks, where you turn left onto a cobbled road running parallel to them; follow this until the sign to the entrance (45min).

OPPOSITE OTAVALO MARKET (P.106) >

ARRIVAL AND DEPARTURE

By bus Regular buses leave from the main terminal in Otavalo (every 20min; 15min) and can be boarded at any of the stops along Roca.

By taxi It's around a $2.50–3 taxi ride from Otavalo to Peguche.

ACCOMMODATION

Aya Huma By the rail tracks up from the waterfall ☎06 2690333, ⓦ ayahuma.com. Friendly hostel in a charming old house with pleasant, simple rooms with hot water in shared or private bathrooms, next to a garden with hammocks. Has a good book exchange, small library and a decent restaurant (mains $7–10) with frequent live music on Saturdays. $35; camping $4/person

La Casa Sol North of the Cascada de Peguche ☎06 2690500, ⓦ lacasasol.com/casaotavalo. Fortress-like main gates belie the warm hospitality of this indigenously owned wood-and-adobe house, set round a courtyard. Brightly painted en-suite rooms have fireplaces, and guests can relax in a lounge or games and television area. Light breakfast included. $62

Parque Cóndor

By the community of Pucará Alto, 3.5km from Otavalo • Wed–Sun & public holidays 9.30am–5pm • $4.50 • ☎06 3049399, ⓦ parquecondor.com • About an hour's walk from Otavalo (45min from the Cascada de Peguche); head uphill on the road to Lago San Pablo, turning off by El Lechero • Buses from Otavalo can drop you at the junction near El Lechero • A taxi from Otavalo costs about $10–12 (including waiting time)

On the top of a high hill between Otavalo and Lago San Pablo you'll find the excellent **Parque Cóndor**, a rehabilitation centre for injured **birds of prey**, which is worth a visit to see a selection of Ecuador's most elegant avian hunters. There are fifteen or so species, including barred hawks, black-chested buzzard-eagles and king vultures, as well as spectacled and other owls, and a couple of sad-looking condors. Trained Harris's hawks and an American kestrel perform flight demonstrations (11.30am & 3.30pm) against a scenic backdrop.

Lagunas de Mojanda

The three brooding lakes of the **Lagunas de Mojanda** are clutched by grassy hills 16km south of, and 1200m above, Otavalo, and the dramatic scenery has made the area a favourite for hikers and horse riders. A cobblestone road winds up from Otavalo to the **Laguna Grande de Mojanda**, by far the largest of the three lakes, more than 2km wide. On the other side of the lake, a clear trail corners eastwards to **Laguna Negra**, while a less-used path continues 1km south to **Laguna Chiquita**. Beyond the ring of ragged peaks encircling the lakes, topped by Fuya Fuya (4263m), is a trail to Cochasquí and a cobblestone track down to Tabacundo. It used to be commonplace for hikers to get mugged in the area and, while the situation has vastly improved in recent years, you should enquire about safety before heading off on a hike.

ARRIVAL AND DEPARTURE

By taxi You can take a taxi from Otavalo to the lakes, and then walk back down to town (3hr 30min) to enjoy the spectacular views. Taxis cost $12 one-way ($15 in a camioneta, which is recommended), plus around $7 per

hour waiting time for the return trip.

Tours You can take an organized tour to the lakes from Otavalo (see p.108) or from one of the nearby hotels (see below).

ACCOMMODATION

★**Casa Mojanda** 3.5km from Otavalo on the Mojanda road ☎0999731737, ⓦ casamojanda.com. A collection of beautiful whitewashed cottages poised on a hillside, with vast windows offering stunning mountain views. The hotel has an organic garden that supplies its excellent, predominantly vegetarian restaurant (meals $22–24). Leisure time can be

spent in the outdoor hot tub, games room or library, on guided horse riding or hiking excursions, or recovering with a massage. Rates include a substantial breakfast. $159

Hostería Rose Cottage 3km from Otavalo on the Mojanda road ☎0997728115, ⓦ rosecottageecuador .com. Scenically located property with seven rather twee houses and a range of good-value accommodation, from a chintzy cottage complete with four-poster bed and private balcony, through doubles, triples, family lodgings, spacious dorm rooms and camping. Facilities include a restaurant, hammocks, games room, tennis court, table-tennis table and a fabulous hot tub with a view ($5/person). Cooked breakfast included. Dorms $14; doubles $40; camping $5/person

★ **La Luna** 4km from Otavalo up the Mojanda road ☎ 0993156082, ⊛ lalunaecuador.info. This attractive, relaxed place with stellar views is a superb budget choice, featuring comfortable rooms with or without private bathrooms and fireplaces, as well as dorm beds and a campsite. There's also a small kitchen available and a restaurant serving modestly priced comfort food. Breakfast included. Dorms $14; doubles $47; camping $8/person

Cotacachi

West of the Panamericana and 11km from Otavalo, the tranquil town of **COTACACHI** is a self-proclaimed "eco-city". It has successfully cut down waste and pollution, and is a pioneering force in participatory democracy, renowned throughout Latin America. It's also a prosperous community thanks to its flourishing leather industry, and dozens of smart boutiques selling every conceivable form of leatherware line 10 de Agosto, the main street running north–south up to **Parque San Francisco**. The park is the focus of the **Sunday leather market**, the best place to pick up a bargain bag, belt or jacket. The town's main plaza is the leafy **Parque Abdón Calderón**, presided over by the white-domed **La Matriz** church. For a good party, make sure your visit coincides with the **Fiestas de la Jora**, two weeks of harvest thanksgiving in early September, which include the usual parades, partying and competitions, including one to judge the best-made pre-Inca *chicha de jora* (fermented maize drink), after which the festival is named.

Museo de las Culturas

García Moreno 13-41 and Bolívar • Mon–Fri 9am–noon & 2–5pm, Sat 1–5pm, Sun 10am–1pm • $1, including guided tour in Spanish

The small **Museo de las Culturas**, set in a cloistered colonial-style building, provides a historical overview of the area from pre-Columbian times, and showcases Cotacachi traditions through colourful costumed mannequins and exhibits on crafts and fiestas. Some signage in English.

ARRIVAL AND INFORMATION   COTACACHI

By bus Buses run between Cotacachi's bus station – at 10 de Agosto and Salinas, at the north end of town – and the bus terminals at Otavalo and Ibarra (daily 6am–7.15pm, every 10–15min; 25min). When heading to and from Quito you need to change buses in Otavalo.

Information The I-Tur office is on Parque Calderón ☎ 06 2915115 (Mon–Fri 8am–noon & 2–5pm). Information and maps are also available in the Casa de las Culturas on Bolívar at 9 de Octubre ☎ 06 2915140 (daily 9am–8pm).

ACCOMMODATION

★ **La Cuadra** Peñaherrera 11–46, between González Suárez and Pedro Moncayo ☎ 06 2916015, ⊛ lacuadra -hostal.com. Spotless modern hostel in the centre of town with friendly bilingual (English and Spanish) owner, offering family and double rooms with private or shared bathroom and plenty of hot water. Also includes use of a kitchen, comfy common areas and a rooftop terrace with great views. $39

Hostal Bachita Sucre and 24 de Mayo ☎ 06 2915063, ✉ hostalbachita@hotmail.com. A cheap hotel whose fourteen decent rooms come with bathrooms and hot water. The place fills up, so book ahead. $22

Land of the Sun Hotel & Spa García Moreno 13-67 and Sucre ☎ 06 2916009, ⊛ landofthesunhotel.com. Aimed squarely at the North American market, this

charming, recently renovated colonial house (previously operating as *Tierra del Sol*) has en-suite rooms – some with balconies – set around a pretty flower-filled courtyard. The restaurant is good and the sauna and massage room are a real boon if you've been for a long hike, while the church bells will ensure you're awake early. Breakfast included. $66

★ **La Mirage** 500m north of town on 10 de Agosto ☎ 06 2915237, in North America ☎ 1 800 327 3573, ⊛ mirage.com.ec. This "contemporary hacienda" is one of the most expensive and opulent hotels in the country, featuring peacock-filled gardens, palatial rooms and suites (with garden patios) sumptuously furnished with fireplaces and four-poster beds, plus a scattering of fresh rose petals. A superior on-site spa offers luxurious treatments. Full breakfast included. Doubles $238; suites $342

2

EATING

Café Río Intag Imbabura on Parque San Francisco. Pleasant split-level café-bar offering intimate tables and (moderately) comfy sofas to enjoy a capuccino and cake or an empanada while chilling out to some mellow sounds. Book exchange too. Daily 8am–9pm, Sat & Sun until 10pm.

La Casa del Turista Bolívar and 10 de Agosto ☎06 2916125. Large brick-and-wood rustic restaurant with a pleasant veranda and garden, which focuses on *parrilladas*, with *carne colorada* the regional and house speciality. Popular lunch stop for tour groups, so time your visit accordingly. Large portions make good-value mains ($7–10) and set-price menus. Daily 8am–10pm.

D'Anita's 10 de Agosto and González Suárez ☎06 2915244. Moderately priced family-run restaurant offering excellent food in a cosy setting that includes courtyard seating. Good for breakfast, lunch or dinner; the shrimp-stuffed whole trout is a treat. Mon–Fri 8.30am–5.30pm, and on weekends and evenings when events are on.

★**La Mirage** 500m north of town on 10 de Agosto ☎06 2915237, ⓦmirage.com.ec. Superb, creative fine dining in one of Ecuador's top restaurants, with prices to match. Enjoy a lovely candlelit ambience for dinner ($43 for three courses), or fine garden views over lunch. Dishes are beautifully presented and there's an extensive wine list. Daily noon–3.30pm & 6.30–8pm.

Reserva Ecológica Cotacachi-Cayapas

Northwest of Otavalo, west of Cotacachi · **Cuicocha Visitor Centre** Daily 9am–5pm · Free

Covering more than two thousand square miles of the western Andes, the **Reserva Ecológica Cotacachi-Cayapas** spans the summit of Volcán Cotacachi (4944m) down to the coastal lowlands (300m), protecting ecological habitats from the páramo grasslands in the east to the dense rainforests of Esmeraldas province. The reserve is part of the **Chocó** bioregion, which extends into southern Colombia, where high levels of rainfall support one of the earth's most diverse ecosystems. Twenty percent of Ecuador's endemic plants are found here, as well as thousands of birds, insects and mammals, including Andean spectacled bears, ocelots, jaguars and river otters.

Cuicocha

From Cotacachi and Otavalo it's easy to get to the centre of the highland section, **Cuicocha** ("Guinea Pig Lake" in Kichwa), a spectacular crater lake at 3060m, located at the foot of the dormant Volcán Cotacachi in the southeastern tip of the reserve. A pair of old volcanic cones that grew up from the floor of a collapsed crater 200m below form two islands, which, according to legend, were used by the Incas as a prison. They're off limits due to on-site research, but you can jaunt across the lake on a **motorboat** ($3/person), or learn more about them in the **visitor centre**.

Better still, you can walk around the rim of the crater on a well-kept, circular **trail**. The 10km hike (best walked anticlockwise) takes 4–5 hours to complete, though your effort is rewarded by wonderful views of Cayambe and Cotacachi on clear days, not to mention orchids and giant hummingbirds, and even a condor if you're lucky.

Volcán Cotacachi

The access to **climb** the snow-dusted peak of Volcán Cotacachi begins at some antennas to its east, at the end of the dirt road heading north from the guard post. It's not a technical climb, but there is some scrambling near the top as well as risk of rock fall. A **guide** is recommended, not least because fog often makes finding routes difficult; ask at *El Mirador* restaurant (see opposite), the Casa de las Culturas office in Cotacachi or tour agencies in Otavalo (see p.108). A camioneta from Otavalo to the antennas costs around $35–40.

Las Lagunas de Piñan

Around 20km, as the condor flies, northwest of Volcán Cotacachi, the little-explored **Lagunas de Piñan** dot the silvery-olive grasslands of the high páramo, presided over by the twin volcanic peaks of Yana Urku (4535m), meaning "Black Mountain" in Kichwa. This desolate region, boasting over 35 lakes of glacial origin, makes for compelling multi-day wilderness trekking, affording good opportunities to spot condors and white-tailed deer, and – should the weather be good – stunning views across the sierra. Although it is possible to hike on your own (IGM *Imantag and Ibarra* and *Cerro Yanaurco* maps would be needed), the community tourism association of the tiny adobe-and-thatch hamlet of **Piñan** offers guided hikes, mules and horse riding, and even operates a well-equipped refuge (☎06 3048996, ⊛pinantrek.com); alternatively, contact a Quito or Otavalo tour operator (see p.79 and p.108).

ARRIVAL AND DEPARTURE

Cuicocha by bus and taxi To get to Cuicocha, take one of the frequent buses from Otavalo or Ibarra to Cotacachi (see p.108 & p.121) or Quiroga, a village about 5min from Cotacachi. From either, go by taxi or camioneta to the lake ($12 return from Cotacachi, including 30min waiting time; $5 one-way taxi from Quiroga). You can also reach

RESERVA ECOLÓGICA COTACACHI-CAYAPAS

cloudforest areas from the Los Cedros reserve (see p.260) to the south.

Las Lagunas de Piñan by bus Transportes Urcuquí runs several buses a day from the bus terminal in Ibarra via Urcuquí, to the village of Irunguicho 4km beyond, and the start of the circular three- to four-day hike.

INFORMATION

The reserve office is in Cotacachi next to the Museo de las Culturas (☎06 2915986; Mon–Fri 8am–5pm). The Casa de las Culturas, at the corner of Bolívar and 9 de Octubre

(☎06 2915140; daily 9am–8pm), also provides information and can help you hire a guide.

ACCOMMODATION AND EATING

Hostería Cuicocha By the jetty ☎06 3017218, ⊛cuicocha.org. Modern hotel with comfortable cabins (with fireplaces) by the shore, two of which have simply stunning views. The price includes breakfast and a two-course dinner in the large restaurant open to the public (daily 9am–5pm). **$110**

El Mirador On the hill above the jetty, overlooking the lake ☎0990558367, ✉miradordecuicocha@yahoo .com. Perfectly placed for an early-morning start on the crater rim trail, with simple, clean cabins affording great views, and a decent restaurant (daily 8am–7pm). **$36**

The Intag valley

West of Laguna Cuicocha, a mainly tarred road climbs to 3300m before twisting into the remote and subtropical **Intag valley**, where only a few isolated settlements sit amid richly forested hills, and the **Río Intag** carves its way coastwards. The area has become a focus of conservation efforts and several private reserves are guardians of these precious portions of **Chocó bioregion cloudforest**, one of the world's ten biodiversity "hotspots". Community-based ecotourism is thriving throughout the region – notably in the isolated villages of **Apuela** and **Junín** – and the reserves near the hamlet of **Santa Rosa** host a cornucopia of birds, butterflies and orchids. Alternatively, soak in the thermal springs at **Nangulví** or visit nearby pre-Inca ruins at **Gualimán**.

Santa Rosa

Blink and you can easily miss the hamlet of **SANTA ROSA**, comprising a handful of houses, a small primary school and an adjacent chapel topped by a bell. Across the road from the bus stop, a friendly *comedor* provides a popular breakfast or lunch stop for truck drivers shuttling produce between the valley's communities and Otavalo, so a good place to hitch a ride if you've missed one of the scarce and unreliable buses.

Apuela

A few meanders down the valley from Santa Rosa, thickly wooded hills enclose the small but growing village of **APUELA**, located at the confluence of ríos Apuela and Azabi. The village consists of little more than a main square and a few simple streets, with a sprinkling of basic shops. While there's not much to interest tourists here in the

2

village, beyond contacting the NGOs based here (see below), hiking **trails** festoon the surrounding hills and a couple of places of interest lie in the vicinity.

Nangulví

Around 6km from Apuela are the **Piscinas de Nangulví** (daily 7am–9pm; $3), which comprise five thermal pools in the hamlet of the same name, set in a gorgeous steep-walled valley. Though busy at weekends, you'll be able to enjoy the scenery from the steaming waters in peace during the week. In the hills above Nangulví, on a spectacular long plateau, stand the scarcely visible **pre-Columbian ruins of Gualimán**. Though there's little to see beyond a few large overgrown pyramid mounds with ramps, the setting alone makes a visit worthwhile. Contact the Red Ecoturística de Intag office (see below), where you can hire a guide to take you there.

Junín

Northwest of García Moreno – at the end of the Intag bus route from Otavalo – a bumpy dirt track leads up to the remote, politically active community of **JUNÍN**, that has repeatedly resisted government and large corporations' attempts (sometimes violent) to foist mining upon them: see ⓦdecoin.org for the latest news. It is hoped that the income generated by a community **lodge** and the thirty-square-kilometre Junín Cloud Forest Reserve (see opposite), as well as by a successful organic coffee-growing cooperative, will help to keep the miners out. There's enormous scope for birdwatching and **hiking** in the surrounding forests, which are streaked with waterfalls, and guiding services are available.

ARRIVAL
INTAG VALLEY

By bus Transportes Otavalo and 6 de Julio operate bus services from Otavalo's bus terminal to Apuela (5 daily, last bus 3pm; 2hr 15min) with most departures going on to Nangulví (2hr 30min) and García Moreno (3hr 30min). A couple of buses deviate after Apuela to head to Peñaherrera, which passes the trailhead for Gualimán, from where it's a 45min walk to the ruins. To reach the community of Junín take the bus to García Moreno, from where it's a 45-minute walk; alternatively, you can arrange with the community lodge to be picked up.

INFORMATION AND TOURS

AACRI (ⓣ 06 2648489, ⓔ aacri@andinanet.net) is a local coffee-producing association, whose agro-tourism projects involve trips to or volunteer placements at nearby coffee farms.

DECOIN (ⓣ 06 2648953, ⓦ decoin.org), a conservation association, can provide information on visiting and volunteering at local reserves.
Red Ecoturística de Intag This eco-tourism

INTAG CLOUD FOREST RESERVE

The **Intag Cloud Forest Reserve** protects five square kilometres of primary and secondary forest ranging from 1800m to 2800m in altitude. High rainfall (2500mm annually) and humidity nurture an incredible array of flora and fauna, including more than twenty types of hummingbird, which you can expect to see zipping around. The owners helped found DECOIN (see above), a local environmental organization that works on regional ecotourism projects, and has so far successfully defended the region's forests and communities from mining interests. In order to minimize the impact of visitors on the environment, they only accept groups of eight and above and reservations are essential.

Intag Cloud Forest Reserve 45min hike from Santa Rosa ⓣ 06 2990001, ⓦ intagcloudforest.com. Take a bus to Santa Rosa (see p.117); onward travel details will be given when you book. Popular with student groups, this simple, informal lodge is equipped with solar-heated showers and composting latrines, and you get to enjoy delicious organically grown vegetarian food. The setting is lush and there's a nearby waterfall. Activities include hiking and birdwatching and learning about the environment in situ. There's a two-night minimum stay, and the price includes full board and activities. $56/person.

organization supports community-based tourism activities, and has an office in the car park at the Nangulví baths (Wed–Sun 9.30am–4pm; ☎06 3016135). They can provide information and help you organize a local guide to go horse riding, or to visit a local waterfall, the ruins of Gualimán (see opposite) or a cock-of-the-rock lek (courtship ground). Rates are inexpensive, though for some activities you may need to provide your own transport. For further information see ⓦintagturismo.com.

ACCOMMODATION AND EATING

JUNÍN

Junín Cloud Forest Reserve ☎06 2648953 or ☎0988871860, ⓦjunincloudforest.com. Large bamboo lodge sleeping 25 people, with six bedrooms (all but one with shared bathroom) and a large common area. The daily rate includes three good meals and a local (Spanish-speaking) guide. Volunteers, who can teach at a local school, build trails, or help farm, pay $20 per person, sharing a room. $̄35/person

NANGULVÍ

Cabañas Río Grande By the Río Intag close to Nangulví baths ☎06 2648296. A collection of clean, flower-draped log cabins (for four) with private bathrooms and electric showers. Two rooms per cabin share a porch with hammocks, yet strangely face the road. Pleasant riverside gardens contain a fair-sized pool, and a decent restaurant provides a varied menu (advanced notice needed). $̄40

Cafetal del Intag 1.6km from Nangulví baths. Book through the *Valle del Amanecer* in Otavalo (see p.109), whose owner can also organize trips to the area. These five simple cabañas can sleep up to five people. $̄20/person

Complejo Nangulví At the Nangulví baths ☎06 2648291, ✉termas.nangulvi@gmail.com. Functional en-suite stone chalets, each containing a double bed and set of bunk beds; use mosquito repellent at night. Rates include entry to the baths. The riverside restaurant (daily 8am–8pm) is delightfully located and serves inexpensive desayunos and almuerzos. There's also a patch of grass by the baths that is set aside for camping. Chalets $̄40; camping $̄5/person

SANTA ROSA

★**El Refugio de Intag** Santa Rosa ⓔelrefugiocloudforest.com. A delightfully restful birdwatching treat, set in a small private reserve traversed by a bubbling stream. A handful of warmly furnished rustic cottages are available, comprising several en-suite rooms (1 and 2 offer the greatest seclusion) with generous showers. Breakfast and access to the trails (with Spanish-speaking guide) are included, and trips further afield can be organized at extra cost. Wi-fi is available in the main lodge, where delicious healthy meals (around $10 for lunch or dinner), made predominantly from organic local produce, are served family-style. $̄110

Ibarra

Some 115km north of Quito, the Panamericana passes around the base of Volcán Imbabura to reveal **IBARRA** (2225m), basking in a broad, sunny valley. Known as the *ciudad blanca* (white city), its low blocks of whitewashed and tiled buildings gleam with stately confidence, interrupted only by the occasional church spire and odd commercial building. It was founded in 1606 to oversee the region's textile workshops, but only a few of Ibarra's original colonial structures survived the great earthquake of 1868, from which the town eventually recovered to become the commercial and transport hub of Imbabura province. Ibarra's population of more than 130,000 people, an unusual blend of mestizos, *indígenas* and Afro-Ecuadorians from the nearby Chota valley, makes it by far the largest highland city north of Quito, but despite this, it still enjoys a relaxed pace of life and an easy-going charm.

Ibarra is a great place to unwind, with good hotels, cafés and bars, a pleasant climate and friendly residents. The more energetic might consider a few lengths of the city's attractive outdoor Olympic-sized swimming pool (Troya and Narváez; daily 9am–5pm; $2) or soaring like a condor with Flyecuador (Villamar and Olmedo ☎06 2953297, ⓦflyecuador.com.ec), which offers paragliding courses for novices and more experienced practitioners, or tandem flights at $75 a day.

On the outskirts of the city, just before the Panamericana, lies the community of San Antonio de Ibarra, a major centre for **woodcarving**. Its plentiful shops and galleries are crammed with a huge array of artefacts in different styles, mostly carved in cedar, from saints and angels to chess sets and life-size carvings of Don Quixote.

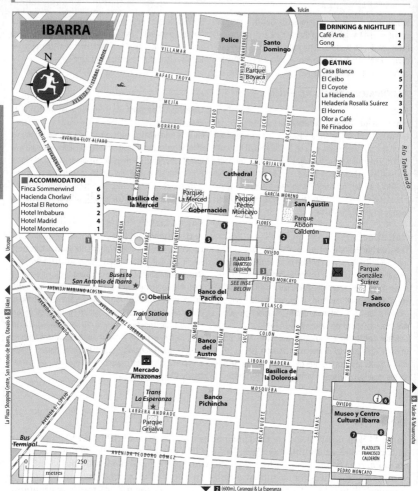

Parque Pedro Moncayo

The best place to start exploring is Ibarra's focal point, the **Parque Pedro Moncayo**, which features a statue of the eponymous nineteenth-century local journalist and politician. The neatly clipped lawns and lofty palms of this grand square are flanked to the north by the **cathedral**, adorned with a golden altar and displaying portraits of the disciples by **Rafael Troya**, one of Ecuador's greatest artists, who was born here in 1845. Along the west side of the park is the **gobernación**, the seat of the province's government, an imposing colonial-style building which looks ravishing under evening floodlights.

Parque la Merced

A quiet central square, Parque Victor M. Peñaherrera is better known as **Parque la Merced** after the **Basílica de la Merced**, an imposing grey-stone church crowned with a weighty statue of the Virgin and housing a towering red and gold altarpiece. Opposite the basilica, on the eastern side of the park, the old **infantry barracks** give the square a distinctly Mediterranean flavour with their impressive Moorish castellations and arches, beneath which **street vendors** sell the sweet Ibarra specialities, *nogadas* and *arrope de mora* (see p.122), from their sunshaded stalls.

Plazoleta Francisco Calderón

A block south of the Parque Pedro Moncayo is the **Plazoleta Francisco Calderón**. A marketplace until the 1960s, it is now the city's cultural focus with occasional performances held on the corner stage. A handful of bar-restaurants line its northern side – during the day it's a pleasant spot to sit in the sun and enjoy a beer or ice cream, while the bars and cafés stay lively late into the night.

La Esquina del Coco

On the corner of Sucre and Oviedo is a lonely coconut tree, known as **La Esquina del Coco**. An unlikely emblem of city pride, it is supposedly the reference point used by President García Moreno for the layout of the new city after its destruction in the 1868 earthquake. A statue of the president poring over his drawing board is tucked away by the railings.

Museo y Centro Cultural Ibarra

Sucre and Oviedo • Tues–Fri 9am–4.30pm, Sat & Sun 10am–4pm • Free

Located just off the Plazoleta Calderón, the engaging **Museo y Centro Cultural Ibarra** concentrates on Ecuadorian archeology from prehistory to the Inca era, particularly in the northern sierra; items include a **gold funeral mask** from the nearby Pimampiro area and a grisly diorama of the bloody war between the Incas and the Caranqui at Yahuarcocha (see p.123). Don't miss the superb ceramics, including the mythological beast of the **Jama-Coaque** culture (350 BC to 1540 AD), with its penetrating eyes, tusked teeth and fish mouth.

ARRIVAL AND DEPARTURE   IBARRA

By bus Most buses use the terminal on Avenida Gómez and Espejo, southwest of the centre, though a couple of local destinations are serviced from points nearby.
Destinations Baños (2 daily; 6hr); Chachimbiro (3 daily, extra at weekends; 1hr 15min); Cotacachi (every 30min; 30min); El Ángel (6 daily; 1hr 30min); Esmeraldas (5 daily; 8hr 30min); Guayaquil (6 daily; 10hr); Guallupe (every 50min; 1hr 30min); La Esperanza (every 20min; 30min); Lita (every 50min; 2hr); Mira (hourly; 1hr); Otavalo (every 10min; 40min); Pimampiro (every 15min; 1hr 15min); Quito (every 10min until 8pm; 2hr 30min); San Antonio de Ibarra (every 20min; 10min); San Lorenzo (9 daily; 4hr); Santo Domingo (18 daily; 6hr); Tulcán (9 daily; 2hr 30min); Urcuquí (every 15min; 30min); Zuleta (hourly; 50min).

GETTING AROUND AND INFORMATION

By bus and taxi Local city buses ply the main thoroughfares, while taxis hang around the main parks, bus stations and downtown streets ($1 for a local ride).
Tourist office The very helpful I-Tur office is on Oviedo and Sucre, at La Esquina del Coco (Mon–Fri 8am–5.30pm; ☏ 06 2608489, ✇ touribarra.gob.ec, ✇ imbaburaturismo .gob.ec), and there's also a small kiosk at the bus terminal; both can provide maps and general information.

IBARRA'S FESTIVALS

Among the most important local **festivals** are the **Fiesta del Retorno**, on April 28, commemorating the return of the town's citizens after the 1868 earthquake; **Independence Day**, on July 17, marking Simón Bolívar's triumph over the Spanish at the Battle of Ibarra in 1823; and the biggest of all, the **Fiesta de los Lagos**, on the last weekend in September, celebrating the city's foundation (Sept 28) with parades and decorated floats rolling through town and motor races held at Laguna Yahuarcocha.

2

ACCOMMODATION

Finca Sommerwind Autopista Km7 at Yahuarcocha ☎0939371177, ⓦfinca-sommerwind.com. Pleasantly situated secure campsite with lake views and plenty of facilities: electricity and hot showers, laundry, BBQ and a great little terrace café. Though only officially open on Sundays (9am–6pm) it will open at other times on request; don't miss the German-style cakes. Cheerful bright cement chalets with private porches also available, and good rates for long-term stays. Chalets $\overline{$35}$; camping $\overline{$5}$/person

★ **Hacienda Chorlaví** Panamericana Sur Km4.5, outside town ☎06 2932222, ⓦhaciendachorlavi.com. Delightful converted colonial hacienda and former Jesuit monastery with whitewashed buildings decorated with painted floral designs set in palm-fringed gardens with pool, spa, tennis courts and even an old disused cockfighting arena. Comfortable rooms and suites with fireplaces have period furnishings and LCD-screen TVs. Tranquil midweek, the place can get noisy at weekends when the renowned but pricey restaurant and live folk music and dancing draw tour groups. Breakfast included. Doubles $\overline{$128}$; suites $\overline{$153}$

Hostal El Retorno Moncayo 4-32 and Rocafuerte ☎06 2958700. Popular budget choice – so often booked up – offering clean en-suite rooms, hot water and cable TV. It also has a restaurant. $\overline{$24}$

Hotel Imbabura Oviedo 9-33 and Chica Narváez ☎06 2950155, ⓔinfo@hotelimbabura-lapitela.com. The most charming of the budget choices (if you don't mind shared bathrooms), with good hot showers and large, high-ceilinged if faded rooms around a pretty courtyard. Breakfast available in the patio café, and there are left-luggage and laundry services. $\overline{$16}$

Hotel Madrid Moncayo 7-41 and Sánchez y Cifuentes ☎06 2956177. Excellent value, offering bright and comfortable en-suite rooms with phone and cable TV – but avoid those without windows. Parking also available. $\overline{$22}$

Hotel Montecarlo Rivadeneira 5-63 and Oviedo ☎06 2958266, ⓦhotelmontecarloibarra.ec. Mid-range, business-oriented hotel with an indoor heated pool, sauna and steam room (open weekends & hols). Comfortable carpeted rooms but they vary in size. The ones at the back have a shared balcony with hammocks. Parking available. Buffet breakfast included. $\overline{$55}$

EATING

All visitors to Ibarra should try the wonderfully smooth, tasty **helados de paila**, sorbets prepared in great copper pans (*pailas*) kept cool on a bed of straw and salted ice, into which fruit, sugar and water are stirred – found at a number of excellent *heladerías* throughout town. Other local specialities are sold at stalls around the Parque La Merced, namely **nogadas** – nougat-style treats made from sugar, milk, egg whites and walnuts, sometimes flavoured with cinnamon, aniseed or vanilla – and **arrope de mora**, a sticky blackberry syrup, usually diluted with water or spirits.

Casa Blanca Bolívar 7-83 and Moncayo ☎06 2952124. Longstanding favourite serving juices, coffees and traditional snacks: *quimbolitos*, *humitas* and the house speciality, hot, crispy empanadas – try the green plantain one with chicken – in an attractive old house set around a courtyard and fountain. Mon–Sat 8am–noon & 4–8pm.

El Ceibo Olmedo 10-15, between Velasco and Colón ☎06 2951946. Popular, inexpensive breakfast ($3) and lunchtime venue ($4) serving attractively presented meals: a skylight creates a clean, bright ambience. Daily 7.30am–4pm.

El Coyote Plazoleta Calderón ☎06 2641959. Easy-going bar-restaurant serving snacks, Tex-Mex (most $5–8) and mulled wine, with a popular heated outdoor seating area – accompanied by non-stop on-screen sports and rock videos – that is really buzzing in the evenings. Mon–Wed 4–10pm, Thurs–Sat 4pm–midnight.

La Hacienda Corner of Oviedo and Sucre ☎06 2605881. Deli, café and bar in a rustic stable-cum-barn complete with hay bales, wooden beams and a stuffed bull's head. Tourist prices but decent breakfasts, deli-

---

CLIMBING IMBABURA AND CUBILCHE

La Esperanza makes an excellent base for climbing Volcán Imbabura and Volcán Cubilche to the west, and **trails** for both begin to the right by the bridge up from the *Casa Aída* hostel. The IGM (see p.48) San Pablo del Lago **map** (1:50,000 scale) is a good resource, and both the town's hostales can provide information and **guides** ($50/day for 1 or 2 people; less for larger groups). Hiking to the summit of **Imbabura** (4621m) is straightforward, except for some loose rock at the top, and the round trip takes about ten hours. Get an early start and don't forget food, water and warm clothing. The less energetic can take a camioneta up as far as an hour's walk from the top, then hike back down, or just spend a day walking through the pastureland around the mountain's base.

Compared with Imbabura, the summit of **Cubilche** (3826m) is an easier proposition (3hr round trip), and offers great views of the lake and Ibarra.

sandwiches and salads for lunch ($4–7), and wine and superior platters of cold cuts and the like for sharing in the evening. Leave room for the tiramisu. Mon–Sat 7.30am–10.30pm.

★**Heladería Rosalía Suárez** Oviedo 7-79 and Olmedo. Although the rival family business across the road may argue its own claim, this is the oldest and most famous place (in business since 1897) to sample tasty *helados de paila* (sorbets), and watch them being made; there are many delicious flavours to choose from. Mon–Sat 7am–6.30pm, Sun 7.30am–6.30pm.

El Horno Rocafuerte 6-38 and Flores ☎ 06 2959019. Very popular restaurant serving up tasty (though occasionally a tad sweet) pizzas (from $8) cooked in a large wood-fired clay oven that dominates the restaurant. Reasonably priced wine

and beer available. Tues–Sun 6–11pm.

Olor a Café Corner of Bolívar and Flores ☎ 06 2954505. This wonderfully restored colonial house is the ideal spot for a leisurely breakfast, lunch or coffee and a cake in a comfortable lounge or interior courtyard, though the food doesn't always live up to the setting. Check out the glorious black-and-white photos of late nineteenth-century Ibarra on the second floor, too. Mon–Fri 8am–10pm, Sat noon–10pm.

Ré Finadoo Plazoleta Calderón ☎ 06 2603033. Enduring bar-restaurant with heated outdoor plant-filled patio and funky glass gazebo plus cosy indoor seating, all of which give this place a mellow, sophisticated feel. A choice spot for a cocktail or a meal. Mains $6–10 plus. Mon–Sat 10am–10/11pm.

DRINKING AND NIGHTLIFE

Avenida Atahualpa is a good bet to trawl for **bars**, restaurants and clubs on a Friday or Saturday night, though some of the bigger **nightclubs** are out by the Panamericana at Yahuarcocha.

★**Café Arte** Salinas 5-43 and Oviedo ☎ 06 2950806. Artist-owned café-cum-art gallery with a warm wooden interior. Intellectual flourishes abound, from the mock triptych menu to the Frida Kahlo cocktail. Live music of all sorts – from Latin rock and pop to jazz, blues and salsa – on Friday or Saturday by national and international artists, for a modest cover charge. Check their Facebook page for details. Thurs 5pm–midnight, Fri & Sat 5pm–2am.

★**Gong** Av Atahualpa 17–102 and Ricardo Sánchez ☎ 06 2640100. This cheerfully decorated bicycle-themed bar draws foreigners and locals alike with its mellow, alternative vibe. Residual energy from the weekly bike ride (Thurs 8pm) can be expended dancing salsa – also on offer Wednesday nights – while Fridays see local or itinerant musicians improvising. Veggie and vegan burgers and light bites are on the menu, with the *plato del día* the most substantial dish. Wash it down with artisanal beer, mulled wine, cocktails or shots. Wed–Sat 5pm–late.

Around Ibarra

On the northern outskirts of Ibarra lies peaceful **Yahuarcocha** – "lake of blood" in Kichwa, recalling the slaughter of the indigenous Cara people here by the Incas under Huayna Capac in 1495. Though the lake's beauty is marred by the tarmac of a racetrack around it, it's a popular weekend getaway for *ibarreños*. The excellent hot springs at **Chachimbiro** are slightly further afield but enjoy a regular bus service from the city. The nearby village of **La Esperanza** makes a sound base for hikes in the surrounding countryside, from a stroll across the folds of **Volcán Imbabura** to a stiff climb to the summit.

La Esperanza and around

At the foot of Volcán Imbabura, 8km south of Ibarra on a cobblestone road, is **LA ESPERANZA**, a tranquil village where Simón Bolívar planned the defeat of General Agualongo and his Spanish forces, thus liberating Ibarra. Forty-five years later, when flattened by the 1868 earthquake, Ibarra again looked to La Esperanza for assistance, its survivors taking refuge here for four years while the city was rebuilt. A century on, La Esperanza briefly attracted magic-mushroom-loving hippies, but today most visitors come for the restful atmosphere, excellent mountain walks and the village's discreet but flourishing artesanía scene, including work in leather, marquetry (*taracea*) for guitar inlays and embroidery (*bordado*).

THE IBARRA TRAIN

Once extending to San Lorenzo on the coast, Ibarra's train now only runs as far as Salinas, an Afro-Ecuadorian community 30km away, on the slopes of the Chota valley. But it's still a fun ride, skirting vertiginous drops, being swallowed by tunnels and clattering across the rickety bridge high above the Ambi gorge. The ticket also includes a guided tour of Salinas, and a visit to a salt museum. It's one of the more popular train excursions, so book in advance (☎ 06 2950390; ☻ trenecuador.com). Departures for the five-hour outing are at 11.20am (Fri–Sun & hols; $28).

ARRIVAL AND GETTING AROUND

By bus Buses to La Esperanza and San Clemente leave Ibarra (every 20min until 6pm; 30min) from Parque Grijalva, a few blocks south of the obelisk.

LA ESPERANZA AND AROUND

By taxi A taxi costs around $5 to La Esperanza from Ibarra, and a camioneta will cost $4–5 to go up Volcán Imbabura from La Esperanza or San Clemente.

ACCOMMODATION

★ **Casa Aída** Main road, La Esperanza ☎ 06 2660221, ☻ casaaida.com. Sra Aída Buitrón has been welcoming visitors – from hippy rock stars to hikers – for around forty years, and her expanding hostel is a travellers' institution, offering simple, clean rooms with shared hot-water showers, and space for camping. Excellent breakfasts, packed lunches and predominantly vegetarian dinners are available ($4), as well as laundry and guiding services. Dorms $16; camping $4/person

Refugio Terra Esperanza La Esperanza ☎ 06 2660228, ☻ refugioterraesperanza.ec. Friendly, brightly painted hostel offering dorm accommodation and private rooms with shared bathrooms. Meals can be arranged or you can use the kitchen, plus there are guided hikes around Imbabura. Dorms $13; doubles $28

Tradiciones San Clemente In the village of San Clemente, near La Esperanza ☎ 06 2660045, ☻ sanclementetours.com. Community-based tourism involving homestays and cultural activities such as embroidery, learning Kichwa, horse riding, mountain biking and guided hikes (at additional cost). It's also possible to volunteer for local development projects or go on a four-day trek in Reserva Ecológica Cayambe-Coca (see p.102). Full board $50

PRIVATE RESERVES IN THE MIRA VALLEY BASIN

A paved road speeds from Ibarra down the parched **Mira valley**, slicing through crumbling hillsides prone to falling rocks as it descends into the warmer, moister climes of the lush lowlands, down to the Pacific coast at San Lorenzo (see p.271). The road is served by buses from Ibarra to San Lorenzo (9 daily until 6pm; 4hr) and Esmeraldas (4 daily; 5hr), though few foreign visitors pass this way; those that do tend to head straight for the beaches, but there are a couple of interesting **private reserves** worth exploring along the way.

Bosque de Paz 300m uphill from the centre of El Limonal, 42km from Ibarra on the San Lorenzo road ☎ 06 2648692, ☻ bospas.org. Transformed from badly eroded landscape into forested hillside, this hospitable working fruit farm – over 20 kinds of fruit and 110 tree species – offers hands-on learning about ecological restoration, permaculture and agroforestry. Several attractive en-suite rooms, each with porch and hammock, command splendid views over the valley. There's also a spacious common area, a lovely stone pool, trails – including an hour-long self-guided bamboo trail open to the public (Tues–Sat; $2) – and the possibility of excursions further afield on foot or on horseback. Meals are inexpensive and volunteers are welcome to work on the farm ($250 contribution for four weeks, or $18 a day; three-month volunteer placement for 5hr/day in exchange for board and lodging). Breakfast included. Dorms $14; doubles $40

Reserva Privada Las Siete Cascadas Alto Tambo, 11km beyond Lita on the San Lorenzo road ☎ 0982611195. This private reserve and lodge consists of a small tract of protected forest, with paths leading to seven glittering waterfalls, which can all be visited in the course of a five-hour walk. Any Ibarra–San Lorenzo bus can drop you off here, where you can explore the forest and go swimming as a day-visitor for $10 per person (more with guide and meals; book in advance), or you can overnight in simple wooden cabañas with hot water in the lodge, or in tents with mattresses on a platform affording views over the forest. Avoid weekends and holiday periods if you want to truly experience the place's tranquillity. Packages include lodging, all meals and guided hikes. $140; camping $70/person

Chachimbiro thermal springs

Squeezed into a steep-sided crater valley, the village of **CHACHIMBIRO** now possesses several complexes with **thermal baths,** which are a real treat if you manage to avoid the weekend crowds. The volcanic waters are rich in sulphur, chlorides, iron, copper and manganese – widely believed to provide relief from neuralgia, arthritis and rheumatism.

ARRIVAL AND DEPARTURE CHACHIMBIRO THERMAL SPRINGS

By bus Buses to Chachimbiro from the Ibarra terminal (daily 7am and 12.30pm, returning at 1pm, 3pm and 5pm, usually with extra buses at weekends; 1hr 30min).

ACCOMMODATION

★**Hostería Pantaví** Tumbabiro, 8km from Chachimbiro, Quito office ☎02 2340601, lodge ☎06 2934185, ⓦhosteriapantavi.com. Gleaming, white-washed hacienda in a lovely setting, with a decent-sized pool, on-site spa and excellent restaurant. Rooms are bright, elegant and laden with original artwork, much of it by the renowned artist-owner Camilio Andrade, giving them a contemporary feel. Breakfast included. $59
Hostería San Francisco 3km from Chachimbiro ☎06 2648442, ⓦhosteriasanfrancisco.com. Attractive, isolated, seventeenth-century hacienda set amid rolling countryside, which can be explored on horseback. It has comfortable rooms, accommodating 1–4 people, painted in warm colours, a heated pool and steam room, plus tennis and volleyball courts. Breakfast included. $75
Santagua ☎06 2936060, ⓦsantagua.com.ec. Now government-owned, this is the largest complex, possessing recreational pools – complete with slides and merry-go-round, popular with young families ($5) – as well as the medicinal pools and spa (daily 6.30am–11pm; $10). Accommodation is comfortable, and rates include full board and use of all facilities. Avoid weekends if possible, when it can be packed, though you'll probably have to put up with disco music any day. $50

Towards the Colombian border

Some 33km north of Ibarra, the Panamericana forks at the village of **Mascarilla**, an Afro-Ecuadorian community with an impressive sideline in clay masks and figurines. To the left the old road to Colombia and Tulcán, via Mira and El Ángel, is little used and in poor condition but affords the easiest access to the remote **Reserva Ecológica El Ángel**, which contains one of Ecuador's most fascinating páramo landscapes. To the right, the busy Panamericana ascends eastwards up the sun-baked Chota valley before veering northwards once again, passing through the villages of Bólivar and La Paz. From the latter a cobbled road leads to the major shrine of **La Gruta de la Paz**, set in an impressive natural cavern. Ten kilometres further north the Panamericana passes through the major farming centre of San Gabriel, then skirts below the rare high-altitude cloudforest and páramo of the Reserva Guandera (see ⓦjatunsacha.org), before completing the final 36-kilometre haul to the border town of Tulcán, and Colombia beyond.

Reserva Ecológica El Ángel

Established in 1992, the **Reserva Ecológica El Ángel**, 15km north of the town of El Ángel, is home to some of Ecuador's most interesting páramo landscapes, a windblown rain-soaked wilderness of rolling grassland hills and lakes, ranging in altitude from 3644m to 4768m. It's most famous for its **frailejones**, peculiar furry-leaved plants endemic to the northern Andes, which grow on dark stems up to seven metres in height and cover 85 percent of the reserve's 160 square kilometres. The reserve's **wildlife** includes foxes, deer and condors, while streams teem with rainbow trout. In a few of its sheltered pockets, forest supplants the soggy moorland, and dense thickets of trees such as the striking papery **polylepis** – draped with mosses, orchids and bromeliads – make the best places to spot hummingbirds and armadillos.

The two glass-like **Lagunas El Voladero** provide the park's most popular destinations, and are the most accessible places to see the extraordinary frailejones up close. A two-hour walk beyond them is the **Laguna de Potrerillos**. Alternatively, head up past the **Cañón El Colorado** from the El Salado entrance to a viewpoint on **Cerro Socabones**, after which the road descends to the hamlet of **Morán**, 37km from El Ángel. Here, you can find simple lodgings and hire a guide and mules to explore the even more remote regions of the reserve.

ARRIVAL AND DEPARTURE   RESERVA ECOLÓGICA EL ÁNGEL

By bus to El Ángel Transportes Espejo buses from Quito (15 daily; 4hr); from Ibarra (6 daily, last bus 1.30pm; last return bus 7pm; 1hr 30min); from Tulcán (4 daily; 1hr 30min).

By taxi Private ($5) or shared taxis leave the main square in El Ángel for Bolívar on the Panamericana, where you can flag down buses heading north and south.

By car (4WD) From the town of El Ángel there are two routes to the reserve. The main one follows the old road from El Ángel to Tulcán for 15km to a guard post, from where a 1km trail leads to the Lagunas El Voladero. The second

route heads northwest from El Ángel through La Libertad to the reserve guard post at El Salado, though taxi drivers are keen to drop you at the nearby polylepis reserve ($10 entry). A third, less used, entrance is off the road heading west out of Tufiño (see p.129), skirting the northern part of the reserve and the Colombian border; enquire before travelling on this road as security is sometimes an issue.

By camioneta From El Ángel's main plaza you can take a camioneta taxi to the reserve ($15 one way, $30 return with one hour's waiting time; $35 to Morán).

INFORMATION

Tourist information The Ministerio del Ambiente office in El Ángel, at Salinas and Esmeraldas, second floor of the Sindicato de Choferes building (☎06 2977597; Mon–Fri 8am–4.30pm), can provide information about

visiting the reserve and put you in touch with local guides (around $15/day). There is also a new, sporadically open I-Tur office on the *parque central* (Mon–Fri 8am–4.30pm; no phone).

ACCOMMODATION AND EATING

Las Orquídeas Morán ☎063012627 or ☎0991374851, ✉castro503@yahoo.com. Located in a small hamlet deep in the park, this basic guesthouse, with shared bathroom and hot-water showers, is owned by highly recommended guide Carlos Castro. Full board, transport and guiding included, but you can negotiate a board-only rate. **$104**

Polylepis Lodge 14km from El Ángel, close to the El

Salado entrance ☎062631819, ✍polylepis.com. Pricey lodge set in a private reserve buffering the national one, comprising snug, though functional, stone-and-wood thatched cottages with fireplaces and private bathrooms – some with jacuzzi. Activities include a night-time stroll through the polylepis forest. Full board and reserve entry included. **$180**

Tulcán and around

TULCÁN (2950m), the provincial capital of Carchi, is a skittish frontier town, shifting people with ruthless efficiency across the Ecuadorian–Colombian border, 7km away. Commerce thrives here as shops crammed with merchandise crowd the narrow streets,

---

LA GRUTA DE LA PAZ

Around 65km north of Ibarra, a couple of kilometres beyond the village of Bolívar, a large road sign directs you 5km east to **La Gruta de la Paz** (Peace Grotto). The grotto plays host to northern Ecuador's most venerated Virgin, **La Virgen de la Paz**, who seems rather lost in her natural chapel – a cathedral-like cavern, home to countless bats and swallows and strewn with stalagmites and stalactites reflected in the dark waters of the Río Apaquí (open access; free). The place draws around a thousand visitors each weekend, and many more during Holy Week and on the Virgin's festival, the first weekend in July. So aim for midweek if you want a more contemplative experience. Water from the heart of the 40-metre deep grotto is channelled down to **thermal pools** (daily 9am–5pm; $2) and there's all the paraphernalia of a major tourist attraction – hotels, restaurants and stands bulging with tacky religious souvenirs. At weekends, buses and camionetas serve La Gruta from the town of San Gabriel, and from Parque Ayora in Tulcán: during the week, you'll need to hire a taxi in Bolívar on the Panamericana for a few dollars.

2

THE AFRO-ECUADORIANS OF THE CHOTA VALLEY

The Chota and Mira valleys are home to a number of **Afro-Ecuadorian communities**, whose ancestors were brought over as slaves from Africa in the seventeenth century to labour on the Jesuit-owned sugar plantations. Though sugar cultivation still features in their livelihoods, beans and other agricultural produce are now of greater importance. Over the years, the communities have developed a **unique culture**, an eclectic mix of African and Andean traditions, best experienced at a cultural performance; check the local press for details or ask at the tourist office in Ibarra (see p.121). Their distinctive **Bomba music** features percussion, guitars and impromptu instruments, such as those made from leaves, while local **dances** involve such feats as balancing a bottle on the head – thought to represent the traditional African way of carrying objects.

Despite a lack of proper pitches or stadiums, the Chota valley is renowned for producing many of Ecuador's best professional **footballers** – seven out of the 23 players in Ecuador's groundbreaking 2002 World Cup squad came from here, even though the first grass pitch only appeared in 2009. Yet, while many *choteños* are proud of their football and music, they are keen to gain recognition in other spheres and escape the racial stereotypes that only associate black success with music and sport.

and the Thursday and Sunday **markets** along Bolívar, Sucre and Olmedo throng with bargain-hunters.

Few travellers linger in Tulcán since it comes across as a cold and bleak town, where the early-morning sun struggles to warm the grey-concrete buildings and dusty streets. But it's worth making time to visit the splendid **topiary gardens** in the town cemetery, and, if the security situation permits (see box, p.129), the isolated **thermal springs**, set high in beautiful páramo near **Tufiño** to the west. The town's two spirited **fiestas** occur on April 11, for the cantonization of Tulcán, and November 19, to mark the day Carchi became a province.

Tulcán is a classic linear settlement strung out lengthways for several kilometres along the original route to Colombia, with the two central streets, **Bolívar** and **Sucre**, home to most of the hotels, restaurants and shops. The **Plaza de la Independencia** marks the centre of town, while the larger **Parque Ayora**, about six blocks north down Bolívar, is a popular open space. One block west, at the corner of Cotopaxi and Panamá, the modest archeological, cultural and art collections of the **Museo Casa de la Cultura** (Mon–Fri 9am–1pm & 2–4pm, Sat 9am–1pm; $1) are worth a peek.

Topiary gardens

Cotopaxi and Avenida del Cementerio • Daily 7.30am–8pm • Free • A 15min walk northeast of the centre or a short taxi ride from the bus station ($1)

Located at the cemetery, Tulcán's resplendent **topiary gardens** constitute the town's highlight. Fragrant cypresses have been snipped with meticulous care into more than a hundred different forms and patterns, including armadillos, turtles and a host of pre-Columbian figures and faces. Known as *escultura en verde* (sculpture in green), the gardens were created by local man José Franco Guerrero, who began working on them in 1936, and following his death – he's buried amidst the glorious greenery – his son, Beningo Franco, has continued to expand them.

ARRIVAL AND GETTING AROUND   TULCÁN AND AROUND

By bus Buses deposit you at the large terminal on Bolívar, from where it's 1.5km uphill northeast to the city centre and most of the hotels. Be prepared for some lengthy, aggressive queuing at weekends, especially public holidays in either Colombia or Ecuador. Buses may leave early when full, or may refuse to take passengers travelling part of the way unless they pay the full fare to the bus's final destination.

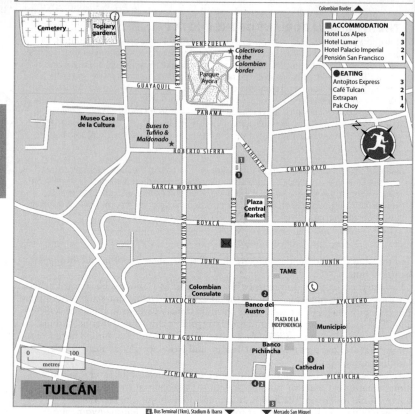

TULCÁN

ACCOMMODATION
Hotel Los Alpes	4
Hotel Lumar	3
Hotel Palacio Imperial	2
Pensión San Francisco	1

EATING
Antojitos Express	3
Café Tulcan	2
Extrapan	1
Pak Choy	4

Destinations Huaquillas (1 daily; 18hr); Ibarra (direct buses every hour, but frequent through buses drop off on the Panamericana; 2hr 30min); Maldonado (1–2 daily; 5hr); Quito (every 15min; 4hr 30min–5hr); Tufiño (11 daily; 45min).
By taxi Taxis cost about $1 around town, and $3.50 to the border.

INFORMATION

Tourist information You can get basic tourist information at the municipal office at the cemetery (Mon–Fri 7.30am–4.30pm; ☎06 2985760, ⦿ carchi.gob.ec), and there's another office at the Rumichaca border (see below).

CROSSING THE COLOMBIAN BORDER

Information Seven kilometres east of Tulcán, the international Rumichaca bridge marks the Colombian border; upstream, by the old stone bridge crossing, there is a tourist information office (Mon–Fri 9am–5pm; ☎06 2984184).
Customs Customs controls on both sides (open 24 hours) are quite efficient and have a telephone office and restaurant.
Entry and exit requirements To cross the border, you'll need an exit stamp from Ecuadorian customs, *Migración*, and an entry stamp from the Colombians on the other side of the bridge; stamps are always required, even if only visiting Ipiales for the day. If you're arriving from Colombia, see Basics (p.46) for more on Ecuadorian entry requirements.
Transport Colectivos from Tulcán to the border leave when full from the corner of Venezuela and Bolívar, in Parque Ayora (10min; $1), and a taxi to the border from anywhere in town should be $3–4. On the other side of the bridge, Colombian colectivos head to Ipiales (every 15min; 10min), a town with plenty of hotels and transport links, while taxis are around $3.

2

Changing money Official moneychangers on both sides offer acceptable rates for cash dollars and pesos, but always check the calculations and money you receive before handing anything over.

ACCOMMODATION

Hotel Los Alpes Arellano and Veintimilla ☎06 2982235. Basic hotel by the bus station, useful if you're arriving late at night, or want an early start. Hard beds but clean and light, with private bathrooms and cable TV. $30
Hotel Lumar Sucre between Rocafuerte and Pichincha ☎06 2980402. Reliable, businesslike hotel offering carpeted, well-furnished en-suite rooms with flatscreen TVs. $37
Hotel Palacio Imperial Corner of Sucre and Pichincha ☎06 2980638, ⊛hotelpalacioimperial.com. A Samurai warrior, a Buddha and vast mock-Ming vases welcome you to this smart, Chinese-themed hotel that has immaculate, modern rooms and suites with all the trimmings. The best hotel in Tulcán also boasts a decent restaurant, a small gym and a rooftop terrace affording panoramic views. Buffet breakfast included. $78
Pensión San Francisco Bolívar and Atahualpa ☎06 2980760. Tatty but cleanish, for budget travellers; it has hot water, cable TV and shared bathroom. Avoid the stale interior rooms and go for something bright and airy upstairs. $13

EATING

Café Tulcán Sucre and Ayacucho ☎06 2980388. For over seventy years, this cheerful, reliable café has been serving a wide range of inexpensive breakfast and lunch dishes plus coffees, juices and cakes. Mon–Sat 8am–6pm.
Extrapan Bolívar and Boyaca ☎06 2985944. The town's best bakery boasts a tempting range of inexpensive buns and pastries, and has an extensive menu of mid-priced chicken, fish and meat dishes ($4.50–6). Daily 7am–midnight.
Pak Choy Corner of Sucre and Pichincha ☎06 2980638. A gleaming tiled floor and golden and scarlet lanterns mark the Palacio Imperial's (see above) popular restaurant, where prices for the tasty Chinese and Ecuadorian dishes are moderate ($4–8). Daily 8am–11pm.

Tufiño and around

Geothermal activity deep below **Volcán Chiles** (4768m) heats numerous thermal springs that bubble along the Colombian border around the village of **Tufiño**, 18km west of Tulcán; some are over the border and you may pass for the day to visit them but formal crossings into Colombia must be made at Rumichaca (see opposite). The best of them are **Aguas Hediondas** ("stinking waters"), set at 3500m in an isolated valley split between Ecuador and Colombia, 6km west of Tufiño. The sulphur-rich waters are thought to be highly curative – you'll leave from a long soak feeling fresh, revitalized but egg-scented. An ascent of the volcano itself offers a more challenging day-trip (3hr up, 3hr down, 3hr back to Tufiño), a technically straightforward, but possibly foggy or snowy climb. Dress for the worst and hire a **guide** in Tufiño (from around $15).

Note that this is a sensitive and potentially dangerous border area (see box above) so you should not travel here without prior enquiries about the safety situation.

ARRIVAL AND DEPARTURE   TUFIÑO

By bus Regular buses run between Tulcán and Tufiño (12 daily; 45min); infrequent buses to Maldonado also pass by the turn-off to the springs, beyond Tufiño.

The central sierra

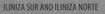

ILINIZA SUR AND ILINIZA NORTE

The central sierra

South of Quito, the two parallel chains of the Andes running the length of Ecuador rise to their most dramatic and spectacular heights in the central sierra, forming a double row of snowcapped peaks the nineteenth-century German explorer, Alexander von Humboldt, memorably christened "the Avenue of the Volcanoes". Eight of the country's ten highest summits are found here, including Chimborazo (6268m), Cotopaxi (5897m) and El Altar (5320m), towering over the region's principal highland towns – Latacunga, Ambato and Riobamba – strung north to south along the Panamericana. On a clear day, the drive south from Quito through this parade of mountains ranks among the world's great road journeys.

3

Frustratingly, though, the highest peaks are often lost in the low, grey clouds so typical of the region, and it's possible to travel right through the central sierra without spotting a single summit. Even so, the landscape can be stunning; dense patchworks of fields stretch up the slopes, formed by alternating strips of maize, barley, potatoes and quinoa, though they are constantly under threat by urban expansion. This deeply rural region is the **indigenous heartland** of Ecuador, a place still brimming with Kichwa-speaking communities whose lifestyles and work patterns have changed little over the centuries. The economic and social focus of these communities – and the best place to get a feel for traditional Andean life – is the weekly **markets** held throughout the region. One of the largest and most exciting is at the small town of **Saquisilí**, near Latacunga, where hundreds of red- and pink-shawled *indígenas* fill the streets, examining mountains of fresh produce or stalls selling anything from rope to soap. Other notable markets include those at the village of **Zumbahua**, also near Latacunga, and the town of **Guamote**, south of Riobamba.

Most visitors stick to the more obvious destinations like **Parque Nacional Cotopaxi**, dominated by the perfect cone of the eponymous volcano, and the easy-going town of **Baños**, whose mild climate, spectacular setting and thermal springs have made it a magnet for Ecuadorians and foreigners alike – despite the renewed activity of nearby Volcán Tungurahua. Another favourite excursion is the famous **Nariz del Diablo** ("Devil's Nose") train ride, a dramatic and thrilling 12km descent off the Andes, from Alausí to Sibambe, though there are other rewarding train trips to be made in this part of the sierra, particularly from Riobamba.

The more remote areas east and west of the Panamericana boast some rewarding outings too, including the stunning crater lake of **Quilotoa**, approached from Latacunga via some

MULE AT LAGUNA QUILOTOA

Highlights

❶ Parque Nacional Cotopaxi The flawless cone of Cotopaxi, one of the highest active volcanoes in the world, dominates the country's favourite highland park. **See p.137**

❷ Quilotoa Loop A grand tour of the sierra's most beguiling rural landscapes, passing vertiginous patchwork fields, isolated indigenous communities and the impressive Quilotoa crater lake. **See p.144**

❸ Baños The ultimate spa resort town, brimming with delightful hotels and restaurants, with plenty to do in the surrounding hills and valleys – not to mention the fabulous hot springs. **See p.152**

❹ Salinas High in the bucolic hills above Guaranda, this small indigenous village is famed for its many cooperatives, which produce everything from cheese to chocolate. **See p.162**

❺ Chimborazo Merely to reach the second refuge of the highest mountain in the world – when measured from the centre of the Earth – will leave you gasping for air and choking with pride. **See p.168**

❻ Nariz del Diablo Ecuador's definitive train journey, a breathtaking switchback descent of an 800-metre rock face, is justly proclaimed "the most difficult railway in the world". **See p.174**

HIGHLIGHTS ARE MARKED ON THE MAP ON P.134

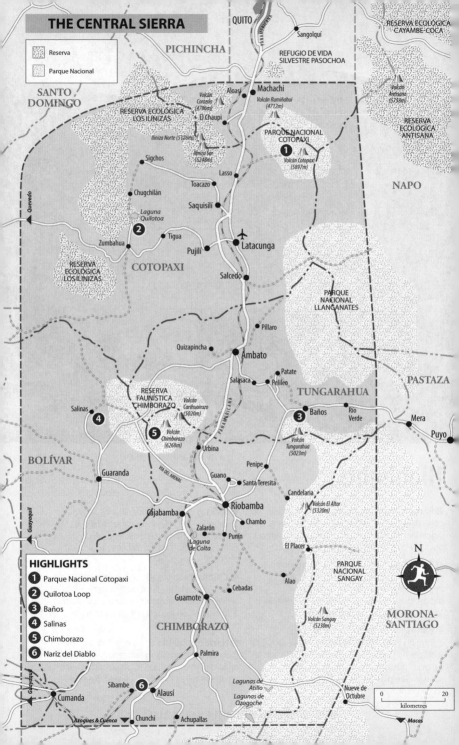

of the most gorgeous scenery in Ecuador; a trip from Ambato to the isolated town of **Guaranda**, then on to the lovely, lost-in-the-hills village of **Salinas**; and an exploration of the valleys, lakes and peaks of **Parque Nacional Sangay**, a sprawling wilderness area east of Riobamba, approached from various access points scattered around the western cordillera.

As for **weather**, expect regular afternoon rainfall and plenty of cloud cover from September to May, with June to September significantly sunnier and drier. At this altitude it can be bitterly cold at any time of year, though when the sun comes out for long spells it's often warm enough for just a T-shirt.

GETTING AROUND   THE CENTRAL SIERRA

By bus Most of the region's highlights can be reached by bus, even some of the more remote villages that lie along dirt roads. Excellent, fast bus services run up and down the main artery, the Panamericana, between Quito, Ambato, Riobamba, and on to Cuenca and Loja in the southern sierra. Latacunga, formerly on the main road, has now been bypassed, but there are still plenty of direct buses. Baños is slightly out on a limb as you turn off east towards the Oriente.

By train As well as the restored luxury train route between Quito and Guayaquil (see p.78), there are various stretches of track open in the central highlands, used more for excursions than for simply getting from A to B. The routes include a stretch of railway from Quito down the Avenue of the Volcanoes to El Boliche, by Cotopaxi (see box, p.140); track from both Ambato and Riobamba to Urbina on the flanks of Chimborazo; a 13km trip down to Laguna de Colta from Riobamba; the longer 120km journey down to Alausí; and the famous 12km descent from Alausí to Sibambe down the Devil's Nose (see box, p.174). Note that the status of Cotopaxi's volcanic activity can affect services on the Avenue of the Volcanoes route. Check ⓦ trenecuador.com for the latest information.

By camioneta Many towns and villages in the sierra have camioneta cooperatives, which either operate as shared taxis or can be hired privately for trips to outlying points.

Reserva Ecológica Los Ilinizas and around

Heading south from Quito, the Panamericana winds its way past a trail of dusty satellite towns, soon emerging into open, cultivated pastures flanked by the eastern and western cordilleras. If you're lucky with the weather, you'll be treated to superb views of Volcán Cotopaxi, its fat white cone dominating the region. A handful of lesser peaks punctuates the surrounding landscape, including **Volcán Corazón**, best explored from the quiet village of **Aloasí**. A little further south stand the two **Ilinizas**, popular with climbers wanting to acclimatize before tackling Chimborazo.

Aloasí

Just south of the turn-off to Machachi – a small, uninspiring town of interest only as a transport hub, and the home of Güitig, Ecuador's most famous bottled water – another side road branches west to the village of **ALOASÍ**, 40km south of Quito and about 1km back from the highway. Apart from its beautiful rural setting, Aloasí's main interest is as a base for climbing **El Corazón**, an extinct volcano sitting immediately west of the village. Its 4788-metre summit can be reached in about five hours on a strenuous but straightforward hike by acclimatized and fully prepared walkers, following the track branching west from the train station, 1.5km west of the village square.

ARRIVAL AND DEPARTURE   ALOASÍ

By bus Frequent buses link Aloasí's central square with Avenida Amazonas in Machachi. Buses to Machachi leave from Quito's Quitumbe terminal (every 15min; 1hr 15min).

ACCOMMODATION AND EATING

El Café de la Vaca Panamericana Km23, south of Aloasí and Machachi ⓣ 02 2315012, ⓦ elcafedelavaca .com. Legendary stop along the Panamericana, feeding all and sundry with a range of Ecuadorian dishes (mains $4–8). Daily 8am–5.30pm.

★ **Hostería-Granja La Estación** Opposite the train

station, Aloasí ☎02 2309246. A nineteenth-century farmhouse with comfortable rooms, polished wooden balconies, open fires and great views of El Corazón, plus a newer annexe with suites featuring private fireplaces. $60

Reserva Ecológica Los Ilinizas

Looming over the west side of the Panamericana is the sharp, jagged outline of the twin-peaked **Ilinizas**, two massive pyramids of rock about a kilometre apart joined by a wide saddle, which are the namesakes of an **ecological reserve** set up in 1996 to protect just under 1500 square kilometres of rugged hilly terrain, páramo, lakes and cloudforest of the western cordillera.

The horseshoe-shaped reserve curves from the Ilinizas and El Corazón around the northern half of the Quilotoa Loop to Zumbahua and beyond (see p.144). The larger **Iliniza Sur** (5248m) dominates the view from the Panamericana; it's an exciting technical climb that only experienced mountaineers should attempt. Strong, confident hill-walkers can manage **Iliniza Norte** (5126m), though there is a demanding scramble near the summit and the altitude can be really debilitating if you're not sufficiently acclimatized. The climbing route on both peaks is difficult to follow in bad weather, so use of a **recommended guide** is strongly advised (see p.80 & below). Both peaks are accessed via the small village of El Chaupi, which sits at the end of a seven-kilometre road signposted off the Panamericana a few kilometres south of Aloasí.

A less strenuous, but enjoyable excursion is to the **Cascada de Cumgyacu**, a "muddy" 20m drop, so-coloured by iron and sulphur, the latter also giving rise to a pleasant natural **thermal pool** nearby. Both are accessible from the village of Pastocalle, where you can hire a local guide to take you there.

ARRIVAL AND DEPARTURE
THE ILINIZAS

By bus Buses run from Machachi to El Chaupi (every 30min; 30min), the access point for climbing the Ilinizas. To reach Pastocalle, take a local bus from Latacunga.

By camioneta A camioneta from El Chaupi to the *Nuevos Horizontes* refuge (see below) costs $10 (arrange through your hostal) and will drop you at the car park known as La Virgen, marked by a shrine to the Virgin Mary, near the base of the Ilinizas, 9km from El Chaupi. From La Virgen the refuge is a 2–3hr hike along a clearly marked trail.

ACCOMMODATION

Hostal Llovizna 50m behind the church in El Chaupi ☎02 3674076, or ☎0979662896, ✉iliniza_blady @yahoo.com. Comfortable, simple rooms downstairs around a large heated room by two central fires, or cramped bunks up in the attic. Also has a kitchen, table tennis and a pool. It's a common departure point for climbing the Ilinizas, and the owner can organize transport, guide, food and equipment for the trip ($90). Breakfast and dinner included. Dorms $19; doubles $38

Neuvos Horizontes Below the saddle between the Ilinizas, a 5–7hr hike from El Chaupi ☎0990504157, office in Chaupi ☎02 3674125, �🌐ilinizas-refuge.webs.com.

CLIMBING THE ILINIZAS

Both **Iliniza Norte** and **Sur** are approached from the *Nuevos Horizontes* **refuge** (see above) at 4765m, just below the saddle between the two peaks. From the refuge count on two to three hours to reach the summit of **Iliniza Norte**. The route is easy to follow, though very steep in parts. The bulk of it involves crossing a rocky ridge – via the unnervingly named Paso de Muerte ("Death Pass"), which requires great care in high winds and snow. The final climb to the summit, marked by an iron cross, involves some scrambling and a head for heights. Coming down is quite fast if you follow the scree slopes below the ridge (1hr 30min).

Climbing **Iliniza Sur** involves a steep ice climb and crossing crevasses, something that is becoming increasingly complicated with the rapidly changing state of the glaciers. You'll need plenty of experience and full mountaineering equipment, including a helmet to provide protection from falling rocks. It takes three to five hours to reach the summit depending on conditions, after an early start from the refuge.

Well-maintained refuge with bunks for 25 people (bring a sleeping bag), fireplace, limited electricity, running water and cooking facilities. Breakfast and dinner included. Dorms $35; camping $15

Nina Rumy At the entrance to El Chaupi ☏ 02 2864688. No-frills wooden rooms with bunks and beds, kitchen and private or shared bathrooms. It's quieter than the neighbouring *Hostal Llovizna* (see opposite). $26

Parque Nacional Cotopaxi and around

Cotopaxi's shape is the most beautiful and regular of all the colossal peaks in the high Andes. It is a perfect cone covered by a thick blanket of snow, which shines so brilliantly at sunset it seems detached from the azure of the sky.

Alexander von Humboldt, 1802

Daily 9am–3pm, last entrance for day-visitors 2pm • Free

Almost opposite the Ilinizas, the snowcapped, perfectly symmetrical cone of **Volcán Cotopaxi** (5897m) forms the centrepiece of Ecuador's most-visited mainland national park, **Parque Nacional Cotopaxi**, which covers 330 square kilometres of the eastern cordillera. With its broad, green base and graceful slopes tapering to the lip of its crater, Cotopaxi is arguably the most photogenic of the country's thirty or so volcanoes, and on a clear day makes a dizzying backdrop to the stretch of highway between Quito and Latacunga. One of the highest active volcanoes in the world, it's also one of Ecuador's most destructive, with at least ten major eruptions since 1742 responsible for repeatedly destroying the nearby town of Latacunga. Following Cotopaxi's first major seismic activity in over a century, in August 2015, the park was closed to the public for several months. Although the lower reaches had reopened to the public at the time of

3

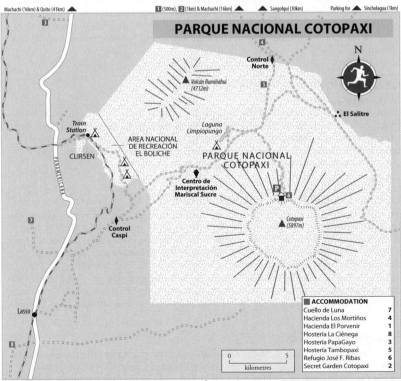

PARQUE NACIONAL COTOPAXI

Machachi (16km) & Quito (41km) ▲   1 (500m), 2 (1km) & Machachi (16km) ▲   ▲ Sangolquí (30km)   Parking for ▲ Sincholagua (1km)

3

Control Norte

Volcán Rumiñahui (4712m)   5

El Salitre

Train Station

Laguna Limpiopungo

AREA NACIONAL DE RECREACIÓN EL BOLICHE

CLIRSEN

PARQUE NACIONAL COTOPAXI

PANAMERICANA

Centro de Interpretación Mariscal Sucre

Control Caspi

Cotopaxi (5897m)

7

Lasso

8

N

ACCOMMODATION	
Cuello de Luna	7
Hacienda Los Mortiños	4
Hacienda El Porvenir	1
Hostería La Ciénega	8
Hostería PapaGayo	3
Hostería Tambopaxi	5
Refugio José F. Ribas	6
Secret Garden Cotopaxi	2

0   5
kilometres

▼ Latacunga (15km)

COTOPAXI: EMERGENCY REGULATIONS

Once the most popular of Ecuador's snowcapped peaks to attempt, Cotopaxi has remained **out of bounds** to climbers since August 2015, when it started to belch forth fumes, and the park was closed to all visitors. Although the park had reopened at the time of going to press, the refuge and any attempt on the summit were still off limits. The future, as with all volcanoes, is uncertain: activity may calm down again and the iconic cone may once again be open to mountaineers; alternatively, it may be like Tungurahua (see box, p.154), whose periodic low-level eruptions have ensured it has remained closed to climbers since 1999. Check its **current status** from reports in the national newspapers, at the SAE (p.79), or from the Instituto Geofísico's (Spanish) website ⓦ igepn.edu.ec, the Cotopaxi website (ⓦ volcancotopaxi.com), also in Spanish, or the Smithsonian's (English-language) volcano-watch website ⓦ volcano.si.edu.

---

going to press, the refuge and summit of the country's most popular climb were still closed (see box above), as the volcano continues to rumble and periodically belch ash; fears remain that it could be due for another major eruption.

Although the volcano dominates everything around it, and the aim of most visitors is simply to get a close-up view before turning home, a number of other attractions make a visit to the park very rewarding – namely the starkly beautiful **páramo**, all rolling moorland streaked by wispy clouds and pockets of mist. At an altitude of some 3500–4500m, the air here is thin and crisp, and the tundra-like vegetation is made up principally of cropped *pajonales* (straw-like grass) and shrubs, lichens and flowers adapted to harsh climates, though some of the area, at the time of going to press, was covered in ash. Over ninety species of **birds** inhabit the park, including the Ecuadorian hillstar and Andean lapwing, while **mammals** include white-tailed deer, rabbits, Andean foxes and pumas, though some animals have been relocated to other reserves by conservationists after the volcano's reawakening in 2015, and others have scarpered of their own accord.

Centro de Interpretación Mariscal Sucre

10km from Control Caspi • Daily 8am–5pm • Free

The **Centro de Interpretación Mariscal Sucre** gives visitors an introduction to the geology, flora and fauna of the park. It also exhibits pieces removed from the remains of the Inca fortress of Pucará El Salitre, located on the northern slopes of Cotopaxi, though there's little to see today at the site itself. Outside the centre there's a short self-guided **trail** to introduce you to the páramo.

Laguna Limpiopungo and Volcán Rumiñahui

Around 5km beyond the museum, a one-hour footpath explores the habitat around the **Laguna Limpiopungo** – a long, shallow lake lying at 3800m, and surrounded by boggy reeds that provide a habitat for numerous birds. When the clouds part, its waters present a striking reflection of the 4712-metre summit of **Volcán Rumiñahui**, looming over it to the northwest, whose lower slopes can be reached by a clear path branching off the north shore of the lake. Then, following an obvious ridge, you can reach the central and the most accessible of the volcano's three peaks, from where it's a precarious scramble over loose rock to the highest one. All this takes around five hours from Limpiopungo.

Refugio José F. Ribas

From Laguna Limpiopungo, the road continues a further 13km to the refuge **parking area** (*parqueador del refugio*), at 4600m on the slopes of Cotopaxi, and the former starting point for mountain-bike tours (see p.80) and ascents to the summit. A steep

ACTIVITIES IN COTOPAXI

There was a time when visitors to the national park were almost exclusively climbers bent on conquering the summit of Cotopaxi; these days there are many more ways to appreciate the park's beauty, either as a **self-drive** – though a guide is now compulsory (see below) – or as part of an **organized tour**; however, some activities have been suspended or curtailed since the volcano's recent activity (see box opposite). Most of the tour agencies are in Quito (see p.80), but there's also a handful in Latacunga (see p.142); the various lodgings in and around the park also offer excursions (see below & p.140), usually at cheaper rates, as they're nearer the action, and allow you to spend more time in the park and less travel time on the Panamericana.

Day-trips (adjusted since the 2015 eruption) usually include a visit to Laguna Limpiopungo and the interpretive centre, a picnic, a little hiking and some mountain biking. At the time of going to press, mountain biking was limited to the main access road, rather than the customary exhilarating whizz down from the refuge, although the authorities were said to be working on a new route. Some horse riding was also allowed, though again, not over the higher, more wilderness sections of páramo. Camping was no longer permitted.

3

footpath leads from the car park up a scree slope to the **Refugio José F. Ribas** (4800m). At the time of going to press, the refuge and its access road were still closed to the public, following the 2015 resumption of volcanic activity.

ARRIVAL AND DEPARTURE

PARQUE NACIONAL COTOPAXI AND AROUND

The park's most commonly used **entry point** is off the Panamericana, about 25km south of Machachi and 7km before the village of Lasso. Here, a signposted turn heads east for 6km to the **Control Caspi** guard post, situated 3km before the park boundary proper. There's a second, little-used access point at **Control Norte** at the north end of the park, reached by an 18km track (mostly cobbled) from Machachi via Pedregal (or a 30km dirt road from Sangolquí).

By bus and camioneta The easiest way to get to the main entrance, Control Caspi, is to take a bus down the Panamericana to the main signposted entrance to Cotopaxi, where camionetas are usually lined up to take you into the park ($30–40/camioneta for a half-day trip for up to four people as far as Limpiopungo; more to go to the refuge). It takes about 40min to get from the Panamericana to Laguna Limpiopungo, and a little over an hour to get to the parking area below the refuge. Camionetas can also be picked up from Machachi or Lasso, or booked to pick you up from nearby hotels.

By car Entering the park in your own vehicle is allowed; make sure it is high clearance, and preferably 4WD, though a saloon car should be allowed in the main entrance along the tarred road as far as Limpiopungo. You will, however, need a certified guide with you; depending on availability, you may be able to hire a Spanish-speaking guide at the gate on the day ($30), though engaging the services of someone via a recognized tour operator in Latacunga or Quito (see p.142 & p.80) in advance would be a better bet.

ACCOMMODATION

At the time of going to press, the basic park **campsites** had been closed to the public since Cotopaxi's volcanic activity recommenced in August 2015 and seemed unlikely to reopen during the lifetime of this guide.

IN THE PARK

★**Hostería Tambopaxi** 2km from the Control Norte ☎0999448223 or ☎02 2220241, ⊛tambopaxi.com. At 3750m high, this hostería offers stunning views of Cotopaxi – hence the price – and has well-insulated rooms with warm duvets and a good restaurant (lunch and dinner around $18, breakfast a hefty $9). Guided hikes, horse and bike rides and transport to and from the park can also be arranged, and there are good camping facilities. Breakfast included for doubles and campers. Dorms $24; doubles $116; camping $16/person

Refugio José F. Ribas Northern flank of Cotopaxi

☎0999902346. The refuge – closed at the time of going to press – has bunks with mattresses (for up to 86 people), lockers, cold running water, a fireplace, limited electricity, and basic cooking facilities as well as a snack bar, where you can order simple meals. Reserve in advance in high season.

AROUND THE PARK

Cuello de Luna Just south of the main turn-off to the park, on the west side of the highway, down a signed 2km track ☎0999700330 or ☎03 3053898, ⊛cuellodeluna.com. Comfortable hotel offering spacious

3

TREN DE LOS VOLCANES

One of the country's most popular full-day train excursions is the **Tren de los Volcanes**, which takes you on a 60km trip from Quito's Chimbacalle station (see p.78) down to El Boliche station in the Área Nacional de Recreación El Boliche, a pleasant, pine-forested family recreational area contiguous with the Cotopaxi National Park, affording great views of the eponymous volcano, and others, along the way. **Departures** from Quito (Fri–Sun and public holidays; $50) are at 8.15am, arriving at El Boliche around 11.15am, in time to wander round the short trails. Lunch and a farm tour at Machachi on the way back are also included in the price. Contact Tren Ecuador for information and online reservations (☎ 1 800 873637, ⌨ trenecuador.com).

---

cabins with private bathrooms and open fireplaces, or semi-private mattresses in the loft. Breakfast included; reasonable rates for half or full board. Lots of transfers and excursions on offer. Doubles $66; mattresses $20/person

Hacienda Los Mortiños A few kilometres north of Control Norte ☎ 02 3342520, ⌨ losmortinos.com. Modern hacienda – though still with whitewashed walls and tiled roof – boasting large windows through which to admire the stunning view. There are bright, comfortable rooms (for 1–5 people) and an on-site restaurant (breakfast from $7; other meals from $18). Also has a climbing wall, horses and mountain bikes, and guided excursions are organized. Dorms $24; doubles $104; camping $10/person

Hacienda El Porvenir 4.5km northwest of the Control Norte on the Pedregal road ☎ 02 2231806, ⌨ volcanoland.com. An ecologically sound adobe lodge – also known as Volcanoland – on the flanks of Rumiñahui with Cotopaxi's summit poking in sight beyond. Comfortable accommodation, good traditional food ($17 for a three-course meal) and plenty of activities, including biking, birding, hiking, riding, abseiling and zip-lining. Breakfast included. Doubles $115; camping $6/person

Hostería La Ciénega Just south of Lasso, 1km west of the Panamericana ☎ 03 2719093 or ☎ 02 2549126, ⌨ haciendalacienega.com. This seventeenth-century hacienda boasts an exquisite private chapel and beautiful gardens. The rooms in the main building have lots of character but are a little faded; those in the modern annexe are enlivened by cosy log fires. Breakfast included. $117

★**Hostería PapaGayo** 500m up a signed turn-off west from the Panamericana at Km26, south of the Machachi toll ☎ 02 231002, ⌨ hosteria-papagayo.com. Charming and popular old farmhouse in attractive grounds, offering a variety of accommodation, plus horses and llamas. There's a stove-heated sitting room and restaurant, tasty food, internet, barn bar and numerous activities arranged by the friendly managers. Rates include breakfast. Doubles $90; camping $17/person

Secret Garden Cotopaxi Via Pedregal, 5km from Control Norte ☎ 02 2956704, ⌨ secretgardencotopaxi .com. Beautifully situated eco-hostel offering great views of Cotopaxi from Pasochoa. Choose from dorms, snug "hobbit homes" – buried into the hillside – with shared bathrooms, or private cabins, most with fireplaces. The restaurant food is good, the vibe relaxed and the jacuzzi a star attraction. Full board included. Dorms $38; hobbit homes $88; cabins $98

Latacunga and around

Some 20km south of the turn-off to Cotopaxi, **Latacunga** (2800m) is an agreeable, mid-sized market town huddled on the east bank of the Río Cutuchi. It's a popular base from which to organize forays into this part of the sierra, in particular to the striking crater lake at Quilotoa (see p.145), or the hectic indigenous market in the nearby village of **Saquisilí**, and even to Parque Nacional Cotopaxi (see p.137). Latacunga's charms are relatively sedate, and can be enjoyed in an afternoon's wander around town, except during its two colourful **Mama Negra** fiestas, when you'll be treated to a riotous display of parades and energetic street dancing (see box, p.142).

Latacunga

Despite its colonial appearance, most of **LATACUNGA'S** architecture dates from the late nineteenth or early twentieth century, due to Cotopaxi's repeated and devastating eruptions, which have seen the town destroyed and rebuilt five times since its foundation in 1534 – most recently in 1877. The focal point of town is the **Parque**

Vicente León, a pleasant, leafy square dominated by the whitewashed **cathedral** and flanked by an austere **municipio** to the east. The twin-towered **Iglesia Santo Domingo**, a couple of blocks north on the small Plazoleta de Santo Domingo, is the most impressive of the town's churches, with its Grecian pillars and extravagantly painted interior covered with swirling blue, green and gold designs.

Opposite the *plazoleta* is the **Casa de los Marqueses de Miraflores** on Sánchez de Orellana and Guayaquil (Mon–Fri 8am–noon & 2–6pm; free), an elegant colonial building and museum with an "archeological-industrial" exhibition displaying pieces recovered from a local textile mill (including the bones of a small boy) that the 1877 Cotopaxi eruption destroyed. The town's main daily **market** is a huge outdoor affair spreading over Plaza El Salto (also known as Plaza Chile), off Avenida Amazonas. A couple of blocks south of the market, on the corner of Vela and Padre Salcedo, is the **Museo de la Casa de la Cultura** (Tues–Fri 8am–noon & 2–6pm, Sat 8am–3pm; $0.50), incorporating the ruins of an eighteenth-century watermill, the Molinos de Montserrat, built by Jesuits but destroyed by a succession of natural disasters. It now houses an ethnographic museum covering popular art, archeology (with over five hundred pieces) and local folklore.

3

ARRIVAL AND DEPARTURE
LATACUNGA

By bus Most buses drop you at or near the large bus station on the Panamericana – on the opposite side of the river from the town – from where you can catch a taxi to the centre ($1), or walk (10min) over the 5 de Junio bridge. Through services from the likes of Riobamba and Cuenca to Quito now bypass Latacunga on the new six-lane section of

the Panamericana but can drop you off at the Latacunga exit. You can then walk up the ramp and catch an onward bus coming from elsewhere. On Thursdays, buses from many local destinations are diverted to Saquisilí market, rather than Latacunga, and leave from there too.

Destinations Ambato (every 15min; 1hr); Baños (every

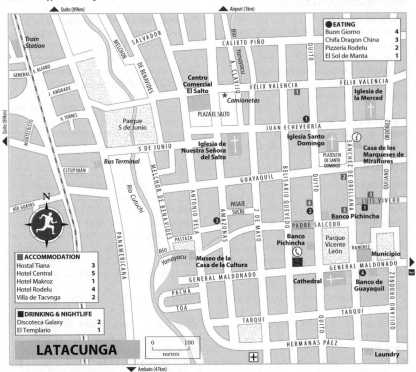

3

MAMA NEGRA FIESTAS

A highlight of the Latacunga year is its renowned **Mama Negra fiestas**, commemorated twice in religious and secular festivals within a few weeks of each other. The fiesta is thought to have derived either from the expulsion of the Moors from Spain or from the astonishment of the local *indígenas* on seeing black people (the slaves that the Spanish had brought here to work in nearby mines) for the first time. The colourful **religious celebration** (also called the *Santísima Tragedia*) is held on September 24, with brightly costumed paraders and various mischief-making characters: the white-robed *huacos*, the whip-wielding *camisonas*, and the belle of the ball, a blacked-up man gaudily dressed as a woman – the Mama Negra. The focus is supposedly the Virgin of the **Iglesia de la Merced** (known as Our Lady of the Volcano because she is believed to have saved the city many times from Cotopaxi's eruptions), who is paraded through the town and up to **El Calvario**, the concrete monument on the hill to the east of town. The flamboyant **secular Mama Negra festival** usually begins on the Saturday before November 11 (though the big parades have been scheduled for the Friday in recent years to discourage excessive drinking) and features the same cheerful costumes and characters, marching bands and street dancing. The festive mood continues with cultural events and bullfights until November 11, the day of Latacunga's **independence**.

15min; 2hr); Pujilí (every 10min; 20min); Quevedo, via Pujilí, Zumbahua and La Maná (every 30min–1hr; 5hr); Quito (every 10min; 2hr); Salcedo (every 10–15min; 15min); Saquisilí (every 5–10min; 30min).
By plane The over-ambitiously named Aeropuerto

Internacional Cotopaxi (☎ 03 2245240) is primarily used to export flowers and agricultural produce to the US and to Europe. However, on weekdays TAME also operates a morning passenger service from and to Guayaquil (1hr; $58 one way).

INFORMATION AND TOURS

TOURIST OFFICES
Information is available at the municipal tourist office by the Casa de los Marqueses de Miraflores on Sánchez de Orellana and Guayaquil (Mon–Fri 8am–1pm & 2–5pm; ☎ 03 2808494). There's also a small desk upstairs at the bus station, which is open irregular hours and keeps brochures, maps and leaflets in Spanish.

TOUR OPERATORS
Neiges Guayaquil 6-25 and Quito ☎ 03 2811199, ⓦ neigestours.wix.com/neiges. Experienced company that

offers climbing and walking trips to Cotopaxi and the Ilinizas, as well as horse trekking, fishing and day-trips to Quilotoa.
Selvanieve Salcedo and Quito ☎ 03 2802529, ⓦ selvanieve.com. Longstanding Scottish–Ecuadorian company offering various climbing and trekking tours as well as canyoning, rafting and multi-day trips.
Tovar Expeditions Guayaquil and Quito ☎ 03 2811333, ⓦ tovarexpeditions.com. Based in *Hostal Tiana* – so a good place to meet others to hike/climb with – and specializes in climbing, but also offers horse riding and mountain biking on one- or multi-day excursions.

ACCOMMODATION

Hostal Tiana Vivero 5-32 and Sánchez de Orellana ☎ 03 2810147, ⓦ hostaltiana.com. Friendly, well-run hostel offering comfortable bunks and private doubles, some with their own bathrooms. The rooftop terrace has great views of Cotopaxi and there's a flower-filled garden, plus semi-open lounge and kitchen areas. There's also book exchange and a café serving great apple pie. Continental breakfast included. Dorms $11; doubles $32
Hotel Central Sánchez de Orellana and Salcedo ☎ 03 2802912, ⓔ hotelcentralatacunga@hotmail.com. Established family-run hotel with clean, spacious, carpeted en-suite rooms and a homely feel. Parking available too. $25
Hotel Makroz Félix Valencia 8-56 and Quito ☎ 03 2800907. Currently the most comfortable place in town,

this modern business-oriented hotel has carpeted rooms, parking and a restaurant. Make sure you get one of the renovated rooms. Breakfast included. $50
★**Hotel Rodelu** Quito 16-49 and Salcedo ☎ 03 2800956, ⓦ rodelu.com.ec. Excellent-value converted old house – formerly *Hotel Rosim* – offering spacious rooms with decent beds, large en-suite bathrooms and parquet-floor corridors. Rooms at the back of the hotel are very quiet. $28
Villa de Tacvnga Sánchez de Orellana and Guayaquil ☎ 03 2812352, ⓦ villadetacvnga.com. Restored colonial-style hotel with courtyard and balconies. The rooms are nicely appointed, if small, though the suites are not worth the extra dollars. Frequent special offers. Breakfast included in the on-site courtyard restaurant. $60

EATING

The classic Latacunga dish that will do little to reduce your cholesterol is **chugchucaras**, a deluxe *fritada* featuring a mixture of deep-fried pork, pork scratchings, popcorn, plantain, *mote* and empanada, and sold at many places along Ordoñez, south of Tarqui. Also popular are *allullas*, biscuits made from pig fat, flour and eggs, and a favourite of vendors in the bus station, often sold together with *queso de hoja* – white cheese wrapped in an *achira* leaf.

Buon Giorno Corner of Sánchez de Orellana and Maldonado, Parque Vicente León ☎03 2804924. A long-established pizzeria in a good location; the dining room is pleasant enough and portions are large, most costing around $6. Daily 1–10pm.

Chifa Dragon China Amazonas and Pastaza ☎03 2800469. Very popular Chinese restaurant with a gleaming tiled floor, serving substantial portions of the usual mixture of Ecuadorian and Asian dishes but in a more homely environment than most *chifas*. Daily 10am–10pm.

Pizzería Rodelu In Hotel Rodelu, Quito 16-31 and Salcedo ☎03 2800956. Tasty pizzas cooked in a wood-fired oven in the hotel dining room. Also a good place for breakfast. Mon–Sat 7.30am–10pm, Sun 7.30am–8pm.

El Sol de Manta Corner of Echeverría and Quito. Fast and efficient *cevichería* serving inexpensive almuerzos, seafood and *encebollados*, but also specialities such as *guatita* (tripe). Usually packed at lunch. Daily 8.30am–3.30pm.

DRINKING AND NIGHTLIFE

Discoteca Galaxy Barrio El Calvario on a hill east of the town. Latacunga's best club – with music pumping out over several floors and plenty of dancing and drinking assured. Cover charge from $3. Fri & Sat 8pm until late.

★**El Templario** Vivero and Sánchez de Orellana ☎0997379154, ⓦes-la.facebook.com/eltemplario latacunga. This mellow café-bar with comfy seats and sofas brews its own beer (lager and stout) and serves up decent, well-priced wraps and sandwiches, plus snacks, coffees and cocktails. Occasional live music at weekends. Mon–Thurs 1pm–midnight, Fri & Sat 1pm–2am.

Saquisilí

A thirty-minute bus ride northwest of Latacunga, **SAQUISILÍ** is a quiet, slightly ramshackle little town of interest primarily for its **market** – one of the biggest in the highlands – which takes place every Thursday morning (see box below). The pleasant main plaza – about the only square not taken over by the market – is also worth a detour, to admire the striking modern interior of the **church**.

ARRIVAL AND DEPARTURE   SAQUISILÍ

By bus Buses leave Latacunga's main bus station (every 5min on Thurs; every 10min other days; 30min) and arrive in Saquisilí on the corner of 9 de Octubre and Barrero, one block west of the main plaza. Return buses leave from Bolívar, three blocks south of the plaza.

ACCOMMODATION AND EATING

It's easy to visit for the morning from Latacunga – though staying overnight on Wednesday allows you to catch the early-morning **market** action.

SAQUISILÍ MARKET

Against the splendid backdrop of the Ilinizas, the sprawling **Thursday market of Saquisilí** makes a worthwhile half-day trip from Latacunga. It spreads over several plazas, each specializing in different types of goods. There's an extraordinary breadth of merchandise on sale, fulfilling just about every consumer need of the hundreds of *indígenas* who journey here from all over the central sierra. Lining the pavements are mountains of vegetables balanced on wooden crates, sacks full of grain, mounds of fluorescent yarns used for weaving shawls, kitchen utensils, finely woven baskets and curiosities, including stuffed animals from the Oriente. About a ten-minute walk north of the centre, dozens of sheep, cows, pigs and the odd llama change hands in the **animal market** (before dawn to around 10am), which is dotted with women clutching tangled cords attached to squealing piglets.

Carmita North side of Plaza 18 de Octubre. Small restaurant stuffed full of folk on market day wolfing down cheap desayunos, almuerzos and meriendas, with *secos de pollo* and *carne* providing the mainstay. Mon–Sat 8am–6pm.

Hostería Gilocarmelo Chimborazo and Bartolomé de las Casas ☎ 03 2721630, ✉ gilocarmelo@hotmail.es. The most comfortable spot to stay in town, with pleasant rooms (most with private bathroom), hummingbirds in the garden and free use of sauna and spa facilities. Breakfast included. **$43**

San Carlos Simón Bolívar and Sucre on the parque central ☎ 03 2721981. Beyond the stuffed monkey staring at you by reception are faded rooms with private bathroom and electric shower; some come with attractive views. **$20**

The Quilotoa Loop

Some 90km west of Latacunga and the Panamericana, in one of the most beautiful parts of the Andes, is the isolated **Laguna Quilotoa**, a spectacular emerald-coloured crater lake. It's most directly approached along the road from Latacunga to Quevedo (see p.268), via the villages of **Tigua** and **Zumbahua**. You can return via a circular route, heading north to the villages of **Chugchilán** and **Sigchos**, perhaps detouring via **Isinliví** then southeast to rejoin the Panamericana near the market village of Saquisilí. This route – totalling around 200km – often referred to as **the Quilotoa Loop** – can just as easily be done in the opposite direction to that described below. If you can, try to time your stay in Zumbahua with the busy Saturday-morning **market**, or with one of the major Catholic festivals like Epiphany or Corpus Christi (see p.34); both are wonderful spectacles. It takes a minimum of two days to do this route on public transport – longer if you want to explore the magnificent countryside on foot (many hostels have rudimentary maps)

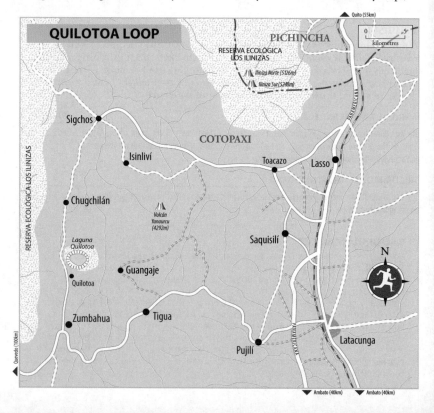

TIGUA NAIVE ART

Perched on the hillside by the main road through Tigua is the **Galería Tigua-Chimbacucho** (daily 8am–6pm, but ask around if closed), Tigua's art gallery cooperative devoted to the **naive art**, originally painted on sheep hide, for which the village is famous throughout Ecuador. The work of around 35 local artists is on display, painted in the characteristic **Tigua style** showing scenes of daily life, legends and village fiestas against a background of brightly coloured peaks and fields. Decorated festival masks, representing characters that feature in local folklore, including wolves, lions, dogs, monkeys and tigers, as well as basketwork and painted boxes, are also available. The prices are higher than you'll pay at Laguna Quilotoa (see below) but reflect the quality of the paintings; expect to pay around $60-plus for a mid-size painting by the more established artists like **Alfredo Toaquiza**, whose father was the first person to begin painting in this style in 1973.

---

or on horseback. In fact, hiking or mountain-biking some of the loop over three to four days – from Isinliví to Quilotoa being the preferred option – is becoming increasingly popular; rudimentary maps and/or guiding services are available at many of the lodgings along the way. Although the villages themselves are unremarkable, the wilderness scenery is stunning and you get to see highland life as it is lived.

The southern loop villages

Around 12km west of Latacunga is the pretty market town of **Pujilí**, whose centre is marked by a beautifully tended plaza, presided over by a handsome church. It's best visited during its Sunday market or the Corpus Christi celebrations (on the first Thursday after Trinity Sunday in June), involving fabulous costumes and masked dancers. Beyond Pujilí, the road ascends, and the temperature drops, until it levels out at the páramo settlement of **Tigua** (3600m) – actually the catch-all name for thirteen local communities, some comprising little more than a handful of *chozas*: the village, about 53km west of Latacunga, is renowned for its artwork (see box above). About 11km beyond Tigua, a turn-off to the right leads 500m downhill to **Zumbahua** (3500m), a small, rather bleak village with a spectacular setting, thanks to the backdrop of sharp peaks covered with patchwork fields. Try and catch the colourful **Saturday market**, which enlivens the otherwise desolate central square, and includes tailors mending clothes on old Singer sewing machines.

Laguna Quilotoa

$3 visitor's fee, payable at the kiosk 300m before the crater rim

Laguna Quilotoa is a breathtaking glass-green lake lying in the crater of an extinct volcano surrounded by steep slopes and jagged cliffs, which remains hidden from view until you're practically on top of it. The burgeoning tourist scene associated with the crater lake – horse rides, guided hikes, handicraft sales – helps to support the impoverished community of **Quilotoa** (3850m), whose meagre shacks huddle by the side of the road up to the lake.

It's possible to **walk down to the lake** from the crater's edge (30–40min) following the path that starts just left of the parking area. It's steep, and not to be undertaken lightly, but the views at the bottom are highly rewarding. You can even hire kayaks for a paddle. Getting back up involves either a stiff one-hour climb, or a 45-minute **mule ride** ($10), which you can organize at the top. The **walk around the rim** (5–6hr; an hour less with mules) is much more challenging and, in places where the path has worn away, rather precarious; you may benefit from the services of a guide ($15) or mules ($25). **Guides** and **muleteers** are available for many other hikes, too, including to the Cueva de los Incas set in cloudforest (5hr; $20), and Chugchilán (6hr; $30).

The northern loop villages

North of Quilotoa, a hair-raising 22-kilometre drive along a narrow dirt road (in the process of being tarred) skirting a cliff edge takes you some 11km through dramatic scenery to **Chugchilán** (3180m), a tiny settlement in a remote rural setting. It's home to little more than a dozen families and a women's **knitting cooperative** selling woollens. Although one of the poorest villages in the region, it's the location of some of the most comfortable places to stay on the whole loop as well as an excellent base for hiking, mountain biking and horse riding.

Popular trips include catching the early-morning bus to Laguna Quilotoa and **hiking** back from the crater via the scenic **Toachi Canyon** (3–5hr); visiting a nearby carpentry workshop a couple of kilometres down the road to Sigchos; and calling in at a **cheese factory** two hours' walk north of the village. Your hotel will be able to help you out with directions, guides, horses or camionetas as required for these and countless other local hikes.

Beyond Chugchilán, the road passes through the small town of **Sigchos**, from where it's worth taking a twelve-kilometre detour southeast to the mainly mestizo village of **Isinliví** (3000m), a small woodcarving centre, whose main attraction is the beautiful setting that offers excellent opportunities for hiking and horse riding. The Saturday-morning animal market at **Guantualo** provides a diverting excursion from here.

GETTING AROUND   THE QUILOTOA LOOP

Planning transport round the loop can be a bit of a nightmare, though the roads are gradually being improved; the worst section – only accessible by 4WD in the rainy season – is the dirt road between Quilotoa and Sigchos, though it is currently being tarred. When planning **bus** transport, note that the section between Zumbahua and Sigchos is the most infrequently serviced and that timetables change frequently and journey times are variable, so always check beforehand. Buses on the loop are often full, especially on market days; get there early and be prepared for a squeeze. **Camionetas** are a good alternative, and there's also an early-morning **milk truck** running between Sigchos and Chugchilán and Isinliví and Sigchos that you can ride on. Camioneta prices given are generally for two to three people. If time's short, consider **renting a car** or going with a Quito- or Latacunga-based **tour company**, many of which offer one- or two-day trips around the circuit. Note also that there are no banks or ATMs in these villages so make sure you have enough cash.

BUSES AROUND THE LOOP

Two Transportes Iliniza buses go all the way round the loop daily, leaving Latacunga main bus terminal at 11.30am (heading anticlockwise, via Sigchos) and noon (clockwise, via Zumbahua). Both overnight in Chugchilán, with the clockwise bus returning to Latacunga via Sigchos at 3am, and the anti-clockwise bus leaving at 4am via Zumbahua. Vivero buses leave Latacunga for Quilotoa at 12.15pm, 1.15pm and 4.15pm, passing through Tigua and Zumbahua en route.

TIGUA

By bus Buses from Latacunga to Quevedo (every 30min–1hr until 7.30pm; 1hr 15min) pass through Tigua. Vivero and Transportes Iliniza buses from Latacunga to Quilotoa also pass by.

ZUMBAHUA

By bus Buses from Latacunga to Quevedo pass the turn-off to Zumbahua (departing every 30min–1hr until 7.30pm; 1hr 45min), a five-minute walk from the village. Return buses to Latacunga from Quevedo do likewise. The clockwise Transportes Iliniza loop bus passes through the village at around 2pm on its way to Chugchilán; the anticlockwise bus

leaves the main square for Latacunga at 5.30am. Vivero buses pass through Zumbahua (2hr) on their way to Quilotoa; a handful return to Latacunga before dawn, with the last one passing Zumbahua between 5.45–6am.

By camioneta Camionetas hanging around the main square can be hired for Laguna Quilotoa ($6) and Chugchilán ($35).

QUILOTOA

By bus The clockwise Transportes Iliniza loop bus (see above) to Chugchilán passes Quilotoa around 2–2.30pm. Vivero buses from Latacunga take 2hr–2hr 30min; a handful leave Quilotoa for Latacunga before dawn.

By camioneta Camionetas to and from Zumbahua cost $6; from Latacunga, bank on paying around $50–60, and to and from Chugchilán $25.

CHUGCHILÁN

By bus The Transportes Iliniza loop bus takes 3hr–3hr 30min to Chugchilán, returning to Latacunga at 3am via Sigchos, and 4am via Zumbahua. There is a school bus to Latacunga via Sigchos weekdays in term time at 6am, as well as the morning milk truck (*lechero*) to Sigchos, plus a smattering of other buses – ask at your accommodation.

OPPOSITE ZUMBAHUA MARKET (P.144) >

By **camioneta** Camionetas to and from Quilotoa ($25), Zumbahua ($35), Sigchos ($20) and Isinliví ($35) leave from the main square.

SIGCHOS

By **bus** Buses leave Latacunga for Sigchos (6 daily, fewer on Sun; last bus 5pm, but 4pm Sat; 2hr 30min), returning to Latacunga (5 daily, 8 on Sat; last bus 2.30pm). The anticlockwise Transportes Iliniza loop bus passes Sigchos around 1.30–2pm.

By **camioneta** Camionetas run between Sigchos and Chugchilán ($25), Isinliví ($15), Latacunga ($60) and Quilotoa ($40).

ISINLIVÍ

By **bus** Buses leave Latacunga for Isinliví (Mon–Wed & Fri at 1pm; Thurs & Sat at 11am; 2–3hr, depending on whether the bus goes via Sigchos), with buses starting from Saquisilí on Thursdays.

ACCOMMODATION AND EATING

You'll find accommodation in Tigua, Zumbahua, Quilotoa, Chugchilán, Sigchos and Isinliví. The most comfortable options are in **Tigua** and **Chugchilán**, while many of the simple hotels in Quilotoa are really just family homes with a few beds for tourists jammed in, with minimal privacy and heating, and many villagers are still wary of outsiders. At this altitude a warm **sleeping bag** is recommended, even with the copious blankets provided.

TIGUA

★ **La Posada de Tigua** Latacunga–Zumbahua road Km49, 800m off main road, 3km before Tigua ☎03 3056103, ✉posadadetigua@yahoo.com. A charming small farmhouse on a working dairy farm, warmed on cold nights by an old wood stove by the front door. Rooms are rustic; the nicest ones are in the house, with cheaper, more basic rooms in an annexe. You can hire horses here to ride to Quilotoa in a couple of hours, or hike there in twice the time. Reservations essential. Breakfast and dinner included. **$80**

ZUMBAHUA

Cóndor Matzi Main square ☎03 2672094. Small, tidy rooms with bunks and clean linen, shared hot-water showers and kitchen facilities, but this place has a slightly abandoned feel to it. If no one's around to let you in, ask in the village for the key. They'll also look after luggage for a couple of dollars while you look round the market. **$16**
Oro Verde Main square ☎03 2802548. Not to be confused with the luxury hotel chain of the same name, this place offers very basic rooms with cable TV and en-suite bathrooms, with unreliable hot water. There's a busy restaurant below. **$14**

LAGUNA QUILOTOA

Hostal Chukirawa By the crater rim ☎03 3055808, ✉hostalchukirawa@hotmail.com. Probably the best of the budget choices, though still offering small, basic rooms – some with good views – with tiny en-suite bathrooms and hot water. The on-site restaurant (daily 7am–8pm) serves spit-roasted guinea-pig among other traditional dishes. Breakfast and dinner included. **$40**
Pachamama By the crater rim ☎0992125962. Simple rooms stuffed full of bunks and beds, with shared hot showers. Double-room and dorm rates include breakfast and dinner. Dorms **$15**; doubles **$30**

CHUGCHILÁN

★ **Black Sheep Inn** 500m east of main square ☎03 2814587, ⊛blacksheepinn.com. Pioneering, award-winning eco-inn comprising a collection of thatched adobe huts, most with wood-burning stoves, spread across a steep hillside affording mesmerizing views; a funky bunkhouse dorm serves those on a tighter budget. There's tasty vegetarian cooking, a lounge with plenty of books, a yoga studio, a hot tub and sauna to keep the highland chill at bay, and composting toilets. A great place to relax for a few days, it's very popular; reservations are advised. Rates include all meals. Dorms **$35**; doubles **$160**
Hostal Cloudforest Main road near the village centre ☎03 2708016, ⊛cloudforesthostal.com. Pleasant, good-value rooms with shared or private hot-water bathrooms, hammocks slung across shared balconies and a restaurant. Rooms are chilly but you can warm up by the fire in the games room, where there are pool and ping-pong tables. They also sell knitwear from the local cooperative. A light supper (not dinner) and breakfast included. Dorms **$15**; doubles **$40**
Mama Hilda's Main road near the village centre ☎03 2708005, ⊛mamahilda.com. A homely place, though possibly overdoing the new buildings, offering a range of cosy, tidy rooms; the pricier ones have fireplaces, others only electric fires, with shared or private bathrooms. The upstairs rooms are quieter. There's also a comfy lounge area with DVD player and honesty bar. Rates include breakfast and a delicious dinner, served family-style. **$70**

ISINLIVÍ

★ **Llullu Llama** Main street ☎0992580562, ⊛llullullama.com. Run by the owners of *Hostal Tiana* in Latacunga, this converted farmhouse is a professional operation, with a relaxed vibe. Recent additions include a small spa and snug cottages with their own fireplace and balcony, affording splendid views. Rates include breakfast and dinner, free-flowing tea and coffee, and luggage storage, plus there are maps and guides to aid your hiking and horse riding, and volunteering opportunities. Discounts for more than a one-night stay. Dorms $19; doubles $23; cottages $39

Ambato and around

Sitting in a fertile agricultural zone some 47km south of Latacunga, San Juan de Ambato – known simply as **AMBATO** (2580m) – is an important and rapidly expanding commercial centre with a bustling downtown core. Though founded in 1570, very little remains of its colonial character due to a catastrophic **earthquake** that virtually razed the city to the ground in 1949. The modern buildings that sprang up in its wake are for the most part bland and unattractive, which is why many tourists bypass the city – except during Carnaval (see box, p.151). However, the capital of Tungurahua province possesses a handsome palm-filled central plaza, a few enjoyable museums, a delightful botanical garden and some good-value hotels and decent restaurants, making it a pleasant place to overnight. If you're around on a Monday, check out the sprawling **market** spread over several sites, including the Mercado Central, next to the Parque 12 de Noviembre, and the Mercado Modelo, a couple of blocks further north.

Ambato is also handy as a jumping-off point for a few neighbouring low-key attractions, including **Quizapincha**, a major producer of leather goods, **Salasaca**, famous for its weavings (and at its best during the Sunday market) and **Patate**, a small village set in a fruit-growing valley. The more adventurous can head for the **Parque Nacional Llanganates**, one of Ecuador's least-explored wildernesses, where the gold meant to pay Atahualpa's ransom was supposedly buried by Rumiñahui, once he had heard of the Inca leader's murder by the conquistadors (see p.384). The park is accessed via the town of **Píllaro**, which is renowned for its flamboyant Diablada, an annual festivity (January 1–6) featuring devils clad in scarlet and black and brandishing whips dancing through the streets.

Parque Juan Montalvo

Ambato's focal point is the leafy central square, **Parque Juan Montalvo**, overlooked by the city's brash modern **cathedral** and monolithic **municipio**. The plaza is named after the locally born nineteenth-century writer (see p.389), the most distinguished of the trio of former residents that gives Ambato its nickname, "the city of the three Juans"; the other two are the novelist **Juan León Mera**, and lawyer and polemicist **Juan Benigno Vela**. Sitting on the north corner of the square, the humble, whitewashed **Casa de Montalvo** (Mon–Fri 9am–noon & 2–6pm, Sat 9am–2pm; $1) was Montalvo's birthplace and former home, and displays a moderately diverting collection of photos, manuscripts, clothes and other personal effects. Adjoining it is the **Mausoleo de Montalvo** (same hours and ticket), an elaborate Grecian-style temple in which the writer's carved wooden coffin is displayed on a platform, forming a kind of morbid altar. Montalvo enthusiasts might consider visiting his summer residence, La Quinta de Montalvo (Wed–Sun 9am–4.30pm; $1), a $2 taxi-ride away in the suburb of Ficoa.

Across the park, the **Casa del Portal** is a handsome survivor of the 1949 earthquake that sports a row of graceful stone arches spanning the width of the square, and now houses the modest **Museo Provincial Casa del Portal** (Mon–Fri 9am–1pm & 2–6pm, Sat & Sun 10am–4pm; free), featuring some regional archeological finds, historical photographs and an art collection, including pieces by the city's most famous artistic son, Oswaldo Viteri (see p.398).

Museo de Ciencias Naturales

Sucre, on Parque Cevallos • Mon–Fri 8.30am–12.30pm & 2.30–6.30pm • $2

Ambato's most compelling attraction, the **Museo de Ciencias Naturales**, is an old-fashioned natural history museum housed in an imposing nineteenth-century building on the city's second major square, Parque Cevallos. The displays kick off with some evocative early twentieth-century photos of the region's volcanoes, including one showing fumaroles spouting dramatically out of Cotopaxi's crater in 1911. The bulk of the collection is formed by stuffed animals, including a jaguar, puma, elephant, boa, spectacled bears, iguanas, monkeys and condors. These are followed by a

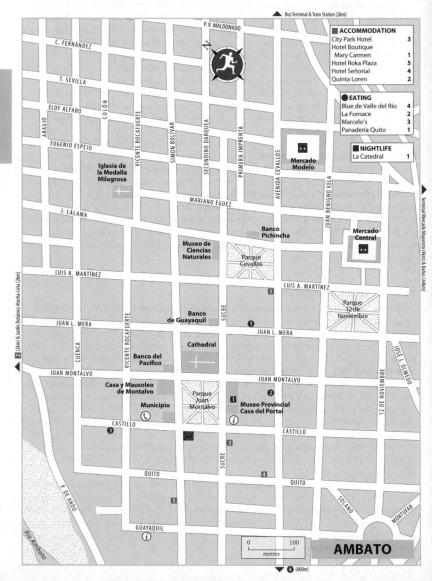

stomach-churning display of preserved "freak animals", including a two-headed calf, a three-legged hen and a lamb with one head and two bodies.

Jardín Botánico Atocha-Liria

Atocha • Wed–Sun 9.30am–5pm • $1 • Walk northwest on Montalvo, across the bridge, and turn right onto Avenida Capulíes, or catch a bus labelled "Atocha" once over the bridge; a taxi will cost around $2

Anyone craving relief from urban Ambato should head for the lush and colourful **Jardín Botánico Atocha-Liria**, only a couple of kilometres north of the city centre. These well-kept themed gardens contain more than two hundred plant species from a range of habitats and the restored country home-turned-museums of two renowned *ambateños*. The more impressive building is **La Quinta de Mera**, home to Juan León Mera, politician, painter, and, above all, prolific writer, who famously penned Ecuador's national anthem. His grand nineteenth-century adobe and clay-tiled house showcases some original period furniture and family personal effects. On the other side of the gardens is the **Museo Histórico Martínez-Holguim** (formerly known as Quinta La Liria), once the fine house of Dr Nicolás Martínez, head of an influential local family at the turn of the 20th century and the person responsible for establishing Ecuador's first botanical gardens here.

ARRIVAL AND DEPARTURE

By bus Ambato's bus terminal is 2km northeast of town. Taxis to the centre ($2) line up outside, or you can walk up to Avenida de las Americas, directly behind the bus terminal (turn right and right again after exiting the bus station) then catch a local bus to Parque Cevallos. Note that buses to Baños don't leave from the main terminal (take a taxi to the "Mayorista" bus stop), while buses to Píllaro leave from the fire station.

AMBATO AND AROUND

Destinations Baños (every 10min; 50min); Cuenca (13 daily; 7hr); Guaranda (16 daily; 2hr); Guayaquil (every 30min; 6hr 30min); Latacunga (every 15min; 1hr); Loja (5 daily; 12hr); Patate (every 20min; 45min); Pelileo (every 10min; 45min); Píllaro (every 15min; 40min); Puyo (every 15–30min; 3hr); Quito (every 5min; 2hr 30min); Quizapincha (every 30min; 40min); Riobamba (every 15–30min; 1hr); Salasaca (every 30min; 20min); Tena (hourly; 5hr).

GETTING AROUND AND INFORMATION

By bus Buses to the botanical gardens leave from 12 de Noviembre and La Quinta. To visit the Parque Nacional Llanganates, take a bus to Píllaro, then a camioneta to the park ($15), or go with a tour operator in Baños (see box, p.157) that offers treks in the park.
By taxi Taxis hang out around Parque Cevallos and Parque Montalvo.
By train Ambato's train station is next to the Terminal Terrestre, 2km northeast of the centre, and offers a day-trip (Fri–Sun and public holidays) by *autoferro* to Urbina, on the flanks of Chimborazo, and a tour of a shoe-factory in Cevallos on the way back. Departures are at 7.15am. Tickets are available at the station or through Tren Ecuador (☎ 1 800 873637, ⓦ trenecuador.com).
Tourist offices For information and a map head for the Ministerio de Turismo office (Mon–Fri 8.30am–5pm; ☎ 03 2821800) at Guayaquil and Rocafuerte, next door to the *Hotel Ambato*, which can also provide information on the Parque Nacional Llanganates (see p.149), though the park is under the administration of the Ministerio del Ambiente in Baños.

ACCOMMODATION

City Park Hotel Sucre 432 between Quito and Castillo ☎ 03 2827266, ✉ cityparkhotel@hotmail.es. Excellent-value spacious rooms with firm beds and gleaming tiled bathrooms in a modern hotel. Parking available. $33
Hotel Boutique Mary Carmen Corner of Av Cevallos and Martínez ☎ 03 2420908, ⓦ hotelboutiquemc.com.

This modern hotel has somewhat in-your-face decor: floors are themed – rhino, zebra, tiger and old-time Ambato – and rooms and suites feature jungle-print fabric, velour wallpaper, eccentric sculptures and circular beds. There's a small spa too. Breakfast included. $100

★**Hotel Roka Plaza** Bolívar between Quito and Guayaquil ☎03 2422360, ⌨hotelrokaplaza.com. Glorious boutique hotel in a renovated colonial mansion (formerly a club) possessing only a handful of unique luxurious rooms and one suite, which blend antique chic and modern elegance. The only niggle is the piped music (until 10pm), aimed at diners in the excellent interior courtyard restaurant. Breakfast included. $78

Hotel Señorial Corner of Cevallos and Quito ☎03 2825124, ✉reservas@hotelseniorial.com. Bright, cared-for and warm rooms (ignore the awful plastic headboards) with gleaming en-suite bathrooms, good showers and cable TV. Some are small, so ask to see a room first; singles offer better value than doubles. Breakfast included. $54

Quinta Loren Av los Guayambos and Taxos ☎03 2461275, ⌨quintalorenambato.com. In a quiet suburb within easy reach of the Quinta Juan Montalvo, this renovated country house offers nine rooms, tastefully furnished in warm colours. The setting is charming: enjoy the views of Tungurahua on a clear day, or the high-quality dining in their cosy restaurant, warmed by a log fire. $79

EATING AND DRINKING

Ambato offers a very respectable choice of places to eat, from budget to fine dining, except on **Sundays** when many are closed. It's particularly strong on cheap **spit-roasted chicken** places and is home to one of Ecuador's most famous highland dishes, **llapingachos** (see p.31).

Blue de Valle del Río 218 Huayna Capac, Cdla San Antonio ☎03 2841967. As the name and the blue neon lighting indicate, seafood is the name of the game here, though its meat dishes are also top-notch, especially the lamb. Discreet, intimate high-end dining (mains from around $10) in a nice stone building, a five-minute taxi-ride from the centre. Wed–Sun noon–10pm.

La Catedral Sucre on Parque Juan Montalvo ☎03 2425590. Nice covered courtyard café-bar in the Casa del Portal; a popular drinking spot in the evening, with occasional live music at weekends. Mon–Sat noon until late.

La Fornace Cevallos 17-28 and Montalvo ☎03 2823244. Intimate, relaxed and very popular place, serving delicious, inexpensive Italian food; pizzas are cooked in a large clay oven in the dining room. Daily noon–10/11pm.

★**Marcelo's** Castillo 02-56 and Rocafuerte ☎03 2828208. Spick-and-span and gleaming with metal and glass, this cheerful café-restaurant serves decent snacks, deli-sandwiches and the like for lunch, as well as delicious, more substantial mains for dinner and fancy ice-cream concoctions for dessert. Mon–Sat 9am–10pm.

Panadería Quito Juan León Mera and Cevallos ☎03 2825475. The city's best bakery-café, which in addition to an array of sweet treats, sells wholemeal buns and loaves. A good place for an early breakfast. Daily 7.30am–8pm.

Baños

Wedged in the narrow Río Pastaza gorge, 44km southeast of Ambato, and 72km northeast of Riobamba, is the small, but ever-expanding resort town of **Baños,** which was founded by the Dominicans in 1553 as a staging post between the sierra and the Oriente, and a base from which to evangelize the Amazonian *indígenas*. At 1820m above sea level, Baños enjoys a mild, almost subtropical climate and a spectacular location, nestled among soaring green hills streaked with waterfalls, though the town itself is gradually becoming overrun with cement-block hotels, neon-fronted tour operators and tacky gift shops. Even so, with the **thermal baths** that give the town its name, a great choice of good-value hotels and restaurants and excellent opportunities for **outdoor activities** such as hiking, cycling, horse riding and rafting, it's easy to see why Baños is one of the most visited destinations in the country – despite the unpredictable condition of the **Tungurahua volcano** towering above the town to the south (see box, p.154). Indeed, Tungurahua's unpredictability is something of a draw in itself, with tourists flocking to high vantage points on cloudless nights to watch it spit lava and igneous rocks into the sky like fireworks.

The **best months** to visit Baños are between September and April; from May to August it can be cloudy and rainy. But avoid the place at all costs during any holiday weekend,

BAÑOS

ACCOMMODATION

Casa Verde	1
Hostel Chimenea	5
Hostal D'Mathias	2
Hostería Isla de Baños	8
Hostería Luna Runtún	11
La Petite Auberge	6
Plantas y Blanco	4
Posada del Arte	7
Posada J	9
Princesa María	3
Villa Santa Clara	10

EATING

Arte Café & Té	2
Café Blah Blah	5
Café Hood	7
Café Mariane	8
La Caña Mandur	4
Dulce Carbón	1
Ricoo Pan	3
Taverna Armenia	6

DRINKING & NIGHTLIFE

Jota Jota	3
Leprechaun Bar	1
Stray Dog Brew Pub	2

when hotel prices are hiked and the streets bulge with 4WDs and throng with folk, as seemingly the entire urban population of the sierra descends on the town to have fun.

Basílica de Nuestra Señora del Rosario de Agua Santa

Calle Ambato • Museum daily 8am–noon & 2–4.30pm • $1

The only eye-catching feature in the town itself is the massive "moderated Gothic" **Basílica de Nuestra Señora del Rosario de Agua Santa**, dominated by a pair of 58-metre spires. It's the latest incarnation of the town's church, which lava has threatened or earthquakes have razed at least half a dozen times in its history. Thousands of pilgrims are drawn here each year, to worship **Nuestra Señora de Agua Santa**, a supposedly miraculous icon credited with rescuing Baños and its citizens from countless calamities over the years, many of them – including volcanic eruptions, fires and collapsing bridges – vividly depicted in a series of paintings inside the church. Faith in the Virgin's powers to intervene in the face of disaster still runs very strong in the community, as was demonstrated in September 1999, when the icon was paraded through the town in a procession attended by thousands of people in an attempt to invoke protection from Tungurahua.

Upstairs from the cloisters, a **museum** houses a fascinating and bizarre assortment of objects including a shrunken head from the Oriente, pickled snakes in jars, priests' robes, the processional wardrobe of the Nuestra Señora and a gruesome collection of stuffed Ecuadorian wildlife put together by someone with a very poor grasp of anatomy.

The baths

Top of the agenda for most visitors to Baños is a loll in one of the town's **thermal baths**. They're all a little institutional-looking, fashioned into rectangular concrete, open-air pools with no-frills changing facilities, but wallowing in yellow-brown waters heated by Tungurahua makes for an irresistible treat. The best time for a soak is an hour or so before sunrise – few foreign tourists manage to drag themselves out of bed at this time, so you'll be sharing the waters with local Ecuadorian families. Plus, the pools are at their cleanest then. It's all very friendly and atmospheric, especially in the thin dawn drizzle.

Piscinas de la Virgen

Eastern end of Avenida Martínez • **Daytime pools** 5am–4pm • $2 • **Evening pools** 6–9pm • $3

The popular **Piscinas de la Virgen** sit at the foot of a waterfall of the same name that tumbles down a rocky cliff; at night they're floodlit to spectacular effect. There are three daytime pools, plus a couple of separate pools only open at night, all of which are touted as being good for stomach and liver ailments; the largest pool is closed at night.

Piscinas Modernas

At the time of writing, the **Piscinas Modernas** were closed for major renovations and due to be combined with the neighbouring Piscinas de la Virgen to make the largest thermal baths in the country, scheduled to reopen at the end of 2016.

Piscinas El Salado

2km west of the centre • Daily 5am–5pm; Fri–Sun also 6–10pm (only the bottom four pools) • $3/4 • Served by local buses every 15min from Rocafuerte and Eloy Alfaro, behind the market, or it's a 30min walk – turn left up a prominently signed fork off the road to Ambato

Without doubt the nicest pools are the **Piscinas El Salado**, nestled in the crook of a ravine leading up to Tungurahua – a gorgeous spot, but, if the volcano is looking active, the last place you want to be. Renovated following the 2006 eruption, the baths comprise five small pools at various temperatures, each heavily mineralized and reputedly highly curative, plus ice-cold hydro-massages. Bath hats are compulsory (and can be hired on the spot) and the place is constantly being doused, making these pools the cleanest in Baños.

VOLCÁN TUNGURAHUA

In October 1999, **Volcán Tungurahua** – the 5023m volcano whose smoking cone lies just eight kilometres south of Baños – resumed activity after almost eighty years of dormancy. Baños and neighbouring villages were forcibly evacuated and roads were sealed off, leaving some 20,000 people homeless. By January 2000, since no major eruption had materialized, 5000 locals (anxious that rogue soldiers were looting their homes) fought their way through military blockades, armed with shovels and rocks. The authorities subsequently agreed to reopen the town, which quickly recovered as a popular resort. But Tungurahua (meaning "throat of fire" in Kichwa) continued regularly to belch gas and lava. Then, in August 2006, activity increased dramatically with a violent, explosive **eruption** that wiped out three hamlets on the volcano's western slopes, accompanied by a ten-kilometre-high ash cloud. Although most residents were evacuated, some refused to leave, and seven people were killed in the eruption.

Volcanic activity continues on a low to medium level, with the latest eruption in 2014 and increased volcanic activity at the end of 2015. However, it's business as usual in Baños, which was unaffected by the 2006 explosion – but be aware that the **risk** is ongoing. Most hotels have evacuation instructions stuck on the walls, and road signs, large yellow arrows and dotted lines on the streets point the way to a designated **safety zone** on the eastern side of town. Before visiting Baños, check Tungurahua's current condition from daily reports in all the national newspapers, from the SAE in Quito (see p.79), from the Instituto Geofísico's (Spanish) website ⓦ igepn.edu.ec, or from your embassy.

SPA TREATMENTS AND MASSAGE THERAPIES

In addition to the baths, a sub-industry of **spa** treatments and **massage** therapies exists in town. Many of the smarter hotels have their own spas, featuring saunas, steam rooms (*turcos*), steam boxes (*baños de cajón*), whirlpools (*hidromasaje*), therapeutic and relaxing massages, facials, aromatherapy, medicinal mud baths and a range of other treatments, which non-residents are generally welcome to use for a fee. El Refugio (W elrefugiospa.com), 1km east of town in the Barrio San Vicente, is a dedicated spa complex in lovely grounds offering most of the above treatments – you can even have your ears or intestines cleaned. Back in town, you can enjoy quality massages (from around $30–35/hour) at the highly rated Stay in Touch Therapeutic Massage (T 03 2740973) at Martínez and Alfaro; at Chakra (W chakramassages.com), nearby on the corner of Martínez and Alfaro, which specializes in Swedish and hot stone massage as well as reflexology; and at Jade Spa (W jadespa-banios .com), on Oriente and Suárez, which features chocolate massage among its treatments.

ARRIVAL AND DEPARTURE BAÑOS

By bus Buses drop passengers inside or right next to the bus terminal, three blocks north of the *parque central*, just off the main road. You can easily walk to most hotels, but you'll find taxis ranked outside ($1 within town). Many buses to major destinations are through buses to be boarded on the main road, Amazonas, by the terminal.

Destinations Ambato (every 10min; 50min); Coca (11 daily; 9hr 30min); Guayaquil (8 daily; 6hr 30min); Puyo (every 30min; 1hr 15min); Quito (every 20min; 3hr 30min); Riobamba, via Ambato (every 30min; 2hr); Río Verde (from Eloy Alfaro and Martínez; hourly, on the hour; 30min); Tena (every15min–1hr; 3hr 30min).

GETTING AROUND AND INFORMATION

On foot Baños is a compact town with most places of interest being within a 10min walk of the main square.
By bus Town buses run every 15min during the day between Agoyán, east of town, to El Salado to the west, stopping in the centre behind the market on Rocafuerte, and returning via San Martín.
Tourist offices The helpful tourist office (daily

8am–12.30pm & 2–5.30pm; T 03 2740483 W banos -ecuador.com, W banios.com) is on the *parque central*, at Halflants and Rocafuerte, and you can pick up maps and leaflets here. If you want to know more about the Parque Nacional Llanganates (in Spanish), consult the Ministerio del Ambiente office in Martínez between Halflants and Eloy Alfaro (T 03 2741662; Mon–Fri 8am–5pm).

ACCOMMODATION

Baños has a huge choice of places to stay, especially at the middle and lower end of the scale, usually offering comfortable accommodation at reasonable prices. Availability is generally not a problem midweek, but at **weekends** and **holidays**, it can be hard to find a room, prices are hiked, and it can be hard to get any sleep. For a more relaxing experience, consider staying just outside town.

★**Casa Verde** Santa Ana, off the road to Puyo, 1.5km from the town centre T 0986594189, W lacasaverde .com.ec. There's nowhere more relaxing than this genuinely eco-friendly retreat, tucked away in lush surroundings above the Río Pastaza, with balconies and decks from which to admire the scenery and hammocks to chill in. Rooms are simple and spacious, using wood and lots of natural light. Enjoy the yoga deck, their fresh food (or use the kitchen) and the peace and quiet. Town is only $2 by taxi. Good long-stay discounts. $50
★**Hostel Chimenea** Martínez and Veira T 03 2742725, W hostelchimenea.com. Efficient, friendly hostel with decent beds and clean bathrooms, plus a great rooftop terrace. Additional attractions include a small pool, a jacuzzi and steam room, and a chilled vibe. Excellent value. Dorms $8; doubles $23

★**Hostal D'Mathias** Espejo and Maldonado T 03 2743203 or T 0986388630, W hostaldmathias.com. Not a party venue, but a spotless, friendly family-run hostal a stone's throw from the bus station, boasting light, well-furnished rooms with polished wooden floors, solid, warm beds, and hot showers. There's a shared living room and well-equipped kitchen, plus a pool table – all for very little. $20
Hostería Isla de Baños Halflants 1-31 and Montalvo T 03 2740609, W isladebanios.com. Appealing, long-standing German-run hostel, set in an attractive garden with riotous greenery around a pond. The rooms are comfortable (firm mattresses), with scrubbed wooden floors and spotless bathrooms, and there are spa facilities and organized excursions. Breakfast included. $66
Hostería Luna Runtun On a hill east of town, 8km by

3

road, turning 2km east of Baños ☎03 2740882, ⓦ lunaruntun.com. This luxury Swiss-run retreat makes a fantastic place to unwind: it's perched on a spur with landscaped gardens and a fully equipped spa centre – open to day-vistors too; you can loll in the infinity pools and soak up spectacular views of Baños and Tungurahua. Rates include breakfast, dinner and use of some spa facilities. $\underline{268}$

La Petite Auberge 16 de Diciembre and Montalvo ☎03 2740936, ⓦ www.lepetit.banios.com. Bags of character in this delightful whitewashed and tiled hotel set back from the road in its own garden. It has a pleasant open-sided lounge area with fireplace and wooden floors, and attractive, if a little careworn, en-suite rooms and split-level suites, many with fireplaces and patios. $\underline{36}$

ACTIVITIES AND TOURS AROUND BAÑOS

Few visitors come to Baños without wanting to strike out into the surrounding countryside to explore its hills, ravines, rivers and waterfalls. There are a number of highly rewarding **hikes**, many of them giving superb views over the town or Volcán Tungurahua. **Cycling** is another great way to explore independently, especially along the descending road to Puyo. In addition, numerous **tour operators** offer a wide range of guided excursions, including **horse riding** in the hills around Baños; **hikes** and treks in the nearby Llanganates and Sangay national parks; and **jungle trips**, which usually mean a bus or jeep ride to Puyo, followed by an hour or two's drive to a base in the rainforest. Adrenaline junkies can take their pick from **whitewater rafting** on Río Pastaza and other rivers (most rapids Grade II–IV depending on the river and time of year); **canyoning**; **rock-climbing**; or **paragliding** (parapente). A few agents also offer **bridge jumps** (also called *puenting*) from the Río Blanco bridge, 8km east of town or closer to home from the San Francisco bridge, across the road from the bus terminal. There's also a vertigo-inducing **swing**, signposted off the hike up to Bellavista, and a number of **zip-lines** slung across the Pastaza gorge, and at Puntzán, up the mountain road to Runtún, all of which you can get to independently. Several companies also offer **climbing tours** of local peaks such as the Ilinizas and Cotopaxi (before its closure), though at only 1820m above sea level Baños is not the ideal base from which to embark on a high-altitude trek or climb.

Do not underestimate the **risks** involved in sports such as rafting, canyoning, *puenting* and climbing, when led by untrained people using substandard equipment. Make sure your guide is properly qualified (AGAR for rafting; ASEGUIM for climbing), and your gear is in good condition. Beware of bottom-dollar operators who may be cutting corners on safety. Note also that the Río Pastaza is polluted.

Lastly, there's Tungurahua itself; party *chivas* (open-sided buses) set out nightly (9–11pm), music blaring, on what is billed as a **volcano tour** but which is usually little more than a cheap, fun mobile disco. But on the rare clear nights when *El Gigante Negro* (The Black Giant) decides to put on a natural fireworks display, it's truly breathtaking. The less actively inclined might consider visiting the low-key local **zoo** at nearby San Martín.

HIKING

There are several interconnecting **footpaths** leading up the mountainside over the south side of town, all clearly marked on the large colour map of Baños available at the tourist office and many local shops. Starting at the south end of Maldonado, a path heads up for around 45 minutes to a large white cross marking a spot called **Bellavista**; the views from the top are breathtaking. From here, you can continue uphill for another kilometre or so to the *Hostería Luna Runtún*, where you can loop west on a downhill path that takes you to the **Mirador de la Virgen**, from where it's an easy downhill walk back to Baños (4hr round trip). The *mirador*, marked by a statue of the Virgin, can be reached directly from Baños (30min) on the path starting at the south end of Juan León Mera. On the opposite side of town, follow the path starting at the corner of Reyes and Amazonas, behind the bus terminal, for about ten minutes down to the **San Francisco bridge** spanning the beautiful Río Pastaza gorge. Across the river, several paths lead steeply up the hillside, as well as east and west along the bank of the gorge, linking up with several other bridges across the river. Another enjoyable walk west is to the **zoo** and waterfall nearby; continuing on from both leads up to the village of Lligua, from where a trail leads to hilltops with fine views. The paths around Baños are generally safe but always check the latest reports before setting out, or hire a local guide.

★**Plantas y Blanco** Martínez and 12 de Noviembre ☏03 2740044, ⓦplantasyblanco.com. Very popular (advanced booking essential) whitewashed hostel offering clean dorms (for 4 or 6), and en-suite rooms with bedside tables – from singles to triples – and lots of services: laundry, luggage storage, DVD rental, massage. Highlights include great breakfasts served on the rooftop terrace and the morning steam bath (both extra). Limited kitchen availability. Dorms $9; doubles $26

Posada del Arte Ibarra and Montalvo ☏03 2740083, ⓦposadadelarte.com. A lovely house adorned with Ecuadorian art in a pretty spot on the edge of town, with a comfy sitting room in which to sip one of their home-brewed ales. En-suite rooms feature polished wooden

---

CANYONING AND ROCK-CLIMBING

Canyoning is a sport that beginners with a good head for heights can have a go at – provided they have an experienced guide with good equipment who knows the route well. The best canyoning area is around the Río Negro (27km east of town), though the San Jorge waterfall (11km east) is a popular, if less spectacular, alternative. **Rock-climbing** takes place closer to home on the basalt cliffs in the Pastaza gorge by San Martín (2km west).

CYCLING

Countless establishments in Baños rent **mountain bikes** for $5–10 per day. You should shop around for the best, and usually pricier, bikes and test the brakes, gears and tyres before committing yourself; also ask for a helmet, pump and basic toolkit. The most popular **cycling route** is the "Ruta de las Cascadas" (see p.159), east along the road to Puyo – paved and mostly downhill, but with a few uphill stretches and substantial traffic at times – returning to Baños on one of the half-hourly buses that trundle along the road (you can store your bike underneath for $1; last bus 7pm). Most people are happy to cycle just the first 15km to the village of Río Verde, near the Pailón del Diablo falls, reached in one or two hours from Baños. The scenery is stunning, but beware of narrow sections, sheer drops and the pitch-black 100m tunnel at Km7, which should be cycled with care and a light if you have one; you can bypass other tunnels on the old road to the side. At the falls, a pick-up can take your bike back to Baños for $2. The whole 61km to Puyo is a more challenging ride (5–6hr) with some stiff uphill stretches along the second half of the journey. Several agencies rent out **motorbikes**, scooters, buggies and **quad-bikes** for around $15 per hour; wear a helmet and ride defensively.

TOUR OPERATORS

Expediciones Amazónicas Oriente 11-62 and Halflants ☏03 2741344, ⓦexpedicionesamazonicas .com. Long-established outfit offering a selection of activities including bridge jumps, canyoning, hiking and a three-day jungle tour.

Flyniton Mideros and Ambato ☏0988030968, ⓦflyniton.com.ec. Paragliding specialist offering tandem flights or full paragliding course.

Geotours Ambato and Halflants ☏03 2741344, ⓦgeotoursbanios.com. Highly recommended operation, offering a vast array of activities, in particular half- to two-day rafting trips on the *ríos* Patate, Pastaza, Palora and Jatun Yacu – $30 for a half day, $60 for a full day – and cloudforest hikes on the flanks of Tungurahua that may afford views of its natural firework display.

Imagine Ecuador 16 de Diciembre between Montalvo and Martínez ☏03 2743472, ⓦimagine ecuador.com. Professional, knowledgeable outfit – specialists in rock-climbing, rafting and kayaking (4-day beginners course for $80/day for a group of four), but they offer a host of other activities too.

José and 2 Dogs Maldonado and Martínez ☏03 2740746, ⓔjosebalu_99@yahoo.com. Small, local, dependable company with friendly guides, known particularly for horse riding and canyoning.

Marberktour Eloy Alfaro between Rocafuerte and Ambato ☏03 2741695, ⓦmarberktour.com. Company specializing in rafting ($60 for a full day) and canyoning ($30), with a reputation for safety and professionalism.

MTS Adventure 16 de Diciembre and Martínez ☏03 2743283, ⓦmtsadventure.com. These canyoning experts even offer night excursions to ramp up the adrenaline level.

El Topo Turismo El Topo ☏0986850757, ⓦeltopoturismo.com. Good community tourism venture just after Río Negro, in a verdant location, halfway along the Puyo road. Nature walks, horse riding, farm visits and river fishing are on offer. Half-day tours (with lunch) for $25, or overnight homestays or camping for modest prices.

3

floors and firm mattresses, the pricier ones having open fires, bathtubs and views of the waterfall. Rooms in the newer Blue House are a little smaller. A great restaurant is attached, with a good number of veggie options. Full breakfast included. $81

Posada J Ibarra and Montalvo ☏03 2740053, ⓦposada-J.com. Good-value, agreeable hotel in a gorgeous spot, right by the tumbling Virgen waterfall. There are splendid views from the light and airy upstairs rooms (all en suite) and the balcony, and discounts in the on-site spa. Continental breakfast included. $50

Princesa María Mera and Rocafuerte ☏03 2741035, ⓦprincesamaria.webs.com. Inexpensive, very friendly family-run hostel in a quiet residential area. Clean en-suite rooms with excellent hot showers and firm beds, plus there's a shared kitchen and living room with cable TV, DVD player and internet. $23

Villa Santa Clara 12 de Noviembre and Ibarra ☏03 2740349, ⓦhotelvillasantaclara.com. Excellent value for money if you plump for the upstairs en-suite rooms, set around the garden, all with cable TV and shared balcony. Safe parking too. The cafeteria offers an impressive array of breakfasts. $34

EATING

Baños boasts a great spread of **international restaurants** offering everything from crêpes to curries, as well as traditional Ecuadorian food and the ubiquitous pizza, at moderate prices. **Sugar cane** abounds in various forms (as juice or sticks to chew). Baños' most famous speciality is *melocha*, a type of **toffee** made from sugar cane, which is hung from the wall and stretched into long, pale-gold strips before being sold in small plastic packets on the street.

CAFÉS

Arte Café & Té 12 de Noviembre 500 and Oriente ☏03 2743488. This place scores on the coffee and tea front, both for variety and quality, and it's a charming spot for a leisurely breakfast: you can swing in hammock chairs on a semi-open patio within a walled garden, or sit inside surrounded by textiles and ceramics. Breakfasts (most $4–5) – try the Colombian – are a delight, as are the crêpes and cakes. Mon–Wed & Fri–Sun 9am–7pm.

★**Café Blah Blah** Corner of Martínez and Halflants ☏0984023466. Small, cheap and cheerful café serving good breakfasts, salads, sandwiches, omelettes, great fluffy pancakes and fruit juices, among other snacks and light meals. 8am–8pm; closes one day a week Mon–Wed.

Ricoo Pan Ambato and Maldonado on the park ☏06 2740387. Busy bakery and café, serving breakfasts ($2.50–6.50), delicious wholemeal bread sandwiches, and a range of snacks, salads and light meals. Also has newspapers. Mon–Sat 7am–7pm.

RESTAURANTS

Café Hood Montalvo and Viera ☏03 2741609. Good food from a mainly veggie menu, featuring Tex-Mex, Indian and Thai dishes (mains $5–6). It has a nice vibe and is in a choice location, with indoor and outdoor seating. Happy hour and occasional live music. Daily 10am–10pm.

Café Mariane Montalvo between Halflants and Eloy Alfaro (set back from the road) ☏03 2741947, ⓦhotelmariane.com. Be transported to the south of France in this romantic dining room – with warm brick walls, embroidered tablecloths and a blazing hearth – and treat yourself with wonderfully indulgent Provençal and Mediterranean cuisine. Mains $9–15. Daily 11am–11pm.

La Caña Mandur Martínez and Halflants ☏03 2742709. One of the top spots in town for Ecuadorian fare, serving a standout *locro de papas* and other firm favourites such as trout, tilapia, ceviche and *churrasco*. Daily noon–10pm.

Dulce Carbón 12 de Noviembre and Oriente ☏03 2740353. Serving cheap, succulent spit-roasted and chargrilled poultry and meat dishes (quarter chicken, salad and chips $6), this friendly, efficient place is understandably popular. Try the tamales in *achira* leaves. Mon, Tues & Thurs–Sun 6pm–midnight.

★**Taverna Armenia** Pastaza and Montalvo ☏0996791903, ⓦtarmenia.com. This family-run restaurant is like nowhere else in Baños, both for the food (Russian, mainly, with Armenian influence) and the ambiance (black-and-white silent films played on screens, accompanied by mellow jazz) and warm hospitality. Tuck into succulent kebabs and *pelmeni* (pasta-like filled dumplings stuffed with meat) – try the llama variety, the house speciality. Tues–Sun 2pm until late.

SPANISH SCHOOLS

A popular place to stay and learn Spanish, Baños has several language schools. Prices for twenty hours of small-group classes are around $100–150 per week. Recommended places include: Baños Spanish Center, Oriente 8-20 and Cañar (☏0987045072, ⓦbanios.com/spanishcenter); Mayra's Spanish School, at Tapia 112 and Oriente (☏03 2743019, ⓦmayraspanishschool.com); and Raíces Spanish School, 16 de Diciembre and Suárez (☏03 2741921, ⓦspanishlessons.org).

DRINKING AND NIGHTLIFE

For nightlife, head to the stretch of **Eloy Alfaro** between Ambato and Espejo, where a cluster of bars and clubs serve cheap cocktails and beers, occasionally with live music (when a small cover charge might apply).

★**Jota Jota** Martínez between Halflants and Eloy Alfaro ☎ 0998373240, ⊛ coffeebarjotajota.com. This intimate open-sided café-bar is a choice spot to while away a wet afternoon, with cushion-laden sofas, fresh flowers, book exchange, ping-pong and pool. By day, enjoy frappés, juices, cakes and light bites; by night, risk your head spinning by sampling the home-brewed spirits ($1 a shot) and cocktails. Tues–Sat 10am–10pm, Sun 1–10pm.

Leprechaun Bar Eloy Alfaro and Espejo ☎ 0999011913, ⊛ facebook.com/leprechaunbarbanios. Vast and usually packed bar and dance venue with several floors offering competing beats, while the upstairs area is more chilled. The big draw, however, is the bar in the back yard (be sure to try a shot of "Flaming Bob Marley"), which occasionally hosts live music and is warmed by a blazing bonfire. Mon–Sat 8pm until late.

Stray Dog Brew Pub Corner of Maldonado and Rocafuerte ☎ 0991036598. The place to come for locally brewed beer on tap (ales and stout), plus some decent American bar food. Mon & Wed–Sat 3–11pm, Sun 11am–7pm.

La Ruta de las Cascadas

East of Baños, the road to Puyo begins its descent towards the Oriente, carving its way through the Pastaza valley, high above the river. It's been dubbed the *Ruta de las Cascadas* for the many **waterfalls** that stripe the verdant valley walls. It's 61km to Puyo, but the star attractions, namely the waterfalls, as well as open-sided, bare-bones **cable cars** (*tarabitas*), zip-lines and most spectacular scenery, are in the upper section, closer to Baños. Frequent buses ply this route, making it easy to visit the various falls by public transport, though the most popular way to explore the area is by bike (see box, p.157).

Manto de la Novia

10km east of Baños • Daily 7/8am–6/7pm • Tarabita $1.50; zip-line $10/15 single/return • Any Río Verde or Puyo-bound bus from Baños can drop you off on the main road

Beyond the impressive Agoyán waterfall, 7km east of Baños, you reach the gorgeous **Manto de la Novia** (Bride's Veil), which in 2011 was split into twin cascades following a landslide. One way to appreciate its splendour is to make the hair-raising 500m trip suspended above the gorge in a *tarabita* (cable car) – the longest and most popular of several such rides across the Pastaza – or to fray the nerves even more by zip-lining there and back, courtesy of Canopy Agoyán. At the other side, there's a small path to a viewing platform and a dilapidated swing bridge that provides alternative access across the river, and allows you to view the falls from below.

Pailón del Diablo

Río Verde • Daily 8am–5pm • $1.50 • Any Puyo-bound bus from Baños can drop you on the main road; from there, walk down to the eastern end of the village, cross the bridge, and follow the steep 15-minute trail down to the falls; local buses for Río Verde leave Baños from Eloy Alfaro and Martínez every hour on the hour

Of the many waterfalls punctuating the Baños-Puyo road, the **Pailón del Diablo** ("Devil's Cauldron"), below the village of **Río Verde** some 15km east of Baños, is justifiably the main draw. It is a brute of a waterfall where the Río Verde, from which the village takes its name, thunders down a gorge into the Río Pastaza. You can observe the falls from a series of viewing platforms and a wooden swing bridge amid swirls of fine spray. Satisfying views of the river below the falls can also be enjoyed from the on-site cafeteria, which serves light meals and snacks. Cabañas are also available.

Manantial del Dorado

Machay • Daily 8am–6pm • $1 • Any Puyo-bound bus can drop you on the main road by the entrance to the falls

The small village of **Machay**, 2.5km east of Río Verde, is gateway to an easily accessible series of pretty waterfalls and a natural swimming pool, including the imposing **Manantial del Dorado**, a 70m cascade that lies at the end of a steep 3km trail, which reaches into glorious cloudforest.

ACCOMMODATION AND EATING

LA RUTA DE LAS CASCADAS

Miramelindo Main road above Río Verde ☎03 2884194, ⓦmiramelindo.com.ec. Hotel and spa with multicoloured roof tiles and cheerily decorated rooms with TV and DVD player, set in orchid-filled gardens. Rates include use of pool and spa facilities plus a buffet breakfast in the excellent restaurant. **$70**

Pequeño Paraíso 2km east of Río Verde

☎0999819776, ⓦpprioverde.com. Good-value, friendly hostel accommodation and camping in a splendid scenic location. There's a shared kitchen/social area (and a restaurant specializing in local trout), small pool, BBQ pits and volleyball court, as well as opportunities for hiking and canyoning. Dorms **$12**; doubles **$30**; camping **$6**/person

Guaranda

Few tourists reach the pleasantly untouristy sierra town of **GUARANDA** (2670m), which sits in a shallow basin surrounded by seven hills – earning it the unlikely sobriquet "Rome of the Andes". Gazing defiantly from one of the hills is the towering statue of **El Indio Guaranga**, the sixteenth-century indigenous chief after whom the town is supposedly named, and Guaranda's only real sight.

To reach here, an extremely scenic two-hour bus ride south from Ambato, or west from Riobamba, skirts the base of Chimborazo, offering dizzying views of the snowcapped summit. It's hard to believe you are in the provincial capital of Bolívar, given the physical isolation and sleepy, small-town air – its narrow, cobbled streets are relatively little traffic. Guaranda hosts a colourful Friday and (larger) Saturday **market** on the Plaza 15 de Mayo, where you'll see *campesinos* from local villages trading wheat, barley and maize for fruit brought up from the coast. The town is also known for its exuberant Carnaval celebrations.

Parque Bolívar

The town's main square is the charming **Parque Bolívar**, lined with old adobe houses with painted wooden balconies and sloping, red-tiled roofs flecked with lichen. The square also houses the grand, twin-towered **Catedral San Pedro de Guaranda**, a striking mixture of bare stone and white stucco, and the gleaming, white-walled **municipio**, looming over the mature palms that give this place a more tropical look than its climate warrants. Guaranda's main services, such as banks, ATMs and the post office, are all huddled around or close to the main square.

ARRIVAL AND INFORMATION

GUARANDA

By bus The bus station is on the outskirts of the town, about ten blocks east, and downhill, of Parque Bolívar; it's served by a few taxis. If coming from Riobamba or Ambato, get off at Plaza Roja – only three blocks east of the park – where the bus drops off passengers before heading out to the bus station.

Destinations Ambato (every 30min; 2hr); Guayaquil (roughly every 30min; 4hr); Quito (20 daily; 5hr); Riobamba (hourly; 2hr); Salinas (2 daily at 6am & noon, though unreliable; 1hr).

By taxi Taxis hang around Plaza Roja, where local buses pull in and out. Most trips around town cost $1.

Tourist office I-Tur is on Moreno and 7 de Mayo (Mon–Fri & public holidays 8am–noon & 2–6pm; ☎03 2980321).

OPPOSITE PARAGLIDING NEAR VOLCÁN TUNGURAHUA (P.157) >

ACCOMMODATION AND EATING

★ **Los 7 Santos** Convención de 1884 and 10 de Agosto, just off the park ☎ 03 2980612. The sunny, interior patio of this friendly, arty café-cum-bar is a pleasant place for brunch and light bites – don't miss the rich chocolate cake – while further back, darker, art-filled recesses provide spots for evening cocktails. Live music at weekends. Mon–Thurs 10am–10pm, Fri & Sat 10am–2am.

La Bohemia Convención de 1884 and 10 de Agosto on the corner of the main park. The tables set in intimate window booths make this a great spot for people-watching. Decent food, too, with plenty of meat and chicken dishes ($6–9), plus less expensive desayunos and almuerzos ($3). Mon–Sat 8am–9pm.

Hotel Bolívar Sucre 704 between Olmedo and Rocafuerte ☎ 03 2980547, ⓦ hotelbolivar.wordpress .com. Bright, light rooms overlook a covered interior courtyard. Comfy sofas are scattered around, and there's a decent restaurant bedecked with Andean instruments. $35

Hotel Ejecutivo Garcia Moreno 803 and 9 de Abril ☎ 03 2982044. No-frills place offering cheap beds, but it has the basics – clean private bathrooms with hot water, and cable TV. Ask for a room with a window. $22

El Mansión del Parque 10 de Agosto and Sucre ☎ 03 2984468, ⓦ guarandaec.wix.com/mansiondelparque. The most comfortable place in the town centre has a good on-site restaurant and a great location overlooking the park. The rooms, however, are small and rather overpriced – pay an extra $20 for a nicer, better-furnished suite. $40

Salinas

The huddled houses of the remote village of **SALINAS** (3550m) enjoy an enviable setting at the head of a picturesque valley, against the backdrop of a dramatic rockface, overlooking rolling pastures. Also called "Salinas de Guaranda", to distinguish it from the coastal resort, the village is named after the abundant supplies of salt that have been exploited here since pre-Hispanic times, though today it is best known for its flourishing **cooperatives** and **hiking** opportunities. If you time your visit for the end of October you can join in the festivities of the relatively new annual **cheese festival**, which is garnering more enthusiasts each year.

The cooperatives

Cooperatives Mon–Sat; visits arranged at the tourist information office • From $3/person depending on group size • **Shop** Mon–Sat 9am–5pm

Salinas' cooperatives were established in 1971 with the help of a Salesian missionary, Father Antonio Polo, who founded **FUNORSAL** (Fundación de Organizaciones de Salinas) to provide locals with training, materials, technical support, bank loans and accounting assistance. It transformed villagers' lives: sheep owners who had previously sold raw wool to middlemen for a pittance began to spin their own yarn and supply directly to the manufacturers for a decent profit, while dairy farmers set up highly productive milk and cheese factories, supplying retailers at a national level. Visiting the village's cooperatives, particularly the **cheese factory**, **wool workshop** and **chocolate workshop**, makes for an enjoyable and enlightening few hours, especially if you take a local guide to show you around. You can also buy their products, including some rather tasty nougat (*turrón*), at the **community shop** on the square. Note, however, that there are no banking facilities in Salinas.

ARRIVAL AND DEPARTURE   SALINAS

By bus There are 2–3 buses daily between Guaranda's Plaza Roja and Salinas (6am, noon and mid-afternoon; 1hr), though they are not very reliable.

By camioneta The quickest and most convenient transport between Salinas and Guaranda is in one of the camionetas run by the Salinas transport cooperative. They leave from Cándido Rada and Eloy Alfaro in Guaranda (five blocks northeast of Parque Bolívar, just north of Plaza Roja) and return from just below the main square in Salinas (approximately every 15min, or when full, until 7pm; 40min; $1).

INFORMATION AND TOURS

Tourist office The community tourist information office is on the main square (Mon–Sat 8am–5pm; ☎03 2210044 or ☎03 2210234, ✉ comunamatiavi@gmail.com).

Guides and tours Community guides – organized via the tourist information office – can show you around the cooperatives, as well as organizing numerous tours, horse rides, bike trips and local hikes ($30/person,

guide and food included). They can also help with visiting the Subtrópico part of the province in the west, such as trips to *Piedra Blanca*, a community ecotourism venture (☎03 2608544 or ☎0980422046, ⊕piedrablanca.org; $80/person for a three-night package) that has a simple lodge and plenty of opportunities to explore its surrounding forests.

ACCOMMODATION AND EATING

La Minga Hostal Main square ☎03 2210234, ⊕laminga-hostal.com. Pleasant, new brick-and-bamboo two-floor hostel built round a light interior courtyard-common room. The place is brimming with pot plants and offers brightly painted small dorms (for 3 or 5 people) and a handful of private rooms. The on-site café, *Pizzería Casa Nostra* (daily 9am–9pm), is a genuine Italian-run joint – also serving desayunos and almuerzos – though the signature llama meat pizza reminds you where you are.

Dorms $̄10; doubles $̄20

El Refugio Vía Samilagua, 300m from the main square ☎0985196031. Cooperative-run rustic hotel with terracotta-tiled floors and rooms with large windows and cable TV; ask for one with views across the valley. Bathrooms are en suite or shared. The hotel also has an inexpensive restaurant, offers Spanish lessons and can organize tours. $̄15/person

Riobamba

The self-proclaimed "Sultan of the Andes", **RIOBAMBA** (2735m) is the liveliest and most attractive city in the central sierra, made up of stately squares, flaking pastel-coloured buildings, cobbled streets and sprawling markets. An important centre since the early days of the colony, the place was dealt an abrupt and catastrophic blow in 1797 when a massive earthquake left it in ruins, though it was quickly rebuilt where it stands today, 20km north of its original site. Located in the centre of the Ecuadorian sierra, 52km south of Ambato (and 66km southwest of Baños), Riobamba is a major trading nucleus, with part of its appeal stemming from the vibrant mix of suited city-dwellers and large numbers of indigenous traders from the countryside. The main **market day** is Saturday, when the city overflows with energy and colour.

With an appealing blend of fast-paced buzz and old colonial charm, Riobamba easily merits a visit in its own right, but can also be combined with worthwhile excursions. First and foremost, it's the main base for visiting **Volcán Chimborazo**, and the starting point for various diverting **train excursions** (see box, p.166). Easy day-trips from Riobamba include **Zalarón**, with its authentic highland Friday market; **Guano**, a rug-manufacturing centre with a modest museum showcasing a mummified monk; and **Santa Teresita** (accessed from neighbouring Guano), where a *balneario* of spring-fed pools offers amazing views of Tungurahua.

Riobamba's main celebrations are **Las Fiestas Abrileñas**, leading up to April 21, which commemorates the victory over the Spanish at the Battle of Tapi in 1822, and November 11 for the **Independence of Riobamba**.

Parque Maldonado

The best place to start exploring Riobamba is the **Parque Maldonado**. This wide square is lined by the city's most impressive nineteenth-century architecture, including the colonnaded **municipio** (where Ecuador's first constitution was signed in 1830) and other flamboyant colonial buildings. On the northwest side of the square is the modest **Museo de la Ciudad** (Mon–Fri 8am–12.30pm & 2.30–6pm; free) in an elegantly restored and stately building, which occasionally hosts art exhibitions. Across the square you'll see the delicately carved stone facade of the **cathedral**, Riobamba's only

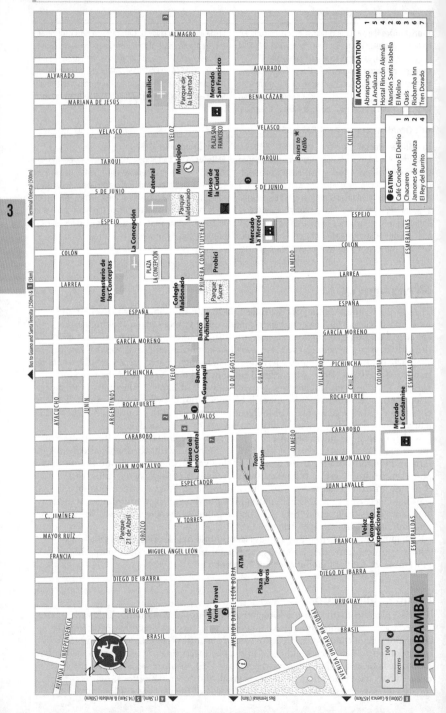

RIOBAMBA

ALMAGRO

ALVARADO

MARIANA DE JESÚS

VELASCO

TARQUI

S DE JUNIO

ESPEJO

COLÓN

LARREA

ESPAÑA

GARCÍA MORENO

PICHINCHA

ROCAFUERTE

CARABOBO

JUAN MONTALVO

ESPECTADOR

C. JIMÉNEZ

MAYOR RUÍZ

FRANCIA

DIEGO DE IBARRA

URUGUAY

BRASIL

AVENIDA LA INDEPENDENCIA

AYACUCHO

JUNÍN

ARGENTINOS

VELOZ

V. TORRES

MIGUEL ÁNGEL LEÓN

OROZCO

Parque 21 de Abril

La Basílica

Parque de la Libertad

Catedral

La Concepción

Municipio

Parque Maldonado

Monasterio de las Conceptas

PLAZA LA CONCEPCIÓN

Colegio Maldonado

Parque Sucre

Banco Pichincha

Banco de Guayaquil

Museo del Banco Central

M. DÁVALOS

Julio Verne Travel

ATM

Plaza de Toros

ALVARADO

BENALCÁZAR

VELASCO

TARQUI

S DE JUNIO

Mercado San Francisco

PLAZA SAN FRANCISCO

Museo de la Ciudad

Mercado La Merced

PRIMERA CONSTITUYENTE

Probici

ESPEJO

COLÓN

OLMEDO

LARREA

ESPAÑA

GARCÍA MORENO

PICHINCHA

VILLARROEL

ROCAFUERTE

CARABOBO

JUAN MONTALVO

JUAN LAVALLE

OLMEDO

FRANCIA

DIEGO DE IBARRA

URUGUAY

BRASIL

Buses to Atillo

CHILE

CHILE

ESMERALDAS

COLOMBIA

ESMERALDAS

ESMERALDAS

Mercado La Condamine

Veloz Coronado Expediciones

Train Station

AVENIDA DANIEL LEÓN BORJA

AVENIDA UNIDAD NACIONAL

ACCOMMODATION

Abraspungo	1
La Andaluza	5
Hostal Rincón Alemán	4
Mansión Santa Isabella	2
El Molino	8
Oasis	3
Riobamba Inn	6
Tren Dorado	7

EATING

Café Concierto El Delirio	1
Chacarero	3
Jamones de Andaluza	2
El Rey del Burrito	4

0 100 metres

Terminal Oriental (500m)

Bus to Guano and Santa Teresita (250m) & (3km)

4 (1.5km), 5 (14.5km) & Ambato (50km)

Bus Terminal (1km)

4 (200m) & Cuenca (457km)

survivor of the 1797 earthquake, painstakingly transported and reassembled here when the town was rebuilt.

Museo del Monasterio de las Conceptas

Entrance on Argentinos • Mon–Sat 9am–12.30pm & 3–5.30pm • $4

The **Monasterio de las Conceptas** houses one of the best museums of religious art and paraphernalia outside Quito. Most of the exhibits date from the eighteenth century, though sadly the museum's most prized possession – a huge gold and jewel-encrusted monstrance – was stolen in 2007, along with other valuable artefacts. Some of these were later recovered, including two golden crosses, which have been stuck, rather pathetically, on top of a life-size cardboard replica of the monstrance that now stands in place of the original. At the time of the robbery, most people in the country – including, crucially, the museum guard – were glued to their TVs watching the Ecuadorian national team play football; to avoid a repeat performance, the museum now remains closed during important home football matches.

Beyond the absent monstrance, the exhibition contains some ornately carved chests and bureaus and a collection of extraordinary antique glass cabinets containing Nativity scenes, which, in their time, were paraded through the city streets on Christmas Eve. In addition to the regular Nativity protagonists, the cabinets are crammed with unlikely casts of characters, from plastic peacocks to toy soldiers and pipe-cleaner animals, accompanied by a wealth of miniature household utensils.

Parque Sucre

The impressive **Parque Sucre** has a fountain of Neptune as its centrepiece, which was erected back in 1913, when piped water was first supplied to the city. However, the square is dominated by the imposing, predominantly Neoclassical facade of the **Colegio Maldonado**; it's worth taking a look inside the college entrance hall to admire its marble staircase.

The markets

On Saturday, an immense **market** bulges out of the streets bounded by calles España, 5 de Junio, Guayaquil and Argentinos, selling products ranging from squawking chickens to rubber boots. **Artesanías** are sold in Plaza La Concepción, in front of the church, where you'll find many *shigra* bags, ponchos, shawls and jewellery. There's a smaller-scale version of the market on Wednesdays, as well as the daily covered **fruit and vegetable market** at La Condamine, and the smaller daily **flower and fruit market** at La Merced, off Colón, between Guayaquil and Olmedo. Something else to look out for are items carved from **tagua nuts** (the seeds of tropical palm-like trees, also known as vegetable ivory); these can be found in a handful of shops on León Borja between Lavalle and Francia.

ARRIVAL AND DEPARTURE	RIOBAMBA

BY BUS

Terminal Terrestre Riobamba's main bus terminal, the Terminal Terrestre (☎ 03 2962005), is a couple of kilometres from the centre, at avenidas Daniel León Borja and de la Prensa. The terminal serves all long-distance routes. Taxis from here into the centre cost $1, or you can take a bus down León Borja to the train station. In the opposite direction, regular local buses go to the Terminal Terrestre along Orozco.

Destinations Alausí (every 30min; 2hr 30min); Ambato (every 15–20min; 1hr); Baños via Ambato (every 20–30min; 2hr); Cuenca (every 30min–1hr, mostly through buses from Quito; 5hr 30min); Guaranda (10 daily; 2hr); Guayaquil (every 15–30min; 4hr 30min); Latacunga (every 15–20min; 2hr); Macas via Atillo (6 daily; 5hr); Puyo (every 30min–1hr; 4hr); Quito (every 15min; 3hr 30min–4hr); Santo Domingo (10 daily; 5hr); Tena (13 daily; 6hr).

Terminal Oriental Infrequent buses to Candelaria (1hr

TRAIN EXCURSIONS

Riobamba's recently renovated **train station** is centrally located on Avenida Daniel León Borja and Carabobo (☎03 2961038; daily 8am–6pm). Though Riobamba is no longer the starting point for the dramatic **Devil's Nose train journey** (see box, p.174), the new **Tren de la Quinua** (Tues–Fri at 6.30am; 5hr; $50 one way) runs to Alausí – after a stop in Guamote – arriving at 11.30am, in time to connect with the afternoon Devil's Nose departure. Alternatively, you can do the return journey from Alausí to Riobamba, departing at 12.45pm. There are two other cheaper diverting half-day excursions by *autoferro* from Riobamba: the **Tren del Hielo 1** (Thurs–Sun 8am; $11), which skirts the eastern flank of Chimborazo to Urbina, where you can check out some llamas and alpacas and visit an interpretative centre that focuses on ice-harvesting; and the **Sendero de los Ancestros** (Thurs–Sun noon; $17), which heads south to the reed-lined Laguna de Colta, stopping at the Iglesia de Balbanera, one of Ecuador's oldest churches.

3

30min) leave from this smaller terminal on the corner of Espejo and Luz Elisa Borja, about 1km northeast of the centre; it's served by plenty of taxis, or you can catch a local bus from the train station.

Terminal La Dolorosa Little more than a parking bay well out of the city centre at Parque la Dolorosa, where some local buses arrive and depart.

Destinations Alao (hourly; 1hr 30min); Atillo (5 daily; 2hr 30min); Guargallá (1 daily; 1.30–2pm, returning to Riobamba 5.30am; 2hr).

GETTING AROUND AND INFORMATION

On foot The centre of Riobamba is very walkable; it'll take you around 15 minutes to reach Parque Maldonado from the train station.

By taxi Taxis hang around Parque Maldonado, Parque Sucre and Parque de la Libertad.

Tourist offices The very helpful Ministerio de Turismo office (Mon–Fri 8am–1pm & 2–6pm; ☎03 2941213) is in the Centro de Arte y Cultura on León Borja and Brasil; there's also a small information booth at the bus terminal.

National park information For basic information on Volcán Chimborazo or Parque Nacional Sangay, take a taxi to the Ministerio del Ambiente (Mon–Fri 8.30am–4.30pm; ☎03 2963779) at 9 de Octubre, by the Quinta Macají, or ask one of the tour operators (see box opposite).

ACCOMMODATION

IN THE CENTRE

★**Mansión Santa Isabella** Veloz 28-48, between Carabobo and Dávalos ☎03 2962974, ⓦmansion santaisabella.com. This lovely restored colonial mansion has gorgeous, beautifully furnished rooms with pretty painted walls, each named after a flower whose perfume pervades the room. Friendly, attentive service, and breakfast included. **$100**

El Molino Ciudad Dulcicela 4213 and Unidad Nacional ☎03 2941372, ⓦhotelelmolino.com.ec. The place may be lacking in character but it's spotless, and you can't fault the rooms: modern, carpeted and earth-toned, with plenty of amenities – especially the suites ($32 extra). Excellent service too. **$98**

Oasis Veloz and Almagro ☎03 2961210, ⓦoasishostelriobamba.com. This friendly family hotel at the quieter end of town is very popular with travellers – so it's a good idea to book. The en-suite rooms are set round a pleasant patio garden (though there is piped music), and there's cable TV. **$30**

Riobamba Inn Carabobo 23-20 ☎03 2961696. Well-run hotel with pleasant, careworn carpeted rooms, all with private bathroom, telephone and cable TV. Has private parking and breakfast is included. **$40**

Tren Dorado Carabobo 22-35 ☎03 2964890, ⓦhoteltrendorado.com. Popular hotel close to the station, with the best rooms at the back, overlooking a patio; all are spotless and en suite, with cable TV and chintzy furnishings. The restaurant is gloomy but does reasonable buffet breakfasts. Local tours on offer too. **$34**

OUT OF TOWN

Abraspungo Km3.5 on the road to Guano ☎03 2944299, ⓦhaciendaabraspungo.com. Upmarket, tastefully designed lodge, offering rustic hacienda style with plenty of modern comforts and attentive service. Spa services and horse riding are on offer. Buffet breakfast included. **$120**

La Andaluza 16km north of Riobamba on the Panamericana ☎03 2949370, ⓦhosteriaandaluza .com. A converted hacienda keeping a degree of historic charm, with antique furnishings and fireplaces, brought up to date with mod cons such as cable TV. It has two good restaurants, a café and bar with karaoke – it's popular with tour groups and conferences. **$97**

★**Hostal Rincón Alemán** Mz H, Casa 9, Romero and Pareja ☎03 2603540, ⓦhostalrinconaleman.com. Great place set in a walled garden in a quiet suburb a $2 taxi ride from the centre. Teutonic touches include goose-down duvets, pine furniture, low firm beds and window boxes brimming with flowers. Rooms are spacious and light – especially the upstairs ones – and there's a fully equipped kitchen and pleasant roof terrace. Healthy breakfasts are included; thereafter, make use of the fully equipped kitchen, pop into town or order a takeaway. **$60**

EATING AND DRINKING

Riobamba isn't exactly heaving with nightlife but the action generally starts to hot up from **Thursday** night, predominantly on **Avenida Daniel León Borja**, from northwest of the station to the park, which forms the ersatz Zona Rosa.

GUIDED TOURS AND CLIMBS AROUND RIOBAMBA

A number of outfits and independent guides offer a range of **tours around Riobamba**. For day-visitors, the most popular target is the refuge at 4800m on the slopes of Volcán Chimborazo (see p.168), from where you can take a strenuous half-hour walk up to the second refuge (5000m). Several hotels in Riobamba offer good-value **day-trips** here, including the *Tren Dorado* (see opposite), though these aren't recommended for serious mountaineering. Dedicated **climbing companies and guides** (see below) concentrate on guided ascents of Chimborazo (6268m), the highest peak in Ecuador and the most popular volcano climb after Cotopaxi; most also offer climbs up neighbouring Carihuairazo (see box, p.169) and other central sierra volcanoes. Some also do multi-day **hiking** programmes around the sierra, providing tents, sleeping bags, food and transport. Rates for a two-day ascent of Chimborazo start at around $250 per person for two people, sometimes less for larger groups. Costs usually include a certified guide, transport, food and equipment rental. Trekking rates are usually lower, from around $110 per person per day. Riobamba is also a great place for **mountain-bike tours** ($40–75), ranging from riding down the slopes of Chimborazo to outings around rural villages along back roads, or tours of the Atillo or Ozogoche lakes.

If you're interested in supporting **community tourism** initiatives in Chimborazo, get in touch with the Corporación de Desarrollo Comunitario y Turismo de Chimborazo, Ramos and Jijón in Los Alamos, Mz E, Casa 6 (☎03 2606774, ⓦfacebook.com/cordtuch).

CLIMBING AND OTHER TOUR COMPANIES

Alta Montaña Posada La Estación, Urbina (see p.169) ☎0999694867, ⓦaltamontanaecuador .com. Well-respected company offering ascents up Chimborazo, Cotopaxi, El Altar and many other peaks, as well as being specialists for logistically difficult climbs, such as Sangay. There are many trekking options, including a five-day hike around Chimborazo, a two-day trek to the Atillo and Ozogoche lakes, plus horse riding, mountain biking and other activities. Recommended. Online booking preferred.

Biking Spirit Mz 2 Ilapo and Tixan ☎03 2612263, ⓦbikingspirit.com. Professional mountain-bike specialists, running a range of day-tours down and around Chimborazo, or to other destinations such as Guano or Guamote. Good bilingual biking guides, excellent bikes and sound back-up.

Expediciones Andinas Urb. Las Abras, 3km along the road to Guano, opposite Abraspungo ☎03 2364278, ⓦexpediciones-andinas.com. A polished outfit run by respected mountaineer Marco Cruz, offering everything from treks (with or without llamas to carry bags), horse rides, ascents up Chimborazo, to multi-climb packages, including a sixteen-day tour taking in five peaks. Uses its own mountain lodge, the comfortable and heated *Estrella del Chimborazo* (see p.169) at 4000m, as base camp for Chimborazo. Book in advance.

Julio Verne Travel Brasil 22-40 and León Borja ☎03 2963436, ⓦjulioverne-travel.com. Reputable Ecuadorian-Dutch operator specializing in adventure tours, including mountaineering, cycling, whitewater rafting, jungle trips and multi-day treks. The multi-day treks include the Inca trail from Alausí to Ingapirca; five days in the páramo around the El Placer hot springs; and around the spectacular El Altar peak. Good equipment.

Probici Primera Constituyente 23-51 and Larrea ☎03 2941880, ⓦprobici.com. (If there's no one there, ask in the fabric shop opposite). Highly recommended and experienced bike-tour operator, offering day-trips for varying levels of experience: whizz down Chimborazo or explore the Atillo and Ozogoche lakes on top-quality bikes, accompanied by a knowledgeable guide.

Veloz Coronado Expediciones Chile 33-21 and Francia ☎03 2960916, ⓦvelozexpediciones.com. Run by Ivo Veloz, an ASEGUIM qualified guide, who comes from a mountaineering family.

3

Café Concerto El Delirio Primera Constituyente 28-16 ☎ 03 2966441. You're paying in part for the history at this beautiful colonial house, once the home of Simón Bolívar, with its flower-filled patio and cosy indoor dining room enlivened by a crackling log fire. Elaborate meat and fish dishes average $8–12, and it can feel a bit touristy, especially with the live *folklórica* music that occurs most nights. Tues–Sun 12.30–9.30pm.

Chacarero 5 de Junio 21-46 ☎ 03 2969292. Popular, family-run restaurant serving decent pizzas; a typical small one goes for around $6. Mon–Sat 4–10.30pm, Sun 5–10pm.

Jamones de Andaluza León Borja 36-04 and Uruguay ☎ 03 2947189. Slightly pricey deli-restaurant, but the patio – sunny by day and heated at night – is great for people watching, even if the food quality is variable. On the menu are breakfasts, salads, deli sandwiches ($4–7) and grilled meats. Mon–Sat 9am–10pm, Sun 9am–2pm & 5–10pm.

El Rey del Burrito Brasil and Colombia ☎ 03 2953230. Inexpensive Mexican restaurant decorated with sombreros and textiles and serving reasonable enchiladas, burritos and all the other standards. Mains from around $8, with some good-value combo platters. Daily 11am–11pm.

Volcán Chimborazo and around

At 6268m, **Volcán Chimborazo** is the highest peak in Ecuador. A giant of a volcano thought to have last erupted some 10,000 years ago, its base spans approximately 20km and its upper elevations are permanently covered in snow and ice. The summit was once imagined to be the highest in the world and still enjoys the distinction of being the furthest point from the centre of the earth and the closest to the sun – thanks to the bulge around the equator.

Facing Chimborazo to the northeast is **Carihuairazo** (5020m), a jagged trio of craggy spires that contrasts with the snowy bulk of its more famous neighbour; it's a very respectable mountain in its own right and a popular preparation climb for a later attempt on Chimborazo. For both you will need to hire a certified guide.

Both mountains form the topographical centrepieces of the 58,560-hectare **Reserva Faunística Chimborazo**, created in 1987 as a haven for alpacas, llamas and especially **wild vicuñas**, which had disappeared from Ecuador around the time of the Conquest. Following a very successful reintroduction programme, there are now more than 2500 vicuñas eking life from the thin air and marginal terrain high up around Chimborazo.

The Chimborazo refuges

The two mountain **refuges** (see below) perched on Chimborazo's slopes make obvious targets for **day-trips** from Riobamba though there's not much to do once there. A fair challenge for most day-trippers is the walk from the lower **Refugio Hermanos Carrel** (which can be reached by car; see below) up to the second **Refugio Whymper** (45min walk), named after Edward Whymper, the British climber who made the first recorded ascent of Chimborazo in 1880 with the Carrel brothers. At an altitude of 5000m, it's only 200m higher than the first refuge, but it can be totally exhausting if you're not acclimatized. With any luck, the views will more than repay the effort, but it's possible that everything will be hidden by clouds. Take plenty of sunscreen, water and very warm gear.

ARRIVAL AND DEPARTURE   CHIMBORAZO

By bus Buses from Riobamba to Guaranda pass the reserve entrance, from where it's an 8km hike to the first refuge.

By camioneta The lower *Hermanos Carrel* refuge can by reached in about 1hr 30min from Riobamba; the easiest way to get there is to take a camioneta from near the train station (about $40 one way, more if you want them to wait). Alternatively, you can arrange transport with your hotel or a tour operator (see box, p.167).

ACCOMMODATION

The **two refuges** in the reserve are not aimed at the general tourist but at hikers who stay there for a night or two before tackling the summit, so they are very basic lodgings with limited facilities.

CLIMBING CHIMBORAZO AND CARIHUAIRAZO

CLIMBING CHIMBORAZO

Although not Ecuador's most technically difficult ascent, the **climb** to the summit of Chimborazo from the Whymper refuge requires large reserves of strength and stamina, previous climbing experience and confidence with full mountaineering equipment. Full **acclimatization** is essential, and climbing several other peaks in advance, such as Iliniza Norte, Carihuairazo and even Cotopaxi, is common preparation. **The best months** for climbing Chimborazo are January and December; between June and October it can be windy, but the climb can be undertaken, weather permitting, year-round.

ROUTES TO THE SUMMIT

There are several **routes to the summit**; fast-changing conditions and the vagaries of the local climate make it imperative to go with a **guide** who knows the mountain well (see box, p.167). Most climbers set off around midnight or earlier, taking seven to ten hours to reach the summit from the Whymper refuge and about three to four to descend. The way up is relentlessly steep, and a long, hard slog, first over unstable rocky terrain, where route-finding is difficult, and then on snow and ice. Along with all the standard mountaineering equipment, you should wear a helmet because of the risk of rock fall in one section. The route tops out at the **Veintimilla summit** (6267m), from where it is a leg-sapping haul across a bowl of snow to the main **Whymper summit** (6268m). The mountain has three other summits – trying to conquer them all in one go (called *La Integral*) is a rarely achieved bravura feat carried off only by the most accomplished mountaineers.

CLIMBING CARIHUAIRAZO

Carihuairazo (5020m) can be approached on a rough track 14km northeast of the crossroads known as the *Cruce del Arenal* on the Ambato–Guaranda road. The track passes through **Mechahuasca**, the area used for rearing vicuñas as part of the reintroduction programme. From here it is about four hours' walk to good camping areas below the rocky slopes beneath the glacier; other scenic camping spots (at around 4300m) can be approached from **Urbina** in the south (see below), after a beautiful day's walk up the Mocha valley. Climbers typically leave around 3am and take about seven hours to get up and down. There's some ice climbing with a messy, mixed terrain scramble towards the top; crampons, ice axe and rope are essential. The true summit, a seemingly inaccessible tower of rock at the end of a precarious ridge, will be out of reach to all but the most experienced climbers.

IN THE RESERVE

★**Estrella del Chimborazo (Chimborazo Lodge)** Chimborazo Base Camp ☎ 03 2364278, ⌨ expediciones-andinas.com. Nicely decorated quasi-Alpine refuge-cum-lodge with traditional thatched roofs and timber beams, set in a grassy valley populated with alpacas, with the glistening glaciers of Chimborazo behind. It has eight double rooms with heating and hot water; bathrooms are shared between two rooms. Primarily lodging mountaineers and trekkers with Expediciones Andinas (see box, p.167), it's also available to other visitors. Book in advance. Half-board included, with lunch extra. **$134**

Refugio Hermanos Carrel With a similar level of facilities as the Refugio *Whymper*, and newly renovated and expanded with around 30 bunks, plus meals for sale as well as a kitchen. **$15**

Refugio Whymper The larger and more comfortable of the two refuges, where most climbers stay, was closed at the time of writing but due to reopen in 2016. It's got two fully equipped kitchens, a fire-warmed living room, bunk

beds, lockers (bring your own lock), cold water and solar-powered electricity. **$15**

AROUND THE RESERVE

Casa Cóndor Pulinguí San Pablo, 32km from Riobamba ☎ 0997580033 or ☎ 03 2606774, ⌨ facebook.com /cordtuch. Simple lodgings (3860m) built in vague avian form, with shared bathrooms, a dorm and a couple of private rooms. It's part of a community tourism project jointly run by two Puruháe villages, which offer guiding services, mountain climbing, bike rides, equipment rental, treks, hikes and camping in community grounds. Prices are inclusive of food and lodging. Dorms **$35**; doubles **$70**

Posada La Estación Opposite Urbina train station, Urbina, 26km north of Riobamba, off the Panamericana ☎ 0999694867. Former train station sitting on high moorland (3620m) converted into an attractive walkers' hostel, with a roaring fire in the dining room, hearty inexpensive meals and a simple shared bathroom with piping hot showers. It's owned by Alta Montaña in

Riobamba (see box, p.167), whose manager, Rodrigo Donoso, is an excellent English-speaking climber and guide, and can arrange hikes, bike rides and horse treks, as well as mountaineering expeditions. $28

Parque Nacional Sangay

Parque Nacional Sangay is Ecuador's largest highland reserve, a sprawling wilderness – and a UNESCO World Heritage Site – covering more than five thousand square kilometres of the eastern Andean cordillera, spilling down into the Amazon basin (see also p.251). The park's stunning sierra scenery takes in three volcanoes (Tungurahua, El Altar and Sangay), over three hundred lakes, pristine páramo and native cloudforest, and provides a habitat for spectacled bears, Andean condors, pumas and deer, among other mammals, while jaguars, monkeys and ocelots inhabit the lower, tropical areas.

There's very little infrastructure for tourists and no marked trail system. Apart from the **Guamote–Macas road**, slicing through the park from the sierra to the Oriente, access to Parque Nacional Sangay is via a number of remote, potholed dirt roads leading to the various *guarderías*, or **ranger stations**, serving the different areas of the park, often situated near local communities that can be reached by bus.

Starting at the northern end of the park, the main attractions begin with **Volcán Tungurahua** (5023m), a snowcapped volcano off limits at the time of writing due to renewed volcanic activity (see box, p.154). To the south is **El Altar**, the highest point in the park and the fifth-highest mountain in Ecuador. Once a volcano, an ancient eruption blew it asunder, leaving a jagged skeleton of rock, now a spectacular semicircle of nine summits teetering over a crater lake; it's a popular target for trekkers. Irascible **Volcán Sangay** (5230m), one of the world's most active volcanoes, is the third great peak in the park, a difficult-to-reach and hazardous climbing proposition. Both it and **El Placer hot springs** are approached from the village of Alao, reachable by bus from Riobamba. Further south, there's wonderful trekking around the **Lagunas de Atillo** and the **Lagunas de Ozogoche**, clutches of beautiful páramo lakes set in rugged scenery; although within the park's boundaries, these are accessed via the village of Guamote, so we cover them in that section (see p.173).

The **best months** to hike in these highland areas of Sangay are November to February, when the weather is at its driest and sunniest, though downpours can occur at any moment, so come prepared. Outside these months the area is prone to cold, wet, windy and sometimes foggy conditions.

El Altar

Some 25km east of Riobamba, **EL ALTAR** (5320m) is an extinct, heavily eroded volcano rising to the south of Volcán Tungurahua. Named Cupac Urcu, or "sublime mountain" in Kichwa, El Altar boasts a breathtaking amphitheatre of jagged, ice-capped peaks studded with hanging glaciers that are constantly rumbling and cracking. The principal of the volcano's nine craggy summits is **El Obispo**, a difficult technical climb not conquered until 1963 and best left to experienced mountaineers. Below, a crater is filled with the murky waters of **Laguna Amarilla** (4300m), sometimes dotted with blocks of ice that have calved off the glaciers above. A wide gap in the west side of the crater opens onto a flat plain known as the **Valle de Collanes**, providing easy access down to the lake.

Hiking to El Altar

El Altar can be reached on a highly rewarding two- to three-day round-trip **hike**, starting from the tiny village of **Candelaria**, a fifteen-kilometre drive down a dirt track southeast from the village of **Penipe**, which sits 22km northeast of Riobamba on the road to Baños. A popular option is to spend the first night at the *Hacienda Releche* (see below) before embarking on the five- to six-hour haul up to the Collanes plain at the foot of the volcano. The hacienda keeps a simple **refuge** (see below) up here, or you can camp. From the plain it's only a couple of hours up to the gap in the crater rim, from where you can scramble down to the edge of the lake in about thirty minutes. Heading back, count on taking about an hour to get back up to the plain and another three to four hours back to Candelaria; some stretches of the path get extremely muddy after rainfall, so consider taking gaiters or rubber boots. An alternative to doing it independently is to join a **guided hike** offered by tour operators in Riobamba (see box, p.167).

ARRIVAL AND DEPARTURE   CANDELARIA AND EL ALTAR

By bus There are five daily buses to Candelaria from the Terminal Oriental in Riobamba (1hr 30min). Alternatively, you can get to Penipe on any of the frequent Riobamba–Baños buses, then hire a truck from the square in Penipe (45min; about $15) – ask around.

ACCOMMODATION

Hacienda Releche 2km from Candelaria towards El Altar ✆ 03 3014067, ⊕ haciendareleche.com. A working farm with comfortable hostel facilities: doubles or bunk beds with shared bathrooms, hot water, fire-warmed living room and kitchen facilities ($10). Meals can be ordered in advance and the place offers guiding services ($50/day) and can hire out mules ($28 per trip, plus $30 for the muleteer). Dorms $13; doubles $27

Refugio Capac-Urcu Valle de Collanes, El Altar. Owned by *Hacienda Releche* (see above) but more basic, with bunks, cooking facilities and cold running water but no electricity; you'll also need your own sleeping bag. $13/person

El Placer thermal springs

About 25km east of the village of Alao, **El Placer** (which appropriately translates as "pleasure") is a fabulous natural pool filled with thermal water. There's a small changing area near the pool and a timber **refuge** (see p.172). It's inaccessible by vehicle, so you'll almost certainly have it to yourself – it's hard to imagine a more rewarding end to your hike than here.

Hiking to El Placer

The well-marked **trail** to El Placer initially follows an abandoned road east from Alao, and takes in some glorious scenery, including wild páramo, alpine forest and humid cloudforest. Just over nineteen kilometres along the road you'll come to pretty **Laguna Negra**, from where it's about a four-hour hike to El Placer. The full walk from Alao to El Placer takes approximately nine to eleven hours – you can camp en route. The terrain is not too difficult when dry, though it's tougher coming back. Note also that in the final section of the trail the path can be indistinct and overgrown, so check conditions in advance. This hike is definitely best done in dry, warm weather; you might still want to carry rubber boots with you to negotiate a few extremely muddy areas. You'll need the IGM maps of Alao, Llagtapamba and Volcán Altar.

ARRIVAL AND DEPARTURE   EL PLACER THERMAL SPRINGS

TO ALAO

By bus Buses leave Riobamba from the Terminal La Dolorosa on Puruhá and 10 de Agosto, eight blocks east of the Mercado San Francisco (Mon–Sat 6 daily, Sun 1 daily at 6.30am; 1hr 30min).

By camioneta From Riobamba to Alao a camioneta will cost around $50 for a one-way journey.

TOWARDS EL PLACER

By 4WD If you have your own transport or have come in from Riobamba by camioneta, it's sometimes possible in the dry season to do the first 15km in a sturdy 4WD, bringing you to within 4km of Laguna Negra.

By horse Horses or mules can be hired from Alao for about $15/day (ask in the village the day before), which can take you some of the way to the springs.

3

CLIMBING VOLCÁN SANGAY

FROM GUARGUALLÁ OR ALAO

Guarguallá has better access to Sangay than Alao, being closer and having better-equipped guides (if you are hiring locally), as well as having a basic hostel ($15). Contact the community tourism organization (☎03 3026688 or ☎0991213205). A daily bus runs to Guarguallá from Parque La Dolorosa in Riobamba at 1.30pm; there's an hourly bus to Alao from Parque La Dolorosa. Ask the park rangers in Alao to put you in touch with a certified guide or ask around in the village.

TACKLING THE SUMMIT

There are a couple of routes to the summit, both taking several days there and back, and you are likely to need a tent, though there are basic shelters along the way. The ascent itself (around 3–5hr up, 2hr down) is not strictly a technical climb but you will need crampons and an ice axe in case there is a lot of snow and ice near the top. It's usually climbed in the dark when it tends to be less cloudy and there's less risk of rock fall.

EQUIPMENT AND ADVICE

As well as your mountaineering equipment, consider bringing rubber boots for the atrocious mud on the way to base camp and a helmet to guard against falling rocks. Sulphur gas emissions can badly irritate the lungs and throat before you realize it, so don't hang around on the summit plateau. Do not underestimate the risks involved in doing this climb; you can get more advice from the SAE in Quito (see p.80), the Ministerio del Ambiente office and tour operators in Riobamba (see p.166 & box, p.167) before embarking on the trip.

ACCOMMODATION

Ranger station The ranger station in Alao has a few beds with use of a kitchen and bathroom. $\overline{\underline{55}}$

Refugio El Placer The refuge has bunks, running water, cooking facilities and a toilet. $\overline{\underline{55}}$

Volcán Sangay

Exquisitely symmetrical **Volcán Sangay** (5230m) is one of the most active volcanoes in the world, being in a state of continuous eruption since 1934. This makes any attempt to climb it a seriously risky undertaking due to frequent rock and ash explosions out of its three craters. Add to this the sheer inaccessibility of the mountain and it becomes clear why it's one of the lesser-climbed peaks in Ecuador. Yet significant numbers of undeterred, adrenaline-hungry climbers pass through determined to have a go – enough for there to be **guide** associations in Alao and Guarguallá. You can also arrange trips through the climbing agencies in Quito and Riobamba (see p.80 & see box, p.167). Due to tricky logistics and route finding, this is not an expedition to be undertaken without a guide.

South to Alausí

South of Riobamba, the Panamericana carves its way through increasingly wild country as it approaches the small town of **Guamote**, the site of one of the most enjoyable indigenous markets in the sierra. Rewarding side roads off this stretch of the highway head east to **Lagunas de Atillo** and **Lagunas de Ozogoche**, high on the páramo in **Parque Nacional Sangay**, while the Panamericana itself sweeps down to **Alausí**, the most southerly town of the central sierra.

Guamote

GUAMOTE (3050m), fifty kilometres south of Riobamba, is an attractive if slightly down-at-heel town sporting a few handsome timber buildings from the railway era in the early twentieth century, with their characteristic balconies leaning on thick wooden pillars. Guamote's main raison d'être is its massive Thursday-morning **market** that almost rivals Saquisilí with its size and vigour – don't miss, too, the chaotic **animal market** up in the field behind the Iglesia de San Vicente, where ducks, chickens, sheep, piglets and guinea pigs (ranked among the most delicious in the country) change hands.

ARRIVAL AND DEPARTURE GUAMOTE

By bus Buses to Guamote (hourly until 4pm; 1hr 30min) regularly leave Riobamba from Unidad Nacional and de la Prensa, close to the Terminal Terrestre. From Guamote they leave from outside the train station. After the last bus at 4pm, you can flag down a through bus on the Panamericana, 600m downhill from the town centre. **By train** The train station is in the middle of town, on the Calle Principal; check ⓦtrenecuador.com for details on the reopening of the Riobamba–Guamote line.

ACCOMMODATION

Chuza Longa García Moreno and Manabí ☏ 03 2916567, ⓦchuzalonga.com. Friendly guesthouse with three simple but spacious en-suite rooms upstairs and an attic dorm, with plenty of blankets to keep you warm. The downstairs restaurant/common area is heated by a fireplace and serves up a decent and varied menu. Dorms $15; doubles $30

Inti Sisa Vargas Torres and García Moreno ☏03 2916529, ⓦintisisa.org. Run by a non-profit organization working for community development, this hostal offers comfortable en-suite rooms or dorm beds and a pleasant communal area. They also organize hiking to the Lagunas de Ozogoche and visits to Chimborazo (both $60) and to local communities ($40), as well as horse riding ($45). Breakfast included; other meals can be arranged ($8–15). Dorms $25; doubles $65

Lagunas de Atillo and Ozogoche

South of the Guamote-Macas road, midway between the two towns, within the confines of Parque Nacional Sangay, lie two remote clusters of paramó lakes. More easily accessible are the **Lagunas de Atillo**, in whose freezing-cold waters the Puruháe people are said to have drowned their most reviled criminals in pre-Hispanic times. The most beautiful lake is **Laguna Magdalena**, dramatically framed by jagged, spiky peaks. A tough hike southwest (6–8hr; IGM map *Totoras and Alausí*) across a high pass takes you to the equally lovely **Lagunas de Ozogoche**, best known as the site of a curious phenomenon no one has been able to explain: periodically, in late September, hundreds of migratory plovers (locally called *cuvivi*) quite suddenly plunge deep into the icy waters of the lakes and kill themselves. Each year the Ozogoche community pays tribute to this little-understood event in a festival of traditional music and dancing, which visitors are welcome to attend; contact the Fundación Cultural Flores Franco on Velasco and Guayaquil in Riobamba for more details (☏03 2943168, ⓦfundacionartenativo.org.ec). Interestingly, the spur of mountain overlooking the lakes is known as Ayapungo – Kichwa for "door of death". If you're happy to overlook these morbid details, the area makes for great wild **camping** and hiking, though both Atillo and Ozogoche also offer some rudimentary accommodation, and places to eat.

ARRIVAL AND DEPARTURE LAGUNAS DE ATILLO AND OZOGOCHE

To Atillo Local buses leave from Olmedo and Velasco, a couple of blocks west of Riobamba's Mercado de San Francisco (Mon–Sat 5.30am, noon & 3pm, Sun 2.30pm; 2hr 30min). Passing buses from Riobamba to Macas also serve the village.
To Ozogoche There's no bus service here, so you'll need to hire a camioneta in Guamote or Alausí (around $35), which is easier on market days, or join a horse riding, hiking or biking tour from Riobamba (see p.167). If you have your own transport (4WD necessary), take the 36km dirt road branching east from the Panamericana at the village of Palmira, 20km south of Guamote, or take a shorter dirt road southwest from the Guamote–Macas road at Atillo.

THE DEVIL'S NOSE TRAIN RIDE

In 1899, after 25 years of frustrated plans and abortive attempts, work finally started on Ecuador's first **railway**, which would link the coastal city of Guayaquil with the capital, Quito, in the highlands – a feat finally achieved in 1908. The greatest obstacle, which prompted the line to be dubbed "the most difficult railway in the world", was met 130km east of Guayaquil at a near-vertical wall of rock, known as **El Nariz del Diablo (The Devil's Nose)**. The ingenious engineering solution was to carve a series of tight zigzags out of the rock, which allowed the train to climb 800m at a gradient of 1-in-18 by going forwards then backwards up the tracks.

Despite frequent delays and derailments, the service from Guayaquil to Riobamba and Quito ran, with interruptions, until 1997, when El Niño-related weather devastated the tracks. The entire Quito–Guayaquil route has now reopened (see p.27, p.78 & p.306), yet the most popular excursion remains the **12-km stretch from Alausí to Sibambe** (also known as Pistishi), at the end of the Devil's Nose descent. Although the inflated price, abandonment of rooftop travel and touristy nature of the trip have undoubtedly diminished the appeal of the journey, it still offers stunning views of Chimborazo and Carihuairazo and a thrilling descent down the Devil's Nose itself.

TAKING THE TRAIN

The train starts at Alausí (Tues–Sun & public holidays at 8am, 11am & 2pm), taking around two and a half hours for the return trip, including a spell in Sibambe, where you are treated to some staged traditional dancing and a small museum-cum-visitor centre, and can pick up some light refreshment. Sit on the right-hand side of the train for the descent, if you can, and take the less busy 8am journey. **Tickets** cost $30 and can be bought on the day at the train station. However, it's better to make an advance purchase by phone, online (☎ 1 800 873637, ⊛ trenecuador.com) or at one of the train stations (Alausí station ☎ 03 2930126; Mon–Fri 8am–4.30pm and before departures), especially if you plan to travel at the weekend or during a holiday period. The carriages have recently been refurbished but it's no longer possible to ride on the roof of the train, which was one of the big draws. Since the service is subject to unpredictable changes, call the station office ahead for the latest news. A connecting rail service between Riobamba and Alausí reopened in late 2015 (see box, p.166).

Alausí

ALAUSÍ (2350m), some 43km south of Guamote, lying far below the highway in a round valley enclosed by hills, is an atmospheric little railway town. Now that the restored **Nariz del Diablo train route** starts here (see box above), more tourists stay, which has helped enliven and smarten the place up, in particular the wide, leafy central boulevard, **Avenida 5 de Junio**, which is home to the town's few hotels, restaurants, banks (including ATMs) and, at the northern end, the main focus of activity, the train station.

ARRIVAL AND INFORMATION
ALAUSÍ

By bus Transportes Alausí on 5 de Junio and 9 de Octubre runs to Riobamba (every 30min until 6pm; last bus from Riobamba 7pm; 2hr 30min); Transportes Patria, on Colombia and 9 de Octubre, goes to Cuenca (6 daily; 4hr), Quito (7 daily; 5hr) and Riobamba (5 daily; 2hr). You can also flag down one of the frequent through buses on the Panamericana, a $1 taxi ride above the town, heading north or south.

Tourist office The I-Tur office on Av 5 de Junio close to the train station (daily 8am–5pm, closed 1hr for lunch; ☎ 03 2930153, ext 307) can provide you with a map and general tourist information, including details about the train at weekends when the station (see box above) is closed.

ACCOMMODATION

Gampala 5 de Junio and Pedro de Loza ☎ 03 2930 138. A modest though overpriced establishment, it is still one of the first to fill up, offering darkish rooms with decent beds,

flatscreen TVs and modern bathrooms. **$49**

Hosteria La Quinta Eloy Alfaro 121 ☎ 03 2930247, ⊛ hosteria-la-quinta.com. One of the best places to stay in town, with nice whitewashed stone walls, wooden beams and balconies, plus large windows to soak up the valley views. Rooms are comfortable, with stylish modern bathrooms, though rates are aimed at foreign tourists. Breakfast included. Cash only. $79

Killa Wasi Barrio Mullinquiz ☎0988603535, ⊛hostelalausi.com. Basic hostel for hardy travellers a 10min walk from town along the train tracks, on the friendly owner's organic farm. Mattresses are comfy and showers hot, but it can get pretty chilly at night once away from the courtyard log fire. Wednesday is pizza and rum night. Dorms $8; doubles $20; camping $5/person

Panamericana Corner of 5 de Junio and 9 de Octubre ☎03 2930156. Adequate rooms with shared or private bathroom and cable TV; there's also a restaurant attached. $15

EATING AND DRINKING

El Mesón del Tren Ricaurte and Eloy Alfaro, by the station ☎03 2930204. Unashamedly aimed at tourists taking the train, this pleasant colonial-style stone-and-brick restaurant right by the tracks can get choked with tour groups. Still, it serves up tasty food (mains $6–9), including decent desserts and some veggie options. Tues–Sun 8am–3pm.

Rincón del Compadre Hotel Gampala, 5 de Junio and Pedro de Loza ☎03 2930138. Probably your best bet for some nightlife: a range of alcoholic and non-alcoholic beverages and a pool table at the back. Mon–Thurs & Sun 1–10pm, Fri & Sat 1pm–midnight.

El Trigal 5 de Junio and Pedro de Loza. A clean and tidy café serving up inexpensive *comida típica*, including $3 almuerzos. Daily 7am–10pm.

3

The southern sierra

INGAPIRCA

The southern sierra

As you head south down the Panamericana from the central highlands, the snowcapped peaks and rumbling volcanoes give way to a softer, gentler landscape of lower elevations and warmer, drier climates. Ecuador's southern sierra – made up of the provinces of Cañar, Azuay and Loja – has a lonely, faraway feel to it, with its relatively sparse population, scarcity of large towns and long stretches of wild, uninhabited countryside. Its charms, however, are considerable, with some of the most rewarding and beautiful pockets of Ecuador tucked away here, including Cuenca, the country's most attractive colonial city, and Ingapirca, its pre-eminent Inca ruins, as well as the two alluring national parks of El Cajas and Podocarpus.

The main urban centre – and only large city – of the southern sierra is **Cuenca**, famed for its stunning colonial architecture and graceful churches and monasteries. It was raised on the site of the ruined city of Tomebamba, built by the **Incas** in the late fifteenth century following their conquest of the region, which had been occupied by the Cañari people for almost a thousand years (see pp.382–385). Virtually nothing remains of Tomebamba, but you can get an idea of the remarkable stonework the Incas were famous for – executed without iron to carve it or wheels to transport it – at the ruins of **Ingapirca**, Ecuador's only major Inca ruins, within easy striking distance of Cuenca. Also on Cuenca's doorstep is an attraction of a very different nature: the starkly beautiful wilderness of the **Parque Nacional El Cajas**, which provides some of the best back-country hiking and trout fishing in the country, though you'll often have to put up with a bit of rain and mist.

South of Cuenca, the sense of remoteness and abandonment increases as you pass mile after mile of largely uncultivated hills and pastures, though the few villages and one-horse towns staggered down the highway are slowly beginning to modernize, with the inevitable breeze-block constructions gradually encroaching on the steep cobbled streets, ageing stuccoed houses and grand old churches. The town of **Saraguro**, some 140km south of Cuenca, is a prime example; while some of the indigenous population maintain the centuries-old tradition of dressing in black, others feel more at home in jeans and baseball caps.

Further south, the small provincial capital of **Loja** is an island of comparative motion and activity, hemmed in by jagged, deep-green hills that soar over the town. It serves as a good jumping-off point for a couple of highly worthwhile excursions: east to the **Parque Nacional Podocarpus**, stretching down from the sierra to the tropical cloudforests of the Oriente, close to the old gold-mining town of **Zamora**; and south to the laidback tourist hangout of **Vilcabamba**, nestled in a peaceful mountain valley. Loja is also the starting point of the region's main direct bus service to **Peru** (see p.201).

Highlights

❶ Ingapirca On a striking hillside perch overlooking idyllic scenery, the best-preserved Inca ruin in the country displays exquisite trademark stonemasonry. **See p.181**

❷ Cuenca Ecuador's third-largest city is regarded as its most beautiful for its dignified architecture, flower-draped courtyards, cobbled streets and leafy plazas. **See p.183**

❸ Museo de Pumapungo This Cuenca museum is without a doubt the region's best, holding the remains of Tomebamba, the great city of the Inca's northern empire, and some stunning ethnographic exhibits. **See p.187**

❹ Parque Nacional El Cajas A stunning and easily accessed wilderness of sweeping páramo views, sparkling lakes and exposed crags caressed by whirling mists. **See p.193**

❺ Parque Nacional Podocarpus This beautiful national park descends from austere páramo into lush cloudforest – a memorable landscape teeming with wildlife and streaked with waterfalls and glinting rivers. **See p.204**

❻ Vilcabamba The slow pace of life in the valley – and the great hiking nearby – has rightly made this village a magnet for many travelling between Ecuador and Peru. **See p.207**

HIGHLIGHTS ARE MARKED ON THE MAP ON P.180

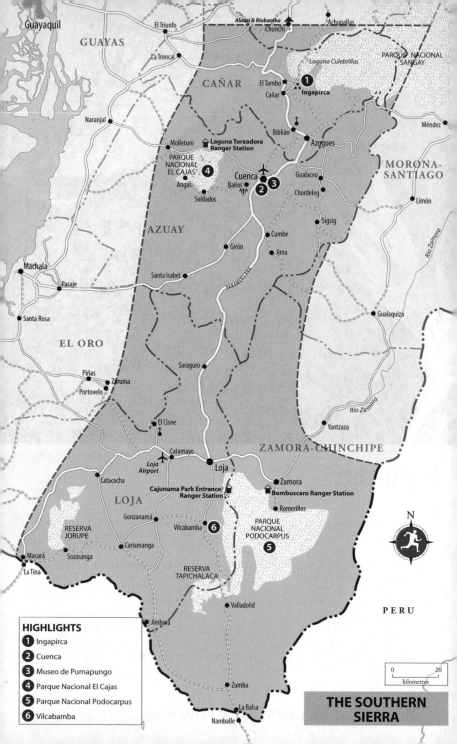

THE SOUTHERN SIERRA

HIGHLIGHTS

1. Ingapirca
2. Cuenca
3. Museo de Pumapungo
4. Parque Nacional El Cajas
5. Parque Nacional Podocarpus
6. Vilcabamba

0   20
kilometres

Ingapirca and around

7km southeast of El Tambo, on the Panamericana • Daily 9am–5.30pm • $6 including guided tour (1.5hr) in English or Spanish • ☎ 07 2217107 • To reach the ruins, turn off the highway in the town of El Tambo, which also provides access to the lesser-known Baño del Inca

Roughly midway between the central sierra town of Alausí (see p.174) and the southern sierra's main city, Cuenca, 79km to the south, stands Ecuador's premier Inca ruin, **INGAPIRCA**. Though not as dramatic or well preserved as the Inca remains in Peru, it is nonetheless an impressive site that certainly deserves a visit, if only to witness the extraordinary mortarless stonework for which the Incas are renowned.

Many of the buildings at Ingapirca have been dismantled, their large stone blocks hauled away by Spanish colonists to be used as foundations for churches and other buildings; however, the complex's central structure – known as the **Temple of the Sun**, or the Adoratorio – remains substantially intact and dominates the whole site.

The rest of the site consists mainly of low foundation walls, possibly the remains of storehouses, dwellings and a great plaza, among other things. There's not a great deal left, but the **guides** can explain various theories about what once stood where. They'll also take you to the nearby **Cara del Inca** ("Inca's Face"), a huge rock face resembling a human profile with a hooked nose, as well as several other rock-hewn curiosities, including the **Casa del Sol** with its circular, supposedly astronomical, carvings, or the **Silla del Inca ("Inca's Chair")**, a large boulder with a chair cut into it – actually a broken piece of a small Inca bath from the hill above. There's also a small **museum** (with attached book and craft shop) displaying Cañari and Inca pots, tools and jewellery, and a skeleton found on the site.

Brief history

Perched on a breezy hill commanding fine views over the surrounding countryside, Ingapirca, which roughly translates as "Inca wall", was built during the **Inca** expansion into Ecuador towards the end of the fifteenth century, on a site that had been occupied by the **Cañari** people for over five hundred years. The Incas destroyed most of the Cañari structures (though a burial site remains), replacing them with their own elaborate complex that probably functioned as a place of worship, a fortress and a *tambo* (or way-station) on the **Inca Royal Road** connecting Cusco to Quito.

The Temple of the Sun

The **Temple of the Sun** is composed of an immense oval-shaped platform whose slightly inward-tapering walls are made of exquisitely carved blocks of stone, fitted together with incredible precision. Steps lead up to a trapezoidal doorway – a classic feature of Inca architecture – that gives onto the remains of a rectangular building within the platform. It is the superior quality of the platform's stonework, usually reserved for high-status buildings, that suggests this was a ceremonial temple.

Baños del Inca

6km from Ingapirca • Daily 8am–5pm • $1; entry includes access to the ruins and a new interpretive centre • The site is a 6km walk from Ingapirca, taking the right fork out of Ingapirca village; alternatively, make the 20min journey in autoferro from El Tambo station (Wed–Sun; $7 return including entry to the ruins)

There's another obscure but interesting ruin near Ingapirca, off the road towards El Tambo near the little village of **Coyoctor**. The **Baños del Inca** is an Inca bathing complex chiselled out of an enormous rock with channels and receptacles eventually leading out onto the adjacent field for irrigation. Restored in the last few years, the site is worth a visit.

4

ARRIVAL AND DEPARTURE	INGAPIRCA AND AROUND

The two access roads for Ingapirca leave the Panamericana at **El Tambo** and **Cañar** (7km south), and meet in the middle at the small village – also known as **Ingapirca** – overlooking the archeological site, which is a 5min walk away.

BY BUS

From Cañar/El Tambo Buses run from Cañar to Ingapirca and back via El Tambo every 15–20min, passing through Ingapirca village. Return buses leave from the village square.

From Cuenca Frequent buses run along the Panamericana between Cuenca, Cañar and El Tambo (daily every 30min; 1hr 30/40min; last bus 6pm), where you can hop on a local

bus to Ingapirca. In addition, Transportes Cañar buses come directly to the site entrance from the Cuenca bus terminal (Mon–Fri 9am &12.20pm, returning 1pm & 3.45pm; Sat & Sun 9am, returning 1pm; 2hr; $3.50).

BY CAMIONETA

Camionetas sit in the main square in Ingapirca ($7 to Cañar, $5 to El Tambo).

ACCOMMODATION

Cabañas El Castillo 100m from the ruins ☎ 07 2217002, ✉ cab.castillo@hotmail.com. Very basic but clean accommodation with five rooms, offering comfortable beds, a bath and shower with hot water, and the best view of the ruins from the front porch. Also has a small restaurant. **$30**

Posada Ingapirca 300m up the road above the ruins ☎ 07 2831120, ⊕ posadaingapirca.com. Lovely

120-year-old farmhouse set in pleasant grounds with splendid views. Rustic rooms offer plenty of natural light, and the place is wonderfully decorated with traditional textiles, hats and utensils. Larger, pricier rooms have their own fireplace – necessary as it's very cold at night – and the decent restaurant is popular with tour groups at lunchtime. Breakfast included. **$105**

THE INCA TRAIL TO INGAPIRCA

The **Inca Trail to Ingapirca** is a three-day hike following a 40km stretch of the route – and in some parts the original path – of the **Inca Royal Road**, which once linked Cusco, the Inca capital, with Tomebamba (where Cuenca now stands) and Quito. The **terrain** you'll cover is mainly wild, open páramo, with some beautiful ridge walks giving fantastic views. Most of it is uninhabited, but the final 8km or so is quite populated with *campesinos*, and you'll probably get a lot of begging from kids asking for sweets, pencils or money. The hike begins in the tiny village of **Achupallas**, where there's a Saturday market.

MAPS AND EQUIPMENT

If you're hiking independently, it's essential to take the IGM maps of Alausí, Juncal and Cañar, as well as full camping equipment and warm, waterproof clothing. Rubber boots or gaiters will be needed for the boggy spots. Try to take as light a bag as possible, though, as you'll be hiking between 3100m and 4400m, which can be quite hard going, though you can hire a mule (and muleteer) for your gear in Achupallas ($30–40/day).

THE ROUTE

The hike is commonly divided as follows: day one takes you from Achupallas up the Tres Cruces valley to the Laguna Las Tres Cruces (6–8hr), though you may want to cut this hard day short and pitch your tent in the páramo a couple of hours short of the lakes; day two takes you from Laguna Las Tres Cruces to a small collection of Inca ruins known as Paredones, by the shore of Laguna Culebrillas (6–7hr); and day three goes from there to the Ingapirca ruins (4–5hr), where there is a campground right by the ruins.

ARRIVAL

Achupallas is an hour's drive from **Alausí** (see p.174). Colectivo trucks and camionetas leave Alausí for Achupallas daily (11am–4pm), except Saturdays; private trucks cost around $15. There's also an unreliable daily bus at around 1–2pm from the corner of 5 de Junio and 9 de Octubre.

ACCOMMODATION

Ingañán Achupallas ☎ 03 2930663. Most hikers set off from Alausí between 5 and 6am (pickup to Achupallas around $15). Alternatively, you could turn up in Achupallas

the day before you want to start walking – there's a small family-run hostel here called *Ingañán*, where you can also order meals. Camping is also possible. **$24**

Cuenca

Santa Ana de los Cuatro Ríos de Cuenca, otherwise known simply as **CUENCA** (2530m), is Ecuador's most seductive colonial city. A classic example of a planned Renaissance town in the Americas, Cuenca's *centro histórico* is a UNESCO World Heritage Site and shares many architectural features with Quito's old town: narrow, cobbled streets, harmonious, balconied houses with interior courtyards and an abundance of gleaming white churches and monasteries – all presented without the pollution, noise and overbearing crowds of the capital.

Despite being Ecuador's third-largest city, Cuenca's colonial centre, which contains most of the city's attractions, is a very manageable size and can easily be explored on foot. You'll need several days here to take in a few churches and museums, sample the city's diverse restaurants and bars and do some shopping and excursions. If possible, try to make your stay coincide with a Friday or Saturday evening, when the town's churches (usually open daily 8am–4pm, but closed for an hour or two at lunch), are illuminated to stunning effect, or a Sunday during the day, when traffic is kept out of the main square.

If you visit during one of Cuenca's multi-day **festivals** – around April 12 for the city's foundation and November 3 for its independence – you'll be treated to plenty of spectacle, no more so than for the "Pase del Niño" on Christmas Eve, a huge colourful procession of children and families, floats, dancers and biblical tableaux.

Brief history

Founded by the Spanish on April 12, 1557, Cuenca was not the first dazzling city to be erected here: the Inca Tupac Yupanqui founded the city of **Tomebamba** here around 1470, which was said to have rivalled Peru's Cusco with its splendour. Its glory was short-lived, however, as the city was destroyed during the Inca civil war that broke out during the second decade of the sixteenth century. By the time Cieza de León (one of the chroniclers of the Spanish conquest) saw it in 1547, Tomebamba was in ruins, but enough remained to evoke its former grandeur: "These famous lodgings of Tumibamba were among the finest and richest to be found in all Peru … The fronts of many of the buildings are beautiful and highly decorative, some of them set with precious stones and emeralds … Today, all is cast down and in ruins, but it can still be seen how great they were". These days, Cuenca's Inca legacy has all but vanished, hinted at only by the foundation stones of some of its buildings, and some modest ruins excavated in the twentieth century.

Parque Calderón

At the heart of Cuenca's colonial centre is the splendid, leafy **Parque Calderón**, filled with tall pines and palms as well as neatly trimmed flowerbeds. It is framed by the city's two main religious landmarks, the Catedral Nueva and Catedral Vieja, making it the most impressive square in Cuenca. It's also the starting point for the popular open-top city bus tour (see p.189) as well as the location of the very helpful tourist office (see p.189), all of which makes the park a good place to start your exploration of the historical sites.

Catedral Nueva

Parque Calderón, Benigno Malo • Daily 8am–4pm, but closed for an hour or so at lunch • Free

Perhaps the most distinctive feature of Cuenca, and clearly visible from most parts of town, are the large, sky-blue domes of the nineteenth-century **Catedral Nueva** (officially called La Catedral de la Inmaculada Concepción). The domes sit towards the back of the building over a jumble of outsized turrets, arches and buttresses, fronted by an immense twin-towered facade looming over the square. Inside, the large central nave is flanked by gorgeous stained-glass windows and pink marble pillars, but the pièce de résistance is the altar set beneath a gleaming baroque baldaquin, dripping with gold leaf.

Museo Catedral Vieja

Parque Calderón, Luis Cordero • Mon–Fri 9am–1pm & 2–6pm, Sat & Sun 10am–1pm • $2 • ☎ 07 2834636

The city's oldest – and now deconsecrated – church, the modest **Catedral Vieja** (or El Sagrario) houses a religious museum. Occupying the site of a mud-and-straw chapel built immediately after the city was founded, and then expanded in 1567 using the stones of the destroyed city of Tomebamba, the present building largely dates from the late eighteenth century, and is characterized by its low, horizontal outline, simple, whitewashed walls, clay-tiled roof and central bell tower, used by La Condamine's geodesic mission as a reference point to measure the shape of the Earth (see p.387). Following a lengthy restoration, original frescos dating back to the late sixteenth century have been uncovered on the walls; most of the other murals are from the early twentieth century.

Plaza de las Flores

Just off the Parque Calderón, on Calle Sucre, is the Plazoleta del Carmen – a tiny square more commonly known as the **Plaza de las Flores** – which is home to a daily **flower market**, presided over by *chola* women wearing blue- or pink-checked aprons, long black plaits and Panama hats. Right behind it stands the **Iglesia El Carmen de la Asunción**, a white-walled, eighteenth-century church with a beautiful carved-stone portico.

Plaza San Francisco

The market square **Plaza San Francisco**, on Córdova and Padre Aguirre, promises a diverse mix of chunky knitwear, wall hangings and cheap clothes and shoes. Plaza San Francisco is overlooked by the peach-and-white **Iglesia San Francisco** (daily 8am–4pm, but closed for an hour or two at lunch; free), which was rebuilt in the early twentieth century in a Neocolonial style, and sports smooth, stuccoed walls embellished with lots of plaster relief. Inside, the only survivors of the original church, built in the eighteenth century, are the high altar adorned by a carving of the Virgin de la Inmaculada by Bernardo de Legarda, the famous Quito School sculptor (see box, p.66), and the gold-leaf pulpit.

Iglesia Santo Domingo

Gran Colombia and Padre Aguirre • Daily, generally 8am–4pm, but closed for an hour or two at lunch • Free

The grey-blue, twin-towered **Iglesia Santo Domingo** is another early twentieth-century church built in the colonial style. It's worth popping inside to admire the intricate geometric motifs covering every inch of the arches and ceilings, and the series of eighteenth-century paintings on the walls, depicting the Mysteries of the Rosary.

Museo Municipal Casa del Sombrero

Arízaga between Luis Cordero and Borrero • Mon–Fri 9am–1pm & 3–6pm, Sat 9am–1pm • Free, including guided tour (in Spanish)

The granting of cultural heritage status to Ecuador's Panama hat by UNESCO in 2012 coincided with the establishment of the **Museo Municipal Casa del Sombrero**, a delightfully restored old Panama hat workshop on a hillside six blocks north of Parque Calderón, whose adobe walls are made from the same straw used in the fabrication of the hats. The "living museum" showcases the city's hat-making history and the production process through old photographs and artefacts – including a $6000 sombrero – as well as offering free instruction to young would-be artisans led by experienced hat-makers. You can watch them at work in the courtyard (Mon, Wed & Fri) or buy a hat from their showroom, but don't forget to climb up to the roof terrace, to take in the superb view of the city centre.

Iglesia San Sebastián

Northwest corner of Parque San Sebastián • Daily 8am–4pm, but closed for an hour or two at lunch • Free

One of the city's oldest churches, the **Iglesia San Sebastián** marks the western limit of Cuenca's *centro histórico*. It was built in the seventeenth century and features a single bell tower over the right-hand side of the entrance, giving the church a slightly lopsided appearance. The quiet little square in front of it was the scene of Cuenca's most scandalous crime of the eighteenth century, when the surgeon of the French geodesic mission was murdered over his love affair with a creole woman.

Museo de Arte Moderno

Parque San Sebastián, Sucre and Talbot • Mon–Fri 9am–5.30pm, Sat & Sun 9am–1pm • Free • ☎ 07 2831027

The single-storey whitewashed building with blue windows spanning the southern side of Parque San Sebastián was built in 1876, and has served as a temperance house, a prison, an asylum for beggars and an old people's home, and currently houses the municipal **Museo de Arte Moderno**. The museum puts on high-quality temporary exhibitions of national and Latin American artists.

Museo del Sombrero

Calle Larga 10-04 • Mon–Fri 9am–6pm, Sat 9.30am–5pm, Sun 9.30am–1.30pm • Free • ☎ 07 2831569

Worth a peek is the Panama hat workshop and shop (see p.192) of Rafael Paredes & Hijos, which incorporates the **Museo del Sombrero**, where you'll be coached through the various stages of hat creation and shown a selection of antique hat-making implements, including a nineteenth-century contraption used for measuring the shape of the head.

Museo Remigio Crespo Toral

Calle Larga 7-07 • Mon–Fri 9am–5pm, Sat 9am–1pm • Free • ☎ 07 2830499

The main reason to visit Cuenca's oldest museum, the **Museo Remigio Crespo Toral**, is to admire the beautifully restored former home of Dr Remigio Crespo Toral, a nineteenth-century intellectual and diplomat. A museum since 1946, it comprises a small but noteworthy collection of pre-Hispanic ceramics and tools, documents dating from the city's foundation, religious paintings and sculpture and a *salón* furnished as it was left by Dr Crespo.

Museo de las Conceptas

Entrance at Hermano Miguel 6-33 • Mon–Fri 9am–6.30pm, Sat 10am–1pm • $2.50 • ☎ 07 2823002

A couple of blocks southeast of the Parque Calderón, the **Monasterio de las Conceptas**, founded in 1599, hides behind the thick white walls that separate its occupants from the outside world. Part of the convent is open to the public as the **Museo de las Conceptas**. The museum houses a large collection of predominantly religious paintings and sculpture from the seventeenth to nineteenth centuries, as well as nineteenth-century toys in room 12, including some small wooden dolls and music boxes, brought here by young novices entering the convent.

While you're here, take a look at the attached **Iglesia de las Conceptas**, giving onto Presidente Córdova, which features a flamboyant steeple, some finely carved wooden doors and an impressive gold-leaf altar.

Museo de las Culturas Aborígenes

Calle Larga 5-24 and Cueva • Mon–Fri 8.30am–6.30pm, Sat 9am–1pm • $2, including guided tour in Spanish, English or French • ☎ 07 2839181

The **Museo de las Culturas Aborígenes** exhibits an excellent, wide-ranging and well-presented collection of pre-Columbian ceramics and artefacts, beginning with Stone Age tools, flints and dinosaur teeth and ending with accomplished Inca earthenware. With over five thousand pieces, this is one of the best private collections in the country. There's also a good shop and café.

Along the Río Tomebamba

The southern limit of old Cuenca is marked by **Calle Larga**, which runs parallel with and backs on to the Río Tomebamba. You can't see the river from the street but a set of **stone steps** at the southern end of Hermano Miguel, known as La Escalinata, leads down to the **riverside**, which affords wonderful views onto the backs of Calle Larga's grand houses, hanging precipitously over the steep riverbank.

Museo de Artes Populares

3 de Noviembre, at the bottom of La Escalinata • Mon–Fri 8am–5pm, Sat 10am–1pm • Free • ☎ 07 2840919, ⓦ cidap.gob.ec

The excellent Centro Interamericano de Artesanías y Artes Populares (CIDAP) has a small but highly enjoyable **Museo de Artes Populares**, bringing together arts and crafts from all over Latin America in changing exhibitions. It also has a fine craft shop, which is a good place to pick up a souvenir (see p.192).

Iglesia Todos los Santos

Calle Larga and Jervés • Daily 8am–4pm, but closed for an hour or two at lunch • Free

Heading east from La Escalinata along the riverbank, you'll come to the white **Iglesia Todos los Santos**, which rises impressively over the Río Tomebamba. It's thought that the first Catholic Mass in Cuenca took place here. The current building dates from the late nineteenth century.

Puente Roto

Half a block east of the Iglesia Todos los Santos is the **Puente Roto** (Broken Bridge), the remains of an old stone bridge, now used as a viewpoint onto the river and the site of a Saturday art fair (10am–5pm) and occasional cultural events.

Museo de Pumapungo

Calle Larga and Huayna Capac • Tues–Fri 8am–5.30pm, Sat & Sun 10am–4pm; last entry 1hr before closing • Free

At the eastern end of Calle Larga is the **Museo de Pumapungo** (formerly the Museo del Banco Central), Cuenca's most polished and absorbing museum. Right behind the main museum building is the **Pumapungo archeological park**, which is where most of the artefacts displayed in the museum's archeological *sala* were found and where the most important religious buildings of Tomebamba were located, though there's little to see now.

The ground floor

The ground floor contains an interactive, and at times overly dark, exhibition devoted to the Inca city of Tomebamba, displaying some beautiful **Inca artefacts** including jewellery, fertility symbols and ritualistic objects, as well as a couple of entertaining dioramas. Much of the information is given in English, Spanish and Kichwa. Also on the ground floor is a collection of **nineteenth-century art**, dominated by religious paintings and sombre portraits, but with some wonderful *costumbrista* (folk art) pieces showing indigenous people dancing, playing the fiddle and roasting a hog.

The Sala Etnográfica Nacional

The highlight of the museum is the **Sala Etnográfica Nacional** extending across the whole of the first floor, which illustrates the diversity of Ecuador's indigenous cultures using everyday objects and reconstructions. Displays include an extraordinary exhibition of Shuar *tsantsas* (shrunken heads) from the southern Oriente; a model of a masked dancer from the southern sierra; a collection of festival costumes; and many musical instruments. Though most of the information is given in Spanish, many of the exhibits are self-explanatory. In the basement there's a collection of coins and notes.

Mirador de Turi

A taxi to the *mirador* costs about $3 each way; daytime buses to Turi leave from the corner of 12 de Abril and Solano, on the southern bank of Río Tomebamba, and will drop you at the bottom of the hill, from where it's a 30min walk up more than 400 steps to the *mirador*; the viewpoint is also the last stop on the city bus tour (see p.189)

The best spot for a panoramic view of the whole city is the **Mirador de Turi**, a lookout point in front of the Iglesia de Turi, perched high on a hill some 4km south of the centre. The **views** are particularly theatrical on Friday and Saturday evenings when the city could almost be mistaken for a lavish Hollywood film set, with all its church steeples floodlit. There's also a good restaurant. Not far from the top is the **Galería Eduardo Vega** (see p.192), well worth a stop for its gorgeous glazed ceramics made on site by Ecuador's leading ceramicist – a good place to pick up a gift or two.

ARRIVAL AND DEPARTURE

CUENCA

BY PLANE

TAME operates daily direct flights between Cuenca and Quito, and Cuenca and Guayaquil. In addition, several international airlines connect Cuenca with international destinations in Latin and North America and even Europe, via Quito or Guayaquil. Aeropuerto Mariscal Lamar (☎07 2862203) is only 2.5km east of the centre along Avenida España. The easiest way to and from the airport is by taxi ($2), or by tram (see below).

Airlines TAME, Florencio Astudillo 2-22, opposite the Millennium Plaza (☎07 4103199) and at the airport (☎07 2866400, ⌨tame.com.ec); Avianca, Miguel Cordero and Paucarbamba (☎07 2455563, ⌨avianca.com/es-ec).

Destinations Guayaquil (2–3 daily; 40min; from $73 one-way); Quito (Mon–Fri 5–7 daily, Sat & Sun 3–4 daily; 55min; from $63 one-way).

BY BUS

Terminal Terrestre The main bus terminal, from which all long-distance and most other buses leave, is 1.8km from the centre, close to the airport on Avenida España. There's an information office (Mon–Sat 8.30am–noon & 2.30–6pm; ☎07 2868482) that's good for travel advice and maps. The easiest way to get into the centre is by taxi ($2) or by tram (see below).

Destinations Ambato (every 30min–1hr, plus numerous through buses to Quito; 7hr); Azogues (every 5min; 30min); Cañar and El Tambo (every 15min; 1hr 30/40min); Chordeleg (every 30min; 1hr 15min); Girón (served by buses to Machala every 15–30min; 40min); Gualaceo (every 15min; 50min); Guayaquil (every 20min via El Cajas, every 25min via Cañar; 4–5hr); Huaquillas (8 daily; 5hr); Ingapirca (Mon–Fri 2 direct daily, Sat & Sun 1 daily; 2hr); Loja (every 30min–1hr; 4hr 30min); Macas (12 daily via Guarumales; 8hr); Machala (every 15–30min; 4hr); Quito (every 30min–1hr; 9hr); Riobamba (every 40min; 6hr); Santo Domingo (10 daily; 10hr); Sigsig (every 30min; 1hr 40min).

Terminal Sur A much smaller bus terminal, Terminal Sur, is 2km west of the city centre by the Feria Libre, the vast open market off Avenida de las Americas. Some transport departs from here, including Transportes Occidental buses to Molleturo, via the El Cajas park entrance at Laguna Toreadora (8 daily; 45min).

GETTING AROUND

On foot The city centre is confined to a fairly compact grid on the northern bank of the Río Tomebamba, and it's easy enough to get to most sights on foot.

By tram At the time of writing, the first line of the city's new tram system was scheduled for completion in late 2016. Extending just over 10km, with 27 stops, it links the airport and bus terminal on Avenida España with the historic centre; heading west in the centre, the line runs along Lamar then out to Avenida de Las Americas. On the return trip to the bus terminal and airport from the centre, the tram runs east along Gran Colombia. Fares had not been fixed, but were likely to be ¢25–50.

TOURS AROUND CUENCA

Most of Cuenca's **tour operators** offer fairly similar trips to Parque Nacional El Cajas, Ingapirca, the craft villages of Gualaceo, Chordeleg and Sigsig, and to the scenic Yunguilla valley and Girón waterfall, with cheaper group excursions or pricier tailor-made private tours. Most operators are closed on Sunday.

Expediciones Apullacta Gran Colombia 11-02 and General Torres (☎07 2837815, ⌨apullacta .com. Well-organized outfit offering a wide array of tours, from guided day-hikes ($68/person) to overnight camping trips to Parque Nacional El Cajas ($210/person), and from local rock climbing and canyoning to multi-day trips all over the country. Camping gear is also available for rent (tent $15/night, sleeping bag $8/night).

Kushi Waira Enquire at the Carolina Bookstore, Hermano Miguel 4–36 and Calle Larga, ⌨kushiwaira .com. Community-based tourism in Tarqui parish. Take a day-trip ($40/person), or stay overnight and learn about village life, from cheese-making to growing medicinal plants, collective agriculture to spinning wool.

Red de Pakariñan Sucre 14-96 Sucre, and Coronel Talbot (☎07 2820529, ⌨pakarinan.com. Works with indigenous communities across five southern provinces, including Saraguro (see p.197), in community-based tourism; can arrange two- or three-day stays.

Terra Diversa Calle Larga 8-41 and Luis Cordero (☎07 2823782, ⌨terradiversa.com. The leading tour operator in Cuenca, and a great place to get tour information, brochures and maps. As well as the usual excursions, it offers horse treks in the countryside around Cuenca ($75/person), mountain-bike rides to Ingapirca ($151/person) and can even organize trips to the Galápagos or to other destinations in Latin America.

Car rental There are several outlets at the airport, or nearby on Avenida España and Elias Liut, including Austral (☎07 286246); Avis (☎07 2860174); Bombuscaro (☎07 2866541); Hertz (☎07 2806147); and Localiza (☎07 4084632).

By taxi You can flag down a metred yellow taxi on any of the main streets, with rides within the city centre costing $1.50, and around $2 to the airport or bus terminal.

INFORMATION AND TOURS

Tourist office The I-Tur office on Parque Calderón, Sucre and Benigno Malo (Mon–Fri 8am–8pm, Sat 9am–4pm, Sun 8.30am–1.20pm; ☎07 2821035, ⓦcuencaecuador .com.ec) has numerous maps and leaflets, including *Agendas Culturales*, which lists the month's cultural events (also on the website). They also have detailed information on Parque Nacional El Cajas.

Bus tours Parque Calderón is the starting point for the city's popular open-top bus tour (Mon–Sat & public holidays 9am–7pm, hourly except 1 & 2pm; Sun 10am, 11am, noon & 3pm; 1hr 45min; $8), which sets off from outside the Catedral Vieja and ends up at the city's top viewpoint, the Mirador de Turi.

ACCOMMODATION

Cuenca boasts a wide choice of mid-priced and upmarket hotels, many of them in restored **colonial-style houses**, while the **budget accommodation** scene is only just beginning to take off. Wherever you plan to stay, it's best to **book ahead** if arriving on a Friday – or any kind of fiesta (see p.183) – as Cuenca is a popular weekend destination with Ecuadorians, and accommodation can fill quite quickly; high season is July–Sept.

★**Alternative Hostel** Corner of Huayna Capac and Cacique Duma ☎07 4084101, ⓦalternativehostal .com. The 15min walk from the centre is more than made up for by this excellent-value, friendly, modern hostel with comfy sofas, TV/DVD player, reading lounge, good kitchen-dining facilities, washing machine, small patio terrace and luggage storage. Dorms $9; doubles $20

El Cafecito Vásquez 7-36 and Luis Cordero ☎07 2832337, ⓦcafecito.net. Popular budget rooms and dorms with shared or private bathrooms, set around an attractive courtyard filled with wooden tables and potted plants. It's also a café-restaurant-bar so can be noisy some nights; the quietest rooms face the back. Dorms $6; doubles $25

★**Casa del Águila** Sucre 13-56 between Montalvo and De Toral ☎07 2836498, ⓦhotelcasadelaguila.com. Lovingly restored nineteenth-century mansion, with gorgeous individually decorated rooms, painted in warm, natural colours with distinctive flourishes – but don't expect modern frills such as high-speed wi-fi, or a TV. Staff are friendly and efficient, and rates include parking and a full buffet breakfast. $80

La Cigale Vásquez 7-80 ☎07 2835308, ⓦlacigale cuencana.jimdo.com. This appealing French-owned hostel is in a lovely restored old building set around a courtyard café-restaurant, which boasts live music most weekends, so it can get noisy. En-suite doubles are neat but small and you can bag a cheap bed in a six-bed dorm for very little. Breakfast included for rooms. Dorms $7; doubles $27

La Cofradía del Monje Córdova 10-33 and Aguirre ☎07 2831251, ⓦhostalcofradiadelmonje.com. Smart timber-floored rooms, some with balconies overlooking Plaza San Francisco and the domes of the new cathedral beyond, others rather small for the price. It also has a café, bar and restaurant. Breakfast included. $60

★**Hostal Macondo** Tarqui 11-64 and Lamar ☎07 2821700, ⓦhostalmacondo.com. Quiet, beautiful old house with waxed wooden floors, high ceilings, spotless rooms – with shared (cheaper) or private bathrooms – and a delightful garden with chairs and hammock. Breakfast included. $61

Hostal Yacumama Luis Cordero 5–66 and Vásquez ☎07 2834353, ⓦhostalyakumama.com. Popular Inca-themed hostel offering bamboo beds in a vast attic dorm, or more conventional beds in smaller dorms. There's also a handful of spacious doubles – well away from the cosy bar-restaurant at the front, but they can get noisy during events or when the skateboard ramp's being well utilized in the pleasant courtyard at the back. Dorms $8; doubles $29

Hotel Cuenca Borrero 10-69 between Gran Colombia and Lamar ☎07 2833711, ⓦhotelcuenca.com.ec. Housed in a distinctive old building, this friendly hotel features recently remodelled rooms of varying sizes with high ceilings, brightly painted walls and a decent amount of furniture. Good reductions in low season and an excellent buffet breakfast included. $70

Hotel Rosamia Machuca 9–43, between Bolívar and Gran Colombia ☎07 2844387, ⓦhotelrosamia.com. A spanking new addition to the budget hotel scene, whose simple, spotless rooms with compact beds are more nicely furnished than you'd expect for the price. Breakfast included. $40

Hotel Santa Lucía Borrero 8-44 ☎07 2828000, ⓦsantaluciahotel.com. Beautiful boutique hotel in a fine old house, tastefully restored with generously furnished en-suite rooms – most come equipped with bathtub, safe, plasma-screen TV, minibar and lots of trimmings. There's also parking, a restaurant and café, and a drawing room complete with grand fireplace. $165

4

Mansión Alcázar Bolívar 12-55 and Tarqui ☎07 2823918, ⓦmansionalcazar.com. Exquisitely renovated colonial building housing one of Cuenca's most luxurious hotels, boasting a grand courtyard converted into a stately drawing room complete with chandelier and fountain, a tropical garden and an outstanding gourmet restaurant. The sumptuous rooms are fragrant with the scent of the freshly scattered petals on the beds – some of which are four-posters – and service is impeccable. $306

La Orquidea Borrero 9-31 and Bolívar ☎07 2824511, ⓦlaorquidea.com.ec. Not a bad deal given its central location. Make sure you get one of the newer rooms upstairs, which are simply furnished and have good-quality en-suite bathrooms and cable TV; some have fridges. Reduced rates if you stay several days. $36

Posada del Ángel Bolívar 14-11 and De Toral ☎07 2840695, ⓦhostalposadadelangel.com. Popular mid-range option with two brightly painted, plant-filled covered courtyards to lounge in, plus comfortable en-suite rooms (for one to four people) boasting plenty of storage space and cable TV. There's a garage too. $80

Posada Todos Santos Calle Larga 3-42 and Ordóñez ☎07 2824247. Well-maintained hostal with nice, carpeted rooms and good en-suite showers. The friendly owners are knowledgeable about sights and activities in the region. $35

Villa del Rosario Vásquez and Mariano Cueva 5-25 ☎07 2828585. Friendly and quiet, this family-owned converted colonial house has basic but prettily painted en-suite rooms set round a flower-filled courtyard. There are shared kitchen facilities and an open-sided dining area with TV, which makes for a chilly social area at night. $24

EATING

Cuenca offers the best choice of restaurants outside Quito, with the usual staple of cheap lunches supplemented by snacks such as crêpes and burritos, as well as fine **international cuisines** in sumptuous surroundings and high-quality *comida típica*. Inexpensive almuerzos can be found at the **comedores** above the Mercado 10 de Agosto, on Calle Larga and General Torres. What follows is only a fraction of a vast array of culinary delights.

CAFÉS

Café Austria Corner of Hermano Miguel and Bolívar ☎07 2840899. Though no longer Austrian-owned, the great corner location, large windows and mellow atmosphere here make this a choice spot for people-watching, though the quality of the food doesn't always live up to the ambience. You need to get here early to catch the famous *apfelstrudel* but there's always happy hour to console latecomers. Daily 9.30am–10.30pm.

Café Nucallacta Hermano Miguel 5–62 between Vásquez and Jaramillo ☎0986190490, ⓦcafenucallacta.com. What started out as a gourmet coffee store has morphed into one of the hottest cafés in town; though the top-notch beans are the main draw, it also offers tasty breakfasts and light lunches and is a favourite spot for weekend brunch. Mon–Sat 9am–6pm, Sun 9am–3pm.

Tutto Freddo Parque Calderón, Benigno Malo ☎07 4031128. Ecuador's answer to Baskin Robbins and seemingly just as popular. Forget the sandwiches and head straight for the great ice creams and cakes. Mon–Wed & Sun 8am–10pm, Thurs–Sat 8am–11.30pm.

Wunderbar Escalinata 3–43, off Calle Larga ☎07 2831274. This vibey café-bar is a great place for lunch on a sunny day, when you can eat in the little garden among the trees and flowers. Serves US-style snacks and light meals (from $4). Mon–Sat noon–midnight.

RESTAURANTS

Café Eucalyptus Gran Colombia and Benigno Malo ☎07 2849157. Enjoyable Anglo-Romanian-run restaurant in a distinguished building, with an eclectic international menu offering everything from Thai green curry to chicken vindaloo to tapas (mains from $6). The place is thriving, and has a blazing fire on cold nights; you'll need to book at weekends. Live music on Fri and Sat in high season (see opposite). Mon–Thurs 3.30pm–midnight, Fri & Sat 3.30pm–2am, Sun 5–11pm.

El Maíz Calle Larga 1-279 and Los Molinos ☎07 2840224, ⓦelmaizrestaurante.com. One of the best places to sample traditional Ecuadorian cooking (goat stew or even *encocado*) with a modern twist, and inventive quinoa concoctions abound (mains from around $10). It also boasts a beautifully painted interior, as well as outdoor seating with river views. Reservations advised. Mon–Fri noon–9pm, Sat noon–4pm & 7–9pm.

Moliendo Café Vásquez 6-24 and Hermano Miguel ☎07 2828710. Fantastic little Colombian restaurant offering inexpensive, authentic cuisine including *arepas* (corn pancakes) with a variety of delicious toppings. Wash it down with a *refajo*, a lager shandy turbo-powered with a hit of *aguardiente*. Mon–Sat 9am–9pm.

★**La Quinua** Beningo Malo 12-73 and Vega Muñoz ☎07 8321370. Excellent, mainly vegan breakfast and lunchtime menus – choose from soups, salads and veggie burgers or more traditional *motepillo*, *llapingachos* or *guatita* – to be enjoyed in a delightful interior courtyard, decked out in textiles, plants and traditional artefacts. A skylight ensures the sun streams in to warm your back. Modestly priced dishes ($3–8) and almuerzos. Mon–Fri 10am–4pm.

★**Raymipampa** Benigno Malo and Bolívar, Parque Calderón ☎07 2834159. The classic place to eat in Cuenca, both for its unbeatable location under the colonnaded arcade of the Catedral Nueva and for its devoted local following. Inexpensive crêpes, pastas, stir-fries, meats and much more are served at a brisk pace. Mon–Fri 8.30am–10pm, Sat & Sun 9.30am–10pm.

★**Tiestos** Jaramillo 4-89 and Mariano Cueva ☎07 2835310, ⦿tiestosrestaurante.com. Larger-than-life chef-owner Juan Carlos makes this Cuenca's hottest dining ticket – evening reservations a must – offering casual, family-style dining with an open kitchen, dishes to share and waiters in Panama hats. Generous portions of creative Ecuadorian and fusion cuisine come in rich sauces, and garnishes, relishes and dips abound – but leave room for the works of art that constitute dessert. Expect to pay around $30–35/person for a three-course meal without

drinks. Tues–Sat 12.30–3pm & 6.30–10pm, Sun 12.30–3pm.

Villa Rosa Gran Colombia 12-22 between Juan Montalvo and Tarqui ☎07 2837944. Upmarket but modern formal dining favoured by Cuenca's bourgeoisie, on an attractive covered patio. The international dishes with Mediterranean flair are well executed but somewhat pricey; there are some Ecuadorian specialities too. Mon–Sat 12.30–3.30pm & 7–10pm.

La Viña Jaramillo 5-101 and Cordero ☎07 2839696. Cosy Italian-owned restaurant producing great thin-crust pizzas and some home-made pasta dishes (mains from around $8), washed down with affordable Italian red wine. There's now a jazz club upstairs too (see below). Mon–Sat 5–11pm.

DRINKING AND NIGHTLIFE

Cuenca's **nightlife** only really takes off on Thurs, Fri and Sat nights, when the city's disco-bars and *salsotecas* fill with teenagers and twentysomethings. If you're short of ideas, have a trawl down **Calle Larga** and see what takes your fancy.

BARS

Jodoco Plaza San Sebastián ☎0988570082. This newish watering-hole sells authentic Belgian craft brews, accompanied by tapas-style snacks and heavier Belgian fare. There are outside tables on one of the town's most delightful squares for sunny afternoons, and an indoor retreat for chill evenings. Mon–Sat 11am until late.

Prohibido Centro Cultural Cruz del Vado, Condamine 12-102 ☎07 2840703. If your musical tastes include gothic, heavy metal and "doom", then you'll find like-minded folk at this bar-cum-gallery, copiously decorated in skulls, writhing succubi and reproductive organs. Not to everyone's taste, but undeniably different, and there's a dressing-up corner too. $1 entry. Mon–Sat 9am–10pm.

Wunderbar Escalinata 3–43, off Calle Larga ☎07 2831274. This relaxed daytime café (see opposite) turns into a vibey bar at night, attracting a good mix of foreigners and locals alike with its stylish interior, large wooden tables, international bottled beers and occasional live music. Happy hour all day Wednesday and much of the rest of the time too. Mon–Sat noon–midnight.

CLUBS AND LIVE MUSIC

Café Eucalyptus Gran Colombia and Benigno Malo ☎07 2849157. Grab a table upstairs and hang over the railings, or sit downstairs by the fire to make the most of the live music on Fri and Sat nights in high season. Good wines and beers, which are free to women on ladies' night

(Wed 6–10pm). The restaurant here is also good (see opposite). Daily 5pm until late, Sun also 11am–2pm.

Jazz Society Café Luis Cordero 5–101 and Jaramillo ☎0939342714. Upstairs at *La Viña* (see above), this intimate venue hosts excellent live jazz from 7.30pm four nights a week, plus you can order good Italian food from the restaurant downstairs, for the same price. Wed–Sat 6.30–10pm.

Velvet Astudillo and 12 de Abril by the Millennium Plaza. Popular club spread over several rooms, with chandeliers, velvet-covered furnishings and dry ice. Heavy on reggaeton and US club music. Thurs–Sat 9pm–3am.

Verde Pintón y Maduro Borrero and Vásquez ☎0994748081, ⦿facebook.com/verdepintonymaduro. Great bar-disco that's big on salsa on Thurs nights, though other tropical beats feature too – merengue, bachata, kizomba and even the ubiquitous reggaeton creeps in later on. Thankfully, salsa makes it onto the menu other nights too, and is often favoured by the national and international artists performing live at weekends. Variable cover charge. Thurs 6pm–midnight, Fri & Sat 6pm–2am.

CINEMA

Millennium Plaza Merchan 2-13 and Peralta ☎07 2888170, ⦿multicines.com.ec. This five-screen multiplex puts on Hollywood blockbusters, many in English with Spanish subtitles, and some dubbed into Spanish.

SHOPPING

With its strong tradition of **crafts**, Cuenca and its environs offer great scope for shopping, being renowned above all for producing some of Ecuador's finest **Panama hats** (see box, p.192) and for hand-woven ikat **textiles** (see p.196), distinctive **ceramics** and intricate filigree **jewellery** (see also p.196). Prices are inevitably lower in the **markets** or in the surrounding towns and villages (see p.196), where the artesanía is actually made, than in the upmarket boutiques of the *centro histórico*.

CUENCA LANGUAGE SCHOOLS

Cuenca is a very popular place to study Spanish, and possesses a number of excellent **language schools**. Recommended centres include: Amauta Fundación, Hermano Miguel 7-48 and Presidente Córdova, whose profits support education for kids from low-income families (☎07 2846206, ⓦamauta.edu.ec); the world-renowned Estudio Sampere, Hermano Miguel 3-43 and Calle Larga (☎07 2849406, ⓦsampere.com), whose four-week crash-course also includes dancing lessons; Sí Centro, Bolívar 13–28 and Juan Montalvo (☎07 2820429, ⓦsicentrospanishschool.com), which offers homestays and activities and runs both Spanish and private English lessons ($160 for a 4-week programme of 20hr/week); and the Yanapuma Foundation, Hermano Miguel 8-59 and Bolívar (☎07 2831504, ⓦyanapumaspanish.org). As well as general classes, the last offers medical Spanish, with profits helping the foundation's work in marginalized indigenous communities.

ARTESANÍA

Casa de la Mujer Torres 7-33, Plaza San Francisco. Also known as CEMUART, this venture organized by the municipality has around 80 small, covered shops on two floors, reflecting a great range of crafts and a similar range of quality, from balsa parrots to indigenous musical instruments and embroidered shirts. Mon–Sat 9am–6pm; some shops open Sun 10am–1pm.

CIDAP (Centro Interamericano de Artesanías y Artes Populares) Escalinata and 3 de Noviembre. Authentic good-quality ceramics, textiles – notably ikat weavings – and woodcarvings in the museum shop (see p.186). Mon–Fri 9am–5pm.

Esquina de las Artes 12 de Abril and Cueva. Houses a handful of smart shops selling superior jewellery, knitwear, textiles, ceramics – including Eduardo Vega (see below) – at suitably high-end prices. Manos del Mundo is the pick of the bunch, focusing on high-quality and innovative Ecuadorian weaving and handicrafts. There's an ice-cream parlour too. Mon 10am–noon, Tues–Fri 10am–7pm; some shops open Sun 10am–3pm.

BOOKS

Carolina Bookstore Hermano Miguel 4-36 and Calle Larga ☎0994748081. This shop has a wide selection of second-hand English-language books, and operates a book exchange. Mon–Sat 10am–6pm.

Libri Mundi Corner of Sucre and Hermano Miguel ☎07 2843782. Though stocking mainly books in Spanish, this bookshop has some nice bilingual coffee-table books on Ecuador and a small English-language section. Mon–Fri 9am–7pm, Sat 9am–6pm.

CERAMICS

Artesa Isabel La Católica 1-102 and Las Américas ☎07 4056457, ⓦartesa.com.ec. One of the country's top manufacturers of fine ceramics, selling a wide range of crockery and other items, hand-painted with beautiful colours and designs. On Fridays you can have a free factory tour and pick up some heavily discounted seconds. There's a much smaller outlet in the town centre. Mon–Fri 8am–1pm & 2.30–5.30pm.

Galería Eduardo Vega Just below the Mirador de Turi (see p.187). ☎07 2881407, ⓦceramicavega.com. Eduardo, the co-founder of Artesa, has his own workshop, and produces decorative items in equally bold colours. Mon–Fri 9am–6pm, Sat 9.30am–1pm.

PANAMA HATS

Homero Ortega & Hijos Ramírez Dávalos 3-86 ☎07 2809000, ⓦhomeroortega.com. A worldwide exporter of hats from the factory behind the bus terminal, where you can see the stages of the hat-making process before ending up at the salesroom – basic Panamas cost around $30 and *finos* from around $80. *Superfinos* are usually from Montecristi (see p.290). Mon–Fri 8am–12.30pm & 2.30–6pm, Sat 8.30am–12.30pm.

Rafael Paredes & Hijos Calle Larga 10-41 ☎07 2831569. A central place with a vast array of hats, from JR-like Stetsons to purple trilbies. Also home to the Museo del Sombrero (see p.186). Mon–Fri 9am–6pm, Sat 9.30am–5pm, Sun 9.30am–1.30pm.

DIRECTORY

Banks Banks with ATMs are plentiful in the *centro histórico*; Vazcorp Casa de Cambios, Av Roberto Crespo and Av del Estadio, changes foreign currency (Mon–Fri 8.30am–5.30pm).
Hospitals Private: Hospital Santa Inès, Daniel Córdova Toral 2-113 (☎07 2817888); state-run: Hospital Vicente Corral Moscoso, El Paraíso (☎07 2822100).

Immigration Ordóñez Lazo and Cipreses, Centro Commercial Astudillo (☎07 2850085), with a new office due to open at the airport in 2016.
Police Luis Cordero, between Córdova and Jaramillo (☎07 2822856).
Post office Main post office at Borrero and Gran Colombia (Mon–Fri 8am–6pm, Sat 9am–1pm).

Around Cuenca

There are several very rewarding day-trips you can make in the area **around Cuenca**.
Top of the list on a fine day should be **Parque Nacional El Cajas**, forty minutes by bus
west of the city, packed with trout-filled lakes, brooding mountains and – almost
certainly by the afternoon – swirling mists, with opportunities for a spot of fishing or
hiking. Then consider soaking those tired limbs in the relaxing thermal baths of **Baños
de Cuenca**, only fifteen minutes out of the city. Heading east, you can enjoy a scenic
bus ride through the hills to the rural communities of **Gualaceo**, **Chordeleg** and **Sigsig**,
and find out more about the crafts produced there. Southwest of Cuenca, just off the
road to Machala, is the impressive waterfall at **Girón**, another worthwhile excursion,
while some 25km northwards along the Panamericana the pleasant hillside town of
Azogues, with its imposing church, also attracts visitors.

Parque Nacional El Cajas

Only 35km northwest of Cuenca, **PARQUE NACIONAL EL CAJAS** is one of the most
beautiful wilderness areas in Ecuador: a wild, primeval landscape of craggy hills and
glacier-scoured valleys studded with a breathtaking quantity of lakes (235 at last count),
glinting like jewels against the mottled earth and rock surrounding them. Spread over
290 square kilometres of high páramo (3000–4500m), the park offers superb **hiking**
and **trout-fishing** opportunities and – despite sitting on the doorstep of a major city –
a tremendous sense of solitude, with visitors kept at bay by the rain and fog that so
frequently plague the area. This inhospitable environment harbours more **flora** and

4

HIKING IN PARQUE NACIONAL EL CAJAS

The best place to start exploring Parque Nacional El Cajas is at the **information centre** (see
p.194) on the edge of the shimmering **Laguna Toreadora**, in the northern sector of the park,
where you can pick up a free 1:70,000 colour **map** of the park and hire a guide if you need to. (If
you want to do some advanced planning, ask at the tourist office in Cuenca, which usually has a
copy you can borrow to photocopy.) The official map details ten **hiking routes** across the park,
ranging from short hops of an hour or two to end-to-end treks of two or three days. You can
supplement this map with 1:50,000 IGM maps covering the area (Cuenca, Chaucha, San Felipe de
Molleturo and Chiquintad). It is driest between June and September but bring warm clothes and
emergency supplies whenever you hike – it can reach freezing when the weather turns bad, no
matter how sunny it is when you set off (see p.36). What's more, don't underestimate the effect
the altitude can have on you; if you've not been in the highlands long, don't try anything too
strenuous. You can rent camping equipment at Expediciones Apullacta in Cuenca (see box, p.188).

LAGUNA TOTORAS AND LAGUNA PATOQUINUAS HIKE

The most popular **day-hike** (a combination of route 2 and part of route 1; 5–6hr) starts at the
information centre, taking you northeast past Laguna Toreadora, through a *quinua* forest and
down southeast past **Laguna Totoras** and **Laguna Patoquinuas**. The hike ends back at the
highway, some 8km east of the information centre, at the Quinuas checkpoint, where you can
catch the bus back to Cuenca; ask the warden to show you the path, which is straightforward
to follow and quite easy-going.

TRES CRUCES HIKE

There's a good hike (5–6hr), which starts 4km further west along the highway from the
information centre, at the **Tres Cruces** hill on the left-hand (south) side of the road. At 4160m,
the hill straddles the continental divide between waters draining west into the Pacific and east
into the Amazon basin – you can scramble up it in about fifteen minutes for great views over
the park. The trail (route 5 on the map) takes you down past a string of three lakes – Negra,
Larga and Tagllacocha – bringing you to the **Ingañán** (paved Inca road) by **Laguna Luspa**,
before heading right (west) back towards the highway.

fauna than first impressions might suggest: native *quinua* trees, with their gnarled and twisted branches, grow alongside the rivers that thread through the park, and many species of shrubs and flowers adapted to harsh climates – such as the orange-flowered *chuquiragua* – survive on the moorland. There's also a tract of dense, humid cloudforest, peppered with orchids and bromeliads, on the eastern edge of the park.

The park is home to wildcats, pumas, deer and some spectacled bears, though you're far more likely to see ducks, rabbits and perhaps some recently reintroduced llamas. Cajas is also rich in birdlife, including woodpeckers, hummingbirds, mountain toucans and Andean condors. Human relics include a scattering of pre-Hispanic **ruins**, probably of former shelters for those travelling between the sierra and the coast, as well as a 4km restored section of the Ingañán, an old **Inca road**, with much of its original paving conserved.

ARRIVAL AND INFORMATION PARQUE NACIONAL EL CAJAS

NORTHERN SECTOR

By bus The paved highway between Cuenca and Guayaquil via Molleturo crosses the northern sector of the park ensuring a frequent bus service (every 35–40min until very late).

Entry checkpoints Ask to be dropped either at the turning (Km15) for the Laguna Llaviucu control (3km walk from the highway) or at the Information Centre at Laguna Toreadora, by the highway, about a 40min drive from Cuenca (Km33.5), or at the Quinuas checkpoint, just over 6km east of the turn-off to the Information Centre. All these places should be able to provide you with a map.

SOUTHERN SECTOR

By bus In addition to the main road through El Cajas, an unpaved road runs along the southern boundary of the park past the communities of Soldados (where there is a checkpoint) and Angas. Transporte Occidental (☎07 2856691) operates a daily 6am bus (returning 4pm; 1hr 20min) from the Terminal Sur in Cuenca (see p.188), which you can pick up at Puente El Vado.

INFORMATION

Centro de Información Laguna Toreadora (daily 8am–4.30pm).

Park head office At ETAPA, the local water and sanitation authority, Edificio Morejón, Presidente Córdova 7-56 and Luis Cordero, Cuenca (☎07 2829853).

ACCOMMODATION AND EATING

There are many **campsites** in the park, which are marked on the official map. You'll need a stove to cook on since fires are not permitted. Both lakes Toreadora and Llaviucu have simple **restaurants**, but these are often only open during busy weekends and holiday periods.

Hostería Dos Chorreras 1km east of the Llaviucu turning, just off the highway ☎07 2853154, ⓦhosteriadoschorreras.com. This upmarket hostería (and now conference centre) has a reasonably priced restaurant, where you can tuck into a range of Ecuadorian and international dishes, including several veggie options, by a blazing log fire. It also has comfortable, heated rooms (some with fireplace), and organizes horse riding, mountain biking and fishing trips. $150

National park refuge Toreadora information centre ☎07 2370127 or ☎07 4049569, ⓔmriquetti@etapa .net.ec. A basic refuge with bunks, cooking facilities and a fireplace, but no wood. You need an advance reservation to stay here, and will need to bring a warm sleeping bag. $4

Baños de Cuenca

Baños is a 15min bus ride (lines 12 and 200) from Cuenca; catch one (every 10min) from Vega Muñoz or the bus terminal, or take a taxi (around $5)

For a relaxing afternoon, head for the pretty village of **BAÑOS DE CUENCA** – not to be confused with the major spa town of the same name in the central sierra (see p.152) – and one of its pleasant **spa complexes**, which issue day-passes and also have places to eat. The nicest are **Balneario Durán** (Mon–Tues & Thurs–Sun 7am–9pm, Wed 7am–2pm; $6; ⓦhosteriaduran.com) and **Piedra de Agua** (Mon–Sat 6am–10pm, Sun 6am–7pm; $10 day-pass for pools, Turkish bath and sauna, $35 for access to the full works; ⓦpiedradeagua.com.ec). Go during the week to avoid the crowds, and two get entry for the price of one on Mondays and Tuesdays.

OPPOSITE HIKING NEAR VILCABAMBA (P.207) >

The Ruta Santa Bárbara

The landscape east of Cuenca is gentle and pastoral, characterized by rippling hills and fertile orchards and fields. From Cuenca, a picturesque paved road leads through these hills to the growing market town of **Gualaceo**, continuing to the villages of **Chordeleg** and **Sigsig**, all of which lie within the canton of Santa Bárbara and are known for their handicrafts; all three places are often visited together on a tour from Cuenca (see box, p.188). Gualaceo and Chordeleg both have enjoyable Sunday-morning **markets**, while Sigsig – which also has a small Sunday market – is best visited during the week when its Panama hat factory-shop is open. This area is also a little-used jumping-off point for the southern **Oriente**, with its scenic roads snaking down from Gualaceo to Limón, and from Sigsig to Gualaquiza (see p.253).

Gualaceo

On the banks of the Río Gualaceo, 36km east of Cuenca, sits **GUALACEO** (2330m), known as the Jardín del Azuay (Garden of Azuay) for its rich agricultural land and mild climate, which make it an important fruit-growing centre; every March the town celebrates the Fiesta del Durazno (Peach Festival) with street parties and peach-tastings. Two of the nearby villages, **Bulcay** and **Bullzhún**, are renowned for their workshops that produce high-quality ikat shawls (*macanas*) – the region's distinctive dyed weavings, some of which can take several months to make and fetch several hundred dollars. Most tourists stop off at the more accessible and more commercialized **La Casa de las Macanas** (⊕casadelamakana.com), 6km before Gualaceo on the road from Cuenca, where you'll pay less for the distinctive weavings than in the boutique shops of Cuenca.

Chordeleg

6km east of Gualaceo, **CHORDELEG** is decidedly smaller and quainter than Gualaceo, though increasingly rather touristy. It is noted for its ceramics – with the largest selection available at the **Centro de Artesanías** on the road into town – and is also famous as a centre of gold and metalwork, including delicately worked filigree **jewellery**, an art that's been practised here since pre-Hispanic times. Numerous shops keep the tradition alive in the village, but a lot of it is made from low-grade gold, so beware of parting with large sums of money.

Museo Municipal

Parque central • Mon–Fri 8am–1pm & 2–5pm, Sat & Sun 9am–4pm • Free

The simple one-room **Museo Municipal** explains the origins and techniques of the various local crafts, from ceramics to textiles, hats to jewellery, with various exemplars on display. Standing head and shoulders above the rest of the exhibits – literally – is the world's largest silver filigree earring (*candonga*); at a height of 1.85m and a width of 1.50m, it weighs in at a hefty 17.5kg, and so is unlikely to be adorning someone's earlobes any time soon.

Sigsig

Some 26km south of Gualaceo, **Sigsig** is a remote agricultural village sitting in gorgeous, hilly countryside near the banks of the Río Santa Bárbara, from whose swaying reeds (*sigses*) it takes its name. It's one of the most important centres of **Panama hat** production in the province, and indeed you'll see many women weaving as they stroll down the street, or separating out the *paja toquilla* fibres on the pavements. A good place to buy a hat at a reasonable price is the **Asociación de Toquilleras María Auxiliadora**, a women's weaving cooperative located in the old hospital next to the river, a 10min walk from the centre on the road to Gualaquiza. Ask around if the place seems shut.

Museo Municipal

Parque 3 de Noviembre • Mon–Fri 8am–1pm & 2–4.30pm • Free • ☎ 07 2266106

On Parque 3 de Noviembre, the upper square with the striking modern church, is the **Museo Municipal**, which shows pieces from the local Talcazhapa culture (500–1470 AD)

and the prehistoric Chobsi culture (10,000–5500 BC), traces of which are also visible in some nearby overgrown ruins and caves, some 6km from Sigsig ($3 by taxi).

ARRIVAL AND INFORMATION   THE RUTA SANTA BÁRBARA

BY BUS

Buses leave Cuenca's main bus terminal to Gualaceo (every 15min; 50min) and Chordeleg (every 30min; 1hr 15min), plus local buses shuttle between Gualaceo and Chordeleg every 10min; there is also a service to Sigsig (every 30min; 1hr 40min), and through buses from Cuenca to Gualaquiza pass through Sigsig (8 daily; 4hr 30min).

TOURIST OFFICES

Gualaceo The I-Tur office is in the *municipio* on the main square (Mon–Fri 8am–1pm & 2–5pm, Sat & Sun 9am–noon & 2–5pm; ☎ 07 2256608).

Chordeleg The I-Tur office is on the corner of Eloy Alfaro and Cobos, a block downhill from the plaza (Tues–Sun 8am–5pm).

Sigsig The I-Tur is in the bus station (Mon–Fri 8am–4.30pm).

ACCOMMODATION AND EATING

The only one of these three places where you are likely to want to stay is **Sigsig**, either on account of the splendid scenery, or as a stopover on a scenic back route down to the Oriente, via Gualaquiza, though inexpensive *hospedajes* and local restaurants are to be found in each place; you just need to ask around.

Saraguro

The remote agricultural town of **SARAGURO** ("land of corn" in Kichwa), 140km south of Cuenca and 64km north of Loja, is home to one of the most distinct highland groups of Ecuador, the **Saraguro indígenas** (see box below). Most Saraguro *indígenas* live as cattle herders in rural farming communities, but just about all of them come into town for the lively Sunday-morning **market** for fresh produce, cattle and household goods, and for Sunday Mass, held in the handsome, honey-stone church on the main plaza.

Most visitors are content to spend a few hours wandering around, but note that the Saraguro community tour operator (see below) can set you up to stay with a family, providing you an opportunity to learn more about this unique culture and to participate in a family's everyday life.

ARRIVAL AND DEPARTURE   SARAGURO

By bus Buses from Cuenca (3hr) and Loja (1hr 15min) pass just above the town centre on the Panamericana at least hourly until late in the day.

By camioneta Occasional camionetas run between Saraguro and Cuenca (Feria Libre), and with greater frequency on market day ($6/person; 2hr).

INFORMATION AND TOURS

Tourist office Information is available at Saraurku (Mon–Fri 9am–5pm; ☎ 07 2200331, ⊛ turismosaraguro.com), the community tourism operator based at the Fundación Kawsay, at 18 de Noviembre and Loja, one block off the main square. They can organize homestays in one of several nearby communities for $35/person, including meals and family activities (take a torch), or day-tours (with a day's advance notice) with a local guide who can show you round the

---

THE SARAGUROS

The Saraguros forebears, originally from the altiplano region of Lake Titicaca in Bolivia, were relocated here by the **Incas** during their expansion into Ecuador, as part of the *mitimae* system used to consolidate colonization. More than five hundred years on, the **Saraguros** are still set apart by their particularly pure form of Kichwa and distinctive clothing. The men wear black ponchos and black knee-length shorts, often over black wellington boots used for their farm work, while the women wear pleated black skirts and hand-woven black shawls, fastened by elaborate silver or nickel brooches called *tupus*. Needless to say, Saraguros have also maintained very traditional forms of celebrating religious **festivals**. Easter, in particular, follows a strict pattern of processions, re-enactments and symbolic rituals, all marked by their great solemnity. Other important festivals include Tres Reyes (January 6), Corpus Christi (early or mid-June) and Christmas.

various neighbouring communities, including a visit to a weaving workshop and an organic garden growing medicinal plants. It is also possible to organize a homestay through a community tourism operator in Cuenca (see box, p.188).

ACCOMMODATION AND EATING

★**Hostal Achik Wasi** Barrio la Luz, Calle Intiñan ☎07 2200058, ⓦturismosaraguro.com. Perched on a hillside overlooking the town, this imposing community-run hostel offers simple but comfortable en-suite rooms. Views from the dining room across the valley are superb, and the wholesome local cuisine is also good – try the local trout – though meals need to be ordered in advance. Breakfast included. **$40**

Mama Cuchara Parque central. Run by a women's cooperative, this place serves basic but tasty and filling dishes for a very reasonable $3–6. Try the *mote pillo* for breakfast. Daily 7am–6pm.

Residencial Saraguro Calle Loja and Antonio Castro ☎07 2200286. Simple rooms with shared or private bathroom, cable TV and hot water – all in a friendly home. **$10**

Loja

Marooned at the bottom of the country, several hours' drive from any other major town, **LOJA** is a remote but thriving little provincial capital undergoing expansion, with some handsome old **eighteenth- and nineteenth-century buildings** and well-cared-for parks and open spaces. Thanks to its isolation, it has long been good at taking care of its own affairs, even dabbling with **self-government** in 1857 – not to mention its distinction of being the first city in the country to generate electricity, in 1897, and the first to host a wind farm – the world's highest – which opened in 2013. With a progressive emphasis on learning and culture, the city boasts two universities, a law school and a major music conservatory, all of which gives the place a youthful, vibrant atmosphere. Spread over a fertile valley at 2100m above sea level, Loja is about 500m lower than most sierra cities, and noticeably warmer (usually 16–21ºC). The city's scenic location is best appreciated from the **Mirador El Churo**, a viewpoint 800m up a hillside east of the city.

Parque central and around

Loja's centre is marked by the large, palm-filled **parque central**, lined by an eclectic collection of buildings competing for your attention. On the north side, the modern **municipio** is a huge concrete monstrosity, with exuberant murals in its courtyard. To the east is the **catedral** with its towering white facade flamboyantly trimmed and topped by a tall spire; it has an ornate, coffered ceiling inside.

Museo de la Cultura Lojana

Parque central • Mon–Fri 9am–5pm, Sat 9am–1pm • Free • ☎07 2573004

The former Casa de Justicia, on the south side of the *parque central*, is a traditional early eighteenth-century mansion with whitewashed adobe walls and clay-tiled roof. Inside, the **Museo de la Cultura Lojana** displays a modest collection of pre-Columbian ceramics and religious sculptures in rooms off a creaking wooden veranda.

Iglesia Santo Domingo

Bolívar and Rocafuerte • Opening hours vary • Free

Two blocks south of the *parque central* along Bolívar sits the imposing **Iglesia Santo Domingo**, whose immense twin bell towers Lojanos cherish as a symbol of their city. Inside, the church is crammed with over a hundred biblical-themed oil paintings hanging amid the swirling floral motifs that cover the walls and ceilings.

Plaza de la Independencia and around

Five blocks south down Bolívar from the *parque central* you'll reach **Plaza de la Independencia**, so called because it was here that Loja's citizens gathered on November 18,

1820, to proclaim publicly their independence from the Spanish Crown. It is undoubtedly the city's most beautiful square, enclosed by colonial-style buildings that look like outsized dolls' houses, with their brightly painted walls, balconies, shutters and doors, and the cheerful **Iglesia San Sebastián** with its pretty blue-and-cream interior. Free concerts featuring traditional music and dance are held in the plaza every Thursday night (8–10pm).

Calle Lourdes

Regarded locally as the jewel of all the town's streets, **Calle Lourdes**, squeezed between Bolívar and Sucre at the southern end of the old centre, has some particularly

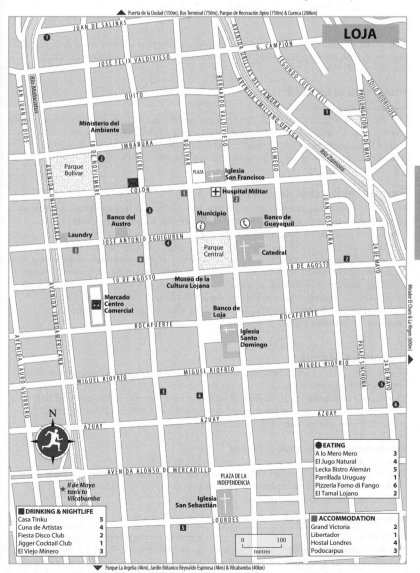

Puerta de la Ciudad (150m), Bus Terminal (750m), Parque de Recreación Jipiro (750m) & Cuenca (208km)

LOJA

4

Mirador El Churo & La Virgen (600m)

Parque La Argelia (4km), Jardín Bótanico Reynaldo Espinosa (4km) & Vilcabamba (40km)

■ EATING

A lo Mero Mero	3
El Jugo Natural	4
Lecka Bistro Alemán	5
Parrillada Uruguay	1
Pizzería Forno di Fango	6
El Tamal Lojano	2

■ DRINKING & NIGHTLIFE

Casa Tinku	5
Cuna de Artistas	4
Fiesta Disco Club	2
Jigger Cocktail Club	1
El Viejo Minero	3

■ ACCOMMODATION

Grand Victoria	2
Libertador	1
Hostal Londres	4
Podocarpus	3

LOJA'S FIESTAS

Loja's most exciting fiesta kicks off on August 20 when the icon of the **Virgen de El Cisne** arrives in the cathedral for a two-month "visit" having been carried on foot from El Cisne (see box, p.203), accompanied by hundreds of pilgrims. The festivities which follow culminate on September 8 with the **Feria de Integración Fronteriza**, a huge craft and trade fair Simón Bolívar established in 1824, in an effort to promote cross-border relations; the fair is still attended by many Peruvians today. The other big party period, comprising an extended programme of parades, concerts, dancing, food fairs and the like, takes place over a couple of weeks from November 18, the commemoration of the declaration of independence from Spain in 1820. Festivities start up again on 8 December, when *lojanos* celebrate the foundation of their city.

well-preserved buildings, following an extensive facelift that saw the woodwork repaired, and the houses and shops spruced up in bright colours to show off the architecture.

Puerta de la Ciudad

Sucre and Universitaria • Daily 8am–9.30pm • Free

The **Puerta de la Ciudad** is a mock early-colonial gatehouse, marking the northern entrance to town. More reminiscent of Disneyland than the Spanish Conquest, it comes complete with tower, crenellations and portcullis, and houses changing art exhibitions and a café. You can climb up the tower for attractive views of the city and the surrounding hills.

Parque de Recreación Jipiro

Between the Río Zamora and Salvador Bustamente, 2km north of the centre • Daily 9am–8pm; swimming pool 8am–6pm • Swimming pool $1; planetarium shows $0.50 • ☎ 07 2583357 • It's a 20min walk from the centre, or take a bus marked "El Valle" or "Jipiro"

Loja's most popular tourist attraction, **Parque de Recreación Jipiro**, lies a couple of blocks northeast of the bus terminal, and is a large, landscaped park with an ornamental lake and a novelty children's playground featuring models of buildings from around the world, such as the Eiffel Tower, an Arab mosque and a truly bizarre replica of Moscow's St Basil's Cathedral, complete with slides. Jipiro is a very popular open space for *lojanos*, who also come to enjoy the heated **swimming pool** here, equipped with retractable glass roof, or the little **planetarium** in the dome of the "mosque", which has regular 30-minute shows at weekends.

Parque La Argelia

Avenida de los Conquistadores, 4.5km south of the city centre • Daily 8am–6pm • $1 • Take a Vilcabamba-bound bus from the bus terminal, or a taxi from the centre for about $2

The **Parque La Argelia** is a mini slice of wilderness on the edge of the city, and has excellent trails running through around one square kilometre of hills, forests and streams; it also affords some brilliant views of the city.

Jardín Botánico Reynaldo Espinosa

Parque La Argelia, 4.5km south of the city centre • Mon–Fri 8am–6pm, Sat & Sun 1–6pm • $1

Part of the Parque La Argelia (with a separate entrance, across the highway) is the **Jardín Botánico Reynaldo Espinosa**, home to a great variety of native and introduced species, including many orchids and medicinal plants.

ARRIVAL AND DEPARTURE   LOJA

BY PLANE

Loja's airport is the Aeropuerto Ciudad de Catamayo (☎ 07 2677306), just outside the town of the same name, 33km west of the city (30min drive). TAME operates direct flights to Guayaquil (Mon–Sat; 40min; $73 one-way) and Quito (daily; 1hr; $82 one-way) and has an office at the airport

(☎07 2677306) and in Loja, on the corner of Ortega and 24 de Mayo (☎07 2570248).

BY BUS

Loja is the hub of Ecuador's deep south, from where you can get direct buses to three border crossings into Peru: Huaquillas (see p.316), Macará (see p.210) and Zumba (see p.211). The one at Macará is the most popular and convenient, and Cooperativa Loja International, which runs three direct buses to Piura in Peru, and picks up in Macará, has an office at the bus terminal and on 10 de Agosto and Guerrero (☎07 2570505). There are also routes east to the Oriente, west towards the coast, and north, up the Panamericana, to Cuenca.

Bus terminal Loja's bus terminal is 2km north of the centre on Avenida Cuxibamba; from here, pick up any local bus heading towards the centre, or take a taxi ($1.50).

Destinations Catamayo (every 30min; 50min); Cuenca (every 30min–1hr; 5hr); El Cisne (5 daily; 2hr); Gualaquiza (15 daily; 5hr); Guayaquil (10 daily; 8–9hr); Huaquillas (6 daily; 5hr); Macará (6 daily via Cariamanga, 2 daily via Catocha; 5hr); Machala (11 daily via Portovelo, 7hr; 4 daily via Chaguarpamba, 5hr); Piñas (2 daily; 4hr 15min); Piura, Peru (3 daily; 8hr); Quito (12 daily; 14–16hr); Saraguro (hourly; 2hr); Vilcabamba (every 15–30min; 1hr); Zamora (every 15–30min; 1hr 30min); Zaruma (6 daily; 5hr); Zumba (12 daily; 5hr).

BY TAXI

The quickest way to reach Vilcabamba is in a shared taxi (40min; $2.25, or $9 for the whole taxi). The taxi company, 11 de Mayo (☎07 2570956), has an office in the street of the same name, near Mercadillo.

GETTING AROUND

On foot The old city centre, the location of most places of interest, can easily be explored on foot.

By bus A new metrobus service opened in 2015, whose most useful line (LC2) runs from Argelia in the south along Avenida Universitaria to Sauces via the bus terminal every few minutes.

By car For journeys further afield, car rental is available at

Arricar, Eguiguren 10-54 and 24 de Mayo (☎07 2575574); Bombuscaro, 10 de Agosto and Universitaria (☎07 2577021, ⓦbombuscaro.com.ec); and Localiza, Nueva Loja and Isidro Ayora (☎07 2581729).

By taxi Taxis charge $1–1.50 for journeys within the city, and can usually be flagged down on the main avenues or around the *parque central*.

INFORMATION AND TOURS

Tourist office The I-Tur office is on the central square, at the corner of Eguiguren and Bolívar (Mon–Fri 8am–1pm & 3–6pm, Sat 10am–2pm; ☎07 2570407 ext 202), with a small kiosk at the bus terminal. The helpful staff should be able to answer most of your questions about Loja, Vilcabamba, Zamora and Podocarpus and its surroundings.

National parks information I-Tur has sufficient information for most tourists' needs. Otherwise, for

information on nearby national parks, you can consult the Ministerio del Ambiente office, on Sucre between Imbabura and Quito (☎07 2571534).

Tour operators Exploraves Birdwatchers, at Lourdes 14-80 and Sucre (☎07 2582434, ⓦexploraves.com) offers birdwatching tours to Podocarpus (see p.204) and further afield, led by extremely knowledgeable bilingual ornithologist, Pablo Andrade ($100/day). For general tour operators, head for Vilcabamba (see p.207).

ACCOMMODATION

Loja offers generally good-value hotels, from the budget to the very comfortable. You're unlikely to need to book unless you're arriving during the festival of the **Virgen de El Cisne** (Aug 20–Sept 8), when prices are hiked (see box, p.203).

★ **Grand Victoria** Valdivieso 0650 and Eguiguren ☎07 2583500, ⓦgrandvictoriabh.com. Loja's finest hotel, as is immediately apparent from the marble-floored atrium with chandelier and the elegant and spacious carpeted rooms and suites with all the trimmings (including a phone in the bathroom). Service is friendly and attentive and there are spa facilities and an excellent fine-dining restaurant. Rates are often negotiable. Buffet breakfast included. $\overline{$92}$

Hostal Londres Sucre 07-51 ☎07 2561936. Well-maintained old house owned by a friendly couple, offering spacious rooms with high ceilings, wooden floors and bare white walls plus spotless shared bathrooms. The best of the cheapies, and one that does not rent rooms by the hour.

Limited wi-fi access. $\overline{$12}$

★ **Libertador** Colón 14-30 ☎07 2560779, ⓦhotel libertador.com.ec. A one-time grand hotel that has been recently renovated, offering spacious, well-furnished rooms with good bathrooms. It also has a decent restaurant, small heated pool, sauna and steam bath. Good value, with buffet breakfast included. $\overline{$65}$

Podocarpus Eguiguren 16-50 ☎07 2584912. Comfortable, modern rooms with spotless en-suite bathrooms, though the walls and furnishings are a little worn. Opt for one of the hotel's back rooms, which are quieter. There's a laundry service, restaurant and parking, and an American breakfast is included. $\overline{$55}$

4

EATING

Once only offering the tasty local specialities such as *repe* (creamy coriander/cilantro-flavoured green banana soup) and *cecina de chancho* (lime-marinated cured pork), Loja's culinary scene is now expanding rapidly to include the likes of sushi and Middle Eastern, Mediterranean and German fare. Many of the new places are popping up along 24 de Mayo.

A lo Mero Mero Sucre and Colón. Cheery café with wooden benches and tables, and sombreros on the wall, serving inexpensive Mexican favourites (most $4–7) and soft drinks. Mon–Sat 9.30am–9pm.

El Jugo Natural Eguiguren and Bolívar ☎07 2575256. Good no-frills place to pick up a freshly squeezed juice, some breakfast and a traditional snack, such as *quimbolitos*, all under $5. Mon–Sat 8am–6pm, Sun 8am–noon.

★**Lecka Bistro Alemán** 24 de Mayo 10-51 between Ríofrío and Azuay ☎07 2563878, ✉eleckabistro aleman@yahoo.es. Run by a German-Ecuadorian couple, this place offers intimate dining – with only a handful of candlelit tables – to a mixed clientele. The small menu comprises delicious, modestly priced Teutonic staples ($5–8): currywurst and goulash with *spätzle* (German noodles), followed by *apfelkuchen* and waffles, washed down by German beer. Cash only. Mon–Fri 5–10.30pm.

Parrillada Uruguay Juan de Salinas and Universitária ☎07 2570260. Friendly, family-run restaurant serving meat cooked over charcoal on a traditional cast-iron *parrilla* (grill). If you're not up to their huge portions, try the steak baguette for a lighter meal. Mains cost $7–10. Mon–Sat noon–11.30pm, Sun noon–4.30pm.

Pizzería Forno di Fango Corner of 24 de Mayo and Azuay ☎07 2582905, ⓦfornodifango.com. Full Italian menu and, most importantly, enjoyable pizzas (from $5) cooked up in a wood-fire oven. Tues–Sun noon–10pm.

El Tamal Lojano 18 de Noviembre and Imbabura ☎07 2582977. On the park, this spotless local favourite is a top place to tuck into its namesake – for which Loja is famed – plus other Ecuadorian snacks and decent coffee. Can get packed with those queuing for takeaways at weekends. Mon–Sat 8.30am–8.30pm.

DRINKING AND NIGHTLIFE

Casa Tinku Lourdes and Sucre ☎0984961903, ⓦes-es .facebook/casatinku. Dark, cavernous venue with flashing lights, which usually has good live rock music on Fri or Sat nights. Otherwise, a DJ pumps out the sounds. Cover charge $8–10. Thurs–Sat 5pm until late.

★**Cuna de Artistas** Bolívar between Rocafuerte and Riofrío ☎0994280390, ⓦfacebook.com/cdaloja. Wonderfully restored, arty colonial building with exhibitions, seasonal poetry readings and live music. Wrap up warm, as the open courtyard that fronts this semi-open café-bar-restaurant can make for chilly dining. Stave off the cold with their heavyweight kebabs, or there's always mulled wine, amid a cornucopia of alcoholic beverages. Mon–Sat noon until late.

Fiesta Disco Club 10 de Agosto and Peña ☎07 2578441. Loja's most popular dance club has been going for years, playing all sorts of music to a clientele of all ages. Fri & Sat from 8pm until late.

Jigger Cocktail Club 24 de Mayo y Segundo Cueva Celi ☎07 2584342. A short hop south of the Zamora river in one of Loja's burgeoning nightlife neighbourhoods, this trendy cocktail bar has swings on a covered patio and occasional live bands. Its signature cocktail is the lethal Jigger Vodka Fizz. Mon–Sat 6pm until late.

El Viejo Minero Sucre 10-76 and Riofrío ☎07 2585878. Cosy, mellow pub-like bar that plays classic rock tracks and brews its own beer. It also occasionally features impromptu live rock music at weekends. Mon–Sat 5pm until late.

Around Loja

Loja sits on the doorstep of the western edge of the **Parque Nacional Podocarpus** (see p.204), a pristine tract of páramo and cloudforest, and is one of the best places to get information on the park or arrange a visit. The eastern part of the park, over the sierra and down towards the Oriente, is approached from **Zamora**, easily reached by bus from Loja.

Loja is also the gateway to **Peru** via two border crossings (see p.210), one of which is a short hop from **Vilcabamba**, an easy-going village that has become an obligatory stop for many backpackers before leaving the country.

Zamora

Nestled in densely forested foothills on the edge of the Oriente, 64km east of Loja, the small town of **ZAMORA** is used by most visitors as a base for visiting the lower section

LA VIRGEN DE EL CISNE

Perched on the mountainside northwest of Loja, the pinnacles and spires of a vast, dazzling pale-blue-and-white neo-Gothic basilica dwarf the carpet of terracotta roofs clustered around it. This is the famous **Santuario de El Cisne**, which resembles an overblown wedding cake, and is home to Ecuador's most revered icon, the **Virgen de El Cisne**. Carved in Quito in the sixteenth century by Spanish sculptor Diego de Robles, this painted cedar effigy immediately confirmed its miracle-performing credentials upon arrival and soon became the subject of a fervent cult of devotion – evident in the numerous and extraordinary range of gifts of thanks brought to the Virgin that are on display in the museum adjacent to the basilica (daily 8am–6pm; $1): from exam certificates, medals and jewellery to model buses and trucks left by drivers in return for her protection. The Virgin attracts pilgrims year-round from southern Ecuador and northern Peru but the devotion reaches its apogee during the **Fiesta de la Virgen**, which begins on August 15. The following day, thousands of pilgrims begin a 70km, five-day trek to Loja, carrying the Virgin on their shoulders – don't attempt to travel that way during that period. The image arrives on August 20, where it is deposited in Loja's cathedral while the partying continues by night across the city. It completes a two-month sojourn in Loja before being carried back to El Cisne.

of the **Parque Nacional Podocarpus** (see p.204). At only 970m above sea level, the town has a subtropical climate, with an average daytime temperature of 21°C, though it can still get chilly at night.

Sitting at the confluence of the Zamora and Bombuscaro rivers, with a backdrop of steep, emerald-green hills rising over its rooftops, Zamora's setting is lovely, yet the town itself is not especially attractive. Despite having been founded by the Spanish in 1549 it's still, at heart, a modern, rough-and-ready pioneer town, its main function being to service the local **gold-mining industry** – which it's been doing on and off for four hundred years. Even so, the place is gradually smartening itself up, with a new riverside malecón and numerous new buildings that have rather overdosed on gaudy paint and reflective glass.

Zamora's principal sight is its **clock** (with a 1600-square-metre face – apparently the largest in the world), up in the hillside above the market, where it glitters like a fairground at night. Otherwise, it's worth casting an eye over the small, neat *parque central*, ignoring the hideous new government buildings that enclose it, but taking in the central fountain that is topped with a painted white-necked parakeet, proud symbol of Zamora, and a common sight in Podocarpus.

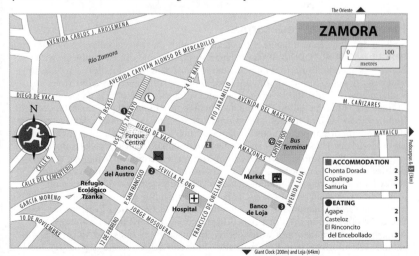

A block from the *parque central*, on Tamayo and Mosquera, is the **Refugio Ecológico Tzanka** (Tues–Sun, 9am–5pm; $2; ☎07 2605692, ✉refugioecologicotzanka@yahoo.es), once the town rubbish dump, but now an animal rescue centre, populated with parrots, sloths and monkeys. It also rents out cheap rooms and takes volunteers.

ARRIVAL AND INFORMATION   ZAMORA

By bus The bus terminal is at the eastern end of town, within easy walking distance of all hotels.

Destinations Cuenca (3 daily; 6hr 30min); Gualaquiza (8 daily; 4hr); Guayaquil (2 daily; 10hr); Loja (20 daily; 1hr 30min); Quito (11 daily; 17–18hr); Yantzaza (20 daily; 1hr 30min).

By taxi Taxis are stationed behind the bus terminal from

5am until late. A taxi to the entrance of the Parque Nacional Podocarpus usually costs $4; the park warden can call a taxi for your return once you're ready.

National park information You can get a map of the Parque Nacional Podocarpus, as well as information, at the Ministerio del Ambiente office (☎07 2606606), just out of town on the road to Loja, or at the park entrance (see p.206).

ACCOMMODATION AND EATING

Ágape Sevilla de Oro and San Francisco. A nice brick-and-bamboo building with covered tables, serving decent breakfasts and lunches, including a *menu del día* from $3.50. Try the *mote de pillo con queso*, a filling dish of sweetcorn kernels fried with onion, garlic, eggs and herbs, plus a slab of cheese. Mon–Sat 10am–9pm.

Casteloz Corner of Tamayo and Diego de Vaca on the main square ☎07 2607991. This pizzeria serves reasonable comfort food – thick-crust pizzas, baguette sandwiches or a plate of nachos – which can be washed down with a chilled beer. Mon–Fri noon–10pm, Sat 4pm–10pm.

Chonta Dorada Jaramillo and Diego de Vaca ☎07 2606384. The spacious en-suite rooms with the usual mod cons make this spot a good-value pick. $20

★**Copalinga** 3km east of town on the road to Podocarpus ☎0993477013, ⊛copalinga.com. A $3 taxi ride from Zamora, this is a lovely, simple wooden lodge with its own hydro-power system, set amid a lush private

reserve aimed primarily at birdwatchers. Most cabins are en suite with a balcony, but there are excellent-value "rustic" cabins with bunks and shared facilities, though still with veranda and hammocks. Dining is communal (meals $13.50–17) and the food good, with breakfast (included) the highlight, to be enjoyed while watching colourful birds at a feeding table. Wi-fi available in the restaurant area. Shared cabins $26/person; private cabins $109

El Rinconcito del Encebollado Corner of Loja and Diego de Vaca. Busy corner café on a raised terrace opposite the market, so great for people-watching. Try one of their signature *encebollados* (fish stew with cassava and pickled onions). Daily 8am–2/3pm.

Samuria 24 de Mayo and Diego de Vaca ☎07 2607801, ✉hotelsamuria@hotmail.com. Modern hotel with nicely furnished, homely, carpeted rooms that have flatscreen TVs and monsoon showers, though they are a little small. Parking is available and breakfast is included. $38

Parque Nacional Podocarpus

Spilling down the eastern flanks of the Andes towards the tropical valleys of the Oriente, **PARQUE NACIONAL PODOCARPUS** presents a spectacular and diverse landscape with high levels of endemism, from high páramo to dense, dripping cloudforest and rushing waterfalls, down to lush tropical forest filled with butterflies and crystalline rivers. Its wide-ranging altitudes (900–3600m), climates and habitats harbour a staggering diversity of flora and fauna, including an estimated three to four thousand plant species, over five hundred recorded **bird species** – hummingbirds, toucans, tanagers and parrots among them, and important populations of mammals such as mountain tapirs, giant armadillos, *pudu* (dwarf deer), spectacled bears, monkeys and pumas. Named after Ecuador's only native conifer (also known as *romerillo*), whose numbers commercial logging have drastically reduced, Podocarpus also includes cinchona (known locally as *cascarilla*), whose bark is the source of **quinine**, which was first discovered in this very region.

There are two **main entrances** to the park, corresponding to its geographical divisions: one is the **Sector Cajanuma** in the Zona Alta (upper section), near Loja; the other is the **Sector Bombuscaro** in the Zona Baja (lower section), reached from Zamora. If you want to visit the more remote, little-visited sectors of Romerillos and Valladolid, you should seek information in Loja from the Ministerio del Ambiente (see p.201), have the relevant IGM maps and engage a certified guide – enquire at the tourist offices in Loja or Vilcabamba, or at one of the Vilcabamba tour operators. The El Palto sector is visited by many of the tours from Vilcabamba, but park facilities and official trails have yet to be developed, though they are on the agenda. You can get basic information and pick up a leaflet at the I-Tur office in Loja (p.201) or at the park entrances themselves.

Sector Cajanuma

Spread over the northern part of the Zona Alta, steep ridges covered with cloudforest and high, lake-studded páramo characterize the **Sector Cajanuma** (near Loja). With average elevations of over 3000m, daytime temperatures usually hover around 12°C, though it can get much colder when the wind whips up and the rains start to fall. Expect high rainfall and muddy trails between February and April; the driest months are usually July to September. The Cajanuma **entrance post** is 15km south of Loja, on the road to Vilcabamba, from where it's 8km uphill to the main **ranger station**, the starting point of a couple of excellent **trails**.

Sendero al Mirador

The **Sendero al Mirador** trail (3.5km) leads steeply uphill to a lookout point, giving stunning views across the deep-green mountainsides poking up through the clouds. This makes a very rewarding half-day hike, and offers excellent **birding** opportunities; look out for the bearded guan, grey-breasted mountain toucan and red-hooded tanager, among others.

Sendero Las Lagunas

The **Sendero Las Lagunas** is a demanding two-day hike leading for 14km (6–8 hours) through cloudforest and high páramo to the eerily beautiful **Lagunas del Compadre**, a network of fourteen lakes at 3200m above sea level, surrounded by bare granite and sharp, rocky peaks. For this trek, you now have to be accompanied by a certified guide (see above). With luck, you may also be able to spot a mountain tapir, which are quite common in this area.

4

ARRIVAL AND TOURS	SECTOR CAJANUMA

By bus Any bus from Loja to Vilcabamba will drop you at the entrance post, by the highway, from where it's 8km uphill (2–3hr) to the ranger station and park entrance.
By taxi Take a taxi from Loja ($12–15) or Vilcabamba

($18–20) and arrange for a return pick-up if you don't want to hike back to the main road.
Tour operators You can also visit the park with a tour operator from Vilcabamba (see box, p.209).

ACCOMMODATION

Camping There are good, free camping spots around the trout-filled lakes, but no facilities.
Ranger station Park entrance ☎ 07 3024862. The ranger station has a refuge and a few basic cabins with

bunk beds (bring a sleeping bag), electricity and kitchen facilities (but without utensils) for overnight visitors. There's hot water in the refuge but not in the cabins. $3/person

Sector Bombuscaro

Down in the Zona Baja, at the foot of the Cordillera Oriental, **Sector Bombuscaro** (near Zamora) is a sensory extravaganza of riotous vegetation, moss-scented air, squawking birds, fluorescent butterflies, gurgling waterfalls and ice-cold rivers. At just under 1000m above sea level, it rarely sees daytime temperatures fall below a very pleasant 18°C, and even during the rainy season (generally March–July) the weather is unlikely to spoil your fun so long as you have waterproofs and a few layers; the driest months are usually from October to December.

From the ranger station, there are a couple of short, signed paths to **waterfalls**, the most impressive being the 90m **La Poderosa** (30min walk). You can also take a refreshing dip in a gorgeous natural pool, signposted "*area de nadar*" from the main path.

RESERVA TAPICHALACA

The **Reserva Tapichalaca**, managed by the Fundación Jocotoco (☎02 2272013, ⊕fjocotoco .org), and signposted on the road north of Valladolid, lies contiguous with the Parque Nacional Podocarpus, and encompasses the same habitats, ranging from high páramo down to subtropical forests. It's an extraordinarily biologically sensitive area, and for a while was thought to be the only habitat of the **Jocotoco Antpitta** – a rare species of bird first "discovered" here in 1997 – until a few more were spotted in northern Peru in 2006. Other rarities include mountain tapirs, spectacled bears, imperial snipe and neblina metaltails, which you might be lucky enough to catch a glimpse of along the trails, which range from 2–8km.

ARRIVAL AND ACCOMMODATION

The reserve and lodge are signposted off the main Loja–Zumba road, 75km south of Loja. To stay in the reserve's simple but comfortable wooden lodge, contact Jocotours (☎02 505129, ⊕jocotoursecuador.com; $280). Five double en-suite rooms lie in the main building, which also has a pleasant lounge-cum-library with fireplace, while an additional cabin contains two further doubles. Day-visitors are also welcome ($15, but $30 if you want to visit the feeding station of the Jocotoco Antpitta, as the cost includes the mandatory guide). Rates include full board and access to the trails; transport and guiding services can also be arranged. There is a nightly mandatory contribution to their conservation fund ($5/person).

Of the several **trails** through the park, the nicest is the **Sendero Higuerones**, which follows the Río Bombuscaro for about 3km through secondary and primary forest, taking an hour or so each way; to stay on this path, ignore the footbridge over the river after 1km. As you walk, you're likely to see an extraordinary number of **birds** such as white-breasted parakeets, copper-chested jacamars and various rainbow-coloured tanagers, among many others. There are also many biting insects, so take plenty of **insect repellent** with you.

ARRIVAL AND DEPARATURE   SECTOR BOMBUSCARO

On foot The Bombuscaro park entrance is a pleasant 6km walk along the unpaved road that leaves from behind Zamora's bus terminal, following the Río Bombuscaro.

By taxi It's a short taxi ride ($4) from Zamora to the parking area at the end of the road. From here, it's a further 20min on foot up to the ranger station.

ACCOMMODATION

Ranger station ☎07 3024862. You can camp by the ranger station or sleep in one of the basic wooden huts nearby (bring a sleeping bag) and use their cooking facilities (bring utensils and food). $̲3̲/person

San Francisco Scientific Research Centre hostel Signposted south 23km along the road to Zamora

☎07 2573691, ⊕naturalezaycultura.org. Managed by NGO Naturaleza y Cultura Internacional in Loja, this basic hostel close to the park boundary comprises three furnished private rooms and dorm bunks (bring a sleeping bag), with use of communal living rooms and kitchen facilities. Dorms $̲2̲0̲; doubles $̲4̲0̲

Sectors Romerillos and Valladolid

Some 25km south of Zamora, the tiny village of **Romerillos** is the starting point for an adventurous but demanding three- to four-day circular hike in the park, through lush, dense cloudforest, with a fair amount of uphill climbing into páramo. Even more remote, and even less visited, is the sector accessed from **Valladolid**, a town 105km south of Loja and 67km south of Vilcabamba, where there is a Ministerio del Ambiente office and a basic hotel. To explore either sector you'll need to bring full equipment and the relevant IGM maps, and have a good guide, or persuade a park warden to accompany you, and should register with the park office before setting out in case you get lost and need rescuing.

ARRIVAL AND DEPARTURE   SECTORS ROMERILLOS AND VALLADOLID

By bus Buses run from Zamora's bus terminal to Romerillos (6.30am, 7.30am & 2pm, returning in the afternoon; 2hr). Buses from Loja via Vilcabamba bound for Zumba near the

Peruvian border, pass through Valladolid (12 daily; 3hr 30min).
By taxi A taxi from Zamora to Romerillos will cost around $25.

Vilcabamba

Just over 40km south of Loja, in a charming valley enfolded by crumpled, sunburnt hills, sits the small agricultural village of **VILCABAMBA**. Synonymous with longevity (see box below), hippiedom and utter relaxation, the village has been attracting travellers for over half a century.

These days Vilcabamba feels like a place not quite grounded in reality – partly because of the myths associated with it, partly because of the high proportion of resident expats – particularly from the US – who've come here in search of the simple life (and, inevitably, have ended up competing vigorously with each other for business, and stirring resentment with local residents), and partly because of the conspicuous presence of foreign tourists. People head here for a variety of reasons. Some come for the hiking and birding in the nearby hills of the **Parque Nacional Podocarpus** (see p.204). Others come for the hallucinogenic cactus juice, **San Pedro**, that the village was once famous for (even though it is now illegal, is locally frowned upon and has therefore been almost completely eradicated from the area), but most – including middle-class *lojanos*, at weekends – come just to relax, enjoy the warm climate and nice views, and maybe take a horse ride or indulge in a massage or steam bath. The **best months** to be here are June to September: October to May can often be rainy. Daytime temperatures usually fluctuate between 18ºC and 28ºC.

There's not a great deal to do in the village itself. The focal point is the leafy **parque central**, presided over by the church and surrounded by a sprinkling of café-restaurants and craft shops of varying quality, which you can happily browse for an hour or so. Don't miss the high-quality silverwork and the artesanal chocolate.

Cerro Mandango

A popular destination for tourists in Vilcabamba is **Cerro Mandango**, which offers fabulous, panoramic views over the valley. The hill resembles a person lying down – with the forehead, nose and chin quite distinct from certain angles – and rises over the village's southeastern side. There is a good trail to the summit (about an hour's stiff climb) and you can return the same way or make a longer, trickier descent via a different route. The tourist office has maps indicating the trail, which is fairly straightforward; alternatively, guides can be engaged via one of the local tour operators (see box, p.209). Muggings have been an issue in the past, although at the time of writing the tourist office was adamant that this is no longer a problem as the perpetrators are now behind bars – but check the current situation before setting out.

ARRIVAL AND DEPARTURE   VILCABAMBA

By bus Buses from Loja's bus terminal (every 15–30min until 9.15pm; last return bus 8.45pm; 1hr 15min) drop passengers off at Vilcabamba's bus terminal on the main road running into town, Avenida de la Eterna Juventud, a couple of blocks from the central square.

By taxi Shared taxis provide a faster way to get between Loja and Vilcabamba (40min; $2.25, or $9 for the whole taxi), though they're not always more comfortable. In Loja head for the taxi office (☎07 2570956) on 11 de Mayo; in Vilcabamba the taxis leave from inside the bus terminal. A taxi to the airport in Catamayo (see p.200) costs $40.

VILCABAMBA: THE VALLEY OF ETERNAL YOUTH?

Vilcabamba first caught the attention of the outside world back in 1955, when *Reader's Digest* published an article claiming Vilcabambans enjoyed a considerably higher than average **life expectancy**, with a very low incidence of cardiovascular health problems. Soon Vilcabamba was being touted as "the valley of eternal youth" and the "valley of longevity", as international investigators unearthed a string of sprightly old people claiming to be up to 120 or 130 years old. More rigorous studies revealed these claims to be wildly exaggerated, and to date no hard evidence has been produced to support theories of an abnormally long-living population in Vilcabamba – though scientists acknowledged that villagers in their 70s and 80s tended to be extremely fit and healthy for their age.

4

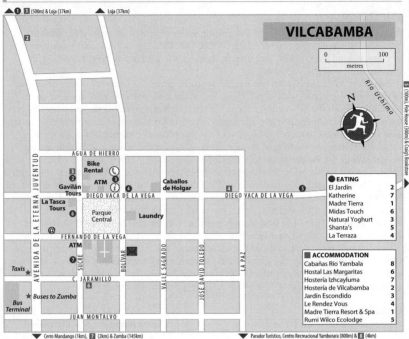

VILCABAMBA

● EATING	
El Jardín	2
Katherine	7
Madre Tierra	1
Midas Touch	6
Natural Yoghurt	3
Shanta's	5
La Terraza	4

■ ACCOMMODATION	
Cabañas Río Yambala	8
Hostal Las Margaritas	6
Hostería Izhcayluma	7
Hostería de Vilcabamba	2
Jardín Escondido	3
Le Rendez Vous	4
Madre Tierra Resort & Spa	1
Rumi Wilco Ecolodge	5

GETTING AROUND AND INFORMATION

On foot Most of the hotels and restaurants are within a few blocks off the main square, easily reachable on foot. A few are 2–3km from the centre, along the main road, which is not particularly pleasant to walk along.

By taxi Local taxis (white camionetas) wait outside the bus terminal and in the main square, and charge up to $2/ trip.

Tourist office The helpful I-Tur office is opposite the church on the *parque central* (daily 8am–1pm & 2–6pm; ☎ 07 2640090).

ACCOMMODATION

There's an enormous amount of **accommodation** to choose from for such a small place, most of it very reasonably priced. Where you stay can make a big difference to your experience of Vilcabamba, so consider whether you want to mingle with lots of other travellers, stay somewhere quiet with a local feel to it or just find somewhere private where you can enjoy the countryside.

★ **Cabañas Río Yambala** (aka Charlie's Cabins) 5km uphill along the road to Yamburara ☎ 0991062762, ⓦ vilcabamba-hotel.com. Delightful, rustic self-catering option for short- and long-term rental, comprising four thatched wooden cabañas in a scenic, secluded location overlooking the Río Yambala and one riverside cottage. The cabins are a very good deal when rented out for the week ($150); no. 2 has the best views. There are one- to three-day horseback and hiking tours (open to non-guests) to their private reserve, *Las Palmas*, that abuts Parque Nacional Podocarpus. Taxis from the village cost $3–4. Cabins $45; cottage $450/month

Hostal Las Margaritas Corner of Jaramillo and Sucre ☎ 07 2640051. This locally owned B&B offers six neat,

modern en-suite rooms with cable TV in a converted house, providing a friendly family environment. There's a small garden pool too. An excellent deal, with breakfast included. $30

★ **Hostería Izhcayluma** 2km south of the centre on the road to Zumba ☎ 07 2640095, ⓦ izhcayluma.com. Popular, friendly German-owned hostel set in pretty gardens overlooking the Vilcabamba valley. Dorms (minimum two-night stay) and rooms have large windows and come with porch, hammock and private or shared bathroom. For a private balcony, you'll pay an extra $13. Plus there's a gorgeous pool, a spa, a table tennis table and board games, as well as a good restaurant serving Bavarian specialities and a decent buffet breakfast ($4). A taxi from town costs $2, and they also offer a shuttle service from Cuenca. Dorms $9; doubles $36

Hostería de Vilcabamba Main road as it enters the village ☎07 2640272, ⓦhosteriadevilcabamba.com. Large modern bungalows set in wooded grounds containing several well-furnished rooms with mirror wardrobes, large plasma TVs and comfortable beds. Also has a pool, sauna, steam baths, whirlpool and an attractive bar-restaurant; it's high-end, but not quite as high-end as it thinks. Breakfast included. $72

Jardín Escondido Sucre, just north of the parque central ☎07 2640281, ⓦfacebook.com/jardin escondido.vilcabamba. Gaily painted three-bed dorms and en-suite rooms, with hard beds set around a beautiful walled garden with a small pool (made even smaller by the presence of its pump), jacuzzi and hammocks and an excellent restaurant, *El Jardín* (see p.210). There are kitchen and laundry facilities too. Breakfast included. Dorms $14; doubles $33

Le Rendez Vous Diego Vaca de Vega 06-43 and La Paz ☎0992191180, ⓦrendezvousecuador.com. Friendly, French-owned hotel offering cheerful rooms for one to four people, with patios, hammocks and shared or private bathrooms facing a pretty, central garden. The price includes a good breakfast, with home-made bread, plenty of fresh fruit and proper coffee brought to your room. Washing facilities, book exchange and board games are also available, and they can arrange Spanish lessons. Prices hiked for festivals. $35

Madre Tierra Resort & Spa 2km before town, above the main road from Loja ☎07 2640269, ⓦmadretierra .com.ec. There's creative use of stone and wood in these individually priced rooms, from a "hobbit hole" through to comfortable mid-priced rooms (some with private bathroom) to stylish suites with fabulous views of the valley. There's also a popular patio restaurant, a renowned spa and a small, attractive pool. It can feel a little cramped if full and the noise from the road does sometimes drift up to disturb the tranquillity. It's always popular, though, so book ahead. $39

TOURS AND ACTIVITIES AROUND VILCABAMBA

Vilcabamba affords great opportunities for **hiking**, **horse riding** and **birding** up to the cloudforests around Parque Nacional Podocarpus (see p.204), and several outfits and guides offer **tours** of the area. Note that horses are not allowed within the park boundaries, so excursions on horseback are in the private reserves adjacent to the national park. If you're keen to go hiking independently, and don't want to go as far as the national park, there are two important private buffer reserves nearby. One is 8km up the valley, belonging to *Cabañas Río Yambala* (see opposite); entry costs $10 and guide services are available. A colour-coded **trail system** leads to swimming holes on the river and viewpoints, with the five-hour "red trail" particularly rewarding. Rumi Wilco Reserve ($2 entry) also has well-signposted trails across the mountainside. If you fancy **mountain biking**, you can rent a bike for $10–15/day from Angel (daily 8am–6pm) on Sucre, just off the park.

If all the above sounds too energetic, you can top up your hammock reading material at Craig's Bookstore (Mon–Fri 7am–6pm, Sat 6–11am), 1km along the road to Yamburara, which boasts a wide range of books (to buy or exchange) in English and fourteen other languages. And given the valley's mythology, there's no end of ways to attend to your wellbeing: in addition to the spas attached to various lodgings, there are opportunities for meditation, yoga, psychic readings, flotation therapy and angelic healing – to name just a few. Check out the Centro de Meditación (ⓦmindfulnessmeditationinecuador.org) and notice boards around the village.

TOUR OPERATORS

Caballos de Holgar Diego Vaca de la Vega and Valle Sagrado ☎0982961238. Leads one- or two-day excursions to the cloudforest (in English, Spanish or German) on foot or on horseback ($50 for one day). The circular tour of Mandango ($35–40) takes in Holgar's family farm en route. Also offers bike tours with Angel (see above).

Gavilán Tours Sucre and Diego Vaca de la Vega ☎07 2640158, ✉gavilanhorse@yahoo.com. Run by New Zealander Gavin Moore, who offers excellent combined hiking and horse riding tours up to the cloudforest bordering Podocarpus from $50/day/person, including food and lodging in the owner's bunk house, or day-rides from $30–45 for 4–6hr, taking in a waterfall.

La Tasca Tours Diego Vaca de la Vega and Sucre ☎07 2640404 or ☎09895562299. Experienced company run by brothers Rene and Alvaro León, who lead a variety of half- or one-day tours involving biking, horse riding and/or hiking – to a waterfall, a *panela* factory or a coffee farm ($35–50 depending on numbers). They also organize highly recommended all-inclusive multi-day excursions in their private reserve (where they have cabins) and to Podocarpus.

★**Rumi Wilco Ecolodge** 15min walk northeast of the centre ⊕07 2640186, ⓦrumiwilco.com. A genuine, simple, low-impact ecolodge set in a private reserve, offering several self-catering accommodation options at varying rates: secluded traditional wooden cabins on stilts (for up to four); a cluster of adobe buildings with shared facilities and outdoor fire-pit, nearer the entrance; and camping, including fire-pit and use of kitchen and bathroom facilities. Guests have free access to the reserve. Discounts are available for long stays, as well as credits for volunteer work. Adobe rooms $8/person; cabins $28; camping $4/person

EATING AND DRINKING

Most hotels offer food as well as rooms, sometimes as a package with the room rate. Vilcabamba offers an appealing range of **international cuisines** alongside the more usual *comida típica*.

★**El Jardín** In Jardín Escondido (see p.209) ⊕07 2640281. Very good Mexican-owned restaurant in the garden of the hotel, serving authentic home-made cooking, including vegetarian dishes using plenty of organic, home-grown produce. Daily 8am–8pm.

Katherine Sucre and Jaramillo. Cheap and tasty Ecuadorian food (mains from $3) and friendly service are offered by this simple local restaurant, with *seco de chivo* (goat stew) at weekends. Mon–Sat 8.30am–4pm & 6–9pm.

★**Madre Tierra** 2km before town, above the main road from Loja ⊕07 2640269. Enjoy tasty, international organic cuisine at *Madre Tierra Resort & Spa* (see p.209) – try one of the Indian and Sri Lankan dishes – while gazing out over the valley from the patio terrace. Only takes outside diners when not full. Daily 8.30am–8.30pm.

Midas Touch Sucre, on the main square ⊕0980970227. *The* place for a long indulgent breakfast ($4–5) – bags of inventive, healthy, mainly organic offerings, including plenty of vegan and veggie fare, served up on their patio. Mon, Wed & Thurs 8am–5pm, Fri–Sun 8am–10pm.

Natural Yoghurt Bolívar and Diego Vaca de la Vega. Tiny café serving excellent-value fresh, organic food: healthy breakfasts, such as yoghurt, fruit and granola, plus soups, sandwiches, and sweet and savoury crêpes at ridiculously low prices. Daily 8am–10pm.

Shanta's Over the bridge on Diego Vaca de la Vega ⊕0985627802. Reliable, inexpensive bar-restaurant, with funky saddle-topped bar stools, serving up trout, frogs' legs, filet mignon and immensely popular pizzas ($7–10). Leave room for the crêpes in chocolate sauce, and down a shot of the house snake liqueur if you dare. Tues–Sun 1–9pm.

La Terraza Corner of Diego Vaca de la Vega and Bolívar ⊕0991667995. Very popular restaurant – even attracting *lojanos* on weekend evenings – with colourful decor and a lively atmosphere, serving well-prepared Mexican, Thai and Italian dishes. Service can be very slow when it's busy. Daily 11am–9pm.

4

South to Peru

The most convenient **border crossing into Peru** from the southern sierra is via a paved road from Loja to the frontier town of **MACARÁ** 190km to the southwest, a much more pleasant and efficient alternative to the frenetic **Huaquillas** crossing on the coast (see p.316), though those based in Vilcabamba or looking for an interesting route into the thick of the Peruvian highlands might consider the remote and adventurous frontier passage at **Zumba**, due south.

Macará

A surprisingly pleasant, though hot, border town, **Macará** sits in a fertile agricultural valley noted for its rice production. The few tourists that pass this way and who are not simply transiting to or from Peru are usually keen bird watchers, drawn by the nearby dry tropical forest populated by giant ceiba trees, and inhabited by the likes of the henna-hooded foliage gleaner, in the **Reserva Jorupe**, 10km along the road to Sozoranga. The reserve is managed by the Fundación Jocotoco (ⓦjocotoursecuador.com) and is open to day-visitors ($15), though it also has a birding lodge there (see opposite).

CROSSING THE PERUVIAN BORDER — MACARÁ

BY BUS

From Loja Regular buses make the journey to Macará from the terminal in Loja; the faster ones (8 daily; 5hr; marked "via Catacocha") travel down the Panamerican highway, while Union Cariamanga buses, via Cariamanga, are slower (around 5hr 30min). In addition, three daily direct buses also go all the way from Loja to Piura in Peru (7am & 11pm; from Piura 1pm & 9pm; 8–9hr; $14, tickets best bought a day before travel), via Catacocha and Macará, operated by Cooperativa Loja Internacional (☎07 2579014, ⓦ cooperativaloja.com.ec).

In Peru In La Tina, the little settlement on the Peruvian side, you'll be whisked away by colectivo to Sullana (2hr), from where there is easy transport to the larger city of Piura (40min further). You could also hop on one of the international buses direct to Piura as they pass through Macará; check for times at the Cooperativa Loja office on Jaramillo and Vaca, Barrio Velasco Ibarra in Macará.

BANKS AND MONEY

The banks at Macará do not change currency but you can find moneychangers with Peruvian *soles* at the border and around the park, where taxis to the border are ranked. The Banco de Loja has an ATM but it is temperamental.

IMMIGRATION

Through buses to Piura from will simply wait while passengers have their passports checked and stamped. Remember you need exit and entry stamps. If you've taken the bus to Macará, and you don't want to wait for one of the international buses, you'll need to get to the international bridge between Ecuador and Peru, a little over 2km southwest of town, which you can walk to in about forty minutes, or you could take a taxi ($2) or colectivo from 10 de Agosto at the park near the market. Either side of the bridge, the Ecuadorian and Peruvian immigration offices, where you get your exit and entry stamps and show proof of onward travel, are open 24hr.

ACCOMMODATION AND EATING

Los Arrozales 10 de Agosto and Amazonas ☎07 2695381. Cheerful new hotel offering the best rooms in town (en suite, with a/c and cable TV) at modest rates. Breakfast included. $32

Caña & Tapa Amazonas, opposite the park ☎07 2694970. This unlikely Spanish–Ecuadorian culinary gem has indoor and outdoor patio seating at nice wooden tables. As well as tapas ($4–8), there are good cakes. Mon–Sat 11am until late.

D'Marcos Jaime Roldos and Amazonas ☎07 2695111. Brightly tiled bar-restaurant on two floors, serving decent, moderately priced mains (around $6) for lunch and dinner.

Daily 8am–10pm.

Terra Verde Vaca A couple of blocks west of the Cooperativa Loja Internacional terminus ☎07 2694540. Respectable budget hotel with clean, air-conditioned rooms (and cheaper ones with fans), private hot-water bathrooms and a rooftop terrace. $16

Urraca Lodge Reserva Jorupe ☎02 505212 in Quito, ⓦ jocotoursecuador.com; 10km along the road to Sozoranga. Six simple wooden cabins in peaceful forest surroundings, with large windows and wraparound verandas from which to watch the birdlife. Reserve entry and all meals included. $280

Via Zumba

There's a less-used border crossing in the tiny village of La Balsa, near **ZUMBA**, over 145km due south of Vilcabamba. The road from Vilcabamba is slowly being paved, but for now you can expect most of the journey to be rough and slow, through you will pass through remote and beautiful scenery.

CROSSING THE PERUVIAN BORDER   ZUMBA

BY BUS AND CAMIONETA

To Zumba Zumba is serviced by regular buses from Loja (8 daily; 6–7hr) via Vilcabamba (5–6hr). Additionally, Transporte Suroriente runs four buses a day.

To the border From Zumba, where there are a few simple hotels, board one of the infrequent *rancheras* (8am, 2pm, and, less reliably, 5.30pm; 1hr 30min) or hire a private camioneta to La Balsa ($20) – it's 15km on a potholed road, which is prone to landslides and closures in the rainy season.

In Peru Shared-taxi camionetas leave for San Ignacio (2hr; $7–15 depending on the number of passengers), a nice enough place to spend the night, and one that has banking facilities with ATMs.

IMMIGRATION

Immigration, not far from the international bridge over the Río Canchis, is open 24hr, though you may have to search around for an official at quiet times.

The Oriente

SANI LODGE

5

The Oriente

No other Ecuadorian habitat overwhelms the senses like the tropical rainforest, with its cacophonous soundtrack of birds and insects, the rich smell of steaming foliage and teeming soil, the glimmer of fluorescent birds and butterflies in the understorey, or the startling clamour of a troop of monkeys clattering through the canopy above. This biodiversity is the Oriente's star attraction, and it's what most visitors are here for – though the region, which occupies a massive area covering almost half the country, contains a good deal more besides. The *alto* (high) Oriente starts on the eastern Andean flank, where the high, windswept páramo steadily gives way to dripping montane forests, swathed in mist and draped with mosses and epiphytes, as the elevation decreases. Waterfalls plunge into broadening valleys and temperatures rise as the mountains descend into the *bajo* (low) Oriente, sinking like talons into the emerald velvet of the vast wilderness: Ecuador's Amazonian jungle, one of the country's most thrilling destinations.

The easiest way of getting into the rainforest – which in places stretches for more than 250km to the borders of Colombia and Peru – is to go on a **jungle tour**. Excursions range from simple day-trips into pockets of forest close to a town, to stays with a rainforest community or at a jungle lodge, to rugged multi-day camping treks into the remotest tracts of primary jungle in distant reserves. **Unguided travel** in the *bajo* Oriente is frowned upon by the Ecuadorian authorities, conservation groups and indigenous communities alike; nor is it recommended, for your own safety (see box, p.217).

Over 15,000 square kilometres of the most pristine tracts of rainforest lie within the confines of the **Reserva Faunística Cuyabeno** and the **Parque Nacional Yasuní**, accessible from the pioneer oil-mining centres of **Lago Agrio** and **Coca** respectively. Yet even from these frontier towns further travel will be needed, by speedboat or motorized canoe, to reach your final destination, which will demand at least four or five days to enjoy properly. Beyond marvelling at the dazzling array of wildlife, excursions deep into Amazonia also offer opportunities to learn about and from the **indigenous peoples** of the region, such as the Siona, Secoya, Cofán and, most notably, the Waorani, many of whom inhabit the vast **Reserva Waorani**, just south of Yasuní.

LAGUNAS DE CUYABENO

Highlights

❶ Staying with an indigenous community
Ecuador has one of the fastest growing
"ethno-tourism" scenes in the world, allowing you
to experience "real life" in the rainforest. **See p.219,
p.227, p.236, p.243, p.249 & p.252**

❷ Jungle lodges Immerse yourself in the sights
and sounds of the rainforest from the relative
comfort of one of the Oriente's many jungle
lodges, most of which are accessed by boat.
See p.220, pp.234–235, p.236, p.246 & p.252

❸ Papallacta's thermal baths Soak up the
steam and gaze at the splendid scenery, in
Ecuador's best-known hot springs. **See p.221**

❹ Lagunas de Cuyabeno Seated in your
dugout canoe, seek out the abundant and

extraordinary wildlife – black caymans, giant
otters, pink river dolphins – that inhabit these
blackwater lagoons. **See p.228**

❺ Parque Nacional Yasuní A World Biosphere
Reserve, harbouring the majority of Ecuador's
mammals and, over a third of all Amazonian bird
species. **See p.233**

❻ Añangu parrot licks It's an extravaganza of
sound and colour when hundreds of parrots
descend on clay banks – called clay licks, salt licks
or salados – and chew off mineral-rich chunks to
aid the digestion of acidic fruits. **See p.234**

❼ Whitewater rafting around Tena The
country's prime destination for rafting and
kayaking, with dozens of runs. **See p.237 & p.239**

HIGHLIGHTS ARE MARKED ON THE MAP ON P.216

5

The meandering descent from the highlands into the northern reaches of the *bajo* Oriente also has its attractions, from the country's most famous hot springs at **Papallacta**, perched on the hilly fringes of the Cayambe-Coca reserve, to the smouldering green-black cone of **Volcán El Reventador**, which watches over the **San Rafael falls**, Ecuador's biggest at 145m.

Further south, and closer to Quito, so favoured by those with limited time, the provincial capitals of **Tena** and **Puyo** afford different rainforest experiences: not being

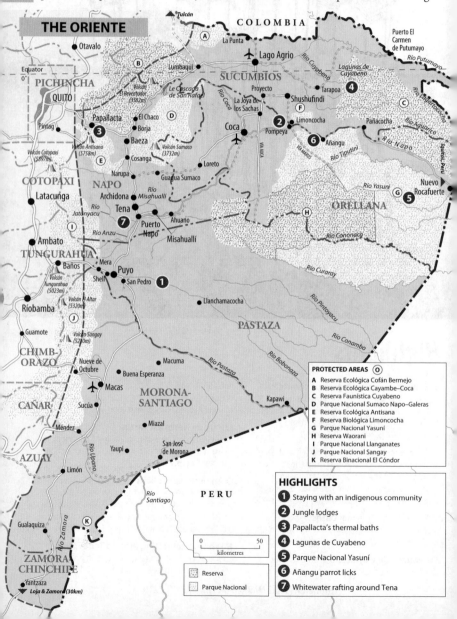

THE ORIENTE

PROTECTED AREAS Ⓞ

A Reserva Ecológica Cofán Bermejo
B Reserva Ecológica Cayambe–Coca
C Reserva Faunística Cuyabeno
D Parque Nacional Sumaco Napo–Galeras
E Reserva Ecológica Antisana
F Reserva Biológica Limoncocha
G Parque Nacional Yasuní
H Reserva Waorani
I Parque Nacional Llanganates
J Parque Nacional Sangay
K Reserva Binacional El Cóndor

HIGHLIGHTS

❶ Staying with an indigenous community
❷ Jungle lodges
❸ Papallacta's thermal baths
❹ Lagunas de Cuyabeno
❺ Parque Nacional Yasuní
❻ Añangu parrot licks
❼ Whitewater rafting around Tena

Reserva

Parque Nacional

0   50
kilometres

SAFETY AND SECURITY IN THE ORIENTE

The region is militarily sensitive and you'll be required to produce your **passport** at regular checkpoints. More so than in other places, it's important that you have original documents rather than copies. As far as security is concerned, at the time of writing the areas adjacent to the **Colombian border** are unsafe due to infiltration of guerrilla and paramilitary units and should be **avoided** (see box, p.226).

as close to such extensive areas of forest, wildlife populations are lower here, though both have more agreeable, slightly fresher climates. Besides, Tena is now a major centre for **whitewater rafting** and other **adventure sports**, while the nearby river port of **Misahuallí** provides easy access to the more affordable cabañas and lodges on the upper Río Napo.

From Puyo, the Troncal Amazónica (Amazon highway), which runs from north to south through the region in the *selva alta*, parallel with the eastern flank of the Andes, runs 129km to the attractive and southernmost urban centre of the Ecuadorian Amazon basin, **Macas**. This highway is virtually the only road in the southern Oriente, which is less developed than the northern region in every way, with fewer roads, fewer towns, fewer colonists, fewer tourists and less oil activity. Access east into the heart of the tropical rainforest, which lacks the protected status of the northern reserves, is possible only by boat along the numerous rivers coiling through the forest, or by chartered light aircraft. **Indigenous groups** – principally the Kichwa, the Shuar and pockets of Achuar – communally own most of this territory.

Tourism in the southern Oriente is considerably less evolved than in the north; with one notable exception, you'll find none of the fancy lodges and cabañas of the kind scattered up the Río Napo. Instead, the southern and central Oriente have excellent opportunities for culturally focused **ecotourism**, offered by tour operators based in Puyo, Macas and Tena in association with host indigenous groups. Guides take tourists on overnight or multi-day trips to indigenous communities – some very remote – often with an emphasis on learning about their customs, mythology and healing rituals while exploring the jungle.

Brief history

The **jungle** – *la selva* – has held a curious place in Ecuador's national psyche since the time of the **conquistadors**. Rumours of the jungle being *el país de canela* ("the land of cinnamon"), a place of abundant fruits and spices, and the legend of El Dorado, the "Golden Man", which later gave rise to the myth of a lost city of gold, drew the early explorers here, suggesting to them a land of staggering natural riches. But the first Europeans to venture here soon found that this fabled earthly paradise had a nightmarish underside; their parties were plunged into an impenetrable green hell (*"el infierno verde"*), teeming with poisonous snakes and biting insects. A string of catastrophic expeditions in the early colonial period quickly discouraged the Spanish from colonizing the Oriente at all. Most people, save for a sprinkling of missionaries and pioneers, kept away, leaving the forests and its inhabitants well alone.

This all changed in the late 1960s following the discovery of large **oil and gas reserves** (see box, p.224), now the country's most important source of wealth. In the space of a few years the Oriente was transformed into a "productive" region and colonists streamed in on the new roads, looking for jobs and levelling still more land for farms. The speed of the destruction was dramatic but the Ecuadorian government, under widespread international pressure, began setting aside large tracts of forest as **national parks and reserves**; the largest four – **Sangay** and **Cayambe-Coca**, which are mainly in the Oriente but most easily accessed from the highlands (see p.170 & p.102), **Cuyabeno** and **Yasuní**, a UNESCO World Biosphere Reserve – were created in the 1970s.

5

AYAHUASCA WARNING

Some tours advertise the opportunity to experience an **ayahuasca ceremony**, a ritual bodily and spiritual cleansing presided over by a shaman, and involving the psychotropic ayahuasca vine, a powerful hallucinogen traditionally used for purifying the mind and body. Since it can have extremely unpleasant side effects (such as vomiting, diarrhoea and psychological distress), it is important that any ceremony is led by a fully trained and experienced shaman with all the right preparations – generally someone with many years of training since childhood – and not a young man with a little shamanic knowledge, used to putting on shows for tourists.

The issues today

Even though there are more than 25,000 square kilometres of protected land in the Oriente – well over half of which is pristine Amazonian rainforest – conservationists are worried that the cash-strapped Ecuadorian government is unable (or unwilling) to make sure it stays that way. The task of balancing the needs of a faltering economy against the obligation to protect some of the most important forests on the planet has been among Ecuador's central problems for the past few decades (see box, p.224).

Meanwhile, oil-mining and drilling activity is ongoing in several crucial protected areas, including Yasuní. While most people would concede that the oil industry has been very much a mixed blessing for the country, the **indigenous peoples** of the region – who include the Siona, Waorani, Secoya, Achuar, Shuar, Kichwa, Cofán and Záparo – have had the most to lose. Many groups, rejecting the Western way of life, have been driven into ever smaller, remoter territories where it becomes increasingly hard to support themselves by traditional means. Their rivers and soil already polluted from industrial waste, most of the communities are under mounting pressure to sell out to the oil industry, both culturally and territorially. In recent years, **ecotourism** has emerged as a

JUNGLE ESSENTIALS

Many organized **tours** supply essential items such as mosquito nets, rubber boots, ponchos, toilet paper, bedding, food and clean water, but always make sure before you go so you know what you need to bring. Check the operator's camping and water purification equipment to see if they work and make sure that tents and nets provide adequate protection from bugs and insects. Put all your belongings in **waterproof bags** (especially valuables and important documents) and make sure that you carry a rain jacket or poncho. There are banks and ATMs in the main centres, but you should take **cash** with you once you venture further into more remote areas. You will also need:

Anti-malarial pills A course of which should be started in advance of your trip as prescribed.

Binoculars Your guide should carry a pair but you'll enjoy the scenery more with a pair of your own.

Camera See the "Photography" section of Basics for more details (see p.50).

Emergency supplies A first-aid kit, compass and whistle.

Insect repellent Lots of it – keeping covered up is a priority. DEET is very effective but it's potent and melts synthetic materials, so store and apply it safely. Sand flies can be more bothersome than mosquitoes, but respond to any kind of repellent.

Light sources A torch or headlamp and extra batteries – electricity is not always available so you'll need these for getting about the lodge or campsite (or spotting caymans) at night. Candles and waterproof matches (or a gas lighter) are also a good idea for evenings in a lodge or cabaña without power.

Passport You'll need one to enter the Oriente; it must be the original, not a copy.

Practical clothing A long-sleeved shirt and lightweight trousers for protection against insects and swimwear for cooling off in rivers; a hat for sun protection on boat trips.

Sun cream Particularly necessary during river journeys.

Vaccinations The "Health" section of Basics (see p.40) has the current recommendations.

Water purifier and bottles For camping trips and basic tours.

great hope for groups seeking to adapt to a life in which external influences are inevitable, bringing in badly needed income, strengthening the case for the conservation of the forests within an economic framework and reasserting cultural identities.

ARRIVAL AND DEPARTURE   THE ORIENTE

The region's oil infrastructure has made the Ecuadorian Amazon one of the most easily accessed rainforest areas in the continent, with its centres of jungle tourism all within a day's bus journey of **Quito**. There are two main routes to the Oriente, while a newer road runs from **Guamote** (south of Riobamba) directly to Macas, slicing through Parque Nacional Sangay, and there are also improving road connections with Macas from **Cuenca** and **Loja**.

From Quito Buses leave from the Quitumbe terminal in Quito and descend into the Amazon basin via the Papallacta pass, which splits at Baeza – north to Lago Agrio (and then Coca), and south to Tena and the faster route to Coca.

From Ambato There is a second main route into the region from Ambato through Baños to Puyo, where it meets the road between Tena and Macas.

TOURS

Taking a **guided tour** is the easiest way to visit the jungle, and often the cheapest. Day-trips range from around $45/person, and usually include transport, guided activities and lunch. Multi-day trips range widely from around $100–280 per person (sharing) per day, and usually include transport from the nearest population centre, **accommodation**, three meals per day, non-alcoholic drinks, some **equipment** (see box opposite), plus guiding services and activities. Travel to the nearest Oriente town, where the tour starts, is usually separate, although most tour operators can help you arrange this if necessary. Visits usually last three to six days and programmes are clearly structured, involving a combination of guided hikes, canoe trips, wildlife-viewing and demonstrations of traditional, indigenous customs. Pricier lodges may have some optional extras, and tips are usually expected for the guide(s), and sometimes the lodge staff. Discounts can often be negotiated in **low season** (Feb to mid-June and Sept–Nov). Tours to high-end lodges are usually booked from abroad or via the lodge office in Quito. Budget-end tours, including many community-based tourism projects to indigenous communities, may be more easily organized through a local travel agent or community organization in one of the Oriente towns (see p.225, p.229, p.237, p.244, p.247 & p.250). Note that much of the first and last day of any tour will be spent travelling to/from your destination and checking in/out, which is why a longer tour usually offers better value for money and a richer experience. Trips to Cuyabeno are generally cheaper than to Yasuní.

ACCOMMODATION

Accommodation ranges from extremely comfortable **lodges** whose adorned en-suite cabañas have ceiling fans, hot water, electricity and private balconies, to simple cabins with shared toilets, containing little more than a bed, mosquito net and four plank walls, to **campamentos** (open-sided camping platforms) or **carpas** (standard tents). No matter how luxurious (and expensive) the lodge, since you are in the rainforest you can expect to encounter some insect life in your lodgings, and there is always the possibility of a power or water outage. Most lodges have a communal dining and social area, constructed in wood and thatch.

GUIDES

A knowledgeable, enthusiastic guide is essential to a good jungle experience. In the most expensive places, they'll be English-speaking naturalists and ornithologists working with a local, "native" guide who will know the area intimately and be able to share their indigenous knowledge of the rainforest. Note that the term "native" may not be synonymous with "indigenous", as it often refers to anyone who lives in the Oriente. All guides should be certified, though this is no guarantee of quality. At the budget end of the scale, it's a good idea to meet your guide in advance as a way of gauging their quality and checking the standard of their English (where necessary). Make sure you find out what the guide-to-tourist ratio is for activities, as larger group sizes minimize

your chance of hearing the guide and seeing the wildlife before it disappears, in addition to having a negative impact on the natural environment.

INDIGENOUS-COMMUNITY STAYS

A growing number of indigenous communities in the Oriente have started ecotourism projects, giving visitors a glimpse of village life in the rainforest by staying with a family, or in simple cabañas just next to a community. A common emphasis is on intercultural understanding, and you're likely to be treated to singing, dancing and folkloric presentations alongside the more standard forest walks and canoe trips. Guides are generally less likely to speak much English, so you'll inevitably get more out of the experience with some Spanish. The income raised from

5

JUNGLE TOUR OPERATORS IN QUITO

There are dozens of **jungle tour operators** in Ecuador competing for your attention; the greatest concentration can be found in the Mariscal area of **Quito**. A selection of recommended Quito-based operators is listed below, but shop around to find the price, guide and itinerary that suits you. All prices quoted below are **per person** (sharing a double room). If you are travelling alone in high season, you are likely to have to pay a single person supplement, or possibly the full cost of a double room.

Advantage Ecuador Ritz Plaza, Gaspar de Villaroel and 6 de Diciembre ☎02 3360887, ⓦadvantag ecuador.com, ⓦmanateeamazonexplorer.com, ⓦanakondaamazoncruises.com. Operates the *Manatee Amazon Explorer*, a popular, relatively luxurious three-tiered air-conditioned river cruiser that navigates the lower Napo on regular four- to eight-day excursions, plus a glamping option; extras can include visits to Yasuní National Park, an observation tower and a parrot lick, plus kayak rental. Also operates the newer, more upmarket *Anakonda* cruise boat. From $1062/person for four days in a twin cabin, with $266/night for additional glamping.

Cuyabeno River Lodge Juan León Mera N24-91 and Foch ☎02 2903629, ⓦcuyabenoriver.com. Economical tours of the Cuyabeno reserve exploring its various black- and whitewater river systems by canoe, and visiting local communities; the longer tours comprise a mixture of camping and nights in the lodge. For a minimum of four people they offer four-day ($250) to six-day ($600) tours, plus a twelve-day expedition that ends in Iquitos, Peru ($1400).

Dracaena Amazon Explorations Pinto E4-360 between Amazonas and Juan León Mera ☎02 2546590, ⓦamazondracaena.com. Friendly, family-run outfit offering four- to seven-day tours on set days ($280–630) to Cuyabeno and further afield, staying within the reserve at their established campsites and *Nicky Lodge*.

Fundación Sobrevivencia Cofán Cardenal N74-153 and Mancheno, Carcelén Alto ☎02 2474763, ⓦcofan.org. The Cofán community of Zábalo offers programmes of four days minimum ($120/day for groups of four, less for larger groups), with comfortable cabañas, and options for trekking, camping and canoeing. They can also put you in touch with other Cofán ecotourism projects.

Jamu Lodge Tamayo N24-96 and Foch ☎02 2220617, ⓦjamulodge.com. Highly rated lodge comprising nine thatched, sub-divided bungalows, ranging from cheaper dorms for up to five with shared facilities and cold showers to private en-suite doubles and triples with hot water, which vary in privacy and tranquillity depending on location. All are connected by a raised walkway, and the main dining and chill area is lighter and airier than in most lodges. Professional guiding, decent food and a well-maintained site make this a popular choice. Three- to five-day tours on offer (dorms $239, doubles $522/dorms $356, doubles $811).

Neotropic Turis Av Los Shyris N36-188 and Naciones Unidas ☎02 2926153, ⓦneotropicturis.com, ⓦcuyabenolodge.com. Operates the pioneering, friendly *Cuyabeno Lodge* on the Laguna Grande, run along sustainable principles, and offering excellent value for money. Most dorms and private cabins are simple, with solar-powered hot showers, though the pricier, lighter and more spacious en-suite rooms in the wonderful observation tower are worth splashing out on. Bilingual naturalist guides are accompanied by Siona guides. A five-day tour costs from around $295 if in a dorm, and from $475 in a private cabin.

Nomadtrek Eloy Alfaro N29-235 between Italia and Alemania, Edificio Fortune Plaza ☎02 3801567, ⓦnomadtrek.com, ⓦtapirlodge.com. Nomadtrek built *Tapir Lodge* in the Cuyabeno lakes area in partnership with a group of Siona. Accommodating up to 32, the lodge consists of a bungalow and a couple of towers housing spacious rooms, with private balcony and hammock. Multilingual naturalist guides lead the rainforest walks; a five-day trip costs $799. They can also organize a longer adventure into Yasuní, trekking, carrying your own gear and camping in Waorani communities.

Tropic Journeys in Nature Pasaje Sánchez Melo OE 1-37 and Galo, Plaza Lasso ☎02 2408741, ⓦtropiceco .com. Award-winning ecologically minded agency that works alongside community-based ecotourism projects throughout Ecuador. They offer exclusive, small-group tours to Yasuní, staying at the Waorani-owned *Huaorani Ecolodge* (see box, p.236), with an emphasis on intercultural exchange and a real wilderness experience. Five days cost from $989; neither the flight into Yasuní from Shell nor the boat-trip out to Coca are included. They also offer a two-day tour to Kichwa communities near Tena, where the focus is on cocoa and *guayusa* tea production; the overnight stay is in *Itamandi Lodge* ($760).

Viajes entre Pueblos Juan León Mera N26-56 and Santa María ☎02 6014132, ⓦturismocomunitario .info. Organization promoting ethical tourism, with community-based projects in numerous villages throughout Ecuador, including with Secoya, Kichwa, Siona and Waorani communities. Five-day tour $450.

paying guests is intended to provide a sustainable alternative for communities to more environmentally destructive subsistence farming, while demonstrating the value of conserving the surrounding forests, though critics point out that these very lifestyles can themselves be corrupted when large numbers of tourists are involved. If you book through a third party (a non-indigenous tour operator) it's crucial that they have the community's permission – ask to see the written *convenio* (agreement) between the community and the operator when booking, which helps emphasize that this is a priority with tourists, and encourages the operator to follow good practices.

MAKING A BOOKING
If you are making a booking directly with a community rather than through a tour operator, allow several days to organize a stay, as the communities need time to make arrangements; it can be difficult to establish contact as internet/and or mobile phone coverage is inevitably erratic in remote areas and email may only be checked when a community member is visiting one of the main towns. Also consider visiting the Federación Plurinacional de Turismo Comunitario, Rumpipamba Oe 1-76, between 10 de Agosto and Atahualpa in Quito (ⓦfacebook .com/feptce); they can advise on where to go and provide community contact details.

The road to Baeza

East of Quito, the road heads steeply up to the **Papallacta Pass** – at 4064m the highest paved road in Ecuador. At its highest point, named **La Virgen** after the simple shrine on the roadside, a track heads north up to some radio masts, the access point for the beautiful **Páramo de Papallacta** grasslands (see box, p.222) at the southwestern corner of the Reserva Ecológica Cayambe-Coca. Crossing the pass takes you over the continental divide, past bare, lake-studded hills eclipsed by the four glacier-streaked peaks of **Volcán Antisana** (see p.242), looming through the clouds to the south at 5758m. After a further winding 18km and a drop of almost a thousand metres, you arrive at the small town of **Papallacta**, home to Ecuador's most famous thermal baths, before descending through increasingly lush greenery to the rolling pastoral landscapes near **Baeza**. Giant oil and supply trucks shudder up and down this eastern flank of the Andes on their way to Lago Agrio and Tena via Baeza, but despite the traffic it's a stunning route, traversing a range of habitats as it plunges more than 2km in vertical height, over 40km.

Papallacta

About 60km east from Quito, **PAPALLACTA** (3120m) is most famous for its steaming **hot springs** – highly ferrous pools reputed to relieve numerous ailments, from kidney trouble to ganglions. The town itself, a string of buildings huddling by the road, isn't of much interest, but lying in a steep, green valley, its location and the surrounding scenery are stunning. Though budget travellers might prefer to stop off at the slightly dilapidated community-run thermal pools in the village – the **Complejo Santa Catalina** (daily 6am–6pm; $3) – it's worth pushing on to the main hot springs, a 2km uphill slog into the crook of the valley.

Las Termas de Papallacta

Valley head, 2km from the village · **Balneario** Mon–Fri 6am–9pm; weekends and public holidays until 11pm · $8.50 · **Spa** Daily 9am–8pm · $22 · ⓦ termaspapallacta.com

Papallacta's best hot spring – and perhaps the best in Ecuador – is **Las Termas de Papallacta**, comprising two beautifully designed, well-managed bathing complexes, both with on-site restaurants and snack bars.

The Balneario

The **Balneario** has nine thermal pools, ranging in temperature between 36°C and 42°C, and three cold pools built in gentle terracotta curves and natural rock, while the heart-stoppingly cold Río Papallacta itself offers a serious cool-off. Don't miss the three small secluded pools up the hill to the left of the restaurant; the top one is over 40°C and is perfect for supine gazing at the mountain ridges.

5

WALKS AROUND PAPALLACTA

There are plenty of good **hikes** in the hills around Papallacta. Make sure that you take a **compass** and the IGM 1:50,000 **map** for Papallacta; it's notoriously easy to get lost in the featureless páramo, which is often wet, cold and, between June and August, snowy. The best time to come is from October to February, but you'll need warm clothes and waterproofs year-round.

Fundación Terra (daily 9am–5pm), at the head of the valley above *Las Termas de Papallacta*, manages a short self-guided trail along the Río Papallacta ($2; free to resort guests) and several longer guided hikes (2–10hr), as well as offering horse rides in fine weather ($8/hr). They can provide guiding services from $6–15/person depending on the trail length, and arrange transport to local birdwatching reserves such as the nearby *Guango Lodge* (ⓦ guangolodge .com; day permits $5), 11km down the main road towards Baeza.

The Spa

The **Spa** has six large pools with water jets and bubble massagers for the exclusive use of guests staying in the complex's accommodation, as well as a "Thermal Club" offering a range of spa treatments.

ARRIVAL AND DEPARTURE   PAPALLACTA

By bus Buses from Terminal Quitumbe in Quito heading for Lago Agrio and Tena, via Baeza, pass Papallacta (every 30–40min until late; 1hr 30min). Some buses will drop you on the paved main road just below the village, from where camionetas (6am–6pm) can take you into the village or to the thermal baths ($2).

ACCOMMODATION AND EATING

Choza de Don Wilson At 'La Y de Papallacta', 500m uphill from the village ☎06 2895027, ⓦ hosteriachozapapallacta.com. Well-prepared trout and chicken staples come with rewarding views of the valley and a lively atmosphere, making this a choice spot for an evening drink. Also offers good-value set menus aimed at tour groups, as well as overpriced rooms (breakfast and pool use included). Daily 8am–10pm. $̶40
Hostal Coturpa Opposite the Santa Catalina baths ☎06 2895000, ⓦ hostalcoturpa.com. Friendly hotel offering warm en-suite rooms with cable TV, a restaurant, social area with blazing fire, and jacuzzi and steam room for guests' use at weekends. $̶35
Hostería Pampa Llacta On the road to the baths, 1.5km from the village ☎06 2895022, ⓦ pampallacta termales.com. With a nice indoor pool, two outdoor pools and spa services, this hotel offers a variety of lodgings, from singles to cabins sleeping six – all with a private fireplace and stone jacuzzi. The restaurant (daily 8am–9pm) serves up tasty Ecuadorian, international and vegetarian meals, including trout from their own pond. Rates include breakfast. Doubles $̶85; cabins $̶129
Termas de Papallacta Spa and Resort At the valley head by the main baths ☎06 2895060, Quito office at Foch E7-38 and Reina Victoria ☎02 2568989, ⓦ termaspapallacta.com. Comfortable rooms or heated, spacious cabins for up to six people, some fitted with sunken bath and a private outdoor hot tub. Also here is the best and most expensive restaurant in the town, with dining rooms in both the bathing complex and the main hotel; it serves excellent food (mains $12–20), with much of the fresh produce grown in its organic vegetable garden. Daily 7–10am, noon–3pm & 7–9.30pm. Doubles $̶158; cabins $̶234; camping $̶6/person
El Viajero Calle Principal ☎06 2895001. No-frills budget hotel with ten basic en-suite rooms that boast thermal-water showers and cable TV. There's also a simple restaurant, serving trout and other dishes at lower prices than most. Daily 7am–9pm. $̶20

Baeza

From Papallacta the road follows the steep descent of the Papallacta and Quijos rivers for 37km before reaching **BAEZA** (1920m), the largest town between Quito and Lago Agrio, though it's still pretty small and there's not much to do. That said, its location in attractive pastoral hills between three large, richly forested reserves – Cayambe-Coca directly to the north, Sumaco Napo-Galeras to the east (see p.243) and Antisana to the southwest (see p.242) – makes it a convenient base for local hikes, as well as expeditions into the more remote depths of these protected areas.

ACTIVITIES AROUND BAEZA

There are several relatively straightforward half-day **hikes** around Baeza – all with good birding potential, allowing you to make the most of its hillside location. Ask at your accommodation, or at the environmental office in Baeza Colonial (see below) for directions. Rodrigo Morales (☎06 2320467; ✉rodrigobaeza1@yahoo.com), at *Casa de Rodrigo*, next to *Gina's*, is a good source of information. He also leads **canyoning** trips and can get you a mountain bike for $15/day.

If you arrive from Quito on a bus bound for Lago Agrio, you'll be dropped at the junction outside Baeza, known as 'La Y', as the main road to Lago Agrio turns northeast. Buses to Tena turn right, taking you through Baeza, and past the rusting corrugated-tin roofs of **Baeza Colonial** first, about 1500m up the hill; the original village still shows traces of its history, with little wooden houses lining a pair of steep, cobbled streets up to a small square and a church. There's a modest local museum at the back of the church, with ceramics and displays on history and tourism in the region. Tickets are available from the Patrimonio Cultural office on the square (Mon–Fri 7.30am–4.30pm; $1) and include a guided tour in Spanish.

Across the Río Machángara, about 800m further along the main Tena road, lies Baeza's new town, confusingly known as **Nueva Andalucía**, which has grown steadily since it was founded in 1987 following an earthquake. Here you can find all of the town's services: the hospital, post and phone office and ATM.

ARRIVAL AND INFORMATION   BAEZA

By bus Buses from Quito to Tena pass though Baeza itself, while those bound for Lago Agrio can drop you at 'La Y', from where regular colectivos ferry people up to Baeza Colonial and Nueva Andalucía ($1). Buses for Borja (20min) and El Chaco (30min) in the Quijos Valley leave from the bus stop on the main road in Nueva Andalucía every 15–20min.

Tourist information For information on the nearby reserves, hikes in the area or hiring a guide, call in at the Centro de Comunicación Ambiental (Mon–Fri 7.30am–4.30pm; ☎06 2320355), on the park in Baeza Colonial.

ACCOMMODATION AND EATING

La Casa de Gina Chimborazo and Jumandi, Baeza Colonial, ☎06 2320471, ✉restaurantgina@hotmail .com. The most popular place to stay, with a choice of simple rooms (shared – only $6/person – or private bathrooms). Also here is the town's best restaurant, which has very slow service when it's busy; tour groups often stop here for its ample trout, meat or vegetarian dishes (most mains $8–10). Daily 7am–9pm. $20

Dido's Main road, Nuevo Andalucía ☎06 2320114. If you can see beyond the chintz, these are decent enough rooms with private bathrooms, fridges and large TVs. Also a reliable source of information on local walks. $18

Hostería Kopal Across the main road from Baeza Colonial ☎06 23200408, ⓦkopalecuador.com. A small place with modest, nicely crafted wooden rooms – containing firm beds – that have porches offering lovely views. Also has an on-site pizzeria serving tasty pizzas, pastas and salads. Daily 5–7pm. $35

El Viejo Main road, Nuevo Andalucía ☎06 2320442. Popular, cosy restaurant with delicious trout the speciality, served every which way, plus a host of other dishes. Daily 8am–9pm.

The Quijos valley

Passing only a handful of settlements on the way, the road heading north from Baeza to Lago Agrio courses through the broad **Quijos valley** for almost 70km. The route may be a principal artery of the oil business, with the Trans-Ecuadorian Oil Pipeline hedging the road like a hard shoulder much of the way to Lago Agrio, but in recent years much work has been done to develop the region's potential for tourism. To the left, the vast **Reserva Ecológica Cayambe-Coca** stretches off high into the northern sierra; on the right, beyond the rocky shores of the Río Quijos, banked by grazing land and fruit farms, the little-explored wilds of the **Parque Nacional Sumaco-Napo Galeras** disappear in knots of cloud-cloaked ridges.

5

The two main settlements in the Quijos valley, Borja and El Chaco, make the obvious bases for exploration, with places to stay and eat. **Borja** has the most comfortable accommodation and is close to the starting point of rafting trips usually organized from Quito. **El Chaco** has a helpful I-Tur office on the main road in town (**☎**06 2329419), and several tour operators specializing in rafting are also based here, plus there are a couple of kayaking lodges. Beyond El Chaco, the two biggest natural attractions of the area, **La Cascada de San Rafael** and **Volcán El Reventador**, stand either side of the road.

ECUADOR'S OIL INDUSTRY

Oil has been mined in Ecuador since 1917, but it wasn't until Texaco struck rich with sites around Lago Agrio sixty years later that the Oriente really figured in the industry. Oil currently accounts for around fifty percent of Ecuador's export income, dominating the economy, but when its value fell in the 1980s, the government signed away increasingly large areas of the Oriente to oil production to make up for the lost revenue; today, virtually all of the Ecuadorian Amazon is available for oil extraction, even indigenous territories and protected areas, since whatever the land's designation, the oil and minerals below belong to the state.

The economy's thirst for oil has been satisfied at considerable cost to the environment. Vast swathes of forest have been cleared and the industry's access roads have unlocked the forest to colonizers who **deforest** large areas of unsuitable land for farming, which then becomes quickly degraded. Huge amounts of toxic waste have been dumped or spilled into the region's soils and waterways, and have been linked to dramatic increases in rates of cancer, miscarriages, skin complaints and birth defects.

The toll on **local populations** has been horrific. In the north, the rivers on which the Cofán, Siona and Secoya relied were polluted beyond use, forcing them to overhunt the forests and move to the cities to work in unskilled and poorly paid jobs – sometimes, ironically, in dangerous oil clean-up work. Other indigenous groups have been victims of aggressive and divisive corporate tactics: leaders bought off or villages bribed with cash and promises to build schools and medical centres (while neighbouring and similarly affected settlements are offered nothing) to obtain permission for oil exploration. When these tactics fail, strong-arm methods – intimidation, restriction of movement, paramilitary activity – have sometimes been used.

Opposition to the oil companies by the indigenous populations has been ongoing. In 1993 and 2003, a lawsuit was filed against Texaco on behalf of 30,000 indigenous people for damages to their environment and health. In 2011 an Ecuadorian court ordered **Chevron** to pay $8.6 billion to clean up the 18 billion gallons of toxic waste the company is alleged to have dumped, a figure which was hiked to $18 billion after the company refused to make a public apology, before being later reduced to $9.5 billion. Maintaining that evidence in the Ecuadorian court case was fraudulent, Chevron itself has turned to the courts to overturn the ruling, though in October 2012, the US Supreme Court refused to block its global enforcement. Even so, since Chevron no longer has significant assets in Ecuador, the plaintiffs are having to appeal to other countries to enforce the ruling; in September 2015 they were given the go-ahead by Canada to sue the company, but the saga – the subject of several books (see p.415) – seems set to run for many more years.

As communities continue to organize resistance to oil exploration, some indigenous groups have opted for **direct action**, such as forcing Petroecuador, the state-owned oil company, to cease production for a week, and to shut down the Trans-Ecuadorian Oil pipeline for several days. However, the failure of the innovative **Yasuní ITT project** in 2013 – an attempt to get foreign governments and bodies to pledge money to the Ecuadorian government *not* to drill for oil in a sector of Yasuní – dealt a further blow to environmentalists and indigenous peoples' rights groups. Unperturbed, however, YASunidos, the umbrella anti-exploitation group, filed a petition with the government in 2014, with well over the requisite number of signatures, to demand a national referendum on the future of Block 43, as the territory is also known. Thus far, the government has refused, questioning the validity of many of the signatures. Amid claims of fraud, intimidation and violence on both sides, tensions have been escalating. In the meantime, though, forests continue to be cleared and indigenous people face an uphill battle to protect their land, as new oil concessions are set to become fully operational in 2016.

La Cascada de San Rafael

Km50 from El Chaco • Daily 8am–5pm • Free • Beside the bus shelter on the south side of the road a tarred road leads downhill a few hundred metres to the guardhouse, where you sign in and will be directed to the falls

Some 50km down the road from El Chaco, the Río Quijos incises a gash between some tree-fringed cliffs before crashing down 145m as **La Cascada de San Rafael** – Ecuador's highest falls – sending great clouds of spray wafting upwards. It's an awesome sight, but one under threat from a controversial hydroelectric dam currently being built 20km upstream and due to be fully operational in 2016. There is a short **trail** (1.5km) that takes you to a fine viewpoint opposite the falls (1hr round-trip).

Volcán El Reventador

On the rare occasions when the cloud lifts you can see **Volcán El Reventador** (3562m) poke its triangular mass through the greenery of the Reserva Ecológica Cayambe-Coca, 9km to the west of the San Rafael falls. El Reventador means "the burster", an apt name as the volcano's been popping away since the first record of its activity was made in 1541. Its 3.5km crater is evidence that a colossal eruption once took place, ripping the volcano apart and leaving it a fraction of its former size.

Its last major outburst was in November 2002, when it spewed more than 200 million cubic tons of ash and rock – the country's largest **eruption** since Tungurahua's in 1886 – over 15km into the sky. The ash drifted as far as Quito, 90km away, where inches of it fell, closing schools and the airport for days. Lava flows spilled down from the breached crater, burning wide streaks through its forested slopes, and a new cone was formed on the eastern slopes of the volcano, 600m below the summit. The eruption also moved the nearby oil pipeline 20m in places – without breaking it, thankfully. There has been other significant volcanic activity periodically since then, which reached high levels in 2015, prompting the authorities to close the summit to climbers.

Hiking on Reventador

At the time of writing hiking to the **summit** was forbidden on safety grounds, though you can still explore the volcano's steep flanks. You should also still engage a guide – enquire at *Hostería Reventador* (see below) and bank on paying around $60 for the day – since the 2002 eruption changed the terrain significantly from what's recorded on the IGM 1:50,000 Volcán El Reventador map. Check **the current condition** of the volcano in advance by consulting the **Instituto Geofísico** website (@igepn.edu.ec) and making local enquiries.

ARRIVAL AND GETTING AROUND   THE QUIJOS VALLEY

By bus Any bus between Quito and Lago Agrio (every 30min–1hr; 2hr–2hr 30min from Baeza or Lago Agrio) can drop you off at the San Rafael falls or at *Hostería Reventador*, if you want to clamber round the volcano.

ACCOMMODATION

Hostería Reventador Km159 Vía Quito–Lago Agrio, 20min walk east of the San Rafael falls ☎06 3020110, @hosteriaelreventador.com. This hostería offers the only accommodation for visiting either the falls or the volcano; it comprises pleasant wood-panelled rooms with large windows, a pool, waterslide, optional tours and rather hit-or-miss service. $49

Lago Agrio and around

LAGO AGRIO, shortened simply to "Lago" by most locals, was once a marginal outpost on the frontiers of the jungle and the country, before it become the black, pumping heart of Ecuador's oil industry, and capital of the province of Sucumbíos. *Lojanos* looking for a new life in the Oriente founded the settlement (whose official name is

5

TRAVEL WARNING: CONFLICT IN COLOMBIA

In recent years, the **conflict in Colombia** has affected Lago Agrio, and armed units are believed to have infiltrated the region (the border is just 21km away). Although this has so far had little impact on tourists, shootings have occurred in the town and there have been **armed robberies** and **kidnappings** in the border areas, including the rare incident of two foreign tourists being kidnapped while on a tour in Cuyabeno (see p.220) in 2012 – though they were released unharmed almost immediately. You should make enquiries with the authorities before travelling here and check postings on your embassy websites. Once in Lago Agrio, do not stray from the central area. If you're heading to Colombia, it is extremely inadvisable to cross here and far safer to cross at **Tulcán** in the northern sierra (see p.126), but if you do decide to take the risk, set out early.

Nueva Loja) only a few decades ago, but in the late 1960s it was used by Texaco as a base for oil exploration, and soon after took its nickname from Sour Lake in Texas, the company's original headquarters. Around 15,000 **Cofán** lived in this area when Texaco arrived, but disease and displacement made them among the worst-hit by the industry (see box, p.224); they now number only a few hundred, squeezed into five small communities, three of which are in the forests on the Río Aguarico, and which can be visited on tours from the town.

Lago Agrio's bustling main street is **Avenida Quito**, where its high-fronted buildings and hotel pavement cafés seem a little out of place in a hard-edged frontier town. Three blocks to the north, a small central park, fronted by a simple church, is about the only gesture to greenery you'll find here, though even here the centrepiece is a nodding donkey. Oil remains Lago Agrio's raison d'être, although the basic infrastructure of hotels, paved roads and transport links the industry brought has also given tourism a foothold, largely in the form of an access point for visits to the vast forested expanse of the **Reserva Faunística Cuyabeno**, one of the Oriente's most beautiful and diverse protected areas and home to various indigenous communities – Cofán, Shuar and Kichwa – some of whom are opening up their villages to tourists (see box opposite).

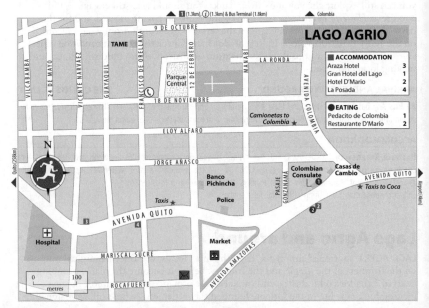

The major party times in Lago Agrio are June 20 and February 13, when the town celebrates its recognition as a canton, and its subsequent elevation to head of the province of Sucumbíos, respectively. Both involve several days of street parades, food stalls, competitions, cultural events, music and dancing, oiled with plenty of alcohol.

ARRIVAL AND DEPARTURE
LAGO AGRIO AND AROUND

BY PLANE

Lago Agrio's airport, served by TAME from Quito (one daily flight; 30min; $80 one-way), is 4km east of the centre; a taxi into town costs $2–3.

Airlines TAME has an office at Francisco de Orellana and 9 de Octubre (☎06 2830113), and one at the airport (☎06 2830500, ⓦtame.com.ec).

BY BUS

Buses will usually drop you on or within a block or two of the main street, Avenida Quito, before heading for the main bus terminal, 2.5km north of the centre. Buses for local destinations such as Shushufindi leave from around the market area. Most destinations, including Quito, are serviced from the bus terminal.

Destinations Ambato (7 daily; 11hr); Baeza (bound for Quito; 36 daily; 4hr); Coca (every 15–30min; 2hr 30min); Cuenca (2 daily; 14hr 30min); Guayaquil (6 daily; 14hr); Loja (2 daily; 19hr); Puyo (2 daily; 8hr 30min); Quito (every 30min–1hr; 7hr); Shushufindi (every 15min; 3hr); Tena (2 daily; otherwise change at Baeza; 7hr); Tulcán via La Bonita – check security (see box, p.226) – (5 daily; 7hr).

CROSSING THE COLOMBIAN BORDER

By camioneta Camionetas to the Colombian border at La Punta (1hr 30min; $2) depart from Eloy Alfaro and Añasco at regular intervals during the morning. There are some security issues at this border crossing, however

(see box, p.226). There are onward pick-up trucks to the Colombian towns of La Hormiga and San Miguel, where you can catch a bus to other destinations.

GETTING AROUND AND INFORMATION

By taxi Taxis – white and yellow pick-up trucks – cost around $1.50 minimum in the daytime, but more at night. For general safety, always take a cab at night – preferably one recommended by a hotel.

Tourist office There's an inconveniently located I-Tur office on Av Quito and 20 de Junio, about midway between the town centre and the bus terminal (Mon–Fri 8am–5pm; ☎06 2833951). You can pick up a map here and get some pointers on community homestays. There's also a shop selling local artesanía.

TOURS FROM LAGO AGRIO

Most operators running tours out of Lago Agrio are based in Quito (see p.220). However, Magic River Tours has an office in Lago Agrio (Primera and Pacayacu; ☎03 2743580, ⓦmagicrivertours .com – also with an office in Baños), and specializes in non-motorized **canoeing trips** on set dates down the various rivers of the Cuyabeno reserve. A five-day package to the Cuyabeno lakes costs $360, while an eight-day package down the Aguas Negras, Cuyabeno and Aguarico rivers costs $900. Accommodation is in tents, in simple huts or at their rustic lodge.

Several **Cofán communities** receive Ecuadorian urbanites at weekends to supplement their agricultural income. Given their proximity to Lago Agrio, and the fact that many can be reached by car, they tend to be very touristy affairs where crafts are sold and dance displays are put on. Most visitors only stay the day, though overnight visits are possible. Currently there are two main villages receiving visitors (though check with the tourist office for the latest news). **Cofán Dureno** (contact Fidel Aguinda on ☎0994145444) is a 400-strong Cofán community 23km from Lago Agrio, on the banks of Río Aguarico. They have a women's cooperative that makes lovely jewellery, and it's a great place to be on April 9 when across Amazonia the various indigenous peoples celebrate the Fiesta de la Chonta, a harvest thanksgiving, championing the *chonta*, one of the region's most versatile palms, which provides food and traditional building material. At the time of writing, overnight visits were not possible as the accommodation was being renovated, but were due to resume again late 2016. **Kichwa Shayari**, approximately 60km from Lago Agrio, a Kichwa Shayari community of only 14 families, offers a less overtly touristy experience, receiving day – ($30) and overnight visitors; a three-day tour costs $156. Contact Guillermo on ☎0986627315, ⓦshayari.ec.

5

ACCOMMODATION

Araza Hotel Quito 610 and Narváez ☎06 2831287, ⓦ hotel-araza.com. The most comfortable place to stay in the town centre, if overpriced, featuring older standard rooms at the front and quieter, though bland, executive rooms with all the accoutrements, plus there's an outdoor pool and jacuzzi. The pleasant bar-restaurant area is under thatch and possesses a pool table, but service is a bit hit or miss. Breakfast included. $62

Gran Hotel del Lago Av Quito and 20 de Junio ☎06 2832415, ⓔ granhoteldelago@grupodelago.com. Spread out in pleasant grounds, the town's top hotel is aimed at oil executives, offering plenty of amenities, including a good-sized pool, gym and sauna. Accommodation ranges from compact, older budget rooms, which are always full, to more business-oriented modern mini-suites (basically good doubles) and spacious upmarket suites. Buffet breakfast included. Doubles $74; mini-suites $134

Hotel D'Mario Quito 2-63 ☎06 2830172, ⓦ hoteldmario.com. Ignore the mustier downstairs rooms and go for the rooms and suites on the middle or top floors, which are fresher and cleaner, with a/c, cable TV, fridge and phone. Note that not all rooms have hot water. Tucked away at the back by the laundry is a small, unappealing pool and jacuzzi. Continental breakfast included. $35

La Posada Corner of Quito and Francisco de Orellana ☎06 2830302, ⓔ laposadahotel@hotmail.es. This good-value budget hotel above a furniture shop has clean, functional rooms with hard matresses and flatscreen TVs, some fan-ventilated, others with new, quiet a/c (for an extra $5). $20

EATING

Pedacito de Colombia Quito and Colombia ☎06 2832212. This simple restaurant dishes up good, cheap Colombian specialities such as *arepas* (stuffed corn pancakes) and *bandeja paisa* (a monster platter of rice, beans, ground meat, fried egg, plantain, avocado and lots more besides), as well as almuerzos, and tamales on Sundays. Daily 6am–8pm.

Restaurante D'Mario Quito 2-63 ☎06 2830172. The restaurant at *Hotel D'Mario* is justifiably the most popular in town by far, with an extensive menu and large tasty portions (most mains $7–10). The passion-fruit tiramisu is an added bonus. Daily 6am–10pm.

SHOPPING

At Lago Agrio's Sunday **market**, between avenidas Quito and Amazonas, some Cofán come to trade their produce and craftwork, including hammocks and bags, and occasionally necklaces made from animal teeth, iridescent insects or birds' beaks. Several shops in town sell their artefacts and those made by other indigenous groups in the area.

Reserva Faunística Cuyabeno

The **Reserva Faunística Cuyabeno**, one of Ecuador's largest reserves, encompasses over six thousand square kilometres of rainforest, holding the Río Cuyabeno basin and much of the watershed of the lower Río Aguarico as far as the Peruvian border. Protecting areas with species that survived the last ice age, Cuyabeno harbours abundant birdlife, with well over five hundred recorded species (a number that continues to grow); 307 tree species were found in a single hectare. The reserve also contains a huge network of lakes and lagoons, including fourteen major interconnected bodies of water and large areas of inundated forest. Among them are two main black-water lake systems: the **Lagunas de Cuyabeno**, which include Laguna Cuyabeno and Laguna Grande, and **Lagartococha**, at the eastern end of the reserve bordering Peru. In contrast to the nutrient-rich whitewater rivers originating in the Andes, blackwater rivers typically form where there is little soil sediment and generally originate in the Amazon basin itself; the water takes on a dark tea-like colour from the vegetable humus that falls into it, which also makes it very acidic and rich in tannins. Some people come to the reserve specifically to see its **aquatic wildlife**, such as pink freshwater dolphins, turtles, black caymans, anacondas, manatees, giant otters, countless colourful frogs and toads and 350 species of fish.

The boundaries of the reserve have changed since its creation in 1979; following major incursions by oil companies and settlers into the western areas around Tarapoa, and subsequent national and international pressure, a vast tract of land on the eastern side was added, almost tripling the size of the reserve. While the reserve is now less accessible to colonizers and far better protected by politically active indigenous communities (including the Kichwa, Cofán, Secoya, Siona and Shuar), who are struggling to defend their cultures and territory against oil company encroachment, oil extraction is still causing problems through toxic waste and spills that have drained into the Cuyabeno basin.

TOURS	RESERVA FAUNÍSTICA CUYABENO

The only way to visit the reserve is on a **tour** or through a lodge, both for environmental and security reasons. Agencies in Quito (see p.220) and Lago Agrio (see box, p.227) offer a range of guided tours. Shorter tours are usually based around the lakes, while longer ones tend to go to the eastern reaches around the Río Aguarico or Río Lagartococha. **Transport** from Lago Agrio to the lodge or community will probably involve a combination of bus and motorized dugout; transport to Lago Agrio from Quito isn't generally included in the price of a tour. **Indigenous-community stays** are also becoming a growing force in the region.

Coca

The booming oil town of **COCA**, capital of **Orellana** province (and officially named Puerto Francisco de Orellana), remained a forgotten outpost in the midst of virgin jungle, cut off from the rest of the world except by boat or plane, until the 1970s. Then, the discovery of black gold led to a speedy influx of oilers and colonists, and the sleepy village soon mutated into an urban nightmare.

It has improved slightly since then, with a spruced up waterfront – where the municipality pipes out non-stop pop music from dawn to dusk, several kiosks sell good-quality Shuar, Waorani and Kichwa *artesanía*, and a sprinkling of bars springs to life at weekends – and a new *parque central*, albeit consisting more of concrete than greenery. Still, with little to see or do, Coca is not a town you'll want to linger in. It's useful mainly as a gateway to the primary forest downstream on the **Río Napo**,

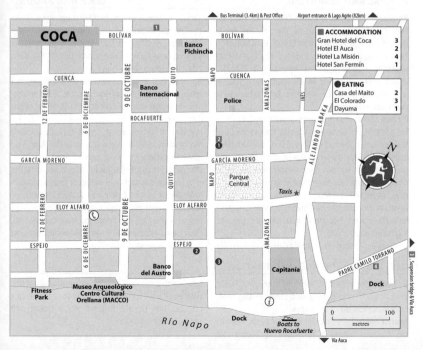

5

a tributary that flows into the Amazon when it reaches Peru, or south along the **Vía Auca**, a newly colonized oil road tearing south through the jungle to the *ríos* Tiputini and Shiripuno.

The town's central streets, Napo and Amazonas, run north–south and are busiest in the few blocks north of the Río Napo, though the town's produce **market**, *municipio* and bus station are a dozen blocks further inland. Most hotels and restaurants lie along the southern end of Napo or around the waterfront.

The town's jetty is the departure point for some of the **lodges** in the lower Río Napo (see box, pp.234–235) and for the lengthy river journey down to **Iquitos** in the Peruvian Amazon, via the border crossing at **Nuevo Rocafuerte** (see p.235).

Museo Arqueológico Central Cultural Orellana

On the Malecón, between 6 de Diciembre and 9 de Octubre • Mon–Fri 8am–noon & 2–6pm, Sat 9am–1pm • $5 • ☎ 06 2881019

Coca's one must-see attraction is the new **Museo Arqueológico Centro Cultural Orellana**, thankfully shortened to **MACCO**. The small collection mainly comprises artefacts from pre-Columbian riverine communities that have been transferred from the former Capuchin missionaries' museum, which lay downriver from Coca at Pompeya. The exhibits are beautifully displayed – though short of labels – and interpreted within a fascinating bilingual textual narrative of what pre-Columbian ceramics can tell us about riverine dwellers' everyday lives and their spiritual beliefs. Don't miss the black and white "magic axes", so smooth they are thought to have been used by shamans for ceremonial or ritualistic purposes, or the extraordinary exhibits related to the Omagua people, who would bind the heads of infants between two wooden boards to flatten their foreheads and produce rounder faces, to look more like the full moon, which they revered.

ARRIVAL AND DEPARTURE   COCA AND AROUND

By plane The airport is about 1.5km down the Lago Agrio road from the town centre. There are three daily weekday TAME flights from Quito (35min; from $74; ☎ 06 2833340, ⊛ tame.com.ec), and one flight a day at weekends. In addition, Aerogal Avianca (☎ 06 2881742, ⊛ aerogal.com.ec; 35min; from $74) operates a flight to and from the capital on weekdays. Both airlines have their office at the airport.

By bus All interprovincial buses leave from Coca's new bus terminal, just under 4km from the town centre (a $2 taxi ride away). The best services to Quito are with Trans Baños (☎ 06 2830330); it's faster to go via Loreto (8hr) than Lago Agrio (10hr), a route also regarded as safer at night. Trans Jumandy has a regular service to Tena and Puyo. Buses and *rancheras* to local destinations south down the oil road to the *ríos* Tiputini and Shiripuno leave from the market, two blocks back from the river, on Alejandro Labaka.

Destinations Ambato (9 daily; 9hr); Baños (3 daily; 7hr);

30min); Guayaquil (4 daily; 16hr); Lago Agrio (every 15–30min; 2hr 30min); Loja (2 daily from Lago Agrio; 22hr); Puyo (9 daily; 6hr); Quito (3–4 daily via Loreto; 12 daily via Lago Agrio; 8–10hr); Santo Domingo (1 daily; 11hr); Tena (every 30min–1hr; 4hr).

By boat Boat arrivals come in at the municipal dock between Napo and Amazonas, but some of the smarter tour companies use the dock at *Hotel La Misión*. Boats (motorized canoes) to jungle lodges are always prearranged for travellers as part of their tour. A daily service downstream to Nuevo Rocafuerte (10–12hr; $15) leaves by 7.30am. It's best to buy your ticket in advance, after midday the day before you intend to travel, and arrive early for a good seat. There is no regular service upstream to Misahuallí, as most people now go there by the Coca-Tena road. If travelling independently downriver, you must register at the Capitanía before you leave Coca by boat. Other destinations include Añangu (4 weekly; 3hr) and Pañacocha (4 weekly; 5hr).

GETTING AROUND AND INFORMATION

By taxi Yellow cars and white pick-up trucks comprise the town's taxis. They're plentiful and cheap, costing rarely more than $1.50 anywhere in town.

Tourist office The I-Tur office on the Malecón, opposite the Capitanía (Mon–Fri 8am–noon & 2–6pm, Sat

8am–4pm; ☎ 06 2880532), has information about the town and Parque Nacional Yasuní, and you can pick up a map too. They can also help put you in contact with certified indigenous guides.

TOURS

Most tours from Coca are organized in advance from Quito (see p.79), though a diminishing number of **local guides** and **tour agencies** operate out of town; some of them offer only a middling standard of guiding and very few speak English. Always make it clear what you expect from your tour and find out whether essential equipment (see box, p.218) and transport is included. Touring out of Coca without a guide is not recommended. A few operators offer the 800km trip down the Río Napo from Coca to **Iquitos** in Peru (see p.236), including Wildlife Amazon and Luis Duarte (see below).

Luis Duarte Ask at La Casa del Maito restaurant ☎ 06 2882285, ✉ cocaselva@hotmail.com. Luis runs two-day trips to Iquitos in Peru in a high-speed twin-engine boat (minimum ten passengers). Trips can also be extended to more gentle seven-day tours, and Luis can help arrange transport for smaller groups too.

Wildlife Amazon Hotel San Fermín, Bolívar and Quito ☎ 06 2880802, ⓦ amazonwildlife.ec. Reliable, professionally run outfit offering a wide range of jungle tours in tents and rustic cabañas (around $380 for four days), including a Coca–Iquitos (Peru) trip (four days; $680, plus $180/day for extra jungle activities).

FRANCISCO DE ORELLANA AND THE "DISCOVERY" OF THE AMAZON

In February 1541, when a band of two hundred Spaniards, four thousand *indígenas* and thousands of assorted horses, dogs and pigs set out from Quito to explore new lands to the east, few of them could have expected that some of their party would end up making the first recorded descent of the Amazon – a journey of over 6000km down part of the largest river system in the world. They were led by Gonzalo Pizarro, younger brother of the ruthless Francisco (the conqueror of the Incas), and soon joined by **Captain Francisco de Orellana**. He had won honour as a young man – and lost an eye – in the battles of Lima and Cusco, and at thirty years old was still hungry for adventure.

Even before the expedition had left the mountains, hundreds of *indígenas* had died in the freezing passes, and as they descended into the uncharted forests they were running desperately low on food. By Christmas, the group had travelled around 400km from Quito, when they stumbled across the **Río Coca**. Having eaten all their pigs and most of their dogs, they decided their only choice was to build a boat and send a vanguard led by Orellana downstream in search of food. Orellana never made it back to his leader and the waiting men – a failure which saw him branded a traitor for centuries afterwards.

Within a couple of weeks, the band of what was by then only sixty men, led by Orellana, was close to starvation. Worse still, the river (they'd now entered the Napo) had become so fast-moving they knew they wouldn't be able to go back upstream, and they were carried down into territory where war drums raged on either side of the river. Yet Orellana was a great diplomat as well as soldier and, unlike most conquistadors, he was well versed in **indigenous languages**, and picked new ones up with prodigious speed – an ability that saved his life many times on his journey. Here, instead of fighting, he embraced a local chief and gave him European clothes, receiving an abundance of partridges, turkeys and fish in return.

Before long, over 1000km from Pizarro's camp, their only concern was to stay alive. By June 1542, they had reached the Río Negro (near what is now Manaus, in Brazil), naming it after its deep-black waters. News of their presence spread before them, and they came across empty villages with severed heads nailed to posts in warning, and were even attacked by a fierce tribe of warrior-women whom they named **Amazons** after the female warriors of Greek mythology. The women were never spotted again, and it has subsequently been hypothesized that they were actually male warriors from the Yagua tribe, who sport pale yellow, grass-style skirts and headgear. On August 26, 1542, the expedition finally came to the mouth of the world's greatest river and named it Orellana, though it soon became known as Amazonas, after the tribe.

Orellana returned to **Spain** in May 1543 but set out for the river again two years later. The ill-equipped expedition lost a ship and more than 220 men before reaching South America. As they entered the Amazon estuary, they'd already run out of food and the remaining ships became separated on the rough tidal waters. Orellana died from illness and grief in November 1546, in the mouth of the river that had brought him fame, but which finally defeated him.

5

ACCOMMODATION

Gran Hotel del Coca Torrano and Esmeraldas ☎ 06 2882405, ✉ granhoteldelcoca@hotmail.com. The town's plushest accommodation, aimed squarely at oil executives, though it's still overpriced and lacking ambiance. It has gleaming tiled suites – some with large windows affording river views – and there's a swimming pool, restaurant, small spa, five-a-side football pitch and fishpond. Buffet breakfast included. $94

Hotel El Auca Napo and García Moreno ☎ 06 2880127, ⓦ hotelelauca.com. A popular hotel offering good service, with a choice of doubles and mini-suites in the main block, plus nicely furnished, smart wooden cabins, with balconies overlooking a large, tree-filled garden. All are en suite with a/c, hot water, cable TV and minibar. There's a busy restaurant too; an average buffet breakfast is

included. Doubles $72; cabins $61

Hotel La Misión Padre Camilo Torrano ☎ 06 2880544, ✉ hotelamision@hotmail.com. One of Coca's better long-established hotels, though you're paying more for the great riverfront location than for the dated rooms – choose one of the upstairs ones – furnished with cable TV, phone, fridge and a/c. There's a restaurant and mini-spa, and guests can cool off in the decent-sized pool, whose appeal is somewhat undermined by an ugly water slide. Room only. $53

Hotel San Fermín Bolívar and Quito ☎ 06 2880802, ⓦ amazonwildlife.ec. Nice, well-priced budget hotel featuring lots of natural wood, cool white tiles and abundant potted plants. Rooms are inexpensive, with fans and shared or private bathroom; a/c costs $7 extra. Wildlife Amazon is the on-site tour operator (see p.231). $25

EATING

There are many cheap and unattractive restaurants dishing up fried chicken and beer to oil-workers in Coca, but the **hotel restaurants** offer better and more varied fare. For a drink, try one of the small bars along the **Malecón**, which really only get going at weekends.

Casa del Maito Espejo, between Quito and Napo ☎ 06 2882285. Specializes in the eponymous *maito*, a delicious traditional fish dish, usually tilapia, which is wrapped up in a banana leaf with a palm heart and chargrilled. Mon & Wed–Sun 7am–10pm.

El Colorado Napo, between Espejo and the Malecón. Cheerful hole-in-the wall joint dishing up a coastal cuisine

of ceviche, encebollados and rice with shrimps. Daily 7am–7pm.

Dayuma Hotel El Auca ☎ 06 2880127. Good, air-conditioned restaurant patronized by tourists and better-off locals, serving well presented international fare. A jar of their delicious lemonade is a good antidote to the heat, and there's also an ice-cream parlour and a lively bar. Daily 7am–10pm.

East of Coca

From Coca, the muddy waters of the lower Río Napo flow in broad curves for over 200km to **Nuevo Rocafuerte** on the Peruvian border. Long motorized canoes ply the

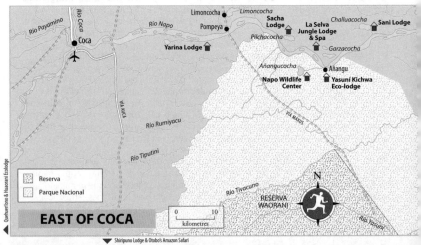

EAST OF COCA

shallow river, searching for the deepest channels between large and slowly shifting sandbanks, while half-submerged logs jostle in the currents. The region is only sparsely populated, and you'll pass just the odd Kichwa homestead linked to the riverbank by steep dirt footpaths. The Río Napo is the region's motorway, and its network of tributaries and backwaters forms the basic infrastructure for remote indigenous communities deep within the remaining tracts of pristine rainforest. In the forests to the south, between the *ríos* Napo and Curaray, lies the **Reserva Waorani** – home to about two thousand people. Their territory acts as a buffer zone to the **Parque Nacional Yasuní**, Ecuador's largest national park, which protects a number of habitats and an extraordinary wealth of flora and fauna.

Since Coca became more accessible in the 1970s, this wild part of the eastern Oriente has been one of the country's top natural attractions, and also the location of several of the best **jungle lodges** (see box, pp.234–235), which provide the most comfortable way of experiencing the rainforest here. Many of them have an observation tower – a high vantage point to see life in the jungle canopy that's all but invisible from the ground – and their own private reserves close to much larger national parks. A couple of less expensive **jungle-tour operators** (see p.231) also run trips down the Río Napo from Coca, some using their own basic accommodation, others making do with tents and campsites. **Añangu**, three hours' drive east from Coca, on the edge of the Parque Nacional Yasuní, is one of the few indigenous communities along the lower Napo that has successfully developed its own ecotourism programme (see box, pp.234–235).

Parque Nacional Yasuní

Parque Nacional Yasuní encompasses just under 10,000 square kilometres of tropical rainforest, forming a giant horseshoe around the basins of the *ríos* Tiputini, Yasuní, Nashiño and Curaray, south of the Napo, and stretching all the way to the Peruvian border. Although a national park, Yasuní is a largely inaccessible tract of rainforest that remains relatively unexplored. Visiting independently is not recommended, as it's potentially damaging, dangerous and costly. Three Waorani groups, the **Tagaeri**, **Taromenane** and **Oñamenane**, have rejected all contact with the outside world and are understandably hostile to the uninvited.

UNESCO was quick to declare Yasuní an **International Biosphere Reserve** in 1979 – two months prior to the park's official creation – to strengthen its protected status before **oil companies** could start prospecting. Despite this, the park is still under

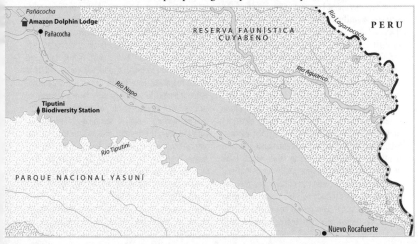

5

constant threat from the oil industry; access roads have been built, including the 150km **Vía Maxus**, which cuts through the park's northern arm. Entry to Yasuní here is monitored to allow access only to oil-workers and members of the three small **Waorani communities** who live inside the park, preventing settlers from colonizing the forest. Even so, the adverse effects of the oil industry on the environment and on the wellbeing of the Waorani have been marked and are ongoing (see box, p.224).

Brief history

Yasuní is part of the "Napo Pleistocene refuge", an area of rainforest thought to have survived the ravages of the ice age, allowing species here to thrive and diversify, generating scores of endemic species. This long period of development is thought to explain why the Amazon rainforest is much more biodiverse than its African and Asian counterparts, which were affected by the ice age. Yasuní claims around half of Ecuador's **mammal species**, including over eighty species of bat, larger animals such as jaguars, ocelots, tapirs and twelve primate species, and aquatic mammals including pink freshwater dolphins, manatees and giant otters. Over six hundred **bird species** have been recorded, including harpy eagles and sunbitterns, and indeed Yasuní currently holds various **world records for**

LODGES ON THE LOWER RÍO NAPO

These **lodges on the lower Río Napo** are reached by a motor-canoe ride from Coca (included in the price), and are usually visited in stays of four or five days, by prior reservation from home or Quito, where most have an office; prices quoted do not include bus or air transport to and from Coca. All prices listed are **per person** sharing.

Amazon Dolphin Lodge Contact Yuturi Conservation Group, Amazonas N24-240 and Colón, Quito ☎02 2504037, ⓦamazondolphinlodge.com. Sited on the lagoon of Pañacocha, this lodge works with a local Kichwa community and offers the usual rainforest walks, plus opportunities for piranha fishing, paddling around in canoes and sighting river dolphins in the wet season. Also offers a four-day trip that includes a day in Yasuní (extra $90). Accommodation is in eleven simple, traditional cane-and-thatch cabañas with wooden floors (sleeping one to four). Tours leave on set days year round. Four days $600; five days $750
★**Napo Wildlife Center** Pinzón N26–131 and La Niña, Edificio Carabelas, Quito ☎02 6005819, ⓦnapowildlifecenter.com. An award-winning high-end lodge owned and managed by the Añangu Kichwa community, the *Napo Wildlife Center* is composed of sixteen beautiful and spacious cabins (including four suites with private hot tub) idyllically situated overlooking Lake Añangucocha. The bungalows have private bathrooms, abundant hot water, electricity (from generators) and hammocks on their porches. Extensive buffets of gourmet international and local cuisine are served in the dining room, which takes up the ground floor of the multi-tiered thatched observation tower, served by an unlikely glass elevator. Wildlife highlights include possible sightings of giant otters, a trip to the 36m canopy tower and visits to parrot licks, where you can observe hundreds (and

sometimes thousands) of blue-headed and orange-cheeked parrots, cobalt-winged parakeets, scarlet-fronted parrotlets and scarlet macaws that feed there in a frenzy of sound and colour (visitors from other lodges can access the hide for $15). Extremely knowledgeable local guides backed up by bilingual naturalists lead jungle walks and non-motorized canoe rides. Four days $1289; five days $1536
★**Sacha Lodge** Julio Zaldumbide 397 and Valladolid, Quito ☎02 2566090, ⓦsachalodge. com. One of Ecuador's most luxurious jungle lodges, 80km from Coca on the marshy fringes of Pilchacocha, *Sacha* is surrounded by 13 square kilometres of its own primary forest reserve. The 26 cabins have screened windows and sealed ceilings (making mosquito nets unnecessary), private bathrooms, ceiling fans and verandas with hammocks, and are connected to a dining room and observation deck. There's 24hr hot water and electricity, plus laundry facilities. Activities include well-marked trails of varying difficulty, wildlife-spotting from a stunning 275m canopy walkway above the treetops, plus a canoe trip to a 43m observation tower soaring over the canopy – 587 bird species have been seen. Tours of the lodge's butterfly farm are also available. Each tour group gets its own English-speaking naturalist and Kichwa guide. Four days $1050; five days $1290
Sani Lodge Roca 736 and Amazonas, Pasaje Chantilly, Quito ☎02 2558881, ⓦsanilodge.com.

species richness in amphibians, reptiles, bats, insects and trees. Most of the park consists of forest on well-drained soil (*tierra firme*), but other life zones include **seasonally flooded forest** (*várzea*) and permanently flooded **swamp forest** (*igapó*). Scientists today believe they've only scratched the surface of identifying all life here.

TOURS	PARQUE NACIONAL YASUNÍ

Several operators arrange adventure tours into the park (see box, p.220 & p.245); if your tour is going into Waorani territory, it's important the operator has **full permission** from the community concerned to do so and is making a satisfactory contribution to it. **Day-trips** are sometimes offered from nearby *Sacha* or *La Selva* jungle lodges (see box below), and it is also possible to stay **inside the park** at the *Napo Wildlife Center* near Añangu (see box below), in its northwestern reaches. Alternatively, there are several options (see box, p.236) for staying in the **Reserva Waorani**, outside the park proper but sharing the same biodiversity.

Nuevo Rocafuerte

Around ten hours downstream of Coca, **NUEVO ROCAFUERTE** is about as far as you can go along the Río Napo before the Peruvian border. It's a small town of limited resources

---

About a four-hour canoe ride from Coca, on the remote Challuacocha, *Sani Lodge* is set in 40,000 acres of community-owned forests, an excellent place to spot some 550 bird species, and wildlife such as the manatee and large black cayman that inhabit the lake. Built, owned and managed by the Sani Isla Kichwa community, it's a comfortable lodge with fourteen screened, thatched cabins (including luxury and family suites), each with private bathroom and solar-power hot showers, and a bar and dining room overlooking Challuacocha. A 30m observation tower provides a fantastic view of the canopy and there are a number of trails accessing different ecosystems, which you can visit with a local expert as well as a multilingual naturalist. The lodge also has a campsite at the end of one of the trails, with dome tents and mattresses on wooden platforms providing a more back-to-nature – and marginally less expensive – experience, though activities are the same. Three- to eight-day tours can be booked. Four days $953; four days camping $811

La Selva Jungle Lodge & Spa Foch 265 and Leonidas Plaza, Edificio Soneisa, 6th floor, Quito ☎02 2550995, ⓦlaselvajunglelodge.com. This award-winning lodge about 100km downstream from Coca has recently upgraded itself into a jungle spa offering massages, honeymoon package extras and romantic sunset cruises on Garzacocha, a freshwater lagoon, in addition to the usual range of activities focused on wildlife and indigenous culture. Accommodation is in nineteen stylish, airy wood-and-bamboo suites, all with private balcony, and some with lake views; family ones also have a private hot tub. It's excellent for monkeys and birdlife, especially at the top

of its nearby observation tower or along the numerous trails; excursions include night walks, cayman-watching and kayak journeys (unaccompanied also possible). Its butterfly farm produces specimens for export. Four days $1215; five days $1510

Yarina Lodge Amazonas N24-240 and Colón, Quito ☎02 2503225, ⓦyarinalodge.com. Only an hour from Coca, so you're less likely to spot the variety of wildlife here that other remoter lodges boast, though there is an animal rescue centre on site. Still, there is *tierra firme* (forest on well-drained soil) nearby, as well as some seasonally flooded and primary forest with a range of trails to explore with Kichwa guides, and opportunities for canoe trips along the Río Manduro to Sapococha, where monkeys are often seen. The twenty simple but comfortable en-suite rooms (accommodating one to four people) have hot water and electricity, at relatively affordable rates. Three days $370; five days $550

Yasuní Kichwa Eco-lodge Edificio Carabelas, Pinzón N26–131 and La Niña, Quito ☎02 547758, ⓦyasuniecolodge.travel. Owned and managed by the Añangu Kichwa community that owns the *Napo Wildlife Center* (NWC), this lodge is located in the village, and is run predominantly by the women, whose empowerment it aims to support. Tours and volunteer programmes emphasize cultural exchange, offering the chance to experience traditional life – including a 4.30am start with a slurp of *guayusa* (herbal tea) – and learn more about the modern developments (such as the school and health centre) that the NWC has enabled within the community. Accommodation is in comfortable thatched cabañas. Volunteers are also welcome. Four days $664

5

LODGES IN THE RESERVA WAORANI

The area of land that is almost enclosed by the giant horseshoe-shaped Parque Nacional Yasuní was made into the **Reserva Waorani** in 1990 for the 21 Waorani communities living here. It is effectively a 6000-square-kilometre buffer zone preventing colonization and oil exploitation from the west. Several of the communities here have become engaged with community-based tourism. Note that visitors at the following lodges usually pay a $20 donation to the Waorani community where they are accommodated, which is usually not included in the price. The following prices are **per person**, sharing a double room.

Huaorani Ecolodge Run exclusively in association with Tropic Journeys in Nature (see box, p.220), Pasaje Sánchez Melo OE 1-32 and Galo, Plaza Lasso, Quito ☎ 02 2408741, ⚈ huaorani.com. Small, Waorani-run lodge consisting of five comfortable, screened palm-thatched cabins on the Río Shiripuno with porches, solar-powered electricity and private bathrooms, reached on a small charter plane from the town of Shell. Learn about the Waorani culture while hiking through the forest searching for peccaries, learning to use a blowgun or paddling down rivers in a dugout canoe. Offers four- to seven-day programmes, which include accommodation and full board. Four days $690; seven days $1350

Otobo's Amazon Safari ⚈ otobosamazonsafari .com. Run by Waorani guide Otobo and family, with the aid of a bilingual naturalist guide, this tour takes you deep into the rainforest, two day's travel from Coca (or a 1hr charter flight from Shell) by motorized dugout down the *ríos* Shiripuno and Cononaco. The tour involves camping on the riverbank en route and on wooden platforms once at the village – fabulous wildlife-viewing and an excellent opportunity to learn about Waorani culture. Six-day tour $1200

Shiripuno Lodge ☎ 02 2271094, ☎ 0995931479, ⚈ shiripunolodge.com. Back-to-nature experiences in eight simple, semi-open thatched cabins on the Río Shiripuno, with private cold-water bathrooms. There's no electricity on site, with all lighting provided by candles. Hikes, piranha-fishing, butterfly-watching, trips to a salt lick and Waorani community visits are all on offer, as well as outstanding birding opportunities. Tours usually leave Tues & Fri. Private tours for two people tailored to your interests are also possible. Adjacent, and managed by the same outfit, is the Shiripuno Research Station (⚈ shiripunoresearch.org), which coordinates research on local wildlife projects. Four days $400; five days $500

with a clear police and military presence. The only reason you're likely to come here is if you're travelling between Ecuador and **Peru**.

CROSSING THE PERUVIAN BORDER NUEVO ROCAFUERTE

TOUR OPERATORS

A couple of agencies and guides (see p.231) offer the trip from Coca to Iquitos, in Peru, among their itineraries, which helps take the hassle and uncertainty out of what can be a difficult and time-consuming journey.

BY BOAT

Boats depart daily from Coca (see p.230) to Nuevo Rocafuerte (10–12hr; $15), but check border conditions at the I-Tur office in Coca before setting out.

From Nuevo Rocafuerte You'll need to get your passport stamped at Immigration in Nuevo Rocafuerte, two blocks back from the waterfront, before taking another boat to Pantoja in Peru (2hr–2hr 30min; around $60–70 flat rate for the boat), where you can get a Peruvian entry stamp and find a cheap place to stay. Kamu Kamu Services (☎ 0981727213, ✉ transportefluvialmakk@gmail.com) offers a weekly direct service from Coca to Pantoja on Sundays, departing at 9am. From Pantoja, boats leave for Iquitos irregularly, but sometimes up to ten days apart. Deck space is cramped and often shared with animals; you'll need a hammock to sleep in. It's not a bad idea to bring spare food, means to purify water, eating utensils, toilet paper and plenty of insect repellent. It's a four-day journey (around $40 – double if you take the fast service) if you get off at Mazán and take a motor-taxi short-cut across a huge river bend, followed by another two-hour boat trip (around $6) to Iquitos; staying on the Pantoja boat and navigating the bend will add another day to your journey. Iquitos is a major Amazon town with plenty of hotels, restaurants and tourist facilities, as well as onward transport by boat or air.

Arriving in Ecuador Those coming into Ecuador at Nuevo Rocafuerte can pick up the daily boat returning to Coca (around 5am; 14hr); contact the Capitanía in Nuevo Rocafuerte (☎ 06 2382169) for information. Kamu Kamu Services' return boat from Pantoja to Coca leaves on Mondays at 1pm.

ACCOMMODATION AND EATING

Nuevo Rocafuerte has a couple of cheap, basic **hotels** ($10–15), back from the river and a few blocks past the military checkpoint, with unreliable electricity and water. There are also a couple of local **restaurants** here serving inexpensive *comida corriente*.

Tena

TENA (500m), the Oriente's largest and most important town for the best part of the last hundred years, is far more agreeable than Coca and Lago Agrio and has plenty for visitors to see and do; within sight of the Andean foothills and cooled off by its two rivers, it also enjoys a slightly fresher climate. The **northern half** of Tena is the oldest and quietest part, with narrow streets, a modest cathedral fronting the central park and the post and phone offices. The main thoroughfare, **Avenida 15 de Noviembre**, divides the more sprawling southern half of the town.

Tena is one of the best centres for **community ecotourism** in the Oriente, and you can easily arrange a stay with local Kichwa families – mostly in nearby villages easily reached by road or river. Since Tena sits at the head of the Napo basin, where a huge number of tributaries converge, it's also the ideal location for a host of **aquatic activities**. A tour from Tena is bound to involve at least one day of swimming, climbing up brooks, bathing in waterfalls or tubing, not to mention **whitewater rafting** and **kayaking**, for which the town is rapidly becoming internationally famous thanks to the scores of runs – from Class I to Class V – all within easy striking distance. A couple of operators have offices down on the waterfront, whose aesthetic appeal has been somewhat undermined by a controversial 2.3-million-dollar cable-stayed pedestrian bridge, which provides access to the town's ecological park (see below) from both sides of the town. While you might question the cost of the bridge and its design, there's no arguing with the stunning panorama from the top of the lofty **mirador** that stands at its centre, which encompasses Volcán Sumaco on a clear day.

Festive occasions to join in include **February 12**, when Tena celebrates the creation of Napo province, and **November 15** for the town's foundation, both of which involve drinking, dancing, partying and the odd parade.

Parque Amazónico La Isla

Between *ríos* Pano and Tena • Daily 8am–5pm • $2 • Access via the new pedestrian bridge

The town's one sight is the pleasant **Parque Amazónico La Isla** – actually the wooded tip of land at the confluence of the rivers. Self-guided paths meander through botanical greenery – over 135 plant species – and past caged animals recovering from injury and abuse, to swimming spots along the river.

ARRIVAL AND DEPARTURE   TENA

By plane Tena's new Aeropuerto Jumandy lies 35km, and a $20 taxi ride, east of the town along the Napo at Ahuano. However, at the time of writing TAME had suspended flights indefinitely on account of lack of passengers.

By bus The bus terminal, roughly 1km south of the centre, is where all long-distance buses stop and depart. Buses from Archidona arrive at and depart from the corner of Amazonas and Bolívar in the northern part of town. Buses for Misahuallí and other local destinations leave two blocks up from the bus terminal on Avenida del Chofer.

Destinations Ahuano (12 daily; 1hr); Ambato (19 daily; 5hr); Archidona (every 20min; 15min); Baeza (26 daily; 2hr 40min); Baños (19 daily; 4hr); Coca (16 daily; 4hr); Guayaquil (2 nightly; 11hr); Lago Agrio (3 daily; 7hr); Misahuallí (every 45min; 45min); Pacto Sumaco (1 daily; 4hr); Puyo (every 30min–1hr; 2hr–2hr 30min); Quito (22 daily; 5–6hr via Baeza); Riobamba (6 daily; 6hr); San Pedro de Sumino (12 daily; 3hr); Santa Rosa (12 daily; 1hr 45min).

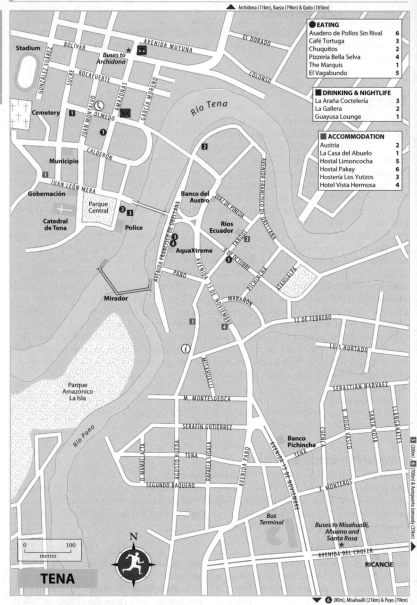

Archidona (11km), Baeza (79km) & Quito (185km)

EATING
Asadero de Pollos Sin Rival	6
Café Tortuga	3
Chuquitos	2
Pizzería Bella Selva	4
The Marquis	1
El Vagabundo	5

DRINKING & NIGHTLIFE
La Araña Coctelería	3
La Gallera	2
Guayusa Lounge	1

ACCOMMODATION
Austria	2
La Casa del Abuelo	1
Hostal Limoncocha	5
Hostal Pakay	6
Hostería Los Yutzos	3
Hotel Vista Hermosa	4

TENA

5 (200m), 6 (700m) & Aeropuerto Jumandy (35km)

RICANCIE

6 (80m), Misahuallí (21km) & Puyo (79km)

GETTING AROUND AND INFORMATION

On foot Tena isn't large and it's easy enough to get around on foot; walking from the central park in the north to the bus terminal in the south shouldn't take more than 20min.

By taxi Yellow or green-and-white taxis – mostly pick-ups

– charge around $1.50 for journeys around town.

Tourist office The I-Tur office is at the intersection of Rueda and 12 de Febrero (Mon–Fri & public holiday weekends 7.30am–12.30pm & 2–6pm; ☎06 2888046); they can provide you with a map.

TOURS

If you don't have time to make the necessary arrangements to stay with an indigenous community (see box, p.243), you might consider a **jungle tour** with an operator who can organize a trip relatively swiftly; several Tena operators are also run by local Kichwa and might include visits to local communities on their itineraries. Many of these tour operators offer **rafting trips** (usually at an additional cost to the basic package), but it is essential you check safety standards first; there should be a kayaker to accompany you and the guide should have accreditation – ideally from AGAR.

TOUR OPERATORS

Agencia Limoncocha Hostal Limoncocha, Sangay 533 ☎ 06 2846303, ⓦ hostallimoncocha.com. Offers a popular two-day jungle trip, including a range of activities ($120), and rafting trips on rivers of varying difficulty ($50–65).

Kallari Huachiyacu Barrio San Jorge ☎ 06 2847050, ⓦ kallari.com. The Kallari office in a suburb of Tena can organize a fascinating day-trip to learn about their gourmet artisanal chocolate-making, or fix up a homestay in one of the cacao-producing Kichwa communities.

Pakay Tours Hostal Pakay, Urb. 30 de Diciembre, Manuel M. Rosales, above the perimetral bypass ☎ 06 2847449, ⓦ ecuadorpakaytours.com. German–Ecuadorian venture running a variety of personalized informative and ethical tours. Day-trips ($45–55 for two people, less for larger groups) take in a variety of activities, from tubing to hiking, peering at petroglyphs to learning about traditional pottery. All-inclusive multi-day trips $45/day.

RICANCIE Av Chofer and Pullurcu ☎ 06 2846262, ⓦ ricancie.nativeweb.org. Association of eight communities offering two- to four-day tours to their villages to learn about and experience life in the rainforest. For groups of up to five people you pay around $180 for a three-day stay (extra for an English-speaking guide).

WHITEWATER RAFTING SPECIALISTS

AquaXtreme Francisco de Orellana, near the entrance to the Parque Amazónico La Isla ☎ 06 2888746, ⓦ axtours.com. Whitewater trips offered on the rivers Jondachi, Jatunyacu and Misahuallí ($63–75), and two days of rafting on the Río Hollín with overnight camping ($255), plus canyoning, horse riding and mountain biking.

Ríos Ecuador Tarqui 230 and Díaz de Piñeda ☎ 06 2886727, ⓦ riosecuador.com. Part of the well-established Yacu Amu Rafting stable (see p.81), offering rafting and kayaking trips on the Jatunyacu, Misahuallí, Jondachi and Anzu rivers. Also does a popular four-day jungle adventure ($412 each for 2/3 people) combining horse riding, hiking, rafting and staying at the *Hakuna Matata Lodge*. Expect to pay $65–87/day.

River People Vía a Inchillaqui, Sector Shaupishungo, just south of Archidona ☎ 06 2865244, ⓦ riverpeopleecuador.com. Professional English-run outfit with good guides, offering a range of river-based tours, including one- and multi-day rafting or kayaking trips ($65–90 for day-trips, including good picnic lunch, or $185–260 for two-day trips), plus kayaking courses; also offers combined rafting and jungle trips.

ACCOMMODATION

Tena offers a far greater choice of places to stay than any other town in the northern Oriente. Most of the hotels are on **Avenida 15 de Noviembre** and near the river on both sides of town.

Austria Tarqui and Díaz de Piñeda ☎ 06 2887205. Convenient yet quiet location whose clean and spacious rooms have cable TV and private hot-water bathrooms, and are set around a pleasant courtyard. $20

La Casa del Abuelo Juan León Mera 628 and Olmedo ☎ 06 2888926, ⓦ tomas-lodge.com. The most comfortable choice in town, with well-designed en-suite rooms in a mock-rustic building of stone and wood, with cable TV, hot water, decent beds and patios; rooms have fans and a/c. Also runs an attractive rustic cabaña complex (*Establo de Tomás*; $40), popular with groups, 4km outside Tena on the Río Lupi, by a forest and lagoon that are good for birdwatching. $37

Hostal Limoncocha Sangay 533, about 300m east of the bus terminal, off Av del Chofer ☎ 06 2846303, ⓦ hostallimoncocha.com. This inexpensive, spotless German–Ecuadorian family-run hostel is set on a hill, with a pleasant river view over the town. You can choose between light, airy fan-ventilated rooms with shared bathroom ($8

cheaper), en-suite ones with a/c and cable TV or a dorm bed. Amenities include a small kitchen, a book exchange and a relaxing hammock-strewn terrace, while good-value jungle and rafting tours are also on offer. Dorms $7; doubles $24

★ **Hostal Pakay** Urb. 30 de Diciembre, Manuel M. Rosales, above the perimetral bypass ☎ 06 2847449, ⓦ en.ecuadorpakaytours.com. A stiff 15min uphill hike from the bus station (or $2 taxi ride), this delightful genuine eco-hostel, complete with composting toilets, is set in lush, tropical forest, giving an out-of town feel, though you'll still hear ring-road traffic during the day. The main lodge, a lovely multi-storey thatched wooden construction, contains dorms and private rooms with shared facilities, plus large verandas, excellent for birdwatching while enjoying breakfast or lolling in a hammock. A wooden terrace of spacious, shady, en-suite rooms with shared porch lies apart. Informative, ethical tours on offer. Breakfast included. Dorms $13; doubles $34

5

Hostería Los Yutzos Rueda 190 and 15 de Noviembre ☎06 2886717, ✉yutzos@outlook.com. This mid-range hotel overlooking the river is Tena's best, with a pretty, peaceful little garden. The rooms are smart and comfortable, with hot water, cable TV and fans or a/c. The more spacious mini-suites with balcony are worth the extra $20. $45

Hotel Vista Hermosa 15 de Noviembre 622 and 12 de Febrero ☎06 2886521. Welcoming place, which, as the name suggests, has fine views over the river from each of its open-air patios, one of which boasts a ping-pong table. All rooms come with fans, a/c and cable TV, but the best are at the top, and the quietest at the back. $27

EATING

Asadero de Pollos Sin Rival 15 de Noviembre and San Miguel, a block and a half south of the bus terminal ☎06 2887284. Straightforward, inexpensive restaurant where you'll find the best barbecued rotisserie chicken in town – *sin rival*. Daily 7am-4pm.
Café Tortuga Francisco de Orellana ☎095295419. This attractive, Swiss-run riverside café does the best breakfasts in Tena; they sell real coffee, great deli sandwiches, salads, fresh juices and desserts. Mon–Sat 7am–7pm, Sun 7am–1pm.
Chuquitos García Moreno, near the footbridge ☎06 2887630, ⍟facebook.com/chuquitosrestaurante. Though bizarrely laid out for banquets, you can't beat the excellent riverside position and tasty, reasonably priced food, including steaks, tilapia, shrimp, chicken and vegetable dishes, plus starters such as *guatita* (tripe stew) and *bolones* (cheese-stuffed mashed plantain balls). Mains $8–10. Daily 7.30am–9pm.

The Marquis Amazonas and Olmedo ☎06 2886513. Formal fine dining characterized by starched table linen and napkins, with prices to match. The professionally trained Colombian owner-chef specializes in Latin American food – particularly steaks and *parrilladas* (mains from $9). There's a good wine selection too. Mon–Sat noon–3pm & 6–11pm, Sun noon–3pm.
Pizzería Bella Selva Francisco de Orellana ☎06 2887964. A decent enough pizza parlour on the waterfront, with a wood-fired oven that is particularly popular with families. Takeaway service and free delivery within town. Thin- or thick-crust pizzas from $6. Daily noon–late.
El Vagabundo Corner of 9 de Octubre and Tarqui ☎0995793242. This bar-restaurant is the new backpacker favourite, with the German owner-chef offering a varied, well-priced menu at cosy candlelit tables. Choose from German, Italian, Mexican and Ecuadorian favourites. Daily 4pm until late.

DRINKING AND NIGHTLIFE

La Araña Cocteleria García Moreno, by the river ☎06 2886884. The town's most popular watering-hole guarantees you a riotous night out, boasting a great riverside location and an extensive cocktail list. Mon–Sat 5pm until late.
La Gallera By Hotel Pumarosa, Francisco de Orellana and Olmedo ☎06 2886320. A lively club that blasts out Latin dance hits into the small hours on its dry-iced dancefloors. Fri & Sat 8pm until late.

★**Guayusa Lounge** Olmedo and Juan Montalvo ☎06 2888561, ⍟facebook.com/guayusalounge. This bar's mellow vibe is occasionally enhanced with live music. Kick back on their comfy sofas and work your way through their inventive cocktails (under $4); start with the Río Napo – dark rum, *guayusa*, ishpingo (local cinnamon) and lime. Tasty fish tacos, salads and the like can be ordered for around $5–6. Tues–Sat 4pm until late.

Around Tena and the upper Napo

Although Tena is most commonly used as a launching pad for jungle tours in the upper Napo region, there are a few places nearby you can visit independently. A fifteen-minute bus ride to the north of Tena takes you to the small, pleasant colonial town – and erstwhile capital of the Oriente – **Archidona**. There's little to detain you, and most visitors merely pass through on their way to visit the **Cavernas de Jumandy**, the most developed and easily accessed of many caves in the area.

Cavernas de Jumandy

4km north of Archidona on the Tena–Baeza road • Daily 9am–5pm • $2; $4 with guided tour • Buses leave from Tena (at the corner of Amazonas and Bolívar) for Archidona, from where there are local buses to Cotundo – ask the driver to drop you off at *las cavernas*; a taxi from Archidona costs around $5

Named after the indigenous general who reputedly hid here before leading an uprising

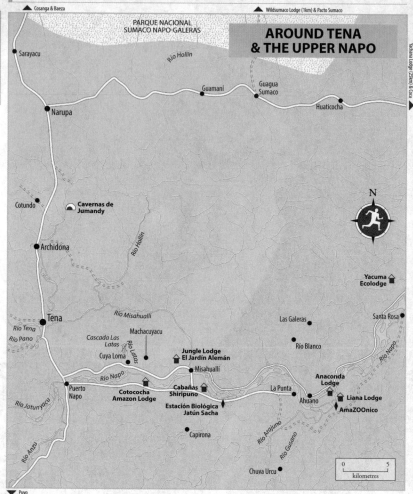

PARQUE NACIONAL
SUMACO NAPO-GALERAS

AROUND TENA & THE UPPER NAPO

Yachana Lodge (25km) & Coca ▶

Sarayacu

Río Hollín

Guamaní

Guagua
Sumaco

Huaticocha

Narupa

N

Cotundo

Cavernas de
Jumandy

Río Hollín

Archidona

Yacuma
Ecolodge

Tena

Río Misahuallí

Las Galeras

Santa Rosa

Río Tena

Machacuyacu

Río Pano

Cascada Las
Latas

Cuya Loma

Río Latas

Río Blanco

Río Napo

Jungle Lodge
El Jardín Alemán

Misahuallí

Anaconda
Lodge

Puerto
Napo

Cotococha
Amazon Lodge

Cabañas
Shiripuno

La Punta

Liana Lodge

Río Jatunyacu

Estación Biológica
Jatún Sacha

Ahuano

AmaZOOnico

Río Anzu

Capirona

Río Arajuno

Río Gusano

0   5
kilometres

Chuva Urcu

▽ Puyo

against the Spanish in 1578, the **Cavernas de Jumandy** have long been venerated by local Kichwa communities. Beyond the rather kitsch touristy entrance and the illuminated main cave, you can explore other dripping, bat-filled passages, which extend for several kilometres underground. A guide can lead you into the dark recesses, through pools of chilly water (for which you'll need your swimming gear) to deep plunge holes, and can explain more (in Spanish) about the caves' history. The guide should have torches, though it's a good idea to take your own too.

North of Tena to Baeza

In the 64km from Tena to Baeza (see p.222) the road snakes its way up through scenery that concertinas into a range of forested gullies and ridges as you pass between two remote protected areas: to the east, the rarely explored **Parque Nacional Sumaco Napo-Galeras** (see opposite) and to the west, the beautiful **Reserva Ecológica Antisana**, its knife-edge ridges rising steadily to prop up the unseen Andean peaks in the far distance – the ice-capped summit of Volcán Antisana (5758m) among them. The main road access into the **highland section** of Antisana – one of the best places in the country to see condors – is on its western side, via the village of **Píntag**, about 30km southeast of Quito. This is also the route mountaineers attempting to climb **Volcán Antisana** take.

Parque Nacional Sumaco Napo-Galeras

Bounded by the Tena–Baeza road to the west, and the Loreto road to Coca to the south, the **Parque Nacional Sumaco Napo-Galeras** harbours over 2000 square kilometres of pristine Pleistocene areas, where there are incredible amounts of undiscovered life; the few scientific forays into its reaches have revealed a staggering forty percent of the plant samples taken to be new species. On clear days you'll see the cleft peak of **Volcán Sumaco** (3732m) soaring upwards from the wooded hills, marking the centre of the park. Dense forests and vertiginous ravines have so far kept human influence at bay, and access is difficult, though not impossible, with one of the main approaches via the tiny village of **Guagua Sumaco**, about 60km northeast of Tena, and nearby **Pacto Sumaco** (see below).

A poor trail from Pacto Sumaco leads past the glassy **Laguna de Pacto Sumaco**, to eventually arrive at the summit of the mist-shrouded **Volcán Sumaco**; if you plan to climb it (three days minimum for a round-trip) or explore any part of the park, be sure to get advance information and hire a guide (see p.244).

ARRIVAL AND DEPARTURE   PARQUE SUMACO NAPO-GALERAS

One of the main entrances to the park is at **Guagua Sumaco**, about 60km northeast of Tena. Just before entering the village, a dirt road shoots 8km north from the main road up to the smaller village of **Pacto Sumaco**, where you'll find the national park office and the **trailhead** for the path to Volcán Sumaco.

BY BUS

To Pacto Sumaco Pacto Sumaco is served by a very slow daily bus (Transportes Expreso Napo) from Tena, leaving Pista de Avionetas at 3.30–4pm and arriving at around 8pm. The return journey leaves Pacto Sumaco at 5am.

To Guagua Sumaco You can get to Guagua Sumaco on one of the Tena–Coca buses (16 daily; 2hr), which leaves you with an 8km uphill hike to Pacto Sumaco. A truck can be hired in Guagua Sumaco to take you there for around $10.

INDIGENOUS-COMMUNITY STAYS AROUND TENA

In addition to the conventional operators (see p.239), Tena has a number of well-established **community ecotourism projects** coordinated by RICANCIE (Red Indígena de Comunidades del Alto Napo para la Convencia Intercultural y el Ecoturismo; Avenida del Chofer and Vasco; Mon–Sat 8am–5pm; ☎06 2846262, ✆ricancie.nativeweb.org) and driven largely by the region's politically active and environmentally aware Kichwa population. In most cases, the whole community is involved, from the building of simple tourist cabañas near the villages to the training of their guides. Tours typically include guided forest hikes, cultural exchanges through music, dance and narration, participation in a *minga* (shared community work), blowpipe competitions, swimming, tubing and canoeing, discussions on the use of medicinal plants and craftwork demonstrations.

Currently eight **Kichwa** communities are involved, mostly based in the upper Napo region around Misahuallí and Ahuano, though they reach as far as Limoncocha.

Accommodation is in fairly rustic cabañas, usually equipped with shared showers and, occasionally, flushing toilets. Some tours allow you to visit more than one community and prices are from around $55 per day per person (two people minimum), including food, lodging, transport from the office in Tena, guides, activities etc. Having a person who can **translate** into English costs around $35 extra per group (make requests at least a week beforehand) and participation in shamanic cleansing rituals (see box, p.218) also costs an extra $30. Drop-ins usually cannot be accommodated and arrangements should be made a few days in advance.

5

INFORMATION AND TOURS

The easiest way to visit is probably to stay in the village of Pacto Sumaco as part of a community homestay arranged by **RICANCIE**, the tourism coordinator in Tena (see box, p.243); at the same time you can arrange for a guide from the community to help you climb Volcán Sumaco or explore other areas of the park. You can also hire a guide through the Ministerio del Ambiente park office (see below), or via *Wildsumaco Lodge* (see below) if you contact them in advance.

National Park office Approximately 200m up the road from Guagua Sumaco to Pacto Sumaco ☎ 06 3018303. The Ministerio del Ambiente park office on the road to Pacto Sumaco is worth calling in at, but to secure a guide

you need to contact José Andi, head of the Pacto Sumaco guides' association (☎ 06 3018324). They need a couple of days' notice and charge $45 per day per person, including food and use of shelters and refuges.

ACCOMMODATION

National Park office Approximately 200m up the road from Guagua Sumaco to Pacto Sumaco ☎ 06 3018303. There are bunk beds available at the park office (free), or you can stay in one of the community cabañas (see below), and there are also beds (but no mattresses) at two other very basic *refugios* along the trail to the summit. All three places have cooking gas and cold water. You can buy basic supplies in the village.

Pacto Sumaco community cabañas Pacto Sumaco ☎ 06 3018324, ⊛ sumacobirdwatching.com. Community-based tourism venture offering inexpensive birdwatching opportunities, and a good chance of spotting chestnut-fronted and military macaws. Lodgings are rustic: a simple

bed, mosquito net, outside shared toilets, and water (with electricity on the way) and shared kitchen. Full board and guide included. $45/person; bunk only $10

Wildsumaco Lodge On the road from Guagua Sumaco, 1km short of Pacto Sumaco ☎ 06 3018343, ⊛ wildsumaco.com. This Swedish/US-run wildlife sanctuary is aimed at birdwatchers, where trails provide outstanding opportunities to spot at least some of the four hundred recorded species here. The lodge itself offers very comfortable accommodation, with a splendid observation deck and hummingbird feeders, or you can access the trails as a day-visitor ($20; book in advance). Full board. $308

Misahuallí and around

Heading 7km south of Tena brings you to **Puerto Napo**, where there's a road bridge over the eponymous river. Along the river's northern bank, a road runs for 17km as far as **MISAHUALLÍ**, a sleepy village-port at the confluence of the *ríos* Misahuallí and Napo, which for many years was *the* place in the Oriente in which to organize a jungle tour. The road linking Tena to Coca, completed in the late 1980s, changed that, slashing the port's commercial trade, while its surrounding forests were cleared or severely disturbed by settlers and oil prospecting. What primary forest remains in the **upper Napo** has shrunk to such an extent that larger animals, particularly mammals, have all but disappeared from the region.

Luckily for Misahuallí, its lingering reputation as a good meeting point for arranging jungle trips at the drop of a hat has kept the port in business. With its constant trickle of foreign tourists and bursts of weekend visitors from Quito, almost every hotel, restaurant, craft shop and racketeer offers forays into the jungle, and the section of the Napo around here has more tourist **lodges** and cabañas than any other part of the river (see box, p.246). What's more, the village exudes an appealingly relaxed atmosphere, has a small beach – frequently overrun by mischievous capuchin monkeys – and is within easy access of the renowned tropical research station **Estación Biológica Jatún Sacha**.

Estación Biológica Jatún Sacha

8km east of Misahuallí · Daily 8am–5pm · $6; $30/group for a guide · Quito ☎ 02 2432240, ⊛ jatunsacha.org · Buses from Tena bound for Ahuano or Santa Rosa pass the entrance (22 daily; 40min)

The other side of the Río Napo from Misahuallí, several kilometres east, lies **Estación Biológica Jatún Sacha**, a prestigious tropical field station protecting almost twenty square kilometres of forest in its own private reserve, which is brimming with hundreds of species of colourful birds and butterflies, and an array of spiders. Day-visitors are welcome to walk the trails or climb the vertiginous, wafer-thin observation tower ladder – not for the faint-hearted. Volunteers are welcome.

Cascada Las Latas

On a hot day, it's worth hopping back on the bus towards Tena, and asking to be dropped off 7km away, at the trailhead of "las cascadas", where you can cool off under the waterfalls and in the refreshing pools of the Río Latas, for a small fee. Closer to Misahuallí, on the same road, is a **mariposario** (butterfly farm), which at the time of writing was closed to the public but due to relocate; enquire at Ecoselva in town (see below).

ARRIVAL AND DEPARTURE MISAHUALLÍ AND AROUND

By air Flights from Quito to Tena's Aeropuerto Jumandy (35km east of Tena) were suspended indefinitely in late 2015 due to lack of passengers.

By bus Buses leave for Misahuallí from two blocks up Avenida del Chofer from the bus terminal in Tena, arriving at and departing from Misahuallí's small main square (every 45min until 8pm; last bus back to Tena at 6pm; 40min). If you're coming from Puyo, get off at Puerto Napo and wait at the north side of the bridge to pick up the bus from Tena.

TOURS

Fierce competition among tour companies has kept **prices** low in Misahuallí; note that there's no ATM in the village, so bring plenty of cash if you intend to go on a tour. Day-trips usually include guided jungle hikes, swimming under waterfalls, panning for gold, canoeing down rivers and visiting **AmaZOOnico** (w amazoonico.org; $4), a rehabilitation centre "zoo" for rescued animals, running the gamut from toucans to tapirs, and coatis to caymans. **Accommodation** on multi-day tours is generally either at campsites or in simple cabins. Unless otherwise stated, prices listed below are **per person per day** – generally from around $45 for a day-trip, including lunch, and from $130 for multi-day excursions, including all meals, transport and lodging, but always make sure you know exactly what you're getting for your money, and how many people are in the group. Most day-trips need a minimum of two people to run; longer trips need four. Check that your guide is licensed and that any guide or agency promising to visit the Waorani can produce written authorization from the community concerned. Tours to the remoter Cuyabeno or Yasuní reserves, the Río Tiputini or more distant rivers are more expensive, and you may be better off arranging a trip that starts from **Coca** (see p.229).

Ecoselva On the north side of the parque central ☏06 2890019 or ☏0998150532, w ecoselvapepetapia.com. Experienced owner Pepe Tapia González speaks good English, leads day- and multi-day tours to the *ríos* Arajuno, Cuyabeno and Yasuní, rents mountain bikes and knows the surrounding jungle well; from $45.

Selva Verde Northwest corner of the plaza ☏06 2890165 or ☏0998215710, w selvaverde-misahualli .com. Ecuadorian–Kichwa company specializing in community- and ethno-tourism, with multi-day trips to Kichwa or Waorani communities, including adventure camping trips to Yasuní (5 days $775; 8 days $1075 for groups of 2–8 people). The highly respected lead guide, Luis Zapata, speaks English, Spanish and Kichwa.

Teorumi José Antonio Santander and Guillermo Rivadeneyra ☏06 2890203 or ☏0987016852, w teorumimisahualli.com. Owner Teodoro Rivadenayra, born in the nearby community of Shiripuno, is a Kichwa guide who studied biology in the UK. With excellent English, decent French and a deep understanding of the region's natural history, his rewarding tours (one to ten days) include hiking through primary forest, visiting waterfalls, swimming and fishing. Longer tours, deeper into the rainforest, involve camping in tents. Day-tours $65; longer tours from $130.

ACCOMMODATION AND EATING

Accommodation in the village is generally aimed at the budget traveller, though there are a few slightly more luxurious places on the outskirts of town, as well as a number of **jungle lodges** in the vicinity (see box, p.246). All of the hotels below have decent **restaurants** as well.

Banana Lodge 400m beyond El Paisano (see p.247) ☏06 2890190, w bananalodge.com. A handful of rooms in an attractive whitewashed building set in a lovely tropical garden overlooking the Río Misahuallí. Spotless en-suite rooms have matching wooden furniture and shutters, plus nicely tiled floors, and the friendly owners

5

JUNGLE LODGES AROUND MISAHUALLÍ

The **lodges** around Misahuallí are easier to get to than those on the lower Napo downstream of Coca, and generally less expensive. Many have small pockets of primary forest attached, but nothing on the scale of the vast reserves in the eastern Oriente. The greater human population, plus habitat clearance and disturbance, mean you are unlikely to see much in the way of mammal life, though for the moment there are still plenty of birds and butterflies, and dripping forest greenery to enjoy. Prices quoted below are per person and include **full board**. You can get close to most of these lodges by road in a private vehicle and sometimes even by public transport.

Anaconda Lodge Anaconda Island, near Ahunao ☎ 06 3017723, ⓦ anacondalodgeecuador.com. Family-friendly rustic lodge on an island in the Napo. Dispersed amid the greenery are ten neat two-room wooden cabins (fan and electric hot-water showers) with shared porch and hammock space. Conscientious service, excellent food, good guiding and a range of activities make this spot really good value. Four-day tour $392; five-day tour $526

Cabañas Shiripuno Comunidad de Shiripuno ☎ 06 2890203, ⓦ shiripuno.weebly.com. Just 2km from Misahuallí (reached by a short boat ride), these rustic bamboo and palm-leaf cabins ($16 for a double room) are run by the Shiripuno community, who also share cultural activities, including cooking and hunting, with guests. You can get more information from Teorumi in Misahuallí (see p.245). All-inclusive tour cost for two sharing $60/day

Cotococha Amazon Lodge Amazonas N24-03 and Wilson, 2nd floor, Quito ☎ 02 2234336, ⓦ cotococha.com. Some 10km along the road to Ahuano, the lodge comprises 22 spacious thatched cabins of traditional Kichwa design – ask for one of the four riverside ones – with smart interiors including private hot-water bathrooms, insect screens, comfortable beds and oil lamps, plus private balconies with reclining chairs or hammocks. There's also a lofty dining area, comfortable social areas and a sparkling pool. Jungle hikes, tubing, kayaking and visits to nearby Kichwa communities are also offered, and rafting also be arranged ($69 extra). Three-day package from $275

Jungle Lodge El Jardín Alemán 3km from Misahuallí on the road to Pusuno ☎ 06 2890122 or ☎ 02 2462213, ⓦ eljardinaleman.com. For those who want the home comforts and the jungle experience: set in spacious, colourful grounds close to its private pockets of primary and secondary forest for jungle hikes, this German-run lodge has en-suite doubles with private bathrooms, a whirlpool, games room and satellite TV/DVD in the

common area. Jungle tours include guided walks, canoe trips and visits to a nearby Kichwa community for cultural presentations. Full board and one daily tour included. $108

Liana Lodge Part of AmaZOOnico (see p.245) ☎ 0999800463, ⓦ lianalodge.ec. Simple but nicely crafted cabins on the Río Arajuno and at the fringes of the forest, draped by vines. Each has a balcony, two spacious, but thinly separated rooms (so be prepared to hear your neighbours' snoring), large screened windows and private hot-water bathrooms, but no electricity. Activities include guided walks, birding, visits to a Kichwa family and shaman, fishing and visiting AmaZOOnico (see p.245), which the profits help support. The staff can also put you in touch with the nearby Kichwa community of Runa Huasi. Prices include transport by motorized canoe from Puerto Barantilla. Three-night inclusive packages $285

★Yachana Lodge Reina Victoria N21-226 and Roca, Quito ☎ 02 2523777, ⓦ yachana.com. This award-winning lodge sits in eight square kilometres of primary and secondary forest and agricultural land, two hours downstream of Misahuallí – boat leaves from Coca (see p.230) – and offers comfortable rooms and family cabins with porches and hammocks, some with river views (an extra $156). Local community members, heavily involved with the running of the lodge, lead guided forest walks, give talks on local culture and take visits to the community development projects the lodge supports; ten percent of your fee goes towards their foundation. Four days $759; five days $1001

Yacuma Ecolodge Baquedano E5-27 and Juan León Mera, Quito ☎ 02 226038, ⓦ yacuma.travel. Aimed at budget-minded travellers, 24 rooms spread across ten thatched wood-and-bamboo cabins and two larger bungalows are set in a tropical garden surrounded by forest up a tributary of the Napo. Combines guided hikes and canoe rides with tubing, swimming, chocolate-making and fishing. Reductions for larger groups. Three days $390; four days $480; five days $595

make you feel at home. Breakfast included. **$36**

Hostal Shaw On the plaza, above the Eko Kafé ☎06 2890019, ⓦhosteltrail.com/hostels/hostalshaw. A good budget choice overlooking the town park, offering simple fan-ventilated en-suite rooms with hot water. The street-level café serves vegetarian food and organic coffee, and features a book exchange and craft store. Tours offered through Ecoselva two doors up (see p.45). Daily 8am–9pm. **$16**

El Jardín 500m from the village centre, across the bridge ☎06 2890219, ⓦeljardinmisahualli.com. Your best, though priciest dining option, offering the most

varied menu (choose from fish, seafood, poultry, meat and vegetarian options). The food is tasty, nicely presented and served in ample portions in an airy semi-open thatched dining area, set in an exuberant tropical garden. Mains around $12. Mon–Sat noon–4pm & 6–10pm.

El Paisano One block north of the square ☎06 2890027, ⓔhotelelpaisano@yahoo.com. Spotless rooms with mosquito nets, a hammock and private hot-water bathrooms, set around a pretty little cobbled garden. There's also a book exchange, internet access and a restaurant, which offers vegetarian dishes and curiosities such as *yuca* omelette. Breakfast included. Daily 8am–9pm. **$34**

Puyo and around

Some 79km south of Tena, and by far the biggest urban centre in the southern Oriente, **PUYO** bears out its name (derived from the Kichwa word for "cloudy") and seems to be permanently suffused with a grey, insipid light that gives the town a gloomy air. Founded in 1899 by Dominican missionaries, it retains very little of its traditional timber architecture. Puyo's focal point is the manicured **Parque Central**, from where you're treated to fine views onto the surrounding countryside; two blocks south, the one-room ethno-archeological **museum** (Mon–Fri 10am–4pm; free) can provide a brief introduction to local history and customs.

 Although Puyo's modern, functional concrete architecture holds little appeal, the town does boast several modest attractions on its outskirts, most notably the fabulous **Jardín Botánico Las Orquídeas**. It also serves as a convenient launch pad for a range of **jungle tours** (see box, p.249), as well as being the **transport hub** of the southern Oriente, with frequent bus connections north to Tena and Coca, south to Macas and west to Baños and Ambato, in the sierra.

Parque Pedagógico Etno-Botánico Omaere

Barrio Obrero • Tues–Sun 9am–5pm • $3, including tour in English or Spanish • ⓦomaere.wordpress.com

At the northern end of 9 de Octubre, a ten-minute walk from the city centre, by the banks of the **Río Puyo**, you'll come to the **Parque Pedagógico Etno-Botánico Omaere** which offers a bite-sized chunk of native forest laced with well-maintained paths, along with a medicinal plant nursery and examples of traditional Shuar and Waorani dwellings. A visit here can be combined with a stroll along the **Paseo Turístico**, a pleasant riverside trail that continues from Omaere for a couple of kilometres as far as the road to Tena.

Jardín Botánico Las Orquídeas

Barrio Los Angeles, 3km along the road to Macas • Daily 8am–5pm • $5 including guided tour • ☎03 2530305, ⓦjardinbotanicolasorquideas.com • A 5min taxi ride ($3) from the centre, or take the hourly bus #2 from opposite Cooperativa San Francisco, on Atahualpa and 27 de Febrero

The not-to-be-missed **Jardín Botánico Las Orquídeas** is an outstanding private botanical garden, with over two hundred species of native Amazonian orchids poking out of a lush tangle of vegetation spread over a couple of hills. At a brisk pace you could get round most of the paths in an hour, but allow at least two to get the most out of your visit. Serious orchid enthusiasts should also consider visiting the **Jardín Botánico Los**

5

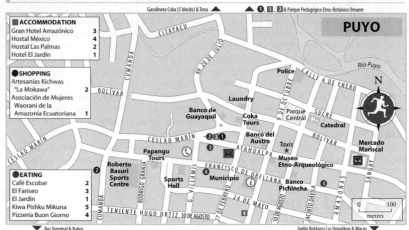

ACCOMMODATION
Gran Hotel Amazónico	3
Hostal México	4
Hostal Las Palmas	2
Hotel El Jardín	1

SHOPPING
Artesanías Kichwas "La Mokawa"	2
Asociación de Mujeres Waorani de la Amazonía Ecuatoriana	1

EATING
Café Escobar	2
El Fariseo	3
El Jardín	1
Kiwa Pishku Mikuna	5
Pizzería Buon Giorno	4

PUYO

Yapas, at Km7 on the road to Tena (Mon–Sat 9am–5pm, Sun 10am–3pm; $4–6, including guided tour; ⓦlosyapas.com); reachable on any Tena-bound bus.

ARRIVAL AND DEPARTURE
PUYO AND AROUND

By bus The bus station is 1km west of the centre, on the road to Baños, from where it's a short taxi ride ($1.50) or 15min walk into town. Some buses drop passengers at the Gasolinera Coka instead, on Avenida 20 de Julio and Cotopaxi, about six blocks north of the centre (also served by plenty of taxis).

Destinations Ambato (18 daily; 2hr 15min); Baños (every 30min; 1hr 15min); Coca (7 daily; 8hr); Guayaquil (10 daily; 8hr); Macas (20 daily; 3hr); Quito (every 30min–1hr; 5hr); Riobamba (16 daily; 3hr); Tena (20 daily; 2hr 30min).

GETTING AROUND AND INFORMATION

By taxi Downtown Puyo is compact and entirely manageable on foot, and there are yellow taxis and white camionetas lined up on 10 de Agosto and Atahualpa that charge under $2 for journeys within the town.

Tourist office The I-Tur office is on the ground floor of the *municipio*, on the corner of 9 de Octubre and Francisco de Orellana (Mon–Fri 8.30am–6pm; closes for lunch; ☎03 2885122). Staff are friendly and can provide a map.

ACCOMMODATION

Gran Hotel Amazónico Ceslao Marín and Atahualpa ☎03 2883094, ⓦhotelamazonico.com. Clean hotel offering decent en-suite rooms with hot showers, though the furnishings are slightly tired. It also has parking, a laundry service, a restaurant and a tour agency. Breakfast included. $34

Hostal México 9 de Octubre and 24 de Mayo ☎03 2885668. Good-value and centrally located hotel, offering comfortable en-suite rooms with excellent hot-water showers, fans, parquet floors and cable TV. Parking available. $24

Hostal Las Palmas 20 de Julio and 4 de Enero

☎ 03 2884832. At a fairly busy junction that generally quietens down at night, this friendly hostal has a small tropical back garden and a few hammocks, as well as bright, clean, comfortable en-suite rooms. Breakfast included. $33

★**Hotel El Jardín** Paseo Turístico del Río Puyo, near Parque Omaere ☎03 2887770, ⓦeljardinrelax.com.ec. This large, lodge-style timber building set in peaceful gardens on the banks of the river is the nicest place to stay, if a little pricey. They offer comfortable en-suite rooms, laundry service, parking, spa treatments and a great restaurant. Rates include breakfast and hot tub use. $90

EATING

★**Café Escobar** Corner of Ceslao Marín and Atahualpa ☎03 2883008. An unlikely find that provides a delightful oasis of rustic chic and a calm and mellow vibe, this bamboo-and-pebblestone bar-restaurant is the place to chill. Upstairs, tuck into

healthy, tasty breakfasts, salads and the like accompanied by fried yuca or *patacones* (mains $5–7), or laze in the café-bar below, sipping fresh juice, craft beer or a cappuccino. Menus in Spanish and Kichwa. Daily 9am–midnight.

El Fariseo Atahualpa and G. Villamil. Café-bar serving all kinds of coffees (including espresso) and hot chocolate, as well as sandwiches, burgers and decent breakfasts. It's also a wi-fi hot spot with a street-side bar counter – good for people-watching. Daily 7am–10pm.

★ **El Jardín** In Hotel El Jardín, Paseo Turístico del Río Puyo ☎03 2887770, ⓦeljardinrelax.com.ec. It's worth making the trip from the centre to this hotel's superior restaurant, where well-prepared chicken, trout, pasta and vegetarian dishes are served in a rustic timber dining room or on a terrace by a babbling stream. Most mains will set you back $11–14. Mon–Sat noon–4pm & 6–10pm.

Kiwa Pishku Mikuna Francisco de Orellana and Jacinto D'Avila. Informal Kichwa restaurant serving traditional dishes such as *maito* (tilapia steamed in palm leaves over hot coals). Daily 8am–8pm.

Pizzería Buon Giorno 27 de Febrero and Francisco de Orellana ☎03 2883841. Modest but spotless little dining room serving delicious, great-value pizzas cooked by a friendly *señora*. Delivery service is available. Daily noon–11pm.

TOURS FROM PUYO

Tourism in the Puyo region is still fairly undeveloped, though a number of opportunities for ecotourism have been opening up in recent years.

The most popular **day-tour** usually involves exploring the **Fundación Hola Vida** (daily 8am–5pm; $1.50), a tract of secondary rainforest 27km south of Puyo near the village of Pomona. This can also be visited independently by taxi from Puyo for about $12 one-way. On a two- to three-hour hike through the forest, you can visit a stunning 30m waterfall, bathe in crystalline rivers and take in splendid views over the Amazonian plain from a *mirador*. Tours here often then continue to the nearby **Proyecto Indi Churis** (☎03 2887309 or ☎03 2887988), an indigenous village, where you can sample traditional Oriente dishes like *maitos* (meat or fish steamed in palm leaves), take part in a blowgun demonstration, hike to a viewpoint, float on a river in a dugout canoe and participate in an evening cleansing ritual using medicinal plants. Your visit can be extended by staying with a local family or sleeping in the project's cabañas. Independent travellers can get here by taxi, or on one of two daily **buses**, which also pass Hola Vida, leaving from the stop by the Mercado Mariscal in Puyo at 6.15am and 1pm (1hr); the last bus returns at 2.30pm.

TOURS TO INDIGENOUS COMMUNITIES

For a more costly but truly off-the-beaten-track jungle encounter, there are a number of far-flung **indigenous communities** (Kichwa, Záparo, Shuar, Achuar and Waorani) that have set up ecotourism projects, which you can visit by making arrangements with Puyo operators. Many of the villages are reached by light aircraft from the small oil town of Shell, but they can also be reached via lengthy motorized canoe rides, with a return trip by plane. You'll need at least four days to make the most of the further communities, even if flying. While facilities are rudimentary, you'll get guided hikes with true experts in pristine forests and be treated to a real insight into authentic rainforest life, which few outsiders experience. Costs given are per person based on two people sharing; costs would reduce with larger groups.

TOUR OPERATORS

Coka Tours 27 de Febrero and Marín ☎03 2886108, ⓔdenisecoka@gmail.com. Offers local trips, tours to Kichwa, Shuar and Waorani communities, and jungle expeditions, including to the black-water systems of Cuyabeno; from $40/day.

Madre Selva ⓦmadreselvaecuador.com. Run by local environmentalist Diego Escobar, this well-established agency offers local two-day tours involving a mix of activities ($119), and longer stays further afield, in Cuyabeno (4 days $250) and Yasuni (4 days $350). Bespoke tours also arranged anywhere in the Puyo, Tena and Baños areas.

★ **Papangu** Tours Orellana, between Manzana and Granja ☎03 2887684, ☎0995504983, ⓦpapangu tours.com.ec. Offers trips (five to fifteen people) to Kichwa villages ($80), particularly the remote Sarayaku community, which is counting on tourism to help win its battle against oil development in its territory (see box, p.224). Cultural activities can include (at extra cost) face-painting, learning how to make chicha or fashioning a dugout canoe. From $640 for a four-day trip, including the 6hr canoe trip in and flight out.

5

SHOPPING

If you've a penchant for **artesanía**, then Puyo is a good place to indulge yourself; prices are modest and you can shop safe in the knowledge too that most of the profits go directly to the Waorani and Shuar artisans themselves.

Artesanías Kichwas "La Mokawa" Cumandá, opposite the Roberto Basuri sports centre ☎03 886918. A large selection of traditional, delicately painted ceramics, including anthropomorphic vessels. They also stock jewellery, chigras ("string" bags from palm fibres) and the like. If shut, enquire next door. Daily 8am–6pm.

Asociación de Mujeres Waorani de la Amazonía Ecuatoriana Grand Hotel Amazónico, Ceslao Marín and Atahualpa ☎03 2883094. You can pick up Waorani jewellery, blowguns, hammocks and chigras here. Mon–Sat 7.30am–6pm (closed one hour for lunch), Sun 7.30am–2pm.

Macas and around

MACAS, 129km south of Puyo, is the most appealing town in the southern Oriente, mainly for its pleasant climate, laidback atmosphere and beautiful views onto the surrounding countryside. There is little to see in Macas itself but the town serves as a base for organizing excursions into the hinterlands to the east or to the lowland sections of the Parque Nacional Sangay to the west. A good place to take in the lie of the land is on the steps of the modern, concrete **Catedral** on the *Parque Central*, giving views across the low roofs of the town onto the eastern flanks of the sierra. On very clear days you can see the smouldering cone of Volcán Sangay, some 40km northwest.

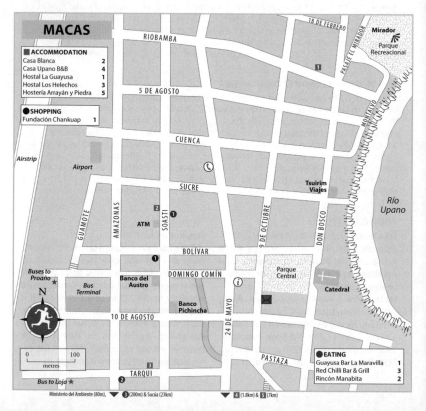

MACAS

ACCOMMODATION
Casa Blanca — 2
Casa Upano B&B — 4
Hostal La Guayusa — 1
Hostal Los Helechos — 3
Hostería Arrayán y Piedra — 5

SHOPPING
Fundación Chankuap — 1

EATING
Guayusa Bar La Maravilla — 1
Red Chilli Bar & Grill — 3
Rincón Manabita — 2

Behind the cathedral, the shelf on which Macas is built drops abruptly down to the **Río Upano**, a sight best appreciated from the **Parque Recreacional** – five blocks north – a small, pretty space with a *mirador* looking down to the seemingly endless blanket of vegetation stretching into the horizon in a fuzzy green haze.

From Macas, the **Troncal Amazónica** road trails down into the southernmost reaches of the Oriente, eventually climbing back up to the highlands at the town of Zamora, 324km away. The charming little town of **Gualaquiza**, 184km south of Macas, provides the most pleasant place for a stopover along this route.

Parque Nacional Sangay

To the west of Macas, the huge **Parque Nacional Sangay** protects over five thousand square kilometres of pristine wilderness, ranging from the ice-streaked peak of Volcán Tungurahua to the steaming Amazon basin. The lowland section is easily accessed from Macas, not least on the new road to Guamote in the sierra (see p.172), which runs across the width of the park, and there's now a new refuge, Tinguichaca, with hot water and electricity beside the main road (ask the park office in Macas for more details). **Independent hiking** here is a challenging undertaking, only suitable for fully self-sufficient hikers with IGM maps, a compass and good orienteering skills. Alternatively you can go on a guided hiking programme with one of the **tour operators** in Macas (see box, p.252); certified guides with an intimate knowledge of the forests and trails usually lead these.

The highland regions of Parque Nacional Sangay are covered in Chapter 4 (see p.170).

ARRIVAL AND DEPARTURE

MACAS AND AROUND

By plane TAME stopped flights indefinitely to Macas airport in late 2015.

By bus Arriving in Macas by bus, you're dropped at the centrally located bus station on the corner of Amazonas and 10 de Agosto, though a new, much larger terminal is planned for 2016/17, to be located outside the town centre.

Destinations Cuenca (22 daily; 8hr); Gualaquiza (6 daily; 8hr); Guayaquil (1–2 daily; 10hr); Loja (one overnight bus leaves at 7pm, from outside the Transportes Loja office, on Guamote); Proaño (hourly; 15min); Puyo (20 daily; 2hr 45min); Quito (5 daily; 9hr); Riobamba (8 daily; 5hr); Sucúa (every 45min; 45min).

INFORMATION AND TOURS

Tourist office A small I-Tur office is on the corner of Comín and 24 de Mayo (Mon–Fri 8am–5pm; ☎07 2700143, ⓦmacasturismo.gob.ec).

National park office Get information on Parque

Nacional Sangay, or arrange to hire a guide for hiking, at the Ministerio del Ambiente, at Juan de la Cruz and Guamote, a couple of blocks south of the bus terminal (Mon–Fri ☎07 2702368).

ACCOMMODATION

Casa Blanca Soasti 14-29 between Bolívar and Sucre ☎07 2700195. Gradually being upgraded, this place offers spacious, clean rooms with tiled or polished wooden floors, private hot-water showers and cable TV, set round a small garden and pool. Breakfast included. **$35**

★Casa Upano B&B Av La Ciudad, Barrio La Barranca ☎07 2702674, ⓔinfo@casaupano.com. Predominantly frequented by birdwatchers, this delightful, airy four-room B&B set in a luscious garden offers two single and two double en-suite rooms (with fans and mosquito nets); bag the one upstairs with the private balcony. Polished parquet floors, French windows and balcony views, topped off with a fine buffet breakfast. **$60**

Hostal La Guayusa Riobamba and Don Bosco ☎07 2704631, ⓦhostallaguayusa.com.ec. Pleasant hostal

down a quiet residential street, with half a dozen brightly painted en-suite rooms and equally bright bedspreads. It also has hot water, cable TV, a small garden and parking. **$28**

Hostal Los Helechos Tarqui and Soasti ☎07 2702964, ⓔhostalloshelechos@hotmail.com. An immaculately maintained budget place with gleaming tiled floors and bathrooms, plus comfortable beds, from doubles to family-sized rooms, with cable TV and phones. **$26**

Hostería Arrayán y Piedra On the road to Puyo, at Km7 ☎07 3045949, ⓔarrayanp@hotmail.com. Across the bridge overlooking the banks of the Upano, this relaxed lodge-like resort has solid, spacious thatched cabins spread around a tropical garden, which has an inviting pool (with bar) at its centre. **$110**

5

TOURS AROUND MACAS

Tourism is in its relative infancy in Macas, so you're likely to encounter fewer tourists. However, the potential is great, with opportunities to explore the indomitable Parque Nacional Sangay, visit both nearby and far-flung Shuar communities in the jungle and navigate the Río Upano by raft or kayak. If hiking in the national park is your main desire, and you speak some Spanish, contact the Ministerio del Ambiente office (see p.251); otherwise consider a tour with one of the operators listed below

The Real Nature Travel Company At Casa Upano (see p.251), Av La Ciudad, Barrio La Barranca ☎07 2702674, ⓦrealnaturetravel.com. Runs high-quality bilingual birding tours in the area or further afield. $180 for a full day for two – less if you have your own transport.

Tsuirim Viajes Don Bosco and Sucre ☎07 2701681, ⓔleosalgado18@gmail.com. The main operator in town, offering a range of scenic, cultural and adventure tours (including rafting and kayaking) around Macas lasting one to eight days, staying with Shuar communities, as well as trips to the Parque Nacional Sangay. Prices are around $75/person/day, and are all-inclusive.

EATING

★**Guayusa Bar La Maravilla** Soasti and Sucre ☎07 2700158. The nicest place to hang out, sip a cocktail or enjoy a meal, in the cosy bar-restaurant area or out on the plant-filled patio. Most mains ($4–8) are served with delicious *yuca* chips and salad. Occasional live music at weekends. Mon–Sat 6pm–late.

Red Chilli Bar & Grill 29 de Mayo and Guamote ☎07 2701575. Char-grilled chicken, wings, ribs and the like (from around $5) are served with cheer in this pleasant bamboo restaurant with patio terrace: a new favourite with meat-lovers. Daily noon–midnight.

Rincón Manabita Amazonas and Tarqui ☎07 2702340. Reliable option serving excellent encebollados, but specializing in seafood from Muisne, as well as good-value set meals ($3–4). Mon–Fri 7.30am–10pm, Sat & Sun 7.30am–4pm.

SHOPPING

The small kiosks along Domingo Comín between Amazonas and Soasti are good places to pick up local souvenirs (irregular opening hours) – or head to Fundación Chankuap (see below).

Fundación Chankuap Corner of Bolívar and Soasti ☎07 2701763, ⓦchankuap.org. Authentic *artesanía* can be bought at this shop, which sells items made by local Achuar communities, including ceramics, woven baskets, bags and blowpipes. Mon–Fri 8.30am–6.30pm, Sat & Sun 8.30am–2.30pm.

KAPAWI ECOLODGE

Due east of Macas, in one of the most remote tracts of the Ecuadorian rainforest, the luxurious **Kapawi Ecolodge** (☎02 6009333, ⓦkapawi.com) is dramatically situated on a lagoon surrounded by primary rainforest, and can only be reached by small plane. Initially created in 1996 by a private operator, it is now wholly owned and managed by the Achuar community on whose land the lodge stands. Care has been taken to minimize the environmental impact: most electricity is solar-powered; only biodegradable detergents are used; and all non-biodegradable waste is flown out for proper disposal.

Eighteen thatched waterfront **cabañas** are built in the traditional Achuar style – without a single iron nail – along with a bar, lounge and dining areas. **Guided hikes** with English-speaking naturalist guides and **canoe trips** in the pristine area around the lodge provide exceptional opportunities for spotting wildlife, including freshwater dolphins, caymans, anacondas and monkeys, as well as over five hundred bird species. Programmes (from four to eight days) also include visits to local Achuar communities. **Prices** start at $929/person for four days, plus $360 for the return flight from Shell to *Kapawi*.

The Troncal Amazónica to Zamora

From Macas, the **Troncal Amazónica** road trails down into the southernmost reaches of the Oriente, eventually climbing back up to the highlands at the town of Zamora, 324km away. The sporadic farming villages and small towns dotted along its length offer little scope for getting into the rainforest further east, and tend to be pretty uninviting places for a stopover.

South of Gualaquiza, the road heads into the tiny province of Zamora Chinchipe, through remote gold-mining territory dotted with macho, rough-edged mining settlements such as **Yantzaza**, before reaching Zamora (see p.202), 120km down the road, where it joins the highway to **Loja** (see p.198) in the sierra.

Gualaquiza

After passing through the small town of **Limón**, about 115km south of Macas, the Troncal Amazónica forks in two: the right-hand fork climbs dramatically up into the sierra to Cuenca, 100km west, while the left one continues 70km south to **GUALAQUIZA**. Its location, sitting at the confluence of the Zamora and Bobonaza rivers against a backdrop of forested hills, makes it the most attractive little town along the road from Macas, but apart from enjoying the views and taking a stroll by the river, there's not much to do here and no compelling reason to stop over, though there are basic lodgings.

The area around town is full of caves, waterfalls and pre-Columbian ruins, but finding them is an adventure best left to well-equipped, self-sufficient souls, preferably with the help of a local guide (see below).

INFORMATION GUALAQUIZA

Tourist office The tourist office on the plaza can help with booking local guides if you're keen to explore the less- visited attractions outside the town (☎ 07 2780109).

The northern lowlands and coast

ROAD TO THE BELLAVISTA
CLOUDFOREST RESERVE

The northern lowlands and coast

The north coast and lowlands, lying west of the Andes and north of the road from Manta to Quevedo, are among the most culturally – and biologically – diverse regions of the country. A few hours by bus away from the highland chill puts you in another universe – one of steaming forests bursting with exotic plants, birds and animals, giving out to long sandy beaches bathed by a warm ocean. You'll notice a much more relaxed atmosphere than in the sierra, further enhanced by a unique blend of Afro-Ecuadorian and indigenous Chachi and Tsáchila cultures.

6

Of the several **routes** to the northern lowlands from the sierra, the old road from Quito to the coast, the **Calacalí–La Independencia road**, passes through some of the best birdwatching territory in the country, including the village of **Mindo** and a handful of excellent private reserves protecting some of the last remaining **cloudforests** in the western Andes. The main arterial route heads from Quito to **Santo Domingo de los Tsáchilas,** set amid a broad sea of banana and oil-palm plantations, but skirts a few tropical wet forests too, including the little-explored **Reserva Ecológica Mache-Chindul**, which protects coastal hills swathed in impenetrable forests. From Santo Domingo a network of paved roads connects the major **coastal centres** of Esmeraldas, Pedernales, Bahía de Caráquez, Manta and Guayaquil via Quevedo. The northernmost coast can be accessed by the fast, paved highway from Ibarra to the isolated port of **San Lorenzo**, lost in a knot of mangrove swamps; this road has largely replaced the famous old railway route, now defunct except for short fragments. Unlike the dry and scrubby shoreline to the south, the much lusher **north** enjoys high levels of rainfall, especially during the wet season (Dec–May), when monthly precipitation averages 300mm, but can easily reach 600mm; this can mean road washouts and travel disruption, so plan ahead.

A hundred kilometres down the coast from San Lorenzo, the rough oil-refining port of **Esmeraldas** lies just north of the area's best-known **beach resorts**, the biggest and brashest of which is **Atacames**, famous for its bars and nightlife, and jam-packed with sun-seeking *serranos* during summer months and holidays. The less-developed beach centres are a bit further afield, including the sand-bar island of **Muisne**, 40km down the coast, the seaside hideaway of **Mompiche** and the laidback surfing zone of **Canoa**, more than 150km south; between them, many tranquil, deserted beaches and secluded hotels dot the coastline. At the southern end of the region is **Bahía de Caráquez**, an elegant resort town and a good base for visiting mangrove and tropical dry forests, and the lively port of **Manta** is the area's economic powerhouse.

At the time of going to print in April 2016 a magnitude 7.8 earthquake struck Ecuador's northwest coast. The area between Manta and Portoviejo in the south and Esmeraldas in the north was the hardest hit. It is expected to take years to rebuild the worst-affected areas, so check ahead before travelling in the region.

SURFER IN CANOA

Highlights

❶ Private cloudforest reserves The most accessible and comfortable places to experience a cloudforest – a misty, half-lit universe of tangled vines, creepers, mosses, orchids, fluorescent butterflies and endemic birds. **See pp.259–266**

❷ Mindo This quiet village set in steep, forested hills has long been a favourite of birdwatchers and nature enthusiasts, though now it offers some fun adventure activities too. **See p.262**

❸ Mangroves Water birds and crabs skulk in the labyrinthine channels of some of the world's tallest mangroves in the Reserva Ecológica Manglares Cayapas-Mataje. **See p.272**

❹ Beach hideaways Holing up in a secluded retreat with its own deserted beach is a great way to recharge your batteries and escape the crowds. **See p.278, p.281, p.283 & p.286**

❺ Surfing at Canoa Powerful breakers relentlessly pound this fantastic stretch of beach, a prime spot for surfing and a superb place to unwind, with cocktail in hand. **See p.283**

❻ Bahía de Caráquez Self-proclaimed "eco-city" of white apartment blocks rising from a slender peninsula – the cleanest and greenest resort town on the coast. **See p.285**

HIGHLIGHTS ARE MARKED ON THE MAP ON P.258

The western Andean cloudforests

Draped across the western flank of the Andes are a number of sizeable and enchanting **cloudforests** – misty worlds of dense, mossy and vine-draped vegetation coloured by orchids, heliconia, hummingbirds and neon butterflies. These are best explored by staying in one of the **private reserves** some 60km northwest of Quito, off the Calacalí–La Independencia road, such as in the **Bosque Nublado Santa Lucía**, or in the **Tandayapa Valley**, which offer great lodgings and superlative birdwatching. Both are within reach of the ruins at **Tulipe,** once a ceremonial site of the ancient Yumbo people. Alternatively, base yourself in the pleasant village of **Mindo**, some 25km further west, which is also an emerging centre for adventure tourism.

These cloudforests make up part of the **Tropical Andes bioregion** that lies adjacent to the equally biologically diverse **Chocó** region (see p.402). Species here were cut off from

the Amazon rainforests to the east by the uplift of the Andes mountains 100 million years ago. Since that time, they have evolved quite differently from their eastern counterparts and the result is an amazing degree of biodiversity and endemism. But with logging, agriculture and human encroachment taking a substantial toll, only seven percent of Ecuador's original western forests remain. The area has been classified by Conservation International as one of the world's biodiversity hot spots – among the planet's most ecologically important and threatened regions.

ARRIVAL AND DEPARTURE

THE WESTERN ANDEAN CLOUDFORESTS

6

BY BUS

Calacalí–La Independencia route The attractive and peaceful Calacalí–La Independencia road leads from north of Quito, passing close to Mindo and various cloudforest reserves, then through the towns of San Miguel de los Bancos and Puerto Quito before joining the main highway between Santo Domingo de los Tsáchilas and Esmeraldas. Trans Esmeraldas buses bound for

Esmeraldas via Los Bancos pass along this route from Quito's Carcelén terminal (15 daily; 6hr), and there are six daily Flor del Valle departures for Mindo, leaving the Ofelia terminal. Most cloudforest reserves on this route are not accessible by public transport alone; you'll need to organize a pick-up from the nearest village, either on the spot or via your accommodation, or be prepared for a strenuous hike.

Reserva Biológica Maquipucuna

20km northeast of Nanegalito · $15 · Contact the Fundación Maquipucuna in Quito, Baquerizo E9-153 and Tamayo ☎ 02 2507200 or ☎ 0994218033, ⓦ maqui.org · You may be able to arrange transport from Quito with staff

Originally oriented towards research but now open to the public too, eighty percent of the 45-square-kilometre **Reserva Biológica Maquipucuna** is undisturbed primary **cloudforest**, ranging from 1200m to 2800m across four ecological zones and bounded by another 140 square kilometres of protected forests. Together the areas are home to a considerable variety of **wildlife**, including 45 mammals, among them pumas, ocelots, tapirs, agoutis and nineteen types of bat. At certain times of the year, the reserve also offers the best chance of spotting the elusive Andean **spectacled bear**.

Traversing the northern end of the reserve are over 30 kilometres of **trails**, offering excursions from fifteen minutes to a couple of days (English-speaking guides available with advance reservation), while near the lodge you'll find an introductory self-guided trail and the cool waters of the **Río Umachaca**, ideal for a quick dip after a long hike. The reserve is also dotted with **archeological sites** relating to the **Yumbo** people, who lived in the area before the arrival of the Incas, including fragments of an ancient trail that once connected the sierra to the lowlands, with path-side walls several metres high.

ARRIVAL AND DEPARTURE

RESERVA BIOLÓGICA MAQUIPUCUNA

By car From Quito the reserve is a 3hr journey; the unpaved section at the end may require 4WD in the wet season (Jan–May). Once through Nanegalito, take the right turn to Nanegal and just before you reach that village, you'll see the turning for Maquipucuna signposted to the right. It's 6km away, past the village of Santa Marianita.

By bus You can catch a Transportes Minas bus to Nanegal from Quito's Ofelia terminal (Mon–Fri noon, 1pm, 3pm, 4.30pm; Sat 7am, 10.30am, noon, 1.30pm & 2.30pm; Sun 8am, 10am, 1.30pm, 2.15pm, 4.40pm) then walk the remaining 6km, or hire a camioneta in Nanegal (around $10).

ACCOMMODATION

Maquipucuna Lodge Reservations through the reserve's Quito office (see above) with at least a week's notice. Rooms in the attractive wood-and-thatch lodge come with shared or private bathroom and have screens rather than walls, allowing the rich forest soundtrack to waft in. Budget travellers can stay in the

research facilities by the organic garden, or camp. Freshly prepared home-cooking included in room rates. Overnight and two-day package, including transport from Quito, meals and bilingual guiding, $406; research station $35/person; camping $5/person

6

Bosque Nublado Santa Lucía

Barrio La Delicia, Nanegal • Day-visitors $10; guides (obligatory on some trails) $50/day or $80 for a birding specialist • ☎ 02 2157242, ⓦ santaluciaecuador.com

The **Bosque Nublado Santa Lucía** is an award-winning community-owned ecotourism project that helps fund the conservation of 6.5 square kilometres of communally owned **cloudforest**. The vast majority is primary forest harbouring over 400 **bird** species, including dozens of hummingbirds such as the rare violet-tailed sylph, as well as leks (courtship display grounds) for golden and club-winged manakins and the cock-of-the-rock; **mammals** such as pumas, ocelots and Andean spectacled bears are also present. There are several forest **trails**, including a six-hour hike along a pre-Columbian path that links Santa Lucía to the neighbouring village of Yunguilla.

The community also takes **volunteers** (two-week minimum) at substantially reduced rates to help with projects for reforestation, organic farming, agro-forestry, conservation monitoring, trail clearance and English teaching.

ARRIVAL AND DEPARTURE   BOSQUE NUBLADO SANTA LUCÍA

By bus and on foot Take a Minas bus from Quito's Ofelia terminal to Nanegal (2–3 a day; 2hr 30min; see under Maquipucuna, p.259). Transport by camioneta can be arranged from Nanegal to the trailhead, from where it's a stiff uphill hike to the lodge (1–2hr).

ACCOMMODATION

★**Santa Lucía Lodge** Barrio La Delicia, Nanegal ☎ 02 2157242, ⓦ santaluciaecuador.com. In a wonderfully isolated mountaintop setting affording superb views, this simple ecolodge (limited solar electricity only in the main lodge, so bring a torch) offers double rooms, dorms with shared hot-water bathrooms or private en-suite cabins. The food is delicious and plentiful (much of it grown in the organic garden). Prices include full board and entrance to the reserve and there are also package deals, including guided hikes. Full board. Dorms $40; doubles $50; cabins $180

Bosque Protector Los Cedros

One of the most remote and exciting reserves in the western Andes, the **Bosque Protector Los Cedros** encompasses 64 square kilometres of pristine rain- and cloudforests contiguous with the Reserva Ecológica Cotacachi-Cayapas (see p.116). Home to hundreds of tropical **birds** inhabiting the misty canopy, the reserve's greenery is a tight weave of vines, lianas, roots, bromeliads, heliconia and more than two hundred varieties of **orchids** (best seen mid-Jan to end Feb), including many newly discovered species. The reserve's also a base for an internationally supported primate research programme into the **brown-headed spider monkey**, Ecuador's only endemic monkey, of which there are only fifty breeding pairs left in the wild, though you can spot howler and capuchin monkeys too. **Volunteers** are welcome for a minimum of two weeks ($300).

ARRIVAL AND DEPARTURE   BOSQUE PROTECTOR LOS CEDROS

By bus Although only 60km northwest of Quito, the reserve is a 3.5hr bus ride followed by a 4- to 5-hour hike or mule ride. From the Ofelia terminal in Quito, take a Transportes Minas bus (5 daily at 6am, 10am, 12.45pm, 3.30pm & 6pm; 6am is best if you want to arrive the same day at the reserve; 3hr 15min) to Chontal, where there are a couple of simple hotels and a few homestay possibilities. There are also two Trans Otavalo buses a day from Otavalo to Chontal (8am & 10am; 5hr) and Contact the office in advance for full details and to arrange transport or mules if necessary.

ACCOMMODATION

Los Cedros Lodge To book, contact the Centro de Investigaciones de los Bosques Tropicales (CIBT), Quito ☎ 02 3612546, ⓦ reservaloscedros.org. The reserve's rustic but comfortable accommodation – a wooden lodge where a nearby mountain stream powers the hydroelectric system and provides fresh water – comes with hot showers and three delicious home-cooked meals a day. $65/person

BIRDWATCHING IN THE TANDAYAPA VALLEY

A left turn off the main **Calacalí–La Independencia road** at Km52 leads to a trio of the country's top destinations for birders, each one set in several kilometres of private reserve among mountains incised by streams and waterfalls, and clothed in dense cloudforests, mosses, bromeliads and orchids. The **Bellavista Cloud Forest Reserve**, neighbouring **Tandayapa Bird Lodge** and **San Jorge de Tandayapa Lodge** are set up primarily to cater for birdwatchers keen to spot some of the well over 300 species here, including the masked trogon, tanager-finch, moustached antpitta, plate-billed mountain toucan and the countless hummingbirds that flock round the feeders. An additional draw is the possibility of sighting an olinguito, a fluffy coati-like creature, "discovered" here in 2013 – the first new carnivorous mammal species to be identified on the continent for 35 years.

Bellavista, which is dominated by a mountaintop, four-storey geodesic dome, tends to attract more casual nature-lovers and researchers, and offers more varied tours and a wider range of accommodation. Day-visitors are welcome and a trail map is included in the entry fee ($8). **Tandayapa** has a hide and a lek (courtship ground) for the ever-popular Andean cock-of-the-rock, and also welcomes day-visitors ($20). Both reserves have a system of trails as well as numerous platforms and viewing points from which to observe the canopy, and guides are available for hire (from $18/person). **San Jorge de Tandayapa Lodge** offers vertiginous views from its rooms and verandas, and forms part of the much-lauded "Magic Birding Circuit", comprising a series of birding lodges in Ecuador (see Basics, p.38).

ARRIVAL AND DEPARTURE

Once off the main road, it's a 6km drive along the Tandayapa Valley to the eponymous lodge, whereas to reach Bellavista entails driving 12km up the mountain through the village of Tandayapa to the reserve. San Jorge de Tandayapa is only 3.5km along the road from the turn-off.

To reach the lodges by public transport, you need to get a bus to Nanegalito (see p.259), where you can hire a camioneta ($15 to Bellavista; $10 to Tandayapa; $6 to San Jorge de Tandayapa).

TOURS

All three lodges offer packages that include transfers to and from Quito, full board and bilingual naturalist guiding. Package rates given are for two people in shared accommodation.

ACCOMMODATION

Bellavista Cloud Forest Lodge ✆02 2232313 in Quito, or ✆02 2116232 for the lodge, ⓦbellavistacloudforest.com. Accommodation here is varied; the geodesic dome has comfortable, light en-suite rooms with balconies, while above, and accessed by ladder, are shared sleeping areas. More private en-suite accommodation is available in three houses, while self-catering bunk-bed dorms offer better value at the nearby research station ($21). Camping is also possible, giving you access to all the facilities, including the on-site gourmet restaurant (breakfast $11, lunch or dinner $26), or you can take a stove. All-inclusive packages include a 3-day stay ($662/person), and day-trips from Quito ($110/person). Accommodation only: dorms $36; doubles $147; camping $8/person

San Jorge de Tandayapa Lodge ✆02 2447520 in Quito, or ✆0999231314, ⓦecolodgessanjorge.com. Accommodating forty people, this exclusive lodge boasts superior rooms with large, comfortable beds and vast windows with stellar views, gourmet meals using produce from their organic gardens and top-notch guiding. Worth paying the extra $60 for the deluxe rooms. Four-day tour including meals, guiding and transfer from Quito (around $1,100/person). Full board $520

Tandayapa Bird Lodge ✆02 2247520 in Quito, or ✆0999231314, ⓦtandayapabirdlodge.com. The lodge has comfortable private doubles and singles, plus a jacuzzi, library and bar, where an ornithologist is always on hand at the end of the day to answer questions over a cocktail. Multi-day packages also available ($1,010 for a 3-day stay). Full board. $520

Tulipe

At Km61 of the **Calacalí–La Independencia road,** 3km beyond Nanegalito, there's a turning north to **TULIPE**, a small village tucked 9km away in a clutch of green subtropical hills, which appears to have once been a ceremonial centre of the Yumbo (800–1660 AD), traders overseeing routes between the Andes and the coast. The area is covered in a network of **culuncos,** tunnel-like pathways made by the Yumbo that have become sunken over time through erosion, and are virtually covered with foliage. Further Yumbo remains lie in the cloudforest reserve and ecolodge a few kilometres further up the valley at Las Tolas.

The ruins
Tulipe • Wed–Sun 9am–4pm • $3 • ☎ 02 3629605

Just below the entrance to the ruins are the **remains** of six "*piscinas*", large sunken areas with steps and channels leading into them, supposed to have been filled with water and used as celestial mirrors to observe the movements of the sun and stars, or to perform rites of worship and purification. An on-site museum here explains the ruins and has displays on the Yumbo culture.

ARRIVAL AND DEPARTURE   TULIPE

By bus Transportes Minas and Transportes Otavalo both operate buses from the Ofelia terminal in Quito that pass through Tulipe (12 daily; 1hr 50min). To reach Las Tolas,

there is a daily direct bus at 5.30pm, or you can hire a pick-up for $10 in Tulipe.

ACCOMMODATION

Urcu de Mindo Cloudforest Lodge 3km from Las Tolas ☎ 02 2873170 or ☎ 0998334489, ⓦ cloudforest ecuador.com. Good choice for those on a tight budget. A friendly family-run enterprise on a small private reserve offering six standard solid stone, wood and bamboo 'tree-houses' containing one double bed and two bunks but no hot water, and four superior cabins with hot water, two with jacuzzis. Also has a pool, small spa and nearby waterfall. Affordable day-trips to Mindo (1hr away). Breakfast included. **$58**

Mindo

Set at 1250m on the forested western slopes of Volcán Pichincha, **MINDO** resembles an Alpine village transplanted to the tropics, with steep-roofed, chalet-like farmhouses punctuating its lush and beautiful landscape. Its pleasant subtropical climate attracts an increasing number of visitors seeking to spend a few days hiking, horse riding, zip-lining or taking part in *regatas* – floating down rivers on inflatable inner tubes. But above all, the town is most renowned as a base for **birdwatching** in the surrounding hills, part of the biologically diverse **Chocó Endemic Bird Area**.

No longer a secret hideaway for bird-lovers, Mindo is expanding rapidly as a popular weekend escape for *quiteños* seeking relief from frenetic city life and the chilly climate of the sierra. Though the place is not yet bursting at the seams, new lodges and hostals are sprouting, some ill-advised developments have occurred, and prices are rising. It's best to avoid weekends and holiday periods if you want a more tranquil, back-to-nature experience.

The town

The town is little more than a village, set round a simple square with a small church and a handful of shops. Though most of Mindo's attractions lie outside in the surrounding mountains and cloudforests (see box, p.267) there are a couple of low-key places in town worth a visit. Of Mindo's two **orquidearios** (orchid gardens; $2), the better one is at the **Cabañas Armonîa**, which has around 200 orchid varieties. **Jardín Nathaly** ($3), a block from the park on 9 de Octubre, exhibits a smaller assemblage of both orchids and butterflies. In each case you can appreciate the blooms for free if you stay at their accommodation.

6

BIODIVERSITY AROUND MINDO

One reason for Mindo's prolific biodiversity is its location in a transitional area between higher-altitude temperate zones and the lower humid tropical forests. This sector encompasses several habitats and harbours some 370 bird species, many of them endemic, including the velvet-purple coronet (one of 33 hummingbirds), yellow-collared chlorophonia and the endangered long-wattled umbrella bird – which resembles a crow and has an unmistakable, dangling black wattle and a large Elvis quiff for a crest. With a good guide, you can spot dozens of colourful birds, including numerous endemics, on a three- to four-day **tour** of Mindo's forests, which also hold several **leks** (courting grounds) for the club-winged manakin and the resplendent Andean cock-of-the-rock – another bird with a quiff, only scarlet this time.

Mariposas de Mindo

About 2.5km along the signposted track from the southwest corner of the town square • Daily 9am–5pm • $6 (free if you stay at the cabins) • Taxi $3

The top spot for butterflies in all of Ecuador is the farm at **Mariposas de Mindo**, which harbours over twenty-five species of colourful *Lepidoptera*, primarily bred for export, though a percentage are released into the wild. The guided tour takes you through the lifecycle of the butterfly, while the star of the show is the electric blue morpho. Over 1200 butterflies will surround you as you wander through the enclosure, and you will even get the chance to feed one.

El Quetzal

Northern end of 9 de Octubre • Daily 9am–5pm hourly (two-people minimum) • $10 • ☎ 02 2170034, ⓦ elquetzaldemindo.com

For chocolate-lovers, **El Quetzal** offers interesting, if overpriced, tours in English or Spanish demonstrating the whole process of their artisanal chocolate-making – "from the bean to the bar"– finishing off with the obligatory sampling of the product, including a piece of their incredibly rich, but addictive chocolate brownie.

ARRIVAL AND DEPARTURE   MINDO

By bus Mindo is 6km down a winding road branching south of the Calacalí–La Independencia highway. Flor del Valle runs daily buses right into the village from the Ofelia terminal in Quito (Mon–Fri 8am, 9am, 11am, 1pm & 4pm; Sat seven buses 7.40am–4pm, Sun 7.40am–2pm four buses; 2hr). From Mindo, buses leave for Quito from Avenida Quito, just off the *parque central*: Mon–Fri 6.30am, 11am, 1.45pm, 3pm & 5pm; Sat & Sun seven buses 6.30am–5pm; 2hr). Alternatively, note that buses bound for Esmeraldas via Los Bancos (15 daily; 1hr 45min) pass the turn-off to Mindo ('La Y'). From here, you can get a ride into town ($3, or less by colectivo), or walk. From Santo Domingo, Transportes Kennedy offers slow daily buses to Mindo; return buses leave from the park (6 daily; 4hr). Alternatively, get a faster Mercedes de la Reina bus (hourly; 1hr30min) to Los Bancos and take a taxi to Mindo ($10), or catch an Esmeraldas bus from the traffic lights to 'La Y'.

GETTING AROUND

By camioneta Central Mindo consists of only a few blocks, which can easily be walked but many of the lodges and activities are several kilometres from the central square so consider hiring one of the taxis that line up beside the church. Prices are regulated, charging from $3 (per cab) to the Mariposas de Mindo, to $8 for the Cascada de Nambillo and $25 (there and back, including waiting time) to Refugio Paz de las Aves; current rates are advertised on the taxi-drivers' hut; alternatively, enquire at the tourist office.

Bike rental Endemic Tours (8am–6pm), half a block off the park, rents bikes for $15/day or $10/half-day.

INFORMATION AND TOURS

Tourist information Limited information is available from the municipal office on the corner of the *parque central* (Tues–Fri & Sun 7.30am–1pm, 2.30–5pm).

Frog concert There's an engaging and surprisingly informative nature walk by torchlight around the pond of Mindo Lago (on the road out of the village towards the highway), peering under leaves and round trees looking for amphibians, creepy crawlies and phosphorescent fungi (daily 6.30pm; 1hr; $5, including a glass of wine; ⓦ mindolago.com.ec).

TOUR OPERATORS

Mindo is now awash with tour operators, all offering more or less the same tours for the same prices, though La Isla (☎02 2170343, ☎0993272190, ⓦlaislamindo.com), whose main office is on the *parque central* and has two outlets in the village, is the most established and has its own private reserve, where many of its activities take place. Prices may differ more with birdwatching tours, which often depends on the quality and renown of the birding guide (see box, p.267).

ACCOMMODATION

Mindo's accommodation continues to expand and as its popularity increases, so prices are rising, though you can often get better deals **midweek** in low season. Rates for all the accommodation listed below include **breakfast**, unless stated otherwise.

IN TOWN

Cabañas Armonía South end of the football pitch ☎02 2170131 or ☎0999435098, ⓦbirdingmindo .com. Has a few modest double rooms with shared bathrooms, and nicer secluded wooden cabins for four with their own facilities – some with porches and hammocks – at the back of the orchid garden, in the midst of the tropical foliage. Doubles $\underline{\$25}$; cabins $\underline{\$36}$

La Casa de Cecilia Northeastern end of Ballén ☎02 2170243 or ☎0993345393, ⓦlacasadececilia .com. Occupying a pleasant riverside location with a nice swimming spot, this friendly, if a little cramped, budget hostal has simple, clean, small rooms, with tiny shared or private bathrooms, mosquito nets and paper-thin walls. Breakfast extra ($3–4). Takes volunteers. Dorm $\underline{\$11}$; doubles $\underline{\$32}$; camping $\underline{\$5}$/person

★**Hacienda San Vicente** 5min walk uphill southeast of the parque central (also known as the Yellow House) ☎02 2236275, ⓦecuadormindobirds.

com. Welcoming, family-run hacienda offering a handful of simple, comfortable rooms with private or shared bathroom, some with a porch, balcony and hammocks. A tasty breakfast is served on a communal balcony with hummingbird feeders. A good option for serious birders, as there are trails on the property and horse riding is also an option. $\underline{\$50}$

Jardín El Descanso Los Colibríes ☎0994829587. An attractive, well-kept wooden house with a bird-filled garden ($2 for non-guests to view the birds), offering neat, well-maintained rooms and a cheaper, shared, open-sided loft with mattresses of varying quality. Doubles $\underline{\$40}$; shared loft $\underline{\$18}$/person.

OUT OF TOWN

Cabañas Bambu 1km on road to the Mariposas de Mindo ☎02 2170216 or ☎0999691213. Relaxed yet efficient budget and mid-range option spread around generous lush garden with pool, volleyball court,

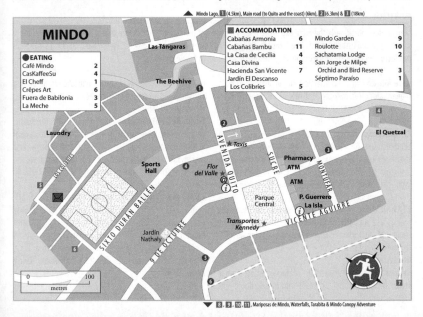

▲ Mindo Lago, **1** (4.5km), Main road (to Quito and the coast) (6km), **2** (6.3km) & **3** (18km)

MINDO

● EATING
Café Mindo	2
CasKaffeeSu	4
El Cheff	1
Crêpes Art	6
Fuera de Babilonia	3
La Meche	5

■ ACCOMMODATION
Cabañas Armonía	6	Mindo Garden	9
Cabañas Bambu	11	Roulotte	10
La Casa de Cecilia	4	Sachatamia Lodge	2
Casa Divina	8	San Jorge de Milpe	
Hacienda San Vicente	7	Orchid and Bird Reserve	3
Jardín El Descanso		Séptimo Paraíso	1
Los Colibríes	5		

Las Tángaras

The Beehive

Laundry

El Quetzal

★ Taxis

Sports Hall

Flor del Valle

Pharmacy
ATM

ATM

Parque Central

P. Guerrero
La Isla

Jardín Nathaly

Transportes Kennedy

VICENTE AGUIRRE

AVENIDA QUITO

SUCRE

MONTUFAR

SIXTO DURAN BALLEN

9 DE OCTUBRE

LOS COLIBRÍES

0   100
metres

▼ **8**, **9**, **10**, **11**, Mariposas de Mindo, Waterfalls, Tarabita & Mindo Canopy Adventure

6

ping-pong table, bar and pleasant semi-open breakfast gazebo. Choose from small en-suite cabins for two with private porch and hammock, or the good-value cheaper rooms with shared facilities ($25). **$50**

Casa Divina signposted off, 1.2km along the road to Mindo Garden ☎ 0990509626, ⊛ mindocasadivina .com. Four beautiful two-storey cabins (sleeping one to four) with porches and hammocks, set in a small, private hillside reserve with hiking trails and lookouts. The comfy en-suite rooms (for one to four) come with proper bathtubs, porches and hammocks. Breakfast and dinner included. **$250**

Mindo Garden 3.5km along the road past the Mariposas de Mindo ☎ 0997223260, ⊛ mindogardens .com. Set in a peaceful garden featuring pleasant cabins near a river, with a games room and a reliable restaurant. **$94**

Roulotte 2km along the road to the Mariposas de Mindo ☎ 0989764484 ⊛ hosterialaroulottemindo .com. Guests are lodged in five compact, cheery, Romany-style coach-cabins – accommodating four in two double-bed bunks. The open-sided restaurant serves excellent food prepared by the Swiss chef – so expect rösti with your mains ($9–12) – while you watch toucans and tanagers feed in the tropical foliage. **$80**

Sachatamia Lodge Km78 on the Calacalí road, just east of the Mindo turn-off ☎ 02 3900907, ⊛ sachatamia .com. Warm and inviting standard and suite rooms within a polished, wooden lodge, and cabañas further in the forest (cabaña 6 is a top choice for location) – including indoor pool, jacuzzi and pool table – with views across its private reserve, which includes a canopy cable traverse. The noise from the main road is noticeable at weekends. Day-visitors $20. **$98**

★**San Jorge de Milpe Orchid and Bird Reserve**, near Los Bancos, 18km northwest of Mindo ☎ 02 2247549, ⊛ eco-lodgesanjorge.com. The jewel in the Magic Birding Circuit's crown (see box, p.38), set in a large reserve awash with waterfalls, rivers, orchids and 22km of trails. Accommodation to suit different budgets. Top billing goes to the fabulous deluxe bamboo cabañas, boasting private balconies with hammocks, and surrounded by forest; the aptly named Cliff Lodge has eight comfortable no-nonsense rooms, and affords breathtaking views across the steep-sided forested Río Chahuaryacu valley from two long communal balconies, a 20-min walk from the main lodge and semi-open dining area, which is crowned with a superb three-tiered observation tower. Full board. Cliff Lodge **$220**; cabañas **$330**

★**Séptimo Paraíso** 500m down a turn-off 4km from Mindo towards the main Calacalí–La Independencia highway ☎ 0993684421, ⊛ septimoparaiso.com. A lovely lodge decorated like a country-house hotel with antique furnishings, artwork and ornaments plus a great pool area – including a semi-open heated one – and separate bar and games room, enlivened by a fire at night. Some rooms are a distance from the lodge, but surrounded by luxuriant forest, with trails open to day-visitors ($13). Doubles **$140**; suites **$185**

EATING

Many hotels, particularly the more expensive ones, have decent restaurants that charge tourist prices, but several more modestly priced establishments line **Avenida Quito**. For picnic items there's a grocer's on the park, stocking some local products, and there are also a couple of mini-supermarkets on the main street.

Café Mindo Quito. An eclectic menu of specialities from Manabí alongside Mexican and vegetarian dishes (mains $7–9). Mon, Tues & Thurs 10am–9pm, Fri & Sat 10am–10pm, Sun 9am–6pm.

CasKaffeeSu Ballén and Quito ☎ 02 2170100. A congenial spot for a frappé or a glass of wine, whether on the shady terrace, or inside by the fire on a damp, rainy evening. Decent, proper coffee. Live Andean music Wed–Sat (cover $3). Sun–Tues 8am–8pm, Wed–Sat 8am–10pm.

El Cheff Quito. A reliable option serving up cheap set menus and a choice of burgers, fish and meat options (mains $4–9), including *lomo a la piedra* – a slab of steak cooked on a hot stone. Mon–Fri 8am–5.30pm, Sat & Sun until 8/9pm.

Crêpes Art Aguirre, opposite La Meche. Sit on the bar stools at this delightful, arty café with mosaic decor, and enjoy a savoury or sweet stuffed pancake washed down with beer and accompanied by mellow music. Noon–8pm; closed Wed or Thurs.

Fuera de Babilonia 9 de Octubre and Montúfar. Rustic, wooden restaurant serving organic food with several veggie options – simple inexpensive almuerzos and meriendas ($3), and a small menu of tasty pasta, salads, steaks, tilapia and trout dishes for around $7. Daily 7am–7.30pm.

La Meche (formerly El Nómada). Aguirre, one block south of the park ☎ 0980574817. Turns out highly praised pizzas from a wood-fired clay oven ($8–10) and home-made pasta dishes, accompanied by wine in elegant glasses. It's also a popular spot for a beer, though service can be desultory midweek. Daily noon–9pm.

ACTIVITIES AROUND MINDO

From its emergence as the hub of Ecuadorian birdwatching, Mindo's menu of **activities** has expanded considerably in recent years to include hiking, horse riding, zip-lining, canyoning, mountain biking and tubing.

ADVENTURE SPORTS

Zip-lining Mindo is gaining a reputation as a good place to go zip-lining. Mindo Canopy Adventure ($8–20; ⓦ mindocanopy.com), halfway up the slope to the *tarabita*, or cable car (see below), offers a good deal and a sustained adrenaline rush with its collection of 11 zip-lines, ranging in length from 75m to 400m, making a total aerial canopy tour of over 3km, plus a fair amount of hiking in between (bring plenty of water). For those who need additional kicks, there's always the vertiginous "Xtreme Tarzan swing".

Tubing Ever-popular tubing ($6/person, four-person minimum; 15–30min depending on water levels), or *regatas*, in rafts of inflated inner tubes down the Río Mindo, is another inexpensive way to increase your pulse rate. Make sure you only go with a reputable operator, like La Isla (see p.265), which provides you with a life-jacket, helmet and guides, and don't be enticed onto the water after heavy rains, when it's much more dangerous. La Isla can also take you canyoning ($15).

BIRDWATCHING

Guides Lodges specifically aimed at birdwatchers have their own birding guides and most places can fix you up with a reliable, qualified guide, who should have binoculars and probably a telescope too. Rates are usually $50–60/person for a couple (less for a larger group) for around five to six hours from dawn, with transport and reserve fees on top. Highly recommended local bird guides who also speak English include the Arias brothers: Marcelo Arias (ⓣ0993406321, ⓔ marceloguideofbirds@yahoo.com) and Irman Arias (ⓣ0991708720, ⓦ mindobirdguide .weebly.com); and Julia Patiño (ⓣ0986162816, ⓦ mindobirdwatching.wordpress.com).

You can spot a fair few birds just wandering round Mindo at dawn; alternatively, consider the private trails ($6/person) of *Hacienda San Vicente* (see p.265), only a short walk out of Mindo. **Spotting the cock-of-the-rock** There are several reserves where you can see the dawn prancing of the male cock-of-the-rock (gallo de la peña) in his lek; the favoured destination is the Refugio Paz de Las Aves ($30/person entry for two or more, ⓣ0987253674, ⓦ refugiopazdelasaves.com), at Km66 off the main highway between Nangelito and the turn-off to Mindo, where you are guaranteed a rich display of colourful birdlife, but given its international reputation you are unlikely to be alone in the forest.

HIKING & WATERFALLS

There are many good hikes around Mindo in the **private reserves** adjoining the larger Bosque Protector Mindo-Nambillo (out of bounds to the general public), which usually have **hiking trails** you can use for a small fee. If you want to venture more off the beaten track, arrange for the services of a **guide**, but make sure they have a licence from the Ministerio de Turismo. Note that after a lot of rain trails inevitably get extremely muddy so get hold of some **rubber boots**.

Cascada de Nambillo One of the most popular hiking trails is to the Cascada de Nambillo waterfall ($3), an attractive spot where you can swim in a cooling river pool. With its concrete changing rooms, a waterslide and plenty of family groups at weekends, don't expect a secret, pristine paradise.

Santuario de las Cascadas Arguably more scenic than the Cascada de Nambillo, the Santuario de las Cascadas ($5 entry, including the *tarabita*) is a private reserve reached by the Tarabita de Mindo ($5), a 530m cable-car ride across a ravine (or a bridge for those averse to heights). The reserve has a circular trail leading you to seven waterfalls over several hours; for tickets and information, go to *Café Mindo* (see opposite) on Avenida Quito.

Cascada de Azúcar Another popular hike (3hr each way) is to the Cascada de Azúcar, inside La Isla's reserve (see p.265), which you can abseil down with a guide for $15 and camp nearby for $5.

HORSE RIDING

Hiring a horse You can hire horses directly at hotels such as *El Carmelo de Mindo* (1km southwest of the football pitch), *Hostal Garceta Sol* (2km from the *parque central*) or *Hacienda San Vicente* or through La Isla (see p.265) for around $12 per person per hour. For something completely different, consider a half-day tour to an apiary ($25); contact *The Beehive* café on Avenida Quito.

The northern lowlands

In contrast to the forest-clad slopes of the western Andes, the major towns in the **northern lowlands**, such as **Santo Domingo de los Tsáchilas** and the transport hub of **Quevedo**, tend to be sweaty commercial centres enveloped by acres of agricultural land that rarely feature on travel itineraries. Still, between Santo Domingo and the main northern coastal city of Esmeraldas lie two important but oft-neglected reserves: **Reserva Biológica Bilsa** and **Reserva Ecológica Mache-Chindul**, isolated fragments of tropical coastal wet forest that form part of the biologically diverse **Chocó Endemic Bird Area**.

Santo Domingo de los Tsáchilas

Getting to and from the major transport hub of **SANTO DOMINGO DE LOS TSÁCHILAS** (formerly Los Colorados) is far easier than finding anything to do once you're there; the main reason to stop here is to book a tour to visit a **Tsáchila community** (see box opposite). You need to keep your wits about you in Santo Domingo, and if you decide to go out at night, make sure you take a **taxi**.

The city is encircled by a ring road linking a number of fast radial roads – east to Quito, north to Esmeraldas, west to Pedernales, southwest to Manta, Bahía de Caráquez and Portoviejo and south to Guayaquil via Quevedo. Beyond the ring road extend vast **banana and oil-palm plantations** that contribute a significant chunk to the national economy, making Santo Domingo by far the most important commercial centre in the northern coastal interior. Its narrow, crowded, sweltering and polluted streets – although recently improved after an injection of civic cash on being made a provincial capital – hold few attractions to sightseers, beyond the **market** along Avenida 3 de Julio, west of the main square of **Parque Zaracay**; it's busiest on Sunday. The streets get even more crowded during the July 3 **fiesta** for Santo Domingo's cantonization, when an agricultural fair packs the *recinto ferial* exhibition hangar opposite the *Zaracay* hotel.

ARRIVAL AND DEPARTURE   SANTO DOMINGO DE LOS TSÁCHILAS

By bus The main route to the northern lowlands starts its descent of the western Andes at Alóag, 40km south of Quito on the Panamericana, heading down towards Santo Domingo de los Tsáchilas (every 10–15min; 3hr), from where there are highways and frequent bus services to all the major coastal centres. Buses for Santo Domingo leave from Quito's Quitumbe terminal. The bus terminal in Santo Domingo, 1.5km north of the town centre along Avenida de Los Tsáchilas, is serviced by dozens of companies with many routes across Ecuador; most buses are passing through. To reach the centre, take a taxi ($2) or one of the local buses, many of which run along the main street and access the terminal.

Destinations Ambato (every 30min–1hr; 4hr); Coca (2 daily; 11hr); Cuenca (5 daily; 9hr); Esmeraldas (every 15min; 4hr); Guayaquil (every 20min; 5hr); Lago Agrio (6 daily; 9hr); Los Bancos (30 daily; 1hr 30min or 3hr, depending on the service); Manta (every 30min; 6hr); Mindo (6 daily; 4hr); Pedernales (27 daily; 2 or 3hr 30min, depending on the service); Quevedo (every 15min; 1hr 30min); Quito (direct, every 10–15min; 3hr).

ACCOMMODATION

Grand Hotel Santo Domingo Río Toachi and Galápagos ☎ 02 2767948, ⓦ grandhotelsantodomingo .com. This immaculate hotel is easily the best place in the centre, with tiled floors and smart rooms. The restaurant (daily 7am–9pm) serves quality food, plus there's a jacuzzi, sauna and pool. Breakfast included. **$112**

Hotel Diana Real Corner of 29 de Mayo and Loja ☎ 02 751384. ⓔ hugo_loaiza@hotmail.com. Reasonable-sized budget option though with dilapidated furnishings; the basic en-suite rooms have fans, hot water, cable TV and phones. **$30**

Quevedo

With no other sizeable community within a hundred kilometres, **QUEVEDO**, south of Santo Domingo, is a major commercial centre – notable for its large Chinese population – amid a sprawling agricultural landscape of rice and banana plantations.

THE TSÁCHILAS OF SANTO DOMINGO

For many years Santo Domingo was known as **Santo Domingo de los Colorados** after the derisive nickname given to the **Tsáchila** people, whom the Spanish labelled Los Colorados, meaning "coloured" or "redheads", due to their bowl haircuts pasted down with bright-red *achiote* dye. These days, however, you're unlikely to see any urban Tsáchila wearing traditional dress or sporting their celebrated hairstyles – except for the stereotypes on local billboards and statues. The destruction of the forests around Santo Domingo has had a deep effect on the Tsáchila, the majority of whom have been forced to abandon their traditional way of life. The seven remaining Tsáchila communities of around 2500 people lie just beyond the city, and are now being encouraged by government and NGOs to take up community-based tourism as a way of improving their economic situation, while helping to preserve their traditional customs. In **Chigüilpe**, for example, money raised through tourism has enabled them to build classrooms where they're now teaching Tsáfiqui (their indigenous language), to young children, in an attempt to prevent its extinction. The Tsáchila's renowned **curanderos**, shamanic healers, are a major attraction, although this raises concerns among older community members that in the rush for the tourist dollar, rituals are losing their cultural significance and becoming corrupted (see also box, p.218).

The main communities that are engaged in tourism are at **Chigüilpe** and **Búa**; both have "living museums", and accept homestays. Several Tsáchila communities now offer a range of cultural activities to tourists, ranging from teaching them about shamanic rituals, body painting and textile weaving, to offering presentations of dance and music or walks in the rainforest, pointing out medicinal plants and demonstrating traditional hunting techniques.

VISITING A TSÁCHILA COMMUNITY INDEPENDENTLY

While tour operators in town can organize day trips to Tsáchila communities, they tend to be rather staged affairs for large groups. If you can muster enough Spanish to get there under your own steam, then you'll have a more personalized and rewarding experience. Both Chigüilpe and Búa can be reached by public transport.

If travelling independently to Chigüilpe, 7km along the road to Quevedo, contact Byron Luis, who speaks English (☎0939733989, ✉cbyronluis@yahoo.es) and can organize various activities from day-tours of the community to overnight stays and camping trips. Located 15km along the road to Chone, Búa welcomes tourists and volunteers (☎0991812011, 🌐shinopibolon .com); volunteering projects here are sometimes organized via NGO Yanapuma in Quito (🌐yanapuma.org).

Given its location at the crossroads of the Portoviejo–Latacunga and the heavily used Santo Domingo–Guayaquil roads, Quevedo is served by many buses, but since the bus terminal was constructed 2km northwest of the town centre, there's little reason for the average visitor to venture into the centre.

ARRIVAL AND DEPARTURE QUEVEDO

By bus There are regular buses to many destinations from Quevedo, including Guayaquil (every 10min; 3hr 30min); Latacunga via Zumbahua (14 daily; 5hr); Manta (every 30min; 5hr); Quito (every 15–30min; 5hr); and Santo Domingo (every 15min; 1hr 30min).

Reserva Biológica Bilsa and Reserva Ecológica Mache-Chindul

In the Mache hills west of Quinindé, 90km northwest of Santo Domingo on the road to Esmeraldas, is one of the last major tracts of Ecuadorian coastal humid tropical forest, the 30-square-kilometre **Reserva Biológica Bilsa** ($6), and the adjoining, enormous **Reserva Ecológica Mache-Chindul** – 700 square kilometres of rarely accessed terrain, though logging, oil pipelines and illegal settlements have made significant incursions over the years. The two protected areas' forests range from 300m to 800m in altitude, high enough for heavy layers of fog to loom over the upper ridges, saturating the vegetation and allowing for great biodiversity and high levels of endemism.

This is one of the few places in the country where the rare long-wattled umbrella bird makes frequent appearances. **Mammals** include jaguars, ocelots and the diminutive jaguarundi, while substantial numbers of mantled howler monkeys bawl across the canopy. In Bilsa, the on-site **Center for the Conservation of Western Forest Plants** produces thirty thousand trees each year for reforestation projects, promotes environmental awareness and teaches land management to local communities. **Volunteers** are welcome ($577/four weeks).

6

ARRIVAL AND DEPARTURE   RESERVA BIOLÓGICA BILSA AND MACHE-CHINDUL

RESERVA BIOLÓGICA BILSA

By bus, taxi and mule The Quito office can help with arrangements to access the reserve, which involves taking a bus to Quinindé, a ranchera to the village of 'La Y' de la Laguna, from where you can hire a camioneta to the research station ($30–35).

Contact details For accommodation bookings (see below) contact the Fundación Jatún Sacha in Quito at Teresa de Cepeda N34-260 and República (☎ 02 2432240, ⓦ jatunsacha.org).

RESERVA ECOLÓGICA MACHE-CHINDUL

From Reserva Biológica Bilsa The easiest access to the park is through the Reserva Biológica Bilsa.

By foot Other access points to the park are quite remote and involve making long hikes, hauling food and camping gear, and hiring a guide or possibly even a mule; you can do so at the village of Boca de Tazones, 15km south of Atacames, the communities southeast of El Salto, 15km east of Muisne and 23km south of Tonchigüe, and Chamanga, halfway between Muisne and Pedernales.

ACCOMMODATION AND EATING

Reserve accommodation On-site basic lodgings are available at the Reserva Biológica Bilsa in wooden cabins (for four to six people; bring your own sheet sleeping bag) with shared baths and latrines. There is electricity but no hot water. Rates include a bed and access to the reserve;

you can either bring in food to cook yourself, or pay someone on site. Jatún Sacha (see above) can also organize package deals, including guide ($30) and transport to the reserve. Advance reservations essential. $24/person

The northern coast

Home to the country's largest Afro-Ecuadorian population, and viewed by many Ecuadorians as the nation's playground, the **northern coast** – part of the Ruta del Spondylus (see p.321) – plays host to dozens of popular **beach resorts**, all within a day's drive of the capital. Busloads of *serranos* pile down from the highlands to fill the resorts during weekends and holidays, making the most of the fun-loving and relaxed *costeño* spirit. However, as unregulated coastal development continues and high-rise concrete blocks continue to sprout, it's getting harder to find a laidback beach vibe. That said, with your own transport and a little time and perseverance, you can still seek out hidden fishing villages, rocky cliffs, tropical wet forests, scrubby tropical dry forests and swathes of mangrove as well as some of the least explored parts of Ecuador outside the Oriente.

At the coast's northern tip near Colombia, **San Lorenzo** can still act as a launching pad for trips to several little-visited destinations, though in recent years security concerns have pushed visitors further down the coast to the small but burgeoning beach resort of **Las Peñas**. On the other side of Esmeraldas, the region's main port, are some of Ecuador's most popular resorts, such as **Atacames**, loaded with beachfront bars, pounding music and cocktails, or the smaller villages of **Tonsupa**, **Súa**, **Same** and **Tonchigüe**, where fishing boats are giving way to beach towels and high-rise hotels.

Past the rocky **Punta Galera** is **Muisne**, an isolated and somewhat neglected outpost on an offshore sand bar, from where a road loops inland and back to the sea at **Pedernales**, and the closest beaches to Quito. Further south, oceanside cliffs and sleepy coves make good geography for a cluster of hideaways, and the long beaches return at the surfing hangout of **Canoa** and extend all the way to the Río Chone estuary. Across the river the gleaming white blocks of **Bahía de Caráquez** herald one of Ecuador's smarter resorts, while further south, **Manta**, the country's exuberant second port, boasts a few beaches of its own.

The area has two distinct seasons, but the **climate** changes slightly the further south you go. Daytime average temperatures hover around 26ºC (79ºF) across the region throughout the year, with greater rainfall and humidity north of Pedernales; to the south there's very little rain from June to November. The **wet season** (Dec–May) features clear skies interrupted by torrential afternoon rains that can wash out roads. **Mosquitoes** tend to be more of a problem at this time, and Esmeraldas province has one of the highest incidences of malaria in the country, so take plenty of insect repellent (see p.42). During the **dry season** the days are a little cooler and consistently cloudy, without as much rain. The most popular resorts get very crowded during **national holidays** and the **high season** (mid-June to early Sept & late Dec–Jan), when hotel rates can be double the low-season prices and rooms are harder to come by.

6

GETTING AROUND
THE NORTHERN COAST

By bus There are regular bus services along the three main roads from the highlands to the north coast: from Ibarra to San Lorenzo, running parallel to the largely disused railway; from Quito via Calacalí or Alóag; and a route from Latacunga via Quevedo.

The Vía del Pacífico Once you're at the coast, it's easy to get around on the paved Vía del Pacífico (E15), which runs its entire length.

San Lorenzo

A small, run-down town at the northwestern tip of the country, surrounded by sea inlets and mangrove swamps, **SAN LORENZO** isn't exactly inviting, with its ramshackle houses and pervasive sense of anarchy and disarray, though a recent injection of government cash has seen the main street paved and the pier area smartened up. Still, the town's considerable number of **Afro-Ecuadorians** – largely the descendants of colonial African slaves and later labourers from the plantations and mines of Colombia – provide a distinct cultural flavour that is refreshingly different from the rest of the country. One of its manifestations is the colourful sound of the **marimba**, the wooden xylophone whose driving rhythms are a key feature of music and dance on the north coast. The town has several groups that stage occasional performances, and it hosts an annual international **marimba festival** during the last week of May. You'll also get plenty of fun and music at the town's main fiesta during the first week of August.

San Lorenzo's fortunes were, for many years tied to the rail line from Ibarra (see box, p.124). When the train opened in 1957, the population of this forgotten port doubled virtually overnight, but the anticipated economic boom never materialized, and hope of further development rather fizzled out when the train service ended in 1998.

Note that because of increasing **drug-related and paramilitary activity** around San Lorenzo, it is not safe to be in the streets after dark (see box below).

ARRIVAL AND DEPARTURE
SAN LORENZO

There are **two routes** from San Lorenzo to Esmeraldas, 110km to the southwest. The fastest by several hours is the new inland road to Esmeraldas via Borbón and Maldonado. The other route involves taking a boat via Limones and La Tola and then a bus along the coast. Although slower and less comfortable, this latter route is far more scenic and passes through the tangled mangrove swamps of the Reserva Ecológica Manglares Cayapas-Mataje.

THE COLOMBIAN BORDER: TRAVEL WARNING

Officially, it's possible for tourists to **cross into Colombia** from San Lorenzo, either by boat to Puerto Palma, and then on to Tumaco, or inland at Mataje, but in light of the increasingly dangerous conditions of remote border areas, it's strongly advised that you **do not enter** Colombia at this point – use the crossing north of Tulcán instead (see p.128). Note also that the town of San Lorenzo too is unsafe after dark. To find out more about current safety precautions, check your embassy's **travel advisories** or ask locally at the **police and immigration** office in San Lorenzo (near the town's entrance).

6

BY BUS

Buses arrive at, depart from or pass near the train station, where most company offices are, except Transportes Esmeraldas on 10 de Agosto, which runs buses to Quito and Guayaquil. Transporte La Costeñita and Cooperativa del Pacífico alternate buses to Esmeraldas.

Destinations Borbón (every 30min; 1hr 30min); Esmeraldas (22 daily; 3–4hr on the express service via Borbón); Guayaquil (3 daily; 10–12hr); Ibarra (19 daily; 4hr); Quito (daily 11pm, or change at Ibarra; 7hr).

BY BOAT

At the dock, Trans Fluvial y Marítimo Pacífico and Transportes San Lorenzo del Pailón each run four daily boats to Limones (6.30am, 7.30am, 10.30am, 1pm & 4pm, returning 7.30am, 10.30am, 2.30pm & 4pm; 1hr 15min; $3), where there are half-hourly connections to La Tola (30min); Playa Cauchal (7.30am, returning 9.30am; 1hr); and to Palma Real (7.30am; 1hr 30min; and on demand for 7–9 passengers by express boat; 45min; $10), from where you can get transport on to Tumaco in Colombia, but note that this is extremely risky (see box, p.271). Boat travel is exhilarating, but sometimes uncomfortable; have a hat and sunblock handy and take something to sit on. From La Tola, there are hourly bus connections to Esmeraldas.

INFORMATION

Tourist office Currently located in the ground floor of the *Hotel Carondelet*, on the *parque central*, with a shared phone number (Mon–Fri 9am–6pm, closed for lunch; ☎06 2781119).

Money The town's one ATM is at the Banco Pichincha on Ponce and Garcés.

ACCOMMODATION AND EATING

El Castibol Eloy Alfaro and Ortiz ☎ 06 2780383. Hotel restaurant that is frequently packed at midday, though folks are drawn as much by the (noisy) a/c as by the tasty and varied seafood dishes. Mon–Sat 8am–9pm.

El Chocó Imbabura and Ortiz. Pleasant, clean, open-fronted restaurant offering inexpensive almuerzos ($3) and other dishes – plenty served in coconut cream. Mon–Sat 6am–9/10pm.

Gran Hotel San Carlos Imbabura and Garces ☎06 2780284. A simple, clean, secure hotel with cheerfully painted rooms that have fans and mosquito nets, private or shared bathrooms (but no hot water) and cable TV. Now also has smarter, pricier rooms with a/c ($5 extra) in an annexe down the street. $20

Tundaloma Lodge Km17 on the Ibarra road ☎0997788743, ⊛tundaloma.com. The nicest accommodation in the area, a 20min taxi ride outside the town, comprises a group of comfortable wooden cabins sleeping four each, equipped with fans, private bathrooms and warm water. They're on a steep hillside overlooking the forest, so the birdwatching is good. Also offers tubing and guided walks. Mains at the restaurant are $8–10 and breakfast is included. $58

Around San Lorenzo

Most travellers bypass San Lorenzo in favour of the beach resorts west of Esmeraldas, skipping the poor and largely comfortless coast on the way, with its rough lumber towns and tumbledown fishing villages. Nevertheless, there are good opportunities here to see the mangroves of the **Reserva Ecológica Manglares Cayapas-Mataje**, and intrepid travellers can also visit the lowland forests of the **Reserva Ecológica Cotacachi-Cayapas** and the fascinating **Chachi** and **Afro-Ecuadorian** communities at its fringes. Community ecotourism projects, such as those in **Playa de Oro** and **San Miguel**, also make good bases, though you'll usually have to give them plenty of notice to prepare for your arrival.

Reserva Ecológica Manglares Cayapas-Mataje

Between San Lorenzo and La Tola • Daily 8am–5pm; guided visits only • $5

The **Reserva Ecológica Manglares Cayapas-Mataje** comprises 513 square kilometres of **mangrove swamps**, a labyrinthine network of natural channels and canals between densely forested islands, stretching from the Colombian border to the estuary at La Tola, and said to be the tallest mangroves in the world at over 60m in height. Five types of mangrove grow here, trees uniquely adapted to the salt water and loose sandy soils of the coast, whose knotted roots give protection from the tides, trap sediments and nurture a wealth of plants, fish, crustaceans and shrimp. Pelicans, frigatebirds, egrets and herons all nest in their branches, taking advantage of this abundance of food.

TOURS

By boat San Lorenzo's two boat companies are Trans Fluvial y Marítimo Pacífico (also Andrés Tours & Wendy's Tours, respectively; ☎ 06 2780161, ask for the very friendly Andrés Carvache, ☎ 0991080108, ✉ andrescarvache @yahoo.es) and Transportes San Lorenzo del Pailón (also Malvinas Tours; ☎ 06 2781058, ask for Julio Moreno).Both operators run half- and full-day excursions, including one or more of the following: mangroves, inland waterfalls and the Isla de los Pájaros. Costs are per boat – usually around $80–100 for a half day; $200–250 for a full day (not including meals) for up to five people, depending on demand and how far you want to go. Midweek it can be difficult and expensive to get a group together. Take plenty of sunscreen, repellent and water and make sure your boat has a roof. Meals can also be arranged. You can also arrange tours from La Tola, or from Las Peñas (see below).

6

Ríos Cayapas and Santiago

Beyond the unprepossessing, ramshackle lumber town of Borbón, which sits on the main road between San Lorenzo and Esmeraldas and at the mouths of the *ríos* Cayapas and Santiago, lies a lush rainforested hinterland that gives way to the remote tropical regions of the vast **Reserva Ecológica Cotacachi-Cayapas** (see p.116). The area is home to vibrant Chachi and Afro-Ecuadorian communities that farm plantains, hunt and fish for survival, but have been under pressure from the logging industry since the 1950s and more recently from multinational agribusiness and mining operations looking to exploit the forests around them. However, **ecotourism** (see below) is now emerging as a good alternative means for these communities to earn income while maintaining their forests.

ARRIVAL AND DEPARTURE   RÍOS CAYAPAS AND SANTIAGO

By canoe Reaching the lodges in this region requires advance notice and travel by motorized dugout canoe. Santa María and San Miguel, up the Río Cayapas, are reached from Borbón (2hr and 5hr, respectively). Boats generally leave Borbón for various destinations up the river between 10am and 11.30am; arrive early to get a place.

There is a daily boat to San Miguel leaving 10–11am ($10). To reach Playa de Oro up the Río Santiago, travel to Selva Alegre on one of the infrequent buses from Borbón – aim to get the 7.30am one – and then travel by canoe (2hr). A private canoe to Playa de Oro costs $50, irrespective of the number of passengers.

ACCOMMODATION

San Miguel Eco Project San Miguel ☎ 02 2528769, ⓦ cayapas-adventures.com. In San Miguel, contact Soyander Orobio ☎ 0992236338. This six-roomed lodge overlooking the village features a very pleasant veranda, and screened bedrooms with mosquito nets and shared bathroom. There are opportunities for guided forest walks, as well as trips to a Chachi village. Rates include transport, accommodation, meals and guiding. $35/person

Tigrillo Lodge 30min upstream from Playa de Oro. Contact Ramiro Buitrón at Valle del Amanecer, Otavalo (see p.109), who can help set up a visit and also organizes group transport to Selva Alegre. You can stay at the two-storey wooden lodge or at cabins in the village, which aren't as quiet, comfortable or secluded. There are jungle tours in the community's reserve ($10 entrance), and you can try your hand at panning for gold or fishing. Rates include meals, guiding and excursions. Advance reservation preferred as there is no regular boat transport to the village. Private transport is $50/boat. $50/person

Las Peñas

When the road from Ibarra to the coast was paved a few years ago, **LAS PEÑAS**, once a quiet fishing village with a few simple huts and wooden boats hauled onto the windswept grey sand, suddenly became the most easily accessed beach from the sierra at just four hours' journey by bus. Now, beach bars and restaurants are dotted among the palm trees along the seafront for hundreds of metres and concrete hotels are sprouting up, strung out along a couple of kilometres of sandy track parallel to the surf. The place still sees few foreign tourists, but fills at weekends and holidays as buses packed with *serranos* from Ibarra park on the beach and room prices lurch upwards. Midweek and out of season, though, Las Peñas has a pleasantly low-key air, and makes a good alternative base for exploring the giant-sized mangroves of the **Reserva Ecológica Manglares Cayapas-Mataje** (see opposite), 18km northeast at La Tola.

6

ARRIVAL AND DEPARTURE

LAS PEÑAS

By bus Hourly buses from Esmeraldas (2hr) bound for La Tola drop off passengers at the scruffy little park in the village centre a stone's throw from the beach, before heading up to La Tola (30min). Return buses from La Tola to Esmeraldas (hourly; 2hr) also pick up. Other, more frequent buses running between San Lorenzo and Esmeraldas (every

20–50min; 2hr either direction) drop off and pick up on the main coastal highway, 2km away, at 'La Y'. Waiting mototaxis will transport you to wherever you want to stay ($1–2). On weekends and holidays there are also direct buses to Las Peñas from Ibarra (5hr 30min).

INFORMATION AND TOURS

Tourist information There is no official tourist office, but William Torres, the village pharmacist, is also a certified guide, has bags of information, and runs Camiteo's, the village tour operator, next to the park on the main road (☎06 2793046 or ☎099418388,

✉ wimatova@yahoo.es). He runs various tours, including boat trips to the Reserva Ecológica Manglares Cayapas-Mataje (see p.272). More information is also available at ⊕ laspenasesmeraldas.com.

Money There is no ATM, so bring sufficient cash.

ACCOMMODATION AND EATING

Cabañas Ecológicas Ronnie's Set back 50m from the beach road, 800m north of the beach entrance ☎0997711111, ✉ jcriollo-31@hotmail.com. The nicest budget option: simple bamboo en-suite cabins with firm beds, mosquito nets and fans, set in a sandy garden with hammocks, deckchairs and a small pool, all surrounded by tropical foliage, including a tree full of parakeets. $25

Cabañas Mikey ☎06 2793101, ⊕ laspeñasesmeraldas .com/cabanas_mikey.html. Three clean, compact two-bedroom family units along a porch with a well-equipped kitchenette (stove and fridge), and there is a tiny pool in the garden. Offers substantial discounts midweek. $84

★ **Donde Stalin** On the beach. The inauspicious name belies a lovely shady beachside garden with seating under

thatch, and hammocks – the perfect spot to enjoy a delicious plateful of fish or shrimp *encocado* with generous accompaniments of rice, salad and lentils (around $8–10). Daily 8am–7pm.

Sabor Costeño On the beach, opposite Cumbres Andinas. Popular, breezy plant-filled veranda, where the bubbly dueña serves up huge portions of seafood accompanied by rice and *patacones*. Try the *bandeja marinera* (seafood platter; $35 for four people) laden with lobster, langostinoes and ceviche plus sides. Breakfasts too are varied: choose from shrimp omelette, fruit salad or *bolones* (stuffed green plantain dumplings with cheese). Daily 7am–10pm.

Esmeraldas

ESMERALDAS is the largest industrial port on the north coast and capital of Esmeraldas province; both town and province derive their name from emeralds the size of "pigeon's eggs" that were supposedly found by the first conquistadors; the moniker stuck despite years of fruitless searches for phantom emerald deposits.

The economy of Esmeraldas is mainly driven by a nearby oil refinery, which links up with the **Trans-Andean oil pipeline**. Little of that wealth has trickled down to much of the population, as evidenced by the city's shaky infrastructure and the slums that fester on the hillsides fringing the centre. It is no surprise then that Esmeraldas is struggling to combat its reputation for **crime**; stick to the busy central areas and don't wander around after dark. That said, the city's lively spirit and warmth is enticing. The tree-filled **parque central** is the focal point of Esmeraldas' population of 150,000, and bustles with street vendors, shoe-shiners and fruit-juice sellers.

Museo de la Arqueología Regional

Parque central, corner of Bolívar and Piedrahita • 8.30m–5.30pm; closed Tues • Free

The city's only real attraction is the **Museo de la Arqueología Regional**, housed within the **Centro Cultural de Esmeraldas**. The ground floor contains a good collection of regional pre-Columbian artefacts, particularly the wonderfully expressive ceramics of the Tolita culture, and some intricate gold jewellery. The second floor hosts interesting temporary exhibitions.

FESTIVALS IN ESMERALDAS

The biggest city **fiesta** is the **Independence of Esmeraldas** on August 5, which includes dancing, processions and an agricultural fair, while around **Carnaval** there's the **Festival Internacional de Música y Danza Afro**, held on Las Palmas beach, in the wealthier northern resort-suburb of the same name, featuring marimba players, and traditional Afro-Hispano-American music and dance.

ARRIVAL AND DEPARTURE ESMERALDAS 6

BY PLANE

Esmeraldas airport is served by TAME flights from Quito (1–2 daily; 40min; from $85 one-way) and Guayaquil (1 daily; 1hr; from $87 one-way). It's 15km by road from the city, or a 30min taxi ride (shared $3; private $10); $25 by taxi to Atacames. Buses to and from San Lorenzo pass the airport at Tachina.

Airlines TAME (ⓦ tame.com.ec) has two offices: in the Multiplaza mall on Maldonado between Estupiñan and Manabí (ⓣ 06 2725203) and at the airport (ⓣ 06 2991640).

By bus All provincial and long-distance traffic uses the large bus terminal at the Codesa roundabout, 4km south of the city centre ($4 by taxi).

Destinations Ambato (11 daily; 8hr); Atacames (every 10–15min; 45min); Borbón (21 daily; 2hr 40min); Chamanga (every 50min–1hr 10min; 3hr); Guayaquil (33 daily; 7–8hr); Manta (4 daily; 10hr); Mompiche (4 daily; 2hr 45min); Muisne (every 20–30min; 2hr 15min); Las Peñas (hourly; 2hr 40min); Quito (24 daily; 6hr); Same (21 daily; 1hr 10min); San Lorenzo (19 daily; 4hr); Santo Domingo (every 15min; 3–4hr); Súa (21 daily every 20min; 1hr); La Tola (hourly; 3hr); Tonsupa (every 10–15min; 50min).

GETTING AROUND AND INFORMATION

By bus In town, city buses travel up Avenida Libertad to Las Palmas.

By taxi Taxis cost $1–2 round the city centre. Make sure you take a licensed one and always travel by taxi at night.

Tourist offices There's basic tourist information at the Ministerio de Turismo office on Bolívar (ⓣ 06 2727340) and there's an I-Tur desk at the airport.

ACCOMMODATION

Costa Esmeraldas Sucre 911 and Piedrahita ⓣ 06 270640. Despite thin mattresses, the ample rooms are all decent value, especially considering they come with ceiling fans, private bathrooms, TVs and phones – though a/c is extra. **$20**

Hotel Cayapas Kennedy and Valdez, Las Palmas ⓣ 06 2721318. Rooms come with a/c, fridge and hot water, though the ones upstairs enjoy better lighting. Also has a neatly pruned garden and a fine restaurant. **$40**

El Manglar Quito between Olmedo and Colón ⓣ 06 2727112. Decent, inexpensive *comida Esmeraldeña*, with seafood featuring large on the menu. Daily 7am–9pm.

Las Redes Bolívar on the parque central ⓣ 06 2723151. An excellent place for breakfast, lunch (when it's packed) or dinner; it's strong on *encocados*, and serves set meals and à la carte dishes. Has a sibling restaurant in Tonsupa. Daily 7am–9pm.

The coast southwest to Muisne

The expanses of pale sand streaking **west of Esmeraldas** sustain some of the country's most popular seaside resorts. During the **high season** (mid-June to Sept & Dec–Jan), a deluge of vacationers descends from the highlands, but the real crush comes during Carnaval, Semana Santa, Christmas and New Year, when the price of a room can double. **Atacames** is the most famous and raucous resort, while others such as **Tonsupa, Súa** and **Same** offer a more tranquil atmosphere, but can be just as busy at peak times. The beaches break around the dry and rocky headland of the **Punta Galera**, whose cliffs and secluded coves provide the quietest and most isolated beaches in the region, giving way to mangrove forests around **Muisne**, one of the more remote seaside resorts of the province.

Although Puerto López (see p.325) is acknowledged to be the best mainland spot for **whale-watching** in Ecuadorian waters, you'll also find enterprising boat owners along this stretch of coastline happy to take you out during the season (June–Sept).

6

ARRIVAL AND DEPARTURE

By bus Regular buses travel along the coast between Muisne and Esmeraldas every 20–30minutes. If you're

THE COAST SOUTHWEST TO MUISNE

heading further south, take one of the hourly buses from Esmeraldas to Chamanga.

Tonsupa

Three kilometres north of Atacames, and soon to be swallowed up in its greedy expansion, tiny **TONSUPA**, for the moment at least, offers a slightly less frantic and safer version of its neighbour's party beach scene, with a small malecón and a handful of loud beach bars and stalls backing a stretch of sand, plus a couple of decent restaurants.

ARRIVAL AND DEPARTURE

By bus Buses between Esmeraldas and Atacames (every 10–15min) can drop you or pick you up at the entrance to

TONSUPA

Tonsupa on the main road, from where it's a 500m stroll down to the beach or $0.50 in a mototaxi.

ACCOMMODATION AND EATING

★**La Pergola** Five blocks back from the beach, on a parallel road one block south of the main access road to the beach ☎06 2465116, ✎ristorantelapergola tonsupa.jimdo.com. A delightful verdant oasis midst the concrete jungle, set in a nice garden with a pergola and semi-open patio shaded by a vine-decorated trellis. The ambiance is great, with authentic Italian food to match: choose from pizzas, pastas, risottos and steaks. Pizzas from $7; most mains $15–20. 6–11pm, closed Tues.

★**VíaVía** Two blocks back from the beach ☎06 2465014, ✎viaviacafe.com. Squeezed in among the condominiums, this congenial hostel will give you a warm welcome. It has eight clean, tidy en-suite rooms of varying capacities, a little-used upstairs terrace and a delightful shady patio garden under a spreading tree, where you can enjoy inexpensive, healthy home cooking and cheap beer though the chatter does drift up to the front rooms. Dorm __$10__; doubles __$24__

Atacames

Heaving with people during the holidays and Carnaval, when it's literally standing room only on its dusky beach, **ATACAMES** is one of Ecuador's top partying beach resorts, though it has suffered from a surfeit of unregulated development, and unless you want your eardrums to suffer assault and battery, it's hard to see the appeal. The town is divided by the tidal waters of the **Río Atacames**, resulting in a slender, sandy **peninsula** connected to the mainland by a footbridge and, further upstream, a road bridge. Most bars, hotels and restaurants compete for space on the peninsula, while shops and services are on the other side of the river, along the main road from Esmeraldas and around the little **parque central**. The beachside **market**, mostly stocked with trinkets and sarongs, sometimes has black-coral jewellery for sale – a species under threat and illegal to take out of the country.

The sea here has a strong **undertow** that has claimed a number of victims, despite the occasional presence of volunteer lifeguards. **Crime** is also an unfortunate element of the quieter beach areas, so stay near the crowds, avoid taking valuables onto the beach and stay off it completely at night.

The Malecón

By the beach, the **Malecón** is the place for night-time action: salsa, merengue, pop and, above all, reggaeton pummel the air from rival speakers, while partiers dance – or stagger – to the beat and knock back fruity cocktails. On weekdays and in low season the crowds evaporate, but you can always count on some bars being open.

ARRIVAL AND INFORMATION

By bus Trans La Costeñita and Trans Pacífico buses run between Esmeraldas and Muisne (every 20–30min; last bus 9.30pm), stopping at the town's central bus stop on Cervantes. Mototaxis ($1–2) can ferry you from the bus stop to your hotel, though they travel via the road bridge,

ATACAMES

so it can be quicker to walk across the footbridge. Long-distance buses usually stop at their own offices; buy your ticket early if you're heading back to Quito (7hr). Trans Esmeraldas, at Juan Montalvo and Luis Vargas Torres, runs three daily buses to Quito (7hr) and Guayaquil (8hr 30min), while other companies, with offices nearby, have less frequent services.

I-Tur office Av Las Acacias, by the road bridge (Mon–Fri 2–6pm; ☎ 06 2731912).

ACCOMMODATION

★**Chill Inn** Los Ostiones ☎ 06 2760477, Ⓦ chillinnecuador.com. Delightfully mellow, friendly hostel with four clean, spacious rooms, and a shared balcony common area with TV, bar and hammocks. Inexpensive breakfasts served. $28

Hotel Cielo Azul South end of 21 de Noviembre ☎ 06 2731813, Ⓦ hotelcieloazul.com. Beachfront location and smart rooms with cable TV, hot water, fridge and mosquito

nets. The pool and hammocks also help make this a comfy, well-sited choice $86

Rincón del Mar South end of beach ☎ 06 2760360. Pleasant low-key cabins with cold water, fans and mosquito nets, set well away from the noise and right on the sand. A few units have fridges and kitchenettes, and there's a small pool too, with hot-water showers. $30

EATING AND DRINKING

The numerous restaurants along the **Malecón** serve up nearly identical seafood meals at tourist prices but wherever you eat, make sure you sample the **local specialities**, such as *encocado*, seafood steeped in spiced coconut milk. Partying generally centres on the various **beachside bars**, some of which have their own dancefloors and DJs. If you make it through the night, be sure to try the traditional Atacames breakfast, reputed to be a great hangover cure – ceviche – freshly prepared at the street stalls on Calle Camarones.

El Alcatraz Main road 300m beyond the road bridge at Unión ☎ 06 2731453. Arguably Atacames' top restaurant, worth the walk from the beach to enjoy the delicately spiced creamy sauces on all types of seafood (most mains $9–12). Daily 8am–9pm.

Paco Foco Los Ostiones ☎ 06 2731076. Restaurant with a reputation justifiably as big as the plates of seafood it serves up (mains from $8). The vast *bandeja de mariscos* (seafood platter, $25) is not to be undertaken lightly, and is best shared. Famous for its coconut milkshakes. 8am–10pm, closed Wed.

Súa

From **SÚA**, the exuberance of Atacames, 4km to the east, shimmers in the distance as a tiny mosaic of colour against the scrolling uniformity of the sand. Set in a cosy bay, with calmer waters than at Atacames, this once-tiny fishing village can get as crowded as its more renowned neighbour in the high season, when inflatable bananas tear through the waves behind powerboats and sputtering jet skis destroy any vestige of tranquillity. Off season, Súa is quieter and more enjoyable.

At the heart of the village, the **Malecón** presents a small strip of hotels, restaurants and shops – though no ATM – overlooking the **beach**, which is diminutive at high tide.

ARRIVAL AND DEPARTURE   SÚA

By bus Buses between Esmeraldas and Muisne (every 20–30min; 1hr 10min) deposit passengers on the main

road, a 5min walk from the beach and Malecón (or you can take a mototaxi).

ACCOMMODATION AND EATING

Anita's 16 de Noviembre, just off the main square before the Malecón ☎ 06 2473113. The large 4WDs parked outside on a Sunday lunchtime attest to this restaurant's reputation in *comida Esmeraldeña*; the ceviches and *encocados* are not to be missed (mains from $8). Daily 7am–6pm.

Hostal Las Buganvillas On the beach ☎ 06 2473008, Ⓦ hostallasbuganvillas.com. Friendly budget choice draped in the eponymous, vivid flowers, with tiled en-suite, fan-ventilated rooms (for two to four people), cold showers and a pool. $30

Same and around

SAME, 11km west of Atacames, is the most exclusive resort in the area, and the least prone to overcrowding, where rows of palms shade a beach of soft grey sand caressed by a warm sea. Developers have long recognized its potential, but strip away their interventions – such as the Jack Nicklaus-designed golf course sitting under the white holiday villas cresting the hills – and Same is just a tiny village with little more than a handful of basic shops.

6

STAYING AT PLAYA ESCONDIDA

A turning off the Vía del Pacífico south of Tonchigüe follows a secondary road 10km along the coast towards the rocky cape of **Punta Galera**, before arriving at the secluded hideaway of **Playa Escondida**. Transportes Costeñita (7am, noon & 4pm; 2hr) and River Taviazo buses (8am & 2pm), marked for Galera, Quingue or Estero de Plátanos, leave Esmeraldas bus station (stopping at all the coastal towns on the way); they can drop you at the main gate.

★ **Playa Escondida** ☎ 06 3027496 or ☎ 0996506812, ⒲ playaescondida.com.ec. This serene, ecologically minded beach hideaway overlooks a pretty cove – effectively a private beach – backed by a tract of semi-tropical, semi-deciduous forest teeming with birds and wildlife, such as guantas and anteaters. On its tawny beach, marine turtles clamber ashore to lay eggs, and whales are occasionally spotted out at sea. There's good walking at low tide among rock pools, and along the craggy shoreline. Accommodation is in charming but rustic cabins, or in a larger self-catering house (for two to five people), with shared or private showers and composting toilets. Campers will find plenty of shade available. The on-site, moderately priced restaurant caters for all tastes. Doubles $50; house $100; camping $10/person

Follow the sands 3km to the south and you'll reach **TONCHIGÜE**, a fishing village where tourism hasn't yet made a significant dent, its beach strewn with blue fishing boats and tangled heaps of netting and frigatebirds wheeling watchfully above. A couple of seafront restaurants serve up the catch of the day with a pile of *patacones*.

ARRIVAL AND DEPARTURE   SAME AND AROUND

By bus Buses between Muisne and Esmeraldas can drop or pick you up at Same and Tonchigüe; ask the driver.

ACCOMMODATION AND EATING

El Acantilado 1km south of Same ☎ 06 30276626, ⒲ elacantilado.net. Lovely clifftop location – so insist on an ocean view – in flower-filled gardens. It has a games room, yoga deck, pool, decent restaurant and cabins (for up to six or eight), and suites (for up to four) with hot-water bathrooms, fridges and fans. Good low-season rates. Suites $120; cabins from $160

Cabañas Isla del Sol Overlooking Same beach ☎ 06 2470470, ⒲ cabanasisladelsol.com. Comfortable wooden cabins comprising doubles and family accommodation, with private porches right on the beach (some with fridges and kitchenettes), hot water, fans or a/c, cable TV, board games and a pool. $90

Seaflower Lateneus (also El Nuevo Seaflower) One block back from Same beach ☎ 06 2470369. One of the best restaurants on the coast serving succulent seafood from a vast and varied menu (mains from $12). Its Aladdin's cave venue – draped with Indian textiles, hanging bottles and indigenous artefacts from across the world – plus great cocktails make this also the beach's best bar. Reservations advised. Daily 8am until late.

Muisne

Those wanting to explore off the beaten coastal track might consider **MUISNE**. Located some 35km south of the big resorts, on a 7km palm-fringed sand bar amid the **mangrove swamps** just off the mainland, the place has a rather abandoned feel, which is further enhanced by its rash of dilapidated buildings and isolated location. It can only be reached by boat from the small town of **El Relleno**, across the Río Muisne. A somnolent spot pretty much year-round, it springs to life momentarily every year on October 3, to celebrate the town's cantonization.

The island itself splits into two distinct parts, connected by the double boulevard of **Isidro Ayora**, which runs 1.5km from the docks, where the town's main shops and services are clustered, to the **beach**, at the boulevard's other end, where crashing breakers and a broad, flat stretch of sand are fronted by a handful of inexpensive hotels, restaurants and the odd bar, all shaded by a row of palms. Tours of the mangrove swamps are worthwhile (see p.280).

For **security** reasons, do not take valuables onto the beach, walk on it at night or venture into deserted areas.

OPPOSITE TSÁCHILA MAN (BOX, P.269) >

6

BRAINS OVER PRAWN

In the last thirty years about 2000 square kilometres of mangroves surrounding **Muisne** have been cut down to create **shrimp farms** – ugly pools resembling sewage treatment facilities – which have dealt a severe blow to the birds, marine life and people who relied on the trees for food and sustenance. A handful of entrepreneurs have become millionaires, but most people have lost their way of life and many now work on the shrimp farms to survive, or have migrated to city slums elsewhere. Government measures to stop the destruction – three to thirty days in jail for felling a mangrove – have largely remained unenforced and ineffective, meaning only about 30 square kilometres of constantly threatened mangrove forests survive.

The organization **Fundecol** (☎06 2480519), which has an office in Muisne just off the main boulevard, attempts to protect the trees through security patrols, political activism and education. The Fundación Jatún Sacha manages the **Congal Biological Station** in five square kilometres of primary mangrove forest 2km from Muisne, developing ecologically sound aquaculture and running reforestation programmes; for **volunteering** work at Congal ($577/four weeks), contact Jatún Sacha in Quito (☎02 2432240, ⓦ jatunsacha.org).

ARRIVAL AND INFORMATION   MUISNE

By boat Boats from El Relleno make the short hop over the Río Muisne to the main town ($0.25; around $5 for a car, or $2 to have the car looked after), where mototaxis can take you from dock to beach.

By bus Buses arrive and depart from El Relleno; there are regular services to Esmeraldas (every 30min; 2hr 30min),
passing the resorts to the north, and El Salto, from where you can catch southbound buses to Chamanga (hourly; 1hr 30min from Muisne), the connecting point for Pedernales (1hr). Buses also depart for both Quito (3 nightly; 8hr) and Guayaquil (2 nightly; 9hr).

Money There is no ATM, so bring all the cash you need.

TOURS

By boat Boat tours of the mangroves leave the ferry dock for around $25/boat.

By mototaxi You can have a tour of the sandbar – which
can include being dropped off (and picked up) for a wallow in some shallow tidal pools for around $5–10.

ACCOMMODATION AND EATING

★**Casa Host** Manabí, several blocks back from the beach ☎06 2480126 or ☎0986186330, ⓦ casahostal muisne.com. The nicest place to stay in Muisne, though overpriced, offering new, simple bright en-suite rooms set round a garden, with a reliable (hot) water supply – rare around here – and fans. Slightly larger rooms with satellite TV also available. $̲8̲4̲

Hotel Galapagos Manabí, several blocks back from the beach ☎06 2480289. Standard en-suite rooms with decent mattresses and cable TV (extra $4); they're a bit
dark but clean and well maintained. $̲2̲0̲

Las Olas On the beach ☎06 8850545. Its prime beachside location is the only draw of this large wooden beachfront hostal offering basic lodgings that desperately needs an injection of cash. The better rooms are on the top floor towards the front. With restaurant. $̲2̲0̲

Restaurante Santa Martha Next to Las Olas. The pick of the restaurants on the beach, serving up succulent shrimp and other seafood dishes. Mains from around $7. Daily 7am–6/7pm.

Muisne to the Río Chone estuary

The turning for Muisne off the Vía del Pacífico is at nondescript El Salto, 11km to the east. From there, the main road speeds south for 56km through land dotted with only the odd stilt hut, passing a turn-off to the low-key surfing resort of **Mompiche,** and then Chamanga (2km from the main road), from where there is regular transport to the uninspiring resort town of **Pedernales**. Protruding northwards from here, a broad 30km sandspit leads up to the tiny fishing village of **Cojimíes**, which is developing into a quiet tourist resort.

Beyond Chamanga and into **Manabí**, the province of the central seaboard, the climate and scenery soon change from the lush greenery of Esmeraldas to an increasingly dry, scrubby landscape. South of Pedernales is a sparsely populated area of small settlements, the largest being Jama, 45km down the road, and a rolling shoreline interspersed with deserted beaches and the occasional secluded hotel. A further 41km away, after turning inland past shrimp farms and through agricultural land, the road rejoins the coast at **Canoa**, an attractive beach resort with good surfing and a mellow vibe. The beaches extend south from here for almost 20km down to the Río Chone estuary, across which gleam the high-rises of **Bahía de Caráquez**, the most upmarket resort on this stretch of coastline.

Mompiche

On the sheltered south side of the Ensenada de Mompiche, where a 7km ribbon of dark sand curls around a broad bay, backed by a shock of emerald-green trees, sits the little fishing village of **MOMPICHE**. Once a peaceful, isolated spot, the village's potholed 6km link road to the Vía del Pacífico has meant that the town's wooden cabins, fishing boats and simple stores have recently been joined by an outbreak of small hotels and hostels. It's now a renowned **surfing** resort with a predominantly backpacker vibe, as there is an excellent left point break at **Punta Suspiro**, at the south end of the bay (best in Dec & Jan), and other good possibilities nearby. Storms in recent years have taken their toll on the beach, however, with most of the sand lying below the waves at high tide.

Isla Portete

Four kilometres south of Mompiche – the turn-off is just at the entrance to the village – a wholly different world exists in the vast all-inclusive Decameron mega-resort, catering to the elite of Latin America. Just beyond the entrance, however, lies the dock for **Isla Portete,** a dreamy island thronging with palm trees that lies a mere 100m across the water. From here you can take a boat tour of the mangroves that line much of the island's protected eastern flank. Alternatively, cross over to the island ($0.50); walk on the fluffy, soft sand, away from the pounding beat of the Decameron's beach club, and you'll eventually come to the tiny relaxed settlement of **Bolívar**, home to fifty odd homes and a few basic rooms or cabañas, from where you can hop across to the even more deserted **Isla Júpiter**.

ARRIVAL AND DEPARTURE
MOMPICHE

By bus Four buses daily (6.40am, 8.30am, 2.40pm and 4.30pm; 2hr 45min) leave Esmeraldas for Mompiche, returning to Esmeraldas at 6.40am, 8am, 10.30am and 1pm. Otherwise, hourly buses passing up and down the coast between Chamanga and Esmeraldas drop off and pick up passengers at the main road, 6km east of Mompiche. Mototaxis can take passengers to Mompiche ($5 private; $1/person colectivo) from the junction; if there is no mototaxi waiting when you get off the bus, you will have to hitch a lift to the village (though some payment will be expected).

ACCOMMODATION AND EATING

DMCA Surf Hostal On the beach and across the road a block back ⓦhosteltrail.com/dmca. Funky surfers' hangout and a good place to chill at rock-bottom rates, featuring basic rooms with private or shared cold-water bathrooms, plus a TV/DVD lounge, kitchen, and hammock terrace. Surf lessons and board rental ($15) available. $6/person; camping $3/person

La Facha La Fosforera, one block back from the beach ☏06 2448024 or ☏0998044604, ⓦlafachahostel .com. Nice vibey hostel with doubles and triples that have shared cold-water showers, plus an en-suite family room. The open-sided upstairs terrace strewn with deckchairs and hammocks also has a TV/DVD area and book exchange. It also offers surf lessons ($25) and tours, including kayaking among the mangroves. The popular bar-restaurant serves decent burgers (around $6) and tasty seafood mains (from $8). $25

★**Hostería Gabeal** On the beach ☏06 2448060 or ☏099696543, ⓦhosteriagabeal.wix.com/turismo ecuador. At the end of the beach strip, this efficient but relaxed budget hotel comprises a few large rustic buildings set in spacious sandy grounds; choose from rooms with tiled floors to simple cabins of bamboo and concrete, with palm-leaf thatched roofs and private bathrooms. Offers whale-watching tours in season (Jun–Sept), boat trips and can arrange horse riding. Doubles $40; camping $3/person

Mud House Opposite the police on the main road, 300m back from the beach ☏06 2448080 or ☏0959688968, ⓦthe-mud-house.com. Small, new hostel – friendly yet organized – with four cosy bamboo-and-thatch bungalows and an eight-bed dorm set in a small tropical garden. It also has a tiny bamboo kitchen and yoga deck and offers inexpensive nature hikes, surf lessons and horse riding. Dorm $8; cabaña from $25

Las Piqualas 3km along the beach on the other side of the bay ☎0999472458. The most romantic and isolated accommodation in the area, whose spacious beach cabins have porches and hammocks, clutched by palms. Breakfast $4; other meals $12. Doubles $40; camping available in low season – rates negotiable.

Restaurante El Sol de Oro At the entrance to the beach. Nice hanging lanterns and a raised deck give this place ambience to match the tasty seafood. *Langostinos encocados* ($15) are the house speciality. Daily 8am–8pm.

★**Suly's** One block back from the beach entrance, to the north of the main road. No phone. The husband-and-wife team offers personalized table service and tasty, freshly made food in this nicely decorated, open-sided bamboo-and-thatch bar-resto, where you can dine by candlelight or enjoy a quiet drink with friends. Choose from burgers, pastas – including three types of lasagne – and a couple of daily specials, from $8. Also sells wine by the glass. Daily 6–10pm.

Pedernales and around

Despite being one of the nearest seaside resorts to Quito, sitting on a 52km stretch of beach, **PEDERNALES**, with its crowded, narrow streets and slightly grubby sands, has remained largely impervious to interest from international travellers, but still has a down-to-earth appeal.

The focus of town is the **parque central**, whose centrepiece is a **stone** that La Condamine engraved in Latin during his 1736 mission to the equator to determine the Earth's shape. The **church** is also worth a look for its colourful stained-glass window and mural overlooking the square. From the park, the streets fall steeply to the sea for a half-kilometre west to the **beach**, where a string of hotels, bars and restaurants catering mainly to national tourists can prove quite lively at weekends. The town's two biggest **fiestas** are for its cantonization, on March 13, and the *fiesta del café*, August 16, honouring the days when coffee was the principal crop.

ARRIVAL AND DEPARTURE
PEDERNALES

By bus The bus terminal is on Juan Pereira, two blocks northeast of the main square, though buses to Cojimíes leave from Calle Roldos, a block and a half from the bus station.

Destinations Bahía (every 40min; 2hr 30min); Chamanga (every 30min, with onward hourly connections up the coast to Esmeraldas; 1hr); Cojimíes (every 30min until 7pm; 30min); Guayaquil (10 daily via Bahía, 6 daily via Santo Domingo; 7–8hr); Quito (11 daily; 5hr); Santo Domingo (every 10–40min; 3hr).

ACCOMMODATION AND EATING

La Choza Malecón and Eloy Alfaro ☎05 2680388. Popular beachfront restaurant serving the usual range of seafood options including a splendid *bandeja de mariscos* (seafood platter). Daily 8am–9pm (later at weekends).

El Costeñito 2 Malecón ☎05 2681404. Brightly lit seafood restaurant with varnished wooden tables, serving an array of fish fillets and shrimp dishes, plus a mountainous *bandeja de mariscos* ($20) and weekend specials. Daily 8am–10pm.

Mr John Plaza Acosta and Malecón ☎05 2680235.

Bright, fresh rooms, with fans, cable TVs and private bathrooms with electric showers. Can be noisy. $25

Royal Hotel Garcia Moreno and Malecón ☎05 2680532. The poshest place in town (it even takes credit cards) is not that great and lies just off the waterfront. It has spacious modern en-suite rooms with a/c, and amazing sea views from the top floor. Make sure the wi-fi and cable TV reception reaches your room. Also has a pool and jacuzzi. $65

Cojimíes

From Pedernales a gorgeous strip of sand unfurls for more than 30km north to the forgotten fishing village of **COJIMÍES,** which is squeezed onto the tip of an ever-dwindling tongue of sand, eroded by water on three sides. At low tide, locals occasionally boat out to the **sandbanks** in the middle of the estuary – the most popular being the Isla de Amor – and use them as private beaches for parties and barbecues. You can also take a boat over the estuary to Bolívar and Daule ($2, generally early morning), from where it's a long walk to the main road, or you could charter a boat to Mompiche.

ARRIVAL AND TOURS

By bus Buses leaves for Cojimíes (every 30min until 7pm; 30min) from Avenida Roldos in Pedernales, a block and a half from the bus station.

Boat tours Ask around at the landing beach north of town

COJIMÍES

for a tour of the estuary ($25/ boat), involving a look at some birdlife on the sandbanks and in the mangroves, plus some time on Isla de Amor; alternatively you can go fishing, or visit a shrimp farm.

ACCOMMODATION AND EATING

Cocosolo Km20 from Pedernales (13km south of Cojimíes). Long-standing windswept lodge enjoying peaceful isolation midst the coconut fronds and pounding surf. Accommodation is in careworn rustic cabañas, or in spacious en-suite rooms in the main house (both with hot water), near the garden, fish pond and uninviting swimming pool. Non-residents should stop by the restaurant and sample the excellent seafood mains ($8–10); rates include a superb buffet breakfast with home-made goodies. Fishing tours and excursions to the estuary mangroves and forested areas nearby available. Daily 8am–8pm (Jul, Aug and holidays); closed Mon & Tues at other times. $60; camping $10/person

Canoa and around

Down the coast from Jama and sitting at the upper end of a huge beach extending 17km south to San Vicente is **CANOA**, which has shifted from sleepy fishing village to laidback beach resort, thanks largely to its fantastic surf and clean sands. With only a single paved street linking its shaded **square** to the sea, the town's low-level hubbub is submerged under the continuous roar of breakers rising and falling on the shore.

It's a lovely place to relax, with long, empty expanses of coastline and ample waves for **surfing** (good from Dec–April, best Jan–Feb; many hotels have boards for rent). At low tide you can take a **horse ride** or a walk to the sandy cliffs rising up through the haze in the north, where there's also a **cave** to explore. It's best done with a local guide for safety; enquire at your lodgings or at the Surf Shak.

ARRIVAL AND INFORMATION

By bus Buses between Pedernales and Bahía pass through Canoa every thirty minutes and stop at the main square. Buses leave the park for Bahía (every 30min until 8pm; 50min).

CANOA AND AROUND

By taxi Taxis between Bahía and Canoa cost $10.

Money Note that the nearest ATM is 17km further south, down the coast at San Vicente.

ACTIVITIES AND TOURS

Tours Excursions to the Río Muchacho Organic Farm can be arranged at their office (see box, p.284). Surf Shak and several of the hotels rent surfboards ($15/day) and/or offer lessons ($20–25 for 2hrs), or offer fishing, mountain biking, sea kayaking or birdwatching trips. Canoa has also become a popular paragliding destination – contact US-certified Greg via Surf Shak, or in his own hotel, *Canoa Beach Hotel*, 15min south of the village. Betty Surf and Yoga (🖥 bettysurfandyoga .com) provides instruction as the name suggests, including a combo yoga and surfing package.

ACCOMMODATION

Being a surfing hangout, most of the accommodation is at the budget end of the scale although on public holiday weekends, when most places hike their prices – some by up to 25 percent – you'll be paying mid-range prices for budget surroundings.

Amalur Hostal San Andrés, overlooking the Plaza Cívica 🕿 0983035038, 🖥 amalurcanoa.com. Great-value new hostel with excellent on-site restaurant (see p.284), boasting bright, spacious rooms, solid bamboo beds with orthopedic mattresses and clean, tiled private bathrooms providing hot-water showers. Plus, you can't beat lying in a hammock on the rooftop terrace while admiring the sea view. Doubles $25; dorms $10

★**Casa Shangri La** 200m north of the park by the old road 🕿 05 2588076 or 🕿 0991468470, 🖥 casashangrila .com. You'll avoid the pounding rhythms of the beach bars at this secluded and secure walled tropical garden with hammocks, plunge pool, bar, BBQ, thatched bar. Plus the clean, homely rooms have pretty blue-tiled bathrooms. $25

Coco Loco Malecón, two blocks south of the beach entrance 🕿 092439613, 🖥 hostalcocoloco.weebly .com. Though the rooms feel a tad damp and the place could do with some maintenance work, this is a friendly spot with a range of accommodation with shared or private facilities. There's hot water, a decent bar and restaurant, and a self-catering kitchen. Offers surfing lessons, riding, fishing and biking trips, yoga and Spanish lessons. Doubles $25; dorms $6

Hostal Baloo South end of the Malecón ☏05 2588155, ⊕baloo-canoa.com. The range of lodgings spread around the palm-filled garden are more substantial and have more furniture than many, with wooden floors, fans and a decent-sized bathroom, though the place is looking a little careworn. There is a choice of three-bed dorms, cabins and doubles, with deck space and hammocks, comfy sofas and coffee tables. Also has a gazebo for yoga, plus a pool table. Doubles $27; dorms $10; camping $3.50/person

★**Hotel Bambú** Malecón, at the north end of the village ☏05 2588017, ⊕hotelbambuecuador.com.

Relaxed but efficient place with appealing rooms – bright and breezy, lacking the musty seaside smell of most hostels here, with little balconies overlooking a garden and the sea, private or shared bathrooms (some with a/c) – plus cabins. You can also sleep in a hammock or camp here. Surfboards available for rent and there's a decent bar and restaurant. Doubles $50; camping $5/person

Shelmar 50m walk back from the beach, on the main street ☏0986448920. Small family-run operation, offering simple, clean wooden en-suite rooms with fans, hammocks and hot water. $16

La Vista Malecón, three blocks south of the beach entrance ☏05 2588106, ⊕lavistacanoa.com. A more substantial thatched and whitewashed brick structure with en-suite rooms, that all boast sea views, wooden floors, decent furniture, glass windows, mosquito nets and balconies – a relief for those tired of flimsy cabins. $38

EATING

Cevichería Saboreame Malecón Popular spot serving tasty, inexpensive ceviches ($4), *encocados*, avocado stuffed with shrimp and also some beef and chicken dishes for those fed up with seafood. Daily 7.30am–9pm.

Koraimar On the beach, opposite Coco Loco. A locally owned beach hut serving superb soups, ceviches and other seafood mains (most $6–7), accompanied by great *patacones*. A choice spot for a cocktail too. Wed–Sun 6am–5pm.

★**Restaurante Amalur** Amalur Hostal (see p.283). Modern-style no-frills decor in this Spanish-run restaurant with the focus firmly on the food: delicious deli-sandwiches in home-made bread, DIY salads, Galician octopus, tortilla and meatballs, tapas, plus plenty of grilled seafood. Mains

from $8. Check out the daily specials chalked up on the board and leave room for the chocolate mousse. Daily 8–11am, noon–3pm, 5pm until late.

Restaurante Bambú Hotel Bambú (see above). Enjoy pancakes or a healthy breakfast in their tree-filled garden, or more conventional dining in their rancho restaurant, where the usual seafood numbers served with rice and salad or patacones are well prepared and start from around $8. Efficient, friendly service. Daily 8am until late.

Surf Shak Malecón. Great place for breakfast – try the French toast with bacon – for a mellow daytime chill or for evening entertainment: pub quiz, poker, NFL and steak nights. Does pizzas, burgers (from around $5) and happy hour drinks (6–8pm). Daily 7.30am–midnight.

DRINKING AND NIGHTLIFE

El Barcito On the beach, north of the entrance. Boat-shaped beach bar with salsa blaring out of vast speakers. The current hot venue for dancing and drinking; dare to sample

their signature cocktail, "*la uña de la bestia*" – a stomach-churning mix of fermented marijuana and coca leaves stuffed with centipedes and the like. Daily noon–late.

RÍO MUCHACHO ORGANIC FARM

About 10km north of Canoa an 8km dirt road leads off to **Río Muchacho Organic Farm** (☏05 2588184, ⊕riomuchacho.com), a leading environmental and ecotourism project in a formerly deforested area, specializing in sustainable agriculture. Visitors can learn about tropical permaculture, milk cows, help with reforestation, pick, roast and grind coffee, fish for river shrimp or opt for more relaxed activities, such as making *tagua* jewellery and utensils from gourds or smearing on local clay for a facial. Accommodation is in rustic eco-cabañas with composting toilets, and the food, naturally, is healthy and organic. Three-day tours are recommended ($162/person all-inclusive, but less for a couple or group), though day-trips ($65) are also possible. The farm also welcomes **volunteers** ($300/month contribution) for farm work, reforestation, teaching in an environmental primary school or learning about organic farming on a month-long intensive course.

There's daily transport to the farm at 9am from their office in Canoa (daily 9am–5pm) on the main street.

Coco Bar Main street a block from the beach. Two-storey joint with downstairs bar and upstairs dance-floor, throbbing with salsa, merengue and reggaeton. Cocktails from $4.50. Mon–Sat 4pm until late.

Bahía de Caráquez and around

BAHÍA DE CARÁQUEZ is one of Ecuador's most agreeable coastal resort towns; it is a smartish place, with spotless, white high-rise apartment blocks, broad tree-lined avenues and sleek yachts bobbing in the marina, though it still has its share of crumbling buildings and unmade streets beyond the waterfront. Sitting on a slender peninsula of sand extending into the broad mouth of the Río Chone, it is connected to the northern mainland at San Vicente via an impressive road bridge, which is illuminated at night. The town's main avenues run north–south, parallel to the estuary on the east side, while the **Malecón** extends around the edge of the whole peninsula.

Following mudslides and a damaging earthquake in 1998, Bahía (as it's called for short) started afresh, proclaiming itself a *ciudad ecológica*, or **eco-city**, and set up a number of ambitious projects, including recycling, permaculture, composting, reforestation, conservation and environmental education programmes.

What's more, Bahía lies near several wonderful natural attractions, including **tropical dry forests**, empty **beaches** and **mangrove islands** teeming with aquatic birds. The vast shrimp farms in the estuary displaced more than sixty square kilometres of mangrove forest during the 1980s and 1990s, with the obvious exception of the world's first **organic shrimp farm**, a pollution-free enterprise that also helps in reforestation. These days, though, Bahía is always at the forefront of national activities to celebrate the Día Internacional del Manglar (**International Day of the Mangroves**) on July 26, which

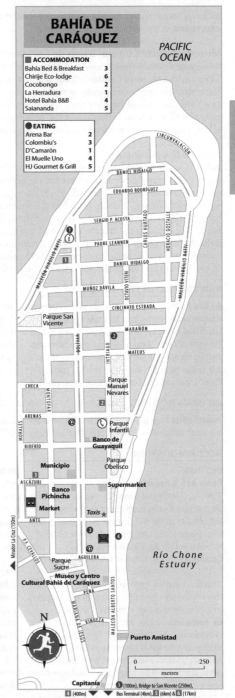

BAHÍA DE CARÁQUEZ

PACIFIC OCEAN

■ **ACCOMMODATION**
Bahía Bed & Breakfast	3
Chirije Eco-lodge	6
Cocobongo	2
La Herradura	1
Hotel Bahía B&B	4
Saïananda	5

● **EATING**
Arena Bar	2
Colombiu's	3
D'Camarón	1
El Muelle Uno	4
HJ Gourmet & Grill	5

CIRCUNVALACIÓN
DANIEL HIDALGO
EDUARDO RODRÍGUEZ
SERGIO P. ACOSTA
CARLOS HURTADO
HORACIO GOSTALLE
PADRE LEANNEN
DANIEL HIDALGO
MUÑOZ DÁVILA
OCTAVIO VITERI
CINCINATO ESTRADA
MARAÑÓN
Parque San Vicente
BOLÍVAR
INTRIAGO
MATEUS
CHECA
MONTÚFAR
Parque Manuel Nevares
ARENAS
MORALES
RIOFRÍO
Parque Infantil
Banco de Guayaquil
Municipio
Parque Obelisco
ASCÁZUBI
Banco Pichincha
Supermarket
Market
Taxis
ANTE
PÍO CEVALLOS
Mirador La Cruz (150m)
AGUILERA
Parque Sucre
Museo y Centro Cultural Bahía de Caráquez
PEÑA
MARIANA DE JESÚS
VINUEZA
MALECÓN ALBERTO SANTOS
Río Chone Estuary
Puerto Amistad
N
0   250
metres
Capitanía
(100m), Bridge to San Vicente (250m),
(400m)   Bus Terminal (4km), (6km) & (17km)

6

6

includes some mangrove planting in the estuary. Lodgings in town can help organize **excursions** in the area (see box opposite).

Museo y Centro Cultural Bahía de Caráquez
Malecón Santos and Ascázubi • Tues–Sat 9am–5pm, Sun 10am–1pm • Free

In town, the **Museo y Centro Cultural Bahía de Caráquez** is one of the best museums on the coast, housing a beautifully presented collection of pre-Columbian artefacts, such as a Valdivian belt of highly prized spondylus shells from 3000 BC, plus a replica balsa raft, as well as a good collection of the striking *gigantes* (giants) of the Bahía culture – large, elaborately decorated ceramic figures, some of which are almost a metre tall.

Around the peninsula
Bahía is a pleasant town for a stroll, following the **Malecón** around the peninsula. There's a pleasant sandy beach near the tip on the eastern side, where you can enjoy a game of late afternoon beach volleyball, do yoga or rent kayaks and water toys to play with in the estuary. Wander round to the west side, and enjoy the bracing wind and the rough rollers coming to shore. Locals surf here, but to find more generous expanses of sand, take a taxi to the **beaches** south of town, such as the favoured surf spot of **Punta Bellaca** (5km south by road; arrange a return journey with the driver). A good complement to the seaside promenade is the short walk up to **Mirador La Cruz**, on top of the hill at the foot of the peninsula, which affords grand views of the city and bay.

ARRIVAL AND GETTING AROUND   BAHÍA DE CARÁQUEZ

By bus The bus terminal is 4km out of the centre on Malecón and Barrio Astillero, from where you can get a taxi ($2) or the #8 bus into town. If you're arriving from the north, it's best to get off the bus immediately after crossing the bridge, if you want to avoid having to take a bus or taxi back into town from the bus station. For Puerto López and the south coast, take a Guayaquil bus and change at Jipijapa.

Destinations Canoa (every 30min; 40min); Guayaquil (13 daily; 6hr); Manta (17 daily, change in Portoviejo; 2hr 45min); Portoviejo (every 30min; 2hr); Quito (4 daily; 8hr).
By taxi There are plenty of taxis ($1 within town) though everything on the peninsula is within walking distance.

INFORMATION AND TOURS

Tourist office Maps and information are available at the municipal tourist office upstairs on Bolívar and Padre Leannen (Mon–Fri 8.30am–5pm, closed 1hr for lunch; ☎ 05 2691044 or ☎ 05 2693240).

ACCOMMODATION

IN TOWN
Bahía Bed & Breakfast Ascázubi and Morales ☎ 05 2690146. Charming but gloomy 150-year-old house (with the plumbing showing its age), enlivened by cheery murals and portraits on the wall. Some of the cheapest beds in town though rooms vary; a few have private bathrooms, hot water and TVs. Breakfast also available. $16
Cocobongo Intriago between Checa and Arenas ☎ 05 2691084, ⓦ cocobongohostel.com. Former hostel in an attractive converted house with polished wooden floors now offering apartments for short-term and long-term lets; still under renovation at the time of writing.
La Herradura Bolívar and Hidalgo ☎ 05 2690446, ⓔ hotelherradura@hotmail.com. Smartish seafront hotel evoking the feel of a hacienda with its wrought-iron furnishings, wagon wheels, barrels, horse harnesses and potted plants. There's hot water, cable TV and many rooms have a/c. $60

Hotel Bahía B&B Punete los Caros, behind El Paseo Mall ☎ 05 2691880 or ☎ 0939050717, ⓦ ecuavacation .com. Not to be confused with the much more downmarket *Bahía B&B* (see above), this conveniently situated and efficiently run place has a handful of small, tidy, tiled en-suite rooms with large sliding glass doors. Decent enough for a short stay. Breakfast included. From $40

OUT OF TOWN
Chirije Eco-lodge 17km south of town ☎ 0999171935, ⓦ chirije.com. Attractive, solar-powered cabañas of varying prices nestled among gardens and greenery, and surrounded by dry tropical forest; activities include forest hikes, birdwatching, snorkelling and surfing (lessons available). A beachside restaurant supplies good local specialities, including *biche*, a peanut and seafood soup. Under renovation at the time of writing.
★**Saiananda** On the main road 5km south of Bahía

TOURS FROM BAHÍA

Among the touring highlights from Bahía is a trip around the **Río Chone estuary** and **Isla Corazón**, where the network of red mangroves supports more than 4000 **frigatebirds** (rivalling the population of the Galápagos Islands), alongside petrels, oystercatchers, sandpipers and the rare **roseate spoonbill**, among many others, as well as crabs and shrimps. A raised boardwalk takes you through the mangroves, and during the mating season (Aug–Dec, sometimes till Feb), it's possible to see the male frigatebirds' characteristic scarlet pouches inflating like balloons to woo circling females. You can organise a two- to four-hour tour (in Spanish) directly with the successful community tourism initiative (☎05 3029316, ⓦislacorazon.com); alternatively, your lodgings can probably make arrangements for you. The four-hour tour ($15/person for two to five people) includes a walk along the boardwalk, some birdwatching and a trip through the mangroves by dugout canoe. Visits to eco-shrimp farms and other attractions are possible add-ons. **Dolphins** are occasionally seen in the estuary, and **humpback whales** can be spotted rolling and diving off the coast (June–Sept).

Further upriver are the Ramsar-protected wetlands of **La Segua**, a small reserve home to at least 164 bird species, including the wattled jacana. In contrast, along the coast south of Bahía Cerro Seco (daily 8am–4pm, but earlier with advance notice; $1.50; ☎05 2693004, ⓦcerrosecobahia.wix.com/cerroseco) is one of the few **tropical dry forests** in the country outside the Parque Nacional Machalilla. Anteaters, sloths and iguanas can be found in this area, which has high levels of endemism and is rich in fragrant *palo santo* trees, barbasco (a plant whose roots yield a poison used for insecticide) and ceiba trees – easy to identify with their great buttressed trunks. There's a self-guided 3km trail, or you can pay for a guide to go birdwatching. Whale-watching trips are on offer in season (June–Sept). During the rainy season (Jan–May), the forests are luxuriant.

Another possible excursion, 17km south of the city, is to the archeological site and small **museum** of pre-Columbian Bahía culture at Chirije, owned by Bahía Dolphin Tours (ⓦbahiadolphintours.com), which also owns *Chirije Eco-lodge* (see opposite)

6

☎05 2398331, ⓦsaiananda.com. Warm hospitality and some lovingly furnished rooms (with fan, or a/c for $20 extra) with bags of varnished wood and character, including a couple of pricier suites with a balcony overlooking the estuary and glass floor panels to watch wildlife in the mudflats below. It has an excellent waterside vegetarian restaurant, and activities include mud baths in a mangrove swamp, massages or kayaking. Doubles $̲9̲0̲; suites $̲1̲7̲0̲

EATING

Arena Bar Corner of Intriago and Marañon ☎05 2692024. Long-time stalwart of Canoa nightlife now in Bahía, losing none of its beach cred: bright colours, tree-trunk tables, surfboards on the wall plus great pizzas, pastas, salads (from around $6) and cocktails all contribute to the vibrant atmosphere. Daily 5pm–midnight.

Colombiu's Bolívar and Ante ☎05 2690537. Features large, delicious and affordable Colombian and Ecuadorian dishes, and good seafood, served on a leafy terrace under a sackcloth awning. Daily 7am–10pm.

D'Camarón Malecón Ratti and Acosta ☎05 08 6623805. Simple, inexpensive seafood restaurant specializing in all things shrimp, enjoying breezy outdoor seating and bracing sea views. Daily 9am–6pm.

★**HJ Gourmet & Grill** ☎098916844, ⓔchefhugoji menez@gmail.com. Culinary heaven at affordable prices (mains $10–15), prepared by Hugo Jiménez, an internationally decorated Peruvian chef, in his own tastefully decorated living room-restaurant, or on his balcony overlooking the estuary. Changing daily menu depending upon what's fresh and available, but you can be guaranteed superb quality and a fusion meal to remember. By reservation only, from 7pm.

El Muelle Uno Malecón Santos, by the dock ☎05 089898927. Fairly priced restaurant with nice estuary views, serving generous, savoury fish and barbecue lunches and dinners, plus simple vegetarian options. Mains $6–12. Daily 9am–11pm.

Manta and around

About 50km south of Bahía de Caráquez, set in a broad bay dotted with freighters, cruise ships and fishing boats is **MANTA**. A city of some 220,000 people and Ecuador's largest port after Guayaquil, this major commercial centre is principally driven by the **seafood industry,** though plans are afoot to build a large oil refinery. Yet Manta is also a popular and lively holiday destination for Ecuadorians, though it attracts few foreign visitors; its main **beach** is relatively clean, regularly patrolled, lined with restaurants and packed at weekends.

Even better beaches are strung out along the coast west of town – with Playa Santa Marianita ($5–6 in a taxi) the pick of them – most of which are more suitable for **surfers** and **kitesurfers** than swimmers.

Excepting the main highways, the city's streets are **numbered sequentially** from the Río Manta, which divides the throbbing commercial centre to the west and the poorer residential area, **Tarqui,** to the east; Manta starts at Calle 1, Tarqui at Calle 101 – while avenues running parallel to the seashore use the coast as the starting point.

Brief history

Fishing has been important to Manta since around 500 AD, when the region was home to the **Manta people**, expert fishermen, navigators and traders, who tattooed their faces and held sway over much of the surrounding coast. This dominance came to an abrupt end in 1534, with the arrival of the Spanish conquistadors. They brutally decimated a one-time population of 20,000, reducing it to a mere fifty inhabitants in only two years.

Playa Murciélago

Manta's tourist focus is **Playa Murciélago**, a broad beach 1.5km north of the town centre, backed by the **Malecón Escénico**, a strip of seafood restaurants and bars.

From December to April the surf is good enough for the town to host international bodyboarding and windsurfing competitions, though swimmers should be wary of the strong **undertow**. There's usually plenty else going on here at weekends, from live music to volleyball.

The police advise against wandering to quiet spots beyond the *Oro Verde*, where robberies have been reported.

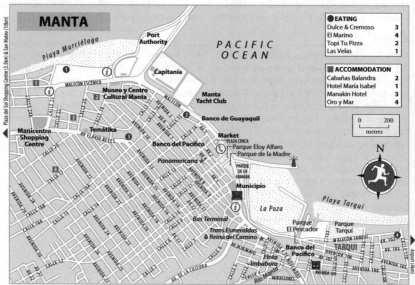

Museo y Centro Cultural Manta

Malecón Escénico • Tues–Fri 8am–5pm, Sat & Sun 9am–1pm • Free

Opposite the Malecón Escénico is the **Museo y Centro Cultural Manta** which has an interesting collection of artefacts from the Valdivian culture, which flourished here 3500–1500 BC, and the later Manteño culture, including fish-shaped ocarinas and beautiful zoomorphic jugs and flasks.

The city centre

As you head east down the Malecón from Playa Murciélago you'll soon pass the **Capitanía** (harbour master's office), by the entrance to Manta's main **port**, frequented by warships, the odd millionaire's yacht and countless container ships. Close to the port, the main square of **Parque Eloy Alfaro** and the **Parque de la Madre** are the town's leafiest spots. Nearby the unremarkable **Plaza Cívica** hosts an artesanía market, which is at its busiest in the cruise ship season (Nov–Feb); stalls stuffed with Otavaleño weavings sit alongside more familiar coastal wares such as *tagua* carvings and Panama hats.

6

ARRIVAL AND DEPARTURE   MANTA

By plane The airport is 4km east of the city centre, and can be reached by taxi for $3–4. TAME and Aerogal operate flights to and from Quito (5 daily; 35min; $78 one way). TAME's main office is at Edif El Vigía, Malecón and Calle 13C (☎05 2622006), with another at the airport (☎05 2380868); Aerogal has an office at the airport (☎05 2626021).

By bus The central bus station at Avenida 8 and Calle 7 near the Malecón is used by all local and long-distance buses, except for those coming from Quito, which have their own offices, in the vicinity. However, the new bus

terminal, 6km from the city centre, should be fully functional by mid-2016.

Destinations Bahía de Caráquez (2hr 30min, change at Portoviejo); Esmeraldas (4 daily; 10hr); Guayaquil (every 30min–1hr; 3hr); Jipijapa (every 30min; 1hr); La Libertad (hourly; 6hr); Montecristi (every 10min; 20min); Pedernales (4 daily; 6hr); Portoviejo (every 10min; 45min); Puerto López (hourly; 2hr via the coastal road, 2hr 30min via the inland road); Quito (hourly; 8hr); Santo Domingo (hourly; 6hr).

GETTING AROUND AND INFORMATION

By bus Local buses service the main thoroughfares and central bus station. If staying in Tarqui you can easily catch one from Avenida 105 into the city centre or to Playa Murciélago.

By taxi Taxis cost around $2 to anywhere in the city.

Tourist office The I-Tur office at Playa Murciélago (daily 8am–noon, 1–4.30pm; ☎05 2624099) is helpful, and the tourism website ⊛ turismomanta.com (in Spanish) is also quite useful.

ACCOMMODATION

Cabañas Balandra Av 7 and Calle 20 ☎05 2620316 ⊛ hotelbalandra.com. Commodious rooms or cabins for four or five, set amid gardens, with a/c, fridges, phones, cable TVs and private bathrooms with hot water, plus a pool. The superior rooms are worth the extra $11. **$109**

Hotel María Isabel Calle 24 and Av M2, Barrio Murciélago ☎05 2625013, ⊛ hotelboutique mariaisabel. Smart boutique business hotel with swish, dark, wooden furniture, elegant furnishings, marble bathrooms and all the trimmings. Some with balcony, jacuzzi and sea view. **$85**

Manakin Hotel Calle 20 and Av 12 ☎05 2620413. Friendly, compact hotel with a handful of neat rooms that have a/c, cable TV and hot water, plus a pleasant patio-bar and restaurant, with the aerobics at the adjacent gym the only occasional disturbance. Breakfast included. **$61**

Oro y Mar Av 24 and Calle 17 ☎05 2623805 or ☎0996928803, ✉ javiergomes2008@yahoo.com. This converted clinic offers spartan, though spacious, budget rooms, with (hottish) electric showers, cable TV and a/c. Very good value. **$20**

EATING

★**Dulce & Cremosa** Flavio Reyes and Calle 16. Extremely popular terrace-café serving an array of gooey cakes, pies and pastries, and sweet and savoury dishes such as *humitas*, quiches, salads and sandwiches (most for

$3–6). To wash it all down there is a good selection of coffees, hot chocolates, juices and home-made lemonade. Daily 7.30am–10pm.

★**El Marino** Malecón Tarqui and Calle 110

6

☎05 2926296. Popular spot at a busy intersection, renowned for its great seafood (mains $9–12) including spicy salads, though the place closes rather early. Daily 8am–5pm.

Las Velas Malecón Escénico ☎05 2629396. The pick of the beachside restaurants, offering the usual array of seafood dishes (mainly $10–14) and the best ocean views. Tuck into the house speciality, *paella de mariscos, cerdo y pollo* (seafood, pork and chicken paella) ($14) while watching the waves. Tues–Sun 9.30am–7.30pm.

DRINKING AND NIGHTLIFE

Manta's nightlife scene mainly gravitates towards **Avenida Flavio Reyes**, which is lined with bars and *discotecas*, though the **Plaza del Sol** mall is also popular with partygoers.

Montecristi

Eleven kilometres inland from Manta, the main road to Portoviejo passes **MONTECRISTI**, a small town nestled at the foot of the green Montecristi hills and founded by beleaguered refugees from Manta after they had lost everything in pirate raids in the early seventeenth century. The central street, **Avenida 9 de Julio**, leads uphill from the highway for almost a kilometre to the main square at the head of the town.

Montecristi might look quite ramshackle were it not for its resplendent white **church** with its elegant double staircase that overlooks the town's attractive **central square**.

WHERE DID YOU GET THAT HAT?

Few injustices can be more galling than having your nation's most famous export attributed to another country, yet this is what Ecuador has suffered with the "**Panama hat**". In the mid-nineteenth century, straw hats from Ecuador were traded in Panama along with vast quantities of other goods and quickly became a favourite with **gold prospectors** and labourers on the **Panama Canal**. It was precisely the question "where did you get that hat?" that started the association with the country of purchase rather than the country of origin – an error that was cemented when it was introduced to Europe at the **1855 World Fair** in Paris as the "Panama hat". The indignant words "Genuine Panama Hat Made in Ecuador" are now stamped on hats in an attempt to reclaim sovereignty over the product without upsetting the world-renowned name.

The tradition of hat-making probably goes back a long way in coastal Ecuador; **Valdivian** ceramic figurines from as long ago as 4000 BC seem to be wearing pointed straw hats. The first **conquistadors** also wrote about the broad, wing-like hats the locals wore, calling them **toquillas**, after *toca*, a Spanish word for a wimple. The Spanish soon began to wear them to stave off the sun's glare, praising their lightness, coolness and even their ability to carry water, due to the hat's ultra-fine weaving, but changed the shape into more conventional European styles. In the 1830s, factories employing more modern methods were set up in the highlands around **Cuenca** and **Azuay** and slowly began to surpass the traditional weavers on the coast. The hat reached its apogee as a fashion icon in the 1940s, when for a short time it became Ecuador's top export.

The toquilla plant that produces the straw, nicknamed **paja toquilla**, grows between Panama and Bolivia, and can grow up to 6m high after three years, but the best leaves are newer shoots harvested from around the base in monthly cycles. The leaves are split, cleaned, boiled, sundried and bleached with sulphur powder, then cut into straw. **Weavers**, mainly rural villagers from Manabí and Azuay provinces, get to work early in the morning or late at night, to avoid the sun, which stiffens the straw prematurely and makes the workers' hands sweaty. The brim is woven, tightened and **trimmed** before the hat is washed, dried and **softened** with a mallet before being further bleached, trimmed and then **blocked** into final shape by hand, which is more of an art than it sounds; most hats are now steam pressed into shape by machine in a few seconds. The making of a highest-grade **superfino** takes several months and as many mastercraftsmen, the last experts in a dying art; perhaps it's no wonder the very best hats can fetch more than $10,000 in the US.

A number of miracles have been attributed to the effigy of the Virgin inside – there's a lively **fiesta** and street markets and processions around November 20–21 in her honour. The town is also the birthplace of **Eloy Alfaro**, the influential Liberal president at the beginning of the nineteenth century; his statue adorns the square, which is backed by a vast mosaic portrait that constitutes the centrepiece of a grandiose frieze lauding his achievements; his house, on Eloy Alfaro and 23 de Octubre, has been made into a **museum** honouring him (daily 8am–12.30pm; free).

Montecristi's claim to fame is as the manufacturing centre of the **Panama hat**, and at one time, almost every house in town had its own workshop. Dwindling demand has driven many locals to more profitable jobs in fishing and canning factories, or other crafts, such as *tagua* carving and straw-basket weaving, which supply the many **craft shops** on Avenida 9 de Julio.

Panama hat workshops

Locals have been producing Panama hats here for well over a century, though the bulk of the weaving work is actually done in villages nearby before being sent for "cutting" and the final touches in Montecristi (see box opposite). Ask at Montecuadorhat, on 9 de Julio between Olmedo and Manta (ⓦmontecuadorhat.com), about visiting villages where you can see toquilla plantations and weavers at work.

Panama hats can cost from a few dollars for a simple model, a *tropical* or *grueso*, to more than $400 for a *superfino* that takes three or four months to make, but this is still cheaper than virtually anywhere else in the world.

ARRIVAL AND DEPARTURE | MONTECRISTI

By bus Buses from Manta marked "Montecristi" go right to the main square (every 15–20min; 15min), while buses between Portoviejo and Manta (every 15min; 30min) stop on the main road, from where it's a 10min walk uphill.

Guayaquil and the southern coast

CERRO SANTA ANA

Guayaquil and the southern coast

Sprawling over the west bank of the murky Río Guayas, the focus of Ecuador's southern coast is the port of Guayaquil, Ecuador's biggest city and an economic powerhouse that handles most of the country's imports and exports. Traditionally considered loud, frenetic, dirty and dangerous, Guayaquil has benefited from a huge injection of cash and a slew of urban regeneration schemes over the last decade or so, and these days is an enjoyable place to spend some time. Its impressive riverside promenade, Malecón 2000, is a particular highlight, and the city's upbeat, urban tempo makes an exciting change of pace from rural Ecuador.

In contrast to this dynamic metropolis, Ecuador's **southern coast**, stretching south to the border with Peru and north to Puerto Cayo in southern Manabí, is largely rural and quiet, comprising a mix of mangrove swamps, shrimp farms and sandy beaches dotted with dusty villages and low-key resorts. Inland, monotonous banana plantations and brittle scrubland hold little appeal, though they do give way to lush forests further north. South of Guayaquil, the coastal highway heads 250km down to Peru, passing a few minor attractions on the way. Just south of town is the bird-rich **Reserva Ecológica Manglares Churute**, protecting one of the last major **mangrove swamps** left on the southern coast. Further south, Machala – capital of **El Oro** province and famous as the nation's "banana capital" – is low on sights and ambience, but serves as a useful launch pad for outlying targets such as the scenic hillside town of **Zaruma** or the fascinating petrified forest of **Puyango**, and is also handy as a stop on the way to the border crossing at **Huaquillas**.

West of Guayaquil, at the tip of the Santa Elena Peninsula, is the aspirational high-rise town of **Salinas** which has the only major resort development in the region, while the nearby transport hub of **Santa Elena** marks the start of the **Ruta del Spondylus**, a 137km stretch of coast sporting a succession of long, golden beaches pounded by surf, and steeped in history. Most are fairly undeveloped and backed by small resorts or down-at-heel fishing villages. Few places see many foreign tourists along here, with the exceptions of laidback **Montañita**, a grungy surfing hangout and serious party spot, and the dusty, tumbledown fishing port of **Puerto López**, a base for summer **whale-watching** and year-round visits to **Parque Nacional Machalilla**. This park is the southern coast's most compelling attraction, taking in stunning, pristine beaches, dry and humid **tropical forests** and, most famously, **Isla de la Plata**, an inexpensive alternative to the Galápagos for viewing nesting blue-footed boobies and frigatebirds.

The **best time to visit** the southern coast is between December and April, when bright blue skies and warm **weather** more than compensate for the frequent showers of the rainy season – the time of year when coastal vegetation comes to life and dry tropical forests become luxuriant and moist. These months count as the high season – except in Puerto López, whose high season coincides with the whale-watching season (June–Sept) – when hotel prices tend to be higher. Outside these months, the dry season features

HUMPBACK WHALE, PUERTO LÓPEZ

Highlights

❶ **Downtown Guayaquil** Boasting fine examples of urban regeneration, Downtown Guayaquil is full of surprises: Malecón 2000 – an impressive 2km waterfront – shady estuarine promenades, striking street art and buzzing nightlife. **See pp.299–304**

❷ **Zaruma** Delightful hilltop town with charming, colonial buildings, a fascinating mining past and fabulous mountain views. **See p.314**

❸ **Bosque Petrificado de Puyango** Set in lovely forested mountain scenery, brimming with birdlife, this collection of immense fossilized tree-trunks – some over 100 million years old – is well worth the detour. **See p.315**

❹ **Partying in Montañita** A surfers' favourite thanks to its great beach and celebrated breaks, but now also a backpacker magnet. **See p.321**

❺ **Whale-watching from Puerto López** See humpback whales breach, roll and call to each other as they swim into warm coastal waters to mate and calve between June and September. **See p.327**

❻ **Isla de la Plata** The only place in Ecuador where the blue-footed, red-footed and masked boobies are found together. **See p.328**

❼ **Playa Los Frailes** Virgin white sands and azure waters, cradled by cliffs and backed by forested hills, make this idyllic beach one of the coast's most beautiful. **See p.329**

HIGHLIGHTS ARE MARKED ON THE MAP ON P.296

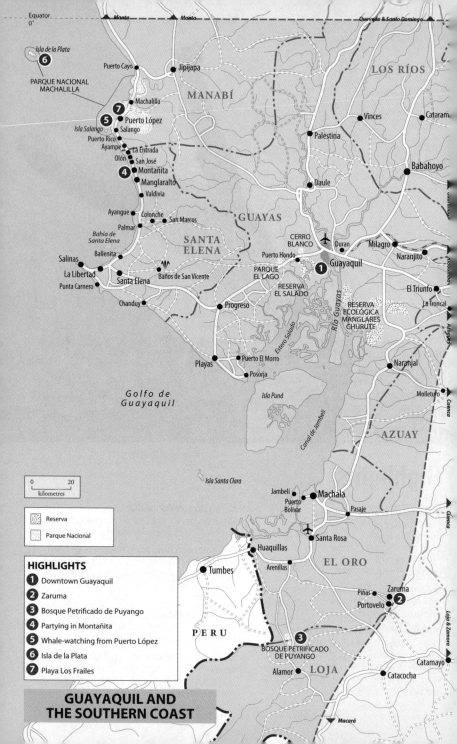

warm weather (around 23°C), but often depressingly grey skies. Not all the south coast's beaches are safe for swimming and many, like Manglaralto and Montañita, have dangerous currents and riptides that should be approached with great caution. Another consideration is the irregular and unpredictable **El Niño** weather phenomenon, when unusually heavy storms can leave the coast severely battered, washing away roads and disrupting communications.

Guayaquil and around

GUAYAQUIL was for years considered one of Ecuador's most dangerous cities, but following major regeneration programmes, public safety campaigns and an ambitious overhaul of public transport, it has dramatically improved: the central district is now an unthreatening and surprisingly likeable place, with a reinvigorated cultural scene. Add to this Guayaquil's natural energy and intensity and you have a winning combination.

Away from downtown, several upmarket, gated residential suburbs reflect Guayaquil's status as the country's wealthiest city, thanks mainly to its massive port that handles major national exports, including bananas, shrimp, cacao and coffee. It's also Ecuador's largest city, with a population of more than 2.3 million people to Quito's 1.6 million, and there is a deep-seated rivalry between the two urban centres. As far as historical attractions go, Guayaquil lags far behind the capital, with only a smattering of colonial buildings still standing (most of the others were destroyed in a 1942 earthquake). Nonetheless, Quito has nothing like Guayaquil's gleaming riverside development, the **Malecón 2000**, that links downtown to the **Cerro Santa Ana**, a once-dangerous slum now ingeniously reinvented as a beacon of urban renewal, and **Las Peñas**, the city's most charming historic district.

Out of the centre, worthwhile excursions include another popular waterside development, **El Malecón del Salado**, and the **Parque Histórico Guayaquil**, an enjoyable exploration of the city's past and its regional environment, as well as the **Jardín Botánico**, which houses a fine collection of orchids. A recent addition to the outdoors scene is the new cycleway-cum-boardwalk around the forested wetlands of **Isla Santay** in the Guayas estuary.

Slightly further afield, the mangroves in **La Reserva Ecológica Manglares Churute** to the southeast (see p.310), and those at **Puerto Hondo**, to the southwest (see p.310) make rewarding **day-trips** from the city.

Brief history

Conquistador Francisco de Orellana founded the city as **Santiago de Guayaquil** on July 25, 1537, its name supposedly honouring the local Huancavilca chieftain **Guayas** and his wife, **Quil**, who killed themselves rather than be captured by the Spanish. From its earliest years it was the most important entry point into Ecuador (known then as the "Audiencia de Quito") and quickly grew into a flourishing little port. Its fortunes were held back by the repeated attacks of pillaging British, French and Dutch **buccaneers**, regular **fires** engulfing its timber buildings and the deleterious mix of **tropical climate** and inadequate **sanitation**, which made it a hotbed of smallpox, yellow fever and typhoid. Nevertheless, during the seventeenth and eighteenth centuries Guayaquil gradually took on the shape of a proper city, with new roads, bridges, schools, hospitals and markets, mostly funded by burgeoning exports of **cacao**, **fruit** and **wood**.

Independence

On October 9, 1820, Guayaquil became the first city in Ecuador to declare its **independence** from Spain, and it was from here that **General Sucre** conducted his famous military campaign, culminating in the liberation of Quito on May 24, 1822. Shortly afterwards, Guayaquil went down in history as the site of the legendary meeting between

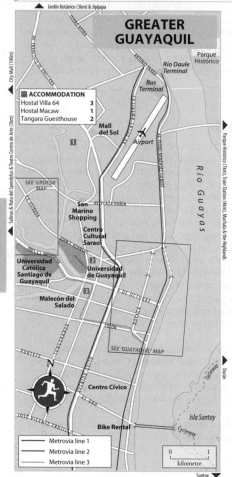

▲ Jardín Botánico (3km) & Jipijapa

GREATER GUAYAQUIL

Parque Histórico

Río Daule Terminal

Bus Terminal

City Mall (100m)

■ **ACCOMMODATION**
Hostal Villa 64	3
Hostal Macaw	1
Tangara Guesthouse	2

Mall del Sol

Airport

Río Guayas

Parque Histórico (1km), Train Station (4km), Machala & the highlands

SEE 'URDESA' MAP

AV PLAZA DAÑIN

San Marino Shopping

Centro Cultural Sarao

Universidad Católica Santiago de Guayaquil

Universidad de Guayaquil

Malecón del Salado

SEE 'GUAYAQUIL' MAP

Salinas & Ruta del Spondylus & Teatro Centro de Arte (3km)

N

Centro Cívico

Durán

Cycleway

Isla Santay

Bike Rental

Cycleway

| Metrovia line 1 |
| Metrovia line 2 |
| Metrovia line 3 |

0 — 1 kilometre

Santay ▼

the two liberators of South America, **Simón Bolívar** and **José de San Martín**, whose campaigns from opposite ends of the continent were then drawing together in the middle (see p.387). In the decades following independence, Guayaquil grew rapidly and asserted its considerable role in the new republic – Ecuador's first bank was founded here in 1859, soon followed by a major public library and university. The tide of success turned in 1896, when the worst **fire** in its history wiped out seventy percent of the city in 36 hours.

The twentieth century and beyond Guayaquil was quickly rebuilt and became prosperous once more in the twentieth century, aided by the dramatic **banana boom**, which began in the late 1940s. The city's pivotal role in the country's international trade (and the huge increase in commerce at that time) funded new port facilities in 1963 and the construction of the massive three-kilometre **Puente de la Unidad Nacional**, the largest bridge on the Pacific coast of South America. In the last couple of decades numerous **shanty towns** have emerged on the city's periphery, as thousands of people have migrated from the countryside in search of work; **crime** levels soared to the point where, in 1998, a state of emergency and nightly curfews were imposed for several months. These measures, along with a stronger police presence, have improved security in downtown areas such as the Malecón 2000 and Cerro Santa Ana, which is now safer than downtown Quito, but vigilance is still required. Having provided the impetus for much of the city centre's renaissance, four-time mayor and former presidential candidate Jaime Nebot is now turning his attention to regeneration projects in Guayaquil's poorer suburbs.

GUAYAQUIL ORIENTATION

Although it can be initially hard to get a handle on the city as a whole, **orientation** in the central area is quite straightforward. The downtown core lies within a compact grid on the west bank of the Río Guayas. The riverside avenue running north–south is called the Malecón Simón Bolívar, usually shortened to the **Malecón**, while three blocks away is the main square of the **Parque Seminario**, sometimes still known by its old name of Parque Bolívar, or more frequently, Parque de las Iguanas, after its famous inhabitants. The principal artery running through the city is **Avenida 9 de Octubre**, running west from the Malecón up to the imposing **Parque del Centenario** and beyond, to the riverside development at **Malecón del Salado**.

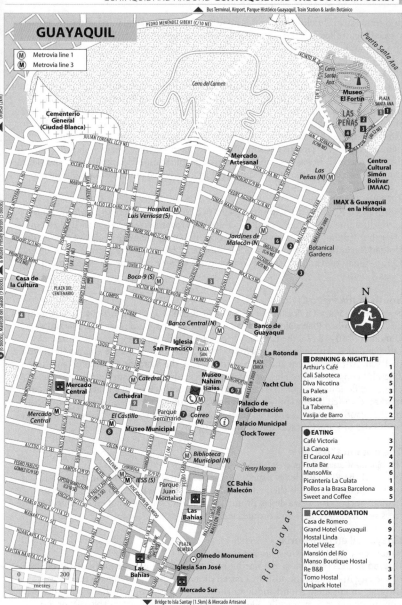

GUAYAQUIL

Ⓜ Metrovia line 1
Ⓜ Metrovia line 3

Cementerio General (Ciudad Blanca)

Cerro del Carmen

Cerro Santa Ana

Museo El Fortín

PLAZA SANTA ANA

LAS PEÑAS

Mercado Artesanal

Las Peñas (N) Ⓜ

Centro Cultural Simón Bolívar (MAAC)

Hospital Luis Vernasa (S) Ⓜ

IMAX & Guayaquil en la Historia

Jardines de Malecón (N) Ⓜ

Botanical Gardens

Casa de la Cultura

Boca-9 (S) Ⓜ

PLAZA DEL CENTENARIO

Banco Central (N) Ⓜ

Banco de Guayaquil

La Rotonda

Iglesia San Francisco

PLAZA SAN FRANCISCO

Museo Nahím Isaías

Yacht Club

Mercado Central

Catedral (S)

Cathedral

El Castillo

El Correo (N)

Palacio de la Gobernación

Palacio Municipal

Clock Tower

Mercado Central Ⓜ

Museo Municipal

Parque Seminario

Biblioteca Municipal (N)

Henry Morgan

IESS (S) Ⓜ

Parque Juan Montalvo

CC Bahía Malecón

Las Bahías

Olmedo Monument

Iglesia San José

Las Bahías

Mercado Sur

Río Guayas

0   200
metres

N

DRINKING & NIGHTLIFE

Arthur's Café	1
Cali Salsoteca	6
Diva Nicotina	5
La Paleta	3
Resaca	7
La Taberna	4
Vasija de Barro	2

● EATING

Café Victoria	3
La Canoa	7
El Caracol Azul	4
Fruta Bar	2
MansoMix	6
Picantería La Culata	1
Pollos a la Brasa Barcelona	8
Sweet and Coffee	5

ACCOMMODATION

Casa de Romero	6
Grand Hotel Guayaquil	9
Hostal Linda	2
Hotel Vélez	4
Mansión del Río	1
Manso Boutique Hostal	7
Re B&B	3
Tomo Hostal	5
Unipark Hotel	8

7

The Malecón 2000

Heaving with traffic, the busy **Malecón Simón Bolívar** skirts the western bank of the wide, yellow-brown Río Guayas; the two-kilometre long pedestrianized section that runs alongside it by the waterfront, known as the **Malecón 2000**, or simply the **Malecón** (daily 6am–midnight), is the most pleasant place to stroll in town. It connects some of Guayaquil's best-known monuments and features a large, paved esplanade filled with trees, botanical gardens, contemporary sculpture and architecture, small shopping malls and restaurants. Enclosed by railings and accessed only via guarded entrance gates, it is regularly patrolled by security guards, making it one of the safest places to spend a day in Guayaquil.

Plaza Cívica

Malecón 2000's centrepiece is the **Plaza Cívica**, reached by gates at the end of 9 de Octubre or 10 de Agosto. As you enter the gates, you're faced with **La Rotonda**, an imposing monument to South America's liberators, José de San Martín and Simón Bolívar, who are shaking hands against a background of tall marble columns topped by billowing South American flags. The memorial, which looks stunning when illuminated at night, commemorates the famous encounter between the two generals here on July 26 and 27, 1822 (see p.387). It was designed so that two people whispering into the two end pillars can hear each other – though the din of the traffic somewhat undermines the effect.

The lookout towers

South of La Rotonda are sculptures dedicated to the four elements, with fire and earth doubling up as timber-and-metal **lookout towers** crowned by sail-like awnings, affording striking views from the top. Looking north, the huge bridge of **Puente de la Unidad Nacional** stretches across to the suburb of Durán, the departure point of the Quito–Guayaquil train. A 23m Moorish **clock tower** marks the southern end of the Plaza Cívica.

South of the Plaza Cívica

South of the Plaza Cívica lie the **CC Bahía Malecón** shopping centre (daily 10am–8pm) and the dignified **Plaza Olmedo**, dedicated to statesman and poet **José Joaquín de Olmedo** (1780–1847), the first mayor of Guayaquil and a key agitator for the city's independence, whose bronze sedentary figure gazes out across the Guayas from atop a pedestal. At the southern end of the promenade, the **Mercado Sur** (daily 9am–8pm), a splendid construction of glass and wrought iron that hosts temporary exhibitions and events, is floodlit at night to dazzling effect. Beyond is a small clothes and **artesanía market**, dwarfed by the sprawling **Las Bahías market** – the place to come for black-market goods – which is sited on several blocks around the pedestrianized streets on both sides of Olmedo, near the bottom of the Malecón.

The botanical gardens

Malecón, between Luzárraga and Aguirre • Daily 6am–midnight • Free

North of the Plaza Cívica is a succession of **botanical gardens**, fountains, ponds and walkways; each garden is themed according to a historical period or Ecuadorian habitat, such as the Plaza de las Bromelias, a lavish concoction of cloudforest-like trees swathed in mosses and bromeliads.

Guayaquil en la Historia

Malecón and Loja, beneath the IMAX • Daily 9am–6pm• $3 • ☎ 04 2563078

Guayaquil en la Historia, at the northern end of the promenade, displays the evolution of the city in fourteen beautifully crafted dioramas that slowly reveal themselves through an engaging sound and light show (in English or Spanish), though the naff pop music grates after a while. Don't miss the marauding pirates (No. 4), or the crackling flames of the great fire of 1896 (No. 11).

Museo Antropológico de Arte Contemporáneo

Malecón and Loja • Tues–Fri 8.30am–4.30pm, Sat, Sun & public holidays 10am–4pm • Free • ☎ 04 2309400, Ⓦ www.museos.gob.ec /redmuseos/maac

At the very northern end of the Malecón is the **Museo Antropológico de Arte Contemporáneo** (more commonly abbreviated to MAAC), the centrepiece of the

GUAYAQUIL FIESTAS

The city's biggest **fiestas** take place on July 24, Simón Bolívar's birthday, and July 25, the foundation of the city, celebrated together in a week of events and festivities known as the **Fiestas Julianas**, complete with processions, street dancing and fireworks. Another important date in Ecuador's fiesta calendar is October 9, for the city's **independence**, which is combined with **Día de la Raza** on October 12, commemorating Christopher Columbus's "discovery" of the New World, in an attempt to cement post-colonial ties between Spain and Spanish-speaking Latin America. In 2011, President Correa renamed the celebration **Día de la Interculturalidad y Plurinacionalidad**, which doesn't exactly slip off the tongue but is thought to be more in tune with contemporary views of the day's significance. New Year's Eve is a raucous affair, celebrated with the burning of the *años viejos*, large effigies, on the Malecón at midnight.

Centro Cultural Simón Bolívar, a flagship arts complex. Space for theatre, cinema (see p.309) and contemporary art is balanced by the museum's excellent collection of over 50,000 items, featuring fine pre-Columbian ceramics – especially zoomorphic pots, as well as golden objects, jewellery made from shells and semi-precious stones, and ceremonial paraphernalia.

Las Peñas

The Malecón ends in the north at the picturesque barrio of **Las Peñas**, at the foot of Cerro Santa Ana. The short, dead-end road – Numa Pompilio Llona – is paved with uneven, century-old cobblestones. Its colourful wooden houses, many of which have been beautifully restored, make this one of the prettiest corners of Guayaquil. A couple of cannons by the entrance point towards the river, honouring the city's stalwart resistance to seventeenth-century pirates, and the street is dotted with a handful of bars and small art galleries.

Cerro Santa Ana and around

Rising above Las Peñas, **Cerro Santa Ana** was a very dangerous slum until a regeneration project transformed a swath of its ramshackle buildings into an eye-catching sequence of brightly painted houses, restaurants, bars and shops built around a winding, 444-step staircase up to the top of the hill. It ends at the **Plaza de Honores**, home to a colonial-style chapel and **lighthouse** modelled on Guayaquil's first, from 1841.

With its discreet balconies, ornate lampposts and switchback streets leading from intimate plazas, the development does a fair job of evoking the image of a bygone Guayaquil – despite the plastic "tiled" roofs, heavy presence of armed guards and large locked gates blocking out the slums at its margins. Yet the spectacular **views** from the Plaza de Honores and the top of the lighthouse are definitely worth the climb, to watch the sun dip on the seething city below.

Museo El Fortín del Santa Ana

Patio El Fortín • Daily 8.30am–late • Free • **Bar** Mon–Sat 6pm–2am

Just below the Plaza de Honores is the open-air **Museo El Fortín del Santa Ana**, which holds cannons, seafaring paraphernalia and the foundations of the fortress of **San Carlos**, built in 1629 to defend the city from pirate attacks. There's also a reconstructed pirate ship, half of which is a bar.

Puerto Santa Ana

Down the steps at the far end of Numa Pompilio pretty Plaza Santa Ana gives way to **Puerto Santa Ana**, a paved riverside promenade dotted with flowerbeds and benches that skirts the base of the hill.

Tucked away behind the plaza are three small, modest **museums** (all Wed–Fri 10am–5pm (closed for lunch hour); Sat & Sun 10am–5pm; free): the Museo de la Música Popular Guayaquileña celebrates Guayaquil's early music scene and most famous and colourful bad-boy musician, Julio Jaramillo; it shares the floor with the Pilsener museum, which narrates the history of Ecuador's most popular lager and its brewing processes – an ironic juxtaposition given that Jaramillo died of cirrhosis of the liver; downstairs is a museum of football, focusing on Guayaquil's two big teams, Emelec and Barcelona.

Parque Seminario

Guayaquil's central square, the **Parque Seminario** (formerly Parque Bolívar) is more popularly known as Parque de las Iguanas, after its impish inhabitants, which make occasional appearances out of the surrounding trees and shrubs, and garner far more attention than the nearby equestrian monument to Simon Bolívar. The huge, gleaming-white **cathedral**, a neo-Gothic confection of spires, arches and lancet windows, dominates the west side of the square; the building dates from 1948 and is built solidly of concrete – fire destroyed the original 1547 cathedral and subsequent incarnations.

Museo Municipal

Sucre and Chile • Tues–Fri 8.30am–4.30pm, Sat & Sun 10am–4pm • Free • ☏ 042594800, Ext 7402, ⓦ museodeguayaquil.com

One block southeast of the Parque Seminario, the engaging **Museo Municipal** focuses on the history of the city and region. Dominating its entrance is an enormous, 600-year-old totem pole embellished with dozens of carvings of human figures, produced by the seafaring Manteño-Huancavilca culture, the first people in what is now Ecuador to have any contact with the Spanish. Other striking pieces include a 10,000-year-old mastodon tooth, some pre-Columbian pottery, a diorama of the great fire of 1896, and displays on the seventeenth-century English buccaneers who attacked the city.

Palacio Municipal and around

Facing the waterfront, roughly opposite the clock tower, is the large, Neoclassical **Palacio Municipal**, one of the most beautiful buildings in the city; its grey walls are set off by dazzling white balconies and stucco mouldings and a central arcade topped by a glass-and-metal vaulted roof. Next door is the smaller, plainer **Palacio de la Gobernación**. Opposite, the well-presented **Museo Nahím Isaías** traces Guayaquil's merchant roots to modern times (in Spanish) (Tues–Fri 8.30am–4.30pm, Sat & Sun 10am–4pm; free).

Parque del Centenario and around

Nine blocks west of the Malecón, along Avenida 9 de Octubre, the **Parque del Centenario** is an immense square landscaped with flowers and trees, but constantly choked with traffic. Its centre is marked by a towering column, the **Monumento a los Heróes de la Independencia** ("Monument to the Heroes of Independence"), crowned by a statue of *Liberty*, arms outstretched, with images of the heroes arrayed around the base.

Museo de la Casa de la Cultura

Moncayo and 9 de Octubre • Tues–Fri 10am–6pm, Sat 9am–3pm • $1 • ☏ 04 2300500

The **Casa de la Cultura**, on the west side of the Parque del Centenario, exhibits a small selection of exquisite polychromatic pots and dazzling gold pieces in an otherwise unremarkable archeological collection. The museum once had over five hundred pieces until a dramatic theft in 1987 reduced the collection to just 63 items.

ESTRADA'S PACT WITH THE DEVIL

Should you pass the main cemetery at the dead of night, and spot a man in full evening dress and top hat astride a white charger, he's probably the ghost of Victor Emilio Estrada Sciaccaluga, or so *guayaquileños* will tell you. According to legend – probably founded on rumours put about by jealous contemporaries – the revered local banker, financier and politician acquired his personal fortune by making a pact with the devil. Upon his death in 1954, at the age of 63, Estrada reneged on the deal by ensuring his coffin was of copper, an apparent satanic deterrent. Understandably peeved at having been cheated out of a soul, the Devil stationed two demons by the tomb to ensure that the incumbent might never rest. And so, at around 11pm every night, unable to sleep, the former statesman can be seen in all his finery, talking to folk at the local bus stop or visiting them in their homes. Some taxi-drivers even claim to have given him a ride back to the cemetery after such outings.

Museo Presley Norton

9 de Octubre and Carchi • Tues–Fri 9am–5pm, Sat, Sun & public holidays 10am–4pm • Free • ☎ 04 2293423

One of the city's standout museums, the **Museo Presley Norton** lies a few blocks west of the Parque del Centenario, in a beautifully restored colonial mansion. Named after a pioneering Ecuadorian archeologist, the museum exhibits over eight thousand artefacts, only some of which are on display upstairs. The bilingual text and labelling take you through the development of pre-Columbian ceremonial and utilitarian pottery from around 4000BC to 1500AD. Highlights include a large polychromatic pot topped with a bird of prey, its beak tucking into a snake, and an extraordinary physically challenged clay man from the Chorrera period.

La Ciudad Blanca

Entrance on Menéndez Gilbert and Coronel • Daily 8.30am–6pm • Free

About a kilometre north of the Parque del Centenario along Moncayo is the city cemetery, the Cementerio General, also known as the **Ciudad Blanca** ("White City") for its many rows of dazzling white tombs and mausoleums housing the remains of the local elite, including five former presidents, though on the west side of the hill you can find the wooden crosses of the poor. For the most part, the funerary sculpture is remarkably indulgent, much of it carved from Italian marble. One of most grandiose tombs is of Victor Emilio Estrada Sciaccaluga (see box above).

The obvious safety measures apply while exploring La Ciudad Blanca – don't wander around in the evening, or on your own during the day, and take a taxi here, rather than walk, since it's a rough area.

Malecón del Salado

Twelve blocks west of the Parque del Centenario, 9 de Octubre meets the green banks of the Estero Salado, a tributary of the Río Guayas and site of another swanky new riverside development, the **Malecón del Salado**, With its sleek, steel pedestrian suspension bridge, large fountains, stylishly designed promenades and observation platforms and the odd café and restaurant, this is a fun place to spend an hour or two. Most nights there is a sound and light show (7–9pm), involving a choreographed display of the fountain's water jets to an eclectic soundtrack, augmented by lasers at weekends. At a dock by the **Puente del Velero** (sailboat), so-named after its sailboat-design, you can rent rowing boats and pedalos.

Circular walk

There is now a very pleasant 3km circular walk along the estuary – popular with *guayaquileño* joggers in the morning – that takes you left (south) from the Plaza

Rodolfo Baquierizo Moreno, at the top of 9 de Octubre, along the Paseo de los Escritores, across the Puente del Velero, doubling back past the fountains and the main bridge, then north along the Parque Lineal to the fun Puente Zigzag, which does just that across the water. From the bridge end, you can either continue northwards into the upmarket neighbourhood of Urdesa, or return southwards along the Malecón Universitario, skirting the western edge of the University of Guayaquil, back to the square where you started. The birdwatching is good too – an assortment of ibis, egrets and kingfishers lurk in the mangroves while parakeets and flycatchers flit through the walkways' treetops.

There's a downloadable map of the route with birdlife information at ⊕turismo .guayaquil.gob.ec/en.

Parque Histórico Guayaquil

Av Esmeraldas and Av Central, Cdla Entre Ríos • Wed–Sun 9am–4.30pm • Free • ☎ 04 2832958 • City buses #97 and #4 pass near the park entrance on Av Esmeraldas, and the #81 comes from the bus terminal • A taxi from downtown costs $5–6

Six kilometres north of the city centre, across the bridge on the headland separating the *ríos* Daule and Babahoyo, sits the **Parque Histórico Guayaquil**, a well-designed and slickly operated park divided into three sections. A **wildlife** zone features walkways through mangroves, spacious enclosures housing native animals including tapirs, caymans, ocelots, spider monkeys, sloths and a harpy eagle, plus an observation tower for birdwatching. The **traditions** zone represents coastal culture and the *montuvio* way of life, with a traditional farmstead (*granja*) and a reconstructed cacao-plantation hacienda. The **urban architecture** zone displays restored fragments of Guayaquil's late nineteenth-century buildings, which now overlook the **Malecón 1900** – the riverside as it might have looked in the early 1900s. At weekends your visit can be further enlivened by theatrical presentations, folk dancing, public talks or short films.

Jardín Botánico de Guayaquil

Francisco de Orellana • Daily 8.30am–4pm • $3 • ☎ 04 2899689 • $6 by taxi from the centre

Perched on top of Cerro Colorado 10km north of the city centre, the **Jardín Botánico de Guayaquil** sits on a peaceful site with great views over the city. It is home to several hundred species of plants, including an excellent collection of orchids. Needless to say, the flora attracts plenty of birdlife too – keep a lookout for whooping motmots, scarlet-backed woodpeckers and pale-legged horneros. There's also a butterfly house, koi pond and geology area with rock and mineral exhibits.

Isla Santay

Pedestrian and cycle access to Isla Santay (in the Río Guayas) via new bascule bridge at Calle El Oro, 1.6km south of the southern end of Malecón 2000 • Daily 6am–5pm; last return 6pm • ⊕ islasantay.info • Free • Take Metrovía Line 1 to Barrio del Centenario, from where it's a 2-min walk to the bridge. There is also a community watertaxi service between the yacht club on Malecón 2000, and Santay • **Bike rental** at the bridge on presentation of ID • 7am–5pm • $4

When you get fed up with concrete and cars in central Guayaquil, there's no better place to escape than via the new 800m pedestrian and cycleway across the Río Guayas to mangrove-covered **Isla Santay.** Turning south at the end of the bridge, 1.8km of raised pedestrian and cycle paths twist through precious wetlands to the former impoverished fishing village of Santay, now turned eco-community. The village's fifty families have been rehoused, practice recycling and have been provided with solar-powered electricity and a water supply – both lacking before. Now able to supplement their fishing livelihoods with income from tourism, they operate a community restaurant, look after a small sanctuary for endangered crocodiles and provide guided boat trips along the river. These internationally recognized wetlands boast over 100 avian species – so are great for morning birdwatching – and some rare mammals: crab-eating raccoons, anteaters and white-tailed deer.

Turning northwards after crossing the bridge from the city, a longer path takes you 4.3km, via a second bascule bridge, to the suburb of Durán, home to Guayaquil's train station (see p.306). Eventually, there will be a 14km circular path for cyclists and pedestrians around the whole island. A hundred bikes (with helmets) are available for rent on the city side of the bridge but avoid the weekend crowds if possible, when the experience more resembles the dodgems.

ARRIVAL AND DEPARTURE

GUAYAQUIL

With its smart new **bus terminal** and **airport**, arriving in Guayaquil is no longer the daunting, chaotic experience it once was and getting to your hotel should be straightforward. That said, guard against **petty theft** by staying alert, not wandering the streets with your valuables and by always taking a taxi at night.

BY PLANE

Airport Aeropuerto José Joaquín de Olmedo is 5km north of the centre on Avenida de las Américas (☎04 2169000, ⓦtagsa.aereo), and is well served by ATMs, internet facilities and an information desk. It serves domestic flights (see below), as well as international flights from various cities across Latin America and the US, including New York and Miami, plus Amsterdam and Madrid (see Basics, p.25).

Destinations Avianca, LAN and TAME all operate daily flights to Baltra and San Cristóbal in Galápagos (daily; 2hr; from $440 return), and to Quito (numerous daily flights; 45min; from $76). TAME also flies to Cuenca (2–3 daily; 40min; from $73); Esmeraldas (1 daily; 1hr; from $87); Latacunga (Mon–Fri 1 daily; 1hr; from $58); and Loja (Mon–Sat 1 daily; 40min; from $73).

Getting to the centre Buses from the airport to the centre (including bus #2) pass outside the terminal on Avenida de las Américas, but when carrying luggage, it's easier and safer to take a taxi ($5–6 to the centre).

BY BUS

Bus terminal Buses arrive at the gleaming three-tiered Terminal Terrestre (☎04 2130166), 7km north of the city centre, beyond the airport, on Avenida Benjamín Rosales Aspiazu, complete with an attached shopping mall and several ATMs. Ground floor for tickets, first floor for long-distance buses and second-floor for regional buses.

Destinations Ambato (hourly; 6hr 30min); Cuenca (every 30–40min; 4–5hr); Guaranda (26 daily; 3hr 30min); Huaquillas (every 30min; 4hr 30min); Jipijapa (every 30min; 2hr 30min); Loja (16 daily; 9hr); Machala (every 30min; 3hr); Manta (every 30min; 4hr); Montañita (10 daily; 3hr 30min, express 3hr); Playas (every 20min; 2hr); Puerto López (8 daily; 3hr 30min); Quito (every 10–20min; 8hr); Riobamba (hourly; 5hr); Salinas (every 10min; 2hr 30min); Santa Elena (every 10min; 2hr); Santo Domingo (every 10min; 5hr); Zaruma (10 daily; 5hr 30min).

Getting to the centre Local city buses use a separate area at one end of the Terminal Terrestre; many (including bus #2) will take you into the centre, as will the Metrovía (see below), opposite the terminal – but it's far easier and much safer to take a taxi to your hotel ($5–6 to the city centre).

International buses There are now daily services offered between Guayaquil's Terminal Terrestre and Lima (26–28hr; $65–70, more for VIP seats), and more frequent departures between Guayaquil and Piura, via the coastal resort of Máncora (9hr; $23–30) in northern Peru. Recommended operators include CIFA International (☎04 2130379, ⓦcifainternacional.com) and Cruz del Sur (☎04 2130179, ⓦcruzdelsur.com.pe).

GETTING AROUND

On foot Most sights in the city centre are no more than a 15–20min walk from the Parque Seminario.

By Metrovía The city's Metrovía ($0.25), an ecofriendly bus system with its own lanes, operates three lines: Line 1 runs north–south through the city between the terminals at Río Daule, opposite the Terminal Terrestre, and El Guasmo, in the south, splitting into two parallel branches in the downtown section, with northbound buses following the axis formed by Pedro Carbo and Vicente Rocafuerte, and southbound buses going down Boyacá. Line 2 runs from Río Daule, past the airport, through the centre of town, down to the southern suburbs. Line 3 branches northwest from the centre (where it connects with Line 1), up to the terminal at Bastión Popular. Top-up swipe cards are used to pay for journeys, available at the main terminals.

By bus Useful bus routes include the #9 and #55, which run along the Malecón, and the #63, which heads out to the Jardín Botánico outside town, from Parque del Centenario. To reach Urdesa, take bus #52 or #54 from the Malecón, or #10 from Parque del Centenario, which also passes the main entrance to the Malecón del Salado.

By car Driving in Guayaquil is rather hairy, but if you want to rent a car for journeys outside the city, you'll find rental

7

companies just outside the airport, including: Avis (⊙04 2169092); Budget (⊙04 2169026); Hertz (⊙04 2169035); Localiza (⊙04 3904523); and Thrifty (⊙04 2169088).

By taxi Many Guayaquil taxi drivers continue to resist the use of taximeters, so haggling is still the norm. The average minimum fare within the city centre is $2 ($2.50 at night). Runs to and from the bus station or airport are usually

$5–6. Otherwise, ask your lodgings for the going rate to your destination, and fix the price with the driver before you get in. It's safest to take a cab belonging to a cooperative whose name and phone number are displayed on the side of the car – you should be able to flag one down easily on most city-centre streets. At night you may prefer to go to the nearest large hotel to find a taxi.

INFORMATION

Tourist office There's an I-Tur at the entrance of the Museo Nahim Isaías, Pichincha 605 between Aguirre and Ballén (⊙04 2324 283; Mon–Fri 8.30am–4.30pm), where you should be able to get hold of a city map and general city information.

Tourist information Of greater use than the I-Tur is the excellent bilingual website: ⓦturismo.guayaquil.gob.ec /en. Although the ever-changing opening hours are rarely up-to-date, there are bags of useful information and several downloadable guides and maps.

TOURS

BOAT TOURS

Pirata Morgan Malecón and Sucre ⊙04 2517228, ⓦfacebook.com/elbarcomorgan. One-hour family outings ($7), serious booze cruises ($15) and themed excursions on a mock seventeenth-century pirate ship ($7). Closed Mon.

TRAIN JOURNEYS

Tren Ecuador has offices at the Malecón between Icaza and Rendón, or at Durán station (⊙04 2154922, ⓦtrenecuador .com). They offer an enjoyable if touristy full day's excursion that heads eastwards by train though rice-fields and banana

plantations towards Bucay, at the foot of the Andes (Thurs– Sun & public holidays; 8am; $28). The 4-hr train journey is followed by a 4-hr sojourn there before a 2-hr return journey by bus. Alternatively, you can go by bus and return by train. Various activities are on offer (at extra cost) once you reach Bucay, such as horse riding, scenic walks, tubing or rafting. Alternatively, if you've time and money to spare, you can now travel the entire historic Guayaquil–Quito route in a luxury train. The fully inclusive four-day trip costs $1524 per person sharing; stops are made along the way at places of interest and overnight accommodation is comfortable.

ACCOMMODATION

Guayaquil is packed with hotels; most are geared towards corporate clients, so are generally cheaper at weekends. High-end and mid-range hotels all come with a/c and hot water, and many are located close to the airport and bus terminal. Most of the budget hotels usually offer some cheaper fan-ventilated rooms but often only have cold-water showers. In the centre, a handful of apartments have been converted into small, affordable B&B-cum-hostels.

DOWNTOWN

Casa de Romero Vélez 501, 7th floor, and Boyacá ⊙04 6036244; see map p.299. Centrally located high-rise flat – some noise drifts up – (with a lift) converted into a B&B, offering a handful of tidy, modern, light, mostly en-suite rooms with a/c, and some with balcony. Also a pleasant TV/DVD lounge, kitchen and laundry. $47

Grand Hotel Guayaquil Boyacá and Ballén ⊙04 2329690, ⓦgrandhotelguayaquil.com; see map p.299. Large, upmarket hotel boasting a gorgeous outdoor pool with a cascading waterfall. Good rooms and furnishings, as well as a roof terrace, sauna, massage rooms, steam baths and a 24hr café open to non-guests. Buffet breakfast and welcome cocktail included. Cheaper deals often available. $179

Hostal Linda Lorenzo de Garaicoa 809 ⊙04 2562495; see map p.299. Smart hostal on the Parque del Centenario containing some mock antique furniture; the immaculate rooms feature cool marble floors, comfortable beds and cable TV. Excellent value. $25

Hotel Vélez Vélez 1021 and Quito ⊙04 2530292; see map p.299. Simple but impeccably clean cell-like singles, doubles and triples (with fan or a/c) with bare walls and en-suite bathrooms with cold water. Worth paying the extra $5 for a window and a/c. Also has its own garage. Service is hit and miss. $12

★**Mansión del Río** Numa Pompilio Llona 120, Las Peñas ⊙04 2566044, ⓦmansiondelrio-ec.com; see map p.299. Beautifully restored colonial mansion replete with antiques, draped curtains and chandeliers, though the rooms have all mod cons such as a/c, minibar, safe and LCD TV. There's a fine restaurant and a terrace-bar overlooking the river. Buffet breakfast and airport transfer included. $204

★**Manso Boutique Hostal** Malecón 1406 and Aguirre ⊙04 2526644, ⓦmanso.ec; see map p.299. Delightful, arty hostal spread over three floors in the heart of the action, comprising a variety of rooms with some decorative touches and private or shared hot-water bathrooms, plus two unisex dorms, all with a/c. There's a café (see opposite), bike rental, the odd performance or tango class, and inexpensive

eco-tours supporting local community-based projects (half-day trips $34/person for 2–4 people). Cheaper if booked online. Breakfast included. Dorms $17; doubles $64
Re B&B Junín 428, 3rd floor, and Córdova ☎ 0987949376, ⓦ rebandb.com; see map p.299. Vibrant retro decoration reigns in this friendly five-room B&B-cum-hostel: four en-suite doubles and an eight-bed dorm with lockers. The kitchen is modern, spacious and well equipped but the TV lounge area is not very homely. Dorms $17; doubles $64
★**Tomo Hostal** Rendon 212, between Panamá and Carbo ☎ 04 2562683; see map p.299. Only a block from the Malecón, this place successfully combines sophisticated, chic minimalist decor – quotations stencilled on gleaming white walls – with a relaxed vibe: lots of sofas for lounging, books to browse, plus the semi-open walled rooftop terrace as a star attraction. En-suite rooms ($12 extra for a window) plus excellent-value deluxe dorm accommodation. Breakfast included. Dorms $17; doubles $65
Unipark Hotel Ballén 406, Parque Seminario ☎ 04 2327100, ⓦ uniparkhotel.com; see map p.299. Large, plush hotel with a vast, marble lobby, pleasant piano bar and modern, well-appointed rooms and suites, many overlooking the park. Private parking. $123

OUT OF THE CENTRE
★**Hostal Macaw** Cdla Guayaquil, Victor Hugo Sicouret Mz. 11 Villa 8 ☎ 042 296799, ⓦ hostalmacaw.com; see map p.298. Superb, friendly, family-run bed and breakfast, in a quiet street near the Mall del Sol, creatively decorated with ceramic mosaic murals. The comfortable en-suite rooms are spotless, the healthy breakfasts plentiful, and the service excellent. $75
Hostal Villa 64 Hurtado 808 between Tulcán and Carchi ☎ 0967768656, ⓦ hostalvilla64.com; see map p.298. Located only a 5min walk from the Malecón del Salado, this cosy B&B comprises ten spotless, themed rooms and a pleasant patio courtyard, where breakfast is served and a small snack-bar operates the rest of the time. The place is secure, and service is excellent. $59
Tangara Guesthouse Cdla Bolivariana, Manuela Sáenz and O'Leary ☎ 04 2282829, ⓦ tangara-ecuador .com; see map p.298. Located in a quiet residential area, this warm family home contains a handful of rooms decorated for bird enthusiasts that are simple, en suite and with cable TV and a/c. Residents share a lounge-dining area, kitchen and plant-laden patio. Interesting day-trips can be arranged. $56

EATING

Downtown restaurants fall into two broad categories: those serving cheap and simple almuerzos, and those (usually attached to the smarter hotels) offering good-quality, but overpriced, menus. You'll find plenty of fast-food outlets at the CC Malecón mall and a couple of café-bars towards the northern end of the promenade. Out of the centre, there's a concentrated collection of restaurants, bars and nightclubs along Avenida Estrada, the main drag in the affluent suburb of **Urdesa**, though the current high-end hotspot is the chic residential area of Sabrondón. Otherwise, the **Mall del Sol** (see "Shopping", p.309) has a handful of smart restaurants, as well as the inevitable huge food court, and the Malecón del Salado offers the odd outdoor bar and seafood restaurant.

DOWNTOWN
Café Victoria Malecón, at the botanical gardens; see map p.299. Down in a shady spot by the duckpond, this café is a popular after-work spot for *guayaquileños* and is stuffed with families at weekends. It's great for coffee and cakes, set lunches or an evening cocktail followed by dinner. Mains $10–17. Try the platter of traditional starters. Daily 11am–11pm.
La Canoa Hotel Continental, Chile 510 and 10 de Agosto; see map p.299. One of the best places to sample proper Ecuadorian cuisine, including ceviche, *caldo de manguera* (pork tripe soup), *bolones* and *guatita*, all at affordable prices and in a spacious, busy dining room. Open 24hr.
El Caracol Azul 9 de Octubre 1918 and Los Ríos ☎ 04 2280461, ⓦ elcaracolazul.ec; see map p.299. This seafood and steakhouse is really all about the gourmet seafood, from shrimps to swordfish, clams to crabs, creatively presented in formal surroundings. Mains from around $23. Mon–Sat noon until late, Sun noon–5pm.
Fruta Bar Malecón and Martínez ☎ 04 2300743; see map p.299. Funky little beach-themed hideaway (with sibling outlet on Estrada, in Urdesa) with painted

chairs and tables (and a/c). Serves refreshing and delicious juices, milkshakes, fruit salads and sandwiches ($6–10). Mon–Sat 9am–midnight.
MansoMix Manso Boutique Hostal, Malecón (see opposite). Healthy, organic, locally produced and predominantly vegetarian light bites served in a pleasant first-floor café – grab the balcony tables overlooking the Malecón. Try *patacones* stuffed with crab ceviche, or quinoa burgers or tortillas with pesto and yoghurt sauce. Most dishes $6–9. Mon–Fri 12.30–10pm, Sat 6.30–10pm.
★**Picantería La Culata** Córdova between Mendiburo and Martínez; see map p.299. With an easy beachside cabaña-style decor, this small Bohemian street café-resto attracts an arty crowd, enticed by its delicious *encocados*, ceviches, *encebollados* and the like with rice or *patacones* (from $6). Also snacks to share. Mon–Sat 8am until late, Sun 8am–4pm.
Pollos a la Brasa Barcelona Sucre and Boyacá; see map p.299. Large, slightly grubby canteen specializing in roast chicken and red meat. No frills but very cheap (all under $5) and popular. Mon–Sat 11am–8pm, Sun 11am–4pm.

URDESA

Lo Nuestro Estrada 903 at Higueras ☎ 04 2386398; see map p.308. A venerable restaurant in an old mansion that reputedly serves up Guayaquil's best Ecuadorian cuisine (most mains from $14) in intimate, dimly lit surroundings – heavy white tablecloths, faded photos, posters of bygone days. Daily noon–10.30pm.

Parrillada del Ñato Estrada 1219 between Laureles and Costanera ☎ 04 2387098; see map p.308. A large fan-ventilated Guayaquil institution that gets carnivores slavering over colossal steaks and enormous portions of grilled meats (mains around $12, but most dishes are for two) – though pizza and seafood are also available. Daily noon until late.

★**Riviera** Estrada 707 and Ficus ☎ 04 2883790, ⊕ rivieraecuador.com; see map p.308. Excellent Italian restaurant, with snappy service and a full menu including fresh pasta, antipasti, risotto, profiteroles and tiramisu. Automatic parmesan graters and mini-chairs for your bags contribute to the air of pampering. Seafood mains from $20. Deli service also available. Daily 12.30pm until midnight.

Sweet and Coffee Estrada and Diagonal; see map p.308. The place is humming after work and at weekends, with frappés, iced coffees and hot chocolates in abundance alongside gooey cakes. Squeeze onto the outside patio or enjoy the blast of a/c inside. There's also a branch downtown on Carbo and Luque. Mon–Sat 8am until late, Sun 10am until late.

DRINKING, NIGHTLIFE AND ENTERTAINMENT

Much of the city's nightlife goes on in the more affluent suburbs north of the centre, though **Cerro Santa Ana** and **Las Peñas** are both good spots for bar hopping, with clusters of inexpensive drinking holes. The **Zona Rosa** is back from the northern end of the Malecón along or around Rocafuerte, while the hip youth tend to hit the discos of the glitzy **shopping malls**. Check **local newspapers** *El Universo* (⊕ eluniverso.com) or *El Telégrafo* (⊕ telegrafo.com.ec) for entertainment listings, or visit ⊕ farras.com to find out about the city's nightlife scene. Check out ⊕ gayscout.com/en/city4177/Guayaquil for the city's listings for gay bars, clubs, saunas and the like.

BARS AND CLUBS

Arthur's Café Numa Pompilio Llona 127, Las Peñas; see map p.299. Popular spot with a rather grubby,

URDESA

0 — 200 metres
(500m)

EATING
Fruta Bar	4
Lo Nuestro	2
Parrillada del Ñato	1
Riviera	3
Sweet & Coffee	5

DRINKING
El Manantial	1

Salado Estero

Central Guayaquil

unatmospheric interior and the potentially fantastic views onto the illuminated Malecón rather undermined by the perspex windows. Also serves average *platos típicos* and traditional snacks. Occasional live music Fri & Sat. Mon–Sat 6pm until late.

Diva Nicotina Escalón 10, at the bottom of the Cerro Santa Ana steps; see map p.299. Large, dark watering hole heaving with folk when there's live music, which is most nights: jazz (Wed), blues (Thurs) and all sorts on Fri & Sat. Fast food and Cuban cigars too. Cover around $10. Tues–Sat 7pm–late.

El Manantial Estrada 520 and Las Monjas, Urdesa; see map p.308. Pleasant and busy bar best enjoyed by sitting outside on balmy evenings and downing a pitcher or two of beer, accompanied by scrumptious seafood snacks. Occasional live music Fri & Sat. Mon–Sat 5pm until late.

★**La Paleta** Numa Pompilio Llona 176, Las Peñas; see map p.299. Arty two-floor bar appealing to a mixed demographic, with good wine, nibbles and tapas on offer, plus chill-out music and a relaxed vibe. Wed–Sat 8pm until late.

Resaca Malecón and Junín; see map p.299. Unmissable faux-Spanish galleon in a great riverside location with outdoor seating on the prow plus large waterfront windows below deck; a prime venue for sipping a beer or cocktail, though food and service can be variable. Live music Fri. Daily noon until late.

Cali Salsoteca Panamá and Martínez, ☎ 0939005298; see map p.299. Legendary *salsoteca* in the heart of the Zona Rosa, attracting national and international artists to the stage. The place to catch hip-swinging salsa and son. Cover charges vary; women often free – check their Facebook page for info. Thurs–Sat usually 8/9pm until late.

La Taberna Plazoleta de los Monjes, Cerro Santa Ana, first left up the steps; see map p.299. Stuffed with memorabilia that pay homage to Barcelona Football Club and Julio Jaramillo (see p.302), this is a great Bohemian hangout, with simple wooden tables and benches – a choice spot to enjoy a drink or two. Sometimes playing Latin rock, at other times classic rock, salsa and the like. Mon–Sat 5pm until late.

Vasija de Barro Halfway up the Cerro Santa Ana steps; see map p.299. Surrounded by a bougainvillea hedge, this breezy patio boasting fine views hosts a down-to-earth bar serving cheap drinks (beer, sangria, shots and cocktails) and snacks (peanuts, *patacones* and empanadas), accompanied by music videos. Karaoke on Saturdays. Mon–Sat 5pm until late.

THEATRE, DANCE AND CLASSICAL MUSIC

Centro Cívico Eloy Alfaro, south of the city centre on Quito and Venezuela ☎04 2444394; see map p.298.

Hosting live theatre and regular performances by the Orquesta Sinfónica de Guayaquil (ⓦosg.gob.ec) plus visiting musicians.

Centro Cultural Sarao Cdla Kennedy ☎04 229 5118; see map p.298. At the cutting edge of contemporary dance.

Teatro Centro de Arte Vía a la Costa 4.5km ☎04 2003699 ext 13, ⓦteatrocentrodearte.org; see map p.298. Shows a range of theatre and dance productions.

CINEMA

Cinemark in the Mall del Sol, Mall del Sur and City Mall ☎1700 CINEMARK, ⓦcinemark.com.ec.

IMAX Cinema Malecón and Loja ☎04 2563078, ⓦsupercines.com/cartelera/imax.aspx.

MAAC Cine at the northern end of the Malecón ☎04 2309400, ⓦochoymedio.net/maaccine-guayaquil. Independent, classic and art-house films.

Supercines in Los Ceibos and San Marino malls ⓦsupercines.com. Both Cinemark and Supercines generally show Hollywood films, with some showings dubbed, and others in English with Spanish subtitles.

SHOPPING

MALLS

City Mall At the junction of avenidas Benjamín Carrión and Felipe Pezo, Cdla Alborado ⓦwww.citymall.com.ec; see map p.298. Shops, cinema, food court and restaurants 10am–10pm.

Mall del Sol At the junctions of avenidas Marengo and Orrantia, near the airport ⓦmalldelsol.com.ec; see map p.298. As well as the usual food court, cinemas and high-end shops, the city's largest mall also has a large number of craft shops. Mon–Sat

10am–9pm, 10am–8pm; food court and restaurants 10am–10pm.

ARTESANÍA

Mercado Artesanal Baquerizo Moreno and Montalvo, near Las Peñas. Numerous stalls with copious weavings, knitwear and other artesanía. Daily 9.30am–6pm.

Mercado Artesanal Malecón 2000 South end of waterfront. Stalls selling artesanía, predominantly from the Sierra.

DIRECTORY

Consulates Australia, Rocafuerte 520, 2nd floor ☎04 6017529; Canada, Janquin Orrantia and Marengo ☎04 2296837; Peru, Edif. Centrum, 14th floor, Av Francisco de Orellana 234 ☎04 2631109; UK, Honorary Consul c/o Agripac General Córdova 623 and Padre Solano ☎04 2560400 ext 318; US, Calle Santa Ana and Av Bonin, ☎04 3717000.

Hospital Clínica Kennedy on San Jorge and La Novena ☎04 2289666.

Immigration Av Benjamín Rosales, opposite Terminal Terrestre, ☎04 2297004.

Money and exchange Downtown banks with ATMs include: Banco Pichincha, Pichincha and 9 de Octubre; Banco de Guayaquil, Icaza 105 and Pichincha; and Banco del Austro, Boyacá and 9 de Octubre. The bus terminal, airport and all large shopping centres have ATMs.

Post office Main office on Carbo and Ballén, just off the Parque Seminario.

Bosque Protector Cerro Blanco

Km16 on the north side of the coast road, west of Guayaquil • Sat & Sun 8am–4pm; Mon–Fri advance booking only • ☎04 2874946, ⓦbosquecerroblanco.org • $4; guides ($12–20/group) obligatory for the two longer trails • Camping or cabin accommodation $25 • Buses from Guayaquil's main bus terminal to Posorja or Villamil (every 10–15min; 40min) will drop you off at the entrance, from where it's a 10-min walk to the interpretive centre

The **Bosque Protector Cerro Blanco** protects around fifty square kilometres of dry coastal forest, providing a vital refuge for **wildlife** such as howler monkeys, collared anteaters, brocket deer, a few jaguars and more than two hundred species of birds – including a group of endangered great green macaw. A major attraction for birdwatchers, the reserve has three **trails** of varying lengths (approximately 1, 3 and 6km) but you can only do the shortest without a guide and your enjoyment of this – and camping – is likely to be undermined by the constant hum of a nearby processing plant.

Puerto Hondo

Km17 on the south side of the coast road, west of Guayaquil • Sat & Sun, you can just turn up; Mon–Fri advance booking only • $15/boat (1–7 people); $4 for a kayak • Contact Sra Zambrano ☎ 0991400186 • Buses from Guayaquil's main bus terminal to Posorja or Villamil (every 10–15min; 40min; ticket counters 90 & 91) will drop you off at the turn-off to the village, from where it's a 5-min walk. Getting back is trickier as buses often don't stop

Strung around the head of a narrow saltwater estuary, the dusty, tumbledown little port of **PUERTO HONDO** has a community-based tourism association that offers tours of the **mangrove swamps** with members of a guide association. You can choose from being shown around in a **rowing boat**, or renting a **kayak** on your own. Either way, it's a far cheaper alternative to the larger and better-known Reserva Ecológica Manglares Churute (see below); the swamps offer the chance to see the same ecosystem and many wetland birds. If you don't want the hassle of navigating public transport, consider taking one of the Manso Boutique Hostal's inexpensive trips (see p.306).

Reserva Ecológica Manglares Churute

Visitor centre Km49 southeast of Guayaquil on the road to Machala • Daily 8am–2pm • ☎ 0939769115 • $10; boat rides through the mangrove swamps (2–4hr; $40 per boat) and guides for hikes must be booked in advance at the visitor centre or at the Ministerio del Ambiente office for Guayas (☎ 04 2320391) • From Guayaquil bus terminal, take any bus to Machala or Naranjal (every 30min; 50min), and ask to be dropped at the visitor centre (*centro de visitantes*)

Hugging the Guayas estuary, the precious **Reserva Ecológica Manglares Churute** protects 500 square kilometres of **mangrove** swamps from being cleared for shrimp farming. Best viewed on a **boat ride** along the labyrinthine channels that thread through the tangled mangroves, they are part of a unique ecosystem that provides a vital nursery for many fish and crustaceans. The reserve also harbours a great variety of **birds**, including the occasionally sighted Chilean flamingos (Jan–Feb), while bottlenose **dolphins** (June–Nov) are frequently seen frolicking around the boats.

Four rewarding **paths** thread through dry and humid tropical forest (ranging from a short stroll to a 3–4hr hike), offering lake or estuary views, a cascading waterfall and the chance to spot howler monkeys. You'll need a guide to explore the trails, or you can visit the reserve on an organized tour from Guayaquil. Take plenty of repellent.

South to the border

On its way **south to the border** 244km away, the major coastal highway from Guayaquil slices through endless plantations as you enter the country's **banana-growing heartland**. Ecuador didn't start exporting the fruit until 1945, but the boom that followed was so dramatic that the crop became the country's most important agricultural export within two years, and has remained so ever since. A large portion of banana cultivation occurs in the province of El Oro, whose capital **Machala** is the industry's main service centre. A busy, workaday town holding little of interest, Machala serves as a launch pad for trips to the charming hillside town of **Zaruma**, 86km east, and the petrified forest of **Puyango**, 100km south, and makes a convenient stop on the way to Peru, a one-hour bus ride south; travellers often choose to spend the night here before crossing the border at the dusty, ramshackle town of **Huaquillas**.

OPPOSITE PLAYA LOS FRAILES (P.329) >

7

BANANA REPUBLIC

Ecuador exports more than five million tonnes of **bananas** yearly, making it the biggest producer of the world's most popular fruit, responsible for almost a quarter of the world's banana exports. Most of the country's banana plantations are effectively controlled by a few huge **companies**, namely US-owned Dole and Chiquita, Del Monte and Ecuador's own Noboa (Bonita).

Ecuador's extraordinary success in this sector is due in large part to the appalling **pay** and **working conditions** of its labourers, who are among the worst paid in the world. For a full day's labour (12–15hr), the typical banana worker can expect a salary of around ten dollars, which also has to cover outlay for the workers' own tools, uniforms, transport to the plantations and drugs should they fall ill or have an on-site accident. Most can't afford **housing** and must share small rooms on the estates or live in squalid, jerry-built shacks.

For many years, hardly any of the 250,000-strong workforce was **unionized**, with most workers effectively denied the right to form unions or bargain collectively. Although this is beginning to change, instant dismissals, intimidation and arrests are still common for active union involvement.

Being so susceptible to disease, the bananas must be regularly sprayed with pesticides and other chemicals. Many workers complain of pesticide **poisoning**; throughout the 1990s, Ecuadorian crops were treated with DBCP, a highly toxic chemical thought to cause birth defects, infertility and liver damage.

To compete with Ecuador, other countries' producers are forced either to degrade conditions for their own workforce or relocate – in other words, Ecuador is winning the race to the bottom. Supermarkets often seem content to turn a blind eye to workers' low pay, non-existent welfare and even **child labour**, which has been documented on Ecuadorian plantations. In Machala, **UROCAL** (ⓦ urocal.org) is the organization most involved with growing and promoting organic and fair-trade bananas and cacao, giving workers a much better deal. At El Guabo, 10km north-east of Machala, on the main road to Guayaquil, a local Fair Trade cooperative of organic banana producers (ⓣ 07 2950088, ⓦ asoguabo.com.ec) puts on a fascinating day-tour in Spanish ($20 per person for 2–3 people, including lunch), which gives insight into the whole process from the planting to the pallet. You can turn up on the day but they prefer an email in advance: ⓔ secretaria@asoguabo.com.ec).

Machala

Despite being founded in the sixteenth century, **MACHALA** looks like a city that's sprung up haphazardly in the last few decades. Beyond the spruced-up **parque central** and its immediate vicinity, shabby concrete buildings covered in flaking white paint line the streets, belying the town's prosperity as the nucleus of Ecuador's banana industry (see box above). If you enter or leave the town via Avenida 9 de Mayo, look out for the **Monumento al Bananero**, a towering statue of a workman carrying a mound of bananas. The crop is also celebrated with the **World Banana Festival**, a huge commercial fair that takes place here over the last ten days of September, with festivities and events, including the World Banana Queen beauty competition.

There's little in the way of tourist attractions, other than the modest one-room **museum** on Bolívar between Montalvo and 9 de Mayo (Mon–Sat 9am–4pm; free), which contains a handful of pre-Columbian artefacts and the odd fossil from the Puyango petrified forest (see p.315). Alternatively, squeeze your way among the overflowing fruit and vegetable stalls where Pasaje meets Montalvo and check out the bustling daily **market**.

ARRIVAL AND DEPARTURE   MACHALA

BY BUS

Machala is planning a new terminal terrestre, due to be completed by the end of 2017, but currently the various bus companies operate out of their own mini-terminals, most of which are clustered a few blocks east of the central square (see map opposite).

Destinations Cuenca, with Transportes Azuay, Rutas Orienses and Express Sucre (every 15–40min; 4hr); Guayaquil, with Ecuatoriano Pullman (from Huaquillas), CIFA and Rutas Orenses (every 10min; 3hr); Huaquillas, with Ecuatoriano Pullman and CIFA (every 10min; 1hr 30min; CIFA express bus every 20min; 1hr); Loja, with Transportes Loja (16 daily; 7hr); Piura in Peru, via Máncora, with CIFA (daily at 9am, 2.30pm, 9.30pm & 11.30pm; 6hr); Puyango

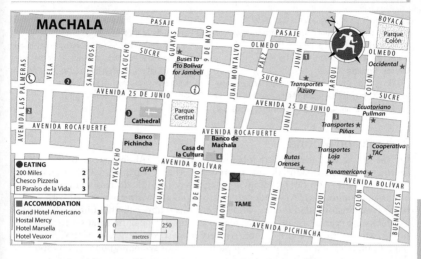

with CIFA (three daily; 2hr); Quito via Santo Domingo, with Panamericana and Santa (24 daily; 10hr); Zaruma, with TAC and Transportes Piñas (every 30min; 3hr).

BY PLANE

Machala's new airport, Aeropuerto Santa Rosa, is actually 28km south of the city at the town of Santa Rosa on the road to Peru. TAME operates daily flights to and from Quito (Mon–Fri 2 daily, Sat & Sun 1 daily; 1hr 10min; from $78). Though they maintain an office at the airport, TAME's main office is in Machala, on Juan Montalvo between Bolívar and Pichincha (☎07 2930129). A new international bus terminal opposite the airport opened at the end of 2015.

INFORMATION AND GETTING AROUND

Tourist office The I-Tur office is on the corner of 25 de Junio and 9 de Mayo on the *parque central* (Mon–Fri 8am–12.30pm, 3–6pm; ☎07 2968480).

By taxi Although Machala's centre is entirely walkable, taxis are abundant and cost $1–2 around the city centre.

ACTIVITIES

Boat trips Trips to the nearby car-free island of Jambelí offer close-up views of mangroves, a wide sandy beach with little shade, and a few basic restaurants and hotels. Boats (every 30min 7am–3.30pm; last boat back 6pm; 30min; $4 return) leave from Puerto Bolívar, Machala's busy international port, which is a mere 15min bus ride from town – catch the #13 bus as it passes along Sucre.

ACCOMMODATION

Grand Hotel Americano Tarqui and 25 de Junio ☎07 2966400. Good mid-range choice with tidy if rather small rooms and bathrooms. Overnight parking and breakfast included. **$59**

Hostal Mercy Junín between Olmedo and Sucre ☎07 2920116. Best budget option in town with eighteen simple, clean rooms set back from the street round a parking area. Cold water, cable TV and fan-ventilated ($4 extra for a/c). **$20**

Hotel Marsella Las Palmeras and 25 de Junio ☎07 2932460. Slightly faded but clean, carpeted en-suite rooms: the beds have hard mattresses, but there's cable TV, a/c and hot water. Rooms at the front are noisy. Breakfast included. **$35**

Hotel Veuxor Montalvo and Bolívar ☎07 2932423. Perhaps taking minimalism a tad too far, this hotel's spacious, gleaming tiled rooms, with a/c and large flatscreen TVs, offer the most comfortable, if overpriced, night's sleep in the city centre. Buffet breakfast included. **$101**

EATING

Outside the decent seafood restaurants along the pleasant malecón at Puerto Bolivar (see above), culinary offerings in Machala are distinctly paltry.

200 Miles 25 de Junio and Santa Rosa ☎07 2937051. Spotless, modern restaurant with attractive decor and ultra-efficient a/c, serving fresh, well-cooked fish and seafood (mains $9–12). Mon–Sat 9am–4pm.

Chesco Pizzería Guayas and 25 de Junio ☎04 2930154, ⓦchescopizzeria.com. Decent enough fast-food pizzas of varying sizes from $4 for a couple of slices to $22 for a vast family-sized pizza laden with toppings. Sat 10am–11pm, Sun from 3pm.

El Paraíso de la Vida Ayacucho between Rocafuerte and 25 de Junio ☎07 2930218. Inexpensive, mainly vegetarian restaurant with a pleasant dining room overlooking a little patio. Most mains $5 or under. Popular at lunchtime and does takeaways too. Mon–Fri 7.30am–8pm, Sat & Sun 7.30am–3pm.

Zaruma and around

Off the tourist trail about 86km inland from Machala, **ZARUMA** is one of the prettiest towns in Ecuador, despite its mining heritage. It has a fine collection of early twentieth-century timber buildings – though they are sadly decreasing in number – and is a charming place to wander around: steep, narrow streets are lined with brightly painted wooden houses, while a gorgeous **timber church**, built in 1912, overlooks the central square. There are also a couple of small **museums** – the municipal one, by the tourist office, is a very modest eclectic affair (Mon–Fri 8am–6pm; free) – and a very inviting public outdoor **swimming pool** (9am–8pm; $1) set in a fantastic hilltop location a ten-minute stroll away, above the town. Further uphill (20–30min) you'll reach the impressive **viewpoint at El Calvario**. For explorations further afield, into the beautiful **surrounding countryside**, contact the local tour operator (see below).

Mina de Sexmo

End of Calle El Sexmo, a 10min walk from the town centre • Daily 8am–5pm • Free

Mina de Sexmo, a small museum on the site of a five-hundred-year-old mine which closed in the late 1980s, is worth a visit. After a short video, you don protective boots and hat and are guided 400m down an old mine shaft by an ex-miner to peer at quartz formations and learn about mining. Zaruma has been associated with mining since conquistadors first established a settlement here in 1549 to exploit the area's large **gold** deposits, and their mines flourished until the eighteenth century when the seams were thought to be exhausted. Yet almost a century later, a Quito geologist analysing local rocks discovered a high gold content, sparking another gold-mining boom in 1880. Artisanal mining continues in the area today but on a vastly reduced scale, though large-scale extraction looms on the horizon once again.

ARRIVAL AND DEPARTURE
ZARUMA AND AROUND

By bus Zaruma's two bus depots are on Honorato Márquez, the main road out of town. If you miss the two direct buses to Loja, take a Machala bus and get off at the junction with the main Machala–Loja road, at Saracay, and catch one of the frequent Loja-bound buses from Machala or Huaquillas.

Destinations Guayaquil (TAC 6 daily; Transportes Piñas 4 daily; 6hr); Loja (TAC 2 daily at 3am & 6am; Transportes Piñas 3 daily at 2am, 8.30am and 12.45pm; 5hr; or last departure from Portovelo at 1.30pm); Machala (TAC 20 daily; Transportes Piñas hourly; 3hr).

By minibus Minibuses to Portovelo, 13km south of Zaruma in the valley, leave from opposite the Ferretería Americana on Sucre, the main street (every 10min; 15min).

INFORMATION AND TOURS

Tourist office A small, helpful I-Tur office is located just off the square on 9 de Octubre (Mon–Sat 8am–noon, 2–6pm) and can supply you with a rudimentary map.

Tour operator Oro Adventure, Plaza de la Independencia (☎07 2972761 or ☎0993094707), is run by the town's most experienced guide, Tito Castillo, and offers a variety of tours (in English or Spanish), taking in waterfalls, rock formations, petroglyphs, old mines and the Reserva Buenaventura (see box opposite).

ACCOMMODATION

★**Hostería El Jardín** Av Isidro Ayora 2km outside town ☎07 2972706, ⓦhosteriaeljardinzaruma.com. This friendly family-run lodging has eight simple, spacious en-suite tiled rooms with large windows, and a delightful patio-café (breakfast only) overlooking well-manicured tropical gardens brimming with birdlife. **$35**

Hotel Blacio Sucre and El Sexmo ☎07 2972045. Hospitable, cheap hotel with fourteen well-kept en-suite rooms (doubles and triples) with hot water and cable TV. Good value. **$20**

Hotel Romeria Plaza de la Independencia

☎07 2972618. In a lovely corner location on the main square, this hotel has bags of character, with uneven creaking wooden floors, old pictures and a communal balcony. Rooms are simple but comfortable. **$30**

Zaruma Colonial Sucre and El Sexmo ☎07 2972742, ⓔhotelzarumacolonial@hotmail.com. Friendly and probably the best value in town, with bright, modern tiled rooms and bathrooms – some on the top floors have great views across the valley; beds have wooden headboards and there are flat-screen TVs. **$34**

EATING AND DRINKING

200 Millas Honorato Márquez ☎07 2972600. The town's best restaurant is down the road from the bus depots; known for its seafood and *tigrillos* (mashed green plantain with onion, cheese, and sometimes meat). Mains $5–8. Daily 8am–9pm.

Imperdible Corner of Bolívar and Plaza de la Independencia ☎07 2973643. Cosy corner coffee shop with an affable Ecuadorian owner and an Italian chef

providing pizza, lasagne and the like ($7–9). Also serves sandwiches, shakes and cakes though there's less choice in the evenings. Mon–Sat 9am–9pm.

Tangobar Plaza de la Independencia. Bar-restaurant that serves inexpensive local specialities during the day – *tamales, bolones, tigrillos, humitas* and almuerzos – and becomes more of a bar in the evening. Mon–Sat 9am–9pm.

Bosque Petrificado de Puyango

Puyango • Daily 8am–5pm (last entry 3.30pm) • ☎07 3096013 • $1 entry, but a tip for the guide is appreciated • Four direct buses a day from Machala bound for Alamor (5.30am, 9.05am, 12.15pm with CIFA; and 1pm with Transportes Loja; 2hr); alternatively take a Huaquillas-bound bus to Arenillas and change to a Loja-bound bus from the border, or a camioneta colectivo bound for Alamor, to the bridge at Puyango, from where a camioneta can take you to the visitor centre for $6–10 return • Camping is possible ($5/tent) but there are no cooking facilities

One hundred kilometres south of Machala, spread over a dusty, semi-arid river valley close to the Peruvian border, the **Bosque Petrificado de Puyango** (Puyango petrified forest) is the largest of its kind in South America. It contains dozens of enormous **fossilized tree trunks** up to 120 million years old, many of which you can see from the 8km of marked paths wending through the mineralized wood. At the **visitor centre**, where you pay and register your visit, you can hire a **guide** to show you around the site; they don't speak English, but will point out many hidden fossils you'd otherwise miss, such as the imprints of ferns concealed by riverside plants. The most impressive relics are the giant tree trunks, types of

---

RESERVA BUENAVENTURA

Signposted off the main road to Machala, 7km west of Piñas, the **Reserva Buenaventura** protects around twenty square kilometres of precious foothill cloudforest. It is home to more than three hundred bird species, including thirty species of hummingbird and the extraordinary-looking long-wattled umbrellabird, as well as being rich in orchids. **Trails** (1hr 30min–4hr) criss-cross the reserve; with advance notice, **day-visitors** ($15 entry fee) can explore them. It's easiest to reach the reserve by private transport, or to visit on a tour from Zaruma (see opposite). The reserve is managed by Jocotours (☎02 505129, ⓦjocotoursecuador.com) affiliated to the Fundación Jocotoco (☎02 2272013, ⓦfjocotoco .org), which offers accommodation at a simple wooden **lodge** that has five en-suite rooms, predominantly with bunk beds, and hot water ($280 for a double, inclusive of all meals and access to trails; guiding services extra).

araucaria, which grew in the region millions of years ago; many are in fragments but a few are almost whole, the largest being 11m long and 1.6m in diameter. The area is also inhabited by more than 120 species of **birdlife**, including beautiful red-masked parakeets.

The fossil museum
Near the visitor centre • Included in entry fee for Bosque Petrificado de Puyango

The small **museum** houses a stash of incredible exhibits, including many marine fossils dating from when much of the region was beneath the sea, now 50km away. The collection includes fossilized pieces of fruit, including a *chirimoya* (a custard apple – you can still see the pips), a ray, a small tortoise and an octopus with clearly visible eyes. Perhaps the most intriguing pieces are the large, perfectly oval stones you can hold in your hands – and which some believe are dinosaur egg fossils.

7 Huaquillas and the Peruvian border

Some 73km southwest of Machala, the border town of **HUAQUILLAS** is a pleasant surprise. After an injection of civic cash, the centre, at least, is fairly easy on the eye: a floral central park with fountains and benches, neatly cobbled streets with pavements and a couple of decent hotels. True, the main commercial street is still crammed with hundreds of hectic market stalls selling cheap clothes, shoes, bags, food and electrical goods but there are worse border towns.

ARRIVAL AND DEPARTURE HUAQUILLAS

By bus All buses arrive at and leave from their company depots within a few blocks of the international bridge (see map below).

Destinations Cuenca (Transportes Azuay 8 daily; 5hr); Machala (CIFA every 10min until 8pm; 1hr 30min; express bus every 20min 1hr); Guayaquil, with CIFA, Ecuatoriano Pullman and Rutas Orenses (every 20–30min; 4hr–4hr 30min); Loja (Transportes Loja 11.30am, 6pm; 5hr); Quito (Panamericana 10 daily; Transportes Occidentales 4 daily; 12hr).

ACCOMMODATION

La Habana Córdovez and Santa Rosa. Sparkling new four-storey hotel with some large rooms offering nice views – all with monsoon showers – above the pleasant open-fronted restaurant that has long been popular for its affordable seafood, grills, breakfasts and almuerzos. Mains from $6. Restaurant open daily 7.30am–9pm.

Breakfast included. __$40__

Hotel Rodey Córdovez and 10 de Agosto ☎07 2995581. Long-standing budget hotel offering basic, clean en-suite rooms with fans, or a/c for a tad more, and satellite TV. __$12__

HUAQUILLAS

ACCOMMODATION		EATING	
La Habana	2	La Habana	1
Hotel Rodey	1		

CROSSING THE BORDER

The Río Zarumilla, hugging the southwestern edge of Huaquillas, forms the border, and the only exit/entry point used to be the old international bridge in central Huaquillas leading to the small town of **Aguas Verdes** in Peru. Once one of South America's most dangerous border crossings, it can now be a relatively stress-free event if you take an international bus (see p.305) that will stop at one of the two brand-new 24-hr CEBAF (Centro Binacional de Atención de Frontera) complexes outside Huaquillas and Zarumilla (Peru), which lie either side of a new road bridge across the river that effectively bypasses the two border towns. Since these twin complexes house both Ecuadorian and Peruvian immigration you only need to visit one of them.

IMMIGRATION

If you do not arrive in your own transport or on an international bus, crossing the border is much more hassle, and costlier. Ecuador's CEBAF is 4km southeast of Huaquillas, and Peru's equivalent is a similar distance outside Zarumilla. Unfortunately, the buses to/from Machala (or Guayaquil) to/from Huaquillas do not pass near immigration, though they can drop you off at a roundabout outside town, where you may be able to flag down a taxi. However, it is better to go into Huaquillas itself, alight at the bus station, and then hop in a taxi (easily available at the *parque central*) to immigration ($3). After immigration procedures, you'll need to take another taxi across the new bridge to the Peruvian CEBAF outside Zarumilla, several kilometres away ($3), and then another taxi back into Aguas Verdes, to catch onward transport. Transportes Flores (@floreshnos.pe) and CIVA (@excluciva.pe) operate onward connections south to towns such as Tumbes, Máncora, Piura and Lima.

INTERNATIONAL BUSES

Several international buses now provide transport between Guayaquil and various Peruvian cities. Recommended operators include Peruvian companies Cruz del Sur (@cruzdelsur.com.pe) and CIVA (@excluciva.pe), which offer services between Guayaquil and Lima, stopping off in Tumbes, Máncora and Piura. Ecuadorian company CIFA International (@cifainternational.com) also operates services between Guayaquil or Machala and Piura, stopping at Tumbes and Máncora. All operators have offices at the Terminal Terrestre in Guayaquil (see p.305). Transportes Azuay (@transportesazuay.com) also runs a nightly bus (9.30pm) between Cuenca and Chiclayo, in Peru, stopping at Piura and Máncora.

MONEY

Change as little money as possible at the border, be it in Huaquillas or Aguas Verdes, as the rates aren't good. Official moneychangers in Ecuador wear IDs, but always check calculations and cash received before handing anything over. Be aware that at the beginning of 2016, Peru changed its currency from Nuevo Soles to simply Soles, though both sets of notes and coins are valid. If you are crossing from Peru into Ecuador, note that there is a Banco Pichincha with an ATM on the corner of calles Machala and Costa Rica in Huaquillas.

West to the Santa Elena Peninsula

West of Guayaquil, the busy E-40 highway heads to the westernmost tip of the mainland, the **Santa Elena Peninsula**. It's an especially busy route on Friday evenings when droves of *guayaquileños* flee the uncomfortable heat of the city for the cooling breezes of the Pacific. Around 65km west, a side road branches south to the easy-going, somewhat shabby little town of **Playas**, the closest beach resort to Guayaquil and always heaving with visitors on summer weekends in high season (Dec–April).

Continuing west along the main road, you enter increasingly dry and scrubby terrain as you approach the Santa Elena Peninsula, whose three main towns – **Santa Elena**, **La Libertad** and **Salinas** – merge into one another almost seamlessly. The peninsula is of great **archeological** interest, as it was originally occupied by the country's most ancient cultures, such as the **Las Vegas** and the **Valdivia**. The most impressive archeological site and museum is the fabulous **Amantes de Sumpa**, near Santa Elena, showcasing the tomb of two eight-thousand-year-old skeletons locked in an embrace. However, the peninsula is best known for its **beaches**, in particular the moderately glitzy and often crowded resort of Salinas.

Playas

About 65km west of Guayaquil along the E-40 highway, in the dreary little town of **Progreso**, a major side road branches 26km south through dry scrubland to the seaside town of **PLAYAS**. As the closest sandy beach to Guayaquil, Playas (whose official but largely ignored name is General Villamil) bulges with city visitors during the summer months and has slowly metamorphosed from a sleepy fishing village into a flourishing holiday resort over the last few decades. Despite the transformation, Playas has a lived-in, unpretentious feel and a slow pace of life. The chief attraction is the long and pleasant **beach**, where fishermen still haul in their nets and you may be able to spot a couple of traditional, single-sail balsa rafts, which were characteristic of the area for many centuries, though most have now been replaced with motorboats.

There's nothing to do in Playas apart from lie on the sands, surf or swim in the sea and enjoy the fresh seafood, though if you feel like exploring you can walk 5km northwest along the beach to the **Punta Pelado**, whose usually deserted sands are backed by rugged cliffs. Alternatively, a thirty-minute bus ride away, in either the fishing villages of **Puerto El Morro** or **Posorja** you can hire a boat to take you out into the mangroves to see bottlenose dolphins (avoid the weekend scrum when the poor creatures are harassed by boats). Boats can also ferry you further afield, to **Isla de Pájaros** (officially Isla Manglecito), where you can see a vast 6000-strong colony of magnificent frigatebirds, as well as pelicans and blue-footed boobies. Boats from Posorja also provide access to the large and as yet undeveloped **Isla Puná**, where small communities of fishermen and shellfish collectors are just waking up to the possibilities of tourism.

ARRIVAL AND GETTING AROUND   PLAYAS

By bus Transportes Villamil and Transportes Posorja buses leave from Guayaquil's bus terminal (every 10min, until 9pm; 2hr) and drop you off in Playas behind the town plaza, just three blocks from the seafront. Local buses for Puerto El Morro leave from just before the municipal market, three and a half blocks from the church (every 20min from 6.30am–7pm, last bus back 6.30pm; 30min). To travel west along the peninsula, take a Guayaquil-bound bus from Playas to the main square in Progreso; here pick-up trucks ($1) will take you 2km west along the highway to a bus stop, where you can catch a west-bound bus from Guayaquil, provided it has space.

By taxi The central area of town is very compact, but if you don't feel like walking, you can hail a mototaxi. For trips further out of town, unsigned pick-up trucks that serve as taxis can be found on Avenida Guayaquil, off the main square.

ACCOMMODATION

Arena Caliente Corner of Paquisha and Estrada ☎04 2761580, ⓦarenacalientehotel.com. Despite the grubby windows this centrally located place is relatively smart, with its pleasant pool and clean, tiled rooms, equipped with a/c, private bathroom and hot water. It also has a popular restaurant and breakfast is included. $70

Hostal Caracol 3 de Noviembre and Malecón ☎04 2760868. A few hundred metres northwest of the centre, this hotel has a communal balcony and rooftop terrace, which overlook the skateboard park and offer great views of the beach. Clean double and family rooms with decent beds, cable TV and fans but only cold water. $25

Hostal Promenade Roldos, half a block from the beach ☎04 2762253. Centrally located and run by a Swiss-Ecuadorian couple, this light, airy hotel has 12 simple, spotless rooms – some with balconies – with tiled, spacious bathrooms, hot water, cable TV, and a/c. Good value for solo travellers ($20/person). $40

★**Posada del Sueco** Km2 on the road to Data ☎0990207629, ⓦposadadelsueco.com. A selection of homely accommodation just off the beach, ranging from a handful of doubles and ocean-view suites to a self-catering family cabin, arranged round a delightful shady tropical garden with plenty of spots to relax: in the hammock house, on the sundeck, or in the small sparkling pool. A real treat. Double $58; self-catering cabin $90

EATING AND DRINKING

Most of the **hotels** out of the centre have their own restaurants specializing in fresh fish and seafood whereas the majority of the *comedores* and *cevicherías* along the **beach** are only open at weekends and in high season.

La Cabaña de Juacho Malecón, southeast of the centre. Pleasant wooden, two-storey bamboo and thatch bar on the beach, serving up serious cocktails or a jug of caipirinha for $30. A few Esmeraldan dishes are also on offer from around $8. 10am–2am; Dec–April Mon–Sat; May–Nov Thurs–Sat.

El Pescadito Roldos. The restaurant that hotels tend to recommend to foreign tourists, so pricier than many

ACTIVITIES AND TOURS AROUND SALINAS

Deep-sea **sport fishing** is very popular around Salinas and can be arranged through Pesca Tours, on the Malecón and Rumiñahui (☎04 2772391, ✉fishing@pescatours.com), who charge $800 for up to six people for a full day, or $450 for a half-day in low season; the best time of year is between November and February but you can fish year-round. Avista Travel on Enríque Gallo (☎0997058171, ✆facebook.com/avistatravelsalinas), works with certified guides and can arrange sport-fishing and **whale-watching** tours from June–Sept (around $25–30). Knowledgeable Dutch naturalist Ben Haase (☎04 2778329, ✉bhaase2012@gmail.com), at the Museo de Ballenas and *Oystercatcher* restaurant, leads **birdwatching** tours to the Ecuasal salt pans south of town ($50) – one of the best places in the country to see the Chilean flamingo and more than 120 other species, including many migratory birds. Ben Haase and Fernando Félix (✉fefelix@hotmail.com) at the museum can also offer advice on organizing **whale-watching** trips.

in the centre (mains from $8) but the quality is consistent. The menu is varied though inevitably with plenty of seafood. Tues–Sun noon–4 or 5pm; Fri & Sat 7–10pm.

La Sason del Cholito#1 Paquisha and Roldos. Very popular *cevichería* and restaurant offering mains from around $7–8 with *ceviche marinera* and *arroz marinera* the house specialities, alongside oysters – try them breaded or au gratin. Dec–April daily 8am–8pm; May–Nov closed Wed.

7

Salinas

The highway ends 170km from Guayaquil at **SALINAS**, Ecuador's swankiest southern beach resort. Arriving at its graceful seafront avenue, the Malecón, feels like stepping into another world: gone are the ramshackle streets characteristic of Ecuador's coastal towns, replaced by a gleaming boulevard lined with glitzy, high-rise condominiums sweeping around a large, beautiful bay. Closer inspection, however, reveals the streets behind the Malecón to be as dusty and potholed as anywhere else, but this doesn't seem to bother anyone – it's the **beach** that counts here, with clean, golden sand and warm(ish), calm waters, safe for swimming, and water toys to rent. In high season (Dec–April) you'll be sharing the sands with droves of vacationing Ecuadorians. The best time to enjoy Salinas is on weekdays in December, early January or March. Around Carnaval and on summer weekends it gets unbearably packed, while from April to November it can be overcast and dreary.

There are also some deserted stretches of coastline to explore around Salinas, such as **La Chocolatera** and **Punto Carnero**, as well as the salt pans of **Escuasal** for bird-watchers, and an impressive archeological museum, **Los Amantes de Sumpa**; all these attractions lie within a $5–6-dollar taxi ride from Salinas.

Museo de Ballenas

General Enríquez Gallo • Daily 8am–5pm by appointment, or when the *Oystercatcher* restaurant is open • No charge, but donations welcome • ☎ 04 2778329, ✆ museodeballenas.org

The small but captivating **Museo de Ballenas**, attached to the *Oystercatcher* restaurant, features a 12-metre skeleton of a humpback whale, skulls and bones of other cetaceans and preserved dolphins, all of which were washed ashore, as well as some informative text on whales.

ARRIVAL AND DEPARTURE   SALINAS AND AROUND

By bus CLP buses from Guayaquil (every 10min; 2hr 30min) via a short sojourn in the sparkling new Terminal Terrestre Regional Sumpa Santa Elena (14km east of Salinas), arrive in Salinas, along the Malecón and continue to the avenue's western end. Arriving from the north, change at Santa Elena and catch a local no. 10 bus bound for Salinas, which leaves right outside the terminal. Catch a bus back to Santa Elena along Avenida General Enríquez Gallo.

INFORMATION AND GETTING AROUND

By bicycle In the high season, bikes can be rented from a couple of places along the beachfront ($10–15/day).

Tourist office There is a sporadically functioning I-Tur kiosk on the beach close to the yacht club.

ACCOMMODATION

Chesco's Almar Malecón by the Banco de Guayaquil, ☎ 04 2770875, ⓦ chescosplace.com. You can't beat the location: bang on the beach with a hammock-hung balcony bar overlooking the action. Nice courtyard seating with more hammocks, plus clean brightly decorated rooms at decent rates. No kitchen but breakfast is inexpensive. Dorms $15; doubles $40

Cocos Malecón and Tomalá ☎ 04 2770361, ⓦ cocos -hostal.com. Friendly though rather faded waterfront

hostal with a lively patio bar-restaurant. Small but nicely decorated en-suite rooms of varying prices, all with a/c, hot water, and cable TV. Laundry and parking facilities. Good low-season discounts. $50

Hotel Blue Marlin del Pacífico Corner of Los Ficus and Nuñez ☎ 04 2773357. Neat and well-maintained hotel offering en-suite doubles, triples, quads and suites. Rooms upstairs are brighter and there's a small pool and patio breakfast area. Good value. $30

EATING

La Bella Italia Malecón at Rumiñahui ☎ 04 2771361. Genuine Italian restaurant serving home-made pasta, crisp pizzas cooked in a wood-fired oven and decent steaks (mains from $7). The dining room is divided into formal and less formal areas. Daily 10am until late.

Café Jazz Fidón Tomala and Gallo ☎ 0980032326. Come here for a breakfast, or a relaxed latte and a muffin later in the day, with the occasional Russian speciality thrown onto the menu. This very pleasant plant-filled patio café has wicker furniture and a mellow jazz soundtrack. Also with rooms to rent. Daily 8am–1pm, 6–9pm.

Cafetería del Sol Malecón next to the Capitanía ☎ 04

2772159. For once in Salinas, you're paying as much for the quality of the cuisine (mains $11–17) – delicious, nicely presented seafood dishes – as for the beachside location. Daily 7.30am–10pm, Fri & Sat until midnight.

Don Kleber's Cevichelandia at Gallo and Las Palmeras. A good bet for a cheap seafood lunch – offering better quality and higher standards of cleanliness than some of its neighbours. Tues–Sun 7.30am–6pm.

Oystercatcher Gallo, by the Museo de Ballenas ☎ 04 2777335. The opening hours may be limited, but it's worth the effort for some of the best oysters in town in this intimate bar-restaurant Fri & Sat 10am–8pm, Sun 10am–6pm.

La Chocolatera and Punta Brava

The rocky headland of **La Chocolatera**, a taxi ride ($5) west of Salinas, is the westernmost point of mainland Ecuador; it's battered by powerful waves that churn the waters chocolate brown at high tide – hence its name. La Chocolatera sits within the perimeter of a naval base where, at the entrance, you'll have to show your passport. Within the base, to the south, **Punta Brava** is home to one of the northernmost colonies of sea lions on the continent.

Punta Carnero and Ecuasal

Some 10km southeast of Salinas, **Punta Carnero** is a lonely, windswept promontory with superb views of the fifteen-kilometre stretch of beach flanking it. Pounding waves and strong currents make swimming at the beach inadvisable, but it's still a fabulous place to treat yourself to some sun and solitude. A few kilometres back towards Salinas along the coast are the salt pans of **Ecuasal**, which are home to thousands of wading and shore birds, but also attract vast flocks of migratory birds, especially in August and September.

Museo Los Amantes de Sumpa

Av Balseca, Barrio Amantes de Sumpa, Santa Elena • Tues–Fri 8.30am–4.30pm, Sat, Sun and holidays 10am–4pm • $1 • ☎ 04 2941020 • From Salinas, take a bus heading east towards Santa Elena and ask the driver to drop you at the turn-off to the museum, signposted to the south of the highway, a couple of blocks away • A taxi from Salinas should cost no more than $6

The museum **Los Amantes de Sumpa**, on the western outskirts of Santa Elena is built on the site of one of the oldest burial grounds in South America, established from 6000 BC by the ancient **Las Vegas** culture. Some two hundred human skeletons were excavated here, including the remains of **the lovers of Sumpa** – the skeletons of a man and woman, about 25 years old when they died, are buried in an eternal embrace. Their tomb, on display at the museum, makes an unforgettable sight, and the accompanying displays on the Las Vegas and other coastal cultures are excellent, ranging from funerary offerings such as shells, knives and colourful pebbles to a reconstruction of a typical *montuvio* house.

Ruta del Spondylus

A paved road runs 137km from **Santa Elena** up the coast to **Puerto Cayo** – a stretch of shoreline that offers fantastic views of long, empty beaches and passes a string of modest fishing villages and resorts. This coastal highway forms part of the **Ruta del Spondylus**, named after the large reddish shell that was of great pecuniary and religious significance to early cultures; the route, which runs the length of Ecuador's coast, spotlights Ecuador's pre-Columbian heritage and cultural diversity, as well as its varied natural attractions.

For much of the way the road runs through arid, featureless landscapes, passing the village of **Valdivia**, after which the ancient Valdivian culture is named (see p.381), bypassing the attractive little seaside village of **Manglaralto** before arriving at hedonistic **Montañita**; initially only frequented by surfers, it is now a full-scale backpackers' beach hangout and the place where young middle-class *quiteños* and *guayacos* come to let their hair down. Beyond this, the road swings briefly inland, skirting the lush fringes of the **Cordillera Chongón-Colonche**, before returning to the sea and the mellow coastal hideaway of **Ayampe**. Further north is **Puerto López**, a base for **whale-watching** trips (June–Sept) and visits to the stunning **Parque Nacional Machalilla**, which takes in a major tract of tropical dry forest, fabulous beaches and the **Isla de la Plata** – favoured by bird lovers as a cheaper alternative to the Galápagos Islands.

7

GETTING AROUND   **THE RUTA DEL SPONDYLUS**

BY BUS
Many buses run up and down this southern section of the Ruta del Spondylus. There are ten direct services a day from Guayaquil bus terminal to Montañita and Olón (3hr) and eight to Puerto López via Jipijapa (3hr 30min). In addition, numerous Transportes Manglaralto buses bound for Jipijapa (every 15–30min; 3hr 50min) and Manta (18 daily; 5hr) run along this stretch of coastline from Santa Elena approximately every 15–20mins during daylight hours, passing Montañita (1hr 30min), Ayampe (2hr 15min) and Puerto López (2hr 50min). They stop and pick up almost anywhere en route. The Terminal Terrestre Regional Sumpa in Santa Elena, 14km east of Salinas and 156km west of Guayaquil, is the main transport hub for the Santa Elena Peninsula and for coastal buses.

Montañita

The surfing resort of **MONTAÑITA**, roughly two-thirds of the way between the Santa Elena peninsula and Puerto López, is like nowhere else on the Ecuadorian coast. Crammed into the centre of a small village are straw-roofed, bamboo-walled hostales and pizzerias advertised by bright wooden signs, while chilled-out backpackers lounge around in shorts and bikinis and surfers stride up the streets clutching boards. Everything is within easy

---

LEARNING SPANISH BY THE SEA
If poring over your exercises while stretched out on a beach towel helps ease the pain of doing homework, then Montañita is the place for you to learn Spanish. Two good language schools operate in in the village, offering twenty hours per week of one-to-one ($180–240) or small group lessons ($140–170), which can also be combined with surfing, yoga and other activities. Montañita Spanish School, El Tigrillo (☎04 2060116, ⓦmontanitaspanishschool.com), is slightly pricier but well established with its own hostel – lovely eco-cabins with a pool, jacuzzi and garden – or homestay, and a greater range of activities. Marazul Spanish School, just north of the river (☎0982511853, ⓦecuador-spanishschool.com), is also reliable and can organize hostel or homestay accommodation for you.

walking distance of the **seafront** and the main street, **Rocafuerte**. There's a certain 1960s, dope-fuelled atmosphere to Montañita that may not appeal to everybody, and it reaches a height during *la temporada* from late December to April. If Montañita's hedonistic scene gets too much, try the attractive village of **Manglaralto**, 4km to the south, which is quieter, with leafy square and long beautiful beach, as well as a handful of inexpensive places to stay: it's easily accessible by bus or taxi ($2–3).

Outside these months, visitors dwindle and the skies cloud over, but the hotels stay open all year catering to the steady stream of surfers who are attracted by some of the best **surfing conditions** in Ecuador – though beware of riptides: waves are strong, consistent and range from one to three metres in height, and there's a long right break lying off the northern end of the beach by the rocky promontory of **La Punta**. The best waves are in the summer months (Jan–April), when the water temperature averages 22–25°C. Every February, an **international surfing competition** is held here over Carnaval, attracting contestants from as far away as the US and Australia.

Around the rocky headland 4km north of Montañita, the village of **Olón** is graced by a long pale beach and gentler waves, and a mellower vibe that can be enjoyed in an increasing array of accommodation.

ARRIVAL AND GETTING AROUND   MONTAÑITA

By bus Manglaralto buses run up and down the coast (every 15–20min) between Santa Elena (1hr 30min) and either Manta (3hr 40min) or Jipijapa (2hr 40min) Puerto López (1hr 40min), dropping and picking up passengers at the entrance to the village, 150m from the beach. More comfortable express CLP buses to and from Guayaquil (3hr–3hr 30min) operate ten times a day; the ticket office and bus stop are on the main road, just north of the

entrance to the village.
By taxi Shared taxis (charging slightly more than the bus fare) shuttle between the village of Simon Bolívar, just north of Valdivia, and Olón, 4km north of Montañita. In Calle Segundo Rosales at the entrance to Montañita, there is a taxi rank with fixed rates to various destinations, including Guayaquil ($80).

ACCOMMODATION

Accommodation is either in the **village centre**, where partying will curtail sleep at weekends and in high season; across the main road up the hill, in **El Tigrillo**; or in calmer **La Punta**, 1km north along the beach. New **hostels** open all the time, with basic rooms, the occasional balcony, hammocks and wi-fi generally standard. Prices are outrageously hiked in **peak periods**, but bargains can be had midweek off-season.

★**Balsa Surf Camp** La Punta ☎04 2060075, ⓦbalsasurfcamp.com. Upmarket surf camp nicely designed in wood, bamboo and thatch with tropical hammock-strewn gardens, a bar-restaurant and TV/DVD area. Spacious en-suite rooms all have nice touches, with surfboard storage and balconies. Don't miss the VW camper van room. Good deals in low season. Breakfast included. $85
Casa del Sol La Punta ☎04 2648287, ⓦcasadel solmontanita.com. Agreeable, wood and thatch rooms with private baths and hot water set round a charming tropical garden. The rooms have small balconies, terraces and hammocks with fans or a/c ($10 extra). There's a TV room and restaurant with wi-fi, and surf lessons and yoga are offered. Breakfast included. Dorm $18; doubles $50
Charo's Hostal Malecón at Rocafuerte ☎04 2060044. Fed up with rustic bamboo and wood? Then try this organized bricks-and-mortar hostal of 26 small, basic tiled double or family rooms with cable TV and a/c, spread over three floors. Upstairs rooms are lighter, though water pressure can be an

issue. Some have sea views and private balconies. All share a small pool with a bar, jacuzzi and tiny garden, dotted with deckchairs and hammocks. Good value. $45
Hotel Hurvínek 10 de Agosto towards the football pitch ☎0985110106. Hostel-like hotel in town comprising brightly painted fan-ventilated rooms (for 2–5 people) judiciously designed in brick, wood and bamboo with a modicum of rustic furniture. Buffet breakfast included. A good choice. $49
Paradise by Dharma Across the river bridge from the centre ☎0967606620, ⓦparadisebydharma.com. Behind the Disneylike Dharma Beach, this quiet spot possesses spacious grounds, dotted with palms and hibiscus, and a pleasant lawn. Rooms are en suite, clean and compact (with fan or a/c for $10 extra), each with hammocks and chairs to lounge in. There's also a communal kitchen. $40
Tiki Limbo Chiriboga and Segunda ☎04 2060019 ⓦtikilimbo.com. Impressive bamboo-and-thatch structure with great social areas: there are sofas, cushions and hammocks to lounge in, plus a vast book

exchange, pool table, buzzing restaurant and on-site surf school and shop. The rooms too are a cut above most cheap-end hostels; even the dorm has a/c. Dorm $\overline{\$22}$; doubles $\overline{\$55}$

EATING

There's a wide choice of average **café-restaurants** in the centre, most moderately priced, offering a seafood menu supplemented by pizzas, pasta, pancakes and tropical fruit juices.

Hierba Buena Rocafuerte and Chiriboga ☎ 0990415179. Well-cooked inexpensive Ecuadorian mains ($6–7); the predominantly seafood dishes are often steamed and accompanied by welcome portions of green vegetables, but you can't escape the vast TV screen. Daily 9am–11pm.

Hola Ola 10 de Agosto and Primera ☎ 04 2060118. Well-established social hub that does everything pretty well, from falafel and hummus to filling breakfasts and substantial salads and pizzas (mains from $9). Turns into a bar-disco in the evening at weekends, occasionally hosting live acts. Daily 8am until late.

Papillón Los Cokteleros and Chiriboga ☎ 0993521551. Psychedelically painted with the eponymous butterflies, this place specializes in sweet and savoury crepes (including a crepe happy hour) and serves up a good variety of breakfasts ($4–6). Watch out for the specials. Mon–Sat 8am until late.

★**Tiburón** Chiriboga and Rocafuerte ☎ 0993592206. Upstairs restaurant serving excellent Thai and Ecuadorian cooking (mains from $7); don't miss the chance to try one of their delicious curries or the substantial lunchtime empanadas. Daily 11am–11pm.

Tiki Limbo Chiriboga and Segunda ☎ 04 2060019 ⓦ tikilimbo.com. Great bamboo lounge-restaurant with large comfy cushions – a place to dine or chill with a drink. Choose from generous portions of Texmex, Italian or Oriental fare (mains from $8), but leave room for dessert and be prepared to wait when busy. Daily 8am until late.

DRINKING AND NIGHTLIFE

All of the café-restaurants listed above are good places to enjoy a cocktail as the sun goes down, while Montañita's nightlife heats up. Those on a tighter budget head for Calle de los Cokteleros, lined with stalls competing to give you the cheapest most lethal mix possible, before filling up with street food to absorb the alcohol.

Caña Grill Los Cokteleros ☎ 04 2060086. This cavernous bamboo construction is a classic party venue with live music most nights – Latin, rock and reggae – drinks specials and a sandy dancefloor. A no-frills Montañita institution. Mon–Sat 5pm until late.

Nativa Bambú Malecón and Primera. Montañita's largest disco – a multistorey bar-restaurant (Tues–Sat 10am–11pm) with breezy top-floor dancefloor offering

7

ACTIVITIES IN MONTAÑITA

There's no doubt that surfing is the signature activity of Montañita – perhaps alongside partying these days – but it is certainly not the only way to spend your time.

SURFING

Although Montañita's waves are best suited to experienced surfers, beginners can learn, when conditions are favourable, by taking one-to-one or small-group **lessons** (around $25 for a 1hr 30min class). Recommended instructors can be found at Balsa Surf Camp (ⓦ balsasurfcamp .com; see opposite), Montañita Surf School at *Casa del Sol* (ⓦ casadelsolmontanita.com; see opposite), Montañita Surf Club at the back of the beach towards La Punta ⓦ facebook.com /MontanitaSurfClub, or Tiki Limbo Surf School, at the hotel of the same name (ⓦ tikilimbo.com; see opposite). Surfboards (*tablas*) can be rented all over the village for about $15 a day, and there are several shops selling surf gear.

TOURS & OTHER ACTIVITIES

There's a growing range of available land-based activities such as mountain biking, horse riding and trekking, often round the inland village of Dos Mangos, as well as whale-watching excursions (June–Sept) and trips to Isla de la Plata from Puerto López, although they're obviously cheaper and easier to organize from Puerto López itself (see box, p.327). Montañitours on the corner of Rocafuerte and Chiriboga (☎ 04 2060043, ⓦ montanitours .com) offers a good selection of these activities whereas Parapente Montañita, on Segundo Rosales and Rocafuerte (☎ 0987011635, ⓦ parapentemontanita.com), specializes in tandem paragliding flights ($35) and courses.

stellar sea views. It hosts themed evenings – Caribbean and Latin – plus ladies' night with big-name DJs and live bands. Generally plays electrónica on the first floor and Latin on the top deck. Variable cover charge. Tues–Sat 5pm until late.

Rosa Mistika Hostal Rosa Mistika, La Punta ☎04 2060171. Right at the back of the beach with mellow music, low seating and large cushions, this is the perfect spot for a relaxing sundowner. Daily 8am until late.

Ayampe

Some 20km north of Montañita, the **Cordillera Chongón-Colonche** begins to rise – a range of 800-metre-high hills, covered by some of the last remnants of coastal forest in the region. After veering inland, the road rejoins the coast at the lush yet unassuming village of **AYAMPE**, home only to a handful of farming families and set back from a huge, empty beach pounded by powerful breakers, its golden sands forming a striking contrast with the deep-green vegetation inland. It's a beautiful, tranquil and little-known surfing spot that has only recently begun to attract visitors to its handful of rustic hideaways and casual restaurants; what's more, the protective community is keen to ensure it remains this way.

ARRIVAL AND DEPARTURE
AYAMPE

By bus Ayampe is 45min north of Montañita and 30min south of Puerto López. Take any of the Manglaralto buses that run up and down the coast road (every 15–20min) between Santa Elena and either Manta or Jipijapa via Puerto López. The bus stop is on the main road by the main entrance to the village.

ACCOMMODATION AND EATING

Cabañas La Iguana Just south of the village, 100m back from the beach ☎05 2575165 or ☎0980163825, ⓦhotelayampe.com. Simple, but attractive, inexpensive double or family cabins of whitewashed stone, wood and thatch, around a pretty garden. Most rooms share facilities, including a barbecue and small kitchen; there are also new tents to camp in. Doubles $33; family cabins $52; camping $8/person.

Cabañas La Tortuga Just south of the village on the beach ☎05 2575163, ☎0993834825, ⓦlatortuga. ec. The only place bang on the beach, though disappointingly only two of the nine small box-like cabins actually overlook the sea ($10 extra). Still, each has a private porch with hammock and chairs, enlivened by decorative touches. There's a pleasant pool and patio area, a mellow open-sided bar-restaurant, and a pool table. A little overpriced. $50

★**Finca Punta Ayampe** 1km south of Ayampe ☎0991285389, ⓦfincapuntaayampe.com. A vast jungle-like property thronging with vegetation and teeming with birdlife. Set on a hill with tremendous views, the main building is a tall open-sided labyrinthine wooden tree-house with seven rooms – most are spacious with ocean-view balconies ($10 more) – a sun deck, hammocks, and a comfy lounge with vast marshmallow sofas round an open fire. Private rustic bamboo cabins – some two-tiered – plus a few newer brick ones with glass sliding doors – all with amazing views – are dotted further down the hillside, where there's a small infinity pool. The restaurant is excellent and local tours are on offer. Breakfast included. Doubles $47; cabins $64/cabin.

★**Los Orishas** Calle La Laguna ☎0999669129, ⓦlosorishasayampe.com. Tucked away at the north end of the village, just back from the beach, this delightful thatched hideaway is a real treat, boasting simple but prettily decorated rooms set round a lovely shady tropical garden. With hammocks and bags of comfy seating to lounge around in, a communal terrace with ocean views and a genuine Italian pizzeria-restaurant to dine in at night (7–10pm, closed Wed), the place is hard to resist. Breakfast included. $36

El Paso Ayampe In the village centre, ⓦrestobaryalojamientoelpaso.com. Friendly local restaurant serving freshly prepared coastal favourites – fish, seafood, rice and plantain feature strongly – at modest prices in a cheerful bamboo and thatch rancho. Mains $7–8 but almuerzos too in high season. Also rents out rooms. 8am–8pm (until 10pm Dec–April); closed one day midweek.

Salango

About 3km north of Ayampe, and 6km south of Puerto López lies the village of **SALANGO**. There's a thriving community-based tourism association here (ⓦsalango .com.ec), which offers a range of inexpensive tours, from horse riding or nature walks, to boat trips out to the avian paradise of Isla Salango ($50/boat), part of Parque Nacional Machalilla (see p.328). The main place of interest in the village itself is the excellent archeological museum.

Museo Arqueológico de Salango

Salango • Daily 9am–5pm • $2.50 • ☎ 05 2574304

The small but well-designed **Museo Arqueológico de Salango** houses a fine collection of artefacts illustrating the area's continuous occupation from Valdivian culture around 3500 BC to Manteño culture up to 1550 AD, including a reconstruction of a single-sail fishing craft.

ARRIVAL AND ACCOMMODATION SALANGO

By bus Salango is 20min south of Puerto López. Take any of the Manglaralto buses that run up and down the coast road (every 15–20min).

Accommodation There are pleasant simple, wooden, thatched beachside cabañas for $18/person. The mattresses are good and each room has a fan and electric shower. Meals are available at the local *comedores* in the village. Contact the community tourism association (see opposite).

7

Puerto López

A small fishing town strung along a wide, crescent-shaped bay backed by steeply rising hills, **PUERTO LÓPEZ** enjoys an undeniably picturesque setting. For many years the place was fairly down-at-heel, with potholed streets, crumbling buildings and a tatty beach. However, its recently acquired status as one of coastal Ecuador's top tourist destinations – thanks to its proximity to an abundance of **natural attractions** – has led

PUERTO LÓPEZ

▲ 🚌 (500m)   Bus Terminal (2km), Machalilla (12km) & Manta (97km) ▲

Rio Pital

MARIA IMMACULADA CONCEPCIÓN

MACHALILLA

Market 🏪

Palo Santo Tours
Laundry

ABDÓN CALDERÓN

Cercapez

GONZÁLEZ SUÁREZ

Machalilla
Tours

ALEJO LASCANO

JUAN MONTALVO

GARCÍA MORENO

Exploramar

ELOY ALFARO

ATAHUALPA

MACHALILLA

JUAN LEÓN MERA

GENERAL CÓRDOVA

P.N. Machalilla
Visitor Centre

ELOY ALFARO

PACIFIC OCEAN

JULIO IZURIETA

MALECÓN

CRISTO DEL CONSUELO

SUCRE

ROCAFUERTE

Banco
Pichincha

Laundry

◼ ACCOMMODATION	
Hostal Los Islotes	7
Hostal Machalilla	5
Hostal Máxima	4
Hostal Sol Inn	6
Hostería Mandalá	1
Hotel Pacífico	3
Itapoa	2

● EATING	
Casa Vecchia	1
Doña Elsie's	3
Patacón Pisa'o	2

N

0 ——— 100
metres

▼ Muelle Turístico (250m)   ▼ Ayampe (18km) & Montanita (46km)

to an acceleration of development: there's a smart new bus terminal, a tourist pier, a tarred road along the beach and a vast malecón that is short on shade and imagination. Yet, come down to the beach by the pier in the early mornings, before the tourist scene gets going, and you can still watch busy fishermen carrying their catch ashore, fending off predatory frigatebirds and pelicans.

Most visitors come to explore the surrounding beaches and forests and **Isla de la Plata**, all part of the nearby **Parque Nacional Machalilla**, whose headquarters and information centre are here in Puerto López. As mainland Ecuador's centre for **whale-watching**, however, the town explodes with tourists between June and September, when hundreds of humpbacks arrive off the coast and tour operators (see box opposite) fight over the droves of tourists who come to witness the acrobatic spectacle of males cavorting in the ocean as they compete for females. A whale festival takes place during the last week of June.

ARRIVAL AND DEPARTURE

PUERTO LÓPEZ

By bus Puerto López is well served by buses, which drop passengers at the new bus terminal 2.5km north of town, where mototaxis queue up to ferry you to your lodgings ($0.50 per passenger, minimum fare $1).
Destinations Guayaquil (8 direct buses daily; 3hr 30min)

or change in Jipijapa (every 15–30min; 1hr); Manta (42 daily, via the coast road (2hr), or via Jipijapa (2hr 30min); Quito (5 daily; 10hr); Santa Elena, via Montañita (every 15–30min; 2hr 50min).

INFORMATION AND GETTING AROUND

By mototaxi Mototaxis are useful for short trips around town ($1–2), though most hotels are within easy walking distance. Camionetas and yellow taxis linger around the town centre for longer journeys.
Tourist office I-Tur is on Atahualpa, between Machalilla and García Moreno ⓦ puertolopez.gob.ec

(daily 8–noon, 1–4.30pm) provides general tourist information and maps.
National park information For information on Parque Nacional Machalilla go to the park's visitor centre (daily 8am–noon & 2–5pm; ☎ 05 2300170) on Eloy Alfaro and García Moreno.

ACCOMMODATION

For a small town, Puerto López offers a fair choice of budget and mid-range accommodation. During the whale-watching season (June–Sept) it can get busy and more expensive – these are the prices given here – so you should book ahead.

Hostal Los Islotes Malecón and Córdova ☎ 05 2300108, ⓔ hostallosislotes@hotmail.com. Tidy good-value option with en-suite rooms of variable quality, with fan or a/c, tiled floors and electric showers. Rooms with a sea view are worth the extra – though you'll get the street noise at weekends – and there's a great upstairs terrace for lounging. $̶2̶5̶
Hostal Machalilla Lascano and Montalvo, ☎ 05 2300155, ⓦ hostalmachalilla.com. Good-value hostel with rooms set around a leafy courtyard with hammocks, a semi-open communal kitchen plus a shady rooftop terrace where you can eat your food. Fan- or a/c-ventilated rooms with TV are decent enough for the price. $̶2̶5̶
Hostal Máxima Suárez and Machalilla ☎ 0999534282, ⓦ hotelmaxima.org. Pleasant Ecuadorian–US hostel set around a nice garden, where you can pitch a tent. Airy accommodation of various sizes, from small to generous-sized double and family rooms with mosquito nets, fans and private hot-water bathrooms. There's also an open kitchen, café, and TV area with a free DVD library. Excellent value. Dorms $̶7̶;

doubles $̶1̶8̶; camping $̶5̶/person
Hostal Sol Inn Montalvo and Eloy Alfaro ☎ 05 2300248 ⓦ hostalsolinn.machalillatours.org. The best backpacker option in town with clean bamboo-sided rooms, mosquito nets and fans (en-suite optional), plus a little garden cum social area with sofas, a pool table, book exchange, a kitchen, and laundry service. Bikes for rent. Small sandy patch to pitch a tent. Dorms $̶1̶0̶; doubles $̶3̶0̶; camping $̶5̶/person
★ **Hostería Mandalá** 1km north of the Malecón ☎ 05 2300181, ⓦ hosteriamandala.info. Head and shoulders above the competition, this hospitable and efficient place has attractively furnished and spacious thatched-roof cabins set in lavish tropical gardens. The main building has a pool table, board games and books, and a lovely wraparound veranda – the perfect place to linger over the restaurant's excellent international cuisine. $̶6̶5̶
Hotel Pacífico Malecón and Suárez ☎ 05 2300234, ⓦ hotelpacificoecuador.com. Long-established hotel featuring clean, simple en-suite rooms set around a swimming pool with an open-fronted restaurant

overlooking the beach. The best rooms have sea-view balconies and a/c ($40 more in high season). Organizes tours too. **$55**

Itapoa Malecón and Calderón ☎09947844992, ⓦitapoareserve.com. Friendly and rustic, with a choice of

jauntily painted cane cabins (some new) in a lovely tropical garden, with spaces to chill. Cabins all have private bathrooms and hot water. There's also a steam room and jacuzzi. Many of the proceeds fund the owners' environmental projects. Tasty breakfast included. **$40**

EATING

Casa Vecchia Eloy Elfaro and Montalvo ☎0988590932. Italian-run restaurant serving sizzling thin-crust pizzas ($8–10) and great home-made pasta dishes plus risottos. Indoor and outdoor patio seating. Daily 6–10pm.

Doña Elsie's Montalvo and Córdova. Freshly prepared – so you may have to wait – modestly priced Esmeraldeñan cuisine served in no-nonsense fashion on plastic tables. *Encocados*, ceviches and plenty of rice and plantain to make your mouth water. Daily 8am–8pm.

Patacon Pisa'o Córdova near the Malecón, ☎0991274206. Tiny Colombian restaurant tucked beneath a mop of thatch and hanging plants. Specializing in its namesake – a crispy base of mashed plantain with various toppings, it also serves kebabs and *arepas* (stuffed cornmeal patties). June–Sept daily 1pm–9.30pm; Oct–May closed Sun.

7

TOURS FROM PUERTO LÓPEZ

There are numerous **tour operators** in Puerto López, almost all of them strung along General Córdova or the Malecón. Most offer the same basic trips in Spanish, at identical prices, and need a minimum of 3–4 people. All boat tours leave from the Muelle Turístico, at the southern end of the Malecón.

The most popular tour is the ninety-minute **boat ride to Isla de la Plata** ($40; see p.328), which lies within the boundaries of Parque Nacional Machalilla. Tours include a moderately strenuous guided hike around the island, followed by a box lunch and snorkelling from the boat. Excursions usually set off at 9/9.30am and return at 5pm, and the crossing can be rough with a biting wind, so take sea-sickness tablets, a warm top and plenty of suntan lotion. From June to September, these trips are combined with some whale-watching en route. Isla Salango, which is smaller and nearer, is a possible half-day alternative as it also affords opportunities to gawp at blue-footed boobies (non-nesting), pelicans and frigatebirds, plus indulge in a little snorkelling.

Whale-watching tours ($30) are an exciting way of seeing humpback whales as they travel up the Pacific coast from the Antarctic to give birth in warmer waters. Sightings are almost guaranteed June–Sept though some operators take boats out in October, when whales are scarce. You can usually get quite close-up views, but try and avoid crowded weekends because when there are too many boats on the water, some practically harass the whales, which can be distressing for the animals and for environmentally conscious tourists.

Other excursions involve half- or full-day tours (from around $25–35) to Machalilla's mainland areas: **kayaking** to Playa Los Frailes (see p.329); **walking and horse riding** along the Sendero Bola de Oro (see p.329) or Sendero El Rocío (p.329); or visiting **archeological sites** at Agua Blanca (see p.328). **Mountain biking**, **diving** and **sport fishing** are also possible.

TOUR OPERATORS

Cercapez González Suárez and Malecón ☎05 2300173, ✉operadoracercapez@gmail.com. Good boats for whale-watching and Isla de la Plata tours, plus they help park officials with conservation work.

Exploramar General Córdova and Malecón ☎05 2300123, ⓦexploradiving.com. Offers scuba-diving two-tank day-tours ($140–160) for certified divers to Isla de la Plata and the three-day practical for open-water courses ($372).

Machalilla Tours Malecón and Eloy Alfaro ☎05 2300234, ⓦmachalillatours.org. Well-established

outfit (but can be overstretched in high season), providing the usual day-trips and many other activities from kayaking, to mountain biking and paragliding. Also rents out kayaks, bikes, plus offers multi-day activity packages.

Palo Santo Malecón and Calderón ☎0992309366, ⓦwhalewatching-ecuador.com. Excellent customer-oriented and environmentally conscious operator, offering bilingual whale-watching trips; also organizes internships for whale researchers.

Parque Nacional Machalilla

Daily 8am–5pm, but last vehicle access to Playa Los Frailes at 3.30pm • Free

Parque Nacional Machalilla, mainland Ecuador's only coastal national park, protects both terrestrial and marine habitats. It includes the country's last major tract of tropical dry forest – now a mere one percent of its original size. The forest is notable for the remarkable contrast between the vegetation at sea level and that covering the hills rising to 800m above the coastline. The **dry forest**, panning in from the shore, comprises scorched-looking trees and shrubs adapted to scarce water supplies and saline soils, including many different cactuses, gnarled ceibas, barbasco trees and algarobbo (able to photosynthesize through its green bark). Also common are highly fragrant *palo santo* trees, whose bark is burned as incense in churches. A short hike east into the hills brings you into the wholly different landscape of **coastal cloudforest**, moistened by a rising sea mist that condenses as it hits the hills, where a dense covering of lush vegetation shelters ferns, heliconias, bromeliads, orchids and bamboos, as well as a great variety of animals and birds. The two different habitats can be observed on some excellent **inland hiking** trails, such as the hike from **Agua Blanca**, north of Puerto López, up to the **San Sebastián** cloudforest area, and the **Bola de Oro** hike. In addition, the park includes a number of pristine **beaches**, of which the most spectacular is **Playa Los Frailes**. Offshore areas include the tiny **Isla Salango** and the famous, bird-rich **Isla de la Plata**, the most popular destination in the park.

Isla de la Plata

Some 37km out to sea, and only accessible with tour companies based in Puerto López (see p.327), **Isla de la Plata** is a small, scrubby island of just eight square kilometres, once the ceremonial centre of the Bahía culture (500 BC to 650 AD). Its name (*plata* meaning silver), comes from the legend that the English explorer Sir Francis Drake buried a chestful of silver here in the sixteenth century – never discovered, of course. Today, the island's fame derives more from its large population of **marine birds**, which are relatively fearless and allow close observation, giving it the sobriquet of "poor man's Galápagos". This hackneyed phrase does not do the island justice as it's the only place in Ecuador – including the Galápagos – where blue-footed, red-footed and masked boobies are found together, though the blue-footed variety, which you can see nesting, are by far the most numerous. You'll also see **frigatebirds**, and, if you're lucky, **red-billed tropicbirds,** though the three breeding pairs of **waved albatross** (April–Oct) are off limits to visitors, and the island's sea lions are rarely sighted. It's also possible to spot dolphins and manta rays on the boat ride, as well as **humpback whales** (June–Sept).

Agua Blanca and around

Agua Blanca museum daily 8am–6pm • Guided tours of the museum, Sangólome site and sulphur pool (in Spanish) cost $5 • Ⓦ comunidadaguablanca.com • Agua Blanca is best reached from Puerto López by camioneta taxi ($6; $14 return including waiting time) or on a guided tour (see box, p.327)

Five kilometres north of Puerto López, at the hamlet of Buenavista, a side road leads east to **AGUA BLANCA**, 5–6km down a dirt road. This humble village stands near the archeological site of **Sangólome**, a former major centre of the Manteño civilization (c.500 BC to 1540 AD), known for its finely crafted and polished black ceramics and large thrones supported by human or animal figures, several of which were found here. A small **museum** in the village displays some beautiful ceramics excavated at Sangólome, which is a forty-minute walk away. While there's little to see at the site, the walk there and back through fragrant forest offers splendid views plus the chance to soak in a pungent sulphur pool.

You can hire **guides** in Agua Blanca ($35 per person per day including use of a mule to carry your gear) to take you on a beautiful, if more strenuous, hike through tropical dry forest with many colourful birds, up to the lush **San Sebastián cloudforest**, home to black howler monkeys, snakes, *guantas* and anteaters. The route, one of the best ways to explore the interior of Parque Nacional Machalilla, is 10km each way, most comfortably spread over two days, **camping** at San Sebastián (come prepared for mud and rain, especially from Jan to April).

Río Blanco and the Bola de Oro hike

9km inland from Puerto López • Best reached from Puerto López by camioneta taxi (45min; $6) or on a guided tour (see box, p.327) • Contact Carlos ☎ 0994188343

The small community of **RÍO BLANCO** (El Pital) is the starting point for a rewarding hike through dense, luxuriant cloudforest, rich in bird and animal life, up to the park's highest point (800m), known as the "**Bola de Oro**", or "gold nugget". You can hire a local guide ($30 per person on horseback; $23 per person on foot) at Río Blanco the day before you plan to hike. The trail, quite hard going in parts, is about a seven-hour round trip, which you can break by camping in a clearing at the Bola de Oro. Come prepared for muddy conditions, especially from January to April.

Playa Los Frailes and around

10km north of Puerto López • Take any bus heading north from Puerto López and ask to be dropped at the turn-off to the beach, by the national park kiosk; from here the beach is a 30min walk down the track • For the Sendero El Rocío hike, stay on the bus for a further 3km and the bus driver can drop you off by the trailhead • Alternatively, take a camioneta from Puerto López ($6) • There is a small community fee to use the Sendero El Rocío trail

Some 10km north of Puerto López, at the national park kiosk on the coast road, just south of the run-down village of Machalilla, a signed dirt track leads to **Playa Los Frailes**, a half-hour walk away. This is one of the most beautiful beaches on the Ecuadorian coast, with dramatic cliffs and forested hills framing its cream-coloured sands. Despite its popularity, the beach still feels like a wild, unspoiled place, particularly if you arrive in the early morning, when you're almost guaranteed to have it all to yourself. The more rewarding approach to Los Frailes involves turning right off the track, 300m after the park entrance, to follow a signed four-kilometre circular trail via the tiny black-sand cove of **La Playita**, rocky **Playa La Tortuguita** and a splendid **mirador** (lookout), giving spectacular views of the coast. Taking your time, you should arrive at Playa Los Frailes a couple of hours later.

About 3km north of the turning off the main road for Los Frailes, you'll see signs for the **Sendero El Rocío**, an enjoyable two-kilometre trail beginning in farmland, and leading up to a viewpoint before emerging at an attractive beach. Locals act as guides for visitors; ask at the farms around the trailhead.

INFORMATION	PARQUE NACIONAL MACHALILLA

Tourist information The park's visitor centre is situated in Puerto López on Atahualpa and Machalilla (daily 8am–noon & 2–5pm; ☎ 05 2300170).

ACCOMMODATION AND EATING

Agua Blanca ☎ 0994434864 (museum community phone). There are simple lodgings in the village in fan-ventilated rustic cabins with shared or private bathroom, tents and a restaurant serving set menus and à-la-carte *comida típica* ($5–8). $20

Río Blanco You can stay with families or in small basic cabañas with shared facilities, mosquito nets over the beds, in the village of Río Blanco. Simple meals also available. $20

The Galápagos Islands

BARTOLOMÉ

The Galápagos Islands

It's quite humbling that thirteen scarred volcanic islands and more than a hundred islets, scattered across 45,000 square kilometres of ocean, 960km adrift from the Ecuadorian mainland, should have been so instrumental in changing humanity's perception of itself. Yet it was the forbidding Galápagos Islands – once feared as a bewitched and waterless hell, then the haunt of pirates and whalers – that spurred Charles Darwin to formulate his theory of evolution by natural selection, catapulting science – and the world – into the modern era. Today the archipelago's matchless wildlife, stunning scenery and unique history make it arguably the world's premier wildlife destination. The animals that have carved out an existence on the dramatic volcanic landscape have a legendary fearlessness which results in close-up encounters that are simply not possible anywhere else on Earth. Witnessing first-hand the mating dance of the blue-footed booby and snorkelling with sea lions, turtles, penguins and sharks are just a couple of the unforgettable experiences that await you.

8

Three years before Darwin's arrival in 1835, Ecuador claimed **sovereignty** over the 13 large islands and 100-plus small islands, islets and rocks that make up the archipelago, but attempts to colonize them were unsuccessful until the mid-twentieth century, and even then only in small numbers. It was inevitable after Darwin's discoveries and the global rise in recreational travel, however, that the Galápagos Islands would start to pull in large numbers of tourists, money and then immigrants.

A total of about 30,000 people live in just four main settlements on four inhabited islands. In the centre of the archipelago lies **Santa Cruz**, site of **Puerto Ayora**, the most developed town, serviced by the airport on nearby Baltra island. **San Cristóbal**, to the east, has the provincial capital, **Puerto Baquerizo Moreno**, and the archipelago's other major airport. Straddling the equator to the west of Santa Cruz is the largest and most volcanically active of the islands, **Isabela**, where tiny **Puerto Villamil** has an inter-island airstrip. **Puerto Velasco Ibarra** on southerly **Floreana** has very little by way of infrastructure but does it have a bizarre settlement history.

These settled sites represent a mere three percent of the total land area of the archipelago. In response to the damage caused by centuries of human interference, the rest of the land – more than 7600 square kilometres – has since 1959 been protected as a **national park** (ⓦgalapagospark.org), with tourists restricted to the colonized areas and 69 designated **visitor sites** spread across the islands (plus 79 water-based sites). Each site has been chosen to show off the full diversity of the islands, and in a typical tour you'll encounter different species of flora and fauna (see p.370 & p.410) every day, many of them found nowhere else on Earth.

Highlights

❶ Puerto Ayora A friendly, bustling little port, home to the islands' best hotels, restaurants and bars – and the Charles Darwin Research Station, the engine of Galápagos study and conservation. **See p.345**

❸ Bartolomé A small island with a spectacular summit vantage point overlooking the landmark Pinnacle Rock, poised above a little bay where you can snorkel among Galápagos penguins. **See p.356**

❷ Punta Espinoza On Fernandina Island, in the far west of the archipelago, Punta Espinoza hosts spectacular gatherings of marine iguanas as well as some of its most unique birds, the tiny Galápagos penguin and the large flightless cormorants. **See p.365**

❹ Waved albatrosses After ranging the oceans, the gentle giants of the Galápagos Islands return to Española between April and December, and enact enthralling courtship displays before breeding with their lifelong partners. **See p.368**

❺ Gardner Bay One of the finest beaches in the islands, a long streak of brilliant white sand lapped by azure waters and populated by playful sea lions. **See p.369**

❻ Genovesa An isolated island formed from a half-submerged crater at the northeastern extreme of the archipelago, where you can snorkel with hammerhead sharks and marvel at the birdlife, including the blood-sucking vampire finch. **See p.369**

HIGHLIGHTS ARE MARKED ON THE MAP ON P.334–335

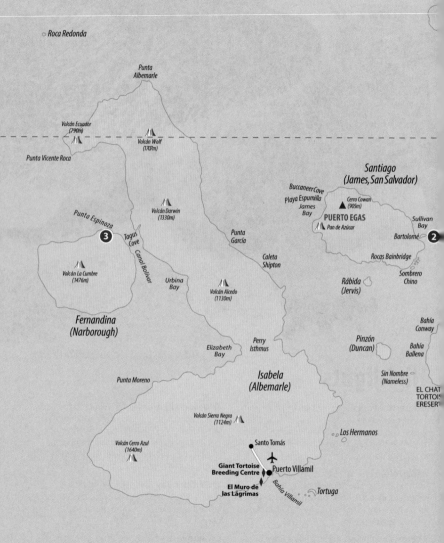

Darwin & Wolf

Pinta
(Abingdon)

Roca Redonda

Punta
Albemarle

Volcán Ecuador
(790m)

Volcán Wolf
(1700m)

Punta Vicente Roca

Santiago
(James, San Salvador)

Buccaneer Cove

Playa Espumilla
James
Bay

Cerro Cowan
(905m)

PUERTO EGAS

Pan de Azúcar

Sullivan
Bay

Bartolomé ②

Punta Espinoza

Tagus
Cove

③

Volcán Darwin
(1330m)

Punta
García

Caleta
Shipton

Rocas Bainbridge

Canal Bolívar

Urbina
Bay

Volcán La Cumbre
(1476m)

Volcán Alcedo
(1130m)

Sombrero
Chino

Rábida
(Jervis)

Fernandina
(Narborough)

Perry
Isthmus

Pinzón
(Duncan)

Bahía
Conway

Bahía
Ballena

Elizabeth
Bay

Punta Moreno

Isabela
(Albemarle)

Sin Nombre
(Nameless)

EL CHAT
TORTOIS
ERESER

Volcán Sierra Negra
(1124m)

Los Hermanos

Volcán Cerro Azul
(1640m)

Santo Tomás

Giant Tortoise
Breeding Centre

Puerto Villamil

El Muro de
las Lágrimas

Bahía Villamil

Tortuga

Post Office Be

Black Beach Bay

Puert
Velasco Ibarr

THE GALÁPAGOS ISLANDS

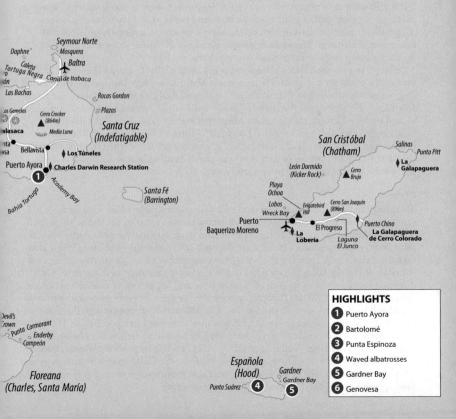

0   20
kilometres

Marchena
(Bindloe)

Genovesa
(Tower)

6 Prince Philip's Steps
Darwin Bay

Equator
0°

PACIFIC OCEAN

Daphne
Seymour Norte
Mosquera
Caleta
Tortuga Negra
Baltra
ón
Canal de Itabaca
Las Bachas
Rocas Gordon
os Gemelos
Plazas
Cerro Crocker
(864m)
nta
Media Luna
Santa Cruz
esa
Bellavista
(Indefatigable)
alasaca
Los Túneles
Puerto Ayora
San Cristóbal
(Chatham)
Salinas
1
Charles Darwin Research Station
Punta Pitt
Santa Fé
La
(Barrington)
Galapaguera
Bahía Tortuga
Academy Bay
León Dormido
(Kicker Rock)
Cerro
Brujo
Playa
Ochoa
Lobos
Cerro San Joaquín
(896m)
Frigatebird
Wreck Bay
Hill
Puerto
Puerto Chino
Baquerizo Moreno
El Progreso
La Galapaguera
La Lobería
Laguna
de Cerro Colorado
El Junco

Devil's
rown
Punta Cormorant
Enderby
Campeón

Española
(Hood)
Gardner
Gardner Bay
Punta Suárez
4
5

Floreana
(Charles, Santa María)

HIGHLIGHTS

1 Puerto Ayora

2 Bartolomé

3 Punta Espinoza

4 Waved albatrosses

5 Gardner Bay

6 Genovesa

GALÁPAGOS TIME

Galápagos time is GMT minus 6 hours, 1 hour behind the Ecuadorian mainland.

It was also in 1959, the centenary of the publication of *On the Origin of Species*, that the Charles Darwin Foundation (CDF) was instituted, which six years later opened the **Charles Darwin Research Station** (CDRS) in Puerto Ayora, whose vital work includes boosting the threatened populations of unique Galápagos species. In 1978 the archipelago was one of the first places to be made a World Heritage Site by UNESCO, which declared it a World Biosphere Reserve six years later. Its position was strengthened in 1998 with the creation of the **Reserva Marina de Galápagos**, protecting 133,000 square kilometres of ocean, making it one of the largest marine reserves in the world.

Brief history

Until the middle of the twentieth century, it was thought that the Galápagos Islands were out of reach of the prehistoric coastal peoples of the continental mainland. In 1947, explorer and archeologist Thor Heyerdahl proved otherwise with his famous voyage from Peru to Polynesia on a balsa raft, the *Kon-Tiki*; in 1953 his excavations on the islands revealed over 130 shards of **pre-Columbian pottery** from coastal Peru and Ecuador, leading him to theorize that the islands were used as a seasonal fishing base.

Other early visitors could have included the great Inca **Tupac Yupanqui**; according to the early Spanish chronicles, Yupanqui may have journeyed to the islands in about 1485 following reports that they held gold, returning almost a year later with "some black men, much gold, a chair made of brass and the skin and jawbone of a horse". This unlikely plunder casts doubts on the story's veracity, handing the prize of first documented visitor to **Tomás de Berlanga**, Bishop of Panama, whose ship ended up here after being swept off course en route to Peru in 1535.

Berlanga and his men spent a desperate week on the islands, before the winds picked up so they could set sail again. He later wrote about how water from a well they had dug "came out saltier than that of the sea" and remarked that the earth was "like dross, worthless". He also noted the islands' "many seals, turtles, iguanas, tortoises", references picked up by a Flemish cartographer, **Abraham Ortelius**, who named the islands "Galápagos" (Spanish for "tortoises") on his 1574 map, *Orbis Terrarum*. The islands' other name at that time, Las Encantadas ("enchanted" or "bewitched"), came from the strong currents and swaths of deep mist that made landing here so difficult, as if the shore itself was being moved by unearthly powers.

Pirates

Their reputation for being haunted made the Galápagos a perfect base for a number of seventeenth- and eighteenth-century **English pirates**, who came to the Pacific to pick off merchant ships as they sailed along the mainland coast. Among the most notorious was **John Cook**, who captured a Danish slave ship and renamed it the *Bachelor's Delight* after 60 female slaves were found in the hold, before using it to take three merchant ships off the coast of Peru in 1684. He then hid out in the Galápagos, only to discover he had a disappointing booty of thousands of sacks of flour and "eight tons of quince marmalade". Among his crew was **William Dampier**, who wrote the first comprehensive description of the islands in *A New Voyage Round the World*, and **William Ambrose Cowley**, the first man to chart the islands, naming them after English notables (see box opposite). In 1709 **Alexander Selkirk**, the inspiration for *Robinson Crusoe*, turned up here after being rescued from the Juan Fernández Archipelago off the coast of Chile by privateer **Woodes Rogers**. Selkirk helped Rogers sack Guayaquil before sailing to the Galápagos to make repairs and stock up on tortoises which, because they were able to survive for up to a year without food or water, were prized provisions for long sea voyages.

Whalers

The buccaneers' secret became well known after **James Colnett**, on HMS *Rattler* in 1793, revealed in a report to the British Admiralty that the Galápagos would be a convenient base for **whalers**. Sperm whales were then one of the major sources of oil, and the cold currents around the Galápagos were guaranteed to attract large numbers. The whalers caused incalculable damage to whale populations and decimated the Galápagos **tortoises** too. Each ship may have loaded as many as 600 of the creatures before setting sail; an estimated total of around 200,000 tortoises were taken during the whaling era, bringing the giant tortoise subspecies to extinction on Floreana, Rábida and Santa Fé islands. In the late nineteenth century, almost every whaling ship in the Pacific called at the islands to stock up. One of them, the *Acushnet*, carried the most famous whaler of them all, **Herman Melville**, who related his experiences in *Las Encantadas*, describing the islands as "five-and-twenty heaps of cinders" where "the chief sound of life... is a hiss."

The first settlers

The first documented **settler**, Irishman **Patrick Watkins**, demanded to be put ashore on Floreana in the early nineteenth century after quarrelling with his captain. It was assumed that he spent all his time on the island drinking rum; in truth, he was hatching a plot to escape, as no captain would take him. After two years, he managed to steal a ship, abduct four people to crew it and sail to Guayaquil, arriving (ominously) alone.

General José Villamil decided to claim the archipelago for the newly founded Republic of Ecuador in 1832. He gave the islands Spanish names and immediately set about colonizing Floreana with eighty soldiers condemned for mutiny, whose death sentences had been commuted to a life of hard labour in the Galápagos. His idea was to start a trade in orchilla moss, used to make a deep-red dye, but the business never took off, and to add to his troubles, the government kept deporting hundreds of criminals and prostitutes to the colony from the mainland. Eventually Villamil gave up and was replaced by the brutal **Colonel José Williams** who, despite keeping a large pack of ferocious dogs for protection, was chased off the islands after the colonists revolted. By 1852 the colony had been abandoned, setting a long-standing precedent of failure.

8

THE NAMES OF THE GALÁPAGOS ISLANDS

Over the years most of the **Galápagos Islands** – officially known as the **Archipiélago de Colón** – have come to own at least a couple of names, usually one given by English pirates, and another official Spanish name given in 1892, marking the fourth centenary of Columbus's discovery of the New World. Many islands have also picked up a number of other names along the way, with some boasting as many as eight. The official names are listed first below, followed by any other commonly used names in brackets; the most frequently used name – which is what we've adopted throughout this chapter – is in bold. Islands that have only ever had one name, such as Enderby, Beagle and Cowley, are not listed.

Baltra (South Seymour)
Darwin (Culpepper)
Española (Hood)
Fernandina (Narborough)
Genovesa (Tower)
Isabela (Albemarle)
Marchena (Bindloe)
Pinta (Abingdon)
Pinzón (Duncan)
Rábida (Jervis)

San Cristóbal (Chatham)
San Salvador (**Santiago**, James)
Santa Cruz (Indefatigable, Duke of Norfolk)
Santa Fé (Barrington)
Santa María (**Floreana**, Charles)
Seymour Norte (North Seymour)
Sin Nombre (Nameless)
Tortuga (Brattle)
Wolf (Wenman)

The infamous **Manuel Cobos** (see p.360) came to a sticky end after a tyrannous rule over a settlement on San Cristóbal, and entrepreneur **José de Valdizán** was murdered in 1878 following a futile eight-year attempt to revive Villamil's colony on Floreana. **Antonio Gil** made a third attempt at the place in 1893, but after four years moved operations to Isabela, founding Puerto Villamil, where he and his group eked out a living by ferrying sulphur from a nearby crater to Guayaquil.

Scientists

While colonists were struggling, **scientists** were visiting in droves, largely thanks to the enormous publicity **Charles Darwin**'s 1835 voyage on the HMS *Beagle* had generated (see box below). Over the next century, scientific expeditions from around the world raced to build up wildlife collections for museums, often contributing to the damage wreaked by the whalers and settlers. In some instances, expeditions claimed that a

DARWIN, THE GALÁPAGOS AND EVOLUTION

When **Charles Darwin** began his five-year global voyage in 1831, he was little more than an enthusiastic amateur naturalist set on a career in the Church. At Edinburgh University he found the lectures stultifying – even those in geology, which later became a passion – and at Cambridge, studying divinity, he only just scraped through without honours. Yet Cambridge Professor of Botany John Henslow recognized a talented mind with a flair for science, and recommended Darwin to Captain FitzRoy, who was seeking a naturalist for an expedition to chart the coast of South America. **HMS Beagle** set sail in December 1831.

On September 15, 1835, the *Beagle* arrived at the Galápagos. "Nothing could be less inviting", Darwin wrote, "the country is comparable to what one might imagine the cultivated parts of the Infernal regions to be". Over five weeks he feverishly set about collecting samples and was taken aback by the "tameness" of the islands' creatures. Darwin noticed countless things previous visitors hadn't, but his experiences only planted the seeds of ideas that would later blossom. Indeed, exhausted from four years of hard travel, Darwin's normally fastidious sampling was somewhat slapdash: he failed to label the source islands of his bird collections, and even misidentified the now celebrated **Darwin's finches**. It wasn't until his return to London, after taxonomist John Gould had examined Darwin's samples and told him about the thirteen closely related species of finch, that the penny dropped. Despite giving acclaimed lectures about his geological discoveries and publishing the *Voyage of the Beagle* in 1839, he only hinted at the big ideas troubling him.

Instead, Darwin started working over his ideas in near secret in his famous **Transmutation Notebooks**. He saw that the volcanic Galápagos Islands were relatively new and that species there bore a resemblance to species in South America but were crucially different. Darwin also realized that life had come to the barren islands by air or sea and adapted to the environment through a process he termed **"natural selection"**. In this, he maintained that at a given time certain members of a species are more suited to their surroundings than others and therefore more likely to survive in it, so passing on their advantageous characteristics to their offspring. Over time an entire population would come to develop those special features, eventually becoming a new species – what Darwin called **"descent with modification"**, rather than "evolution". In his groundbreaking model, change was without direction and could result in a number of new species from a single ancestor.

It pained Darwin to know his ideas would upset the public and the Church, and he sat on his theory for nearly twenty years, quietly amassing the information to back it up. It took a letter from **Alfred Russel Wallace**, who had arrived at a similar conclusion (though without Darwin's intellectual rigour), to jerk him into action. In 1858 they offered a joint paper to the Linnaean Society in London and a year later Darwin published **On the Origin of Species**. It sent shock waves throughout the Western world and intense debate followed, but by the time of Darwin's death in 1882, the notion of evolution was well established. The most important, original and far-seeing part of his theory – natural selection – was still highly controversial; it was only in the 1930s that it received the full recognition it deserved, forming the basis of modern biology and forever changing humanity's view of itself.

GALÁPAGOS ESSENTIALS

- Take sufficient cash; you need to pay the $100 park entrance fee in cash on arrival and tip guides and boat crew.
- The islands' only banks and ATMs are in Puerto Ayora and Puerto Baquerizo Moreno.
- Prices are higher than on the mainland, and there are usually high service charges for using credit cards. Shops and agencies generally prefer MasterCard, then Visa, though American Express and Diners are sometimes accepted.
- You'll need to bring shorts, t-shirt, hat and sunglasses, trousers and long sleeves; a lightweight raincoat; sturdy boots or shoes; and swimwear and sandals.
- Earplugs, seasickness medication for sufferers, sunscreen, lip protection, skin creams and insect repellent are all essentials too. A small dry bag, a day pack and a torch (flashlight) are also handy. Be sure to buy plenty of sunscreen at home, as taxes make it painfully expensive in Ecuador.
- A zoom or telephoto lens is a big bonus for more dramatic photos. A polarizing filter helps maintain vivid colours in harsh sunlight. Binoculars are useful, even though most of the time you'll be watching wildlife from close quarters.
- It's worth bringing your own mask, snorkel and fins, and from July to December, a wet suit. Scuba divers should bring as much of their own equipment as practical (see box, p.343).

species was on the verge of extinction, so justifying the removal of the last few specimens they could find – only for future expeditions to do the same with any survivors. The 1905 voyage of the *Academy* gathered the largest collection, taking over 8500 bird specimens and 266 giant tortoises, including 86 from Pinzón and one from Fernandina, the only tortoise ever recorded on this island.

The early twentieth century

In the early **twentieth century**, European colonists began appearing on the islands, the most extraordinary of whom were involved in the so-called **Galápagos affair** (see box, p.367). During this period, international powers were starting to regard the islands as a place of considerable strategic importance, especially as a base from which to guard the entrance to the **Panama Canal**. By the time the canal was completed in 1914, a bidding war over the islands had already begun between several countries, including the US, Britain and France. However tempting the US's $15 million offer in 1911 for a 99-year lease was, Ecuador stuck firm – by this time the islands were a part of the national identity. After the Japanese attacked Pearl Harbor in 1941 it was clear the Panama Canal would need protection, and the Ecuadorian government granted the US permission to use Baltra as an air base. It was returned after the war and the runway there remains one of the island's main points of access.

Tourism, immigration and other challenges

Ever since regular flights began in the late 1960s, organized tourism has grown at a phenomenal rate to reach annual overseas visitor figures of almost 216,000 in 2014 – up from about 70,000 in 2000 and a fourfold increase in twenty years, despite strict controls. The industry's success has also encouraged immigration to the islands, with the current population estimated at around 30,000, surging from a little over 1000 in the 1950s. Immigration control does happen, leading to deportations to the mainland, but birth rates are high and the population is still growing fast.

The success of tourism has been both a boon and bane. Revenues have undoubtedly helped insulate the Galápagos from terrible economic crises on the mainland, and provided a financial motive and backing for the crucial and highly successful conservation effort, as well as raising the profile of the islands around the world. But the wealth has also attracted large numbers of national migrants, and both tourists and residents put pressure on the islands' stretched resources and infrastructure. Then there are the imported goods; building materials, oil, agricultural fertilizers and produce are all part of the surge in cargo traffic that has resulted in a sharp increase in harmful alien species (see box below).

Economic migrants who work outside the tourist industry can also create problems. **Farmers** cultivate a variety of introduced species, many of which have "escaped" into the wild, while **fisherman** do their best to make a living from the waters of the marine reserve within the regulations of the 1998 **Special Law for the Galápagos**, which allows only "local artisanal fishing" within it. The law did not go down well and the imposed quota on **sea cucumbers**, a delicacy in Asia, led to violent clashes with park authorities. Overfishing has had a lasting impact, and some poachers, both Ecuadorian and international, use outlawed methods, such as **long-lining**, which kills large numbers of sea birds as well as endangered fish. The Ecuadorian navy and park wardens still detain illegal fishing boats, occasionally finding hundreds of **shark fins** (used in shark-fin soup) on board; the non-commercial part of the catch – sea lions, turtles, dolphins, pelicans, boobies and the shark carcasses themselves – are simply dumped at sea.

8

CONSERVATION IN THE GALÁPAGOS

No species has done more to upset the delicately balanced ecosystem of the Galápagos than **humans**. In one study, it was found that nearly every extinction of native species followed the arrival of Tomás de Berlanga, the first recorded visitor, in 1535. From then onwards, the hunting of tortoises, whales and other animals has brought populations to the brink. Although our depredation of native species within the park has ceased, and fishing in the marine reserve is strictly controlled, a concerted conservation effort will always be needed to offset the impact of human colonization. Since the national park was declared in 1959, protection of the environment has indeed improved significantly.

FOREIGN SPECIES

By far the worst human legacy has been the catastrophic introduction of **alien species**. When settlers arrived they brought with them plants, and domestic and farm animals that soon went wild, overrunning the islands and out-competing native species. **Pigs** trample vegetation, snaffle up bird hatchlings and young tortoises and devour turtle eggs. Feral **dogs** have attacked iguanas, and **black rats**, thought to be responsible for the extinction of endemic rice rats on four islands, also killed every tortoise hatchling on Pinzón for most of the twentieth century. Biologists have recently succeeded in the daunting task of ridding Pinzón of black rats, enabling tortoises to hatch there again. Wild **goats** are regarded as one of the biggest threats, denuding entire islands of vegetation, causing plant species to become extinct, as well as depriving native animals of food and encouraging soil erosion. Among some 490 accidentally introduced insect species are about 55 highly invasive types; these include two species of **wasp** and the **fire ant**. Introduced plants are also a major threat, disrupting the food chain from the bottom up – 60 percent of native plants are thought to be under threat.

The Galápagos National Park Service (GNPS) and the Charles Darwin Foundation (CDF) have taken a varied approach to the problem of introduced species. **Eradication programmes** have done enough to allow some threatened native species to recover. For example, feral pigs, donkeys and goats have been eliminated from Santiago, and goats have been eliminated from six of the islands and islets. There has been a series of **repopulation programmes**, such as the one for giant tortoises, where eggs are gathered, incubated, hatched and raised until large enough to survive predatory attacks before being repatriated. A **quarantine system** in ports and airports has inspectors checking incoming cargoes for alien pests and seeds and the usual stowaway frogs, rats and insects.

FRIENDS OF GALÁPAGOS

The best thing visitors can do to help the conservation effort is to join the **Friends of Galápagos**, a network of international organizations which provide vital funding for conservation efforts. In the UK, contact the Galápagos Conservation Trust (☏ 020 7629 5049, ⓦ savegalapagos.org); in the US, contact the Galápagos Conservancy (☏ 703 383-0077, ⓦ galapagos.org). Both websites list other national Friends organizations, or you can join up in the islands at the CDRS (see p.346).

A new Galápagos law in 2015 led to **peaceful street protests**. The law implied that the park limits, almost unchanged in over half a century, might be modified, causing concerns among environmentalists and local residents that hotels could start opening on current parklands. The Correa administration says that any new hotel construction will be limited to 30 new rooms and will be subject to tough environmental standards.

The Galápagos at risk

The combined threats to the Galápagos are so acute that in 2007 UNESCO declared it a **World Heritage Site in Danger**. The response of president Rafael Correa was to declare the conservation of the archipelago a "national priority", and in 2010, UNESCO voted to remove the islands from its endangered list, citing improved efforts by Ecuador to protect the biodiversity of the Galápagos. However, this decision was criticized by many international conservation groups who warned that the islands continue to face risks from alien plants and animals. Still, since 2009 the number of visits has increased at a much slower rate, relieving pressure on the environment.

When to visit

The Galápagos has a two-season **climate** governed by the strong **ocean currents** – notably the cold Humboldt current – that swirl around the archipelago. The islands are relatively dry all year, but during the **warm-wet season** (Jan–June) there are short and heavy bursts of rain while air temperatures nudge 30°C (86°F). Sea temperatures are between 20°C and 26°C (68–79°F), reaching perhaps as high as 29°C (84°F) around the northeastern islands. In the **cool-dry season** (July–Dec), the air temperature drops to around 22°C (72°F), the oceans become choppier and the skies are more consistently overcast, though very little rain falls on the lowlands. Sea temperatures can dip as low as 16°C (61°F), especially in August and September, so consider bringing a wet suit. At this time of year, the *garúa* mists linger over the oceans and bathe the uplands in a near-perpetual fine drizzle, occasionally descending to sea level. The transitional months between seasons can show quite changeable weather combining any of these elements.

For tourism, the Galápagos **high season** begins around mid-June and lasts till August, starting up again in December and carrying on until mid-January. Exact times vary, usually according to demand, with some operators only counting May to mid-June, and September, as **low season**. Wildlife-spotting is good throughout the year, but some species are only seen at certain times: check our wildlife guide for details (see pp.370–379).

8

ARRIVAL AND DEPARTURE   **THE GALÁPAGOS ISLANDS**

Boats from mainland Ecuador are not allowed to take tourists to the Galápagos, so the only way to reach the islands is by **plane**. High air fares and park entrance fees mean that just getting to the Galápagos is a relatively pricey undertaking – and that's before stumping up for a cruise.

BY PLANE

Flights There are several daily flights from Quito via Guayaquil; the journey takes around three hours in total, though can be longer depending on how long the stopover in Guayaquil takes. Avianca (☎02 2942800, ⓦavianca .com), LAN (☎1800 842 526, ⓦlan.com) and TAME (☎1800 500 800, ⓦtame.com.ec) all fly to Baltra (for Puerto Ayora on Santa Cruz) and Puerto Baquerizo Moreno on San Cristóbal.

Fares Return flights from Quito cost $455–510; flights from Guayaquil are a bit cheaper; students with an ISIC card can get a fifteen percent high-season discount. In high season it can be difficult to get a seat, so make sure you're not being put on the waiting list. Reconfirm inward and outward

flights two days in advance. The baggage allowance is 20kg.

Transfers Having flown in from the mainland, those with a pre-booked cruise – the vast majority of tourists – will be given free transfer to their boat. If arriving in Baltra, your boat will either be waiting at the island's dock nearby, or at Puerto Ayora on Santa Cruz, a short hop by ferry from Baltra over the Canal de Itabaca to a connecting bus on the other side (45min). In Puerto Baquerizo Moreno, San Cristóbal, buses will take you the few minutes to the harbour.

FEES

Park entrance fee On arrival in the Galápagos you have to pay a $100 park entrance fee in cash at the airport. There are discounts for under-12s ($50) and under-2s (no charge).

Hold onto the receipt, as your tour operator will need it. **Transit card** You will also need to pay $20 for the Galápagos Transit Card; usually it's bought at point of departure, or tour companies can sort this out for you prior to arrival.

GETTING AROUND AND TOURS

Cruise boats, which mostly sail between islands by night, are undoubtedly the best way to see the Galápagos, though **land-based tours** are also available. **Independent travel** around the Galápagos is possible, using **inter-island flights and boats**, though these largely restrict you to the colonized areas, which rather misses the point of a trip here. Still, there are attractive visitor sites close to the main settlements that you can reach on your own without a licensed

GALÁPAGOS CRUISES

Galápagos cruises sail between visitor sites that are specially chosen to show off a representative portion of an island. Lasting anything from a few days to several weeks, most cruises combine a variety of sites – usually stopping at two a day – but the popularity of the Galápagos does mean that even on longer tours to remoter islands, you'll probably be sharing the sites with several other groups. Maximum group sizes for visitor sites are sixteen, and authorities strictly control the total number of allowed visitors per site; for shore excursions, this means that you will probably share spots with the same number of people regardless of whether you're travelling on a small or larger vessel. Eighty **boats** currently have licences to tour the Galápagos; these are divided into several categories of comfort and range from converted fishing boats for a handful of people to luxury cruisers for a hundred. Most carry between ten and twenty passengers and almost all rely on engine power, though several boost their speed with sails. See p.344 for a list of recommended cruise operators.

BOATS AND COSTS

Economy boats can cost as little as $100–120 per person per day in the low season and around $150–170 in the high season. Many of these boats are poky, often having tiny bunk-bed cabins and shared bathrooms, as well as uninspiring food and Class-I guides, who are Galápagos locals with the lowest level of naturalist training and only a fair amount of English. The boats are slower, tend to stick to the central islands and generally suffer most from rocking and rolling.

Tourist boats (around $170–350 per person per day) should be a bit more spacious with slightly better facilities and Class-II guides, Ecuadorians with good education, often in related fields, who have at least five years' experience and can speak English, French or German fluently. **Tourist-superior boats** (roughly $350–450 per day) usually have more comfortable cabins still, sometimes with a/c, better food and Class-III guides, the highest level of accreditation, who have at least eight years' experience, degrees in biology, tourism or similar, and can speak fluent Spanish and English plus French or German, and sometimes Italian or Russian.

Many of the boats in the Galápagos are **first-class** or **luxury boats** ($450 plus per day), enjoying the best food, service, comfort and guides, who are always Class-III and invariably very highly qualified naturalists. Cabins typically have beds rather than bunks, private bathrooms and a/c. They also tend to be faster, and a few have stabilizers to lessen the effects of rough seas. While the largest boats may have extra facilities and treat wastewater, an important environmental concern, groups can take longer to disembark, giving you less time on shore. Tours on first-class and luxury boats are most often arranged in your home country (see Basics, p.266 for details of specialist operators).

If you're travelling alone you may be asked to pay a hefty **supplement** for your cabin, unless you're prepared to share. The *Santa Cruz II* has a few single-passenger cabins. Other hidden costs include alcohol and tips; as a general rule an economy guide and crew will expect around $15–30 per cabin per day, while operators of some luxury boats suggest $100 plus per person per week for the crew and $50 plus per person per week for the guide. Many boats provide their own tipping guidelines. If you can give the tip directly to the deserving, so much the better, as this avoids the possibility of unfair distribution of a general tip by unscrupulous captains or guides.

BEFORE YOU BOOK

Before you choose a tour, inspect the **itinerary** and make sure it takes in islands with the creatures you want to see. A week-long tour will give you a good overview, but you still

guide, and you can also take **day-trips** from the larger towns, namely Puerto Ayora and to a lesser extent Puerto Baquerizo Moreno, to a handful of sites around the central islands.

INDEPENDENT TRAVEL BETWEEN THE ISLANDS

By plane The most efficient but costly means of inter-island travel is by flying with EMETEBE (ⓦ emetebe .com); see relevant town accounts for phone numbers.

There are daily services (Mon–Sat) between San Cristóbal, Baltra and Isabela; a one-way ticket for foreigners costs $170–190. The luggage allowance is just 9kg (20lbs), but fees for additional kilos are reasonable.

By boat Cooperative-run *lanchas* or *fibras* (fibreglass

won't see everything, so make sure your choice covers species you most want to see. To give you as much time at the sites as possible, don't pick tours that include more than a night in a single port, sail during the day (which means less time on the islands) or stop at too many sites you can visit independently without a guide anyway. On the lower-end tours in particular, you should check exactly what is included: ask about what **food** you can expect (especially if you're vegetarian); if drinking water is free; whether there are **masks and snorkels** available; if the **guide** speaks decent English; how much you will see on the first and last days; how many nights will be spent ashore; what the bathrooms and cabins are like; whether you'll have to share with strangers; and whether the boat will sail at night. Most importantly, make sure your boat has adequate **safety equipment**, like life jackets, rafts and fire extinguishers. Boats carrying more than fifteen passengers are required to hold an International Safety Management (ISM) certificate, which should be available for you to inspect on request.

BUDGET DEALS

Cruising the Galápagos Islands is not an activity well geared to **budget** travellers, but it is possible to minimize costs by getting a **last-minute deal**, especially in low season, when you can often save up to fifty percent off the listed price. Checking out the tour operators online and based in Quito is a good place to start, with the cheapest deals almost always found via companies that own their own boats. You'll get the best prices if you book at Puerto Ayora, but you risk waiting for several days or even weeks for a space; at busy times of year (July, August and over Christmas and the New Year), it's virtually impossible to get one.

THE DAILY ROUTINE

Except for the most basic boats, life aboard a ship is relaxed and well organized. After an early breakfast, you'll set out in a dinghy (*panga*) for the visitor site and disembark with either a **wet landing** (wading ashore) or **dry landing** (on rocks or a dock). After a few hours on the island, you'll return to the boat for lunch and a siesta before another visit in the afternoon; most days, there'll be the chance to swim or snorkel once or twice. The boat usually sets sail for the next site after dinner, arriving early next morning; the engine noise and rocking of the boat may be disturbing on the first night, but even those without sea legs tend to get used to it. Earplugs will help you get a good night's rest.

PROBLEMS

Most tours pass without incident, but occasionally **problems** occur. Economy boats are usually the worst offenders; things that can go wrong include overbooking, petty theft, annoying engine noise and smells, food and water supplies running out, changes of itinerary, breakdowns and sexual harassment from the guide or crew. One trick of operators is to swap boats at the last moment; your contract should stipulate a refund if the category of boat changes and you should try to get a receipt from the agency and boat owner so it's clear what you've paid for. Even if the operator breaches the contract, getting a reimbursement can be hard work; if you feel wronged, report the operator to the Ministerio de Turismo and Capturgal (see p.348), who may be able to impose a fine and get you a **reimbursement**. You can also tell South American Explorers in Quito (see p.79), which keeps a file of cruise operators. In rare cases, irresponsible guides have disobeyed park rules, perhaps erring from the path, touching animals or bringing food onto the islands. This kind of behaviour should be reported to the Galápagos National Park Service.

8

motorboat) make daily trips from San Cristóbal to Santa Cruz (usually departing 7am, returning 2pm; 2hr), and from Isabela to Santa Cruz (usually leaving 6am, returning 2pm; 2–3hr). Tickets ($30 one-way) are sold at local travel agents. The ride can be rough and uncomfortable; bring plenty of water and sunscreen, check there are life jackets, pack seasickness pills and, ideally, take a boat with more than one engine. *Lanchas* do not make scheduled trips to Floreana and chartering is expensive, but tour operators in Santa Cruz and San Cristóbal offer $75 day-trips.

DAY-TRIPS

An inexpensive way to see the islands is to arrange day-trips, especially from Puerto Ayora. Costing around $60–140/person, these usually include a guide of varying quality, lunch and a visit to one island. They're easy to organize as they're offered by many of the travel agencies in town, though you'll be limited to a handful of islands within striking distance of the port, namely Plaza Sur, Seymour Norte, Santa Fé and Floreana (if the boat leaves from Baltra, you may get to visit Bartolomé too).

LAND-BASED TOURS

Some operators also offer land-based tours, where you sleep at night on shore and sail out to nearby visitor sites during the day – effectively a string of day-trips packaged together as a multi-day Galápagos tour. While this has the advantage of comfortable hotel accommodation and is usually less expensive than a conventional cruise (depending on the level of hotel used), sailing in the day makes for less time at the sites and means you'll be restricted to the busiest sites nearest to the population centres.

CRUISE OPERATORS

This list gives a good selection of boat owners rather than general operators (see p.80) who can make bookings on boats from a range of companies but sometimes charge an extra commission; some are also agents for other companies. Unless stated otherwise, prices listed are for an eight-day cruise in high season, per person, based on two sharing a cabin, excluding airfares and park entrance fees.

Aida Maria Travel Amazonas N23-31 and Veintimilla, Quito ☎02 2546028, ⊚aidamariatravel.com. One of the less expensive operators, with a fleet of motor yachts ranging in comfort from economy to first-class, including the mid-range *Eden*, a diving boat (*Deep Blue*) and a sailing catamaran (*Valkiria*) for tours between the settled areas. From $1450.

Andando Tours/Angermeyer Cruises Moreno Bellido E6-167, Quito ☎02 3237330, ⊚visitgalapagos.travel.

The environmentally minded Andando is owned by a branch of the Angermeyer family, who came to the Galápagos in the 1930s. It has two good-looking first-class sailing yachts (*Mary Anne* and *Sagitta*) and also represents the owners of several other vessels. From $2337 (for a five-day itinerary).

Ecoventura Almagro N31-80, Edificio Venecia, Quito ☎02 2297396, ⊚ecoventura.com. This company operates three first-class motor yachts, *Eric*, *Flamingo I* and *Letty*, as well as a specialist diving boat, *Galapagos Sky*. From $4300.

Enchanted Expeditions De las Alondras N45-102 and De los Lirios, Edificio Floralp, Quito ☎02 3340525, ⊚enchantedexpeditions.com. A reliable and recommended operator running the luxury *Beluga* motor yacht and the first-class *Cachalote I*, an attractive 96-foot schooner. A good standard of service and guiding is complemented by some excellent cooking. From $2960.

Haugan Cruises Sonelsa Tower 6th floor, Foch 265 and 6 de Diciembre, Quito ☎02 2226612, ⊚haugancruises .com. Norwegian-owned operator of the luxurious, sixteen person catamarans *Cormorant*, *Ocean Spray* and *Petrel*. Cruises 4–15 days. From $3090.

Klein Tours/Go Galápagos Av Eloy Alfaro N34-151 and Catalina Aldaz, Quito ☎02 2267000, ⊚gogalapagos .com. Long-standing operator with two mid-sized first-class boats, *Coral I* and *Coral II*, as well as the luxury hundred-person cruiser, *Galápagos Legend*. From $2990.

Metropolitan Touring 6 de Diciembre and Julio Moreno, 1st floor inside the mall (among other branch agencies), Quito ☎02 2988200, ⊚metropolitan -touring.com. One of the pioneers of tourism in the Galápagos, Metropolitan operates three first-class boats: the ninety-person *Santa Cruz II*, the forty-person *Isabela II* and the 48-person *La Pinta*. It also offers land-based tours from its luxury hotel *Finch Bay* (see p.348). From $3195.

Quasar Expeditions Ponce Carrasco E8-06 and Av Diego de Almagro, Quito ☎02 3825680, ⊚galapagos expeditions.com. This well-respected, highly professional company offers top-level Galápagos tours on first-class and luxury yachts. Guiding, service and accommodation are all excellent, and the boats *Grace* (which was once owned by Grace Kelly) and *Evolution* are among the most comfortable in the islands. From $4800 (including flights).

Rolf Wittmer Tip Top Foch E7-81 and Diego de Almagro, Quito ☎02 2563098, ⊚rwittmer.com. Rolf Wittmer, credited with being the first recorded native of Floreana island and son of the famous pioneering Wittmer family (see box, p.367), owns four first-class motor yachts, *Tip Top II - IV* and *Nortada*, each with a sixteen-person capacity. From $3395 (including flights).

8

Santa Cruz and around

The archipelago's centre and tourist hub, **SANTA CRUZ**, is a conical island of just under 1000 square kilometres, whose luxuriant southeastern slopes are cloaked in *garúa* drizzle for much of the year. Reaching an altitude of 864m, the island supports all Galápagos vegetation zones (see p.413), from cactus-strewn **deserts** around the coast, to tangled scalesia and miconia **forests** wreathed in cloud in the highlands, and sodden grassy **pampas** at the summit.

Santa Cruz's central location and proximity to the airport on Baltra have helped make it the most populated island in the Galápagos. The majority of the 30,000 or so islanders live in the archipelago's largest town, **Puerto Ayora**, which is also the nerve centre of the conservation programme, headquarters of both the **Charles Darwin Research Station** and the **Parque Nacional Galápagos**. Home to more boats, tour brokers, hotels and restaurants than anywhere else in the islands, Puerto Ayora is also the best place for budget travellers to find last-minute places on cruises. There's plenty to do in the meantime, such as visiting **Bahía Tortuga**, the **Chato Tortoise Reserve** or exploring the island's several **lava tunnels**. Those itching to get to the wildlife can take day-trips by boat to the nearby islands in this central group, namely **Santa Fé**, **Plaza Sur** and **Seymour Norte**.

Puerto Ayora

Lying around the azure inlets of Academy Bay's rocky shore, **PUERTO AYORA**, on the southern coast of Santa Cruz, was home to fewer than a couple of hundred people until the early 1970s. Now, laden with souvenir shops, travel agents, restaurants and hotels, the current denizens enjoy a higher standard of living than any other province in the republic, giving it a distinct aura of well-appreciated privilege. There's a relaxed atmosphere to the place; tourists meander down the waterfront in the daytime, browsing through shops stuffed with blue-footed booby T-shirts and carvings of giant tortoises, while fishermen across the street in little **Pelican Bay** build boats and sort through their catches, watched by hungry pelicans. In the evenings, locals play volleyball outside the Capitanía (an Ecuadorian naval base) and as it gets darker, the restaurant lights cast a modest glow over the bay and the bars fill with locals, tourists and research scientists, a genial mix that ensures Puerto Ayora has the best **nightlife** in the Galápagos.

Brief history

The first record of human habitation in what is now Puerto Ayora is of a group of **sailors**, shipwrecked in 1905. They survived for three months by drinking sea-lion blood and chewing cactus pads, before discovering brackish water collecting in rock pools in Academy Bay, named after the California Academy of Sciences boat which – unbeknown to them – had moored here only a few weeks earlier; they languished in the bay for a further three months until their rescue.

Puerto Ayora itself was founded in the 1920s by a small group of **Norwegians**, lured to the Galápagos by ruthless promoters trading on the popularity of William Beebe's 1924 book, *Galápagos, World's End*, an account of his trip there with the New York Zoological Society. They promised the Norwegians – who gave away all their savings to go – a secret Eden where the "soil is so rich that 100,000 people could easily find homes", noting that gold and diamonds were probably around too. Under an agreement with the Ecuadorian government they landed on Floreana, but within a few months of back-breaking work some had died and many more given up. In 1926, others went to **Academy Bay** and built houses, a fish cannery and a wharf, so founding the port. For a time, things went uncharacteristically well until the cannery blew up, killing two and injuring several others. To rub salt into the wound, the government

PUERTO AYORA

ACCOMMODATION
Darwin	11
Finch Bay	12
Galapagos Suites	2
Lirio del Mar	10
Mainao	7
La Peregrina	8
Red Mangrove Aventura Lodge	5
Royal Palm	3
Semilla Verde	4
Silberstein	6
Solymar	9
Verdeazul	1

● EATING
Angermeyer Point	6
Galápagos Deli	4
La Garrapata	3
Il Giardino	2
Hernán	5
La Tintorera	1

■ DRINKING & NIGHTLIFE
Bongo Bar and La Panga	1
The Rock	2

seized their boat and all their remaining equipment, claiming the settlers had not built the harbours, roads and schools as laid out in their previous agreement. By 1929, only three Norwegians were left on Santa Cruz, but through superhuman determination, they built the foundations for the largest and richest city in the Galápagos.

Charles Darwin Research Station

At the northern end of Av Charles Darwin, a 20-minute walk from the town centre • Mon–Fri 7.30am–12.30pm & 2–5pm • Free • ☎ 05 252 6146, ⍵ darwinfoundation.org

Even though it is primarily a science and conservation facility, just about every tour sooner or later washes up at the **Charles Darwin Research Station** (CDRS). Past the **information booth** at the entrance, a path leads between some giant cacti to the **Van Straelen interpretation centre**, exhibiting information on geology, climate, conservation and many related aspects of Galápagos nature. A short video about the CDRS and the islands, introduced by a staff member, can be seen on request; details are available here about joining Galápagos conservation organizations (see box, p.340).

The tortoise-rearing pens

Beyond the interpretation centre are the **tortoise-rearing pens**, where predator-proof enclosures hold batches of miniature giant tortoises divided by age. Since 1965, a programme of tortoise repopulation has been ongoing, with eggs being carefully extracted from the wild and incubated here. After two or three years the hatchlings graduate to larger enclosures with the kind of terrain they might find in the wild; after four to six years they are deemed to have grown to an uneatable size (as far as predators are concerned) and repatriated to their home islands. **Land iguanas** and critically endangered **mangrove finches** are also bred here.

The tortoise corrals

From the pens, a raised boardwalk weaves past the **tortoise corrals**, which house fully grown giant tortoises. This is the best place to take photos, though make sure you don't touch the tortoises. Until his death (aged an estimated 100) in June 2012, this was the home of **Lonesome George** (*Solitario Jorge*), the last surviving tortoise of the Pinta island subspecies, who was considered by many to be the rarest animal in the world. From 1906 until 1971 (when George was found) it was thought that Pinta tortoises were extinct. Numerous efforts to mate him with female tortoises from elsewhere in the islands failed, though this only seemed to enhance his popularity with the public.

Beyond the tortoise corrals, just before the exit, is a kiosk selling T-shirts, videos and souvenirs; this is the only place on the islands you can buy CDRS logo clothing, the proceeds of which go straight to the station. Near the exit you'll see a sign for a little **beach**, a hidden spot for lazing about and looking across the bay.

Bahía Tortuga

3km southwest of town • The bay is only accessible on foot (a 40min walk): head west out of Puerto Ayora on Charles Binford, which continues as a dirt road to a cliff, at the top of which is a national park guardhouse; from here a paved trail leads to the beach

Bahía Tortuga is a beautiful beach of soft, white sand unfurling for almost a kilometre, washed by luminescent blue waters. People swim here but it's not safe, as the currents are very strong and there are no lifeguards around. A better spot for a dip is at the western end of the beach, beyond the rocky outcrop of lava, where there's a lagoon wrapped in mangroves; you may see marine iguanas, brown pelicans and even flamingos. Kayaks can be rented here for $10. There are no facilities or shops here so bring water with you.

Playa de los Alemanes

A short water-taxi ride across the bay from town, near the *Finch Bay* hotel

Just over the bay from Puerto Ayora are two popular swimming spots in an area surrounded by lagoons and saltbush teeming with birdlife. From the dock, a path leads to an attractive protected beach ideal for swimming and snorkelling, the **Playa de los Alemanes**, named after the early German settlers who made their homes here.

Las Grietas

Beyond the beach, a gravel path leads for fifteen to twenty minutes to **Las Grietas**, stunning inland saltwater canyons surrounded by high lava walls, which are very popular with locals at weekends for bathing; on weekdays the pools are quiet.

ARRIVAL AND DEPARTURE
PUERTO AYORA

BY PLANE

Flights The airport (☏ 05 2521165) is on the neighbouring island of Baltra, with daily flights from Quito via Guayaquil, as well as around six weekly services from Puerto Baquerizo Moreno, on San Cristóbal, and Puerto Villamil, on Isabela. The airlines have offices in Puerto Ayora, as well as at the airport: Avianca, San Cristóbal and General Rodríguez Lara (☏ 05 2526797, ⊛ avianca.com); EMETEBE, Av Charles Darwin above the post office (☏ 05 2526177, ⊛ emetebe .com); LAN, Av Charles Darwin (☏ 1800 101 075, ⊛ lan .com); TAME, Av Charles Darwin and 12 de Febrero

(☏ 05 2526527, ⊛ tame.com.ec).

Airport transfers From the airport, free shuttle buses run to the dock where the cruise boats wait, or to the Canal de Itabaca, the narrow stretch of water between Baltra and Santa Cruz. Here, a passenger ferry ($0.80) connects with buses ($3.50) on the other side, which take you over the highlands to the bus terminal just outside Puerto Ayora; the buses only connect with incoming flights from the mainland, so at other times you'll have to get a camioneta or taxi to Puerto Ayora ($15–20).

GETTING AROUND

By boat There are daily boats (called *fibras* or *lanchas*) to Puerto Baquerizo Moreno (about 2hr) and Puerto Villamil (around 2–3hr), usually departing at 2pm from the dock; tickets cost $25–30.

By taxi Taxis cost around $1–2 to most local destinations,

and about $10 for a trip to Santa Rosa (see p.351).

By water taxi Water taxis (yellow dinghies with blue awnings) are useful for trips across the bay, or for day-and-night runs between the shore and your tour boat (around $1/person).

INFORMATION

Tourist offices Capturgal (the Galápagos Chamber of Tourism), on the corner of Darwin and 12 de Febrero (☏ 05 2526609, ⊛ galapagostour.org), and the Ministerio de Turismo on Charles Binford near 12 de Febrero (☏ 05 2526174), stock

simple maps and brochures of the islands and population centres: both open Mon–Fri 8.30–5.30pm. The Charles Darwin Research Station (see p.346) has all the nitty-gritty facts and figures of Galápagos wildlife and natural history.

TOURS AND ACTIVITIES

Galápagos Alternative ☏ 0994655018, ⊛ galapagos alternative.com. American-Ecuadorian-run company offering a wide range of customizable tours and activities.

Galápagos Sub-Aqua Av Charles Darwin near the entrance to the Charles Darwin Foundation ☏ 0999198798, ⊛ galapagos-sub-aqua.com. Long-standing outfit offering introductory dives at Academy Bay, day-trips and diving cruises, plus PADI courses.

Macarrón Scuba Dive Av Charles Darwin across from the fishermens' pier ☏ 05 2524080, ⊛ macarronscubadiver.com.ec. Run by friendly Juan Carlos Moncayo ("Macarrón"), a fisherman turned diver and environmentalist, this reputable agency offers diving throughout the central island, including beginners' courses.

Moonrise Travel Av Charles Darwin 160 ☏ 05 2526403, ⊛ galapagosmoonrise.com. Another established agency

with a reputation for finding last-minute places on the more reliable tour boats quickly; it also runs day-trips, glass-bottomed boat tours and excursions to the highlands, including to their private ranch, where you can see wild tortoises.

Scuba Iguana Av Charles Darwin ☏ 05 2526497, ⊛ scubaiguana.com. Highly professional, Ecuadorian-German diving operator, offering trips and courses throughout the central islands, as well as Floreana and, for advanced divers, Gordon Rocks.

We Are The Champions Tours Av Charles Darwin ☏ 05 2526951, ⊛ wearethechampionstours.com. Ecuadorian-German-run company offering a range of day-trips around Santa Cruz, longer excursions to Isabela and Floreana and a selection of cruises, plus diving and snorkelling.

ACCOMMODATION

Accommodation prices are higher than on the mainland, yet even the thriftiest backpackers should find something to suit them; in the **low season** you may be able to bargain down to the rate nationals pay, though many hotels insist on one price throughout the year. The smarter hotels can quickly fill up in the **high season**, so reserve well in advance. Some budget hotels don't have hot water.

IN TOWN

Darwin Av Herrera and Tomás de Berlanga ☎05 2526193. One of the better budget options in Puerto Ayora, this pleasant hotel has a collection of clean, no-frills rooms with private bathrooms (with hot water) set around a small courtyard. Staff are friendly and breakfast is included. $30

★ **Finch Bay** Punta Estrada, a water-taxi ride across the bay from town ☎05 2526297, ⊛finchbayhotel.com. This award-winning, luxury eco-hotel is in a private location surrounded by mangroves. It has its own large pool, open-air hot tub, beach access and excellent restaurant, as well as a desalinization plant and rubbish processing and recycling programmes. The comfortable en-suite rooms, renovated in 2015, have a/c and private terraces with views of the garden or the sea. Breakfast included. $345

Galapagos Suites Cucuve s/n and Floreana ☎05 2526209, ⊛galapagossuites.com. This superior B&B has six airy, minimalist en suites with modern bathrooms and a/c; those on the upper floors have sea views. Staff are friendly and helpful, there's a tranquil patio garden, and the included breakfast is one of the best on the island. $152

Lirio del Mar Islas Plaza between Darwin and Berlanga ☎05 2526212. This budget hotel has reasonable, if very basic, rooms: each has a private bathroom with hot water and a fan (but no a/c). The rooms on the upper floors are the best, and there's a rooftop terrace from which to admire the views. Breakfast included. $45

Mainao Matazarnos near Indefatigable ☎05 2527029, ⊛hotelmainao.com. Blazing whitewash and little red awnings evoke the Mediterranean at this quiet back-street hotel, featuring comfortable, clean en suites with a/c; some also have private balconies. Free internet access is available, and Rough Guides readers get a ten percent discount. Breakfast included. $118

La Peregrina Av Charles Darwin and Indefatigable ☎05 2526323, ⊛laperegrinagalapagos.com.ec. This peaceful B&B has good-value rooms with private bathrooms, hot water and a/c; they vary in size, so ask to see a few. There's also a pleasant garden area strung with hammocks, and tours and day-trips are on offer. Breakfast included. $75

Red Mangrove Aventura Lodge Av Charles Darwin and Las Fragatas ☎05 2526564, ⊛redmangrove.com. Set at the water's edge amid mangroves, this secluded hotel was designed and built by its artist owners and has many idiosyncratic flourishes. Rooms are bright and fresh, with views of the bay or mangroves; there's a whirlpool on the veranda. Day-trips, windsurfing, kayaking, horse riding, mountain biking and tours to their highland camp and lodges on Isabela (see p.361) and Floreana (see p.366) can all be arranged; breakfast included. Minimum five-night stay. 2–7 night packages from $1049

Silberstein Av Charles Darwin and Seymour ☎05 2526277, ⊛hotelsilberstein.com. Attractive, traditional hotel catering to divers. The a/c en suites are large and comfortable (if a bit overpriced), and there's an appealing swimming pool in the garden area, as well as a decent restaurant and a reliable in-house travel agency. Breakfast included. $239

Solymar Av Charles Darwin ☎05 2526281, ⊛hotelsolymar.com.ec. The highlight of *Solymar's* bright and spacious en-suite rooms are the private balconies overlooking the bay. As well as a mid-sized pool and hot tub, there's a restaurant and bar located right on the water (a romantic evening spot if you find it on a quiet night); breakfast included. Its similarly styled, slightly cheaper *Isla Sol* is across the street. $328

Verdeazul Petrel and Marchena ☎05 2524262, ⊛hotelverdeazul.com. Run by the family behind the *Mainao*, *Verdeazul* is another decent, lower-cost option away from the waterfront. The rooms here are pretty spartan, but all are clean, and have a/c and private bathrooms; be sure to ask for one with a sea view. Breakfast included. $95

OUT OF TOWN

Royal Palm 18km north of town ☎05 2527409, ⊛royalpalmgalapagos.com. One of the most expensive hotels in Ecuador, the swanky *Royal Palm* counts Brad Pitt and Angelina Jolie among its past guests. Set in an exclusive estate in the highlands with gorgeous views over the islands, the hotel provides smart service, a full range of amenities (including its own art gallery) and lavish accommodation (even the cheapest "Veranda" rooms have their own private hot tubs). Breakfast included. It has an exclusive, even more luxurious private bayside option in town, the *Villa Escalesia*. From $350

★ **Semilla Verde** 12km northwest of Puerto Ayora on the road to Baltra ☎0987103006, ⊛gps.ec. This tranquil British-Ecuadorian-run guesthouse, a 15min drive from Puerto Ayora, is a real find: beautiful en suites, personalized service and a lovely forest setting, which is home to giant tortoises, among numerous other species. A proportion of the room rate is used to fund a reforestation project. Breakfast included. $185

8

EATING

Along Avenida Charles Darwin are a good proportion of relatively expensive restaurants (most of which double as bars) aimed at tourists, as well as a few simpler and less expensive places aimed more at locals. For good-value seafood, head to Calle Charles Binford, where a string of *kioskos* (kiosks) cook simmering cauldrons of *encocados* (seafood in a sauce of coconut milk, tomato and garlic – an Esmeraldas speciality) and serve up plates of fish and rice, cooked in the style of the mainland coast, as well as good, inexpensive lobster in season. Lobster season is roughly the second half of the year, but the precise dates are set annually by the island authorities. The *kioskos* block becomes pedestrianized in the evening.

Angermeyer Point On a private dock just south of town ☎ 05 2527007. Built on decks over a rocky promontory, where marine iguanas live, this popular restaurant is just a water-taxi ride ($1) from the dock. The rather pricey menu ranges from steaks to seafood (with sushi on Friday nights), and while the dishes ($15–30) don't always match the superb setting, *Angermeyer Point* is still well worth a visit. Reservations recommended. Tues–Sun 5–10pm.

Galápagos Deli Tomás de Berlanga between Baltra and Islas Plaza ☎ 05 3014981. Pleasant, modern café-restaurant featuring excellent home-made ice cream and sandwiches and Puerto Ayora's best thin-crust pizza, as well as fish and chips for those nostalgic for the UK. Tues–Sun 10.30am–10.30pm.

La Garrapata Av Charles Darwin and Tomás de Berlanga ☎ 05 2526264. This popular open-air restaurant has candlelit tables and a relaxed atmosphere. The menu features delicious fish, seafood and grilled meat (mains around $7–20), although service can be hit or miss. Mon–Sat 9am–4pm & 6.30–10/10.30pm.

Il Giardino Av Charles Darwin and Charles Binford ☎ 2526627. This smart, predominantly Italian restaurant serves well-prepared seafood (including octopus carpaccio and fresh lobster), pasta, crepes and steaks (mains $10–28). There's also an appealing ice-cream parlour attached, that serves authentic gelato. Use insect repellent as mosquitoes love ice cream too. Tues–Sun 8am–10/10.30pm.

Hernán Av Baltra at Charles Darwin. In a location ideal for people-watching, *Hernán* serves up decent thin-crust pizzas, pasta dishes and seafood at pretty reasonable prices for Puerto Ayora: mains cost around $8–18. The coffee and juices are both very good too. Daily 7/7.30am–9/10pm.

La Tintorera Av Charles Darwin and Isla Floreana ☎ 05 2524141. This relaxed restaurant-bar, close to Pelican Bay, has a more varied menu than most of its competitors. Although not all the dishes hit the spot, most tastes are catered for – including sushi, numerous vegetarian options, tapas, coconut curry and fresh tuna cooked on a lava rock. Mains $6.50–14.50. Mon–Fri 8.30am–10.30pm, Sat 9.30am–10.30pm.

DRINKING AND NIGHTLIFE

Bongo Bar and La Panga Av Charles Darwin near Tomás de Berlanga. The most popular nightclub in town, *La Panga* tends to fill up quite late in the evening with both locals and foreigners. Upstairs is the *Bongo Bar*, a rooftop venue with open-air seating, a pool table and a small dancefloor. Wed–Sat 7pm–2/3am.

The Rock Av Charles Darwin at Islas Plaza. Named after the first Galápagos bar established on Baltra in the 1940s, this charming place serves up a a wide variety of juices, shakes and cocktails, plus good food, from Mexican quesadillas to teriyaki fish fillets ($6–10). Tues–Sun 2pm–12am.

DIRECTORY

Banks There are several ATMs in town, including at Banco del Pacífico, on Av Charles Darwin at Charles Binford, which also changes dollar and euro travellers' cheques.

Hospitals The public hospital is on Av Padre Julio Herrera and Av Charles Darwin (emergencies ☎ 05 2526103). A better-staffed and -equipped private clinic is Protesub (☎ 05 2526911, ⓦ sssnetwork.com) on 18 de Febrero and General Rodríguez Lara, which primarily provides medical services for submarine and aquatic activities, and has a hyperbaric recompression chamber, but also offers general medical care.

Language school Instituto Superior de Español; contact via the Quito office at Darquea Terán 16-50 and Av 10 de Agosto (☎ 02 228 5657, ⓦ islas-galapagos.com).

Post office The post office is on Av Charles Darwin, next to the Proinsular Supermarket.

The Santa Cruz highlands

The flora and fauna of the **highlands** of Santa Cruz are quite distinct from the parched coastal areas. From Puerto Ayora the main road over the island ascends from the lowland scrub and cactus fields, and by the time it reaches Bellavista, introduced elephant grass, plantains, papayas and avocados grow from the fertile red soil. The highland sites are relatively easy to get to for independent travellers, though it's a good idea to hire a guide for trails up Cerro Chato or Cerro Crocker.

Hiking to Cerro Crocker

Six kilometres north of Puerto Ayora is the little village of **Bellavista**. From here a trail leads north through farmland, miconia forests and pampa grass for about 8km (a 2hr

30min trek) to the summit of the island, **Cerro Crocker** (864m); when the mists disperse, the panoramic **views** are spectacular. About 5km into the walk you'll reach the crescent-shaped **Media Luna** and nearer the summit, **Puntudo**, both old volcanic cones grown over with thick vegetation. The trail can get very muddy and hard to follow in places, so getting a guide is a good idea. Note that flash floods destroyed the bike route in January 2016 check on; conditions before attempting to cycle here.

Chato Tortoise Reserve

Around 9km northwest of Bellavista, the farms of **Santa Rosa** sit amid abundant fruit orchards and cedar trees that dwarf the native vegetation. From here, a track leads through three kilometres of farmland dotted with white cattle egrets and smooth-billed anis to the edge of the **Chato Tortoise Reserve** on the southwestern corner of the island – t's among the best places in the Galápagos to see giant tortoises in their natural habitat. Here, the trail forks between a branch heading west through endemic scalesia forest up to **Cerro Chato** (about 3km), and east to a small lagoon (2km), where tortoises wallow in the company of white-cheeked pintails. Vermilion and Galápagos flycatchers are common sightings, but you'll need more luck to spot the secretive Galápagos rail. A **guide** is strongly recommended for visiting the reserve, not least because it is dangerously easy o get lost here; bring plenty of water, sturdy shoes and wet-weather gear.

Los Gemelos

A couple of kilometres beyond Santa Rosa on the way to Baltra, the road passes between **Los Gemelos**, a pair of yawning, forest-swathed pit craters, formed when lava collapsed into underlying magma chambers. Trails lead from the road to viewpoints overlooking each, and **finches** and **flycatchers** inhabit the surrounding forests.

8

GETTING AROUND	SANTA CRUZ HIGHLANDS
By bus Buses going to Santa Rosa (20min; stopping at Bellavista after 10min) leave Puerto Ayora hourly from the market on Avenida Padre Julio Herrera and Isla Duncan. The last bus back from Santa Rosa is at 9pm.	Traffic is sporadic, so allow plenty of time to hitch a lift back to town if necessary.
By taxi or shared taxi Wait at Puerto Ayora market to catch a ride in a shared taxi ($2–3 to Bellavista; $4–5 to Santa Rosa); a normal taxi will cost around $10 one-way.	**By tour** Travel agencies in Puerto Ayora can arrange a guided trip for around $30/person, depending on the size of the group. If you're on a cruise, the itinerary may give you a half-day to explore the highlands.

Northwest Santa Cruz

On the northwest side of Santa Cruz there are several sites worth visiting. **Las Bachas** gets its name from the barges the US abandoned on the beach here during World War II, and

---

SANTA CRUZ LAVA TUBES

Huge underground **lava tubes** perforate Santa Cruz, and in places extend for several kilometres, enclosed by high jagged walls that disappear into the gloom. The tubes were formed when cooler outer parts of lava flows hardened into thick rock walls, providing insulation to keep a flow going inside; eventually the flow subsided, leaving long empty tunnels easily big enough to walk down. As they're on private land, you don't need an official guide to explore these volcanic curiosities, though tours can be arranged in Puerto Ayora. The floors can be slippery and rubble-strewn, so a flashlight and sturdy shoes are a good idea.

One of the easiest to get to is near Bellavista (follow the "*los túneles*" signs from the village), where you can rent a flashlight ($0.50) to explore a tunnel ($2) several hundred metres long. Another set, known as El Mirador, is within walking distance, 2.5km from Puerto Ayora ($1–2 by taxi). You can also visit the Salasaca tunnels ($3), 5km northwest of Santa Rosa on the farm of Señor Arias; contact him through one of Puerto Ayora's travel agencies to arrange a visit.

you can still see the rusting skeletons poking through the sand. It's a popular place for a swim, but also has a good selection of wildlife, including marine iguanas, hermit crabs, black-necked stilts and great blue herons, as well as flamingos in the nearby saltwater lagoon. To the west is **Caleta Tortuga Negra**, a cove where Pacific green turtles (despite the cove's name) come to breed at the beginning of the warm-wet season. White-tipped reef sharks and rays can be spotted year-round, and the lagoon itself is fringed by mangroves, where herons and pelicans nest. **Cerro Dragón**, on the northwestern tip of the island, is accessed via a gravel path winding up from flamingo lagoons to the top of the hill, passing land iguanas.

ARRIVAL AND DEPARTURE	**NORTHWEST SANTA CRUZ**
By boat The only way to visit these sites is by boat. Occasionally, day-trips (around $100) sail there, but more	commonly cruise boats call at these spots having left the harbour at Baltra.

Islands around Santa Cruz

Among the small islands and islets surrounding Santa Cruz, there are five visitor sites, most of which can be reached on day-trips from Puerto Ayora (around $120–200). Those close to **Baltra** are often visited at the beginning or end of a cruise, while tour boats frequently call at **Seymour Norte**, **Plaza Sur** and **Santa Fé**, though few stop at the tiny lava reef of **Mosquera**. **Daphne Mayor** is one of the most restricted sites in the archipelago, due to a difficult landing on steep rocks prone to erosion.

Baltra
Stunted scrub and cactus growth, dry air and a parched landscape dotted with abandoned buildings isn't much of a welcome to one of the world's natural wonders, but **BALTRA** is many visitors' first taste of the Galápagos, before being whisked off to the dock to join a tour boat or catch the Santa Cruz ferry. The US Air Force occupied the island during World War II, blasting an airstrip into the rock so planes could swiftly be mobilized to defend the Panama Canal, but today it's controlled by the Ecuadorian Air Force. Except for **pelicans** and **sea birds** around the dock, there's not much to see on the island. The population of **land iguanas** was wiped out during the US occupation, though fortunately seventy specimens had been experimentally transferred in the early 1930s to Seymour Norte, immediately to the north. Following a repopulation programme by the CDRS, captive-bred iguanas were repatriated to Baltra in 1991.

Mosquera
Lying in the channel between Baltra and Seymour Norte, the tiny island of **MOSQUERA** is a shock of coral sand heaving with sea lions. You have free rein to walk about the island, enjoying the company of **herons** and **lava gulls**, and you can swim with the playful sea lions – but keep away from the bull males.

Seymour Norte
SEYMOUR NORTE, directly north of Baltra (other name, South Seymour), is a small, low, flat island created by geological uplift, and makes frequent appearances on tour-boat itineraries. Passengers come ashore on black lava, where a trail leads past large colonies of **blue-footed boobies**. The island is also one of the best places in the Galápagos to see the **magnificent frigatebird**. Along the shore you'll also find **sea lions** and **marine iguanas**; take care where you put your feet as the latter nest here. An endemic variety of the *palo santo* tree, smaller than its relative with hairier, greyer leaves, borders the inland loop of the trail, and **land iguanas** (introduced here from Baltra in the 1930s) can occasionally be spotted tucked away in the vegetation.

Daphne Mayor

Visible about 10km to the west of Baltra and Seymour Norte, **DAPHNE MAYOR** (the larger of the two Daphnes) is composed of a tuff cone embedded with two craters. At present, only scientific boats are allowed to stop here. Since the early 1970s the island has been the focus of research into **Darwin's finches** by two British scientists, Peter and Rosemary Grant, who have weighed, ringed, measured and photographed every finch on the island – about 25,000 altogether – and so documented evolutionary processes at work; Jonathan Weiner's book *The Beak of the Finch* tells the story of their studies (see p.416). A slender trail leads up to the rim of the island; here you can gaze down into the craters. Colonies of **blue-footed boobies** nest in the furnace heat of these natural cauldrons, and **red-billed tropicbirds** tenant the crevices in the cliff walls.

Plaza Sur

Less than a kilometre from the eastern coast of Santa Cruz, the two tiny Plaza islands, dramatically tilted to form sheer cliffs on the southern side, were formed by seismic uplift, when sections of the sea floor were thrust out of the water. Only **PLAZA SUR**, the larger of the two at less than 1.5km long and under 250m at its widest point, is open to visitors. Being within range of Puerto Ayora day-trippers, the little island can get crowded. Vociferous members of the thousand-strong colony of **sea lions** here see this as a territorial boundary, so take care boarding and disembarking; snorkelling and swimming are also better around neighbouring Plaza Norte, out of the sea-lion war zone. A rather more subdued group of elderly bachelors languishes on a corner of lava (polished smooth over the years by their tired, defeated bodies) up on the cliffs, a tortuous climb over the rocks away from the macho action of the main colony.

The island has striking vegetation, a covering of juicy *Sesuvium* plants that turn crimson in the dry season, punctuated by chunky *Opuntia* cactus trees. When the succulent cactus pads fall to the ground, **land iguanas** wriggle out of their torpor for a bite to eat. Before park rules were enacted, visitors often fed the iguanas fruit, and they subsequently learned to dash to the dock whenever a party landed; they're still often seen lurking around newly arrived groups, waiting in vain for a banana or orange.

A trail leads up to sheer cliffs, an excellent vantage point to spot **noddy terns**, **swallow-tailed gulls**, **Audubon's shearwaters** and **red-billed tropicbirds**, as well as the occasional **blue-footed** and **Nazca boobies**, **frigatebirds** and **pelicans**. Looking down into the swell, you may see yellow-tailed mullet, surgeonfish, manta rays and dolphins.

Santa Fé

Visitors to **SANTA FÉ**, about 25km southeast of Puerto Ayora, disembark for a wet landing on the northeastern side of the island, at a stunning cove with brilliant-blue water and white sand, protected by a partly submerged peninsula. The bay is good for swimming – though give the bull sea lions here a wide berth – and snorkelling may yield up **spotted eagle rays** and **stingrays**, **white-tipped reef sharks** and other colourful reef fish.

IMPORTANT RULES OF THE GALÁPAGOS

- Do not touch, feed, disturb or chase any animal. Do not approach them within two metres.
- Do not move plants, rocks, shells or any natural objects.
- Do not take food onto the islands.
- Make sure you're not carrying soil or seeds from one island to another on your clothes or shoes.
- Never throw litter overboard or on the islands.
- Do not buy souvenirs made of plant or animal products from the islands.
- Declare any organic products in your possession to the quarantine services on arrival.
- Plants, fresh flowers and live animals may not be brought to the islands.

There are two trails on Santa Fé. The first is short and easy, circling through a forest of giant *Opuntia* **cacti** (a variety found only on the island), many reaching 10m in height with trunks 4m in circumference. The second is more strenuous, heading up a steep hill that affords spectacular views of the island. On both, you have a fair chance of seeing a species of **land iguana** unique to Santa Fé, having a paler colour and longer spines on its back than its counterparts on the other islands. With luck, you might also see one of the three surviving endemic species of **rice rat** rustling in the scrub – unlike on Fernandina, the only other island where they are found, this species often appears in the daytime. This is a good island to spot several other endemic species, including the **Galápagos hawk**, **dove** and **snake**. Giant tortoises were reintroduced here in 2015.

Santiago and around

About 25km northwest of Santa Cruz, **SANTIAGO** – officially San Salvador – is the fourth-largest island in the Galápagos at 585 square kilometres, and the last unpopulated one to have been abandoned by human settlers. In the early nineteenth century, Captain Porter (p.367) is reputed to have set four goats free on the island, which swiftly set about multiplying, soon causing extensive damage to the island's native wildlife. Before trained hunters, aided by dogs and satellite tracking systems, could get to work on the island's 100,000 goats, its rampant feral pig population had to be eradicated, a mammoth task that took 28 years and was finally completed in 2001; the last goat was killed in 2005. As well as Santiago's four visitor sites, there are some interesting satellite islands, such as **Rábida**, **Bartolomé** and **Sombrero Chino**, and its proximity to Santa Cruz means the majority of cruise boats stop somewhere in this area. Day-trips from Puerto Ayora also occasionally call at Bartolomé.

Puerto Egas

Puerto Egas, in James Bay on the western side of the island, is Santiago's most visited site, good for snorkelling and spotting a healthy cross-section of wildlife. A few derelict buildings of the old port litter the bay, the relics of failed salt-mining operations from the 1920s and the 1960s, when Héctor Egas, the namesake of the port, left three men here to look after the property, vowing to return with more money to rekindle his bankrupt industry. One of his employees waited four years in vain for his boss to return, and became a minor attraction for early tourists – the vision of a castaway, with shaggy hair and a long, unkempt beard, who scoured the island for food.

A trail leads east from the port area to the old salt mine, a crater where flamingos are occasionally spotted. Along the shore to the west, the bay is an expanse of cracked and weathered black basaltic lava, with enough pools and crevices to sustain a wealth of intertidal wildlife. The **Sally Lightfoot crabs**, **seaurchins**, **anemones**, **eels** and **octopuses** here make a handsome smorgasbord for a number of shore birds, **herons**, **oystercatchers**, **ruddy turnstones** and **noddy terns** among them. At the far western end of the trail, erosion has formed the **fur seal grottoes**, shimmering turquoise pools and inlets worn from lava tubes by the waves. Natural rock bridges straddle the breaches where **marine iguanas**, **fur seals** and **marine turtles** swim. The sloshing of water in one has earned it the title of "Darwin's Toilet". The tuff cone of Pan de Azúcar (Sugarloaf) volcano (395m) overshadows scrub and acacia trees often used by **Galápagos hawks** as perches.

Playa Espumilla

North of Puerto Egas, on the other side of a lava flow, lies **Playa Espumilla**, a tawny beach couched in mangroves, favoured by **marine turtles** as a nesting ground. Feral pigs

that dig up and eat turtle eggs have been a serious problem here in the past, but a recovery is expected following the completion of the eradication programme. A trail leads inland from the beach, weaving through the mangroves alongside a salty lagoon into thick vegetation, home to **Darwin's finches** and **flycatchers**.

Buccaneer Cove

Many boats cruise by **Buccaneer Cove**, roughly 8km north of Puerto Egas and a favourite hide-out of the seventeenth- and eighteenth-century freebooters. Fifty-metre tuff cliffs, spattered with guano, taper down to a short, dusky beach and then rise in the north forming pinnacles and spurs. Pre-Columbian pottery shards discovered here led archeologist and explorer Thor Heyerdahl to suggest that mainland fishermen had used the cove as a campsite long before the arrival of the pirates, probably in the wet season when a freshwater stream ran down to the beach.

Sullivan Bay

On the eastern side of Santiago, **Sullivan Bay**, named after Bartholomew James Sullivan, a lieutenant on the *Beagle*, is one for **lava** fans. A trail leads across a vast, century-old flow of pahoehoe lava, a petrified lake of rumpled ooze, intestinal squiggles and viscous tongues, punctuated by oddities like *hornitos*, solidified pimples made by bursts of gas, and moulds of tree trunks that vaporized in the heat. Two large tuff cones dominate the lava field, and in the cracks and crevices you'll see the layers of previous flows beneath. In this barren landscape, the pioneering *Mollugo* and the **lava cactus** *Brachycereus* are the only plants that can eke out life.

Bartolomé

BARTOLOMÉ, positioned a few hundred metres off the east coast of Santiago, holds the best-known landmark of the Galápagos, the teetering dagger of **Pinnacle Rock**, a jagged remnant of an old tuff cone overshadowing a streak of pale sand at the southwestern end of the island. The many tours that come here usually combine a hike to the island's summit (114m) and a refreshing swim beneath the Rock, where you'll get some fine snorkelling and perhaps catch a glimpse of **Galápagos penguins** zipping by schools of colourful fish. If you don't see them here, you've a better chance of spotting them from a *panga*, on the shaded cliffs each side of the bay.

The **trail to the summit** begins at the man-made dock on Bartolomé's northern point, before crossing a parched landscape relieved only by a scant covering of silvery *Tiquilia* – just about the only plant that can survive such dry, ashy soil – and the infrequent slitherings of a **Galápagos snake**. The trail loops round to the east and climbs up several hundred wooden steps to reach the top of the hill, from where there's the famous view of Pinnacle Rock. On the opposite side a stunning moonscape vista unfolds, with large spatter cones and **lava tunnels** dropping to the southeast to reveal the Daphnes, Baltra, Seymour Norte and Santa Cruz in the distance.

Bartolomé's second trail begins at the beach and leads through the mangroves and dunes across the island's isthmus to a second beach, patrolled by sharks and rays and out of bounds for swimmers. **Marine turtles** nest here at the outset of the warm-wet season.

Sombrero Chino

Barely 100m from the southeastern tip of Santiago, the volcanic cone of tiny **SOMBRERO CHINO** does indeed bear more than a passing resemblance to a Chinese hat. Only small boats are allowed to call here, mooring in the blazing-blue channel between the islands, a terrific spot for snorkelling and where **Galápagos penguins** are occasionally seen. A trail on the island follows a white-coral beach, past a **sea-lion** colony to a cliff vantage point surrounded by scuttling **Sally Lightfoot crabs** and **marine iguanas**. The pockmarked lava landscape is dashed with brighter blotches of **lava cactus**, while around the beach you'll find **saltbush** and colourful **Sesuvium**.

Rábida

Five kilometres south of Santiago is **RÁBIDA**, less than five square kilometres in area. A wet landing at the north of the island onto a russet, sea-lion-strewn beach brings you to a trail leading through saltbush to a saline lagoon; **pelicans** sometimes build nests in the saltbush, while **white-cheeked pintails**, bachelor **sea lions** and **stilts** are lagoon residents. It's possible to see the odd **flamingo** sifting the murky waters for food here as well. A path rises up through **palo santo** and **Opuntia cacti** to a viewpoint above the carmine cliffs. There's good snorkelling near the cliffs or at the landing beach and plenty of colourful fish, diving **boobies** and pelicans to see.

San Cristóbal and around

Out on the eastern side of the archipelago, with a shape resembling a "shrivelled appendix" according to 1940s travel writer Victor von Hagen, is **SAN CRISTÓBAL**, the administrative seat of the Galápagos and at 558 square kilometres its fifth largest island. **Wreck Bay**, at its western tip, is the site of the peaceful provincial capital, **Puerto Baquerizo Moreno**. Attractions here include the excellent **interpretive centre**, which concentrates on the human and natural history of the islands, plus the nearby islets **León Dormido** (Kicker Rock) and **Lobos**, which often feature in local excursions. On the rest of the island, points of interest include the highland town of **El Progreso**, site of Manuel Cobos's tyrannical colony, **Laguna El Junco**, the largest freshwater lake in the Galápagos, and **Punta Pitt**, the archipelago's easternmost point.

8

   Cerro San Joaquín (summit measurements range from 730m to 896m), whose windward slopes are fertile enough to be farmed, dominates the southwestern half of the island. The northeastern area has the characteristic volcanic landscape of the archipelago, a collection of lava flows, spatter cones and other volcanic features.

Puerto Baquerizo Moreno

Founded by the colonist General Villamil in the mid-nineteenth century, **PUERTO BAQUERIZO MORENO** was named after the first Ecuadorian president to visit the islands, in 1916. Despite being the capital, it's a sleepy town, virtually lifeless in the heat of the early afternoon, only coming alive fully when the sun sets over the bay. It may not get as many visitors as Puerto Ayora, but there is a burgeoning industry here: along the waterfront promenade, a glut of travel agents, cafés, restaurants and souvenir shops all show a town keen to cut itself a larger slice of the tourism pie. Puerto Baquerizo Moreno is a bit short of things to do but there's enough on the island to keep visitors busy for a few days, not least the spectacle of hordes of grunting sea lions on the town's beaches.

Centro de Interpretación

A 20min walk north of the centre along Av Alsacio Northia • Daily 9am–noon & 2–5pm • Free

The town's stand-out attraction is the **Centro de Interpretación**, the Galápagos National Park's exhibition centre. The displays cover everything from geology, climate and conservation, to attempts at colonization in the 1920s, and have detailed explanations in Spanish and English. Impressive installations include a reconstruction of a ship's hold stuffed with overturned giant tortoises as they would have been stored by the pirates and whalers. Talks, lectures and concerts are also held regularly here.

8

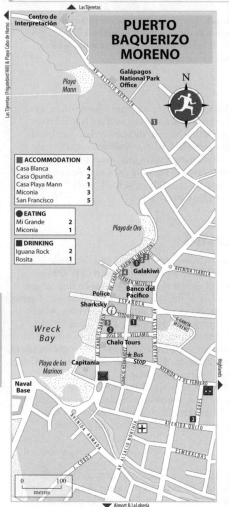

Cerro de las Tijeretas

Behind the last exhibition room at the Centro de Interpretación, a path leads up to **Cerro de las Tijeretas**, or **Frigatebird Hill**. It's only 20 minutes' walk through fragrant *palo santo* forests to a viewpoint, where you'll have a fine panorama of Wreck Bay, Lobos to the north and León Dormido to the northeast. Below, a rocky cove echoes with **sea lions** while **frigatebirds** circle in the air above. They nest here in March and April and are seen less frequently during the cool-dry season. Snorkelling is possible here. A series of paths network around the hill, so you can do a circuit: one trail leads to the **Tijeretas cove**, where you can snorkel, while others go down to the road back to town past the interpretation centre. Heading away from town to the north, you'll come to a secluded beach, the **Playa Cabo de Horno**.

Tongo Reef

At the weekends **surfers** make their way to the shoreline west of town to catch the waves. **Tongo Reef**, a 25-minute walk south of town, is one of the more popular places, but others include **Punta Carola** (beyond the Playa Cabo de Horno) and **El Cañón** (just northeast of Tongo Reef). You'll need to leave identification at the base, as this is a military area, and it's best to be with someone who knows the place as currents can be strong. The waves are best from December to February at the beginning of the warm-wet season, when the water is also warmer.

La Lobería

A good place to spot wildlife is **La Lobería**, a 30-minute walk to the southwest of Puerto Baquerizo Moreno. Here, a trail leads along a rugged coast of pitted black lava buffeted by ocean spray to a small beach, where you'll find sea lions, marine iguanas and a number of shore birds.

ARRIVAL AND GETTING AROUND   PUERTO BAQUERIZO MORENO

By plane There are daily flights to and from Quito via Guayaquil, as well as around six weekly services to Baltra and Puerto Vilamil. Avianca (wavianca.com), EMETEBE (wemetebe.com), LAN (wlan.com) and TAME (wtame .com.ec) all have offices at the airport. A taxi to the town centre costs $1.

By bus Buses (30min) to El Progreso pick up on Av 12 de Febrero and Alsacio Northia; the service is irregular so ask locals for departure times.

By boat *Fibras* and *lanchas* head to Puerto Ayora (2hr)

from the town's dock at around 7am.
By camioneta or taxi Camionetas and taxis can be caught on the Malecón (the town's promenade) and charge $1–2 for journeys around town.

INFORMATION AND TOURS

Tourist office The helpful Cámara de Turismo (Capturgal) on Av Charles Darwin and Wolf (Mon–Fri 7.30am–noon & 2–5.30pm; ☎05 2520592, ⍟galapagostour.org), has leaflets and advice on all aspects of visiting the islands.
Tour operators Several agencies offer local excursions, diving, kayaking, surfing lessons, and bike and snorkelling equipment rental, including: Chalo Tours, Av Charles Darwin and Villamil (☎05 2520953); Galakiwi, Av Charles Darwin (☎05 2521864, ⍟galakiwi.com); and Sharksky, Española at Charles Darwin (☎05 2521188; ⍟sharksky.com).

ACCOMMODATION

Puerto Baquerizo Moreno has enough hotels to house its modest flow of tourists throughout the year, though prices are quite high for what you get. The budget places can fill up with South American surfers from **December to February**, when you'll need to book in advance. Rates for all include taxes.

Casa Blanca Av Charles Darwin and Melville ☎05 2520392, ⍟casablancagalapagos.com. A charming, family-run B&B with seven en-suite rooms, each with a/c, fan and individual artistic decor. Several have lovely views of the harbour, and one has its own private roof terrace. There's a café-restaurant out front. Breakfast included. **$100**
Casa Opuntia Av Charles Darwin and Isabela ☎05 3010209, ⍟opuntiagalapagoshotels.com. This reliable hotel has spacious rooms with whitewashed walls, tiled floors, a/c, safes and modern bathrooms, as well as lovely sea views and their own hammocks. To cool off, there's also a small pool at the back. Breakfast included. **$126**
Casa Playa Mann Via a Playa Mann ☎05 2521971. Just south of Playa Mann, this six-room hotel near the national park entrance is still just a short walk from the waterfront.

The white rooms with dark wood furnishings are large, with TVs and a/c. Its welcoming service and environmental efforts distinguish it. Breakfast included. **$135**
Miconia Av Charles Darwin near Melville ☎05 2520608, ⍟miconia.com. One of the smartest hotels in town, with a great location overlooking the bay. The comfortable en-suite rooms have a/c and fridges, and there's a small pool, gym and jacuzzi, as well as a good restaurant (see below). Breakfast included. **$213**
San Francisco Av Charles Darwin near Villamil ☎05 2520304. One of the better shoestring options, the central *San Francisco* is particularly popular with surfers. The simple en-suite rooms are reasonable value for the price, though the pipes snaking over the colourful indoor courtyard reflect the rather erratic plumbing. Breakfast included. **$20**

EATING AND DRINKING

Restaurant menus in town are rather similar, concentrating mainly on **seafood**, with the usual chicken and meat courses as backup. Keep an eye out for the local **organic coffee**. General opening times are provided below, but most places take a flexible approach depending on how busy they are.

Iguana Rock Flores and Quito ☎05 2520418. If you fancy a drink in the evening, head over to *Iguana Rock*, a friendly little bar located a few blocks back from the front where a cold beer or cocktail costs around $3–5. Mon–Sat 6/7pm–1/2am.
Mi Grande Villamil near Charles Darwin. Up on the first floor, this basic restaurant named for its friendly, tall, former basketball-player owner serves up well-priced local fare and fast food from breakfasts to burgers ($3–7). Opening times are erratic, but usually Mon–Sat 8am–9.30pm.

★**Miconia** Miconia hotel ☎05 2520608. The best restaurant in town, Miconia's first-floor dining area overlooks the bay and specializes in fresh seafood (the ceviche is well worth a try), pizzas and pasta. Mains cost $7–29, or there's a good-value $8 "económico" set menu for lunch/dinner. Daily 7am–9.30pm.
Rosita Ignacio de Hernández and Villamil ☎05 2521581. Flags and football shirts from around the world hang from the ceiling of this restaurant-bar. Most of the dishes are overpriced, but the set lunch (around $5) is a good choice. Mon–Sat noon–10pm, Sun noon–3pm.

DIRECTORY

Bank Banco del Pacífico, on the promenade by Av Charles Darwin, has ATMs that accept MasterCard, Cirrus and Visa.
Hospital Alsacio Northia and Quito (☎05 2520118 in emergencies).
Police Av Charles Darwin and Española (☎911 in emergencies).

8

San Cristóbal highlands

The road heading east from Puerto Baquerizo Moreno rises swiftly into the misty highlands. Among the attractions in this region is the sleepy village of **El Progreso**, **El Junco lake**, the **Galapaguera tortoise habitat** and **Puerto Chino beach**.

El Progreso

About 8km east of Puerto Baquerizo Moreno, along a road lined with orange groves, you come to **El Progreso**, a peaceful village of wooden, stilted houses, banana plants and fruit trees. It was founded in the 1870s by **Manuel Cobos**, an entrepreneur who tried to colonize the place with a hundred convicts. They planted orchards, sugar cane and vegetable gardens, built a sugar mill and enjoyed modest success for a short period – but, far away from the gaze of authority, El Progreso began to slip into brutal tyranny. Cobos paid his workers in his own invented currency only redeemable in his shop; he also owned the island's only boat, effectively making his workers prisoners and slaves. An increasingly savage overlord, he regularly beat them, once flogging six to death, and abandoned a man on Santiago and another on Santa Cruz, leaving them for dead. The Santa Cruz castaway survived for three years eating iguanas and cacti, and might have been rescued sooner had Cobos not left a sign visible to passing boats but inaccessible to the hapless victim, reading "Do not take this man away. He is twenty times a criminal". The bloody retribution came in 1904 when desperate colonists hacked Cobos to pieces on the spot where he'd just had five people shot.

ARRIVAL AND DEPARTURE

EL PROGRESO

By bus There's an irregular bus service from Puerto Baquerizo Moreno to the village (ask in town for the current departure times).

By taxi A taxi can take you to El Progreso for $2–3.
By bike Alternatively, you can cycle there in less than an hour (though it's uphill all the way).

ACCOMMODATION AND EATING

La Casa del Ceibo Just outside the village ☏ 05 2520248. This place takes the prize for being the most peculiar hotel in the archipelago. A precarious bridge of rope and wire takes you 14.5m up into San Cristóbal's biggest tree – a 300-year-old ceibo – to a tree house equipped for three people, with sleeping mats, fridge, cooker, bathroom, hot water and a fireman's pole for the shortcut to the ground. Beneath, in a cave, is the video room. The restaurant, which is open at weekends, is no less eccentric, with walls constructed from over 20,000 bottles of beer, while the kitchen and paths are made of plastic crates. **$25**

Laguna El Junco

A taxi from Puerto Baquerizo Moreno costs around $20 return with waiting time; Puerto Baquerizo Moreno tour operators also run trips here

Laguna El Junco, ten kilometres beyond El Progreso, is a caldera lake at about 650m, often shrouded in mist in the dry season and surrounded by ferns, miconia, brambles and guava bushes. The quiet is occasionally broken by the squawk of a **moorhen** or splash of **white-cheeked pintails** and **whimbrels**. This is one of the few freshwater lakes in the Galápagos, and if the clouds lift as you follow the **trail** around the rim you'll have some wonderful views over the island. Bring sturdy shoes and a waterproof jacket.

La Galapaguera de Cerro Colorado and Puerto Chino

Daily 6am–6pm • Free • It is best visited with a Puerto Baquerizo Moreno travel agency, who can also organize camping trips here • Alternatively, a taxi from Puerto Baquerizo Moreno costs around $25 return to La Galapaguera; $30 return to Puerto Chino.

Beyond El Junco, the road descends to the southern shore, passing **La Galapaguera de Cerro Colorado**, one of two places to see **giant tortoises** on the island; the other is on the island's north side and visited from Punta Pitt on a cruise (see opposite). This colony is the focus of a tortoise repopulation programme, and there's an **information centre** for visitors. The area is rich in *Calandrina galapagosa*, a critically endangered endemic plant. Continuing the descent, the road meets the coast at **Puerto Chino**, where there's a beautiful beach.

Punta Pitt and La Galapaguera

Tour boats rarely visit the northeastern extremity of San Cristóbal, so it's best visited with a Puerto Baquerizo Moreno tour company (see p.359). After a wet landing into a tight sandy cove, a fairly strenuous trail leads between thorny scrub and tuff cones, climbing to a pass with panoramic views. The real treat of **Punta Pitt** is that it's the only place in the Galápagos where all three species of booby are seen together. **Red-footed boobies** cling to *muyuyo* trees, while **blue-footed boobies** mark their patches on the ground with a ring of guano. **Nazca boobies** prefer spots closer to the cliffs, and **frigatebird** nests are also found in the *palo santos*. A trailhead at Salinas, west of Punta Pitt, leads to **La Galapaguera** after about 90 minutes' hike, a good place to see **giant tortoises** in the wild.

Lobos and Playa Ochoa

Tour operators in Puerto Baquerizo Moreno (see p.359) can organize day-trips here

Thirty minutes' sail north of Puerto Baquerizo Moreno, **Lobos** is a tiny island of rocky lava shores, covered with *palo santo* and speckled with **candelabra cacti**. It's heaving with **sea lions**, but you'll also spot **blue-footed boobies** and **frigatebirds**. Opposite, on the shore of San Cristóbal, is **Playa Ochoa**, a fine white beach with a colony of **sea lions** and backed by a tidal lagoon nurturing **flamingos** and the endemic **Chatham mockingbird**; newly arrived tour groups are often taken here first for a snorkel.

León Dormido and Cerro Brujo

8

Tour operators in Puerto Baquerizo Moreno (see p.359) can organize day-trips here

Another hour by boat to the northeast of Playa Ochoa brings you to **León Dormido** (it's said to resemble a sleeping lion), known as **Kicker Rock** in English. Dizzying tuff cliffs rise out of the ocean, cleft at one end by a narrow waterway, wide enough for a dinghy to go down. There's no landing site, but a cruise around the cliffs should reveal plenty of sea birds, including **frigatebirds**, **red-billed tropicbirds** and **Nazca and blue-footed boobies**. It's a popular site for scuba diving and snorkelling. Visits to León Dormido sometimes return via **Cerro Brujo**, about 30 minutes to the east. On the west coast of San Cristóbal, this cone stands over a white beach alive with **sea lions**, **pelicans** and **waders**.

Isabela

Straddling the equator, **ISABELA** is the largest island in the Galápagos at 4558 square kilometres, accounting for well over half the total land surface of the archipelago. The island comprises six **volcanoes**, fused together over time: from north to south, Ecuador (790m), Wolf (1707m), Darwin (1330m) and Alcedo (1130m) make up a narrow volcanic chain that tapers into the inaccessible **aa lava** flow of the Perry Isthmus, on the southwestern side of which Sierra Negra (1124m) and Cerro Azul (1640m) compose the squat base of the island. Several of the volcanoes are still active, the most recent eruptions being Wolf, right on the equator in 2015 Cerro Azul in 2008 and Sierra Negra in October 2005.

Much of Isabela's huge landmass is impassable, riven by fissures, blocked by jagged lava flows or tangled thickets and the rocky shores mean that there are few landing places on the island. Most of the visitor sites – **Urbina Bay**, **Elizabeth Bay**, **Punta Tortuga**, **Punta Moreno**, **Punta Vicente Roca** and **Tagus Cove** – are on its far western side, putting them in range only of the longer tours and faster boats. But it's worth the effort, because the upwelling of cold waters off the coast makes for a nutrient-rich zone, supporting such oddities as the **Galápagos penguin** and the **flightless cormorant**, also frequently spotted on nearby **Fernandina**. Plentiful stocks of fish also attract **whales**, large schools of **common dolphins** and gregarious **bottle-nosed dolphins** – an unexpected highlight of the western islands.

Puerto Villamil, on the island's southeastern coast, is far less developed than either Puerto Ayora or Puerto Baquerizo Moreno, but makes a quiet retreat away from the tour boats. From the town, you can also visit several interesting sites, as well as take a horse ride through the verdant highlands up to the awesome crater of **Sierra Negra** – provided it's not spitting ash and lava.

Puerto Villamil

PUERTO VILLAMIL, sitting under the cloud-draped slopes of the huge Sierra Negra volcano, was founded at the beginning of the nineteenth century and named after the general who annexed the islands for Ecuador in 1832. Now home to most of Isabela's 2200-plus settlers, the sleepy port isn't well developed for tourism, and visitors are infrequent enough to be conspicuous. Just a small town of sandy roads and simple houses with fences of woven branches and cactus, fronted by a beautiful palm-fringed **beach**, it is nevertheless one of the most pleasant off-the-beaten-track places to stay on the islands, boasting several good attractions nearby that can be seen without guides.

A small dusty square, fronted by the *municipio* and a simple church, fixes the centre of town a block back from the waterfront, dock and Capitanía. Heading north of the square takes you towards the airport and highlands. There's not much going on in town, but plenty to see nearby. To the east is a path to **Concha de Perla**, a quiet and sheltered little bay with reasonable snorkelling.

Giant Tortoise Breeding Center

A 20-minute walk north of the town centre • Mon–Fri 7.30am–12.30pm & 2–5pm • Free

From the town centre, Avenida Antonio Gil heads west and passes small, secluded lagoons (*pozas*) – where you can spot waders, shore birds and sometimes flamingos – before a signposted track branches off north to the **Giant Tortoise Breeding Center**. Work is ongoing to breed the island's five unique tortoise subspecies, each based around the five largest volcanoes. On show are the rearing pens for the hatchlings, and corrals for adult tortoises taken from the wild, including Cerro Azul tortoises rescued from the volcano when it erupted in 1998 and others saved from a serious forest fire on Sierra Negra in 1994.

Playa de Amor and around

The westward road along the coast (ignoring the turn-off to the tortoise centre) continues past several peaceful beaches, including the **Playa de Amor**, where there are some scenic trails perfect for local wildlife-spotting.

El Muro de las Lágrimas

After about two hours' walk from Playa de Amor, you'll come to **El Muro de las Lágrimas** (The Wall of Tears), a testament to the suffering of three hundred prisoners who toiled here in the 1940s and 1950s; they had to build their own prison using sharp-edged lava boulders. Many died making the wall, which was some 190m long, 9m high and 6m wide at the base when the prison colony was abandoned after a revolt in 1959.

Las Tintoreras

A short boat ride ($15–20) from Puerto Villamil

The best nearby place to see marine life hereabouts is at **Las Tintoreras** (also known as **Las Islas de los Tiburones**), a handful of ragged black-lava grottoes poking out of the sea. From the natural dock a trail leads past scuttling **marine iguanas** to a lagoon and a narrow channel, where a "viewing gallery" allows you to see the sleek shapes of white-tipped **reef sharks** cruising back and forth. You can swim and snorkel in the lagoon – though don't swim in the channel itself, as it's not big enough for both you and the sharks – or back at the landing site.

Los Túneles

Hotels in Puerto Villamil can organize half-day trips here

The top wildlife spot near Puerto Villamil features **penguins, sea horses, rays, sea turtles and many other species** in the gin-clear waters at **Los Túneles** (Cabo Rosa), about an hour's ride away by boat from the port, where semi-submerged lava tunnels have created a striking, otherworldly landscape. The water is shallow here, so the approach is sometimes difficult in the dry season.

ARRIVAL AND DEPARTURE   PUERTO VILLAMIL

By plane EMETEBE flights arrive daily Mon–Sat from San Cristóbal via Baltra. Their office is on Av Antonio Gil, opposite the police station (☎05 2529155, ⍟emetebe .com.ec). The airport is 3km outside town; there's no bus service and taxis rarely wait here ($2–3). The hour-long walk along the road across the lava wastes is hot,

uncomfortable and best avoided if you can.
By boat *Lanchas* leave for Puerto Ayora daily at 6am ($25–30; 2hr). "Independent travel between the islands" has more information on *lanchas* (see p.343). Note that there's a $5/person docking charge.

ACCOMMODATION

The hotels in Puerto Villamil are generally of a good standard and cater to a range of budgets. Most can provide **meals**, given some advance notice, and arrange **local tours**.

Caleta Iguana (Casa Rosada) Av Antonio Gil at the western end of town ☎05 2520484, ⍟iguanacove .com. A surfers' place a cut above the norm, with seven pleasant white or colourful rooms right on a beach frequented by marine iguanas. Doubles start at $40
★**Casa de Marita** Just east of town ☎05 2529301, ⍟galapagosisabela.com. This stylish beach house, shaded by palms on a gorgeous stretch of sand, has very tasteful rooms, all bright, individual and equipped with a/c, mini-fridge and private bathrooms. Bicycles and snorkelling equipment are available, and tours around the island can be arranged; breakfast included. $153
Hospedaje Las Gardenias Las Escalecias and Tero Real ☎05 2529115, ⍟geocities.ws/gardeniasisabela /indexenglish.htm. A couple of blocks back from the beach in a peaceful spot, this shoestring hotel has three en-suite rooms and a triple with shared facilities, plus a well-stocked kitchen and a TV lounge. Meals and packed lunches are available on request. Breakfast included. $20

Red Mangrove Isabela Lodge by the beach ☎05 2526564, ⍟redmangrove.com. In a lovely beachfront location, this hotel has airy rooms, each with beamed ceilings, two queen-size beds, private bathrooms and a/c. The food – a buffet breakfast is included – is pretty good, and staff can organize an extensive range of trips. $335
Rincón de George 16 de Marzo and Flamingos ☎05 2529214, ⍟vacacionesengalapagos.com. Also known as *George's Corner Inn*, this small, whitewashed hotel is bang in the centre of town. Rooms are nothing special, but represent reasonable value – each one is en suite, and has hot water, a TV and a/c. There's a roof terrace, and guests can use the kitchen. $40
San Vicente Cormorán and Las Escalecias ☎05 2529140, ⍟sanvicentegalapagos.com. Popular with groups, this hotel is decent value, with neat and bright en-suite rooms (with a/c and TVs) set around a little garden. Bikes are available for rent, and the owners can arrange horse riding, kayaking and snorkelling trips. Breakfast included. $80

EATING AND DRINKING

Most restaurants in Puerto Villamil cluster around the main square, but some of the best food on offer is at the smarter **hotels**, notably *Casa de Marita* and *Red Mangrove Isabela Lodge*.

Bar de Beto On the beach ☎05 2529015. This laidback bar, right on the beach, is perfect for a cold beer (from around $3) or a cocktail at sunset. There's often food (particularly seafood) available too, and the owner, Beto, will put on a barbecue if there's enough demand. Opening times vary but generally Mon–Sat 4/5pm–1/2am.

El Encanto de la Pepa Conocarpus ☎05 2529284. Overlooking Puerto Villamil's main square, *El Encanto de la Pepa* is one of the better restaurants in town, with a fine selection of fresh fish and seafood. Mains $7–20. Opening times vary but generally Mon–Sat noon–9/9.30pm.

8

Internet Most hotels have (fairly slow) internet or wi-fi connections. Otherwise, try *Easy Cybercafé* in town.

Money Bring all the cash you need, as there are no banks or ATMs on the island and few places accept credit cards.

Sierra Negra

If you have a day to spare in Puerto Villamil, you can't do much better than go to the summit of **Sierra Negra** (1124m), which reveals a monstrous **crater** some 10km in diameter and 200m deep. It's best reached by horse from **Santo Tomás**, a highland farming community 14km northwest of the Puerto Villamil, from where a muddy trail leads uphill over rugged terrain frequently cloaked in thick mist during the cool-dry season. Once at the rim, the heavy clouds curl dramatically over the southern lip before evaporating, leaving the gaping black crater stretching out in full view. On the north side of the rim you can walk to **Volcán Chico**, a collection of hissing volcanic cones that last erupted in 2005. The striking red and black lava coloured by wispy sulphur deposits is virtually lifeless, except for the odd candelabra cactus and a few hardy shrubs clinging to the walls of the fumaroles to suckle on the volcanic steam. This side of the volcano is usually in the sun and gives stupendous views of Fernandina and Isabela's four volcanoes beyond the Perry Isthmus.

ARRIVAL AND DEPARTURE — SIERRA NEGRA

By horse Most hotels in town can organize a trip to Sierra Negra, including guide and horse, costing around $30–35 for a half-day or $45–50 the whole day. Getting to the crater from Santo Tomás takes about 90min by horse and it's a further thirty minutes' walk to Volcán Chico. Sheets of rubber and plastic sacks will probably serve for saddles if they're not wooden, so you can expect to get pretty sore. Wear long trousers for the ride and take a long-sleeved top and rain jacket.

Tagus Cove

A secluded cove of tuff cliffs on the Bolívar Channel, at the foot of Volcán Darwin, **Tagus Cove** is Isabela's site most visited by cruise boats. It's also a convenient anchorage that has been used for many years, as testified by the dozens of boat names etched and painted onto the cliffs; many are those of millionaires' yachts that stopped here on grand world cruises in the 1930s, but the oldest is from 1836, only a year after Darwin's visit.

From the landing point, a trail leads steeply up a breach in the cliffs into the scrubby vegetation typical of the dry coastal regions, including **lantana**, **lechoso**, **Galápagos cotton** and an endemic variety of **palo santo**, which provides a good habitat for a number of **Darwin's finches** and **flycatchers**. The path rises around the rim of **Darwin's Lake**, eventually giving wonderful views of its emerald surface. Strangely, this crater lake has both a higher salinity and water level than the sea, and no one knows exactly why; one theory is that sea water is absorbed upwards through porous rocks and concentrated in the "crucible" of the crater. The trail leads further up to a tuff cone from where you can see a maroon carpet of **aa lava** extending off to Volcán Wolf and Volcán Ecuador in the distance.

Around the cliffs by Tagus Cove, made stripy by thousands of compacted layers of ash, **blue-footed boobies**, **noddy terns**, **pelicans**, **penguins** and **sea lions** can all be seen. To its north, **marine turtles** make nests on the black-sand beach of **Punta Tortuga**. Mangroves back the beach, making it one of the few places to see the endangered **mangrove finch**.

Urbina Bay

Around 25km south of Tagus Cove, **Urbina Bay** shows one of the most dramatic results of tectonic activity. In 1954, a 1.5-square-kilometre section of sea reef was shunted up out of the water, an uplift of almost 4m in places. Skeletons of fish, lobsters and turtles strewn about the rocks told of the violence of the movement; you'll see some sun-bleached brain corals, shells and urchins, several hundred metres from the water's edge.

The trail here forms a long circuit, heading inland from a wet landing on a black beach to where **land iguanas** lurk beneath poison-apple trees (**manzanillo** – don't touch it), **palo santo**, **Vallesia** and **cordia**. In the rainy season, **giant tortoises** descend from Volcán Alcedo to the lowlands to lay eggs; feral goats have caused damage to the tortoises' habitat in this area. The trail then loops back along the shore, over the twisted black lava, home to **marine iguanas** and a few pairs of **flightless cormorants**.

Elizabeth Bay

On the west coast of the Perry Isthmus, it's possible to explore the narrowing, mangrove-crowded inlet of **Elizabeth Bay** by *panga* from your cruise boat. This is a great place to spot marine wildlife; **turtles**, **reef sharks**, **sea lions** and **rays** all favour the cold, nutrient-rich waters. **Herons** look on from their perches in the tangled mangroves as **blue-footed boobies** dive-bomb the secluded channels, and **shearwaters** skim the surface of the sea. Tour boats usually anchor at the tiny Mariela islands at the mouth of the bay, a good place to see **Galápagos penguins**.

Punta Moreno

Around 30km west of Elizabeth Bay, **Punta Moreno** is one of the remotest and least-visited sites in the islands. An enormous flow of **pahoehoe lava** unfurls into the distance, broken by fissures and peppered with brackish water holes ringed by reeds and buzzing with insects. These are the few sources of life in a virtually sterile landscape, supporting **flamingos**, **herons**, **moorhens** and **white-cheeked pintails**.

Punta Vicente Roca

Punta Vicente Roca, on the northwestern corner of the island is a spectacular geological extremity of the collapsed Volcán Ecuador. There's nowhere to land in this stunning blue cove, but a *panga* ride close to the shore reveals breathtaking streaked tuff cliffs and a half-submerged cave, home to **blue-footed** and **Nazca boobies**, while flightless cormorants make good on less vertiginous patches. In the water, huge **ocean sunfish**, weighing around a tonne, feast on the jellyfish that congregate here – reason to take care when snorkelling in this otherwise enthralling spot, where dolphins, turtles and even whales are regulars.

Punta Albemarle

Punta Albemarle marks the northernmost tip of the island and was a US radar base during World War II. As such, the military detritus doesn't look that inviting as you approach, but you'll also see (usually from the boat as it's a rough landing rarely attempted) **flightless cormorants** and what are thought to be the largest **marine iguanas** in the islands. It's also a good area for **whale** sightings.

Fernandina

FERNANDINA, west of Isabela and dominated by the brooding shape of **Volcán La Cumbre** (1476m), is the youngest island in the archipelago, thought to be between 60,000 and 400,000 years old.

Punta Espinoza, a spiky finger of lava at the northeastern tip of the island, is Fernandina's only visitor site. It's home to a sizeable colony of **marine iguanas**, their ashen

8

bodies crammed head to foot on the black rocks. They lay eggs in pockets of sand and you'll see **Galápagos hawks** in the trees nearby waiting to pounce on any stray hatchlings. This is one of the best islands for **flightless cormorants**, which stand at the water's edge after a foray underwater for food, to dry out their useless wings. **Galápagos penguins** can also be seen floating around the point, competing for fish with **sea lions**.

A trail here leads over rippled **pahoehoe lava**, studded with clumps of lava cacti, to a series of tide pools, a great place to spot **crabs**, **octopuses** and a range of shore birds, including **whimbrels**, **herons** and **oystercatchers**. A final trail heads eastwards to an imposing wall of **aa lava**, a jagged barrier to the slopes of Volcán La Cumbre.

Fernandina has so far escaped the introduced species that have so damaged other islands, leading to the claim that it's the world's largest pristine island; take care not to inadvertently transport any organisms, such as seeds, on your clothes or soles of your shoes.

Overall, Fernandina is one of the most volcanically active islands, erupting ten times in the twentieth century alone, and most recently in April 2009. La Cumbre is crested by a huge caldera, 6km wide and 900m deep, the floor of which exploded in 1968, sending it crashing down by 300m.

Floreana

One of the most regularly visited islands (by cruise boats, rather than island-hopping tourists), **FLOREANA** is also among the oldest, weather-beaten and eroded over several million years. The sixth-largest island in the Galápagos (173 square kilometres), and just some 50km south of Santa Cruz, it has a small settlement on its western coast, **Puerto Velasco Ibarra**, now home to around a hundred people. Apart from that, it's a very quiet island, with little to see and do – beyond hiking in the highlands and visiting **La Lobería** (sea-lion colony) – but it's an unbeatable place to get away from it all.

Brief history

Arriving at the beginning of the nineteenth century, Patrick Watkins (see p.337) was the first in a long line of colonists here. Since the island was favoured for its good supply of both tortoise meat and fresh highland water, General Villamil began Ecuador's first official colony here, the **Asilo de la Paz** ("Haven of Peace"), using convict labour in 1832. He gave up after five years, handing the settlement over to the brutal Colonel José Williams, who kept a pack of vicious dogs to keep his unruly charges at bay, but the hounds weren't protection enough and Williams fled the island after a rebellion in 1841. Almost thirty years later, José de Valdizán sought to rekindle the ill-fated venture, but after eight years his desperate settlers armed themselves and fought each other. Valdizán and several others were killed and the settlement fell apart. All this human interference has not been without effect on Floreana: its tortoise population is extinct, and feral cats so severely preyed on the **Charles mockingbird** that it's now only found on the islets Enderby and Campeón, off the northeastern shore.

Punta Cormorant

At **Punta Cormorant**, on the northernmost tip of Floreana, you'll land by *panga* on a beach made green from deposits of the mineral olivine. You won't actually see cormorants here, but a trail to the lagoon behind the mangroves leads to a variety of wading birds, including **ruddy turnstones**, **whimbrels**, **stilts**, **white-cheeked pintails** and **phalaropes**; above all, this is the best place in the islands to see **flamingos**. Around this site are two species of plant found nowhere else in the world, the **cutleaf daisy** (*Leocarpus pinnatifidus*) and a type of **scalesia**.

THE GALÁPAGOS AFFAIR

In the 1930s, a string of deaths and disappearances among a curious group of European settlers on Floreana – which became known as the **Galápagos Affair** after the book by John Treherne – attracted global attention. The story began with the arrival in 1929 of two Germans, **Dr Friedrich Ritter** and his mistress **Dore Strauch**. Ritter was pumped up on Nietzsche and Lao-tze, and had pretensions to being a great philosopher. Dore fell under his spell as his patient in Berlin, and they eventually conspired to run off to the Galápagos, the perfect place to found a dark utopia. Seeing himself as a Nietzschean *Übermensch*, Ritter refused to bring any morphine with him, welcoming the test of beating pain "by the power of the will". He had also had his and Dore's teeth removed, preferring the reliability of a shared set of steel dentures. Ritter refused to show his mistress any love, and even beat her, but Dore claimed that her devotion never faltered.

The couple lived alone on the island until 1932, when the **Wittmer family** arrived from Cologne. They were a far more practical bunch and largely stayed out of the way of their strange neighbours. A couple of months later, an Austrian calling herself the **Baroness Wagner de Bosquet**, stormed onto Floreana with her two German lovers, Rudolf Lorenz and Robert Philippson. She planned to build a luxury hotel, but it soon became clear that she was a compulsive liar and a sadistic megalomaniac. She treated Lorenz like a slave and regularly got Philippson to beat him; intercepted the mail of the other settlers; stole supplies; and declared herself "Empress of Floreana".

In 1934, the Baroness and Philippson disappeared. According to Margret Wittmer, the Baroness said a friend was taking them to Tahiti, a story backed by Lorenz, who had managed to escape the household shortly before. But Dore claimed she heard a "long-drawn scream" and Ritter seemed unusually sure they had gone for good – even though all the Baroness's belongings were where she'd left them. Neither the Baroness nor Philippson was ever seen again.

After their disappearance, Lorenz grew increasingly desperate to leave and persuaded a visiting Norwegian, Nuggerud, to sail him to San Cristóbal. Four months later, the bodies of both men were found on Marchena Island. A few days later, Ritter fell gravely ill after eating a poisoned chicken cooked by Dore. In his final message to Dore he wrote: "I curse you with my dying breath". Dore returned to Berlin, where she died, shortly after telling her story in the book, *Satan Came to Eden* (see p.416). Margret Wittmer, the last survivor of the original settlers, died in 2000 aged 95, but the Galápagos Affair is no closer to being solved.

8

The trail passes a viewpoint looking out to a tuff cone, and finishes at **Flour Beach**, so called for its very fine, white sand of ground coral. **Marine turtles** nest here, but it's better known for the schools of **stingrays** that settle in the shallows. Note that you can't swim here.

Devil's Crown

Opposite Punta Cormorant is **Devil's Crown** (also called Onslow), a submerged cone sheltering beautiful coral reefs from the currents outside, which makes for excellent snorkelling and scuba diving. In addition to **surgeonfish**, **angelfish**, **parrotfish** and **wrasse**, you may see **white-tipped reef sharks** and even **hammerheads**.

Post Office Bay

A few kilometres west of Punta Cormorant is **Post Office Bay**, named after a barrel near the beach that has been used as a makeshift mail drop since the end of the eighteenth century. British whalers, who left letters here to be picked up by homeward-bound vessels, began the practice, which was cleverly exploited during the Anglo-American war of 1812, when the canny US Navy Captain, **David Porter**, intercepted communications here, allowing him to round up one million tons of shipping in the region's waters.

The original **barrel** has long been replaced, but post is still left and delivered free of charge by visitors to the bay. The "post office" is now marked by a shrine of planks, with the names of yachts etched onto them, animal bones, driftwood and many other bits and pieces left by the regular tour boats and numerous day-trippers who visit. Nearby are the remains of a fish-canning factory that Norwegian colonists set up and then abandoned in the 1920s, and a short trail leading to a lava tube, for which you need caving gear to descend.

ARRIVAL AND DEPARTURE   FLOREANA

Unless you're on a **cruise**, it's not straightforward to get to Floreana. The best way to get here is to organize transport through one of the **travel agencies** in Puerto Ayora (see p.348) or Puerto Baquerizo Moreno (see p.359).

ACCOMMODATION

Floreana Lava Lodge Just south of Puerto Velasco Ibarra ☎05 2526564, ⓦfloreanalavalodge.destinationecuador .com. On an old lava flow close to the shore, this is the island's top lodging option, with clean but spartan pine cabins with private bathrooms and a/c. Meals can be provided, and it's a short walk from the town and a sea-lion colony. $153
Pensíon Wittmer Right on Playa Negra ☎05 2520150. For many years this lodge was the only place to stay on the

island. It used to be run by Margret Wittmer, but after her passing has been run by her daughter Ingeborg and granddaughter Erika, who'll insist you just read the book if you ask about the "Galápagos Affair" (see box, p.367). The en-suite rooms are comfortable, and as well as providing meals for guests, the Wittmers can give advice on the hikes around the island. $80

Española

8

ESPAÑOLA, in the far southeastern corner of the archipelago is a remote island featuring regularly on tour-boat itineraries, a favourite for its sea-bird colonies and native wildlife. Isolation has given rise to a number of endemic species: Española's mockingbirds, lava lizards and colourful marine iguanas are found nowhere else in the world, while the **waved albatross**, the star of the island when in residence between April and December, has only one other home – even then in small numbers – at the Isla de la Plata off the mainland coast. Española's **giant tortoises** were nearly wiped out (down to only 14 specimens in the 1970s) because of feral goats, which have since been eradicated. Under a long-term repopulation programme, the thousandth Española tortoise reared in captivity was successfully repatriated to the island in March 2000.

Punta Suárez

Española's two visitor sites offer very different experiences. At **Punta Suárez**, on the western end of the island, noisy **sea lions** welcome visitors landing on a small beach. On the rocks, **marine iguanas**, unusual because of their rusty colorations that erupt into turquoise and red during the mating season, bask in the sun. **Hood mockingbirds**, even more gregarious than their relatives on other islands, will hop to your feet and tug at your shoelaces. From the beach, a long, looped trail heads up to a large plateau covered in **muyuyo**, **croton**, **lycium** and **atriplex** (salt sage), a scrubby costume of plants that bursts into green during the rainy season. The **waved albatross** nests among these bushes from April to December; it's a giant of a bird that flies alone above the seas for three months, before returning to the island to find its lifelong mate, perform its alluring courtship dance and breed (see also p.372). When it's time to hunt, the adults waddle to the high cliffs at the southern end of the island to launch themselves off, unfurling their 2.5-metre wings. Along the cliffs you'll also find **Nazca boobies**, **swallow-tailed gulls** and **red-billed tropicbirds**; in the west, a blowhole sends a tall jet of spray gushing through a fissure in the lava. The trail then heads back across the plateau, through a field of **blue-footed boobies**, high-stepping and sky-pointing at each other in a cacophony of whistling and honking.

THE NORTHERN ISLANDS

Of the five islands that make up the remote northern group, only **Genovesa** is open to visitors. The tiny islands of **Darwin** and **Wolf**, at the far northwestern reaches of the archipelago, and **Marchena**, some 90km north of Santa Cruz, are occasionally visited by scuba divers, but only for offshore exploration, while **Pinta** is out of bounds to all but authorized scientists.

Gardner Bay

The second visitor site on Española, **Gardner Bay**, on the northeast side of the island, holds one of the most spectacular beaches in the archipelago, a lightly curling strip of soft, white, coral sand, lapped by a dazzling blue sea. Bull **sea lions** energetically patrol the water while their many consorts doze on the sand. As an open site, you can walk the length of the beach without the rest of your group or the guide. It's a good spot for some swimming, but snorkelling is better around the offshore islets nearby, especially **Tortuga**, where **eagle rays** and **white-tipped reef** and **hammerhead sharks** can be seen.

Genovesa

Lying approximately 95km northeast of Santa Cruz, and reached after a night of sailing, **GENOVESA** is usually only visited by faster boats or as part of longer itineraries. It's well worth the extra effort, however, as it's one of the best **bird** islands in the Galápagos and home to the world's largest colony of **red-footed boobies**. Captains align solar-powered beacons on Genovesa to find the safe route into **Darwin Bay**, formed by a pincer of imposing cliffs rising to 25m over the sea, the remnants of a large, sunken caldera.

A wet landing onto a small beach brings you face to face with **Nazca boobies, frigatebirds, swallow-tailed gulls, mockingbirds** and **red-footed boobies**. Birds rule the roost here; there are no introduced species and very few reptiles. The **marine iguanas** on the rocks are among the smallest in the islands, and the absence of land iguanas and giant tortoises means Genovesa's **prickly pear cacti**, free from major predators, grow with soft spines. As a trail heads west along the shore past red-footed boobies, you'll also see **great** and **magnificent frigatebirds** nesting in saltbush and red mangroves, with **lava herons** and **Galápagos doves** hopping around the rocks searching for food. **Yellow-crowned night herons** loiter near the tide pools watching for chances to snatch **wrasse, blenny** and **damselfish**. Four types of **Darwin's finches** also inhabit the *palo santo* and *croton* scrub, including the vampire finch, which can feed on the blood of seabirds and was recognized as a separate species in 2015. Snorkelling in the bay can be thrilling for the schools of **hammerhead sharks** that sometimes congregate at its western arm.

Among the crevices and protrusions at the eastern end of the bay inhabited by **fur seals, swallow-tailed gulls** and **red-billed tropicbirds** is a natural dock and a gully, named **Prince Philip's Steps** after the Duke of Edinburgh's visit in the 1960s. **Nazca boobies** greet you at the top and another trail takes you through a *palo santo* forest, past more red-footed boobies and frigatebirds. On the far side you come out of the vegetation to stand above a broad lava flow overlooking the sea. Clouds of **storm petrels** swarm in the sky above their nests hidden in the lava fissures. They're the smallest of the sea birds – a perfect-sized meal for the superbly camouflaged **short-eared owls** which prey on them.

8

Galápagos wildlife

Uniquely evolved and remarkably tame, the astonishing wildlife of the **Galápagos Islands** is, for many, Ecuador's greatest attraction. These thirteen volcanic islands (and hundred-plus islets and rocks) are home to some of the world's most extraordinary creatures – including giant tortoises, waved albatrosses and magnificent frigatebirds – and helped inspire Charles Darwin to formulate his theory of evolution. This **field guide** helps you identify the more common birds, reptiles, mammals and marine invertebrates in one of the world's most unmissable wildlife destinations. Further details on the islands' wildlife can be found in **Contexts** (see pp.410–413).

BIRDS

BLUE-FOOTED BOOBY *SULA NEBOUXII (PIQUERO PATAS AZULES)*

Of the three species of boobies in the Galápagos, the blue-footed booby is the most widespread but least numerous, occupying small colonies all over the islands (though they prefer to breed on those south of the equator), where you'll hear the limp whistle of the males and boisterous honking of the females. Their wonderful courtship display of "sky-pointing" and "high-stepping", to show off the blueness of their feet, happens throughout the year. The female lays up to three eggs in the nest and incubates them with her feet. If food is scarce, the first-born hatchling will tuck into its less fortunate siblings, a way of guaranteeing that at least one will survive. The islands hold three-quarters of the global population of the birds. Incidentally, the name, booby, probably comes from the Spanish *bobo*, meaning "fool", perhaps a reference to the birds' ungainly waddle and relaxed attitude to being caught.

NAZCA BOOBY *SULA GRANTI (PIQUERO DE NAZCA)*

The Nazca booby (formerly called the masked booby, but now considered a separate species) has rather lacklustre feet compared to its relatives, though makes up for it with its dazzling white plumage. They are common throughout the islands and, like the blue-footed booby, nest on flat areas marked by a ring of guano. Colonies have their own yearly breeding cycle. Of the two eggs that are laid, only one will survive; the stronger chick will force the other out of the nest if it hatches. Outside of the nine-month breeding cycle, adults leave the colony scouring the seas for food.

RED-FOOTED BOOBY *SULA SULA (PIQUERO PATAS ROJAS)*

The world's largest colony of red-footed boobies is on Genovesa (though you can also spot them on San Cristóbal,

Seymour Norte and Española), and despite numbering around a quarter of a million pairs in the archipelago, the red-foots are the least seen of the boobies, as they tend to inhabit the remoter islands. They're also the only branch-nesting booby, and have a slow breeding cycle that lasts over a year.

GREAT AND MAGNIFICENT FRIGATEBIRDS

FREGATA MINOR (FRAGATA COMÚN), FREGATA MAGNIFICENS (FRAGATA MAGNÍFICA)

The two frigatebird species in the archipelago, the great frigatebird and the magnificent frigatebird, are among the most commonly seen sea birds, often spotted manoeuvring in the sky, blotting out the sun with their huge wingspans (up to 2.4m), while their twitching scissor tails keep them on course. The two appear similar at first, but are easy to tell apart: male magnificent frigatebirds have a purple sheen on their feathers, whereas great frigates have green; female magnificent frigatebirds have a blue eye-ring, whereas female great frigates have a red eye-ring and a white chest.

Once called man-of-war birds, they have a reputation for aggression, harrying other sea birds to disgorge their catch, which they'll skilfully intercept before it hits the water. Their own fishing technique involves a deft flicking with their long hooked beaks on the surface of the water, whipping out their prey while ensuring that their feathers stay dry (they can't oil their plumage, and will drown if they get too wet). In the mating season, the males inflate their brilliant red gular sacs, or throat pouches, to attract passing females. At times, dozens of males will be competing for a mate when the colonies, freckled with colour, resound with their wavering calls. You can see the spectacle throughout the year at Seymour Norte or during March and April at Genovesa and San Cristóbal, though you may also be lucky at other times.

8

GALÁPAGOS PENGUIN *SPHENISCUS MENDICULUS* (PINGÜINO DE GALÁPAGOS)

The Galápagos penguin is another endemic sea bird and the only penguin found north of the equator. It's related to Humboldt and Magellan penguins and, like its relatives, it also prefers the cold water, largely colonizing in cracks and caves around Isabela and Fernandina islands (elsewhere, snorkellers often encounter them beneath Pinnacle Rock, Bartolomé or at Sombrero Chino and Rábida). Using its small, muscular wings as paddles and its feet as rudders, Galápagos penguins can propel themselves at up to 40km per hour through the water. Active before sunrise, they spend most of the day swimming, with occasional breaks basking in the sun on rocky shores. If the water is cold and fish plentiful, they hunt in packs.

FLIGHTLESS CORMORANT *NANNOPTERUM HARRISI* (CORMORÁN NO VOLADOR)

Among the endemic sea birds, the flightless cormorant is one of the most peculiar-looking on the islands. Unable to fly, these blazing-blue-eyed birds have developed large webbed feet and a sturdy lower body better suited to diving for food. Without an oily plumage, the birds hold their useless, bedraggled wings out to dry after each fishing expedition. Their snake-like necks can reach into nooks and crannies for eels and octopus, and play a prominent part in their courtship ritual in which partners swim past each other while snaking their necks and making throaty gurgles. Their nests are exotic collections of seaweed, twigs, fish bones, starfish and whatever else the male offers to the nest-tending female during the incubation and brooding times. There are only around 500 pairs of flightless cormorants in the world, all found on the rocky shores of Fernandina and northern and western Isabela.

LAVA AND SWALLOW-TAILED GULLS *LARUS FULIGINOSUS* (GAVIOTA DE LAVA) AND *CREAGRUS FURCATUS* (GAVIOTA TIJERETA)

The threatened lava gull is perhaps the rarest gull in the world, numbering only around 200 pairs. The dusky-coloured bird with white eyelids scavenges the ports, bays and beaches of the population centres, particularly at Puerto Ayora. The other endemic gull, the swallow-tailed gull, is far more attractive, having large black eyes set off from its black head by bright red eye-rings. It's one of the world's only nocturnal gulls, flying up to 35km out to sea and picking out phosphorescent shapes of squid in the darkness with its huge eyes, then turning home to locate land by the echo of its strange clacking call.

WAVED ALBATROSS *PHOEBASTRIA IRRORATA* (ALBATROS DE GALÁPAGOS)

The waved albatross is the largest bird of the archipelago with a wingspan of 2.5m, weighing 4kg and living for up to 40 years. Save for a few pairs that nest on the Isla de la Plata (see p.328), the waved albatross is endemic to Española, and each year more than 12,000 pairs come to nest and breed there from March to January. This bird chooses a mate for life (although recent research has shown it isn't always faithful) and roams the island after months alone at sea to find its partner. Its beguiling courtship display (best observed towards the end of the breeding season), a lengthy mix of "bill circling", "sky-pointing", "gaping", "clunking" and "sway-walking" among other manoeuvres, is thought to cement the marriage bond.

RED-BILLED TROPICBIRD *PHAETON AETHEREUS* (RABIJUNCO PIQUIRROJO)

The largest colonies of red-billed tropicbirds are found on high ledges or in crannies on steep cliffs on Genovesa, South Plaza, Daphne and Seymour Norte. As suitable nesting areas are limited, there are often fights for space. Once a bird finds a site, it will start breeding, which means there's no fixed annual cycle.

LAVA AND STRIATED HERONS *BUTORIDES SUNDEVALLI* (GARZA DE LAVA) AND *BUTORIDES STRIATUS* (GRACILLA ESTRIADA)

The diminutive, dark-coloured lava heron is a common sight along Galápagos shorelines. It lives in intertidal areas, mangroves and saltwater lagoons where it catches small fish, crabs and lizards. The lava heron usually breeds from September to March. It is often confused with the striated heron; the latter has a black cap and a paler neck and breast. The striated heron nests on Santa Cruz, Pinta, Pinzón, Isabela and Fernandina. A solitary predator, it usually waits to strike from a perch by the water's edge.

1 LAVA HERON; **2** FLIGHTLESS CORMORANT; **3** WAVED ALBATROSS; **4** RED-BILLED TROPICBIRD; **5** LAVA GULL; **6** GALÁPAGOS PENGUIN; **7** SWALLOW-TAILED GULL; **8** STRIATED HERON >

GALÁPAGOS HAWK *BUTEO GALAPAGOENSIS (GAVILÁN DE GALÁPAGOS)*

The fearless, inquisitive Galápagos hawk is found on the lowlands of most of the islands, with the exceptions of San Cristóbal, Baltra, Seymour Norte, Daphne, Floreana, Wolf, Darwin and Genovesa. It has an unusual breeding practice of "cooperative polyandry" in which four males pair with a single female, and team up to defend the territory and look after the young.

GALÁPAGOS MOCKINGBIRD *NESOMIMUS PARVULUS (CUCUVE DE GALÁPAGOS)*

The Galápagos mockingbird that fascinated Darwin is widespread on Genovesa, Wolf, Darwin, Isabela, Fernandina, Santa Cruz, Santiago, Pinta, Marchena and Santa Fé, with separate species on the islands of Floreana (*Nesomimus trifasciatus*), Española (*Nesomimus macdonaldi*) and San Cristóbal (*Nesomimus melanotis*). Juveniles help their parents to patrol territory and care for newborn offspring. The birds are very confident and will often hop right up to you to take a look.

GALÁPAGOS DOVE *ZENAIDIA GALAPAGOENSIS (PALOMA DE GALÁPAGOS)*

The Galápagos dove lives on the drier lowlands of most of the islands; the doves on Darwin and Wolf are much larger than those on the other islands and are classed as a separate subspecies. The peak breeding season is between February and June; the birds nest in sheltered spaces under rocks or use old mockingbird nests.

CACTUS FINCH *GEOSPIZA SCANDENS (PINZÓN DEL CACTUS)*

The cactus finch, one of the 15 species of Darwin's finches, lives on all the islands except Genovesa, Wolf, Darwin and Española. It has a proportionately longer bill than the other Darwin's finches, and is specially adapted to feed on *Opuntia* cacti.

VAMPIRE FINCH *GEOSPIZA DIFFICILIS SEPTENTRIONALIS (PINZÓN VAMPIRO)*

The sharp-beaked vampire finch lives only in the far northwest of the archipelago, on Darwin and Wolf islands. Their taste for the blood of boobies during dry season has made them notorious, probably developed as an adaptation to their homes' extremely arid environment. They do prefer bugs and seeds when they're available in the rainy season.

WOODPECKER FINCH *CAMARHYNCUS PALLIDA (PINZÓN ARTESANO)*

The woodpecker finch is mainly found on the highlands of Santiago, Santa Cruz, San Cristóbal, Isabela and Pinzón; it is sometimes spotted by the coast and in transitional areas of these islands. It uses twigs or cactus spines to pick grubs, larvae and insects from their holes.

GALÁPAGOS SHORT-EARED OWL *ASIO FLAMMEUS (BÚHO OREJICORTO)*

The Galápagos short-eared owl lives in the highlands and on the coast next to sea-bird colonies (such as the storm petrel colonies of Genovesa) of most of the islands except Fernandina, Wolf and Darwin. A diurnal hunter that picks off small birds, this owl cedes the skies to the Galápagos hawk when it's present, and hunts at dusk.

GALÁPAGOS FLYCATCHER *MYIARCHUS MAGNIROSTRIS (PAPAMOSCAS)*

The Galápagos flycatcher is found on all the islands except Genovesa, Darwin and Wolf. It likes to nest in the rainy season (December–May) in holes in trees and cacti, and will sometimes even eat from the palm of your hand.

8

REPTILES

GIANT TORTOISE *CHELONOIDIS SPP. (TORTUGA GIGANTE)*

Found on Isabela, Santa Cruz, Santiago, San Cristóbal, Santa Fé, Española and Pinzón, giant tortoises have come to symbolize the islands – and indeed, are the origin of their name. The lumbering and hoary beasts weigh up to 250kg and are the world's largest tortoises. Only one other island on the globe, in the Seychelles, has a giant-tortoise population. The Galápagos once had 14 subspecies of giant tortoise, and numbers could have been as high as 250,000. Unchecked slaughter during the height of the whaling era in the nineteenth century brought the population down to 15,000 and made three subspecies extinct. One other was recently lost, too, when Lonesome George – thought to be the last Pinta tortoise – died in 2012 at the Charles Darwin Research Station on Santa Cruz. Some hope has emerged that both the extinct Floreana and Pinta species might be resurrected within a matter of years, thanks to genes in some tortoises near Wolf Volcano on Isabela, analysed in 2015.

Giant tortoises can be identified by two basic types of shell shape: the dome-shaped tortoise is found in moister areas with thicker vegetation, while the saddleback shape allows a greater reach for the scarcer food on the drier islands. Giant tortoises are vegetarians and eat more than 50 plant species. When food is abundant they eat heartily, but it takes as long as three weeks to digest a meal, and even when it finally passes through, it's easy to see what they've been eating. Their somewhat coarse digestion does allow them to gorge on the highly toxic poison apple and prickly *Opuntia* cactus pads, despite the spines.

Tortoises are thought to live for more than 150 years, though no one knows for sure as they always outlive the research projects. They only become sexually mature around their twenty-fifth birthday. The mating season begins as the warm-wet season nears its end, when males compete for females by extending their necks – the highest head wins. The male mounts the female, fitting perfectly on her back due to the concave shape of his underside, and mates in a cacophony of grunts, wheezes and sighs lasting hours. Females then retreat to coastal areas to lay their billiard-ball-sized eggs, which can take up to eight months to hatch. It's the temperature of the nest that determines the sex of the hatchlings, rather than any specific chromosomal information. Apart from mating, tortoises are virtually silent unless alarmed, when they retreat into the shell and force air out of their nostrils with a sharp hiss.

PACIFIC GREEN TURTLE *CHELONIA MYDAS (TORTUGA VERDE)*

Although you may spot leatherback, hawksbill or olive ridley turtles in Galápagos waters, only the Pacific green turtle is a resident, regularly nesting on the islands' beaches. The green turtles weigh up to 150kg and are graceful swimmers, motored by their large front flippers. They make regular journeys between the islands and the mainland and can stay submerged for several hours. The peak mating and nesting season is November to February. Females mate with a succession of males inshore at the surface and dig large holes on sandy beaches to lay clutches of up to 100 eggs. Within two months, the hatchlings dash to the sea avoiding mockingbirds, frigatebirds, herons, ghost crabs and a host of other hungry predators. They break out at night simultaneously to keep the number of casualties down to a minimum, but even when they've reached the sea they swim nonstop to avoid predators lurking inshore.

MARINE IGUANA *AMBLYRHYNCHUS CRISTATUS (IGUANA MARINA)*

The cracked volcanic shores of the archipelago house demonic-looking colonies of marine iguanas, the world's only seagoing iguana. They feed on small tufts of seaweed or algae in rocky, intertidal areas, while the larger males supplement this with underwater weeds. Using their flattened tails to swim, they can dive to 12m and stay submerged for up to an hour, while they feed. Special glands above the eye allow the marine iguana to blow excess salt out of its nose in a fine spray, hence the salt crystals caked to their heads. They'll often "sneeze" at you if you get too close to them. In the mating season (January to March on most islands) marine iguanas take on a fiery red coloration. On Española they have a blotched black-and-red appearance during the year and burst into bright red and turquoise in the months of breeding.

LAND IGUANA *CONOLOPHUS SUBCRISTATUS, C. PALLIDUS ON SANTA FÉ; C. ROSADA ON WOLF VOLCANO, ISABELA (IGUANA TERRESTRE)*

Larger than marine iguanas, land iguanas can live up to 60 years and prefer the drier areas of the central and western islands, as they rely on cactus pads and fruits for much of their food. Three endemic species inhabit the Galápagos, one of which is confined to Santa Fé island; and another, identified as a new species only in 2009, is a pink iguana found only near the summit of Wolf Volcano on Isabela. Introduced species have been very harmful to land-iguana populations: the creatures are now extinct on Santiago and were almost finished off on Baltra during World War II, though fortunately some had been moved to Seymour Norte previously and have since been reintroduced to their home island.

LAVA LIZARD *TROPIDURUS (LAGARTIJA DE LAVA)*
Seven types of endemic lava lizards dart around the island coasts (except on Genovesa, Darwin and Wolf), hunting for insects and spiders. The males can grow up to 30cm in length and are larger than the females, which are distinguished by the vivid-red coloration on their head or throats. They mark their territories by doing sequences of "press-ups" on their forelegs, and each island has its own unique pattern.

GALÁPAGOS SNAKE *PHILODRYAS BISERIALIS, ALSOPHIS DORSALIS AND A. SELVINI (CULEBRA DE GALÁPAGOS)*
The three species of Galápagos snake are common on all the islands apart from Genovesa, Darwin and Wolf. Non-venomous constrictors, they grow to about a metre in length and devour geckos, lava lizards, finch chicks, rats and marine iguana hatchlings. The snakes are not dangerous to humans.

MAMMALS

GALÁPAGOS SEA LION *ZALOPHUS CALIFORNIANUS WOLLEBACKI (LOBO MARINO)*
A relative of the larger Californian sea lion, the Galápagos sea lion never fails to charm visitors to the islands. Sometimes boisterous, sometimes lazy, the sea lions' yelping, sneezing, coughing and whooping has an unnerving human quality to it. You'll commonly see sleepy females piled together on the beach, while the large dominant bull, weighing up to 250kg and identifiably male for the pronounced bump on its forehead, aggressively patrols its territory barking loudly above and below the waves.

Lesser males have no place at these heavily guarded "harems" and form colonies in less favourable locations, where they build up strength and size to make a successful challenge. The bull spends so much of its time guarding its territory that it doesn't feed, and eventually has to give way to a fitter male. These inquisitive, graceful and friendly animals will often check you out if you're swimming nearby, staring into your mask or tugging at your flippers. The bulls should be given a lot of space, though – they have a nasty bite and don't take kindly to humans who appear to be muscling in on their territory.

GALÁPAGOS FUR SEAL *ARCTOCEPHALUS GALAPAGOENSIS (FOCA)*
Galápagos fur seals are more shy and difficult to see than sea lions, choosing the shade of craggy cliffs and rocks, where they can find a nook to keep out of the sun's glare. They are usually encountered at James Bay, Santiago and Darwin Bay, Genovesa. In spite of their name, fur seals are in the same family (*Otaridae*) as the sea lion, having protruding ears and the ability to "walk" on their front flippers, unlike the *Phocidae*, the true seals. They're related to the southern fur seals of Antarctica and the southern mainland, and have thick coats like them, though in the heat of the Galápagos they must take care not to overheat. In the nineteenth century, their warm, double-layered pelt was highly sought after, and numbers declined from overhunting. They are now protected, and colonies have recovered to around 5000–6000.

MARINE INVERTEBRATES

SALLY LIGHTFOOT CRAB *GRASPUS GRASPUS (CANGREJO DE LAS ROCAS)*
The distinctive Sally Lightfoot crab is found in intertidal areas, particularly rocky shorelines. They follow the movements of the tide, scavenging for scraps and spooning up pieces of algae on specially adapted pincers. The crabs are skittish if approached, but if you wait they will often come to investigate.

WHALE- AND DOLPHIN-SPOTTING

One of the most thrilling moments during a Galápagos cruise is a sighting of **whales** or **dolphins**. Amiable **bottle-nosed dolphins** frequently surf the bow wave, jockeying for position and jumping high in synchrony. Huge schools of dark-grey and white **common dolphins** occasionally pass boats, skipping through the waves in long lines, while **striped** and **spinner dolphins** are seen less frequently. Whalers hunted the waters west of Isabela and Fernandina exhaustively during the first half of the nineteenth century, until populations all but disappeared around the 1860s. Today several whale species are found hereabouts and the **sperm whale** is known to have breeding grounds in the area. The **humpback whale** is the most easily spotted, sometimes "breaching" – hurling its 16-metre body out of the water before crashing down in an avalanche of spray. Other baleen whales, those that sift for plankton and shrimp such as the **sei**, **minke**, **Bryde's** and **finback**, are more usually seen as a fin and a puff of spray in the distance. **Orcas** or **killer whales** feed on dolphins, fur seals, penguins and sea lions.

LA ROTONDA ON PLAZA CÍVICA, GUAYAQUIL

Contexts

History

Exactly how and when the Americas were populated is still debated, but most authorities accept that humans first migrated from Asia over the Bering land bridge, formed by low sea levels during the last Ice Age, or along the coast aided by prevailing currents, between 40,000 and 12,000 years ago. The earliest evidence of human presence in Ecuador was discovered east of Quito at the El Inga archeological site and dates back to around 8000 BC.

Early cultures

Around this time, small **hunter-gatherer communities** collected seeds, berries, roots, insects and reptile eggs from the valley forests and roamed the high grasslands for bigger game. On the coast at about this time other hunter-gatherer groups of the **Las Vegas** culture were emerging around the Santa Elena peninsula, and by 6000 BC they began seasonal cultivation of food crops and cotton – becoming Ecuador's first known **agriculturists**.

The Formative Period

Semi-permanent settlements and the fashioning of tools from polished stone laid the basis for the **Valdivia** culture, which blossomed around 3500 BC and spread across the coast to southern Esmeraldas and beyond over the next 2000 years, dominating the early **Formative Period** (4000–400 BC). The Valdivia culture is best known for its ceramics – among the oldest found in South America – especially its **Venus figurines**, stylized miniatures of women. They lived in oval, wood-and-thatch houses surrounding a central square, in villages strung along the coast and around river plains, where the soil was fertile enough to grow maize, cotton, cassava, peppers and kidney beans.

The **Machalilla** culture (1500–800 BC) that followed preferred rectangular structures on stilts and practised skull deformation as a sign of status. They were more expert than their Valdivia counterparts at fishing and had surplus stores for trading with neighbouring groups. Their ceramic flasks are similar to those made by the Cotocollao, Cerro Narrío and Upano cultures, suggesting there was contact between them. Based around the Quito area, the **Cotocollao** people traded agricultural produce for coastal cotton, while the **Cerro Narrío** site in the southern sierra was an important trading centre between the coast and the Upano group based around Volcán Sangay in the upper Amazon basin. This communication across the regions seems to have intensified with the **Chorrera** culture (900–300 BC), which flourished on the coast at the close of the Formative Period. They were sophisticated people who crafted some of the most beautiful ceramics of that age, distinctive for their iridescent sheen.

The Regional Development Period

The subsequent **Regional Development Period** (300 BC–800 AD) saw a splintering of cultures and the appearance of highly stratified societies. The driving force behind

40,000–12,000 BC	6000 BC	3500 BC
Humans migrate from Asia to the Americas	The Las Vegas culture around the Santa Elena peninsula become Ecuador's first known agriculturists	The Valdivia culture blossoms and spreads across the coast to southern Esmeraldas and beyond

these changes was a burgeoning economy and the related interaction between cultures. As trading routes sprang up along the coast, seafaring cultures such as the **Bahía** (from south of Bahía de Caráquez, dating from 500 BC to 650 AD), **Jama-Coaque** (north of Bahía, from 350 BC to 1540 AD) and **Guangala** (Guayas coast from 100 BC to 800 AD) transported their wares on balsawood rafts with cotton sails. The merchants of these cultures were part of the elite, acting as diplomats and facilitators securing necessary goods from afar. The merchants' most treasured possession was the deep-crimson **spondylus** (thorny oyster) shell, harvested from a depth of 20–60m by highly skilled fishermen. Prized ornaments and symbols of fertility, the shells were also a kind of universal currency. Such was the range of these traders that ceramics representing them – sitting **basketmen** figures, often adorned with necklaces, bracelets and earrings, with outsized baskets on their backs – have been found on the Pacific coast from Ecuador to Central America.

Meanwhile, in northern Esmeraldas and stretching into Colombia, the culture of **La Tolita** (500 BC–500 AD) occupied one of the prime religious and trading centres on the South American coast, thought to have been on the island of La Tolita, in the mangroves near present-day San Lorenzo. Traders, craftsmen and worshippers from different regions swarmed to the site, and the cross-fertilization of ideas led to the creation of exquisite ceramic and metalwork.

The Integration Period

In the **Integration Period** (800–1480 AD), when political leaders and chiefs (*curacas*) of local territories, defined through frequent skirmishes, exacted tribute and levied taxes from their communities, agricultural productivity surged through improved techniques in irrigation and terracing, and trading continued to boom. On the coast the **Manteño-Huancavilca** culture (500 BC–1540 AD), occupying land from the Gulf of Guayaquil to Bahía de Caráquez, continued the seafaring traditions of their coastal forebears, while also producing distinctive artefacts like ceremonial U-shaped chairs supported by human or animal figures, and black ceramics. To their north, people such as the **Nigua**, **Chachi**, **Campaz**, **Caraque** and **Malaba** continued to live by hunting, fishing and farming small agricultural plots. Inland, to the south, the **Chono** – the ancestors of the Tsáchila (or Colorados) of today, defined archeologically as the **Milagro-Quevedo** culture – were known for fine weavings and gold adornments such as nose rings, headbands and breastplates. They also frequently warred with the fierce **Puná**, who occupied the island of the same name in the Gulf of Guayaquil.

The highlands

In the highlands at this time, the major population groups occupied the elevated valley basins between the western and eastern cordilleras of the Andes, each basin separated from the next by mountainous *nudos*, "knots" where the cordilleras tie together. From north to south these were the **Pasto**, occupying southern Colombia and Carchi; the **Cara** (or Caranqui), living around Ibarra, Otavalo and Cayambe, and responsible for enormous ceremonial centres such as the one at Cochasquí; the **Panzaleo** (also called the Quito), who inhabited the Quito valley, Cotopaxi and Tungarahua, and did much trade with the **Quijo** in the Oriente; the **Puruhá**, of the Chimborazo region; the **Cañari**, great gold and copper craftspeople who dominated the southern sierra; and the **Palta**, a

1500–800 BC	From 500 BC	800–1480 AD
The Machalilla culture follows on from the Valdivia culture	As trading routes spring up, the merchants of seafaring cultures such as the Bahía, Jama-Coaque and Guangala become an elite	The Integration Period sees political leaders and chiefs levying taxes, a surge in agricultural productivity and a boom in trade

tribe whose major centre was Saraguro near Loja and who had strong links with the Amazonian group, the **Shuar**.

The Incas

In around 1200 the **Incas** were an unremarkable sierra people occupying Peru's Cusco valley. After a string of military victories over neighbouring tribes in the fifteenth century, they grew into one of South America's most sophisticated civilizations. In about 1450 the **Tupac Yupanqui**, son and later successor of the Inca **Pachacutec**, set out to conquer present-day Ecuador with a force of 200,000 men. He brushed aside the Palta in the south, but met fierce resistance from the Cañari, and the fighting devastated the whole region. The Cañari had been so impressive that when they were beaten many were recruited into the Inca professional army. The Cara in the north were even more bellicose, and managed to keep the invaders at bay for years before a terrible massacre at Laguna Yahuarcocha around 1520, led by **Huayna Capac**, Tupac Yupanqui's son.

At its height in the early sixteenth century, the Inca Empire extended from Chile and the Argentine Andes to southern Colombia, a total area of some 980,000 square kilometres. It was a highly organized and efficient society that built great stone palaces, temples, observatories, storehouses and fortresses using masonry techniques of breathtaking ingenuity. Just as impressive was its administrative system, allowing a relatively small number of people to hold sway over huge areas.

Inca rule

Indirect rule was imposed on the conquered regions, with the local chief allowed to remain in power as long as he acknowledged the divine sovereignty of the Inca emperor. Lands were divided between the Incas (for the king, nobility and army), the religious establishment (for sacrifices, ceremonies and the priesthood) and the local communities, and tribute was paid in the cultivation of the imperial lands. Each year, subjects also had to honour the **mita**, a labour obligation requiring them to spend time working in the army or on public works. A shrewd policy stipulated that the community could not be taxed on its own produce, a measure that did much to ensure contentment and stability. Any troublesome subjects were forcibly resettled hundreds of miles away, with indoctrinated and acculturated colonists brought in as replacements.

Considering that the Incas were rulers in what is now southern Ecuador for no more than seventy years, and in northern Ecuador for only thirty years, they had an enormous impact on the region. New urban and ceremonial centres were built, such as **Tomebamba** (now buried beneath Cuenca) and **Quito**, with roads connecting them to the rest of the empire, and fortresses were erected at strategic points across the country, as at **Ingapirca**. The language of the Incas, **Kichwa**, was imposed on the defeated population and it's still spoken in various forms (as Quichua or Kichwa) by the majority of Ecuador's *indígenas*. The Incas also introduced sweet potatoes, peanuts and other crops, and drove large herds of llamas north from Peru for their wool and meat.

Civil war

By 1525 Huayna Capac was looking to establish a second capital at Quito or Tomebamba. Before he had a chance to act he was struck down by a virulent disease –

1200 AD	1450–1493	C.1520
The Incas occupy Peru's Cuzco valley	Incas under Pachacutec and Tupac Yupanqui conquer present-day Ecuador	The Cayambe and Caranquis, after years of resistance, are massacred by the Incas under Huayna Capac at Laguna Yahuarcocha (Blood Lake)

probably **smallpox**, which had been brought to Central America by the Spanish and had swiftly spread southwards. Huayna Capac's likely heir also died from the disease and in the resulting confusion two other sons took charge of the empire: **Huáscar**, who, ruling the south from Cusco, claimed he was the chosen successor; and **Atahualpa**, who asserted he'd been assigned the north and governed from Quito. Within a few years, friction between the two brothers erupted into a full-blown **civil war**, but Atahualpa had the advantage as the bulk of the imperial army was still in the north and under his command. Their forces clashed at Ambato, a pitched battle where more than 30,000 soldiers from both sides were killed. Atahualpa drove his brother south, laying waste to Tomebamba and the Cañari lands in revenge for their support of his enemy. With his superior troops, Atahualpa eventually got the upper hand, but even before he had heard of his generals' final victory over Huáscar in Cusco, news reached him of a small band of bearded strangers that had landed on the coast nearby.

The Spanish Conquest

In 1526 the Spanish pilot **Bartolomé Ruiz** sailed down the Ecuadorian coast on a reconnaissance mission and, near Salango, captured a large Manta merchant vessel laden with gold, silver and emeralds. His report convinced **Francisco Pizarro** that there were great riches to be had on the continent. After obtaining royal approval, Pizarro set sail from Panama in December 1530 with 180 men and 37 horses, landing at **Tumbes** in northern Peru in May 1532, with a few more troops brought by two other hardy campaigners, Sebastián de Benalcázar and Hernando de Soto. The Inca city, which marked the northernmost limits of the empire on the coast, lay in ruins from the civil war. The Spanish, learning that the civilization had been in the grip of a terrible conflict, saw the perfect opportunity for conquest.

The massacre at Cajamarca

Pumped up by his victory over Huáscar's army, Atahualpa didn't regard the Spaniard's straggly band of a few hundred as much of a threat – even with their horses, an unknown quantity to the Incas. In a fatal miscalculation, the new emperor invited them to a meeting at **Cajamarca**, letting them past countless guardposts and strongholds and over mountainous terrain that would have been too steep for cavalry attacks. A day after his arrival in Cajamarca, Pizarro launched a surprise attack, taking Atahualpa hostage and massacring thousands of Inca soldiers and nobles. Atahualpa offered to fill a room with gold and two huts with silver, in return for which Pizarro promised to restore him to his kingdom at Quito. Within a few months, six metric tons of gold and almost 12 tons of silver had been melted down, making rich men of the conquistadors. Nevertheless, they broke their promise and, fearing a counterattack, swiftly condemned Atahualpa to be burnt alive – a terrifying prospect for someone who believed his body must be preserved for passage into the afterlife – unless he became a Christian. In July 1533 the weeping Inca was baptized and then garrotted.

The race to Quito

The Spanish quickly took Cusco and southern Peru, and then turned their attention to Quito and the northern empire, (modern Ecuador) – a race was on to find the

1525	1526	1528–1530
At its height, the Inca Empire extends from central Chile and the Argentine Andes to southern Colombia	Bartolomé Ruiz captures a valuable Manta merchant vessel; his report convinces Francisco Pizarro of the south's great riches	Huayna Capac dies; his sons – Huáscar and Atahualpa – divide the empire between themselves but slide into civil war

suspected treasures of its cities. In March 1534, the merciless governor of Guatemala, **Pedro de Alvarado**, gathered a formidable army and landed on the Ecuadorian coast in the Manta area. Despite torturing natives to find the best route into the highlands, he ended up going over the highest and most treacherous pass near Chimborazo, losing many men along the way, as well as the race to Quito.

Sebastián de Benalcázar, meanwhile, had got wind of Alvarado's expedition early on, and swiftly summoned his own forces together, riding across the bleak Peruvian coast onto the Inca highway to Quito. In Tomebamba he forged an alliance with the Cañari, who were bent on exacting revenge for years of Inca subjugation. A couple of large Inca armies were still mobilized in the north, and in the cold páramo grasslands at Teocajas above Tomebamba, the tenacious Inca general **Rumiñahui** prepared his 50,000 troops for attack. They fought bravely but it was clear it would take a miracle to beat the Spanish and their horses. Rumiñahui battled with Benalcázar all the way to Quito and before the Spanish could get there he removed the treasures and torched the palaces and food stores. Then, joining forces with another general, **Zopozopagua**, he launched a night attack on the Spanish encamped in the city, but was again thwarted. Eventually both Rumiñahui and Zopozopagua were caught, tortured and executed. **Quisquis**, the last of Atahualpa's great generals, valiantly fought his way from southern Ecuador to Quito, but when he found the city had already been taken, his army mutinied, hacking him to pieces rather than facing death on the battlefields.

The founding of San Francisco de Quito
In August 1534 the Spanish founded the city of **San Francisco de Quito** on the charred remains of the Inca capital, and a few months later they had conquered all of the northern part of the Inca Empire. The inaccessible north coast and much of the Oriente were deemed too difficult and unproductive to colonize and stayed out of their control for much of the colonial era. Still, the conquest had a devastating effect on the native populations of Ecuador through war, forced labour and Old World **diseases**. Smallpox, measles, the plague and influenza cut the aboriginal population to 200,000 by the end of the sixteenth century, down from 1.5 million.

The Colonial era
The Spanish were quick to consolidate their victories, with the Crown parcelling out land to the conquistadors in the form of **encomiendas**, grants that entitled the holders, the **encomenderos**, to a substantial tribute in cash, plus produce and labour from the *indígenas* who happened to live there. In return, the *encomenderos* were entrusted with converting their charges to Christianity, a task that was only a partial success; in many cases the *indígenas* merely superimposed Catholic imagery onto their existing beliefs, but eventually the two traditions fused in a syncretism that can still be seen today.

The *encomienda* system grafted easily onto the old Inca order, and the *encomenderos* were soon the elite of the region, which became the **Audiencia de Quito** in 1563. Roughly corresponding to modern-day Ecuador, the *audiencia* had rather vague boundaries, but included a huge swath of the Amazon following Francisco de Orellana's voyage (see box, p.231). It also enjoyed legal autonomy from Lima and direct links to Madrid, even though it was still a part of the Viceroyalty of Peru. During the early

1532	1533	1534
Pizarro lands in northern Peru with 180 men and 37 horses. He is joined by campaigners Sebastián de Benalcázar and Hernando de Soto	Atahualpa invites the Spanish to a meeting at Cajamarca; Pizarro attacks, taking Atahualpa hostage and massacring hundreds of Incas	The conquistadors break a promise to free Atahualpa, and garrotte him

1600s, there were more than 500 *encomiendas* in the *audiencia*, run on the labour of about half the region's *indígenas*, who were effectively serfs on these estates.

Another quarter of the area's *indígenas* deserted the productive *encomienda* lands for the undesirable páramo and lowland forests, but they were rounded up at the end of the century and resettled in purpose-built "Indian towns", or **reducciones**, where colonists could more easily collect tribute and exploit their labour.

The mita and the rise of haciendas

The Spanish also borrowed – and corrupted – another Inca institution, the *mita*, a system that required these supposedly free *indígenas* to work for a year according to the needs of the colony. These workers, the **mitayos**, received a small wage but it was invariably less than the amount they owed their employers for subsistence purchases. Soon the *mita* system descended into debt slavery, as the *mitayos* worked indefinitely to pay off their unending deficits – which their children would inherit, so trapping them, too. The *audiencia* had such poor mineral resources – the small gold and silver deposits around Cuenca and Loja were exhausted by the end of the sixteenth century – that the *mitayos* were at least spared the agonies of working in mines: millions of their contemporaries died in mines in Peru and Bolivia. Instead, most of the indigenous labourers were involved in **agriculture** and **textiles**.

Events of the 1690s saw an abrupt halt to the economic success, as another wave of epidemics wiped out a third to half of the indigenous population, droughts destroyed harvests and severe earthquakes shook the region. This triggered the demise of the *encomiendas*, which were replaced by large private estates, or **haciendas**, but for the *indígenas* the new system of **huasipungo** brought little relief. In return for their labour on the haciendas, they were entitled to farm tiny plots of land in their spare moments, where they were expected to grow all their own food.

Life on the coast

Around a quarter of the remaining indigenous population escaped the rule of the Spanish altogether by living in the inaccessible tropical forests of lowland Oriente or the north coast, the latter area under the control of a **black** and **zambo** (mixed black and indigenous) population, largely the descendants of escaped slaves, brought to work on the coastal plantations or fight in the Spanish army. The south coast had only a tiny workforce available, as more than 95 percent of the natives had been wiped out by disease, but even so, **Guayaquil**, founded by Benalcázar in 1535, was developing into an important trade and shipbuilding centre.

Shifting attitudes

In the early 1700s the **Bourbon** kings of Spain, who had replaced the Hapsburg dynasty, were determined to tighten their grip over their American territories. They embarked on a strategy of economic and administrative reform intended to boost productivity, such as transferring the Quito *audiencia* to the newly established Viceroyalty of **Nueva Granada**, with its capital at Bogotá, Colombia, in 1717 (an arrangement that lasted three years), and then again in 1739. The expulsion of the **Jesuits** in 1767 by Charles III only damaged further the weak highland economy. The Jesuits – as well as teaching Christianity to the *indígenas* – had run the best

1534	1563	1690s
The Spanish take the Inca site of Quito and found the new city of San Francisco de Quito. Within months, the northern Inca Empire has been captured	The Audiencia de Quito is formed	A wave of epidemics, droughts and earthquakes end a period of economic success

schools and most productive and profitable workshops in the *audiencia*, but their very success had made them unpopular with the Crown. Yet while the highland textile economy suffered severe depression, the **cacao** industry on the coast was flourishing, with the commodity becoming the colony's largest export.

By the middle of the eighteenth century, the **criollos** – Spanish born in the colonies – were nursing a growing resentment against the motherland that wasn't helped by the economic situation. High taxes, continual interference from Spain and the fact that all the best jobs still went to the **peninsulares** – Spanish-born newcomers – only added to the discontent. At the same time, the **Enlightenment** was opening up new lines of political and philosophical thought in Europe, which filtered down into the upper-class households of the *audiencia*, and sharply contradicted the colony's semi-feudal organization. Scientific expeditions were a source of new knowledge, such as **Charles-Marie de La Condamine**'s mission (1736–45) to discern the shape of the Earth, which he did by measuring a degree of latitude on the equator north of Quito.

One of the first to articulate the new influences was **Eugenio Espejo**, an exceptional man who, despite being born of *indígena* and mulatto parents in a deeply racist society, obtained a university degree and became an outstanding doctor, lawyer, essayist and satirist. His outspoken views on republicanism and democracy cost him his life – he died in jail in 1795 – but he's still honoured as the progenitor of the country's independence movement.

The birth of the republic

Napoleon's successful invasion of Spain in 1808 sent shockwaves throughout its New World colonies. On August 10, 1809, a short-lived junta in support of the deposed king, **Ferdinand VII**, was established in Quito, but it failed in a matter of weeks when the backing of the rest of the *audiencia* was not forthcoming. Despite assurances of pardons, those involved were rounded up and sentenced to death. In August 1810, an incensed public stormed the prison but the guards massacred the junta's leaders before they could be freed. Even so, the disturbances led to a new **junta**, which ambitiously declared the independence of the *audiencia* in 1811, whether the rest of the colony was ready for it or not. With a band of ill-disciplined troops, the new government launched a foolhardy attack against the well-trained Spanish forces and were consequently routed at Ibarra in 1812.

After that defeat, it wasn't until 1820 that the independence movement regained momentum – this time in Guayaquil, led by **José Joaquín de Olmedo**, an intellectual and shrewd politician – and **independence** was declared on October 9. Urgent requests for assistance were immediately sent to the Liberator **Simón Bolívar**, who was marching south from Venezuela, and **José de San Martín**, who was sweeping north from Argentina, crushing the Spanish armies as they went. Bolívar quickly dispatched his best general, **Antonio José de Sucre**, with a force of seven hundred men. Sucre scored a great victory at Guayaquil, but was thwarted at Ambato, until reinforcements sent by San Martín enabled him to push on to Quito. On May 24, 1822, he won the decisive **Battle of Pichincha**, and five days later the old *audiencia* became the **Department of the South** in a new autonomous state, **Gran Colombia**, roughly corresponding to the combined territories of Ecuador, Colombia, Panama and Venezuela today.

1736–1743	1795	1809–12
Charles-Marie de La Condamine discerns the shape of the Earth by measuring a degree of latitude on the equator near Quito	Eugenio Espejo, outspoken advocate of republicanism and democracy, dies in jail	A short-lived junta is established in Quito in support of Ferdinand VII, who was deposed by Napoleon

A time of turbulence

The early years of the republic were turbulent, and disagreements over the border with Peru escalated into armed conflict in 1828. Guayaquil suffered extensive damage, but Sucre and **General Juan José Flores** defeated the Peruvian forces at the Battle of Tarqui in 1829. A year later, on May 13, following Venezuela's split from Gran Colombia, Quito representatives also decided to declare their own republic, naming it **Ecuador**, after its position on the equator, and **General Flores**, a Venezuelan by birth who had married into the Quito aristocracy, became the first president.

The new nation didn't gel well at all. In the sierra the **Conservative** land-owning elites were happy to keep the colonial system in operation, while on the coast the **Liberal** merchant classes, rich on the country's sole export commodity, cacao, wanted free trade, lower taxes and a break with the old order. This dualism between the regions – and their great cities, Quito and Guayaquil – has coloured the country ever since.

Flores soon found his heavy-handed and Quito-oriented administration desperately unpopular on the coast, and cannily arranged for the *guayaquileño* politician **Vicente Rocafuerte** to take the second term. Meanwhile Flores lurked in the background, pulling the strings as head of the military, and became president again from 1839 to 1845, when he was ousted by a junta from the coast. For the next fifteen years, the country descended into a political mire, with bitter fighting between the regions and the seat of government moving from Quito to Guayaquil to Riobamba and then back to Guayaquil. Eleven presidents and juntas followed each other in power, the most successful being led by the Liberal **General José María Urbina**, who ruled with an iron fist from 1851 to 1856 and managed to **abolish slavery** within a week of the coup that swept him to the presidency. Moreover, he had strongly encouraged his predecessor, **General Francisco Robles**, to axe the tribute the *indígenas* were still being forced to pay after three centuries of abuse.

The Terrible Year

The turmoil of the era culminated in 1859 – later known as the **Terrible Year** – when the strain between the regions finally shattered the country: Quito set up a provisional government, Cuenca declared itself autonomous, Loja became a federal district and, worst of all, Guayaquil, led by General Guillermo Franco, signed itself away to Peruvian control. Peru invaded and blockaded the port, while Colombia hungrily eyed the rest of Ecuador for itself.

Conservative rule: 1861–95

Aiming to set the republic right, **Gabriel García Moreno** quashed the various rebellions with the help of Flores and seized power as president in 1861. Born into an elite but economically struggling family in Guayaquil, García Moreno was educated in Quito and Europe and was both fiercely Conservative and a devout Catholic. He saw the country's salvation in the Church, and set about strengthening its position, establishing it as the state religion, signing control over to the Vatican, founding schools staffed only by Catholics, dedicating the republic to the "Sacred Heart of Jesus" and making **Catholicism** a prerequisite for citizenship. He was also ruthless with his many opponents, crushing them and several coup attempts.

1822	1822–29	1829	1830
Battle of Pichincha leads to definite independence from Spain	Ecuador forms part of Gran Colombia	Armed conflict with Peru: Guayaquil suffers extensive damage, but Peruvian forces are defeated at the Battle of Tarqui	Ecuador declares independence: Juan José Flores becomes its first president

His presidency helped foster growth in agriculture and industry, initiating a much-needed programme of road-building and beginning the Quito–Guayaquil railway, as well as creating the first national currency. Nevertheless, he was hated by the Liberals for his authoritarianism and for strengthening the Church. One of the loudest critics was the writer, **Juan Montalvo**, who vilified his policies from the safety of self-imposed exile. In 1875, just after García Moreno had been elected to his third term of office, an assassin murdered the president on the steps of the Palacio de Gobierno.

An export boom

After García Moreno's death, Conservative power waned and an uprising brought to power the military dictator **General Ignacio de Veintimilla**, a man who was surprisingly popular, perhaps for his large-scale public works programmes and boisterous public fiestas. From 1884 to 1895 the country returned to constitutional governments, overseen by three progressive Conservative presidents who navigated between radical Conservatism and Liberalism. Yet their success in bridging the divide was limited, and all the while the Liberals were accruing power and influence as the late nineteenth and early twentieth centuries saw phenomenal growth in Ecuador's **exports**. For a time, the country was the world's leading producer of cacao, and coffee, tagua nuts and Panama hats were also doing well – products all based on the coast around Guayaquil – and much of the money filled Liberal coffers.

The Liberal era: 1895–1925

A committed revolutionary and Liberal, **Eloy Alfaro** had been involved in guerrilla skirmishes with García Moreno's Conservative forces since his early 20s. He'd already fled the country twice before Liberal cacao lords sought his return and funded a military coup that brought him to power in 1895. Alfaro immediately set about undoing García Moreno's policies and began measures that would permanently weaken the Catholic Church. In his two terms as president (1897–1901 and 1906–11), Alfaro defined the radical Liberal position, secularizing the state and education, expelling foreign clergy, instituting civil marriage and divorce and cutting links with the Vatican. Like García Moreno however, he ploughed money into public works and saw through the completion of the Quito–Guayaquil railway.

Yet he was under attack from both Conservatives and Liberal party factions sympathetic to his rival **General Leonidas Plaza** (president 1901–05 and 1912–16). To fend off the revolts, largely instigated by Conservative rebels with the backing of the Church, Alfaro allocated forty percent of his entire budget to military expenditure. The split within the Liberal camp worsened, and when Alfaro's chosen presidential successor, Emilio Estrada, died suddenly just after his inauguration in 1911, the country fell into a bloody **civil war**. A year later, Plaza's forces defeated Alfaro, and he and his supporters were transported to Quito, where they were murdered, dragged through the streets and burnt in the Parque Ejido. One good thing to come out of this period was the 1918 scrapping of debtor imprisonment that ended the colonial system of **debt peonage** for the *indígenas*.

1851	1859	1861–75
In a coup, José María Urbina becomes president, ruling with an iron fist but ending slavery	The "Terrible Year" sees the country split between governments in Quito, Guayaquil, Cuenca and Loja	Fiercely conservative Gabriel García Moreno dominates this period, strengthening the Church and ruthlessly suppressing opponents

The rise of La Argolla

The civil war had left the state weakened and cash-strapped, allowing power to shift to **la argolla**, a "ring" of wealthy cacao merchants and bankers, underpinned by the private Banco Comercial and Agrícola in Guayaquil. The bank provided loans to a succession of ailing administrations at the expense of rocketing inflation rates, and became so influential that it was said that any politician needed its full backing to be successful.

In the 1920s Ecuador descended into an **economic crisis** (a symptom of this arrangement) as well as crippling inflation and a severe slump in cacao production. A devastating blight damaged the crop, and cacao prices plunged as the market was swamped by new producers, especially British colonies in Africa. The poor were hit very badly, and uprisings – one in 1922 by workers in Guayaquil and another in 1923 by *indígena* peasants on a highland estate – were suppressed with massacres. The bloodless **Revolución Juliana** of 1925 effectively marked the end of the old Liberal–Conservative tug-of-war and ushered in a disoriented era of coups and overthrows.

Political crisis: 1925–47

After two swift juntas, the military handed power to **Isidro Ayora** in 1926, who embarked on a programme of reforms, including the creation of the Banco Central in Quito to smash the influence of *la argolla*. The new bank couldn't temper the rate of inflation, and popular discontent forced Ayora's resignation in 1931. Fuelled by the woeful economic condition at home and the Great Depression worldwide, the country's political cohesion finally crumbled away. During the 1930s a total of fourteen men took the presidency, and from 1925 to 1948 Ecuador had a total of 27 different governments.

Out of the turbulence of this era came the first of populist **José María Velasco Ibarra**'s five presidential terms, which began in 1934 and lasted less than a year, thanks to his removal by the military when he tried to assume dictatorial powers; in his career, he was to be overthrown by the army three more times. He went into exile until the 1940s, and chaos reigned.

The Rio Protocol

In 1941, while pro-government troops were tied up in Quito defending the presidency of **Carlos Arroyo del Río**, Peru invaded, marching north and west through the Amazonian jungle and occupying the provinces of El Oro and Loja in the south. The occupation only ended after the nations signed the **Rio Protocol** of January 1942, forcing Ecuador to cede 200,000 square kilometres – almost half the land it claimed. Although much of the disputed territory was effectively already under Peruvian rather than Ecuadorian control, the loss was a huge blow to national pride. The move continued to be disputed by Ecuador, thanks to an irregularity in the treaty, and the territory was included on all Ecuadorian maps until a peace treaty of 1998 between the two countries finally brought the issue to a close.

Velasco ousted the disgraced Arroyo in 1944, but was deposed by the military in 1947. Three presidents soon came and went before Galo Plaza Lasso took the helm in 1948, adding some much-needed stability.

1883–95	1895	1911
Following military rule, the country returns to civilian government. Ecuador becomes the world's leading cacao producer	Liberal Eloy Alfaro's becomes president, secularizing the state and much of society	Divisions in the Liberal party and Ecuador result in bloody civil war. Alfaro is defeated, arrested and killed

Prosperity and decline: 1948–72

Galo Plaza Lasso was the son of the former Liberal president Leonidas Plaza, but he also had strong links with the powerful Conservative families in the sierra and so was well placed to form a stable government. Committed to democracy, he strove for freedom of speech and of the press, and as a fair and popular president, he was the first since 1924 to complete his term of office.

The banana boom

The stability Plaza had helped foster was due in large part to economic prosperity brought on by the **banana boom**. After World War II the world demand for bananas rocketed, and while the traditional exporters in the Caribbean and Central America had trouble with crop diseases, Ecuador had huge parcels of ex-cacao land ready to be given over to bananas – and soon the country became the world's largest exporter, a position it retains today. Government reserves brimmed over and money was invested in infrastructure to open up more areas of the countryside to banana farms. Large areas around Santo Domingo were cleared for agriculture, and **colonists** flooded to the coast – between 1942 and 1962, the population in the region more than doubled. As the industry was dominated by small and medium-sized farms, the new wealth spread through a wider portion of society than it had during the cacao boom.

Unemployment and strikes

The prosperity and wellbeing was such that Velasco even managed to complete his third term in office (1952–56), the only one that he did. His successor **Camilo Ponce Enríquez** also saw his term through, but in the late 1950s, as world demand for bananas slumped, **unemployment** began to rise and people took to the streets in protest.

Once again, the master-populist Velasco was elected, thanks to his oratory and promise of support for the urban poor. Exploiting the popularity of the recent Cuban revolution, he laced his speeches with anti-US attacks and won the support of the Ecuadorian left. Before long, pressure from the US on Latin America to cut ties with Cuba heightened tensions between leftists and anti-communists. Hopes that the country had at last achieved political maturity were dashed as Velasco's coalition disintegrated under the strain, and rival groups resorted to violence. In a desperate search for revenue, Velasco put taxes on consumer items, sparking **strikes** across the whole country.

The military junta

As a Cuba-style revolution threatened, the military (with probable CIA interference) installed Velasco's vice–president, **Carlos Julio Arosemena Monroy**, in 1961, but he soon became unpopular with the establishment for refusing to sever links with Cuba and was branded a communist. The damage to his credibility had been done by the time he relented in 1962, but by then he was a broken man. A year later a **military junta** took power, jailing the opposition and suppressing the left, though it did pass the **1964 Agrarian Reform Law**, which at last brought the *huasipungo* system to an end, even if it didn't achieve a far-reaching redistribution of land. As banana prices plummeted in 1965, the junta ran up against serious cash-flow problems and was forced to step down the following year.

1920s	**1925–47**	**1941**
Ecuador descends into economic crisis: power shifts to the *la argolla* collection of merchants and bankers	A bloodless revolution ushers in economic reform, but the Great Depression triggers instability, with a total of 27 different governments	Peru invades, forcing Ecuador to recognize Peruvian sovereignty of 200,000 square kilometres in the Amazon

Velasco returns

Elections in 1968 brought Velasco back to power by the slenderest of margins. The economic situation was so serious that he was forced to devalue the sucre (Ecuador's then currency) and raise import tariffs, but to temper these measures, he seized US fishing boats found inside Ecuador's territorial limits, the so-called **tuna war**. After two years, he assumed dictatorial powers and clung to power until his overthrow by the military in 1972.

Military control and the oil boom: 1972–79

The military, led by **General Guillermo Rodríguez Lara**, seized control because it was anxious that the flighty populist, **Assad Bucaram**, former mayor of Guayaquil, would be victorious in the upcoming elections, and because it aimed to be the custodian of the large **oil reserves** found in the Oriente. Texaco's explorations in 1967 had struck rich, locating high-quality oil fields near Lago Agrio, and by 1971 more than twenty international companies had swarmed to the Oriente on the scent of a fortune.

The junta was aggressively leftist-nationalist and determined that the state should get as much from the oil boom as possible. Contracts with foreign companies were renegotiated, a state-owned petroleum company was set up, and in 1973 Ecuador joined **OPEC**. Money flooded into the public sector, stimulating employment, industrialization, economic growth and urbanization. The Oriente infrastructure was revolutionized, and in 1971 Texaco built a road to Lago Agrio, the first to leave the eastern Andean foothills. To keep Colombia or Peru from getting ideas about the oil-rich lands, colonists such as military conscripts were encouraged into the region by the thousands. The huge **environmental cost** of all the colonization and oil-industry activity is still being felt today.

Debts and taxes

The junta pushed its nationalist stance too far when it declared that the state's stake in Texaco operations should be upped to 51 percent, thus discouraging further foreign investment and prospecting. Oil production fell by a fifth, but this was temporarily offset by a sharp rise in global prices. Yet even with the huge increases in revenues and booming economy, the government managed to overspend and rack up some significant **debts**. Trying to redress the balance, it slapped sixty percent duty on luxury imports, upsetting the private sector and sparking a failed coup. Rodríguez Lara's position was weakened enough for a second, bloodless coup in 1976, led by a triumvirate of military commanders, who sought to return government to civilian rule, but on their terms.

The return to democracy: 1979–87

In August 1979, the military could no longer deny power to the young centre-left coalition candidate, **Jaime Roldós Aguilera**, after his landslide election victory three months earlier and heavy pressure from US President Jimmy Carter. Since the oil boom, the **economic landscape** of the country had transformed: per-capita income was now five times greater than before 1972, employment was up by ten percent, and a new urban middle class had emerged. Despite the new wealth, inequality remained

1948	1961	1968
Ecuador becomes the world's biggest banana exporter, the boom bringing political stability through the 1950s	The military installs Carlos Julio Arosemena as president, later replacing him with a repressive junta	Populist president José María Velasco Ibarra is re-elected for the fourth time and devalues the sucre

entrenched. Roldós's plans for wide-ranging structural reforms fell through as a bitter rivalry developed between him and his party associate and the uncle of his wife, Bucaram, the leader of congress.

By 1981 the economic situation was again precarious, with an enormous budget deficit, in large part due to overspending by Bucaram's congress. Worse still, trouble flared up on the Peruvian border, adding to the financial burden. Then, in May, three months after a ceasefire with Peru and only weeks after the presentation of a revolutionary law that would redistribute oil wealth to the people, Roldós was killed in an airplane crash near Loja. Many suspected it was an assassination, and, in the eyes of the Roldós family, the accident has never been satisfactorily investigated.

A period of austerity

Roldós's vice-president **Osvaldo Hurtado Larrea** stepped in and tried to push on with the reform programme, but the economic situation rapidly deteriorated. Oil prices fell sharply, and gross domestic product shrank by more than three percent; **inflation** soared, **unemployment** climbed, and there were four **general strikes**; **El Niño** floods caused $1 billion of damage, while **blight** ravaged highland potato crops. Still, Hurtado managed to take unpopular austerity measures to combat the $7 billion **foreign debt**, and secure constitutional elections and the transition of power to a second democratically elected government – the first time in almost 25 years.

The impact of neoliberalism

León Febres Cordero Rivadeneira and his centre-right coalition won the 1984 general election. Inspired by Reagan and Thatcher, the new government embarked on a neoliberal programme favouring free markets, foreign investment, exports and the roll-back of state power. Yet the government was plagued by allegations of **corruption** and **human rights abuses**, and as living costs rose, public disquiet grew. In 1986, shortly after a failed coup attempt by air-force general **Frank Vargas**, Febres Cordero was held hostage by Vargas supporters and threatened with death unless the general was released. The president immediately complied, an act perceived as cowardly by the public. To add to the country's woes, in March 1987 a serious **earthquake** rocked the Oriente, killing hundreds, leaving tens of thousands homeless and destroying 40km of the Trans-Andean oil pipeline. The economy was crippled as oil production stopped for six months, and Febres Cordero was forced to default on payment of foreign debts totalling more than $10 billion.

The Democratic Left

The failure of right-wing politics led to social democrat **Rodrigo Borja Cevallo** winning a convincing victory with his *Izquierda Democrática* party (Democratic Left) in 1988. Borja's reform programme (**gradualismo**) steered the country away from the policies of Febres Cordero and aimed to protect human rights and press freedom, boost literacy rates and improve relations with Peru. Yet runaway inflation led to a wave of strikes, and in 1990 an umbrella organization of the nation's indigenous peoples, **CONAIE**, staged an uprising, calling for rights to land and territories, the right to self-government and creation of a multinational Ecuadorian state. The same year, twelve Waorani communities received territorial rights to land bordering the Parque Nacional Yasuní in the Oriente.

1970	1972–79	1979	1981
Velasco assumes dictatorial powers	The military retakes power and rides an oil boom, but racks up serious debts	Civilian rule returns with centre-left politician Jaime Roldós Aguilera	Roldós is killed in a suspicious airplane crash

The return of the right

Desperate to fix the economy, the public switched its support back to the right, voting in **Sixto Durán Ballén** in 1992. He strove for modernization, privatization and reduction of state bureaucracy, but his administration was dogged by hostility from labour unions and CONAIE, as well as **corruption** scandals, and in 1995 his vice-president, Alberto Dahik, fled the country to avoid prosecution over mismanagement of intelligence funds.

Off the rails: 1996–2006

The 1996 elections brought a shock when outsider **Abdalá Bucaram** – the nephew of Asaad Bucaram and known as **El Loco** (the Madman) – won with an informal populist style, promising increased subsidies and a stronger public sector. His publicity stunts included releasing his own CD ("Madman in Love"), shaving off his Hitler-style moustache (he was an admirer) in an auction, and offering to pay Diego Maradona $1 million to play a football match in Ecuador. Before long, Bucaram betrayed his supporters with austerity measures that made utility prices skyrocket, and rumours of large-scale mismanagement of funds and **corruption** also began to circulate. In just a year, his popularity plummeted and trade unions called a general strike. Congress voted him out of office on grounds of "**mental incapacity**", but Bucaram stubbornly clung on. For a few days in February 1997, Bucaram, vice-president Rosalía Arteaga and congressional leader Fabián Alarcón all claimed to be the rightful president. Meanwhile huge crowds gathered around the presidential palace calling for Bucaram's removal. Ultimately, he fled to Panama, allegedly carrying suitcases stuffed with embezzled cash – reportedly he may have robbed the country of nearly $100 million.

Economic disarray

Fabián Alarcón muddled through the commotion as interim president, faced with economic stagnation and corruption allegations, and in 1998 the Harvard-educated mayor of Quito, **Jamil Mahuad**, beat Alvaro Noboa, Ecuador's wealthiest banana baron and candidate of Bucaram's party. After an amazing start, signing a peace treaty with Alberto Fujimori, ending decades of tension and hostility with Peru, nothing went right. The country's finances were in disarray and even the government claimed it to be Ecuador's worst **economic crisis** in seventy years, with inflation at around fifty percent, oil more expensive to produce than to sell and $2.6 billion of El Niño damage to deal with, including the devastation of the banana harvest.

Despite paralysing strikes, Mahuad still pushed on with neoliberal **austerity measures**, terminating fuel subsidies – almost doubling the price of petrol, and quadrupling the cost of electricity. Just as it seemed the banking system was on the brink of collapse, he froze more than $3 billion of bank deposits – a measure that didn't save banks from folding or stop a run on the sucre. Facing a **foreign debt** of $16 billion, Ecuador defaulted on a Brady-bond interest payment, the first country ever to do so.

The removal of Mahuad

By January 2000, Ecuador's economy had shrunk by seven percent from the previous year, inflation was running higher than sixty percent and the sucre had devalued by

1987	1996–97	1998–2000
A major earthquake kills hundreds and snaps an important oil pipeline. Ecuador defaults on foreign debts worth over $10bn	Populist "El Loco" Abdalá Bucaram comes to power, ushering in a decade of instability; he soon flees Ecuador	Amid a severe economic and banking crisis prompted by the plunge in oil prices, Ecuador replaces the sucre with the US dollar

almost three hundred percent. In a desperate bid to save his presidency and stop the economy from completely falling apart, Mahuad announced the resignation of his entire cabinet and plans to **dollarize** the national currency. CONAIE mobilized its supporters, and tens of thousands of *indígenas* filtered into Quito. On January 21, 2000, the military unit guarding Congress stepped aside and the indigenous groups stormed the building and announced the removal of Mahuad and the dissolution of Congress and the Supreme Court.

Only hours later, the military junta called for vice-president **Gustavo Noboa** to take up the presidency; Mahuad went into exile. Noboa forged ahead with dollarization, implementing it in 2001 with the help of a $2 billion aid package. Though it helped economic stability and stopped hyperinflation, it came at the cost of rising prices and worsening conditions for the ever-increasing poor.

The rise and fall of Gutiérrez

In the 2002 elections, another outsider, **Lucio Gutiérrez**, an ex-colonel involved in the 2000 coup, won with the backing of indigenous groups and unions by pledging to root out corruption and reverse monetarist reforms. Once in power, it wasn't long before he turned his back on his leftist supporters by cutting food subsidies and spending large chunks of oil revenue on servicing debt. As his national popularity plummeted, he managed to cling to power only through mercurial coalitions with a range of unlikely political groups.

His unconstitutional dismissal of the Supreme Court in late 2004, with the aim of replacing judges with cronies who would drop criminal charges against Abdalá Bucaram, was widely criticized as a "dictatorial act" and led in April 2005 to mass demonstrations and the withdrawal of support by the armed forces. Congress voted to remove him from office, and he fled by helicopter, eventually finding asylum in Brazil. Claiming he had been illegally removed from power and that he would follow constitutional channels to get it back, he returned to Ecuador in October, whereupon he was arrested and imprisoned, only to be released in March 2006. His vice-president, **Alfredo Palacio**, was sworn in as interim president and held together the many pieces of the fractious political system as best he could until the 2006 elections.

Correa's rule

After such instability, Ecuador sought a strong leader, like **Rafael Correa**, who became the country's 56th president in 2007 after winning run-off elections the previous year. Describing himself as a humanist and socialist Catholic, Correa is a populist firebrand in the mould of Hugo Chávez of Venezuela and Bolivia's Evo Morales – anti-neoliberal, against foreign and particularly US interference in sovereign affairs, sceptical about the motives of the World Bank and IMF, and strongly in favour of social justice, redistribution of wealth and the welfare state. In 2008, Ecuadorians voted by a two-thirds majority to approve the country's **20th constitution**, which aimed to redress structural inequalities and bolster civil rights, allowing civil union for same-sex couples and free health care for the elderly. It also made Ecuador the first country in the world to extend "inalienable **rights to nature**", in the declaration that nature "has the right to exist, persist, maintain and regenerate its vital cycles, structure, functions and its processes in evolution".

2003	2007	2011
A dispute over control over the judiciary leads to massive street protests and the fall of populist former coup-leader, Lucio Gutiérrez	Leftist firebrand Rafael Correa is elected president amid a pledge for renewal and a new constitution	A referendum grants the president greater powers over the judiciary and the media

Dealing with debt and foreign relations

The president, who trained as an economist in Belgium and the US, has not been afraid to throw his weight around. In December 2008, he claimed that foreign loans taken by previous regimes were "illegitimate" and defaulted on $3.2 billion in sovereign debt, but afterwards embarked on an aggressive borrowing programme, much like the 1970s military ruler. He renegotiated Ecuador's contracts with oil multinationals, and expropriated numerous companies including two television channels from a group that also owned Filanbanco, one of the collapsed banks from the Mahuad era, but failed to privatize them to compensate those who lost their savings.

Thanks to the unprecedented price of oil plus his borrowing, he embarked on a massive plan to pave and widen roads, build hydroelectric plants and new schools and universities. He has increased social spending, not least for the indigenous poor; having spent a year at a Salesian mission in Cotopaxi, he is a rarity as a Kichwa-speaking president. If relations with the **US** have been predictably strained, they could hardly be worse than those with **Colombia**. Correa cut diplomatic relations with Colombia after the Colombian military bombed a FARC base over the Ecuadorian border, unheard of even during wars with Peru (these have been since restored).

A second and third term

Correa's populist, no-compromise stance and freewheeling spending pressed the right buttons at home. He was **re-elected** early in April 2009 with a majority vote, something that hadn't happened in a first round for thirty years. It has not been plain sailing however. In September 2010, he dared protesting police to kill him, only to flee to a nearby hospital, from where he was extracted by the army. He insists in calling the event, which left several dead, a coup attempt, while coming up short on evidence.

In 2011, a narrowly won referendum gave the president greater powers over the judiciary and to regulate the media, and a proposed constitutional reform was drafted to allow him to stand for election again. After spending some $250 billion over ten years in office, with the price of oil plummeting and debt payments accumulating, Correa backpedalled on the reform in November 2015, raising questions over who might succeed him in the 2017 elections.

Since introducing the dollar, Ecuador has made important strides in reducing poverty and improving infrastructure. However, clouds over emerging market economies raise questions as to how sustainable progress will be.

The 2016 earthquake

In April 2016, a magnitude 7.8 earthquake struck Ecuador's northwest coast – the deadliest natural disaster to hit the country in decades. The area between Manta and Portoviejo in the south and Esmeraldas in the north was the hardest hit, but there was damage to buildings and a highway bridge as far south as Guayaquil. It is expected to take years to rebuild some of the worst-hit areas, so check ahead before travelling in the region.

2012	**2013**	**2015**
Ecuador grants asylum to WikiLeaks founder Julian Assange in its London embassy, leading to frosty diplomatic relations	Correa is re-elected president for a third term, continuing massive infrastructure spending	Amid a severe fall in the price of oil that weakens the economy, Correa announces that he won't stand for re-election in 2017

Art

In many ways, pre-Columbian art in Ecuador resembles modern artesanía, in its combination of function and aesthetic. What we understand as fine art didn't make an appearance until after the Spanish conquest, when it was employed in the process of converting the native population to Catholicism, being central both as a means of religious instruction and to provide icons for worship in place of indigenous pagan idols.

The Quito School

The engine of artistic production in the new colony was the **Quito School** (see box, p.66), founded by Franciscan friars in the 1530s, which taught indigenous people how to paint and carve in order to provide decoration for the new churches and monasteries. One of the key early exponents of painting was **Fray Pedro Bedón** (1556–1621), who had studied under the Italian Jesuit artist, Bernardo Bitti, himself the main source of the Renaissance and Mannerist styles of Spain, Flanders and Italy, Bedón taught local *indígenas* and mestizos to reproduce famous compositions from the Old World. The artworks were not mere copies, however, but imbued with a clearly discernible Andean flavour, reflecting the need to adapt images to local tastes.

The rise of secular painting

The last major Quito School artist, **Manuel Samaniego** (c.1767–1824), formed the bridge from religious to **secular** painting. He forsook the sombre, tenebrous tones of his predecessors, preferring a fresher, brighter and more colourful palette, and paid special attention to background landscapes. The career of his apprentice **Antonio Salas** (1795–1860) was bookended by religious commissions, but his most famous works define the early **Independence** period, being potent and striking portraits of the heroes and leaders of the age, including Simón Bolívar.

He was also the patriarch of a large and accomplished artistic family, including **Ramón Salas** (c.1815–80), an early proponent of **costumbrismo**, where the focus is on everyday life. Such studies were a part of a growing interest in Ecuador itself, and a burgeoning pride in its land and people, which was beginning to find expression in the paintings of nineteenth-century artists. Ramón's better-known half-brother, **Rafael Salas** (c.1824–1906), who was sent to be trained in Europe at an early age, was a leading figure in this direction, and among the country's first to make **landscape** a subject in its own right. His works were surpassed only by **Joaquín Pinto** (1842–1906), a prodigy with little formal training, whose unrivalled eye for the unusual and charming repeatedly triumphed in landscapes and *costumbrista* tableaux. Landscapes achieved new heights of technical finesse under the brush of **Rafael Troya** (1845–1920), who studied under visiting German artists and draughtsmen and owed much to the naturalistic traditions of that country in his broad and idyllic panoramas.

The indigenismo movement

In the early **twentieth century** the picturesque *costumbrismo* sketches of local people, particularly of *indígenas*, took on much stronger political and social overtones, developing into the **indigenismo** movement, which articulated native culture and imagery in terms of social protest. Its leaders were **Camilo Egas** (1899–1962), **Eduardo Kingman** (1913–98) and **Oswaldo Guayasamín** (1919–99). Of this trinity of modern Ecuadorian masters, Guayasamín, the son of an *indígena* and a *mestiza*, now figures as the nation's favourite and most famous artist, regarded as the true champion of the oppressed.

Avant-garde art and the Grupo VAN

Guayasamín's domination of the art scene over the last few decades belies the richness of modern art in Ecuador, which has had links to a plethora of artistic movements and currents of thought. **Manuel Rendón** (1894–1982) grew up and trained in Paris and was exposed to new ideas, the avant-garde and non-figurative art from an early age. He won praise from artists as eminent as Matisse, Braque and Modigliani, and his exhibitions in Quito and Guayaquil in the late 1930s had a huge influence on later generations, along with the work of **Araceli Gilbert** (1913–93), an early Ecuadorian proponent of abstract and geometric art, and one of the country's few female artists.

Following their line, **Enrique Tábara** (b.1930) became a leader of the avant-garde and non-figurative art in Ecuador, a man who rubbed shoulders in Barcelona with Dadaists and Surrealists, and back home founded the influential Grupo VAN with the likes of **Aníbal Villacís** (b.1927), **Estuardo Maldonado** (b.1930), **Hugo Cifuentes** (1923–2000) and **Luis Molinari** (b.1929–94) in opposition to the heavy political social realism of Guayasamín and others. Other important figures include **Juan Villafuerte** (1945–77), whose prolific but short career included the celebrated "Transmutation Series" of monstrous and deformed figures designed to unsettle; **Oswaldo Viteri** (b.1931), who uses a wide variety of materials to explore *mestizaje*, the cultural mix of Ecuador; and **Gonzalo Endara Crow** (1936–96), whose distinctive paintings blended myth, folklore and naturalism.

The contemporary scene

More recently, the **Artefactoría** collective was founded in 1982 by Xavier Patiño, Jorge Velarde and Marcos Restrepo, loosely inspired by Surrealism. While native culture has been very important to modern Ecuadorian art, it's notable that there have been relatively few well-known indigenous artists. One of them is **Ramón Piaguaje** (b.1962), a Secoya from the Cuyabeno area, who drew from childhood with his fingers in the sand and had no idea it was possible to create pictures in colour until an anthropologist supplied him with oils. He shot to fame after winning a major international prize with a beautiful depiction of his rainforest home.

The mainland: geography and wildlife

In terms of wildlife and geography Ecuador is one of the most diverse countries in the world. No larger than the US state of Nevada and around the same size as the UK, this diminutive country is home to more than 1600 species of birds, over 300 different mammals, 680 amphibians and reptiles, twenty thousand flowering plants and more than a million types of insect. The mainland comprises three geographical regions and an extraordinary variety of habitats and ecosystems. In the sierra, mountain páramos (high-altitude grasslands), volcanoes and the Andean mountains form the north–south spine of the country. To the east, the mountains slope down through primeval cloudforests into the tropical rainforests of the Amazon basin. On the west of the Andes, more cloudforests cloak the mountainsides down to the coast (*costa*, or *litoral*), which comprises agricultural lands, dry and tropical forests, lowland hills, beaches and mangrove swamps.

The sierra

Around 100 million years ago, the westward-moving South American tectonic plate collided with the eastward-moving Nazca plate, which holds the southern Pacific Ocean, and the **Andes** mountains rose along the edge of the South American landmass. In Ecuador, they consist of two parallel mountain chains, or cordilleras, separated by a broad central valley – which German explorer Alexander von Humboldt named the "Avenue of the Volcanoes" in 1802. This central valley is itself divided into a series of fertile basins, cut off from one another by "knots" of intermediate hills. The basins have been populated for hundreds of years – in several cases, thousands of years – and even today are home to almost half the country's population.

A relatively young mountain range, the sharp, jagged peaks of the Andes, reaching almost 7000m in places, are not yet rounded by erosion and are still growing as the two underground giants continue to rumble against each other, making Ecuador geologically unstable and volatile. **Earthquakes** and **tremors** are common, and Ecuador also has a number of active **volcanoes** – Cotopaxi, at 5897m, is one of the world's highest. Ten volcanoes exceed the snow line (4800m), and the summit of Chimborazo, at 6268m, actually surpasses Everest as the point furthest from the centre of the Earth by more than 2km, thanks to the planet's bulge around the equator. Eruptions of active volcanoes cause occasional disruption.

Páramo

Below the snow line of the highest Andean peaks is a slender margin of tundra-like *gelodifitia*, where little else than mosses and lichens can survive the freezing nights and frigid soils. From around 4700m down to 3100m, the climate of the **páramo** is less harsh, allowing for a wider range of life. The vegetation of the páramo, covering ten percent of Ecuador's total land area, is dominated by dense tussocks of *Festuca* or *Calamgrostis* grasses, along with terrestrial bromeliads and ferns. In the wetter páramo, pockets of *Polylepis* forest grow, one of the few trees that can survive at this altitude. Plants tend to have small thick leaves to resist the nightly frosts and waxy skins to reflect the intense ultraviolet radiation during cloudless spells. Páramo soil is sodden, and excess water collects in the hundreds of lakes that spangle the undulating scenery. The first signs of **wildlife** also emerge in the páramo with mammals such as the Andean spectacled bear and birds like the Andean condor.

Cloudforests

Lower than the páramo are the **cloudforests**, clothing the sierra in dense vegetation between 1800m and 3500m. Wet, green, vibrant and extraordinarily beautiful, cloudforests feel like the prehistoric habitat of dinosaurs. Streaked by silvery waterfalls, the forests are shrouded in heavy mists for at least part of each day. It's this dampness that creates such lush conditions, giving rise to an abundance of **epiphytes**, such as **lichens**, **mosses** and **ferns**, which drape over the trees. Many **orchids** are epiphytes, preferring moss-covered branches or exposed bark to normal soil. With more than 3500 species, Ecuador is thought to have more orchids than any other country in the world.

Cloudforests are also home to an incredible range of animals such as woolly tapirs, spectacled bears and pumas, and they have an exceptional level of bird endemism – species unique to a place and not found anywhere else. At higher altitudes, the cloudforest is called **elfin forest** because the trees are restricted in growth by the permanent mist that blocks out the sunlight. Elfin forests are an impenetrably dense tangle of short, twisted, gnarled trees barely two metres tall.

The Oriente

The **Oriente** represents Ecuador's own piece of the **Amazon rainforest**, the largest tropical rainforest habitat in the world, with the greatest diversity of plants and animals on the planet – its unidentified varieties of beetles and insects alone are thought to outnumber all of Earth's known animal species. One study has even found that a single hectare of Amazonian forest can contain up to 250 tree species, whereas in Europe and North America only ten different kinds of tree would occupy the same space. The rivers and their banks, too, are home to a fantastic array of animals, including nearly two thousand species of fish, plus freshwater dolphins, giant otters, anacondas, caymans and many unique birds. One reason for this extraordinary diversity is the Oriente's **climate** – it never suffers from a lack of heat or water, with high levels of precipitation all year round, particularly from April to July.

Rainforest types

The different types of soil, terrain and rivers of the Amazon basin have allowed various kinds of rainforest to evolve. In the Oriente – and the Amazon as a whole – the majority comprises **tierra firme rainforest**, with well-drained, nutrient-rich soils. Trees typically have huge, flaring buttress roots, tall slender trunks and branches radiating out at the top. Most grow to 25–30m, although some, such as the ceiba or kapok, exceed 50m, with the forest canopy creating a dark, permanently shaded and enclosed space underneath.

Because trees are often interconnected by vines, one falling tree can bring some of its neighbours down with it. Sunlight floods in, creating a different microclimate for the shadowy world under the canopy. Initially, fast-growing plants are favoured, and a dense tangle of competing shrubs, vines and spindly trees proliferates. Areas of disturbed forest, with an undeveloped canopy but dense ground cover and undergrowth, are known as **secondary forest**. Over time, it matures into fully developed **primary forest**, as the slower-growing trees out-compete and dwarf the pioneers and the canopy closes over, once again blocking sunlight from the forest floor, allowing only a sparse scattering of low-level plants.

The Oriente also holds large areas of flooded forest around different river systems, providing important alternative habitats for plants and animals. **Whitewater rivers** flow down from the Andes carrying great amounts of suspended sediment, enriching the soil during floods. Over time, accumulated sediment on the riverbanks forms ridges, or levees, which help prevent regular flooding, meaning the plants that thrive here have to withstand years without a flood. These areas of intermittently flooded forest are known as **várzea**, characterized by a dense understorey (a low layer of vegetation), a middle layer of *Cecropia* and a high layer of trees reaching over 35m.

Black-water rivers usually originate within the rainforest area itself, so contain very little suspended sediment, but do have a lot of decomposing organic matter. The result is an acidic, tannin-rich water that looks like strong black tea. The open floodplains around black-water rivers give rise to the haunting **igapó forests**. *Igapó* trees are relatively short and have adapted to floods, with roots that can survive underwater for long periods. Many trees here have developed a seed-dispersal strategy that relies on fish: their fruit falls into the water during floods, and their seeds germinate after having passed through the creature's digestive system.

The lush and palm-dominated **moretal** habitat occupies swampy and poorly drained areas near rivers and lakes, which often flood after localized rains. The most striking tree is a palm, *Mauritia flexuosa*, which grows to 30m, and the understorey is filled out with thick bursts of *Scheleea brachyclada* and *Croton tessmannii* among others.

Rainforest trees and plants

Rainforest trees usually have broad leaves that thin to a narrow point at the end to facilitate water run-off. **Palm trees**, a good example of this, are extremely common and are used by indigenous peoples to make thatch, ropes, weavings, hunting bows, fishing lines, hooks, utensils and musical instruments, as well as food and drink.

Many trees are cauliflorous, so their flowers and fruits grow from the trunk, rather than the canopy branches, enabling terrestrial animals to access their **fruits** containing large seeds, a source of energy for monkeys, tapirs, rodents and peccaries. Other food simply falls to earth. Many palms, such as the **coconut palm**, produce large, hard fruits encasing the seeds. Meanwhile, in the canopy, birds such as curassows, toucans and parrots eat smaller fruits and seeds.

Plants that don't rely on animals and birds for reproduction have developed **protective measures** to counter the attentions of hungry animals. Some plants produce drugs, or **defence compounds**, and many tropical leaves are generously dosed with poisons such as curare, caffeine and cyanide. The **monkey pot tree**, for example, deters foragers by producing rotund "cannonball" fruits, each containing up to 50 long, thin seeds laced with toxic selenium. Other plants grow spines on their trunks to impale voracious caterpillars, while, less vindictively, the sap of the **rubber tree** congeals on exposure to air, so any insects that have gone to the trouble of chewing through the bark are only rewarded with an inedible goo.

Epiphytes flourish on, around and over the vegetation, and sometimes the treetops are so laden with squatters seeking access to the sun that it's hard to define the host under all its house guests. In the competitive world of the cloudforest, even epiphytes can have their own epiphytes. Many bromeliads' leaves arrange themselves in overlapping rosettes, forming a bowl that catches and holds rainwater. Birds bathe in it, monkeys drink from it, and tree frogs, mosquitoes, flatworms, snails, salamanders and crabs can all complete their entire life cycle in these miniature aquatic habitats.

Lianas (a woody vine that roots in the ground) dangle downwards from trees, elaborately draping and entwining around their trunks. **Trunk-climbing vines** start at the bottom of tree trunks and grow upwards, while **strangler vines** start at the top and grow down, encircling the tree and squeezing it tightly enough to choke it: the tree inside dies and decomposes, and the vine claims its place on the forest floor.

The coast

The western slopes of the Andes fall away to the **coastal region**, beginning with a large, fertile lowland river plain that extends for 150km to a range of hills, which rise up to 900m and form a ridge about 20km inland from the sea. The region has a very warm **climate**, with temperatures fluctuating between 25°C and 31°C (77–88°F) throughout the year.

The northern coastal region

The northern coastal region was once thickly forested and included within it the **Chocó bioregion**, an area of extraordinary biodiversity extending into Colombia. When the Andes were formed, the Chocó region in the west was cut off from the Amazon rainforests to the east. Since then, these highly humid western forests survived the Ice Age and followed an evolutionary path that diverged from that of their eastern counterparts, and it is thought that anywhere between one-fifth to a half of the nine thousand estimated plant and animal species here are endemic, such as the glorious scarlet-and-white tanager.

Unfortunately, less than five percent of Ecuador's Chocó forests have survived the twentieth century. Since the 1950s the destruction started apace with new roads leading to unplanned **colonization** and rapid **deforestation**. The region's fertility has given it the dubious honour of being Ecuador's most intensively farmed area, with banana, rice, cacao, coffee and sugar-cane plantations. The latest threat to the Chocó comes from **oil-palm plantations**, which have felled about 1000 square kilometres of native forest. Numerous animal species are in danger of extinction in the Chocó. Limited areas are protected, with the western part of the Ilinizas and Cotacachi-Cayapas the largest among them.

The southern coastal region

The southern coastal area forms part of the **Tumbesian bioregion**, which continues down into Peru. Originally, much of this distinctive landscape comprised **dry tropical forests** suited to the arid southern climate, but almost all of this habitat has now been cleared for agriculture, save a few pockets such as at the Parque Nacional Machalilla and the Bosque Protector Cerro Blanco. Trees and spiny shrubs grow in abundance, as do some otherwise disappearing native trees, such as balsam and *tillo colorado*, long coveted for their fine wood. Plants in the region have adapted to the desert-like environment, and many trees lose their leaves when water is scarce during the height of the dry season (July–Oct). Fewer birds live here than in the wet forests, but there are a significant number of range-restricted, endangered species endemic to this area, such as the grey-backed hawk and the ochre-bellied dove. Mammals include mantled howler monkeys, capuchins, ocelots and pumas.

Long, empty beaches fringe about one-third of Ecuador's 2000km of **coastline**, the rest comprising mangrove swamps, marshes, sandy cliffs, river deltas and estuaries. **Mangrove trees**, growing in shallow salt or brackish waters, are found especially along quiet shorelines and in estuaries. The mangroves build up rich organic soil in the knotted network of their roots and branches, supporting many other plants and wildlife. Frigatebirds, boobies and brown pelicans nest among the tangled branches and many types of fish, molluscs and crustaceans make homes in the protective shelter of the roots.

Mangroves play an essential role in the ecology of coastal areas, but most of Ecuador's mangrove treasury has been squandered, cut down to make way for the construction of profitable **shrimp farms**; only a few patches have been conserved. Around San Lorenzo near the Colombian border, the **Reserva Ecológica Cayapas-Mataje** harbours the tallest mangrove forest in the world as well as lovely coconut forests, teeming bird colonies and rare mammals such as the miniature tree sloth, while **Manglares Churute**, south of Guayaquil, is home to flamingos, pelicans and occasionally bottlenosed dolphins. Other nationally protected mangrove forests are at the estuary of the Río Muisne and Salado.

Wildlife

Few countries in the world come close to Ecuador for **wildlife**. Blessed with many thousands of colourful **birds** and **animals** crammed into a small area, Ecuador is a naturalist's dream – birdwatchers alone can rack up a list of several hundred after only a few days in the forests. To top it all off, a good number of species are found nowhere else – making Ecuador one of the most biologically important countries on Earth.

Birds

Ecuador is home to just over 1600 different **bird** species, a sixth of the planet's total. Because of its small size, the country also has the world's highest **diversity** of birds – even though Brazil is thirty times larger, the two countries are home to about the same number of bird species.

Cotingas

The most famous **cotinga** is the fabulous **Andean cock-of-the-rock**, which inhabits lower to mid-montane cloudforest, where several dozen birds gather in **leks** (courtship display areas) to reproduce. The chunky males, with spectacular scarlet-orange plumage outlined by black wings and tail and a showy crescent of feathers running over their heads, preen and pose for the females. Relationships are brief, lasting for only one or two couplings, after which the male continues to strut his stuff in the search for more mates. The **screaming piha** is another cotinga that lives in the rainforest, but its mating appeals are auditory – its piercing call is one of the forest's most distinctive sounds.

Eagles

The **harpy eagle** is one of the world's largest, at over 1m in height, with sturdy, powerful legs as thick as human wrists and claws the size of human hands. Their wings and back are black and their faces and bellies are grey. Remarkably agile despite their size, harpy eagles twist and turn through the canopy, making swift strikes at monkeys and sloths, plucking them off trees with their legs. They tend not to soar, but **crested eagles** and three species of **hawk-eagle** are easier to see circling high over the rainforest canopy.

Hummingbirds

Hummingbirds' names accurately reflect their beauty: **garnet-throated**, **sparkling-tailed** and **velvet-breasted**, to name but a few. Highly active, hummingbirds' wings can buzz at eighty beats per second as they dart backwards, forwards and hover on the spot to sip nectar with their bills. They're quite feisty and compete aggressively for flowers. Females flirt with dominant males and will mate with them even during the non-breeding season to gain access to the flowers in their territory. Hummingbird habitats range from the jungle to the páramo, with some species such as the sword-billed and the booted racquet-tail found in the cloudforests. Cloudforest lodges with hummingbird feeders are the best places to see them up close.

Oropendolas

Trees favoured by the crow-sized **oropendolas** can be spotted at a distance because they tend to be out in the open and have pendulous, basket-like nests. The birds pick isolated trees to avoid egg-stealing monkeys, which don't like to traverse open ground. These birds come in two colour types – one displaying greenish hues, the other mostly black and russet, with yellow on the bill and tail. They are great singers, producing a wide range of sounds and songs.

Owls and potoos

The **spectacled owl**, one of Ecuador's largest, is dark brown with a brown-yellow lower breast and belly and bright yellow eyes ringed by white. The **black-and-white owl** has a horizontally black-and-white striped breast and feeds almost exclusively on bats.

The **common potoo**, another large nocturnal bird, is a visual challenge to detect in the daytime – it sits completely still in trees and, with its colouring and artful physical pose, looks exactly like the end of a branch.

Parrots and macaws

Most **parrots** are well camouflaged in the rainforest, but their banshee-like screeching makes them easy to locate. They usually mate for life, and it's possible to pick out the pairs by watching a flock. They crack tough nuts and seeds using strong jaws, while the upper jaw also functions as an extra limb for climbing and manoeuvring.

Macaws are the most spectacular members of the parrot family and their rainbow plumage, ranging from the magnificent **scarlet macaw** to the brilliant **blue-and-yellow macaw**, is easily seen even in the densest forest. About 30 percent of the South American parrots are at risk of extinction because of habitat loss and the highly profitable trade in exotic pets.

Tanagers

These small, gloriously colourful birds feed on fruit, nectar and insects and live in a variety of habitats, from lowland jungle to highland cloudforest. Montane species include the **golden tanager**, **beryl-spangled tanager** and **blue-winged mountain-tanager**. In the Amazon you can't miss the flocks of exotic **paradise tanagers** with their neon-lime heads, purple throats, crimson lower backs, black upper backs and turquoise rumps.

Toucans

With their flamboyant oversized bills and colour-splashed bodies, **toucans** are easy to spot. The largest is the **white-throated toucan**, which has a black bill with a yellow stripe running down the middle, and baby-blue framed eyes. This species lives in the jungle along with **araçaris**, smaller, more colourful toucans. The highlands are where to find the wonderful **mountain toucans**.

Vultures and condors

Vultures thrive everywhere that other animals die, as they eat only carrion. **Black vultures** are common around urban rubbish dumps, while the **greater yellow-headed vulture** dominates the rainforest niche.

The **Andean condor**, Ecuador's national bird, is the world's heaviest bird of prey, with a wingspan of 3m. Adults are black with a ruff-like white collar and bald pinkish head. Hunting has reduced their population to a maximum of around a hundred individuals. They live near and above the tree line, with the largest number soaring over the páramo around Volcán Antisana in the northeast.

Mammals

Ecuador is home to 317 species of **mammals**, about eight percent of the world's total. Many live in the forests and are shy of human presence, making them difficult to spot, though most jungle trips are rewarded with sightings of monkeys skipping through the canopy. The holy grail of the mountain forests is the Andean spectacled bear, but few visitors are lucky enough to see one.

In 2013 the olinguito, a fluffy coati-like creature, was 'discovered' in the Tandayapa Valley – the first new carnivorous mammal to be identified in South America for 35 years.

Anteaters

Giant anteaters can weigh up to 40kg and amble along the rainforest floor looking for ant nests; when they find one, they poke their long tongues inside and trap the ants with gluey saliva. The other three species, including the tiny **pygmy anteater**, live in trees, where they live on ants, bees and termites.

Bats

Tent-building bats live in the rainforest and create homes by selecting a large leaf and nibbling a line down each side so that the leaf flaps droop downwards. Small groups can be seen huddling together in a close-knit scrum underneath their protective tent.

The **common vampire bat** lives in the rainforest and subtropical forests of the Andean slopes up to 1500m, feeding entirely on the blood of mammals. They bite with sharp incisors, rarely waking their victims, and lick up the drops of blood dripping from the wound – vampire-bat saliva contains special anticoagulants so that the blood flows freely. There are very few cases of bats feeding on humans.

Wild cats

Felines aren't easy to find, but they do scratch logs to proclaim their presence, so look for telltale marks, as well as paw prints and faeces.

Ocelots are mid-sized cats, with tawny fur and black spots, stripes and rosettes, and live in a range of habitats with good cover, from rainforest to desert scrub, sometimes raiding chicken coops in villages. Pale-grey or yellow **pumas** also live in dry areas, while those in the rainforest are yellow-brown to dark red-brown. **Jaguars** are tawny yellow with black spots. They've adapted to a range of habitats, hunting at any time of day for capybaras, deer, turtles, caymans, birds or fish.

Wildcat attacks on humans are very rare. If you meet a jaguar or a puma, don't run: stay facing it, make a lot of noise and wave your arms about.

Dolphins and manatees

Pink river dolphins, or *botos*, hunt for fish, turtles and crabs. Although nearly blind, they navigate and locate prey using a sonar system housed in a large bulge on their foreheads. Curious and intelligent, they'll approach swimmers but won't attack.

Amazonian manatees are highly endangered due to hunting. These large, hairless, cigar-shaped herbivores are docile, browsing on aquatic plants and living under the water, only breaking the surface with their nostrils to breathe.

Monkeys

Ecuadorian **monkeys** live in trees and only hit the ground running to cross open space. **Marmosets** and **tamarins** are the smallest of them and sport flamboyant facial hair, ear tufts, tassels, ruffs, manes and moustaches. They communicate with chirps and bird-like whistles, and can be seen in villages and towns.

Howler monkeys are more often heard than seen. At dawn and dusk they band together for deafening howling sessions which carry across the canopy for kilometres. A male usually starts off with an escalating grunting session, which segues into long, deep roars. Females join in with their higher-pitched voices. **Red howlers** favour tall riverbank trees, so they're most easily spotted from a boat.

Otters

There are two **otters** in Ecuador, the **neotropical river otter** and the **giant otter**, which can grow up to 1.5m in length, not counting its metre-long tail. They have sleek reddish-brown coats, huge, fully webbed feet and intelligent, canine-type faces (their local name is *lobo del río*, or river wolf).

Rodents

Rats and **mice** thrive in urban environments, **squirrels** leap acrobatically through the trees and **porcupines** root around on the rainforest floor. The **capybara** is the world's largest rodent, weighing some 55kg, and has a stocky body and thin hind legs – they often sit on their haunches like dogs. Small herds live along Amazonian lakes, rivers and swamps, feeding on water lilies, water hyacinth, leaves and sedges.

Sloths

Sloths live in the rainforest and feed on canopy leaves, digesting them in a multi-chambered stomach. Algae flourishes in tiny grooves on their body hair, turning them an alien green and camouflaging them in the trees. They're hard to see from the ground, but eagles are masters at swooping in to pick them off the branches. Once a month, sloths climb down from their trees and dig a hole in the ground in which to defecate.

Spectacled bears

Ecuador's only **bear** lives in forested mountain habitats from 1000m to 4000m. They're mostly black or brown, mottled white or cream with distinctive "spectacles" encircling part of each eye. By bear standards they're small – the males weigh about 80kg and the females 60kg. Each paw is equipped with powerful claws for climbing or tearing apart trees. Up in the trees they build platforms of branches, on which they rest or feed on fruits and honey.

Tapirs

Tapirs, the region's largest terrestrial mammals, have stocky bodies, muscular necks, elongated, overhanging upper lips and short tails, and spend about ninety percent of the day eating a calorie-poor leaf diet. Their droopy upper lips are used to reach out and sweep food into their mouths.

The **Brazilian tapir**, the size of a Shetland pony, varies in colour from black to red to tan. They hang out in swamps in the rainforest and in grassy habitats up to 2000m, and if afraid leap into the nearest water and swim away – though if you can imitate their loud whistle, they will answer you. The extremely rare brown, shaggy **mountain tapir** lives in the montane forests and páramo.

Reptiles and amphibians

There are about eight hundred **reptile** and **amphibian** species living in Ecuador. They thrive in the Amazon and also in the Andean foothills, where many are endemic.

Caymans

Crocodilian **caymans** lie motionless along riverbanks waiting for fish and other water-dwelling animals, such as capybaras, snakes and birds, to come within striking distance of their powerful jaws. The best way to see them is from a boat at night. Hold a torch at eye level and scan the riverbank; the caymans are easy to find because their eyes shine red in the beam.

Frogs

Frogs thrive in the Amazon where the hot, damp conditions keep them warm and hydrated. Over 75 percent are nocturnal and a deafening chorus wafts each night from ponds, lakes, riverbanks and the depths of flooded forests, as the males compete to attract females with their throaty tones.

The **leaf dweller**, which looks just like a dead leaf, is fairly common but only visible when on the move. Fast-flowing streams are where to look for **glass frogs**, which are completely transparent, revealing their tiny beating hearts and other organs under the skin. The **poison-dart frog** is small, brightly coloured and only active in the day.

Lizards and geckos

Many **lizards** and **geckos** live in the Amazon, such as the common **iguana**, which, with its heavily scaled head and spiny back, looks like a miniature dinosaur. The **basilisk**, or

Jesus lizard, can be seen scurrying across still rivers, but it isn't really walking on water – the hind feet are just under the water's surface and are sprung upwards and onwards by an air bubble trapped beneath its webbed feet.

Snakes

Plenty of **snakes**, both harmless and poisonous, slither through Ecuador's forests, but they are encountered only rarely. **Pit vipers** locate prey with heat receptors between their eyes and nostrils that can register changes in temperature of only 0.003°C. The teeth usually lie back horizontally but are erected to strike, bite and inject venom. Tan-coloured with dark diamond patterning, the two-metre-long, highly venomous **fer-de-lance** is the most notorious viper, an aggressive snake with a very painful bite that can kill. The **bushmaster** is the world's largest viper at up to 3m in length.

The **boa constrictor**, which can reach 4m in length, is found in a variety of habitats from wet lowland forest to arid grassland. Another constrictor, the **anaconda**, is the largest snake in the world, occasionally growing to over 8m and weighing in at more than 200kg. Highly intelligent, it lies in wait by rivers for unsuspecting capybaras, tapirs, large birds and peccaries, watching their drinking habits for weeks at a time before striking.

Turtles

Aquatic side-necked turtles are frequently seen in the rainforest, sunning themselves on branches sticking out of the water. When defending themselves, they tuck their heads sideways into their shells. Turtles build nests of rotting debris, which incubate their eggs at a constant temperature.

Insects

In Ecuador there are at least a million different types of **insect**, and the rainforest is the best place to find them. At nightfall, they produce the unmistakeable rainforest soundscape – a cacophony of cheeps, clicks, trills, screeches and wheezes.

Ants

Many rainforest **ants** make their homes on plants, which provide shelter, protection and food via nectar. **Acacia ants**, for example, pay for their board on the acacia tree by defending it from unwelcome visitors and will attack beetles, caterpillars and other ants that try to land or climb on it. They also prune back other plants that grow too close or shadow their tree from the sunlight.

Army ant colony members can number over a million. Squadrons run eight to ten abreast along forest trails and cooperate to overpower other invertebrate creatures far larger than themselves. **Leaf-cutter ants** are highly visible as they move in lengthy columns bearing relatively huge leaf clippings. The leaves are transported back to their vast underground nests, but instead of consuming them the ants chew them into a soft pulp to make compost on which to grow a special fungus – their favourite food.

Avoid the **conga** or **giant hunting ant**, a large, aggressive-looking black creature whose sharp sting can cause pain and fever, lasting from a few hours to a few days.

Beetles

One of the most common beetles is the **giant ceiba borer**, its outer skeleton gleaming like iridescent metal. **Hercules**, **rhinoceros** and **elephant beetles** are hard to miss, as they're the little giants their names suggest. The **headlight beetle** of the bioluminescent **pyrophorus** genus is also easily spotted: two round, light-producing organs behind its head give it the appearance of a toy car. The beautiful **tortoise beetle** looks as though it's been dipped in liquid gold.

Butterflies

Ecuador is home to around 4500 species of **butterfly**. The most striking are the **morphos**, huge tropical visions in electric blue. Their brilliant colour derives from the way light is reflected and refracted by their complex wing scales. **Owl butterflies** have owl-like eyespots on their wings to direct hungry birds away from crucial body parts. **Clearwings** look like tiny fairies; with transparent wings, they're hard to see when motionless. **White-and-sulphur butterflies** are highly visible from rainforest rivers. Droves gather on riverbanks to lick nutrients from the ground.

Fish

Ecuador has more than eight hundred species of **freshwater fish**, with an incredible diversity in rainforest rivers. The **pirarucu**, one of the world's largest freshwater fish, lives here – the real giants have all been fished out, but specimens of up to 2m are still caught. Watch for **leaf fishes** which are hard to discern from dead leaves on account of their crumpled, blotchy appearance and lower jaw, which mimics a stem.

Forty percent of the fish are either **catfish** or **characins**. Many characins are fruit-eaters and wait for fruit to fall from trees in the flooded forests. The notorious **red piranha** is also a characin. Small but ferocious, they are only a danger to human swimmers in large groups when water levels are low and food supplies poor. Far more dangerous is the **electric eel**, which grows up to 1.8m and can produce a jolt of 650 volts.

The catfish to watch out for is the tiny **candiru**, which usually parasitizes other fish, but is also thought to follow urine currents of human swimmers, entering the urethra on occasion. Once inside, it lodges itself securely with an array of sharp spines and causes unmentionable discomfort. The offending fish is so firmly wedged it has to be surgically removed.

The Galápagos: geography and wildlife

The thirteen large islands and over forty small islands, islets and rocks making up the Galápagos Archipelago cluster around the equator 960km west of mainland Ecuador. The total land area of the archipelago is 7882 square kilometres; Isabela, the largest island, takes up well over half of this.

The origins of the archipelago

The archipelago is **volcanic** in origin, and remains one of the most volatile such regions on the planet; the most recent eruption was on Fernandina in 2009. Unlike most of the world's volcanic areas, the islands don't lie on the borders of two tectonic plates, a fact that has puzzled scientists. The **hot spot theory**, in which a fixed area of extraordinary heat in the magma occasionally bubbles up to form a volcano, offers the most plausible explanation. The archipelago sits on the **Nazca plate**, which is moving eastwards and downwards to South America at a rate of 3.4cm a year: as the plate shifts, the volcano comes off the hot spot, becomes extinct and is eventually eroded by the elements and submerged beneath the sea. Meanwhile, new volcanoes appear over the hot spot. This would explain why the most easterly islands are the oldest and most weathered; San Cristóbal is thought to be between 2.3 and 6.3 million years old. In the west, Isabela and Fernandina are thought to have been created less than 700,000 years ago and are the most volcanically active. Two chains of extinct and eroded underwater mountains and volcanoes – the Cocos and Carnegie ridges – are evidence the hot spot has been working for millions of years.

VOLCANIC FORMATIONS

The beautiful **volcanic formations** on the Galápagos Islands are often quite different from those found on the mainland. This is due to **basaltic lava** which, rather than producing high cones such as Cotopaxi, makes **shield-shaped volcanoes**. The broad tops of these can collapse into empty magma chambers below, leaving enormous **calderas**, huge depressions many times the size of the original vents, or **craters**, circular basins rimmed by lava walls at the volcano's summit; Volcán Sierra Negra on Isabela has a crater 10km across, one of the world's largest. Like steam vents on the volcanoes, sulphur-encrusted **fumaroles** send puffs of gas into the air.

Much of the Galápagos landmass consists of **lava flows**, and you'll find two particularly interesting types on several islands. **Pahoehoe lava**, from the Hawaiian word meaning "ropey", describes the rippled effect caused when molten lava in contact with the air begins to solidify, but is then ruffled up by molten lava passing beneath it into tongue or rope-like shapes. **Aa lava**, named after the Hawaiian for "hurt", occurs when the surface of the lava flow buckles, breaks and then gets bulldozed by the continuing movement of the flow, resulting in layers of small, sharp rocks. If a lava flow hardens on the outside, and then the strength of the flow decreases, **lava tubes** are sometimes formed; there are several large enough to walk down on Santa Cruz.

Cones of various sizes and types frequently appear on the islands: **hornitos** (less than 1m high), resemble burst pimples solidified on a lava bed; the larger **spatter cones** give Bartolomé its spectacular lunar landscape; and the impressive **tuff cones** are often made up of stripy layers of rock-hard compacted ash. The **uplift** at Urbina Bay, on Isabela, is one of the more startling products of volcanic activity. In 1954, a 5km stretch of reef was shunted 4m into the air by movements of magma beneath the crust, leaving its marine inhabitants drying in the sun. Islands including Plazas, Baltra and Seymour Norte are entirely the result of uplifts.

Wildlife

In contrast to the diversity of life found on the mainland, few species have managed to make the 960km journey to the Galápagos. But it's the islands' small number of species in isolation that has fascinated generations of scientists. Like a self-contained puzzle, life on the Galápagos can be unravelled in a way impossible for the tangled mass of mainland biological relationships. Our Galapagos wildlife field guide (see pp.370–379) has further detailed information on the animals, birds and reptiles that you are likely to see on the archipelago.

The origins of Galápagos life

The Galápagos Islands came into being as barren, lifeless heaps of lava cut off from the rest of the world by vast expanses of ocean. It's thought that the first life to make the crossing were seeds and spores of mosses, lichens and ferns, blown from the continent on the prevailing **winds** and deposited on the islands through rainfall. Insects, snails and spiders could also have been carried thousands of kilometres in the air, and when the winds were fierce enough they may also have blown land birds, as well as bats to the archipelago. Many of the sea birds routinely fly long distances and need no vegetation for nests, making them likely candidates for early pioneers. As the unforgiving lava broke down into soil patches, a larger number of plants would have been able to colonize the island, in turn supporting more animals. It's thought that up to sixty percent of plant species were brought to the islands by **birds**, either as undigested seeds in guano, or regurgitated, or attached to their feet and feathers.

The last route was **by the sea** – several currents converge on the islands, and may have brought species from the Pacific, Central and South American coasts. Swept up in the flow, marine turtles, penguins, seals and sea lions could all have swum to the islands, while giant tortoises – not natural swimmers – are buoyant and can survive for long periods without food or water. The only satisfactory explanation for the arrival of other reptiles and rice rats (the only native land mammal) is on tree trunks and logs, or on floating rafts made of matted vegetation set adrift after storms. Such a journey would have taken a couple of weeks, too long for most mammals and amphibians to survive without fresh water, but well within the capabilities of reptiles such as iguanas.

The arrival of **humans** in the Galápagos provided a new means for foreign species to colonize the islands, and those, such as dogs, rats, ants and goats, as well as plants like blackberry, red quinine and elephant grass, now pose one of the greatest threats to the delicate ecology of the islands (see box, p.340).

Separated from the rest of their kind, the marooned denizens of the Galápagos **evolved** as they adapted to their new environment, often ending up as quite different species from their mainland counterparts. These new plants and animals, found nowhere else in the world, are termed **endemic** species. Sometimes a single common ancestor has brought about a number of new species – as with Darwin's finches, a process known as **speciation**. In the Galápagos, though, the story doesn't end there: not only is the archipelago far from the continent, but the islands and islets comprising it are distant enough from each other to bring about their own endemic species. In a few instances, even the isolated habitats *within* an island can provoke speciation: for example, the five main volcanoes of Isabela are each populated by their own subspecies of giant tortoise.

Many Galápagos animals have evolved without the threat of **predators**, which accounts for their unusual fearlessness.

Birds

The Galápagos Islands are an incomparable treat for birdwatchers. Despite a relatively small number of **bird species** for the tropics (there are sixty types of resident birds, and another 81 migratory species visit the islands), about half of the residents are endemic, and visitors are often able to get within a metre of many of them. The naturalist William Beebe, who made two expeditions to the islands in the 1920s, tells of frantically searching for a flycatcher with his camera, only to find it perched on the lens "pecking at the brass fittings".

Sea birds make the most of good fish stocks in the cool-dry season, and migrants are in evidence from around October to February. Most **land birds** breed in the rainy season, when food is more abundant.

Sea birds

Since most **sea birds** are naturally strong long-distance fliers that thrive in island environments, only six out of the 19 resident species are endemic. Sea birds are also among the most prevalent of Galápagos fauna, numbering almost a million. Some of the best-known species are **boobies, flightless cormorants, frigatebirds, Galápagos penguins, gulls** and **waved albatrosses** (see pp.370–373). Other residents of the archipelago include the graceful **red-billed tropicbird**, the widespread **brown pelican**, the **brown noddy** and **sooty tern**, the **Galápagos petrel, Audubon's shearwater** and three species of **storm petrel**.

Shore and wetland birds

Rock pools, mangroves, beaches and shallow salty lagoons are common features of the Galápagos coast, providing habitats for as many as fifty bird species, many of them migrants such as the **wandering tattler**, which commutes from the Arctic. Only one shore bird is endemic, the **lava heron** (see p.372), though several residents have shown enough of the slow signs of evolution to have earned endemic subspecies status, such as the **yellow-crowned night heron**. **Striated herons** (see p.372) and **great blue herons** are the other resident heron species frequently seen around the coastal waters, gazing into pools with beady eyes. **American flamingos** tiptoe about the saltwater lagoons, sifting the silt and surface for water boatmen and shrimp. During the breeding season, care must be taken not to disturb these elegant birds, as they may abandon nests if startled. There are fewer than 250 pairs in the Galápagos.

As well as resident waders such as the **American oystercatcher** and **black-necked stilt**, a number of familiar migrants are in evidence, including **turnstones, sandpipers, yellowlegs, sanderlings, whimbrels, phalaropes** and **plovers**. The **white-cheeked pintail duck** is equally at home by the coast or at the freshwater lagoons in the highlands, where the **purple** or **common gallinule** (moorhen) make their home. **Cattle egrets**, nesting in the mangroves, are more usually seen in the highlands in large flocks near livestock. This striking white bird has now managed to colonize much of the world, though it was found only in West Africa till the late nineteenth century.

Land birds

The **land birds** of the Galápagos have been of enormous interest to scientists ever since Darwin's discoveries. Unlike most strong-winged sea birds, which are accustomed to making long journeys, the land birds can only have been brought to the archipelago blown on the winds of freak storms. And yet, of the 29 resident species, a phenomenal 22 are endemic, so such abnormal bird-carrying gales must have occurred no less than fourteen times – quite a feat considering that none strong enough to achieve this has yet been recorded.

Most famous of the Galápagos birds are **Darwin's finches**, the fifteen endemic and subtly different finches that proved to be of enormous importance to their namesake. These dowdy, sparrow-sized birds can be difficult to tell apart, despite the all-important differences in beak size and feeding habits. Since the finches are so similar, more like each other than any other kind of finch, Darwin suspected that they were all descendants of a common ancestor. No doubt the archipelago's grouping of isolated islands allowed for this remarkable speciation, even though many of them now inhabit the same islands.

The **large ground finch** has the biggest beak and is able to crack open large, hard seeds, while the **warbler finch** probes plants and flowers with its sharp and slender bill and has been called "more warbler than finch". The **woodpecker finch** (see p.374) and critically endangered **mangrove finch** are celebrated for their ability to use tools, often fashioning a twig or a cactus spine to wheedle larvae and grubs from tight spots. On remote Wolf and Darwin islands, the **vampire finch** is named for its pecking at the backs of Nazca boobies and feeding off their blood. The **small ground finch** has better interspecies relations, preening tortoises and iguanas for parasites.

The archipelago has four endemic **mockingbirds**: the **Galápagos mockingbird** (see p.374) is fairly widespread, while the **Chatham mockingbird** only inhabits San Cristóbal, the **Hood mockingbird** Española, and the rare **Charles mockingbird** a couple of islets around Floreana. They are confident and inquisitive birds, with no qualms about hopping around the feet of large groups of tourists.

Galápagos hawks (see p.374) are almost as fearless, having no natural enemies, and are content to let humans get to within a few metres of them. The Galápagos hawk practises a breeding system whereby the female has as many as four mates, who help her incubate the eggs and tend to the young. With the hawk, the **Galápagos barn owl** and the **short-eared owl** (see p.374) make up the archipelago's birds of prey. The last is the more commonly seen, particularly on Genovesa, where it swoops on the young of the large sea-bird colonies. Other endemics include the elegant **Galápagos dove** (see p.374), the secretive and miniature **Galápagos rail**, the **Galápagos flycatcher** (see p.374) and the **Galápagos martin**, the archipelago's only non-migratory member of the swallow family.

For all their intrinsic interest, the endemics can be a drab bunch, and indeed, the archipelago's two most colourful birds are residents. The **yellow warbler** and the dazzling male **vermilion flycatcher**, boasting a smart red-and-black plumage, are common favourites brightening up the dour scenery.

Reptiles

Above all fauna on the Galápagos, it's the **reptiles** that give the islands their prehistoric flavour. Although their appearance is antediluvian, the Galápagos reptiles have undergone the same evolutionary processes as the islands' other creatures, resulting in a high level of endemism. Of the 23 reptile species, 21 are unique to the Galápagos and several of these are specific to particular islands. Five reptile families are represented on the archipelago: **tortoises**, **marine turtles**, **iguanas** (including lizards, see pp.376–378), **geckos** and **snakes**.

Being **ectothermic** animals, reptiles cannot regulate their body temperature through physiology, such as sweating or dilating and constricting blood vessels as humans do. They need to heat their blood up to a certain level before they can become properly active – which is why you'll commonly see iguanas splayed on rocks absorbing the sun's rays for many hours, only moving into the shade if they get too hot. This system also allows them to survive on less food and water than other animals.

Mammals

The travails of making the crossing from the continent have proved too much for most **mammals**, and there is a noticeable absence of them on the islands. Just six native species inhabit the Galápagos, and of them only the **rice rats** made the gruelling sea journey on a vegetation raft (like many of the reptiles, which are far better suited to this kind of transport). Four of the seven rice-rat species are now extinct, wiped out by the introduced black rat, which out-competes them. The remaining three species are found on Santa Fé and Fernandina islands, islands that have so far been spared invasion by the black rat.

The **bats** took the air route: the ancestors of the endemic *Lasiurus brachyotis* were most likely blown over from the mainland like land birds, while the other native species, the **hoary bat**, is a known migrant and widespread throughout North America. There's nothing to stop mammal populations flourishing once they get to the Galápagos, as has been demonstrated by a number of **introduced species**, such as feral goats, cats, dogs and rats, which have been doing terrible damage to native wildlife, all brought to the islands by another late and supremely harmful mammalian arrival, *Homo sapiens*.

Fish and marine invertebrates

Bathed in cold upwelling currents and warm tropical waters, the Galápagos harbours 306 fish species, with 51 endemics. Plenty of interesting fish can be spotted with a snorkel and mask, but the most thrilling to swim with are the **sharks**. Regularly seen species include **white-tip reef sharks**, **hammerheads** and **black-tip sharks**, none of which is usually dangerous to humans. You'll generally need to scuba dive to see the **Galápagos shark**, which prefers deeper waters. There have been very few reports of shark attacks in the Galápagos, certainly none fatal, but follow the advice of your guide all the same. The colossal 18m **whale shark** is the world's largest fish and feeds on plankton.

The **rays** include the **stingray**, the **golden ray**, the beautiful **spotted eagle ray** and the **manta ray** (which can grow up to 6m across). The larger rays are frequently seen flipping out of the water before landing in clouds of spray. Among the more commonly seen bony fishes are the **blue-eyed damselfish**, the stripy **sergeant major**, the **Moorish idol**, the **hieroglyphic hawkfish** and the **white-banded angelfish**, as well as several **blennies**, **wrasses** and **parrotfish**. The **four-eyed blenny** is so called because each eye has two facets, allowing it to see both in and out of the water. It can spend two hours flapping about the rocks as it hunts for insects and small crabs.

Octopuses lurk in rock pools, but can be difficult to see because of their ability to change colour. Among the most visible intertidal animals are the more than one hundred **crab** species. The brightest is the **Sally Lightfoot crab** (see p.378), whose red casing gleams against the black lava. Its name comes either from a Jamaican dancer or its ability to zip over a tide pool. Young Sally Lightfoots are dark in order to blend in with the background. **Ghost crabs** live in holes dug in sandy beaches, while the soft-bodied **hermit crab** occupies abandoned shells, moving as it grows. **Fiddler crabs** are easy to identify by their outsized claw. **Sea urchins**, **sea cucumbers**, **starfish**, **anemones**, **molluscs** and **sponges** can also be found.

Land invertebrates

There are more than two thousand species of **land invertebrates** – animals without a backbone, such as insects and spiders – in the Galápagos, over half of them endemic. It sounds a huge number, but compared with more than a million species found in mainland Ecuador, it's clear that land invertebrates found the archipelago difficult to colonize.

The arid climate has meant that many **insects** are nocturnal, escaping the noonday heat in dank and shaded hideouts. For this reason many are drably coloured. **Beetles** account for more than four hundred species, **bugs** eighty or so and **flies** around a hundred, including the bothersome **horsefly** and **midge**. The **carpenter bee** is the only bee, an important pollinator of native plants. Of the butterflies and moths, the yellow **Galápagos sulphur butterfly** and the **green hawkmoth**, which has a proboscis twice the length of its body, are among the most commonly seen of the two groups. The **Galápagos silver fritillary** has sparkling silvery patches on its wings, but perhaps the most colourful insect outside the eight butterfly species is the **painted locust**, frequently spotted around the coast in black, red and yellow. There are two **scorpions**, both of which can sting but are not dangerous, and more than fifty **spiders**, including a venomous relative of the black widow and the **silver argiope**, which weaves a silky "X" into the centre of its web. A 30cm, crimson-legged **centipede**, the poisonous endemic *Scolopendra galapagensis*, has a very painful bite, normally reserved for unlucky insects, lava lizards and small birds.

Ticks and **mites** annoy reptiles rather than humans, and tortoises and iguanas rely on finches to remove them. Of the tiny **land snails**, the *Bulimulus* genus has enjoyed extraordinary speciation with more than sixty known endemics descended from a single ancestor – putting Darwin's finches quite in the shade.

Plants

There are more than six hundred plant species in the Galápagos, around forty percent of which are endemic. Botanists have divided the islands into **vegetation zones**, each of which contains certain groupings of plants. Levels of rainfall play an important part in determining these zones and, generally speaking, the higher the altitude, the more moisture is received, allowing for a greater number of plant species. Usually the southern, windward side of an island receives far more rain than the leeward, so in many cases the zones differ from one side to another.

Coastal and arid zones

Going by altitude, the first zone is the **coastal** or **littoral zone** around the shore, dominated by salt-tolerant plants, the most notable of which are four species of **mangrove** (red, black, white and button), which make important breeding sites for many sea and shore birds. When water is scarce, **sea purslane** (*Sesuvium*) turns a deep red, covering shorelines in a crimson carpet, reverting to green in the wet season. **Beach morning glory** is a creeper that helps bind sand dunes together and produces large lilac flowers.

The **arid zone** is one of the largest zones, and is the most familiar to island visitors for its scrubby and cactus-filled semi-desert landscape. The **candelabra cactus** (*Jasminocereus*), whose distinctive barrel-shaped fingers can grow to 7m, and the **lava cactus** (*Brachycereus*), growing in small yellow clumps on black lava flows, are both endemic. The widespread **prickly pear cactus** (*Opuntia*) comes in fourteen endemic types on the islands and forms a major food staple for many birds and reptiles. The most striking of them has developed into tall, broad-trunked trees up to 12m in height, in part an evolutionary response to browsing tortoises. The lower shrubby forms are mostly found on tortoise-free islands, and in the northern islands, where pollinating insects are absent, the spines are softer to allow birds to do the job.

The ubiquitous tree of this zone is the **palo santo**, recognizable for its deathly grey appearance. Its name translates as "holy stick", both because its fragrant resin is burnt as incense in churches (it can also be used as an insect repellent) and because its off-white flowers appear around Christmas. When the rains come, green leaves start sprouting on its branches. Virtually waterless ashy or sandy soils support the low-lying grey *Tiquilia*, as seen scattered around the dry slopes of Bartolomé. The genes of the **Galápagos tomato**, one of the world's only two tomato species, whose seeds germinate best having passed through the giant tortoise's digestive system, have been used to develop drought-resistant tomatoes in other countries. **Lichens** are also common in the arid zone, requiring very little moisture or soil, and grow on trees, rocks and even tortoise shells.

Transition and highland zones

The **transition zone** links the dry zone to the more humid areas of **highland zones**. It's dominated by **pega pega** (meaning "stick stick"), so called for its sticky leaves and fruit; **guayabillo**, an endemic that produces fruits similar to the guava; and **matazarno**, a tall tree used for timber.

The humid area starts at around 200m and is divided into four zones. The **scalesia zone** is lush and densely forested, perpetually soaked in *garúa* mist during the cool-dry season. It's dominated by **lechoso** (*Scalesia pedunculata*), a 15m-tall tree with a bushy leafy top which is among the tallest members of the daisy and sunflower families, most often seen by visitors in the highlands of Santa Cruz. From one ancestor the *Scalesia* genus has developed into twenty forms according to the various environmental nuances of the islands. As in a cloudforest, the trees are covered with **epiphytes**, mainly **mosses**, **liverworts** and **ferns**, but also a few **orchids**, and one **bromeliad** (*Tillandsia*). At the higher end of this zone, the smaller **cat's claw** tree begins to take over; it is also hung heavy with epiphytes, which appear brown in the dry season, so giving this level the name the **brown zone**.

On Santa Cruz and San Cristóbal islands, the **miconia zone** is made up of a belt of **cacaotillo** (*Miconia robinsoniana*), an endemic shrub growing to about 5m, producing dark blue berries and resembling the cacao. Beginning at about 700m, the **pampa zone** is the highest and wettest zone, made up of **grasses**, **sedges** and other plants adapted to boggy environments. The **tree fern**, reaching a height of 3m, is the tallest plant in this zone.

Books

With the possible exception of the Galápagos Islands, foreign writers have paid less attention to Ecuador than to its South American neighbours, and few Ecuadorian works are translated into English. That said, there's a reasonable choice of books available in English, though not all are easy to find. Those books marked (o/p) are out of print, and those marked with ★ are particularly recommended.

ART AND POPULAR CULTURE

★ **Dawn Ades** *Art in Latin America: The Modern Era 1820–1980*. Excellent and lavishly illustrated general history of Latin American art from Independence, with discussions of a number of Ecuadorian artists.

Christy Buchanan and Cesar Franco *The Ecuador Cookbook: Traditional Vegetarian and Seafood Recipes*. A bilingual cookbook with delightfully illustrated and easy-to-follow vegetarian and seafood recipes.

Thomas Cummins *Ecuador: The Secret Art of Pre-Columbian Ecuador*. Fantastic illustrations of Ecuador's greatest and most unusual pre-Columbian artwork, plus essays from expert archeologists.

Gabrielle Palmer *Sculpture in the Kingdom of Quito*. Meticulously and thoughtfully researched study of the development of colonial sculpture in Quito, illustrated by some gorgeous photographs.

FICTION

★ **Demetrio Aguilera-Malta** *Don Goyo*. A spellbinding novel, first published in 1933, dealing with the lives of a group of *cholos* who eke out a living by fishing from the mangrove swamps in the Gulf of Guayaquil, which are in danger of being cleared by white landowners.

Kelly Aitken *Love in a Warm Climate*. Collection of short stories by a Canadian writer, all set in Ecuador and told by a series of North American female narrators.

Susan Benner and Kathy Leonard (ed) *Fire from the Andes*. The eight Ecuadorian stories in this anthology of contemporary Andean women writers touch on themes such as patriarchy, racial prejudice, poverty and ageing.

William Burroughs *Queer*. Autobiographical, Beat-generation novel about a morphine addict's travels through Ecuador in an abortive search for *yagé*, a hallucinatory drug from the Oriente.

Jorge Icaza *Huasipungo* (*The Villagers*). Iconic *indígenista* novel written in 1934, portraying the hardships and degradation suffered by the Andean *indígena* in a world dominated by exploitive landowners.

Benjamin Kunkel *Indecision*. Enjoyable coming-of-age novel about a 20-something trying to find direction in his life, who travels to Ecuador to see an old high-school crush.

Adalberto Ortiz *Juyungo*. A 1940s novel set in the tropical lowlands, about the life of a black labourer who kills two white men in self-defence. An atmospheric read, full of evocative detail.

Luis Sepúlveda *The Old Man Who Read Love Stories*. Captivating and deceptively simple story of an itinerant dentist's twice-yearly voyages into a Shuar community in the Oriente – vividly evoking the sensations of travelling in the rainforest, while raising environmental questions.

Kurt Vonnegut *Galápagos*. A darkly comic novel which, turning natural selection on its head, has a handful of passengers on a Galápagos cruise ship marooned on the islands as the only survivors of a war and global pandemic.

GALÁPAGOS

Johanna Angermeyer *My Father's Island*. The author uncovers the hidden past of her relatives through lyrical reminiscences on the Angermeyer family's struggle to settle on Santa Cruz, Galápagos.

Carol Ann Bassett *Galápagos at the Crossroads*. Provocative book dissecting the colliding forces that threaten to destroy what is special about the islands.

William Beebe *Galápagos: World's End*. This book brought the Galápagos to the attention of a new generation of travellers in the 1920s, and its popularity sparked a number of ill-fated attempts to colonize the islands. Beebe, director of the New York Zoological Society, went to the Galápagos as head of a two-and-a-half-month scientific expedition, but problems meant that he spent only "six thousand minutes" there.

Isabel Castro and Antonia Phillips *A Guide to the Birds of the Galápagos Islands*. Comprehensive bird guide with colour illustrations and detailed descriptions to help identification.

Charles Darwin *Voyage of the Beagle*. A hugely enjoyable book with a chapter devoted to the Galápagos; original insights and flashes of genius pepper Darwin's wonderfully vivid descriptions of the islands' landscapes and wildlife.

Adrian Desmond and James Moore *Darwin: The Life of a Tormented Evolutionist*. The enormous, definitive and best-selling biography of Darwin, so thorough and wide-ranging that it also serves as a compelling study of Victorian Britain as a whole.

Julian Fitter, Daniel Fitter and David Hosking *Wildlife of the Galápagos*. A great, portable wildlife guide with photos of more than 250 Galápagos species accompanied by succinct and informative text, plus coverage of history, climate, geography and conservation too.

★ **John Hickman** *The Enchanted Islands*. A succinct, well-researched and entertaining history of human life on the islands, especially strong on the many episodes concerning pirates and castaways.

Michael H. Jackson *Galápagos: A Natural History*. The most complete guide to the natural history of the Galápagos, containing a broad and readable overview of geography, geology, flora and fauna, and conservation.

Henry Nicholls *Lonesome George*. Everything you wanted to know about the world's most famous tortoise in a spirited and entertaining biography. Nicholls has also penned the well-written *The Galápagos: A Natural History* adding the trials and triumphs of human settlement to the well-organized presentation of land, sea and wildlife of the archipelago.

Dore Strauch *Satan Came to Eden*. The other first-hand account of the torrid and violent Galápagos affair on Floreana, remote even for the Galápagos. This book became the basis of the eponymous crime thriller meets Darwin documentary released in 2013.

★ **Andy Swash and Robert Still** *Birds, Mammals and Reptiles of the Galápagos Islands*. Excellent compact field guide with colour photos and sketches, including a fin guide to aid the identification of dolphins and whales.

Jonathan Weiner *The Beak of the Finch*. The fascinating work of two British scientists who have spent twenty years cataloguing Darwin's finches – in effect, witnessing the processes of evolution at first hand.

Margret Wittmer *Floreana*. One of Floreana's original colonists describes how she conquered the privations of Galápagos life and gives her version of events in the Galápagos affair.

HISTORY AND SOCIETY

★ **Carlos de la Torre** (ed.) *The Ecuador Reader: History, Culture, Politics*. Enthralling compilation of voices, opinions and writings by Ecuadorian politicians, authors, artists, intellectuals and activists, interspersed with essays on Ecuador by outsiders.

John Hemming *The Conquest of the Incas*. Marrying an academic attention to detail with a gripping narrative style, Hemming's book is widely regarded as the best account of this devastating conquest.

Peter Henderson *Gabriel García Moreno and Conservative State Formation in the Andes*. This mould-breaking biography explores the life of a leader who helped Ecuador survive its deepest crisis and launched modernization, but who is still a figure of controversy more than 120 years after his murder.

Osvaldo Hurtado *Portrait of a Nation: Culture and Progress in Ecuador*. Thrust into the presidency at a young age following the death of Jaime Roldós, Hurtado sets out to explain Ecuador's stumbling development over five centuries, with insights from his own experience as leader.

Wilma Roos and Omer van Renterghem *Ecuador in Focus*. A short introduction to Ecuador, with chapters on history, people, environment, economy and culture.

Mary Weismantel *Cholas and Pishtacos: Stories of Race and Sex in the Andes*. Brilliantly explores the relationship and tensions between the races and sexes, set against the vivid backdrop of the Andes.

MEMOIRS AND TRAVEL

Ludwig Bemelmans *The Donkey Inside* (o/p). Classic narrative based on the author's travels through Ecuador in the 1940s. A little old-fashioned and conservative, but masterfully written and a lively read.

Toby Green *Saddled with Darwin: A Journey through South America*. Elegantly written and loaded with wonderful anecdotes, an account of a madcap undertaking to follow Darwin's travels across South America on horseback.

★ **Peter Lourie** *Sweat of the Sun, Tears of the Moon*. Gripping account of the modern-day treasure-seekers intent on retrieving Atahualpa's ransom from the Llanganates mountains.

★ **Henri Michaux** *Ecuador: A Travel Journal*. Beautifully written impressions of Ecuador, based on the mystical Belgian author's travels through the country in 1977, and presented in a mixture of prose, poetry and diary notes.

Tom Miller *The Panama Hat Trail*. Blending lively travel narrative with investigative journalism, an engaging book tracking the historical and geographical course of the Panama hat (which, despite the name, originated in Ecuador).

Karin Muller *Along the Inca Road: A Woman's Journey into an Ancient Empire*. The author searches for the Royal Inca highway that once linked Ecuador to Chile and has dozens of adventures on the way.

Neville Shulman *Climbing the Equator: Adventures in the Jungles and Mountains of Ecuador*. A writer and explorer journeys through rainforests, meets indigenous people and attempts to climb Chimborazo, in a compelling and informative narrative.

★ **Paul Theroux** *The Old Patagonian Express*. A cranky but entertaining account of the author's train odyssey through the Americas, including a chapter on the time he spent in Quito (which he liked) and Guayaquil (which he hated).

★**Moritz Thomsen** *Living Poor*. An American Peace Corps volunteer writes lucidly about his time in the fishing community of Río Verde in Esmeraldas during the 1960s, and his mostly futile efforts to haul its people out of poverty. Thomsen never left Ecuador and followed up with three other autobiographical works – *Farm on the River of Emeralds*, *The Saddest Pleasure* and *My Two Wars* – before dying in a squalid apartment in Guayaquil in 1991.

Celia Wakefield *Searching for Isabel Godin: An Ordeal on the Amazon, Tragedy and Survival*. Fascinating account of the story of Isabel Godin, the Peruvian wife of Jean Godin, one of the key scientists on La Condamine's mission.

Robert Whitaker *The Mapmaker's Wife*. The story of Isabela Godin again, but with more of the science and history surrounding La Condamine's mission.

MOUNTAINEERING AND HIKING

Darcy Gaechter, Larry Vermeeren and Don Beveridge *The Kayaker's Guide to Ecuador*. Updated in 2014, this is the definitive guide to Ecuador's world-class kayaking options, describing dozens of runs throughout the country.

Robert and Daisy Kunstaetter *Trekking in Ecuador*. Includes almost thirty beautiful, well-chosen routes, and plenty of maps, photos and elevation profiles.

Rob Rachowiecki, Mark Thurber and Betsy Wagenhauser *Ecuador: Climbing and Hiking Guide*. A long-standing climbing and hiking guide to Ecuador, which details more than 70 routes throughout the country.

Richard Snailham *Sangay Survived*. Brisk account of the attempt of six British soldiers to climb Volcán Sangay in 1976, when an unexpected eruption left two dead and the rest seriously injured and stranded.

★**Edward Whymper** *Travels Amongst the Great Andes of the Equator*. Exploits of the pioneering nineteenth-century mountaineer, who managed to rack up a number of first ascents, including Chimborazo, Cayambe and Antisana.

THE ORIENTE

Paul Barrett *Law of the Jungle*. For more than twenty years, the case of Amazon villagers versus oil giant Chevron continues unresolved. While the divisive lawsuit for as much as $18 billion carries on in courtrooms around the world, thousands still live in a contaminated swath of Ecuador.

Philippe Drescola *The Spears of Twilight: Life and Death in the Amazon Jungle*. Drescola, a French ethnologist, spent two years living among the Achuar of the Oriente in the 1970s, a time vividly and intelligently recounted in this memoir.

Gines Haro *Yasuní Green Gold*. Coffee-table book with a conscience, celebrating Yasuní and explaining the issues as part of a campaign to "keep oil underground" there.

Joe Kane *Savages*. An affecting and sensitive book on the protests of the Waorani against "the Company", the monolithic multinational oil industry and its supporting agencies. It's sprinkled with a poignant humour generated from the gap in cultures between the author and his subjects.

José Toribio Medina (ed.) *The Discovery of the Amazon*. The most detailed account of Francisco de Orellana's voyage down the Amazon, with half the book given to the original source documents, translated into English.

Suzana Sawyer *Crude Chronicles*. The deepest exposition on the flowering of the indigenous and environmental movements in Ecuador against the ravages of neoliberal politics and global economics. A benchmark work in this field.

★**Anthony Smith** *Explorers of the Amazon*. An entertaining introduction to the exploration of the Amazon, streaked with wry humour. Includes chapters on Francisco de Orellana, La Condamine and Alexander von Humboldt. *The Lost Lady of the Amazon*, is about the epic journey of Isabela Godin (see above).

Randy Smith *Crisis Under the Canopy* (Abya Yala, Ecuador). An in-depth look at tourism in the Oriente and its effect on the Waorani people.

WILDLIFE AND THE ENVIRONMENT

John Eisenberg and Kent Redford *Mammals of the Neotropics: Ecuador, Peru, Bolivia, Brazil*. Useful guide to more than 650 species, including distribution maps, colour and monochrome photographs and background information on ecological and behavioural characteristics.

★**Alexander von Humboldt** *Personal Narrative of Travels to the Equinoctial Regions of the New Continent during the Years 1799–1804*. Written by perhaps the greatest of all scientist-explorers, who composed 29 volumes on his travels across South America. The sixth volume of his *Personal Narrative* touches on Ecuador, and includes the ground-breaking botanical map of Chimborazo.

David L. Pearson and Les Beletsky *Ecuador and the Galápagos Islands*. Substantial wildlife guide including 96 colour plates, which gives a good overview of much of the flora and fauna you're likely to stumble across on your travels.

★**Robert S. Ridgely and Paul J. Greenfield** *The Birds of Ecuador*. Monumental two-volume book (available separately) including a field guide with glorious colour plates of Ecuador's 1600 bird species. The country's definitive bird guide, and an indispensable resource for anyone interested in South American avifauna.

Language

The official language of Ecuador is Spanish, though at least twenty other first languages are spoken by native Ecuadorians, including nine dialects of Kichwa (also known by its Spanish spelling of "Quichua") and a further eight indigenous languages of the Oriente. English and some other European languages are spoken in tourist centres, but otherwise you'll need to know a bit of Spanish.

It's an easy language to pick up, especially in the Ecuadorian **sierra**, whose inhabitants are known for speaking fairly slowly and clearly, usually pronouncing all the consonants of a word. On the **coast**, the accents are much harder to decipher, with the "s" sound frequently dropped and whole word endings missing, so that "arroz con pescado", for example, becomes "arro' con pe'ca'o". Many beginners spend a week or longer getting to grips with the basics at one of Quito's numerous **language schools**, most of which offer great-value lessons (see box, p.89). Popular alternatives to Quito include Baños (see p.158) and Cuenca (see p.192).

Those who already speak Spanish will have no trouble adjusting to the way it's spoken in Ecuador, which conforms to standard textbook **Castilian**, spoken without the lisped "c" and "z". That said, it does have its own idiomatic peculiarities, one of which is the compulsive use of the word "nomás" ("just" or "only"), which crops up all over the place ("siga nomás" for "go ahead", or "siéntate nomás" for "sit down", for example). Something else that sets Ecuadorian Spanish apart from Iberian Spanish are the many indigenous words that pepper its vocabulary, particularly **Kichwa** words such as *guagua* (baby), *mate* (herbal infusion), *pampa* (plain), *soroche* (altitude sickness) and *minga* (communal labour). Ecuador also readily borrows from **English**, resulting in a slew of words regarded with horror by Spaniards, such as *chequear* (to check), *parquear* (to park), *rentar* (to rent), *sánduche* (sandwich) and *computador* (computer). This somewhat flexible approach makes Ecuadorians more than willing to accommodate a foreigner's attempts to speak Spanish.

Pronunciation

The rules of **pronunciation** are pretty straightforward and, once you get to know them, strictly observed. Unless there's an accent, words ending in d, l, r, and z are **stressed** on the last syllable, all others on the second last. All **vowels** are pure and short.

A somewhere between the "a" sound of back and that of father

E as in get

I as in police

O as in hot

U as in rule

C is soft before E and I, hard otherwise: cerca is pronounced "serka".

G works the same way, a guttural "h" sound (like the ch in loch) before E or I, a hard G elsewhere – gigante becomes "higante".

H is always silent

J is the same sound as a guttural G: jamón is pronounced "hamon".

LL sounds like an English Y: tortilla is pronounced "torteeya".

N is as in English unless it has a tilde over it, as with mañana, when it's pronounced like the "n" in onion.

QU is pronounced like an English K.

R is rolled, RR doubly so.

V sounds more like B, vino becoming "beano".

X is slightly softer than in English – sometimes almost SH – except between vowels in place names where it has an "H" sound – for example México (meh-hee-ko).

Z is the same as a soft "C", so cerveza becomes "servesa".

If you're using a dictionary, remember that in Spanish CH, LL, and Ñ count as separate letters and are listed after the Cs, Ls, and Ns, respectively.

Words and phrases

We've listed a few essential **words** and **phrases** below, but if you're travelling for any length of time a dictionary or phrasebook, such as the *Rough Guide Dictionary Phrasebook: Spanish*, is a worthwhile investment.

BASICS

yes, no	sí, no	with, without	con, sin
please, thank you	por favor, gracias	good, bad	buen(o)/a, mal(o)/a
where, when	dónde, cuándo	big	gran(de)
what, how much	qué, cuánto	small	pequeño/a, chico
here, there	aquí, allí	more, less	más, menos
this, that	este, eso	today, tomorrow	hoy, mañana
now, later	ahora, más tarde	yesterday	ayer
open, closed	abierto/a, cerrado/a		

GREETINGS AND RESPONSES

Hello, Goodbye	Hola, Adiós	I (don't) speak Spanish	(No) Hablo español
Good morning	Buenos días	My name is…	Me llamo…
Good afternoon/night	Buenas tardes/noches	What's your name?	¿Cómo se llama usted?
See you later	Hasta luego	I am English	Soy inglés (a)
Sorry	Lo siento/discúlpeme	…American	…norteamericano (a)
Excuse me	Con permiso/perdón	…Australian	…australiano (a)
How are you?	¿Cómo está (usted)?	…Canadian	…canadiense (a)
I (don't) understand	(No) Entiendo	…Irish	…irlandés (a)
Not at all/You're welcome	De nada	…Scottish	…escosés (a)
		…Welsh	…galés (a)
Do you speak English?	¿Habla (usted) inglés?	…New Zealander	…neozelandés (a)

ACCOMMODATION

twin room	una habitación doble	…a room	…una habitación
room with double bed	una habitación matrimonial	…with two beds/ double bed	…con dos camas/cama matrimonial
single room	una habitación sencilla	…for one night/one week	…para una noche/una semana
private bathroom	baño privado	It's for one person	Es para una persona/
shared bathroom	baño compartido	/two people	dos personas
hot water (all day)	agua caliente (todo el día)	It's fine, how much is it?	¿Está bien, cuánto es?
cold water	agua fría	It's too expensive	Es demasiado caro
fan	ventilador	Don't you have anything cheaper?	¿No tiene algo más barato?
air-conditioned	aire-acondicionado		
tax	impuesto	Can one…?	¿Se puede…?
mosquito net	tolda/mosquitero	…camp (near) here?	¿…acampar aquí (cerca)?
key	llave	Is there a hotel nearby?	¿Hay un hotel aquí cerca?
check-out time	hora de salida	I want	Quiero
Do you know…?	¿Sabe…?	I'd like	Querría
I don't know	No sé	What is there to eat?	¿Qué hay para comer?
There is (is there)?	(¿) Hay (?)	What's that?	¿Qué es eso?
Give me…	Deme…	What's this called in Spanish?	¿Cómo se llama este en español?
(one like that)	(uno así)		
Do you have…?	¿Tiene…?		

DIRECTIONS AND TRANSPORT

bus terminal	terminal terrestre	aisle	pasillo
ticket	pasaje	window	ventana
seat	asiento	luggage	equipaje

How do I get to…?	¿Por dónde se va a…?	What time does the bus leave?	¿A qué hora sale el camión?
Left, right, straight on	Izquierda, derecha, derecho	What time does the bus arrive?	¿A qué hora llega el bus?
Where is…?	¿Dónde está…?	How long does the journey take?	¿Cuánto tiempo demora el viaje?
…the bus station	…el terminal de buses	Is this the train for…?	¿Es éste el tren para…?
…the train station	…la estación de ferrocarriles	I'd like a (return) ticket to…	Querría pasaje (de ida y vuelta) para…
…the nearest bank	…el banco más cercano	What time does it leave (arrive in…)?	¿A qué hora sale (llega en…)?
…the post office	…el correo		
…the toilet	…el baño		
Where does the bus to… leave from?	¿De dónde sale el camión para…?		

NUMBERS

1	un/uno/una	50	cincuenta
2	dos	60	sesenta
3	tres	70	setenta
4	cuatro	80	ochenta
5	cinco	90	noventa
6	seis	100	cien(to)
7	siete	101	ciento uno
8	ocho	200	doscientos
9	nueve	201	doscientos uno
10	diez	500	quinientos
11	once	1000	mil
12	doce	2000	dos mil
13	trece	first	primero/a
14	catorce	second	segundo/a
15	quince	third	tercero/a
16	dieciséis	fourth	cuarto/a
17	diecisiete	fifth	quinto/a
18	dieciocho	sixth	sixto/a
19	diecinueve	seventh	séptimo/a
20	veinte	eighth	octavo/a
21	veitiuno	ninth	noveno/a
30	treinta	tenth	décimo/a
40	cuarenta		

DAYS AND MONTHS

Monday	lunes	March	marzo
Tuesday	martes	April	abril
Wednesday	miércoles	May	mayo
Thursday	jueves	June	junio
Friday	viernes	July	julio
Saturday	sábado	August	agosto
Sunday	domingo	September	septiembre
		October	octubre
January	enero	November	noviembre
February	febrero	December	diciembre

Food and drink terms

The following should more than suffice as a basic menu reader for navigating restaurants, food stalls and markets throughout the country.

BASICS

aceite	oil	huevos	eggs
ají	chilli	mantequilla	butter
ajo	garlic	merienda	set-menu dinner
almuerzo	lunch, set-menu lunch	mermelada	jam
arroz	rice	miel	honey
azúcar	sugar	mixto	mixed seafood or meats
la carta	the menu	mostaza	mustard
cena	dinner	pan (integral)	(wholemeal) bread
comida típica	traditional food	pimienta	pepper
cuchara	spoon	plato fuerte	main course
cuchillo	knife	plato vegetariano	vegetarian dish
la cuenta	the bill	queso	cheese
desayuno	breakfast	sal	salt
galletas	biscuits	salsa de tomate	tomato sauce
hielo	ice	tenedor	fork

COOKING TERMS

a la parrilla	barbecued	duro	hard-boiled
a la plancha	lightly fried	encebollado	cooked with onions
ahumado	smoked	encocado	in coconut sauce
al ajillo	in garlic sauce	frito	fried
al horno	oven-baked	picante	spicy hot
al vapor	steamed	puré	mashed
apanado	breaded	relleno	filled or stuffed
asado	roast	revuelto	scrambled
asado al palo	spit roasted, barbecued	saltado	sautéed
crudo	raw	seco	stew (also means dry)

SOUPS

caldo	broth	sopa	soup
caldo de gallina	chicken broth	sopa de bolas de verde	plantain dumpling soup
caldo de patas	cattle-hoof broth		
crema de espárragos	cream of asparagus	sopa del día	soup of the day
locro	cheese and potato soup	yaguarlocro	blood-sausage soup

MEAT AND POULTRY

aves	poultry	cuy	guinea pig
bistec	beef steak	jamón	ham
carne	beef	lechón	suckling pig
cerdo/carne de chancho	pork	lomo	steak of indiscriminate cut
chicharrones	pork scratchings, crackling	pato	duck
chuleta	cutlet, chop (usually pork)	pavo	turkey
churrasco	beef steak with fried egg, rice and potatoes	pollo	chicken
		res	beef
conejo	rabbit	ternera	veal
cordero	lamb	tocino	bacon
cuero/cueritos	pork crackling	venado	venison

OFFAL

chunchules	intestines	menudos	offal
guatita	tripe	patas	feet, trotters
hígado	liver	riñones	kidneys
lengua	tongue		

SEAFOOD AND FISH

anchoa	anchovy	corvina	sea bass
atún	tuna	erizo	sea urchin
bonito	Pacific bonito (similar to tuna)	langosta	lobster
		langostino	king prawn
calamares	squid	lenguado	sole
camarón	prawn	mariscos	seafood
cangrejo	crab	mejillón	mussel
ceviche	seafood marinated in lime juice with onions	ostra	oyster
		pescado	fish
concha	clam, scallop	trucha	trout

SNACKS

bocadillos	snacks	quimbolitos	Sweet cornmeal sponge wrapped in leaf and steamed
bolón de verde	baked cheese and plantain dumpling	salchipapas	chips, sausage and sauces
canguil	popcorn	sánduche	sandwich
chifles	banana chips/crisps	tamales	ground maize with meat or cheese wrapped in leaf
empanada	cheese or meat pasty		
hamburguesa	hamburger		
humitas	ground corn and cheese wrapped in leaf and steamed	tortilla de huevos	omelette (also called omelet)
		tortilla de maíz	corn tortilla
patacones	thick-cut fried banana/plantain	tostada	toast
		tostado	toasted maize

FRUIT

cereza	cherry	manzana	apple
chirimoya	custard apple; cherimoya	maracuyá	passion-fruit
		mora	blackberry
ciruela	plum	naranja	orange
durazno	peach	pera	pear
fruta	fruit	piña	pineapple
frutilla	strawberry	plátano	plantain
guayaba	guava	tomate de arbol	tree tomato
higo	fig	toronja	grapefruit

Vegetables

aceitunas	olives	legumbres	vegetables
aguacate	avocado	lentejas	lentils
alcachofa	artichoke	menestra	stew, typically beans and lentils
arvejas	peas		
cebolla	onion	palmito	palm heart
champiñón	mushroom	papa	potato
choclo	maize, sweetcorn	papas fritas	chips (french fries)
coliflor	cauliflower	pepinillo	gherkin
espinaca	spinach	pepino	cucumber
frijoles	beans	tomate	tomato
hongo	mushroom	verduras	vegetables
lechuga	lettuce	zanahoria	carrot

DESSERTS

cocados	coconut sweets	flan	crème caramel
ensalada de frutas	fruit salad	helado	ice cream

manjar de leche	very sweet caramel, made from condensed milk	**pastel**	cake
pastas	pastries	**postres**	desserts
		torta	tart

DRINKS

agua (mineral)	(mineral) water	**café con leche**	coffee with milk
con gas	sparkling	**caipiriña**	cocktail of rum, lime,
sin gas	still		ice and sugar
sin hielo	without ice	**cerveza**	beer
al clima	at room temperature	**chicha**	fermented corn drink
aguardiente	sugar-cane spirit	**cola/gaseosa**	fizzy drink
aromática	herbal tea	**jugo**	juice
hierba luisa	lemon verbena	**leche**	milk
manzanilla	camomile	**limonada**	fresh lemonade
menta	mint	**mate de coca**	coca leaf tea
batido	milkshake	**ron**	rum
bebidas	drinks	**té**	tea
café	coffee	**vino (blanco/tinto)**	(white/red) wine

Kichwa (Quichua)

Up to 20 percent of Ecuador's population are **Kichwa**-speakers, the language of the Inca Empire, which in one form or another is spoken by indigenous communities from southern Colombia all the way to northern Chile. There are many regional differences, however, so that a speaker from Ecuador would have as much difficulty understanding a Peruvian, as a Spanish-speaker would have understanding Italian. **Dialects** also differ between areas of Ecuador, with noticeable variations between speakers of the highlands and of the Oriente, and again between highland areas such as Cañar, Chimborazo and Imbabura.

Though there are regional differences, the basic **phrases** below should be understood by Kichwa-speakers throughout the country. Spellings do vary; you may see "c" written for "k", or "hua/gua" for "wa", for instance. Most people will also know Spanish, but exhibiting an interest in speaking Kichwa can only help increase pride in a language that has long been stigmatized and suppressed by the Spanish-speaking establishment. It's little wonder that many speakers are rejecting the Spanish spelling of their language, "Quichua", which you'll still see commonly used. The effort spent taking some time to **learn** Kichwa will be repaid many times over in the access it will give you to Kichwa communities and the friendships you'll make. Lessons are offered at EIL, Hernando de la Cruz N31-37 and Mariana de Jesús, Quito (☎02 2551937, ⓦeilecuador.org), or you could try indigenous tour operators, such as Runa Tupari of Otavalo (see p.108), who will be able to fix you up with homestays. You could also make enquiries and pick up resource materials at Abya Yala, a cultural centre in Quito dedicated to protecting and promoting indigenous culture, at 12 de Octubre 1430 and Wilson (☎02 2506251, ⓦabyayala.org), or check the notice boards of the SAE (see p.79).

USEFUL WORDS AND PHRASES

Hello	Imanalla	**I am fine**	Allillami kapani
Good morning	Alli puncha	**Please**	Jau man
Good afternoon	Alli chishi	**Thank you (very much)**	Pagui (shungulla)
Good evening/night	Alli tuta	**Yes**	Ari
See you tomorrow	Kayakama	**No**	Manan
See you later	Asha kashkaman	**I, my**	Ñuka
Let's go	Akuichi	**You (informal)/(formal)**	Kan/kikin
How are you?	Imanalla kangui?	**Excuse me**	Kishpi chigway

It's so cold!	Achachay!	Please sit down	Tiyaripay
It's so hot!	Araray!	Say it again please	Kutin nipay
What's your name?	Ima shuti kangui?	How old are you?	Mashna watata
My name is	Ñuka shuti mikan		charingui?

NUMBERS

1	shuk	11	chunka shuk
2	ishki	12	chunka ishki
3	kimsa	20	ishki chunka
4	chusku	21	ishki chunka shuk
5	pichka	100	pachak
6	sukta	1000	waranka
7	kanchis	2345	ishki waranka kimsa
8	pusak		pachak chuksu
9	iskun		chunka pichka
10	chunka	1,000,000	junu

COMMON WORDS IN NAMES AND PLACES

alli	good	pakarina	sunrise
allpa	earth, soil	pichu	chest
chaka	bridge	pirka	wall
chullpi	corn	pishku	bird
churi	son	rasu	snow
huarmi	wife	raymi	fiesta
huasi	house	ruku	old
inti	sun	rumi	stone
jaka	abyss	runa	indigenous person
jatun	big	sacha	forest
kari	man	sara	corn
killa	moon, month	sisa	flower
kincha	corral	sumak	beautiful
kucha (cocha)	lake	tayta	father, polite term for
llakta	village, community		an older man
makui	hand	tullu	bone
mama	mother, polite term for	uma	head
	an older woman	urku	mountain
ñan	path, street	warmi	woman
ñaña	sister	wawa (guagua)	baby
pacha	hour, weather	wayna	lover
pachamama	nature, mother earth	yaku	water, river

Glossary

Adobe Sun-dried mud brick

Aguas termales Hot springs

Ahigra A bag made of tightly woven straw, often dyed in bright colours

Apartado Postal box

Artesanía Traditional handicraft

Balneario Thermal baths resort

Bargueño Colonial wooden chest, inlaid with bone, ivory and other decorative materials in geometric patterns

Barrio District, quarter or suburb

Buseta Small bus

Cabaña Cabin

Calle Street

Camioneta Pick-up truck

Campesino Literally from the countryside, used to describe mestizo rural farmers

Canoa Dugout canoe

Casilla Post box

C.C. abbreviation of *centro comercial*, or shopping centre

Chicha fermented maize drink

Chiva Open-sided wooden bus mostly found in rural areas

Cholo Coastal fisherman, but also used in the sierra to refer to mestizo artisans and traders in the Cuenca region, most commonly applied to women ("la chola Cuencana")

Choza A rough-thatched hut or shack

Colectivo Collective taxi

Cordillera Mountain range

Criollo "Creole": used historically to refer to a person of Spanish blood born in the American colonies, but nowadays as an adjective to describe something (such as food or music) as "typical" or "local"

Curandero Healer

Fibra Open fibreglass boat used as transport between islands in the Galápagos

Finca Small farm

Flete Small boat for hire

Folklórica Andean folk music

Gringo Slightly (but not always) pejorative term for an American specifically, but also used generally for any foreigner from a non-Spanish-speaking country

Guardaparque Park warden

Hacienda Farm or large estate

Indígena Used adjectivally to mean "indigenous", or as a noun to refer to an indigenous person

Lancha Launch, small boat

Lek Bird courtship display area

Local "Unit" or "shop" in a shopping centre

Malecón Coastal or riverside avenue

Mestizo Person of mixed Spanish and indigenous blood

Minga Kichwa term for collective community work

Mirador Viewpoint

Montuvio Mestizo farm worker in the coastal interior

Mototaxi Motorbike powered taxi with passenger seats

Municipio Town hall or town council

Nevado Snowcapped mountain

Pampa Plain

Panga Dinghy, usually with a motor

Páramo High-altitude grassland, found above 3000m

Peña Nightclub where live music is performed, often folk music

Petrolero Oil-worker

Plata Silver; slang for money

Pucará Fort

Quebrada Ravine, dried-out stream

Quinta Villa or fine country house

Ranchera Open-sided wooden bus mostly found in rural areas

Sala Room or hall

Selva Jungle or tropical forest

Serrano From the sierra or highlands

s/n used in addresses to indicate "*sin número*", or without a number

Soroche Altitude sickness

SS HH Abbreviation for *servicios higiénicos*, toilets

Tambo Rest-house on Inca roads

Tarabita Simple cable car

Termas Thermal baths, hot springs

Triciclero Tricycle-taxi driver

Small print and index

A ROUGH GUIDE TO ROUGH GUIDES

Published in 1982, the first Rough Guide – to Greece – was a student scheme that became a publishing phenomenon. Mark Ellingham, a recent graduate in English from Bristol University, had been travelling in Greece the previous summer and couldn't find the right guidebook. With a small group of friends he wrote his own guide, combining a highly contemporary, journalistic style with a thoroughly practical approach to travellers' needs.

The immediate success of the book spawned a series that rapidly covered dozens of destinations. And, in addition to impecunious backpackers, Rough Guides soon acquired a much broader readership that relished the guides' wit and inquisitiveness as much as their enthusiastic, critical approach and value-for-money ethos.

These days, Rough Guides include recommendations from budget to luxury and cover more than 120 destinations around the globe, as well as producing an ever-growing range of ebooks.

Visit **roughguides.com** to find all our latest books, read articles, get inspired and share travel tips.

Rough Guide credits

Editors: Greg Dickinson, Natasha Foges, Rebecca Hallett
Layout: Jessica Subramanian
Cartography: Deshpal Dabas
Picture editor: Aude Vauconsant
Proofreader: Jennifer Speake
Managing editor: Mani Ramaswamy
Assistant editor: Divya Grace Mathew

Production: Jimmy Lao
Cover photo research: Aude Vauconsant
Editorial assistant: Freya Godfrey
Senior DTP coordinator: Dan May
Programme manager: Gareth Lowe
Publishing director: Georgina Dee

Publishing information

This sixth edition published September 2016 by
Rough Guides Ltd,
80 Strand, London WC2R 0RL
11, Community Centre, Panchsheel Park,
New Delhi 110017, India
Distributed by Penguin Random House
Penguin Books Ltd, 80 Strand, London WC2R 0RL
Penguin Group (USA), 345 Hudson Street, NY 10014, USA
Penguin Group (Australia), 250 Camberwell Road,
Camberwell, Victoria 3124, Australia
Penguin Group (NZ), 67 Apollo Drive, Mairangi Bay,
Auckland 1310, New Zealand
Penguin Group (South Africa), Block D, Rosebank Office
Park, 181 Jan Smuts Avenue, Parktown North, Gauteng,
South Africa 2193
Rough Guides is represented in Canada by DK Canada, 320
Front Street West, Suite 1400,Toronto, Ontario M5V 3B6
Printed in Singapore
© Rough Guides 2016
Maps © Rough Guides

440pp includes index
A catalogue record for this book is available from the
British Library
ISBN: 978-0-24124-574-3
The publishers and authors have done their best to ensure
the accuracy and currency of all the information in **The
Rough Guide to Ecuador & the Galápagos Islands**,
however, they can accept no responsibility for any loss,
injury, or inconvenience sustained by any traveller as a
result of information or advice contained in the guide.
1 3 5 7 9 8 6 4 2

MIX
Paper from
responsible sources
FSC™ C018179
www.fsc.org

Help us update

We've gone to a lot of effort to ensure that the sixth
edition of **The Rough Guide to Ecuador & the Galápagos
Islands** is accurate and up-to-date. However, things
change – places get "discovered", opening hours are
notoriously fickle, restaurants and rooms raise prices
or lower standards. If you feel we've got it wrong or
left something out, we'd like to know, and if you can
remember the address, the price, the hours, the phone
number, so much the better.

Please send your comments with the subject line
**"Rough Guide Ecuador & the Galápagos Islands
Update"** to mail@uk.roughguides.com. We'll credit all
contributions and send a copy of the next edition (or any
other Rough Guide if you prefer) for the very best emails.

Find more travel information, connect with fellow
travellers and plan your trip on ⓦ roughguides.com.

ABOUT THE AUTHORS

Sara Humphreys is a freelance researcher, writer and educator, who has toiled, travelled and tarried in various countries in Latin America, Africa and Europe and when not travelling or sitting hunched over a laptop, can be found swinging in a hammock in Barbados.

Stephan Küffner, a German-Ecuadorean who grew up in the US, has been working as a foreign correspondent in South America for well over a decade, writing for the likes of *The Economist*, *Bloomberg*, *Time Magazine* and energy newswire *Platts*. He lets off steam about politics and economics by playing ice hockey in Quito and travelling as much as possible.

Acknowledgements

Sara Humphreys Muchísimas gracias a Mauro Quito and Katrin Kubber for warm hospitality, insights and early morning dog-walking in the Parque Metropolitano, and to Christian Oquendo for entertaining debates on the meaning of life, and other such trivia. In Guayaquil, I'm indebted to Ricardo Cevallos of *El Manso* for sharing his knowledge and for a memorable trip to Trinidad, and in Puerto López thanks are due to Maya Steiner of *Hostería Mandalá* for copious info and red wine. I'm also grateful to Amelia Peñaloza Bur for her rapid recce of Cojimíes and surroundings. Across the country, staff in the various I-Tur offices were exceedingly helpful, especially in Cuenca, where Fabiola Jadan provided outstanding assistance. Back at *Rough Guides*, appreciation is due to Greg Dickinson, Natasha Foges and Rebecca Hallett for helping panel-beat the text and maps into shape, and to Andy Turner and Mani Ramaswamy for project oversight. Last but not least, thanks to Adrian for troubleshooting laptop emergencies, and providing home support.

Readers' updates

Thanks to all the readers who have taken the time to write in with comments and suggestions (and apologies if we've inadvertently omitted or misspelt anyone's name):

Xavier Amigo, David Anderson, Maria Teresa Barragán, Tim van Beek, Fabian Bonilla, Agi Boronkay, Nathalie Bridey, Annechien ten Brink, Betsy Clark, Elizabeth Clark, Dan Cohen, Carolin Collmar and Stefan Schulze, Kevin Geary, Diane Green, Marc Griffith, Robert Zachary Haas, Inge Van den Herrewegen, Olaf Hestvik, Seth W. Howard, Sarah Howe, Juan, Kyra de Keyzer, Maureen Klovers, Andrés Larsen, Mark, Ted McKen, Michel Leseigneur, Hannah Lupien, Phoebe Mason, Christian Mesía Montenegro, Mirco, Leslie Moore, Ana Maria Naranjo, Patricio Ledesma Nuñez, Carmen Ortega, Ken Pennell, Caroline Pierron, Maggie Reniers, Robbie Ripamonti, Rosa, Sandra Rosenfeld, Dag Saunders, Steve Skinner, Harriet Smith, Anika Stevens, Karen Story, Christof Tononi, Marije van Vilsteren, Anne Webber.

Photo credits

All photos © Rough Guides except the following:
(Key: t-top; c-centre; b-bottom; l-left; r-right)

Index

Maps are marked in grey

G

Map symbols

The symbols below are used on maps throughout the book

	International boundary	Ⓜ	Metrobus stop		Zoo		Swimming pool
	Provincial boundary	Ⓔ	Ecovía stop		Ruin		Waterfall
	Chapter division boundary	Ⓣ	Trole stop		Campsite		Lighthouse
	Road		Boat		Volcano		Spring/spa
	Pedestrianized road	@	Internet café/access		Border crossing		Museum
	Unpaved road	ⓘ	Information office		Mountain lodge		Church (regional maps)
	Steps	Ⓟ	Parking		Cave		Building
	Path	Ⓒ	Telephone office		Bridge		Church (town maps)
	Railway	✚	Hospital	▲	Mountain peak		Stadium
	Ferry route		Post office		Mountain range		Beach
	Cable car		Market		Cliff		Park
✈	Airport	♦	Place of interest		Crater		Cemetery
★	Bus stop	☉	Statue		Viewpoint		

Listings key

■ Accommodation

● Eating

■ Drinking/nightlife

● Shopping

San Jorge Eco-Lodges &
Botanical Reserves
Ecuador, S.A.

George Cruz

THE MAGIC BIRDING & HIKING CIRCUIT

- Birdwatching & Natural History
- Wildlife Photography
- Hiking & Natural History
- Pre-scheduled or Custom Tours
- English speaking specialized Guides
- Trip Advisor Traveler's Choice Awards

- 6 Private Nature Reserve
- 5 Beautiful Eco-Lodges
- Birds – Hummingbirds – Butterflies - Orchids
- Visit 11 diversified eco-systems
- Andes Highlands, Cloud Forest
- Tropical Rainforest, Pacific Coastal + more

Trips of a Lifetime!

www.eco-lodgesanjorge.com   info@eco-lodgesanjorge.com